Compliments of Verl A Teeter

DATE DUE

WHO'S
WHO
IN
FOOTBALL

WHO'S WHO
IN
FOOTBALL

Ronald L. Mendell
Timothy B. Phares

University of Tulsa
McFarlin Library
Tulsa, Okla.

ARLINGTON HOUSE   New Rochelle, New York

Library of Congress Cataloging in Publication Data

Mendell, Ronald L   1943-
   Who's who in football.

   1. Football--Biography--Dictionaries. I. Phares,
Timothy, joint author. II. Title.
GV939.A1M46   796.33'2'0922   74-17336
ISBN 0-87000-237-6

EDITOR'S NOTE

The records of athletes and coaches are sometimes in dispute, and human error can play a role in the compilation of any work. For these reasons the authors would appreciate it if every reader would pass along any corrections. Beyond that, if the reader can think of any significant omissions, the authors would like to hear your opinions.

This volume is likely to become one of the established sources on the subject of football. It you have any suggestions or corrections please write to the authors in care of Arlington House, New Rochelle, N.Y. 10801. Everyone who helps will be making a significant contribution to sports research. Those whose suggestions, or corrections, are used will be given a credit line in the revised, enlarged and updated edition we hope to bring out in the late 1970's.

FOREWORD

Vigorous young men at play, lusty cheering in crowded stadia, and crisp autumn afternoons help give football its unmistakable flavor. Football's magic captured my imagination long ago, and it has mesmerized millions of others in its glorious 105 year history.

Who's Who In Football is a book that gives the game its due. It includes over 1,400 biographical sketches of players, coaches, officials, administrators and owners. The book spans the collegiate and professional levels, since the game's inception in 1869.

The authors have given the student of the game an invaluable reference tool, as well as hours of enjoyment for the ordinary buff.

Tim Cohane*

Boston
August, 1974

*Former sports editor of
Look; currently
Professor of Journalism,
Boston University.

PREFACE

Football's growth, from the 200 or so spectators who attended the first intercollegiate game in 1869, has been staggering. It is today almost the national religion.

Over 31 million people attended college football games in 1973. That was 15 million more than a decade ago. The volume of other devotees, who played or saw games at any or all levels in 1973, is left to the imagination.

Television has certainly played a prominent role in football's growth, especially in the 1960s and 70s. It has taken the game into every household, and football, seizing the opportunity, has proselytized the family.

Even without TV, growth was almost assured. The sport has a magnetic appeal for the spectator. It is violent and fast, characteristically American. It is rich in fact, lore and legend. And it has been blessed with dedicated disciples.

Walter Camp, the "Father," gave definition and inspiring leadership. Coaches such as Alonzo Stagg, Knute Rockne, George Halas, were men of integrity, perfectly suited to carrying the game's gospel throughout the land. The players, like Red Grange, Sammy Baugh, Bronko Nagurski, O. J. Simpson, provided essential ingredients — speed and power. And men of letters, such as Tim Cohane, Grantland Rice, Allison Danzig, have educated the masses to the finer points of gridiron warfare.

Owing to football's storied past and present buoyancy, this volume seems particularly appropriate. In it will be found biographies of over 1400 men. They all helped the sport achieve its present station. Football history should unfold in these pages, and hopefully, many of the great moments will come alive.

Consideration was given to those persons directly involved with the game, meaning players, coaches, officials, owners, administrators. Included are those who starred or participated for a long time, others who partook only briefly. The unique or unusual individual, hero for a day, is also considered. For the most part, longevity of service and performance were primary criteria. Both collegiate and professional are included.

Unfortunately, only vague and suspect information was available on certain noteworthy individuals. These men had to be sacrificed for accuracy, and are not included. Every possible means, it can be truly stated, was enacted by the authors to secure complete information.

A partial bibliography would include the following: *Football's Greatest Coaches, The Saga of American Football, College Football All-Time Record Book, College Football All-Time Galaxy, College Football Modern Record Book* (1973), *Who Was Who in American Sports, Good Clean Violence, College Football U.S.A. 1869-72, The Yale Football Story, Football Immortals, The Big Ten, The Big Nine, The History of American Football, Great College Football Coaches of the Twenties* and *Thirties,* The *Sporting News,* The New York *Times, Sports Illustrated.*

We would like to acknowledge cooperation of sports information and alumni offices of the following universities and colleges: Alabama, Arizona, Arizona State, Arkansas, Auburn, Baylor, Brigham Young, Brown, Bucknell, California, UCLA, U. of Chicago, Clarion State, Clemson, Colgate, Colorado State,

Colorado, Columbia, Cornell, Dartmouth, Delaware, Drake, Georgia, Georgia Tech, Grambling, Hardin-Simmons, Harvard, Hillsdale, Hobart, Holy Cross, Houston, College of Idaho, Illinois, Indiana, Iowa, Iowa State, Kansas, Kentucky, Lafayette, Louisiana State.

And: Memphis State, Miami (Fla.), Michigan, Michigan State, Mississippi, Missouri, Minnesota, Nebraska, Nevada (Las Vegas), New Mexico State, Notre Dame, Oklahoma State, Oklahoma, Princeton, Rice, Rutgers, U. of the South, South Dakota State, Southern California, Southern Methodist, Stanford, Syracuse, Tennessee, Texas A. & M., Texas Christian, Texas, Tulane, U.S. Air Force Academy, U.S. Military Academy, U.S. Naval Academy, Vanderbilt, Virginia Military Institute, Virginia Tech, Washington & Jefferson, Washington, Washington State, Wesleyan, West Texas State, West Virginia, Williams, Wisconsin, Wyoming, Yale.

We would also like to thank for their help, publicity directors of the 26 National Football League teams; also the offices of the National Football Foundation, the Fellowship of Christian Athletes, and the National Football League. Gratitude must also be expressed to the men included in the book, too numerous for mention individually, who supplied direct information by personal interview or questionnaire.

Two men warrant special acknowledgement, for they provided material not readily available from other sources. They are: William R. Schroeder, managing director, Citizens Savings Athletic Foundation; and James Campbell, librarian-researcher, Professional Football Hall of Fame.

Ronald Mendell
Tim Phares

May 24, 1974

ABELL, EARL C. (Toughey) Tackle. B. 5/29/92, Portage, Wis. 5'11", 204. Colgate, 1912-15. All-America, 1915. Captain of 1915 team. That season kicked two FGs, one for 42 yds. and other for 40, to beat Yale and Army. Served in World War I, advancing to army Capt. Coached at Colgate, VMI, Mississippi State, Virginia before entering private industry. National Football Foundation Hall of Fame.

ABRAMOWICZ, DANIEL (Abe; Danny) End. B. 7/13/45, Steubenville, Ohio. 6'1", 195. Played for Xavier (Ohio), 1965-67. Although interviewed by many scouts, Danny was not drafted until 17th round by New Orleans Saints. Made team on determination, courage and moves, becoming regular after injury to Kent Kramer. Made sensational TD reception on skin part of Anaheim Stadium infield in 1967 exhibition game. Led NFL in pass receptions with 73, 1969, for 1015 yds. and 7 TDs. Thus became third man in NFL history to have 50 or more receptions each of first three seasons (50 receptions in 1967, 54 in 68). Also caught more than 50 (55) in 1970. In six seasons, 1967-72, caught more passes (307) than any other wide receiver (for 4856 yds., 37 TDs). Added 37 receptions in 1973. Traded to San Francisco 49ers, 10/73. Cousin of Tom Franckhauser, cornerback of Minnesota Vikings, who suffered severe brain injury.

ADAMLE, MIKE Running Back. B. 10/10/49, Kent, Ohio. 5'9", 197. Played at Northwestern, 1968-70. Set 11 Northwestern and six Big 10 records. Established conference mark for yds. rushing, season, with 1053 in senior year. Played in

11

College All-Star game, 1971. Kansas City Chiefs, 1971-72; New York Jets, 1973. Drafted originally on 5th round by Chiefs. Gained 303 yds. rushing, 185 on kickoff returns in 1972. Traded to Jets for Gerry Philbin. Son of Tony Adamle, who played linebacker for Cleveland Browns.

ADAMS, ANTHONY L. (Touchdown Tony) Quarterback. B. 3/19/50, San Antonio, Tex. 6', 198. Attended Ramona H.S. in Riverside, Calif., and Utah State. In 1970-72 collegiate career, Adams completed 456 of 867 passes for 6228 yds., 52 TDs. Total offense was 6587 yds. Passed for 561 yds. vs. Utah State, 11-11/72, setting NCAA one-game record. Responsible for 62 career TDs. Majored in political science. Drafted No. 14 by San Diego Chargers, 1973.

ADAMS, PETE Tackle. B. 5/4/51, San Diego, Calif. 6'4", 260. All-America at Southern California, 1972. Trojans were 11-0, won national championship. In Rose Bowl they crunched Ohio State, 42-17. Popular among teammates. His dog, Cosmo, attended all practice sessions and home games. One of two 1st-round draft choices of Cleveland Browns in 1973, other being Steve Holden. USC coach John McKay wished pupil well and commented, "If Pete can't play for the Browns, they must have some football team." Capable at offensive tackle and guard.

ADDERLEY, HERBERT A. Defensive Back. B. 6/8/39, Philadelphia, Pa. 6', 205. Attended high school in Philadelphia. Graduated from Michigan State in 1961. No. 1 draft pick of Green Bay Packers same year. On 10/31/66, vs. Philadelphia Eagles, recorded 6th TD by interception in one year. Thus, broke own record thrice in same season. Record had been three. In 1967 Super Bowl made 60-yd. TD run after intercepting pass by Daryl Lamonica. In 1970 traded to Dallas Cowboys, though Adderley had previously announced retirement. On 7/3/73 traded to Los Angeles Rams. Released by L.A., 8/7/73, in contract dispute. Pro Bowl, 1964, 65, 66, 67, 68. NFL championship games, 1961, 62, 65, 66, 67. Only man to play in four Super Bowl games, in 1966, 67, with Green Bay and in 1971, 72, with Dallas.

AGAJANIAN, BENJAMIN (Automatic) Kicker. B. 1919, Long Beach, Calif. 6', 215. Graduated from New Mexico, 1945. One of only two men to play in AAFC, NFL, AFL. Broke in with Pittsburgh Steelers, 1945. Before season ended became Philadelphia Eagle. Inactive in 1946. Joined Los Angeles Dons of All America Conference in 1947. Led AAFC in FGs that year with record 15. Joined New York Giants, 1949, playing one season. In 1953 played for Los Angeles Rams, then traded to Giants. Played thru 1957 in N.Y. In 1956 title game kicked five PATs and two FGs. Came out of retirement in 1960, becoming kicker for Los Angeles Chargers. Kicked 38- and 22-yd. FGs to give Chargers 6-0 lead in 1st quarter of first AFL championship game. Added another for 27 yds. in 2nd quarter, kicked 3 PATs. Dealt to Dallas Texans, 1961. Released, signed with Green Bay Packers. Oakland Raiders, 1962; San Diego Chargers, 1964. Son, Larry, picked by Green Bay on 7th round of 1969 draft.

AGANNIS, HARRY (Greek) Quarterback. B. 4/20/30, Lynn, Mass. D. 6/27/55, Boston, Mass. Fatal illness struck down Harry Agannis in prime of brilliant athletic career. Famous for baseball and football. Boston U., 1949, 51-52. Was southpaw quarterback. Threw 15 TD passes in 1949, then joined marines. Played at Camp Lejeune, N.C. Received dependency discharge in 1951 to support his mother. Returned that year to B.U. In final two seasons completed 226 of 418 passes for 2930 yds., 34 TDs. Also averaged better than 40 yds. as punter. Received 1951 Bulger Lowe Award, signifying New England's outstanding player. Still holds 15 B.U. records. Played 59 minutes and tossed two TD strikes, winning Senior Bowl MVP honors in 1952. Signed with baseball's Boston Red Sox, 1953, for $60,000 bonus. Had been No. 1 draft choice of NFL Cleveland Browns. Batted .261 (157 games) as Red Sox first baseman, 1954. Was hitting .313 when stricken with viral pneumonia in mid-May, 1955. Thought to be recovering, he suffered relapse and died of pulmonary embolism before ever returning to uniform. Over 30,000 New Englanders filed past altar to pay final respects to "Golden Greek." National Football Foundation Hall of Fame.

AGASE, ALEXANDER Guard. B. 1922, Evanston, Ill. 5'10", 195. One of few players to win Consensus All-America honors at two schools: Purdue in 1943, Illinois in 1946. Began collegiate career at Illinois. Won All-America mention there, 1942. USMC then transferred him to Purdue for military schooling. Served in Pacific theater during World War II, then returned to Illinois. Standout in 1947 Rose Bowl. MVP in Big 10, 1946. Los Angeles Dons (AAFC), 1947; Chicago Rockets (AAFC), 1947; Cleveland Browns (AAFC), 1948-49; Browns, 1950-51; Baltimore Colts, 1953. Named head coach at Northwestern in 1964, succeeding Ara Parseghian whom he had served eight years as assistant. Coached Wildcats thru 1972; record of 32-58-1. National Football Foundation Hall of Fame.

ALBERT, FRANK C. (Frankie) Quarterback. B. 1/27/20, Chicago, Ill. 5'9", 175. Played for Stanford, 1939-41. Consensus All-America, 1940,41. Citizens Savings Player of the Year, 1940. Under Clark Shaughnessy switched from unimpressive single-wing tailback, to fine T-formation QB. Southpaw. Superb ball-handler, passer and kicker; "a magician with the ball," according to Shaughnessy. George Byrnes, football scout, stated Albert was best faker and ball-handler he had ever seen. In 1941 Rose Bowl threw 41-yd. TD pass and kicked 3 PATs as Stanford beat Nebraska, 21-13. Finished collegiate career 9th in passing yds. (1795), tied for 6th in TD passes (15), 10th in TDS-accounted-for (24), 4th in interceptions (37). Served in Navy during World War II. Played QB for San Francisco 49ers, 1946-52. Runnerup to Otto Graham in all-time AAFC passing with 6948 yds., completing 515 of 963 passes, percentage of 53.5, 88 TDs. Retired as player in 1953, and succeeded by Y.A. Tittle as QB. Head coach of 49ers, 1956-58 (19-16-1). Citizens Savings Hall of Fame, National Football Foundation Hall of Fame.

ALCOTT, CLARENCE R. End. D. 10/23/57, East Hampton, N.Y. 5'9", 175. Yale All-America, 1907. On receiving end of long forward passes that decided 12-

0 victory over Harvard, 1907. On third down, 12 yds. to go, he leaped high in air, grabbed ball and was downed on Harvard's 4 for gain of 21 yds. Yale then punched across score. Played in famous 1907 come-from-behind victory over Princton, assisting Tad Jones and Ted Coy in drive by nabbing two passes from Jones. Part of Veeder-to-Alcott, one of earliest pass combos. Yale end coach under Tad Jones, 1916.

ALDERMAN, GRADY C. Tackle. B. 12/10/38, Detroit, Mich. 6'2", 240. Played at U. of Detroit, 1957-59. Drafted on 10th round by Detroit Lions, hometown team, 1960. In 1961 went to Minnesota Vikings in expansion draft. Is now last original Viking. Serves on kickoff return squad in addition to regular offensive tackle duties. Smart, tough on pass protection. Makes up in wisdom what he lacks in speed. Played in NFL championship game, 1969. Super Bowl, 1970, 74. Pro Bowl, 1965, 66, 67, 68, 69. Is certified public accountant.

ALDRICH, CHARLES C. (Ki) Center. B. Temple, Tex. 5'11", 215. Texas Christian, 1936-38. Consensus All-America, 1938. Best center in TCU history. Greatest game was 1939 Sugar Bowl, TCU winning over Carnegie Tech, 15-7. Called one of the greatest by his coach, Dutch Meyer. Also included in Meyer's list of three best pupils, others being Sammy Baugh and Davey O'Brien. 1936 teammate of Baugh, with whom he later played at Washington (Redskins). Houston newspaperman called him greatest linebacker Southwest Conference had ever known. Drafted on 1st round by Chicago Cardinals, 1939. With Cards, 1939-40; Washington, 1941-42, 45-47. Citizens Savings Hall of Fame, National Football Foundation Hall of Fame.

ALDRIDGE, LIONEL Defensive End. B. 2/14/41, Evergreen, La. 6'4", 245. Played for Utah State, 1960-62. Co-captain and All-Skyline tackle, 1962. Drafted by Green Bay Packers on 4th round in 1963. Packers were NFL champions, 1965, 66, 67. Did not miss single game during first three pro seasons, nor in five seasons, 1968-72. In 1972 traded to San Diego Chargers for tackle Jim Hill. Brought to San Diego by former Packer coach, Phil Bengston, now assisting at New England. Super Bowl, 1967, 68. Master of defensive end craft. In off-season is Milwaukee sportscaster.

ALEXANDER, JOSEPH A. Guard. B. 4/1/98, Silver Creek, N.Y. 6', 210. Syracuse, 1917-20. All-America, 1918, 19; 2nd team, 1920. Described by Walter Camp as "one of the greatest defensive guards ever seen on the gridiron." During years that Alexander starred, Syracuse record was 19-6-1 and opponents were scoreless in 13 games. In 14-0 victory over Colgate made 11 consecutive tackles. In 1920 game vs. Dartmouth (Big Green's first loss in 16 games), made tackle on initial three downs and intercepted pass on fourth, returning it past midfield. Syracuse won, 10-0. Rochester Jeffersons, 1921-22; Milwaukee Badgers, 1922; New York Giants, 1925-27. Coach for Giants, 1926. Later physician in New York City. Citizens Savings Hall of Fame, National Football Foundation Hall of Fame.

14

ALEXANDER, KERMIT J. Defensive Back. B. 1/4/41, New Iberia, La. 5'11", 187. UCLA All-America and MVP, 1962. Played both offensive and defensive back. 1st-round draft pick of San Francisco 49ers, 1963. Returned 32 kickoffs for 741 yds., 1965. Returned one punt for TD, 1966, NFL leader that year. Runnerup in interceptions with nine, 1968. At San Francisco in seven seasons, 1963-69, had 36 interceptions for 499 yds., 49er career records. In 1970 traded to Los Angeles Rams. Rams switched him from cornerback to safety. Also used on punt and kickoff returns. Made 82-yd. TD run with interception against Redskins, 1971. Philadelphia Eagles, 1972-73. Has 43 career interceptions. Pro Bowl, 1969. Was vice president of NFL Players Association. Looking to law career.

ALEXANDER, WILLIAM A. Coach. B. 6/6/1889, Mud River, Ky. D. 4/23/50, Atlanta, Ga. Graduated from Georgia Tech, 1912. Assistant coach at Tech under John Heisman, 1912-1920. In 1920 succeeded Heisman. Remained until 1944, except for part of 1942 season when he quit due to heart ailment. Established series with Notre Dame, 1922, which gained permanence. 1928 was best year as Tech defeated every opponent. Defeated California 8-7 in Rose Bowl, 1/1/29, one of most famous games in history; it featured Roy Riegels' wrong-way run. First coach to send teams to all four major bowl games: Rose Bowl, 1929; Orange Bowl, 1940 (defeated Missouri, 21-7); Cotton Bowl, 1943 (lost to Texas, 14-7); Sugar Bowl, 1944 (defeated Tulsa, 20-13). Resigned in 1944 and became athletic director, head of physical education dept. Record: 131-93-15. In all, spent 44 years at Tech: six as player, eight as assistant coach and math professor, 25 as head coach, five as athletic director. Coach of the Year, 1942. Amos Alonzo Stagg Award, 1946. Touchdown Club of New York Award, 1948. Many years member of Rules Committee. Citizens Savings Hall of Fame, National Football Foundation Hall of Fame.

ALLEN, CHARLES R. (Chuck) Linebacker. B. 9/7/39, Cle Elum, Wash. 6'1", 225. Played at Washington, 1958-60. San Diego Chargers, 1961-69; Pittsburgh Steelers, 1970-71; Philadelphia Eagles, 1972-73. Was drafted No. 28 by Chargers in 1961. Intercepted 28 passes for 352 yds., 1 TD in 12 pro seasons. Intercepted five rookie season. AFL All-Star game, 1963, 64. Played in AFL championship games, 1963, 64, 65.

ALLEN, GEORGE H. Coach. B. 4/29/22, Detroit, Mich. Played end at Alma and Marquette. At Michigan played baseball and was on wrestling team. Graduated from Michigan in 1947, received M.A. degree from Stanford, 1948. Also did graduate work on doctorate at Southern California. Assistant coach at Ann Arbor (Mich.) H.S., 1947. Head coach at Morningside College, 1948-51. Head coach, Whittier College (alma mater of President Richard Nixon), 1952-56. In 1957 assisted Los Angeles Rams. Defensive coach of Chicago Bears, 1958-65. In 1963 received game ball after Bears' title-game victory over New York Giants. In 1965-66, after decision to join Rams as head coach, involved in litigation brought by George Halas and Bears. Won suit in 1966 and became head coach of Rams. Won 1967, 69 divisional titles. In 1965 Los Angeles had 4-10 record, but Allen jumped mark to 8-6 in 1966 with basically same personnel. Fired by Rams, 1970, but rehired on demand of players.

In 1971 became head coach of Washington Redskins and established motto, "The future is now." Also general manager. Swung 19 trades, 1971, involving 24 draft picks, 33 players, 8 of them Rams. Author of six books. Had 9-4-1 record, 1971, to finish 2nd in division. Coach of the Year, 1971. Was visited in clubhouse by Pres. Nixon, 11/71. Guided team to NFC title, 1972, and into Super Bowl. Has had eight consecutive winning seasons, making him winningest active NFL coach. Record: 79-28-5. In 1973 hired Dick Myers as assistant general manager, who in previous capacity as NFL player personnel coordinator, caught Allen twice for trading already traded draft picks.

ALWORTH, LANCE D. (Bambi) End. B. 8/3/40, Houston, Tex. 6', 184. Extremely swift, efficient receiver. Arkansas, 1960-62. In 1960, 61 led NCAA in punt returns. Drafted on 2nd round by Oakland Raiders in 1962. Offered baseball contract by New York Yankees and Pittsburgh Pirates. Traded by Raiders to San Diego Chargers. Played with Chargers, 1962-70. Set several AFL records, including consecutive games scoring TDs (9); seasons leading league in TDs (3); consecutive games, one or more pass receptions (96), breaking Don Hutson's record of 95; games making TD reception (9). Also tied two AFL records: game TD receptions (4), game receptions (13). In 1963 returned 10 kickoffs for 216 yds., 21.6 average. Leading AFL pass receiver, 1968, 69. Only player in league history to gain more than 1000 yds. receiving seven consecutive seasons. In 1963 gained 1205 yds. on 61 receptions, leading league with average of 19.8 and 11 TDs. Averaged 20.2 yds. per catch, 1964, and made 13 TD catches. In 1965 gained 1602 yds., average of 23.2 yds. and 14 TDs.

Played with two broken hands in 1966, but didn't miss game until suffered hamstring injury late in season. Caught 73 passes that year for 1383 yds. and scored 13 TDs. Led AFL pass receivers in each category. In 1967 made 52 receptions for 1010 yds. and nine TDs. Led league with 68 receptions for 1312 yds. and 10 TDs, 1968. In 1969 led AFL with 64 receptions for 1003 yds. and 4 TDs. Ranks 4th among all-time receivers. In 11 years had 542 receptions for 10,266 yds., average of 18.9, and scored 85 TDs. On 5/19/71 traded to Dallas Cowboys for wide receiver Pettis Norman, tackle Tony Liscio, defensive tackle Ron East. Chargers retired uniform number (19). Played in seven AFL All-Star games. Played in AFL championship games, 1963, 65. Played in Super Bowl following 1971 season (scored one TD). All-AFL flanker, 1963, 69. Announced retirement, 7/2/73. Named to All-Time AFL team.

AMECHE, ALAN D. (The Horse) Running Back. B. 6/1/33, Kenosha, Wisc. 6'1", 217. Played for Wisconsin, 1951-54. Starter in freshman year. Unanimous All-America, 1954; All-America, 1953, MVP in Big 10, 1954. Heisman Trophy, 1954. Academic All-America, 1953, 54. Gained 3212 yds. rushing on 673 carries, scored 25 TDs over 4 seasons (37 games). Net gain of 2463 yds. rushing and 20 TDs in 25 games of Big 10 competition. Played in Rose Bowl, 1953. Baltimore Colts, 1955-60. Led NFL rushers with 961 yds., 1955. In first three years with Colts gained 2313 yds. In 1958 NFL championship vs. New York Giants, regarded by many as football's greatest game, scored two TDs, including winner in pro's first-ever overtime period. Rookie of the Year, 1955. All-Pro, 1955. Pro Bowl, 1956, 57, 58, 59. Once wrote magazine article, "College Football Is for Boys."

AMES, KNOWLTON L. (Snake) Running Back. B. 1868, Chicago, Ill. D. 12/23/31, Chicago, Ill. Princeton fullback, 1886-89. All-America, 1889. Clever at spinning, changing direction, faking. Against Yale, 1889, used fake kick to great advantage; was pioneer in this field. High point of career was 1889 game vs. Harvard — he caught punt, then made great broken-field run for 70 yds. and TD. Caught punt behind crossbar, ran to 20 before he slipped and fell. Arthur Cumnock, Harvard captain, promptly leaped at Ames but Snake shook him off, regained footing and sprinted on to 5-yd. line. There, he again lost balance but went ahead to score. On next punt return put Princeton in TD position. Evasive runner, could not be tackled around legs; "Go for his neck" was opponents' cry. Great spiral punter. Holds record for most points scored in career with 730. Scored 62 TDs (4 points each), kicked 176 PATs (2 points each) and 26 FGs (5 points each). In final three years scored 645 points, consisting of 46 TDs, 168 PATs and 25 FGs. Coached Purdue to 12 straight wins, 1891-92. National Football Foundation Hall of Fame.

ANDERSON, BILLY GUY Quarterback. B. 2/17/41, Palme, Tex. 6'½", 195. Graduated from U. of Tulsa, 1966. Had spectacular senior season, 1965. Was NCAA total-offensive leader, involved in record 580 plays in 10 games; gained record 3343 yds.; and record yds. per game, season, with 334.3. Also 1965 passing leader with 509 attempts (record) with 296 completions (record) and 14 interceptions, totaled 3465 yds. (record). Was responsible for 35 TDs. Holds record for passes completed per game, season, with 29.6. Holds record for passes completed, game, with 42 in 65 attempts, for 477 yds., 10/30/65 vs. Southern Illinois. Shares record for consecutive passes completed, game, 11/25/65, vs. Colorado State, with 15. Compiled 502 total offense yds. in that game. On 10/9/65 vs. Memphis State completed 39 of 65 passes for 477 yds. Selected as future by Los Angeles Rams on 19th round of 1965 NFL draft. On Los Angeles taxi squad, 1966, 68. Houston Oilers, 1967. Played in AFL championship game, 1967.

ANDERSON, DON (Donny) Running Back. B. 5/16/43, Borger, Texas. 6'3", 210. Attended Texas Tech. Consensus All-America, 1965; All-America, 1964. Leading collegiate runner in 1964, gaining 1710 yds. in 10 games (966 rushing, 320 on kickoff returns, 424 other). Drafted on 1st round as future by Green Bay Packers, 1965; reported to them, 1966. Played in NFL title games and Super Bowl games, 1966, 67. In 1967 Super Bowl scored 1 TD, on 5-yd. rush, 4 FGs and 3 PATs. Played with Pack thru 1971. In 1972 traded to St. Louis Cardinals for running back McArthur Lane. Returned punts and kickoffs first two years for Green Bay. Led Packer rushers twice. Runnerup in TD scoring in 1973 with 13 (10 rushing, 3 passing). Rushed for 679 yds. that year, added 409 on 41 pass receptions. Talented, versatile player. Scored 50 TDs during eight seasons as pro. Pro Bowl, 1969.

ANDERSON, EDWARD N. (Eddie) Coach. B. 11/13/00, Oskaloosa, Iowa. 5'10", 149. Played under Knute Rockne at Notre Dame, 1918-21. Captain in 1921. Fine end. Played for 1922 Rochester Jeffersons, 1922 Chicago Cardinals, 1923 Chicago Bears, 1926 Chicago Bulls. Coached Loras to record of 16-6-2, 1922-25. De Paul coach, 1926-32 (21-22-4). Received medical degree from Rush Medical College while serving as De Paul coach and playing for Bulls. In 1933-38 coached at Holy Cross, compiling record of 47-7-4. 1935 record was 9-0-1, 1937 team also undefeated (8-0-2). Iowa head coach, 1939-43. Led one of finest clubs in Iowa history, 1939, and was named Coach of the Year. Took over team which had 22-50 nine-year record and only five Big 10 victories. Among members of 1939 "Iron Men" were Nile Kinnick, Erwin Prasse, Mike Enich. Ironically, in 1939, Anderson defeated alma mater, previously unbeaten Notre Dame, first time teams had met since own playing days. Most satisfaction gained from 1938 Holy Cross and '39 Iowa squads. In 1939 barely missed Sugar Bowl.

Maj., U.S. Army Medical Corps, 1943-45. Returned to Iowa for 1946-49 stint; had 16-19-1 record, making 35-33-2 overall with Hawkeyes. Resigned in 1950, and returned to Holy Cross to revive sagging club. Stayed at Holy Cross thru 1964 and had 15-year record of 82-60-4, giving him 129-67-8 overall there. Winner of 201 games, one of only six coaches ever to win 200 or more games. He lost 128, tied 15 for .606 percentage. Used much from Rockne in coaching system. Never abandoned medical practice during Holy Cross-Iowa years; takes satisfaction from fact that many of his players became doctors, dentists, lawyers. Cited influence of Rockne in staying in medical school. One of his friends, player he cut at Loras, was actor Don Ameche. Citizens Savings Hall of Fame, National Football Foundation Hall of Fame.

ANDERSON, HEARTLEY (Hunk) Coach. B. Tamrack, Mich. Notre Dame guard, 1919-21. Teammate of George Gipp, on Rockne's unbeaten 1919, 20 teams. Is reported to have told students at 1921 pep rally: "You do the best you can and I'll do the best *we* can," which became part of Notre Dame tradition. Played for Chicago Bears and served as a line coach, 1922-25. Assistant coach for Notre Dame's "Four Horsemen" team, 1924. When Rockne went to see Army-Navy game in Chicago, he left Hunk to coach Notre Dame; result was dramatic upset victory by Carnegie Tech, 19-0. This was considered great boner by Rockne. Anderson served as N.D. head coach, 1931-33, succeeding Rockne after death in plane crash 3/31/31. Three-year record: 16-9-2. Co-coach, Chicago Bears, 1942-45. Considered by Grantland Rice one of best line coaches. Combined coaching with profession in engineering. Now in steel business, still called upon by Irish coaches for advice.

ANDERSON, KENNETH A. Quarterback. B. 2/15/49, Batavia, Ill. 6'2", 210. Attended Augustana College. Selected by Cincinnati Bengals on 3rd round of 1971 draft. Completed 171 of 301 passes and had lowest interception total, with seven, in NFL, 1972. On 12/16/73, vs. Houston Oilers, Anderson passed for three TDs, two to Isaac Curtis, for 77 yds. and 67 yds., and other to Bob Trumpy for 10 yds. In 1973 was 3rd in AFC passing efficiency with 81.5, broke five club records: 2523 yds. total offense, 2428 yds. passing, 18 TD passes, 186 completions, 329 attempts. His longest pass was 78 yds., 12 were intercepted. Holds degree in mathematics.

ANDERSON, RICHARD Defensive Back. B. 2/10/46, Midland, Mich. 6'2", 200. Played for Colorado, 1965-67. Consensus All-America, 1967. Miami Dolphins, 1968-73. In six years had 32 interceptions for 757 yds. and 3 TDs. On 37 punt returns gained 291 yds. In '71 AFC title game ran 62 yds. for TD. On 12/3/73, vs. Pittsburgh Steelers, set club record of four interceptions, including two for TDs and another for 31 yds. that set up TD. Was 1973 NFL co-interception leader with 8, for 163 yds., 2 TDs. All-AFC, 1973. Played in AFC championship games, 1971, 72, 73. Super Bowl, 1972, 73, 74. Enjoys snow skiing, golf, tennis. President of Pro Financial Services.

ANDERSON, ROBERT C. (Bobby) Running Back. B. 10/11/47, Midland, Mich. 6', 208. Attended Boulder (Colo.) H.S., then U. of Colorado in 1967-69. Consensus All-America, 1969. Shifted from QB to halfback as senior. Rolled up 4564 yds. in three years and finished 20th in total offense yds. Longest play was 69-yd. rush vs. Iowa State in 1969. Scored two TDs in Astro-Bluebonnet Bowl in 1967, rushed for 108 yds., completed 5 passes. In Liberty Bowl, 1969, rushed for game record of 254 yds., scored 3 TDs. Selected by Denver Broncos on 1st round of 1970 NFL draft. Broncos, 1970-73. Active in Fellowship of Christian Athletes.

ANDERSON, ROBERT P. Running Back. B. 3/31/38, Cocoa, Fla. 6'2", 198. Won 15 letters at Cocoa (Fla.) H.S. Army, 1957-59. Consensus All-America, 1957. That year rushed for 963 yds. to break Glenn Davis' West Point record. Ranked 2nd nationally with 14 TDs. Could run, pass, placekick, tackle, defend. In 1958 overshadowed by backfield mate Pete Dawkins, who won Heisman Trophy. Resigned army as 1st Lt., 1963.

ANDERSON, WALTER W. End. B. 7/16/36, Hendersonville, N.C. 6'4", 225. Graduated from Tennessee, 1958. Sugar Bowl and Gator Bowl, 1957. Selected by Washington Redskins on 3rd round of 1958 draft. Played with 'Skins thru 1964. Traded to Green Bay Packers, 1965. Retired after 1966 season. In eight-year pro career played in 98 games, caught 178 passes for 3048 yds., averaged 17.1 yds. per catch, scored 15 TDs. Pro Bowl, 1960, 61. NFL championship games, 1965, 66. Super Bowl, 1967.

ANDRIE, GEORGE J. Defensive End. B. 4/20/40, Grand Rapids, Mich. 6'7", 255. Marquette, 1959-60. Marquette dropped football after his junior season. Dallas Cowboys, 1962-72. In 1964, vs. Cleveland Browns, Andrie roughed up Frank Ryan, and then Jim Brown attacked Andrie. Before scrap was over, fans had spilled onto field and police intervened to prevent riot. Scored TD on fumble recovery, 1964. Made interception for 6-yd. TD, 1965. Pro Bowl, 1966, 67, 68, 69, 70. NFL championship games, 1966, 67, 70, 71, 72. Super Bowl, 1972, 73. Strong tackler. Fine golfer — he and Ron Santo of Chicago Cubs teamed to win Astrojet Golf Classic at Phoenix, 1970.

ANDRUS, HAMLIN F. Guard. B. 3/30/1886, Yonkers, N.Y. D. 7/9/57, Greenwich, Conn. 6'1", 208. Yale All-America, 1909; 2nd team, 1908. Starred in 1909 "Battle of the Lines" vs. Harvard. 1909 team produced six All-Americas, Cooney, Hobbs, Kilpatrick, Philbin, Coy, Andrus, four of whom were linemen. Andrus was strong blocker.

ANTWINE, HOUSTON (Twine) Tackle. B. 4/11/39, Louise, Miss. 6', 270. Attended Southern Illinois. NAIA heavyweight wrestling champion. Played in 1961 College All-Star game, then signed as free agent by Boston Patriots. All-AFL, 1963, 66. Selected to AFL All-Star game, 1963, 64, 65, 66, 67, 68. Played AFL title game, 1963. Strong tackler, fierce player. Played for Boston, 1961-70; New England Patriots, 1971; Philadelphia Eagles, 1972. Traded by Patriots to Eagles for linebacker Bill Hobbs. Attended same college that produced QB Jim Hart, basketball star Walt Frazier. Cited by President Nixon for his work against drug abuse.

APPLETON, G. SCOTT Tackle. B. 2/20/42, Brady, Tex. 6'3", 260. Texas, 1961-63. Unanimous All-America, 1963. Outland Trophy, 1963. Great tackler. With linemen Pat Culpepper and Johnny Treadwell sparked Texas to unbeaten season in 1962 (9-0-1), perfect season in 1963 (10-0-0). Helped Darrell Royal win Coach of the Year award in 1961 and 1963. Played in Cotton Bowl, 1963 (lost to LSU, 13-0); and 1964 (beat Navy, 28-6). Drafted by Houston Oilers on 1st round, 1964. Played with Oilers thru 1966. Had two interceptions for 11 yds., 1963. Traded with linebacker John Baker, to San Diego Chargers for defensive back Miller Farr, 1967. Retired after 1968 season to devote full-time to ranching.

ARBANAS, FREDERICK V. (Fritz) Tight End. B. 1/14/39, Detroit, Mich. 6'3", 243. Played 1958-60 at Michigan State. Drafted on 7th round by Dallas Texans in 1961, but suffered back injury and couldn't play. Texans, 1962; Kansas City Chiefs, 1963-70. Strong blocker and pass receiver. Played in AFL championship games, 1962, 66, 69. 1962 game was longest ever, until K.C. - Miami Dolphin contest in 1972. AFL All-Star games, 1963, 66, 68. Selected for 1964 and '65 teams but didn't play. All-AFL, 1963, 64, 66. In 1967 Super Bowl scored one TD on pass from Len Dawson. Also 1970 Super Bowl. Continued to play despite losing vision in one eye in 1966 when struck by assailant on Kansas City street. Now, Kansas City advertising executive and city councilman.

ARMSTRONG, IKE J. Coach. B. 6/8/95, Seymour, Iowa. Coach at Utah, 1925-49. In high school made varsity football team in eighth grade. Fullback at Drake, 1920-22. Played against Cornell, Washington, other powers. 1921 team was undefeated, won conference title. As coach led unbeaten teams in 1926, 28, 29, 30, 41. Sun Bowl, 1938; Pineapple Bowl, 1946. Shared conference titles, 1938, 40, 41; won title outright, 1947, 48. 1939 club won nine games, scored 258 points which led nation. Overall record: 140-55-15, .702 percentage. Was also basketball, track coach. Citizens Savings Hall of Fame, National Football Foundation Hall of Fame.

ARMSTRONG, NEIL End. B. 3/9/26, Tishomingo, Okla. 6'2½", 196. Played end for Oklahoma State, 1943-46. As freshman was collegiate pass-receiving champion with 39 catches for 317 yds. In 1946 made 52 receptions for 513 yds. and 8 TDs in 10 games. Philadelphia Eagles, 1947-51. Played in NFL title games, 1947, 48, 49. Later, assistant coach for Minnesota Vikings.

ARMSTRONG, OTIS Running Back. B. 11/15/50, Chicago, Ill. 5'11", 196. Played for Purdue, 1970-72. Consensus All-America, 1972. During 31-game career rushed for 3315 yds., scored 17 TDs. Averaged 106.9 yds. per game, 4.95 yds. per play. As senior carried ball 243 times for 1361 yds., 9 TDs. Holder of every Purdue rushing record and most Big 10 marks. In final collegiate game gained 276 yds. on 32 carries in mud vs. Indiana. Denver Broncos, 1973.

ARNETT, JON D. (Jaguar Jon) Running Back. B. 4/20/34, Los Angeles, Calif. 5'11", 203. Southern California halfback, 1954-56. One of best backs of 1955; scored 108 points, 2nd best in country. All-America that year. Scored one TD in 1955 Rose Bowl vs. Notre Dame. Los Angeles Rams, 1956-63; Chicago Bears, 1964-66. Drafted No. 1 by Rams in 1956. Uncommon broken-field runner. Gave lessons in gymnastic football, specializing in front- and back-flips. Almost always regained balance. During career rushed for 3833 yds. on 964 carries (4.0 average), scored 26 TDs. Greatest years with Rams. Returned kickoff 105 yds. for TD vs. Detroit Lions, 10/29/61. All-Pro, 1958. Pro Bowl, 1958, 59, 60, 61, 62.

ATKINS, DOUGLAS L. Defensive End. B. 5/8/30, Humboldt, Tenn. 6'8", 230. Graduated from Tennessee. Cleveland Browns, 1953-54; Chicago Bears, 1955-66; New Orleans Saints, 1967-69. Was 1st-round draft choice of Browns. With Bears ordered by George Halas to study films of Gino Marchetti. Often would say on way to film room, "Here I go. Another chapter of 'The Gino Marchetti Story.'" Scored safety in 1963. Three-time All-Pro. Pro Bowl, 1958, 59, 60, 61, 62, 63, 65. 1958 Lineman of the Game. In 1962 Pro Bowl switched positions with tackle Henry Jordan of Green Bay Packers, and was excellent. Gun collector. Played in title games, 1953, 54, 56, 63. Played in 205 NFL games.

ATKINSON, ALAN E. (Hombre) Linebacker. B. 7/28/43, Philadelphia, Pa. 6'2", 230. Villanova, 1962-64. All-America and All-East, 1964. Played in 1962 Liberty Bowl vs. Oregon State. Voted outstanding defensive lineman in Senior Bowl. Appeared in Coaches All-America game. 3rd-round draft choice of Buffalo Bills, 1965. Waived to New York Jets prior to season opener. Became starter in final two games of '65 season. Twice voted "most underrated" defensive player in AFL. In 1968 season played in AFL All-Star game, AFL championship game and Super Bowl III. Played in Super Bowl with separated shoulder. Defensive captain for Jets since 1969. Received nickname from teammate Jim Hudson, because of toughness. Hobbies are country music, collecting coins. In

1970 retired, stating he could "no longer play with Joe Namath." Came out of retirement shortly thereafter. Active member of Fellowship of Christian Athletes. Institutional broker in off-season.

ATKINSON, GEORGE HENRY (Butch) Defensive Back. B. 1/4/47, Savannah, Ga. 6', 182. Earned four football letters, three in track at Morris Brown College. Had best time of 9.6 in 100-yd. dash. Oakland Raiders, 1968-73. Was 7th-round draft choice. AFL defensive Rookie of the Year. Set all-time record with 205 yds. on punt returns against Buffalo Bills, 9/15/68. AFL leader in kickoff returns with 25.1-yd. average. Intercepted 20 passes in six seasons. Fine strong safety. AFL All-Star games, 1968, 69.

BABARTSKY, ALBERT J. (Ali Baba) Tackle. B. 4/19/1895, Shenandoah, Pa. 6', 225. Fordham, 1935-37. All America, 1937. One of "Seven Blocks of Granite" line that was not penetrated for one score in 1937. In spite of ankle injury and bad knee, still managed to make All-America. Teammate of Vince Lombardi. Played tackle for Chicago Cardinals, 1938-39, 41-42 and for Chicago Bears, 1943-45. Played on Western Conference championship team and in title game vs. Washington Redskins, 1943 (Bears won, 41-21).

BACH, JOSEPH Tackle. B. 1/17/01, Tower, Minn. D. 10/24/66. Played at Notre Dame. One of "Seven Mules" who blocked for "Four Horsemen." Other Mules were ends Chuck Collins and Ed Huntsinger, tackle Rip Miller, guards Noble Kizer and John Weibel, center Adam Walsh. Occasionally, Knute Rockne would replace his starting line with scrubs to test Horsemen's mettle. "See?" Rockne chided when backfield efficiency decreased. "Without the Mules, you Horsemen are just turtles." Bach coached Duquesne, 1934; Niagara, 1937-41; St. Bonaventure, 1950-51. Served two 2-year stints as Pittsburgh Steeler head coach, 1935-36, 52-53. Pro record was 21-27. He also was assistant pro coach seven years and pro scout.

BACHMAN, CHARLES W. (Charlie) Coach. B. 12/1/92, Chicago, Ill. At Notre Dame won letters as right guard, fullback, left guard. Was teammate of Knute Rockne and Gus Dorais. All-America 2nd team guard, 1916. As senior coached high school team. Youngstown Patricians, 1917. In 1918 played at Great

Lakes Naval Station where he was roommate of George Halas; next door was Paddy Driscoll, later his assistant at Northwestern. Assistant coach at DePauw, 1917. Coached Northwestern, 1919; Kansas State, 1920-27; Florida, 1928-32; Michigan State, 1933-42, 44-46; Hillsdale College, 1953. In 1919 stormed Michigan dressing room to accuse Fielding (Hurry Up) Yost of unethical practices. Yost threatened to throw him out. "Nobody will throw me out of here," Bachman retorted. "I came in on my own and I'll go out on my own." Then, he left. In 1922 lost Big 6 title by one game. 1928 loss to Tennessee deprived Florida of Rose Bowl appearance. Tennessee coach was Bob Neyland, Bachman foe while playing at Army. His 8-1-0 record in 1928 was best in first 65 Florida seasons. Developed Johnny Pingel, member of Michigan State's all-time backfield. Called Pingel "best quick-kicker I ever coached." At Michigan State beat Michigan four straight years, 1934-37. Lost Orange Bowl, 6-0, to Auburn 1937. Solid, sound instructor. Learned much from Chicago's Amos Alonzo Stagg, and Snake Ames. His .613 percentage (137-82-24) is higher than that of Stagg, Eddie Anderson, Bill Alexander, Dutch Meyer, Clark Shaughnessy, all Hall of Fame members. In 28 seasons, only six times lost more than won. Although never defeated, five times lost only one game. Pioneer of 6-2-2-1 defense. In food, real estate business when not coaching, until retirement.

BACON, CLARENCE E. Quarterback. B. 8/18/1890, Westbrook, Conn. 5'10", 155. Wesleyan (Conn.), 1909-12. Great runner, passer, kicker, defensive player. Led team to 16 wins, 9 losses and 2 ties. All-America 3rd team and *New York Sun* All-Eastern 1st team, 1912. Also selected to official All-New England squad. Pioneer of forward pass. Expert kicker of punts, dropkicks; fine punt receiver. Captained tennis team and pitched four years on varsity baseball team. Became prominent investment banker in New York City and trustee of Wesleyan, Atlanta U., Morehouse College, Spellman College, Bennett College. Citizens Savings Hall of Fame, National Football Foundation Hall of Fame.

BACON, LANDER M. (Coy) Tackle. B. 8/30/42, Cadiz, Ky. 6'4", 265. Graduated from Jackson State, not selected in NFL draft. Signed by Charleston of Continental Football League where he played, 1965-66. In 1967 signed as free agent with Dallas Cowboys and was member of taxi squad. In 1968 dealt to Los Angeles Rams for draft choice. Played with Rams thru 1972. Traded with running back Bob Thomas, to San Diego Chargers for QB John Hadl. Played in Pro Bowl, 1972, 73. Fine defensive player, capable of playing tackle or end. Hobbies are bowling and horseback riding.

BAGNELL, FRANCIS (Reds) Running Back. B. Philadelphia, Pa. 6'0", 178. Pennsylvania, 1948-50. All-America, 1950. At age 12 was Penn waterboy. Raised in shadow of Franklin Field. In 1949, vs. Navy, returned punt 74 yds. On 10/14/50, vs. Dartmouth, accounted for 490 yds., setting NCAA one-game record. Set NCAA record by completing 14 consecutive passes in one game, 1950. Finished collegiate career with 289 rushes for 904 yds; 147 pass completions in 300 attempts for 2018 yds., 13 interceptions, 18 TDs; made eight interceptions for 143 yds.; returned 18 punts for 228 yds.; returned eight kick-offs for 98 yds.; scored 13 TDs. Maxwell Trophy, 1950. Citizens Savings Player of the Year, 1950.

BAIRD, JOHN Running Back-Quarterback. D. 5/25/18, New York, N.Y. 5'9½", 163. Princeton All-America fullback, 1896; 3rd team QB, 1897. 1896 team undefeated, tied by Lafayette. Excellent dropkicker, fine broken-field runner. Also excellent punter. Against Yale ran 65 yds. for TD. Made FGs vs. Army and Cornell.

BAKER, EUGENE V. B. 12/21/1855, New York, N.Y. D. 9/42, Los Angeles, Calif. Yale, 1873-76. Captain in 1876. Played in game vs. English team, Eton Players, which converted him to idea of 11-man teams. In 1876, Yale defeated Harvard in first Rugby game played between two American colleges with 11 men per side. TDs did not count in scoring. Yale won by 1 goal to 0. Walter Camp played on this team as freshman. Same year attended meeting at Massasoit House at which Intercollegiate Football Association, forerunner of present Ivy League, was established. Also adopted modification of Rugby Union Code. Yale did not join association for three years as Baker disagreed with decision to have 15 men on team and to count TDs as score. He insisted on 11 men and scoring only kicked goals. Walter Camp wrote: "Eugene V. Baker was the man to whom Yale owes this innovation, and his efforts laid the foundation for his future remarkable record in this branch of sport."

BAKER, LORIS H. (Sam) Kicker. B. 11/12/29, San Francisco, Calif. 6'1", 210. Attended Oregon State. Drafted on 11th round by Los Angeles Rams as future in 1952. In 1953 traded to Washington Redskins for draft choice. Played for Skins, 1953, 56-59. Was NFL FG leader with 17, 1956. Tied with Lou Groza for NFL scoring championship with 77 points, 1957. 1958 NFL punting leader with 45.4-yd. average. In 1960 traded to Cleveland Browns for tackle Fran O'Brien and placekicker Bob Khayat. Stayed with Browns, 1960-61, then traded to Dallas Cowboys for defensive back Tom Franckhauser. Played for Dallas, 1962-63. Following '63 season traded to Philadelphia Eagles, with two other players, for wide receiver Tommy McDonald. Played with Philadelphia until retirement, 1970. At retirement was Eagles' all-time scorer, runnerup to Lou Groza as all-time NFL scorer with 898 points. Formerly held record for most punts, lifetime, with 703. Pro Bowl, 1957, 64, 65, 69.

BAKER, RALPH (Moon) Running Back. B. Rockford, Ill. 5'10", 172. Attended Northwestern. Consensus All-America, 1926. One of most famous Wildcat players. Northwestern put up game fight vs. Notre Dame that year, but finally lost by 13-6 score. 1926 yielded school's best season to that time; Wildcats shared Big 10 title with Michigan. Baker was one of greatest backs of year, triple-threat man.

BAKER, TERRY Quarterback. B. 5/5/41, Pine River, Minn. 6'3", 195. Notable scholar-athlete. Oregon State, 1960-62. Unanimous and Academic All-America,

1962. In '62 won Heisman Trophy, first Far West player so honored. Won Maxwell Trophy same year. Led NCAA in total offense with 2276 yds., 1962. Also led in passing with 112 completions in 203 attempts for 1738 yds. and 15 TDs. Also led NCAA in TDs-accounted-for with 24. Ended collegiate career with 233 pass completions in 454 attempts for 3476 yds. and 23 TDs; on 753 plays gained 4979 total-offense yds. and accounted for 39 TDs. Citizens Savings Player of the Year, 1962. Played in 1962 Liberty Bowl vs. Villanova, setting record with 99-yd. rush. Chosen 1st in entire 1963 NFL draft, by Los Angeles Rams. Played with Rams, 1963-65. Now practicing law in Portland.

BAKKEN, JAMES L. (Bak) Kicker. B. 11/2/40, Madison, Wis. 6', 200. Wisconsin, 1959-61. Drafted by Los Angeles Rams in 1962, released, signed by St. Louis Cardinals. NFL FG leader, 1964, with 25, and 1967 with 27. On 12/13/64 scored five FGs vs. Philadelphia Eagles. NFL scoring leader in 1967 with 27 FGs and 36 PATs, total of 117 points. On 9/24/67 set record of 7 FGs in one game (18, 24, 33, 29, 24, 32 and 23 yds.). In same game missed 2 FGs (50 and 45 yds.) to set record for FG attempts (9). Established record for consecutive games kicking FGs with 19, 1966, 67. Kicked five FGs vs. Atlanta Falcons, 1973. In '73 season kicked 31 of 31 PATs, 23 of 32 FGs for 100 points, bringing career point total to 1002. Pro Bowl, 1966, 68. With Cards, 1962-73. Past president of NFL Players Association.

BALDWIN, BURR End. B. Bakersfield, Calif. 6'1", 196. UCLA, 1944-46. Unanimous All-America, 1946. Co-captain of 10-1 team, 1946, which played in Rose Bowl. Fine receiver, blocker, defensive player. One of finest players in UCLA history. Los Angeles Dons (AAFC), 1947-49.

BALLIN, HAROLD R. Tackle. B. 10/16/1893, New York, N.Y. 6'1", 194. Princeton, 1912-14. All-America, 1913, 14. Played varsity football for three years, was captain as senior. Also participated in track and wrestling. Prepped at Lawrenceville School before enrolling at Princeton. Received degree in engineering, 1915. Served in Marine Corps, World War I. Princeton line coach for two years, at Lafayette one year before becoming field engineer in Pittsburgh. Then was head coach at Duquesne for two years. Later associated with U.S. Steel, and Pitomar Corp. before retirement in 1959. National Football Foundation Hall of Fame.

BALLMAN, GARY J. End. B. 7/6/40, Detroit, Mich. 6'1", 215. Michigan State, 1959-61. All-America honorable mention, 1961. All-Big 10, 1961. Hula Bowl, East-West Shrine games, 1961. Drafted on 8th round by Pittsburgh Steelers in 1962. In 1964 amassed 47 receptions, 935 yds., 7 TDs. In 1965, 17 rushes for 46 yds. and 3 TDs, 40 receptions for 859 yds. and 5 TDs. Traded to Philadelphia Eagles, 1967. Injured in 1967. Eagle MVP, 1970. Among top 10 active NFC receivers. Suffered knee injury in 1971, missed eight games. Traded to New York Giants, 1973. Great hands. Pro Bowl, 1964-65. In career had 66 kickoff returns for 26.6-yd. average.

BARBER, STEWART C. Tackle. B. 6/14/39, Bradford, Pa. 6'2", 250. Penn State, 1958-60. In 1961 drafted on 4th round by Buffalo Bills, playing with them thru 1969. Excellent blocker, also served on special teams. In 1961 three pass interceptions for 30 yds. AFL All-Star games, 1964, 65, 66, 67, 68. Played in AFL championship games, 1964, 65, 66. In 1974 joined New York Stars of WFL as offensive line coach.

BARNES, ERICH (E) Defensive Back. B. 7/4/35, Elkhart, Ind. 6'3", 212. Graduated from Purdue, 1958, and chosen on 4th round by Chicago Bears. Played with Bears thru 1960. Traded with QB Zeke Bratkowski, to Los Angeles Rams for QB Bill Wade, 1961; Rams then traded him to New York Giants with linebacker John Guzik, for defensive back Lindon Crow. On 10/22/61 tied NFL record for longest TD interception return, 102 yards, vs. Dallas Cowboys. In 1964 traded to Cleveland Browns for linebacker Mike Lucci and draft choice. Pro Bowl 1960, 62, 63, 64, 65, 69. Played in NFL championship games, 1961, 62, 63, 65, 68.

BARNES, STANLEY N. Tackle. B. Baraboo, Wis. 6'1", 186. Moved to San Diego as youngster. Played on 1916 national championship high school team. U. of California (Berkeley), 1918-21. All-Pacific Coast center, 1918. All-Coast tackle, 1920-21. 1920, 21 "Wonder Teams" unbeaten and went to Rose Bowl. President of his class. Went into legal profession after graduation and became lawyer, judge. President of Federal Bar Association, 1951-53. Has been judge in U.S. Court of Appeals, 9th Circuit Court, since 1956. Chairman of the Section of Judicial Administration of American Bar Association, 1967-68. Fellow of American College of Trial Lawyers of the American Bar Foundation and of American College of Forensic Science. Has served as superior court judge in Los Angeles and as assistant attorney general of U.S. National Football Foundation Hall of Fame.

BARNEY, LEMUEL J. (Lem; Stroll) Defensive Back. B. 9/8/45, Gulfport, Miss. 6', 190. Jackson State, 1964-66. Averaged 41.6 yds. as punter. Named All-Conference three times. Starred in 1966 Blue-Gray game. Drafted on 2nd round by Detroit Lions, 1967. At first training camp given only slim chance of making club. In first game intercepted Bart Starr pass for TD. As rookie tied existing NFL record for most TD pass interceptions, season, with three. Named NFL defensive Rookie of the Year, 1967. NFL co-leader in interceptions that season with 10, for 232 yds., longest 71 yds. In 1968, vs. Chicago Bears, made three interceptions. Averaged 26.8 yds. on kickoff returns and scored 2 TDs, one on 98-yd. run, 1968. Led league in TD interceptions with two, 1970. In seven seasons, 1967-73, made 38 interceptions for 774 yds. and 6 TDs; returned 107 punts for 804 yds. and 2 TDs; returned 49 kickoffs for 1246 yds. and 1 TD; scored 60 points. All-NFC cornerback, 1968, 69, 72. Pro Bowl, 1968, 69, 70, 73, 74.

BARNHILL, JOHN H. Coach. B. 2/21/03, Savannah, Tenn. D. 10/21/73, Fayetteville, Ark. Won nine letters at Tennessee, 1925-27. Played guard in football. Twice voted Tennessee's Athlete of the Year. In 1927 played in Los Angeles All-Star game, forerunner of East-West Shrine. Coached Tennessee, 1941-42, 44-45; Arkansas, 1946-49. 54-22-5 record, including four bowl games. 35-5-2 at Tennessee. Arkansas athletic director, 1946-71. In 1972 named to National Association of Collegiate Directors of Athletics Hall of Fame.

BASS, MICHAEL T. Defensive Back. B. 3/31/45, Ypsilanti, Mich. 6'0", 192. Michigan, 1964-66. Regular defensive back last two years. Member of 1965 Rose Bowl team, '67 College All-Star squad. Detroit Lions, 1967-68; Washington Redskins, 1969-73. Drafted originally on 12th round by Green Bay Packers. Spent most of two years with Lions as free agent. Signed by Redskins on taxi squad. Became starting right cornerback in training camp, 1969, and has remained there. In 1971 intercepted eight passes, 3rd best in NFL and best for Redskins since 1964. Scored Washington's only TD in Super Bowl VII, when he grabbed desperation pass by Garo Yepremian and ran 49 yds. to score. His father, Thomas, is M.D., was track star at Lincoln U. (Mo.). Mike is investment consultant in off-season.

BASS, RICHARD L. Running Back. B. 4/15/37, George, Miss. 5'10", 200. Played for U. of Pacific, 1956, 58, 59. All-America, 1958. Same year led NCAA in scoring (116 points), rushing (1361 yds. on 205 tries), average yds. rushing (6.6), total offense (1440 yds. on 218 plays). Scoring, rushing, total offense titles gave him collegiate "triple crown." Also gained 164 yds. on punt returns, 227 yds. on kickoff returns, for all-purpose running total of 1878 yds. in 10 games. In 1959 drafted by Los Angeles Rams on 1st round as "future", marking first time future was ever drafted on 1st round. As rookie with L.A., 1960, gained 604 yds., second on club to Jon Arnett. Averaged 6.4 yds. per carry which led team. Also led team in kickoff returns with 11 for 246 yds. In 1961 led league in average yds. on kickoff returns with 30.3 (698 yds. on 23 kickoffs). Became first Ram to break 1000 yds. in season as he gained 1033 yds. rushing, 1962. Played with Rams thru 1969. In 10 seasons gained 5417 yds. rushing, becoming 6th runner to gain over 5000 yds. in career. Also gained 1841 yds. on pass receptions, 263 on punt returns, 1415 on kickoff returns, scored 252 points. Now TV sportscaster. His brother Norm pitched for Kansas City Athletics. Pro Bowl, 1963, 64, 67.

BASTON, ALBERT P. (Bert) End. B. 12/3/1894, St. Louis Park, Minn. 6'1", 170. Minnesota, 1914-16. All-America, 1915, 16. First Minnesota player to make All-America team two consecutive years. Favorite receiver of Arnold Wyman, famous as part of Wyman-to-Baston aerial circus. Spearheaded Dr. Henry Williams' 1916 "perfect team", which was upset 14-9 by Coach Bob Zuppke's more-than-40-point-underdog Illinois squad. After graduation became auto dealer, first in Minneapolis, later in St. Cloud, Minn. Assistant to Bernie Bierman at Minnesota, 1932-50. National Football Foundation Hall of Fame.

BATEMAN, MARV Kicker. B. 4/5/50, Salt Lake City, Utah. 6'4", 213. Utah, 1969-71. All-America punter, 1971. 1970 college punting leader with 45.7-yd. average. Also college punting leader in 1971 with 48.1-yd. average, NCAA record for minimum 50 punts. In 1971, vs. Utah State, kicked 59-yd. FG. Holds NCAA record for career punting with 46.9-yd. average. Selected by Dallas Cowboys on 3rd round of 1972 NFL draft. In rookie year, 51 punts, average of 38.2 yds. in 14 games. That performance was disappointing after collegiate success. Averaged 41.6 yds. in 1973, drilling 55 punts for 2190 yds.

BATTLE, MICHAEL L. Defensive Back. B. 7/9/46, Southgate, Calif. 6'1", 180. Played collegiate football at Southern California, 1966-68. 1967 NCAA punt-return leader with 570 yds., 47 returns for 12.1-yd. average. Played in 1969 Rose Bowl game. Excellent defensive back. New York Jets, 1969-70. Showed great promise but injuries, lack of size shortened career. Gutsy player.

BATTLES, CLIFFORD Running Back. B. 5/1/10, Akron, Ohio. 6'1", 195. West Virginia Wesleyan, 1929-31. All-America halfback, 1931. Rhodes Scholarship candidate. Fast starter, excellent speed. Made at least 14 TDs on runs of 50 yds. or more. In 1930 made three TDs on dashes of 90, 96 and 98 yds. In 1932, signed with Boston Braves, whom he chose over Portsmouth Spartans and New York Giants because team sent representatives and George P. Marshall, Boston owner, was from West Virginia. During first season beaten in home opener by Portsmouth, made up of many Boston castoffs. 1934 team shifted to Fenway Park from Braves Field, became Redskins. On 10/18/33, vs. Giants, gained 215 yds. rushing on 16 attempts. In 1936, after Marshall spat with press, "Homeless Redskins" played last two home games at New York's Polo Grounds. Moved with team to Washington in 1937. Played with two divisional champions, 1936, 37. Scored first TD in 1937 NFL title game which 'Skins won. League-leading rusher in 1933 with 737 yds., in 1937 with 874. In 1932-37 career gained 3403 yds., averaging 4.1. After 1937 season went on barnstorming tour with Chicago Bears. In 1938 became assistant to Lou Little of Columbia, stayed until end of Little regime in 1956. Currently works for General Electric in Washington, D.C., and serves as president of Washington Touchdown Club. All-NFL 1933, 36, 37. Citizens Saving Hall of Fame, National Football Foundation Hall of Fame, Pro Football Hall of Fame.

BAUGH, SAMUEL A. (Slingin' Sammy) Quarterback. B. 3/17/14, Temple, Tex. 6'2", 180. All-America for TCU, 1935, 36. Consensus choice in '36. Threw 599 passes in three varsity seasons, completed 274. One of finest punters of era, kicking 198 for 8108 yds. In 1936 Sugar Bowl, vs. LSU, made 14 punts, 48-yd. average. Washington Redskins, 1937-52. Led NFL in passing, 1937, 40, 43, 45 (shared), 47, 49. Led NFL in punting, 1940, 41, 42, 43. Average of 51.0 yds. in 1940, still all-time record. Led league in interceptions (thrown), 1943. Led Skins to five divisional titles, 1937, 40, 42, 43, 45; two championships, 1937, 42. Twice passed for 6 TDs in one game. Superior defensive player, highly unusual for QB. Led NFL in interceptions with 11, 1943. In 1938 went to spring training with St. Louis Cardinal baseball team, was cut. When retired in 1952 to Texas ranch, Baugh held NFL records for most passes (3016), completions (1709), TD passes (187), highest career efficiency (56.5 percent), single-season efficiency (70.3 percent). All-Pro, 1937, 40, 48. Coached New York Titans, 1960-61. Coached

Houston Oilers, 1964. Named to Modern All-Time All-America team. Citizens Savings Hall of Fame, National Football Foundation Hall of Fame.

BAUGHAN, MAXIE C., Jr. Linebacker. B. 8/3/38, Forkland, Ala. 6'1", 230. Played center for Georgia Tech, 1957-59. Consensus All-America, 1959. Drafted on 2nd round by Philadelphia Eagles, 1960. In 1966 traded to Los Angeles Rams, for linebacker Fred Brown, defensive back Willie Molden, draft choice. In 1968, despite injuries, made 63 tackles, intercepted 4 passes. In 1960-70 career intercepted 17 passes for 215 yds. Played in Pro Bowl, 1961, 62, 64, 65, 67, 68, 69. NFL championship game, 1960. Appointed assistant coach for New York Giants, 1974. Was Georgia Tech assistant, 1972-73.

BAUSCH, JAMES Running Back. B. Wichita, Kan. 210. Kansas, 1929-30. Left Wichita University (now Wichita State) for Kansas, angering Wheatshocker officials. They accused Jayhawks of tampering. Regarded by many as greatest all-round athlete in Kansas history. All-Big 6, 1929, 30. Starred in basketball, was 1932 Olympic decathlon champion. First Kansas player ever in East-West Shrine game at San Francisco, 1930. In 1930, vs. Kansas State, returned opening kickoff 95 yds. for TD and scored 60-yd. TD rushing. Big 6 shotput champion, also winner at Drake and Texas Relays. Two-time decathlon champ at Kansas Relays. Also Big 6 javelin, pole vault titlist. 1932 Sullivan Award winner for throwing javelin 203' 3½". National Football Foundation Hall of Fame.

BEAGLE, RONALD G. End. B. 2/7/34, Hartford, Conn. 6'0", 186. Played three years at Navy, 1953-55. Receiving end of Welsh-to-Beagle pass combo. Consensus All-America 1954; unanimous All-America, 1955. In 1954 led team to Lambert Trophy, symbolic of Eastern championship. New Year's Day, 1955, led Middies to 21-0 win over Ole Miss in Sugar Bowl. Maxwell Trophy, 1954. Great blocker, receiver. Bothered by injured hand in 1955. In final collegiate game, 1955 vs. Army, fumbled to aid Cadet win. During career caught 64 passes for 840 yds., average gain of 13.1 yds., 8TDs. Didn't play pro ball.

BEALS, ALYN R. Wide Receiver. B. 4/27/21, Marysville, Calif. 6'0", 190. Attended Santa Clara. Signed with San Francisco 49ers, 1946. As rookie led All America Football Conference in scoring, made All-League. Was also All-AAFC, 1948, 49. In 1948 set AAFC season record for TDs receiving with 14. Set AAFC career records for TDs receiving with 45, points with 278, and consecutive games catching pass with 45. Remained with 49ers thru 1951.

BEATHARD, PETER F. Quarterback. B. 3/7/42, Hermosa Beach, Calif. 6'1", 205. Southern California, 1961-63. In 1962 led Trojans to national championship. In 1964 drafted by Kansas City Chiefs on 1st round. Traded to Houston Oilers, 10/8/67, for defensive tackle Ernie Ladd, QB Jackie Lee, 1st-round draft pick. In 1965 scored two-point conversion. Missed four games due to appendectomy in 1968. In 1970 involved in first ever AFC-NFC trade, going to St. Louis Cardinals with defensive back Miller Farr for cornerback Bob Atkins, QB Charley Johnson. Traded to Los Angeles Rams, 1972. Year later traded back to Chiefs. AFL championship game, 1966. Super Bowl, 1967. Never achieved pro stardom which was predicted for him by some observers.

BEBAN, GARY J. Quarterback. B. 8/5/46, Redwood City, Calif. 6'1½", 195. Played QB for UCLA, 1965-67. Unanimous All-America, 1967. Heisman Trophy, 1967. Fine passer. In 1965 completed 79-yd. pass vs. Syracuse, 78-yd. pass vs. California, 66-yd. pass vs. Stanford, 60-yd. pass and made 60-yd. rush vs. Washington. In 1966 Rose Bowl rushed for two TDs. In college career rushed for 1257 yds., completed 235 of 444 passes for 3940 yds. and 23 TDs, scored total of 202 points. Drafted on 2nd round by Los Angeles Rams, 1968, but draft rights traded to Washington Redskins. 'Skins switched him to wide receiver, and he stayed with them thru 1969. In 1968 caught only pro pass, for 12 yds. Citizens Savings Hall of Fame. Now television sportscaster in Los Angeles.

BEDNARIK, CHARLES (Chuck) Linebacker. B. 5/1/25, Bethlehem, Pa. 6'3", 235. Pennsylvania center, 1945-48. Consensus All-America, 1947-48. Named to 33 All-America teams. Citizens Savings Player of the Year, 1948. Maxwell Trophy, 1948. Entered Penn at age 20 after World War II service, played on varsity as freshman. During war flew 30 combat missions over Germany as B-24 aerial gunner. Won Air Medal with five Oak Leaf Clusters, five Battle Stars. 1949 No. 1 draft choice of Philadelphia Eagles. 1949 Rookie of the Year as center. Year later moved to linebacker where he stayed until 1954. Again played center, 1954-60; linebacker again, 1961-62. Won 1960 John Wanamaker Award. Eight times All-NFL, eight Pro Bowls. Son of immigrant steel worker from Czechoslovakia; aided father's second job, chopping trees. As child played football with stocking stuffed with rags. Made high school varsity as fullback in freshman year, later switched to center and was All-State honorable mention. Also All-State 2nd team in basketball, was baseball catcher. In 1960 led Eagles to NFL championship. 1960 season marred by unfortunate accident, Bednarik's tackle resulting in brain concussion to Frank Gifford of New York Giants. It kept Gifford out for entire 1961 season. Some fans accused Bednarik of deliberate, brutal tactics. Accusation probably unfair, though Chuck was extremely hard tackler. Retired from pros in 1962 after 14 years. Modern All-Time All-America 2nd team, National Football Foundation Hall of Fame.

BEDSOLE, HAROLD (Hal) End. B. 12/21/41, Chicago, Ill. 6'5", 230. Attended Roseda H.S. in Los Angeles and Piercy (Calif.) J.C. before enrolling at Southern California. Played three years under John McKay, 1961-63. Consensus All-America, 1963. Was prep and juco QB but converted to end at USC. Proved to be natural; had instinctive moves and great physical qualities. Best year, 1962, caught 33 passes for 827 yds. and 11 TDs. That season gave pass-and-run performances of 46, 51, 59, 73, 79 yds. Caught two TD passes, starred on defense and singled out for three roughness penalties in 1963 Rose Bowl victory over Wisconsin. Confident, outspoken; admitted to lackadaisical attitude, hated practice — "I'm a Saturday ballplayer." Minnesota Vikings, 1964-66.

BELL, DE BENNEVILLE (Bert) Commissioner. B. 2/25/1895, Philadelphia,

Pa. D. 10/11/59, Philadelphia, Pa. Graduate of Pennsylvania. In 1933 bought Frankford Yellowjackets and moved them to Philadelphia. Team was renamed Philadelphia Eagles. Eagles president, 1933-40. Coached Eagles, 1936-40. In 1941, Philadelphia and Pittsburgh Steelers swapped franchises. Served as coach first two games of '41 season. In 1946 elected NFL commissioner serving until death at game between Philadelphia and Pittsburgh, two teams he had coached. Inaugurated pro draft, 1936. Came from wealthy Philadelphia family, is father of executive Upton Bell. His television policies of home team "blackouts" and one-league, one-network led to NFL's financial growth. Both concepts have been changed in recent years. NFL Player Pension Plan, instituted in 1962, named for him. Pro Football Hall of Fame.

BELL, MADISON (Moanin' Matty) Coach. B. Fort Worth, Tex. Went to Centre College from "schoolyards district" of Fort Worth, along with Bo McMillin, Bill James, Red Weaver. They helped school gain national football prominence. Graduated from Centre in 1920. Coached at Haskell, 1920-21; Carroll (Wis.), 1922; TCU, 1923-28; Texas A. & M., 1929-33; SMU, 1935-41, 45-49. 154-87-17 lifetime record. Known for making predictions of disaster each week, primarily for psychological advantage. Also took opposite extreme if he felt that was to his advantage. In 1934 became SMU line coach, moving up to head coach in '35. 1935 team had 12-0 record, scored 288 points, allowed only 32 and was national co-champion. Lost 1936 Rose Bowl, 7-0, to Stanford. Among his All-Americas were Doak Walker, Kyle Rote and Iron Man Wetsel. Devoted full-time to duties as SMU athletic director after 1949. Was president of American Football Coaches Association longer than any other man. Citizens Savings Hall of Fame, National Football Foundation Hall of Fame.

BELL, ROBERT L. (Bobby) Linebacker. B. 6/17/40, Shelby, N.C. 6'4", 228. Great scholastic athlete, winning All-State honors as quarterback in North Carolina. Played for Minnesota under Murray Warmath, 1960-62. All-America tackle, 1961; unanimous, 1962. Outland Trophy, 1962. Played on 1963 College All-Star team that defeated Green Bay Packers. Kansas City Chiefs, 1963-73. All-AFL, 1965, 66, 67, 68, 69. All-AFC, 1970, 71, 72. AFL All-Star games, 1964, 65, 66, 67, 68, 69. Pro Bowl, 1970, 71, 72. Has been linebacker throughout pro career. In 11 years intercepted 25 passes. Played in Super Bowl I, 1967, and Super Bowl IV, 1970. Absolutely fearless player. Vicious tackler, fast, versatile. Probably could have been standout at any position. Snaps on punts and field goals. Hobby is working on old cars, owns '41 Chevrolet and '28 Oldsmobile. Member All-Time AFL team.

BELLINO, JOSEPH Running Back. B. 3/13/38, Winchester, Mass. 5'8", 185. Immortal Navy halfback. Built like fireplug; fast, tough, elusive. Also outstanding baseball catcher. Had major league potential. Played for Navy, 1958-60. Unanimous All-America, 1960. 1960 Heisman Trophy winner. In 1960, vs. Virginia, made 90-yd. rush. In college career carried 330 times for 1664 yds. average of 5.0; caught 45 passes for 602 yds. average of 13.4, and 7 TDs; returned 15 punts for 256 yds.; returned 23 kickoffs for 577 yds.; scored 198 points on 31

TDs and 12 PATs. Played in Orange Bowl, 1961. Boston Patriots, 1965-67.

BEMILLER, ALBERT D. (Tombstone) Center. B. 4/18/39, Hanover, Pa. 6'3", 238. Syracuse, 1958-60. Graduated with degree in biology. Received nickname because he intended to become mortician. Buffalo Bills, 1961-69. Played in three consecutive AFL title games, 1964, 65, 66. AFL All-Star game, 1965.

BENTON, JAMES End-Running Back. B. 9/25/16, Carthage, Ark. 6'3", 206. Played at Arkansas, 1935-37. As senior was NCAA receiving champion with 47 receptions. In 1938 joined Cleveland Rams and played thru 1940. In service, 1941, and returned to Rams, 1942. In 1943 traded to Chicago Bears, but again returned to Rams in 1944. Moved with them to Los Angeles in 1946 and played thru 1947. Received 29-yd. TD pass from Sid Luckman in 1943 title game against Washington Redskins. Received 10 passes for 303 yds., one-game yardage record, 11/22/45, vs. Detroit Lions. In 1945 title game, vs. Washington, received 37-yd. TD pass from Bob Waterfield. Led NFL receivers, 1946, with 63 receptions, for 981 yds. and 6 TDs.

BERRY, CHARLES F. (Charlie) End. B. Phillipsburg, N.J. D. 9/6/72. 6', 185. Lafayette, 1921-24. All-America, 1924. Had one of most unusual and varied careers in history of American sports. One of Lafayette's greatest, playing on Jock Sutherland's 1921 team that Sutherland referred to as his "masterpiece." After college played two years with Pottstown Maroons of NFL. Played for Philadelphia Athletics (baseball) as catcher in 1925. Played for Portland and Dallas in 1926, 27, and then went to Boston Red Sox until 1932; then to Chicago White Sox who traded him back to A's in 1934. Played until 1938, coached with A's until 1940. Compiled batting average of .267 in 13 seasons, 709 major league games. Managed A's farm team, Wilmington, in 1940. Coached football at Grove City College for five years during baseball off-season. Umpire in minor leagues, 1941, and part of 1942 before joining American League. For next 19 years worked in both AL (baseball) and NFL (football) as umpire. When retired from active participation, Berry continued working for Joe Cronin as special representative in AL matters and did some football scouting. Umpired at 3rd base because of major league umpire strike, during 1st game of major league playoffs in 1970 (Baltimore vs. Minnesota). Died at age 69.

BERRY, RAYMOND End. B. 2/27/33, Corpus Christi, Tex. 6'2", 187. Played under father at Paris (Tex.) H.S. Also attended Schriner J.C., Kerrville, Tex., before playing end at Southern Methodist. Graduated in 1955. Played for Baltimore Colts, 1955-67. Had one leg shorter than the other, suffered from poor eyesight (wore contacts) and back condition (used canvas support strap). Nevertheless, became excellent receiver and holder of many records. NFL receiving leader, 1958, 59, 60. Shared title with Pete Retzlaff in '58. In 1958, 56 receptions, 794 yds., 9 TDs; in 1959, 66 receptions, 959 yds., 14 TDs; in 1960, 74 receptions, 1298 yds., 10 TDs. Suffered knee injury in game vs. San Francisco 49ers. In 1964 reached career total of 506 receptions, breaking existing all-time NFL record of 503. Eventually retired with 631 receptions, 9275 yds., 68 TDs.

Now ranks 2nd to Don Maynard. During West Coast games wore sun goggles. Squeezed "silly putty" to strengthen fingers and help prevent injuries, occasionally wore surgical gloves to keep hands from getting stiff on cold days. Played on 1958, 64 NFL championship teams. Assistant coach, Dallas Cowboys, 1968-69. Served as Arkansas assistant, 1970-72. In 1973 became Detroit Lion assistant. Pro Football Hall of Fame. Active in Fellowship of Christian Athletes.

BERRY, ROBERT Quarterback. B. 3/10/42, San Jose, Calif. 5'11", 185. Played at Oregon, 1962-64. All-America, 1964. Threw for 37 TDs and over 4000 yds. in college. Played in Hula Bowl, East-West Shrine, Coaches All-America games. Minnesota Vikings, 1965-67, 73; Atlanta Falcons, 1968-72. Played under Norm Van Brocklin, both with Vikings and Falcons. Was regular with Falcons. Completed 60.2 percent of passes (136 of 226) in 1971. Threw for 2158 yds., 1972. Was traded back to Vikings in 1973 for QB Bob Lee.

BERTELLI, ANGELO B. (Accurate Angelo) Quarterback. B. West Springfield, Mass. 6'1", 173. Notre Dame, 1941-43. All-America, 1942; Consensus All-America, 1943. Heisman Trophy, Notre Dame's first winner, 1943. Citizens Savings Player of the Year, 1943. Masterful passer, fine defensive player and kicker. Entered marines after six games of 1943 season. Johnny Lujack then took over at QB, and Irish went on to win national championship. They came within 30 seconds of undefeated season, losing only to Great Lakes Naval Training Station. Bertelli, Creighton Miller, Jim White, John Yonakor, Pat Filley gave N.D. five All-Americas in one season. Bertelli's three-season passing totals: 169 of 324 attempts, 2582 yds., 21 TDs. Los Angeles Dons (AAFC), 1946; Chicago Rockets (AAFC), 1947-48. Citizens Savings Hall of Fame, National Football Foundation Hall of Fame.

BERTELSEN, JAMES Running Back. B. 2/26/50, St. Paul, Minn. 5'11", 205. Played for Texas Longhorns, 1970-72. In career gained 2510 yds., averaging 6.0 yds. per carry and scoring 33 TDs. Los Angeles Rams, 1972-73. Was 2nd-round draft choice of Rams. Rookie performance was so good that L.A. traded running back Willie Ellison to Kansas City Chiefs following 1972 season. Bertelsen gained 581 yds. rushing in 1972, 854 in '73. Dangerous pass receiver, on kickoffs and punts. Pro Bowl, 1974.

BERWANGER, J. JAY Running Back-Quarterback. B. 3/19/14, Dubuque, Iowa. Attended U. of Chicago, 1933-35. In 1934 became first Chicago All-America in 10 years. Consensus All-America, 1935. Citizens Savings Player of the Year, 1935. Silver Football, 1935. First winner of Heisman Trophy, also in 1935. Gained 4108 yds. in three varsity seasons. Good placekicker. Often played entire game. In 1936 drafted on 1st round by Philadelphia Eagles, thus becoming first player ever drafted by professional football team. However, didn't sign. Modern All-Time All-America team. Citizens Savings Hall of Fame, National Football Foundation Hall of Fame.

BETTENCOURT, LAWRENCE (Larry) Center. B. 9/22/07, Newark, Calif. St.

Mary's (Calif.), 1924-27. Competed in football, baseball, track. Ran 440-yd. dash in 52 seconds. Was devastating roving center under Edward (Slip) Madigan. His play revealed possibilities of mobile defense, contributed to eventual introduction of linebackers into modern football. Captained Galloping Gaels in 1927. Blocked kicks in six consecutive games that year. Following graduation, Bettencourt became first man to play pro baseball and football simultaneously. Baseball with St. Louis Browns, football with Memphis Tigers and Green Bay Packers. Was Packer in 1932. Superintendent in Avondale Shipyards, New Orleans. National Football Foundation Hall of Fame.

BEZDEK, HUGO F. Coach. B. 4/1/1884, Prague, Czechoslovakia. D. 9/19/52. Nicknamed "Thirteen-Inch Shell" by high school classmates. Only man to coach major-college football and manage big-league baseball. Played for U. of Chicago, 1902-05. Prize pupil of Amos Alonzo Stagg. Coached Arkansas, 1908-12; Oregon, 1906, 13-17; Penn State, 1918-29; Delaware Valley, 1949. As player, pile driver on offense but weak tackler. At Bezdek's request, Stagg bawled him out over tackling just before each game. 3rd-team All-America fullback, 1905. 1905 team won Western Conference (Big 10) championship, handing Michigan's Fielding Yost first defeat in 56 games. At Oregon, in first year of coaching, Bezdek led team to unbeaten season. 1916 Oregon club undefeated, beat Penn 14-0 in Rose Bowl. In addition to coaching chores, managed Pittsburgh Pirates, 1917-19. Managerial record: 166-187. Penn State record was 65-29-9; overall: 127-57-14. In 1922 lost Rose Bowl, 14-3, to Southern California. Coached NFL Cleveland Rams, 1937-38 (5-17). Was demanding, belligerent, autonomous. Pittsburgh sportswriter Chet Smith wrote: "Hugo lived a strenuous life, which included a good many triumphs and a number of lickings. If he was inclined to brag a bit over one, you have to admit also that he never cried about the other." Citizens Savings Hall of Fame, National Football Foundation Hall of Fame.

BIBLE, DANA X. Coach. B. 10/8/91, Jefferson City, Tenn. Attended Carson-Newman. Coached Mississippi College, 1913-15; LSU, 1916; Texas A&M, 1917-28; Nebraska, 1929-36; Texas, 1937-46. Winner of 14 conference championships; overall record: 205-73-20. Known for quoting scripture, Bible on Bible. Believer in basic, fundamental football, disapproving of fancy formations and plays. Pet play was fake punt on 3rd down. Author of book, *Championship Football,* on how to mold winning team. Good chapter on scouting. Went to great lengths to find out about future opponents. Scouts had to fill out 50-page form on every assignment. Went into great detail about each player. Began coaching high schools at age 21, while still attending college. Follower of Amos Alonzo Stagg, Dr. Henry Williams, Pop Warner, Fielding Yost, Bob Zuppke. In 1918 served in Air Corps as flight instructor. On return led Texas A. & M. to unbeaten season. Under his leadership Aggies didn't have losing season. At Nebraska lost but three conference games. At Texas won two Cotton Bowls 1943, 46, tied another, 1944. Served 27 years on National Football Rules Committee. Bestowed with every possible football honor. Citizens Savings Hall of Fame, National Football Foundation Hall of Fame.

BIDWILL, CHARLES W. Owner. B. 9/16/95, Chicago, Ill. D. 4/19/47, Chicago, Ill. Attended Loyola (Chicago). In 1933 became owner-president of Chicago Cardinals. Served in that capacity until his death. Close friend of George Halas, owner of rival Chicago Bears. Before becoming Cardinal owner, Bidwill loaned Halas money so that he could buy out partner, Dutch Sternaman. Assembled 1947 Dream Backfield — Christman, Goldberg, Harder, Trippi — which won NFL title, first for Cards. Unfortunately, Bidwill had died few months before. Placed team in Comiskey Park, and later in Soldiers Field. Pro Football Hall of Fame.

BIELSKI, RICHARD End-Kicker. B. 9/7/32, Baltimore, Md. 6'1", 218. Fullback and placekicker at Maryland, 1951-54. Member of national championship team, 1953. That year Terrapins finished regular season 10-0, then lost to Oklahoma in Orange Bowl. Also played in 1952 Sugar Bowl. Philadelphia Eagles, 1955-59; Dallas Cowboys, 1960-61; Baltimore Colts, 1962-63. Was taken by Cowboys in 1960 expansion draft. Caught two-inch TD pass, shortest ever, from Eddie LeBaron on 10/9/60. As pro caught 107 passes for 1035 yds., 12 TDs. Also kicked 58 PATs, 26 FGs. Receiver coach for Colts, 1964-72. Joined Washington Redskins in similar capacity, 1973.

BIERMAN, BERNARD W. (Bernie) Coach. B. 3/11/1894, Waseca, Minn. Tabbed "Silver Fox of the Northland." Minnesota captain, 1915. Ran 100-yd. dash in 10 seconds. Awarded Big 10 Medal of Honor. Dedicated, austere coach. Coached Montana, 1919-21; Mississippi State, 1925-26; Tulane, 1927-31; Minnesota, 1932-41, 45-50. Minnesota record: 93-35-6. Overall: 146-62-12. Recorded six Big 10 titles, four National Championships, five unbeaten seasons. Coach of the Year, 1941. Bierman admitted "... never made an emotional speech in my life." Produced 12 All-Americas at Minnesota. Primarily, as coach, used single-wing formation, rather than Minnesota shift. Had about 500 different plays, yet frequently accused of having "dull" offense. Modifications necessary, he felt, to take advantage of material. Favorite story was from 1935 Stanford-Southern Cal game. When USC player was hurt, Stanford's Jim Coffis rushed over and massaged injured player's leg. Asked why he had done so Coffis replied, "Listen, I didn't want to see that guy leave the game. He's the easiest fellow to block I've ever played against." Citizens Savings Hall of Fame, National Football Foundation Hall of Fame.

BIGGS, VERLON Defensive End. B. 3/16/43, Moss Point, Miss. 6'4", 270. Attended Jackson State, 1962-65. NAIA All-America, 1965. New York Jets, 1965-70; Washington Redskins, 1971-73. AFL All-Star games, 1967, 68, 69. Named game's outstanding defensive player, 1967. Super Bowl, 1969, 73. Won 1970 Heede Award as Jets' most improved and dedicated player. Played out option with Jets in 1970, then signed with Redskins. Scored first pro touchdown in 1972: recovered fumble of former teammate Joe Namath and ran 16 yds. to score. Excellent defensive end; strong, rough tackler.

BILETNIKOFF, FREDERICK End. B. 2/23/43, Erie, Pa. 6'1", 190. Played flanker for Florida State, 1962-64. Consensus All-America, 1964. In 1963, vs. Miami (Fla.), returned interception for 99 yds. In 1965 Gator Bowl caught major bowl record 13 passes, for Gator record 192 yds. and four TDs. In three seasons received 87 passes for 1463 yds., average of 16.8 yds., and 16 TDs; scored 104 points overall. Oakland Raiders, 1965-73. Drafted on 2nd round in 1965. Set AFL championship game record, 1968, for yds. on pass receptions with 190. Same game tied record for receptions with 7. NFL's leading pass receiver in '68 with 61 receptions, 929 yds., 9 TDs. In nine-season pro career has caught 408 passes for 6512 yds., average of 16.0 yds. Has scored 49 TDs. Great moves to get open, tremendous hands, tough in clutch. All-AFL, 1969. All-AFC, 1972, 73. AFL All-Star games following 1967, 68, 69 seasons. Super Bowl, 1968. Brother, Bob, was minor league baseball player and football star at Miami (Fla.). Father was national AAU boxing champion. Off-season involved in public relations work.

BIRD, RODGER P. Defensive Back. B. 7/2/43, Corbin, Ky. 6', 200. Played at Kentucky, 1963-65. Oakland Raiders, 1966-68. Was 1st-round draft choice. On 10/29/67, vs. San Diego Chargers, Bird made 78-yd. punt return for longest AFL return that year. Set AFL season record for punt returns, 46, 1967. Also set AFL season record for yds. on punt returns with 612. In 1967 set AFL game punt-return record with 9, gaining record 143 yds. Same year set AFL playoff game punt-return record with 5; AFL career playoff punt-return record with 7; career playoff record, yds. on punt returns, 87.

BIRDWELL, DANIEL L. Tackle. B. 10/14/40, Big Spring, Tex. 6'4", 250. Attended U. of Houston, 1959-61. Drafted on 6th round by Oakland Raiders in 1962. Played with Oakland thru 1969. AFL title games, 1967, 1968. Super Bowl, 1968. All-AFL defensive tackle, 1968. AFL All-Star game, 1968.

BLACKMAN, ROBERT L. Coach. B. 7/17/18, Desoto, Iowa. Bout with polio in freshman year ended playing career at Southern California. Immediately turned to coaching as student assistant to USC's Howard Jones. Graduated from Southern Cal in 1941, later earned master's degree. Head coach at Pasadena City College, 1949-52; Denver, 1953-54; Dartmouth 1955-70; Illinois, 1971-73. Won two national juco championships with Pasadena. Outstanding success at Dartmouth, winning three Ivy League titles and two Lambert Trophies. Big Green were thrice unbeaten, untied. Dartmouth record: 104-37-3; overall collegiately: 129-63-5. Great strategist, teacher. Many of his former assistants are now head coaches.

BLAIK, EARL H. (Red) Coach. B. 2/15/97, Dayton, Ohio. Played four years at Miami (Ohio), 1914-17, and two at Army, 1918-19. All-America, 3rd team, 1919. Also played baseball, basketball. First Cadet to play three sports vs. Navy. Joined Cavalry in 1920. Resigned three years later to enter real estate-building business in native Dayton. Assistant coach at Army, 1923-34. Head coach at Dartmouth, 1934-40; Army, 1941-58. Developed five undefeated Army teams. Felt that championship football requires merely hard work. At Dartmouth produced 22-game unbeaten string. Overall record there: 45-15-4. Coach during 1940 game in which Cornell was given five downs in final moments, using last to score 7-3 win; Cornell later forfeited, 3-0. In 1941 inherited Army team which had 1-7-1 record year before. Finished 5-3-1 first season. Composite Army record: 121-33-10. Was 3-4-2 vs. Notre Dame, 8-8-2 vs. Navy. In 1951, lost 44 of 45 varsity players in "cribbing" scandal. Three national championships, 1944, 45, 46; six Lambert Trophies, 1944, 46, 48, 49, 53, 58; three unbeaten, untied teams, 1944, 45, 49.

From 1944 thru 1947, won or tied 32 consecutive games, longest Army unbeaten streak. Possessed in words of George Trevor, "methodical brilliance." Did not believe in luck. Known for axioms such as, "Inches make a champion, and the champion makes his own luck." Coach of the Year, 1946, 53. In 1956, honored as "most congenial and co-operative figure in college football." Received Gold Medal from National Football Foundation, 1966. Produced 33 All-Americas. Twenty-four of his assistants became head coaches, including Vince Lombardi. Father of Bob Blaik who holds Army record for longest punt (74 yds.) in 1950 vs. Michigan 166-48-12 overall. Citizens Savings Hall of Fame, National Football Foundation Hall of Fame.

BLANCHARD, FELIX A., Jr. (Doc; Mr. Inside) Running Back. B. 12/11/24, Bishopville, S.C. 6', 210. Army, 1944-46. Unanimous All-America, 1945, 46. Never played pro. Great tackler and blocker, in addition to running ability. Also on track team. Surpassed 50' in shot-put. Only man to break 50' in first collegiate season. Felix Sr. was fine player for Tulane. Felix Jr. became half of famous Blanchard and Davis team, "Mr. Inside" and "Mr. Outside." Originally enrolled at North Carolina, against whom he played his first game for Army. Never played in losing game at Army. Called "greatest fullback ever" by Northwestern coach Pappy Waldorf. 1945 NCAA scoring champion with 115 points, on 19 TDs. In first varsity game played only 17 minutes, yet averaged 58 yds. on kickoffs, punted once for 40 yds., carried ball 4 times for 4.5 average. Often punted 50-60 yds. In 25-game career scored 231 points on 38 TDs and 3 PATs, averaging 9.2 points per game. Could run 100 yds. in 10 seconds. In 1945 won Sullivan Award, Walter Camp Trophy, Maxwell Trophy, Heisman Trophy. He's now Lt. Col. Citizens Savings Hall of Fame, National Football Foundation Hall of Fame.

BLANDA, GEORGE F. Quarterback-Kicker. B. 9/17/27, Youngwood, Pa. 6'2", 215. Football's ageless wonder. Kentucky, 1946-48. Drafted on 12th round and signed by Chicago Bears, 1949. Played with Bears thru 1958. Traded in 1949 to Baltimore Colts, but returned to Bears. In 1960, after year's absence from football, signed as free agent by Houston Oilers. In 1967 dealt to Oakland Raiders. Played in every AFL game for Houston and Oakland. Has played more seasons than any other pro player (24 thru 1973). Holds many records, more than any other player, among them are: seasons as active player (24); games played (312); consecutive appearances (196, shared with Jim Otto); lifetime points (1842); seasons leading with PATs (5); lifetime PATs attempted (865); lifetime PATs (855); lifetime FG attempts (600); lifetime FGs (311); consecutive games scoring (40), 12/11/60 to 11/10/63; season TD passes (36, 1961); lifetime passes had intercepted (276); season passes intercepted (42, 1962); season PATs (64, 1961); season PATs attempted (65, 1961); game passes attempted (68) and completed (37), 11/1/64.

Holds nine championship game records, including game passing yds. (301) and longest pass completion (88 yds.). Led AFL in numerous passing categories. In 1967 led league in points with 116, on 56 PATs and 20 FGs, first man to achieve honor on kicking alone. In 1956 led in PATs with 45, FG attempts with 28. Led in FG attempts, 1960, with 34. Led in PATs: 1961 with 64; 1962 with 48; 1967 with 56; 1968 with 45; 1972 with 44. On 11/8/70 kicked FG with three seconds remaining to beat Cleveland Browns, 23-20. At end of 1973 season had 1909 pass completions in 4000 attempts for 26,881 yds., average of 6.72 yds., 235 TDs, had 277 passes intercepted, had kicked 855 PATs, missing only 10, made 211 of 600 FGs. 1973 was one of his most accurate seasons, scoring 23 of 33 FGs and 21 of 31 PATs. His four FGs broke Miami Dolphin 15-game winning streak, 12-7. AFL Player of the Year, 1963. AFC Player of the Year, 1970. AFL All-Star game, 1962, 63, 64, 68. Has played in title games in both leagues (NFL, 1956; AFL, 1960, 61, 62, 67, 68, 69). Super Bowl, 1968. Oldest active player in pro football. Was 46 on 9/17/73. National sales representative for REA Express during off-season.

BLANKS, SIDNEY Running Back. B. 4/29/40, Del Rio, Tex. 6'1", 200. Graduated from Texas A.&I. In 1964 drafted by Houston Oilers; in rookie year had 1 reception for 8 yds. Spent six years with Oilers. In 1969 dealt to Boston Patriots with Charlie Frazier, Ron Caveness, Larry Carwell, for Leroy Mitchell and draft choice. On 12/13/64 ran 91 yds. from scrimmage, AFL record. Remained with Patriots thru 1970. AFL All-Star game, 1964.

BLUE, FORREST M., JR. Center. B. 9/7/43, Marfa, Tex. 6'5½", 255. Grew up in Tampa. Played for Auburn, 1965-67. Drafted by San Francisco 49ers on 1st round, 1968. 49ers, 1968-73. Played in every game since joining club. Hobbies are golf, cards, fishing. NFC Pro Bowl starter, 1972, 73, 74. All Pro 1971, 72, 73. Wants to be lawyer, attending law school.

BOCK, EDWARD Guard. B. 9/1/16, Fort Dodge, Iowa. 6', 210. Iowa State, 1936-38. Consensus All-America 1938. Started every game for Iowa State during career and played many full games. In 1938 graduated from Iowa State with degree in mechanical engineering; in 1940 received master's degree. 1938 team had 7-1-1 record. Joined Monsanto Co. of St. Louis in 1941, is currently president and chief executive officer. Named to *Sports Illustrated* Silver Anniversary All-America team in 1963. Past national president of Iowa State Cyclone Athletic Club. National Football Foundation Hall of Fame.

BOMAR, R. LYNN End. B. 1904, Gallatin, Tex. 6'2", 215. Played for Vanderbilt, 1921-24. All-America, 1923; 2nd team, 1922. On offense, Commodore's leading receiver. Defensively, South's leading linebacker. One of first Southerners on Walter Camp's All-America team. Won varsity letters in football, baseball, basketball. New York Giants, 1925-26. All-Pro. Later, chief of Tennessee Highway Patrol and commissioner of safety for State of Tennessee. Citizens Savings Hall of Fame, National Football Foundation Hall of Fame.

BOMEISLER, DOUGLASS M. (Bo) Tackle. B. 6/20/92, Brooklyn, N.Y. D. 12/28/53, Greenwich, Conn. 5'11", 190. Competed in track, basketball, football at Yale. All-America, 1911, 12. Invented knee brace of leather strips connected by steel hinges, 1911, which is still used today. Felt he had to do something or wouldn't be able to play. Knee injuries began in 1910, causing him to miss most of season. Injured again in 1911, and played 1912 with braces on both knees. Also bothered by dislocated left shoulder which "popped out" against Harvard in 1911. Was relentless defender, excellent on covering punts. Vice president of Empire Trust Co., New York City, at death. National Football Foundation Hall of Fame.

BOOTH, ALBERT JAMES, JR. (Albie) Running back. B. 2/1/08, New Haven, Conn. D. 3/1/59. 5'6", 144. "Little Boy Blue" played halfback for Yale, 1929-31. Led Bulldogs to 15 wins, 5 losses, 5 ties with excellent running, passing, punting and dropkicking. On 10/26/29 entered game vs. Army in 2nd quarter. Cadets were leading, 13-0. Proceeded to score all Eli points as Yale pulled 21-13 upset. Carried ball 33 times for 233 yds. In three seasons gained 1428 yds. rushing on 344 carries; made 8 interceptions for 135 yds.; returned 63 punts for 718 yds.; returned 13 kick-offs for 420; scored 137 points on 17 TDs, 23 PATs and 4 FGs. Performance against Army actually did him disservice. Such brilliance was thereafter always expected, but it set standard that he or no other back could have lived up to. Nevertheless, was outstanding throughout career. Secret was shiftiness, ability he shared with such escape artists as Red Grange, Tom Harmon, Glenn Davis. Honored with four captaincies at Yale: freshman football, basketball; varsity football, basketball. In final athletic appearance for Bulldogs, Booth hit grand-slam home run to beat Harvard. Also called "Little Albie," "The Mighty Mite," "Number 48," "Mighty Atom." National Football Foundation Hall of Fame.

BOOZER, EMERSON (Billy Boo) Running Back. B. 7/4/43, Augusta, Ga. 5'11", 207. Maryland State, 1962-65. Twice Little All-America. In college gained 2537 yds. on 374 carries, scored 22 TDs. New York Jets, 1966-73. Was 6th-round draft choice. As rookie ranked 10th in league in rushing. Excellent blocker, also serves as receiver. Has played despite injuries. In 1967, hampered by knee injury, scored 13 TDs, six short of AFL record. Had excellent season, 1970, despite bruised rib cartilage, with back-to-back 100-yd. days vs. Oakland Raiders, Miami Dolphins. In 1971 home opener vs. Buffalo Bills, 31 carries for 116 yds.; that season gained 618 yds. AFC leader in TDs with 14 (11 rushing, 3 receiving). Gained 831 yds. on 182 carries, for 4.6-yd. average. His 4441 yds. rushing, thru 1973, represents Jet career standard. AFL All-Star games, 1967, 69. Has worked for Census Bureau. Also radio announcer in New York City.

BORRIES, FRED JR. (Buzz) Running Back. B. 12/13/11, Louisville, Ky. D.

1/3/69, West Orange, Fla. 6', 175. Played at Navy, 1932-34. Consensus All-America, 1934. Basketball All-America same year. Great runner, passer, punter, blocker, defender. One of best halfbacks ever to play for Navy. Lou Little once said that "Borries beat my Columbia team almost singlehanded — and that was the only game we lost in 1934." Scored 18 career TDs, 3 conversions. Won Navy A.A. sword for excellence in athletics. Fighter pilot during World War II. Awarded Bronze Star. National Football Foundation Hall of Fame.

BORYLA, MICHAEL J. Quarterback. B. 3/6/51, Denver, Colo. 6'4", 200. Big, rangy quarterback. Son of Vince Boryla, former pro basketball great and now executive with ABA Utah Stars. Injured in first varsity game at Stanford, 1970. As result was granted another year of eligibility by Pacific Conference. Played sparingly in 1971, backing up Don Bunce who took Indians to Rose Bowl. In 1972 finished 4th nationally in passing and 12th in total offense. Threw for 2284 yds., 14 TDs. Final season, 1973, averaged 12.7 yds. per completion, compiling 1629 passing yds.

BOSLEY, BRUCE L. Center. B. 11/5/33, Fresno, Calif. 6'2", 240. Attended high school in Green Bank, W. Va. Then West Virginia U., 1953-55. Consensus All-America, 1955. Teammate of Sam Huff. Enjoyed long, prosperous career with San Francisco 49ers, 1956-68. Played final season with Atlanta Falcons, 1969. Was pro center. Pro Bowl, 1960, 65, 66, 67.

BOTTARI, VICTOR, JR. Running Back. B. 12/21/16, Vallejo, Calif. 5'9", 177. California, 1936-38. Consensus All-America, 1938. Called signals from left halfback position and handled most kicking duties. One of few players of era to dropkick conversions. Short in stature, had huge shoulders and legs. Seldom hit squarely by tacklers because of unique talent for sliding off for extra yardage. Crushing blocker and tackler, fine passer. In 1937 sparked Bears to unbeaten season and 13-0 Rose Bowl win over Alabama. Lost only once in college; 13-7 to Southern California, in 1938. Named to *Sports Illustrated* Silver Anniversary All-America team in 1963. Now insurance broker in Oakland.

BOWDITCH, EDWARD, JR. (Pete) End. B. 10/29/81, Albany, N.Y. D. 4/6/65. 6', 173. Harvard, 1900-02. All-America 1902; 2nd team, 1901. Supreme end in pre-forward pass era. Played for 1900 Crimson squad which beat Yale, 28-0. Combined with teammate Soup Campbell to form one of Harvard's greatest end combinations.

BOYD, ROBERT D. Defensive Back. B. 12/3/37, Garland, Tex. 5'10½", 195. Oklahoma QB, 1957-59. Drafted on 10th round by Baltimore Colts in 1960. Switched to cornerback in Colt training camp. Became safety in 1963. Led NFL in interceptions, 1965. Pro Bowl, 1964, 68. Super Bowl III, 1969, was his last game. Four-time All-Pro, 1964, 65, 66, 68. Intercepted eight passes in 1968, giving him 57 for career. Now ranks 5th on all-time list. In 1969 became Colt defensive backfield coach. His charges led AFC in interceptions with 28 in 1971.

In 1972 coached Jack Mildren, also former Oklahoma QB. Exited after 1972 season in mass firing of Baltimore coaches.

BOYETTE, GARLAND D. Linebacker. B. 3/22/40, Orange, Tex. 6'1", 235. Played for Grambling, was Little All-America. Signed as free agent with St. Louis Cardinals in 1962. Tried for 1960 Olympic decathlon team, barely missed qualifying. In 1964 joined Montreal Alouettes of Canadian League. All-Canadian, 1965. MVP in CFL, 1965. In 1966 jumped to Houston Oilers, playing with club thru 1972. Returned three kickoffs in 1966 for 42 yds. Two career interceptions. Played in 1968 AFL All-Star game. Played guard, defensive end. outside linebacker, middle linebacker. Uncle of Ernie Ladd, former football player, wrestler.

BOYNTON, BEN L. Quarterback. B. 12/6/1898, Waco, Tex. D. 1/23/63. 160. Williams, 1917, 19-20. 3rd-team All-America, 1919, 20. Led team to 18-5-1 record, including upsets over Columbia, Cornell. Swift, elusive, strong passer. Known as "Purple Streak." Tied collegiate record by returning punt 110 yds. in 1920. Rochester Jeffersons, 1921-22; Buffalo Bisons, 1924. During 1921 game dived over defensive lineman, landing on head and shoulders. Got back on his feet and ran 70 yds. for TD. At Rochester was teammate of Elmer Oliphant. Paid $250 per game. Later, he was Texas amateur golf champion. National Football Foundation Hall of Fame.

BRADLEY, BILL Defensive Back. B. 1/24/47, Palestine, Tex. 5'11", 190. Texas, 1966-68. Lettered three years. Played QB, wide receiver and defensive back. Played in Hula Bowl and Coaches All-American games. Selected by Philadelphia Eagles on 3rd round of 1969 draft. In 1969, vs. Dallas, returned interception 56 yds. for TD. Led NFL in interceptions, 1971, with 11, for 248 yds; longest was 51 yds. Repeated as interception leader with nine, 1972. Hobby is painting. All-NFC, 1971, 72, 73. Played in Pro Bowl following 1971, 72, 73 seasons. Also punts, returns punts, holds on placekicks.

BRADSHAW, JAMES (Rabbit) Quarterback. B. 6/23/1898, Greene County, Mo. Football, track, tennis star in high school. Attended U. of Illinois and Nevada. Graduated from Nevada in 1922. Participated in football, basketball, track while in college. Was great open-field runner. All-Pacific Coast in football, 1920, 21. Captain of basketball and track teams. Olympic Club, 1922, 25. One year professional ball with Wilson Wildcats, 1926. Toured in exhibition games with New York Yankees, coached by Red Grange. Player-coach of San Francisco Tigers, 1927. Coached high school football seven years. Freshman and/or backfield coach at Stanford under Pop Warner seven years. Head coach at Fresno State eight years. Freshman and assistant varsity basketball coach at Stanford, 1928-35. Citizens Savings Hall of Fame.

BRADSHAW, TERRY P. Quarterback. B. 9/2/48, Shreveport, La. 6'3", 214. Exceptionally strong-armed quarterback. Louisiana Tech, 1966-69. 1968 college-division champion in total offense, gaining 2987 yds. on 426 plays in 10 games. His career total offense yardage was 6664. 1970 1st-round draft pick of Pittsburgh Steelers. As rookie had most passes intercepted (24) to lead league, 1970. Threw 22 interceptions in 1971 but had good completion record of 54.4 percent. In 1972 had only 12 passes intercepted; threw for 12 TDs., 1887 yds., 47.7 percent. Averaged better than five yds. per carry through first four pro seasons. In 1972 playoff game vs. Oakland Raiders, combined with Franco Harris on 60-yd. TD pass play. Ball bounced off Oakland's Jack Tatum, Harris grabbed it and ran for winning score as time expired. Played infrequently during 1973 season due to injury but compiled record of 89 completions in 180 attempts for 1183 yds., 10 TDs. In '73 playoff game vs. Oakland completed 12 of 25 passes. Owns 400-acre ranch in Grand Cane, La. Wife is former Miss Teen-Age America.

BRADY, PATRICK Defensive Back-Kicker. B. 9/7/28, Seattle, Wash. 6'3", 210. Nevada, 1949-51. Made 99-yd. punt in 1950 against Loyola (Calif.), longest in modern college football history. Pittsburgh Steelers, 1952-54. Led league in 1953 with 43.2-yd. punting average, again in 1954 with 46.9 average.

BRAHANEY, THOMAS F. Center. B. 10/23/51, Midland, Tex. 6'2", 225. Twice consensus All-America at Oklahoma, 1971, 72. Sooners were 11-1 both years and climaxed seasons with Sugar Bowl victories. One of eight finalists for 1972 Lombardi Trophy. Named to College All-Star and Coaches All-America game rosters. St. Louis Cardinals, 1973. Was 5th-round draft choice.

BRAMLETT, JOHN C. (Bull) Linebacker. B. 7/7/41, Memphis, Tenn. 6'1", 210. Attended Memphis State. Played football and baseball. Signed as pro baseball player in 1963. Earned nickname "Bull" by running through wood fence. Played at Winnipeg and Billings, 1963; Tulsa and Raleigh, 1964. In 1965 switched to football, signing with Denver Broncos as free agent. Broncos, 1965-66; Miami Dolphins, 1967-68; Boston Patriots, 1969-70; Atlanta Falcons, 1971. Returned attempted field goal for TD in 1966. Holds degree in industrial technology.

BRATKOWSKI, EDMUND R. (Zeke) Quarterback B. 10/20/31, Danville, Ill. 6'2", 210. Georgia, 1951-53. Easily discouraged and lacking maturity, he was held out of competition in 1950 (scheduled to be sophomore season) by Bulldog coach Wally Butts. Wound up throwing for 4863 yds. and 360 completions, both SEC three-year records. Led NCAA in interceptions thrown with 29, 1951; again in 1953 with 23. Set career record by throwing 68 interceptions on 734 attempts. In 1952 led nation in passing yds. with 1824. NCAA punting leader twice, 1952, 53. Received nickname as youngster because he wore baseball uniform bearing name of Zeke Bonura. Chicago Bears, 1954, 57-60; Los Angeles Rams, 1961-63; Green Bay Packers, 1963-68, 71. Played briefly in Super Bowl I and II. Came out of retirement to play 1971 season. Excellent backup quarterback. Assistant coach, Chicago Bears, 1973.

BRENNAN, TERRANCE P. (Terry) Running Back. B. 6/11/28, Milwaukee,

Wis. Notre Dame, 1945-48. Father, brother both played football for Notre Dame; father, Martin, as center, 1909; brother, Jim, as halfback, 1944, 46-47. Attended Milwaukee's Marquette H.S. Was on track team four years, won three letters in football and played hockey. Enrolled at Notre Dame, 1945, at age 17. Played 1945 for Hugh Devore; 1946-48 for Frank Leahy, whom he would succeed as coach in 1954 at age 26. Teammate of George Connor, Johnny Lujack. In 1947, vs. Army, ran back opening kickoff 97 yds. for TD. Irish were 1947 national champions. Earned varsity letters in football, track, hockey. 1947 statistics: 11 TDs, 87 carries, 16 receptions for 191 yds., 11 punt returns for 115 yds. — led team in each category for second straight year. Earned degree in pre-law and then attended Loyola and De Paul, both in Chicago. Received law degree in 1953. Coached Chicago's Mt. Carmel H.S. while earning law degree and won city championships 1950, 51, 52. Coached Notre Dame, 1954-58. Leahy called him "a very talented young man who borders almost on the genius as a coach." In 1954 lost only to Purdue, led by QB Len Dawson. 1954 team ranked No. 4 in nation. 1955 squad shattered by 42-20 defeat to Southern California, but still had 8-2 record. In 1955, Brennan converted Paul Hornung from fullback to QB. 1956 record was 2-8-0; 1957, 7-3-0; 1958, 6-4-0. Replaced by Joe Kuharich at end of 1958 season. Was dismissed for "failing to fulfill Notre Dame's commitment to excellence."

BREWER, CHARLES Running Back. B. Honolulu, Hawaii. D. 1959. 5'9", 150. Harvard, 1892-95. All-America halfback, 1892, 93. Excellent runner, fine blocker. Probably would have been All-America in 1894 except for injury. Led Harvard to 48 wins in 54 games. Served as Harvard rusher in first "flying wedge" play, 1892 vs. Yale, after receiving ball from captain Bernie Trafford. Was banker. National Football Foundation Hall of Fame.

BREWER, JOHN L. (Tonto) Linebacker. B. 3/8/37, Vicksburg, Miss. 6'4", 230. Mississippi, 1958-60. Drafted by Cleveland Browns, 1961. Pro Bowl, 1966. Nicknamed because of Indian ancestry. NFL title games, 1964, 65. Intercepted two passes for 75 yds., 1 TD in 1967. In 1968 dealt to New Orleans Saints, stayed thru 1970. Strong linebacker. Defensive end as pro rookie.

BRICKLEY, CHARLES E. Running Back. 11/24/1898, Boston, Mass. D. 12/28/49. 5'10", 186. Harvard All-America halfback, 1912, 13. In 1913 drop-kicked 13 FGs. Same year dropkicked five FGs against Yale for 15-0 victory. Kicked 34 career FGs, 1911-13. Citizens Savings Player of the Year, 1913. Citizens Savings Hall of Fame.

BRIGHT, JOHN Halfback. B. 6/11/30, Ft. Wayne, Ind. 6'0", 195. Drake, 1949-51. All-America, 1950. Was major college total-offense leader in 1949, gaining 1950 yds. Repeated in 1950 with record 2400 yds. Accounted for 30 TDs that season, another record. In 1950 game vs. South Dakota, made 86-yd. rush and set game record of 15.2 total-offense yds. per play. In 25-game career scored 40 TDs, 240 points, for 9.6 average points per game. Set additional season records in passing yds. per attempt (9.3), rushing yds. per carry (6.7), pass completion percentage (.591). Finished career 1st in total-offense yds. (5903), 1st in total-offense yds. per play with 7.16 (5903 yds. on 825 plays), 1st in TDs-accounted-for (64), 2nd in rushing yds. (3134), 2nd in rushing yds. per carry (6.1). Did not play in NFL.

BRILL, MARTIN (Marty) Running Back. D. 4/30/73, Los Angeles, Calif. Outstanding blocker, adept runner. Played for Notre Dame 1928-30. All-America, 1930. Reached peak in 1930 win (60-20) over Penn, where he originally enrolled. Switched to Notre Dame as sophomore after clashes with coach Lud Wray. Coach Rockne allegedly told QB Frank Carideo to let Brill loose for revenge vs. Penn, but all involved denied it. In 1931 went to Columbia as assistant coach, staying two seasons. LaSalle head coach, 1933-39. Head coach at Loyola (Los Angeles), 1940-41. In 1943 joined USMC. At time of death was sales manager for liquor distributing company.

BRISCOE, MARLIN (Magician) End-Quarterback. B. 9/10/45, Oakland, Calif. 5'11", 180. Graduated from Nebraska (Omaha). Set 22 school passing and total offense records. NAIA All-America, 1967. Drafted on 14th round by Denver Broncos, 1968. Played with Broncos, 1968; Buffalo Bills, 1969-71; Miami Dolphins, 1972-73. In 1968, Briscoe became first Black to play QB on regular basis for pro team. Gained 1897 yds. total offense that year, 1589 passing and 308 rushing. Has been wide-receiver, almost exclusively, ever since. 1970 AFC pass-receiving leader with 57 (1036 yds.). Was traded by Bills prior to 1972 season with defensive tackle Jim Dunaway; Dolphins gave up linebacker Dale Farley and 1st-round draft choice. All-AFC, 1970. Pro Bowl, 1971. AFC championship games, 1972, 73. Super Bowl, 1973, 74.

BROCKINGTON, JOHN Running Back. B. 9/7/48, Brooklyn, N.Y. 6'1", 225. Played for Ohio State, 1968-70. Veteran of Rose Bowl, Hula Bowl, College All-Star games. All-America, 1970. In 1971 drafted by Green Bay Packers on 1st round. 1971 NFC rushing champion with 1105 yds., highest ever for rookie. 1971 NFC Offensive Rookie of the Year. In 1972 became first player in seven years (since Jim Brown) to gain 1000 yds. or more two years in row, and first ever to do so first two years in league. Had NFC's leading total of 1114 yds. in 1973, becoming first player in NFL history to rush for 1000 or more yds. in each of first three pro seasons. In last regular-season game, 12/16/73, gained 142 yds. on 22 carries. All-NFC, 1971, 72, 73. Pro Bowl, 1972, 73, 74. Teams with MacArthur Lane to form outstanding running combination. Durable and consistent, Brockington should make Packers strong offensively for years to come.

BRODIE, JOHN R. Quarterback. B. 8/14/35, San Francisco, Calif. 6'1", 210. Played QB for Stanford, 1954-56. Consensus All-America, 1956. In 1955 made 62-yd. pass vs. California. Led NCAA in passing, 1956, with 139 completions in 240 attempts for 1633 yds., percentage of .579, 12 TDs. Also led that year in total offense plays with 295, for 1642 yds. Finished collegiate career with 296 completions in 536 attempts for 3594 yds., 37 interceptions, 19 TDs. Gained 3560 yds. on total offense on 652 plays. MVP in College All-Star game, 1957. Selected by San Francisco 49ers on 1st round of 1957 draft. First four seasons backed up Y. A. Tittle, becoming regular in 1961 when "Bald Eagle" was dealt to New York Giants.

In 1958 led league in passing percentage with 59.9 (103 completions in 172 attempts, 13 interceptions, 1224 yds.). Led league in average yds. per pass completion, 1961, with 9.14 (155 completions for 2588 yds.). In 1965 led in passing attempts with 391, completions with 242, passing percentage with 61.9, yds. with 3112, TDs passing with 30. In 1968 vs. Atlanta Falcons made 17 completions in 20 attempts. In 1968 completed 234 of 404 passes for 3020 yds., had most interceptions with 21. NFL passing leader, 1970, with 223 completions for 2941 yds. and 24 TDs. Jim Thorpe Trophy, 1970. Retired after 1973 season. Finished 17-year career with 55 percent completion average with 2469 completions on 4491 attempts for 31,548 yds., 214 TDs, 224 interceptions. One of four players to pass for more than 30,000 yds. Joined NFL Management Council Committee on artificial turf and player safety. Appeared with teammate Gene Washington in premiere episode of TV's *Banacek*. All-NFC and NFC Player of the Year, 1970. Pro Bowl, 1966, 71. In 1970 NFC championship game threw TD pass to Dick Witcher. Extremely talented, confident. Became richest pro player in 1966 when he signed contract worth more than $1,000,000.

BROOKE, GEORGE H. Running Back. B. 7/9/1874, Brookville, Md. 5'9", 174. Pennsylvania, 1893-95. All-America halfback, 1894; fullback, 1895. Played for Swarthmore, 1889-92, before attending Penn. Thus played seven years of college football. When first made All-America was 19 years old. Powerful runner, excellent kicker. Known for long, low, spiraling punts which were hard for receivers to handle. Good football sense. Served in Spanish-American War. Head coach at Stanford, 1897; Swarthmore, 1898-1911. Fine football official, tennis player. National Football Foundation Hall of Fame.

BROOKER, WILLIAM T. (Tommy) End-Kicker. B. Demopolis, Ala. 6'2", 230. Alabama, 1959-61. Dallas Texans, 1962; Kansas City Chiefs, 1963-66. In 1962 AFL title game vs. Houston Oilers, kicked 25-yd. FG to win what was then longest game ever. Boot came at 12:56 of 2nd overtime period. It was only overtime title game in AFL history and remained longest pro contest until 12/24/71 when surpassed by Miami-Kansas City playoff. In 1966 played on AFL championship team; lost in Super Bowl I to Green Bay Packers, 35-10.

BROOKSHIER, THOMAS Defensive Back. B. 12/16/31, Rosewell, N.M. 6'1", 194. Played at Colorado, 1950-52. Philadelphia Eagles, 1953, 56-61. Inactive in 1954-55. Smart defensive back. Played with Philadelphia's world championship team, 1960. Pro Bowl, 1960, 61. Currently, analyst on CBS-TV football telecasts.

BROSKY, ALBERT Defensive Back. B. Chicago, Ill. 5'11", 172. Illinois, 1950-52. All-America, 1951. Played on Illinois' undefeated 1951 team. He and halfback Johnny Karras led Illinois to Big 10 championship and Rose Bowl. In 1950 vs. Iowa Brosky had 61-yd. interception return; 31-yd. interception return in 1952 Rose Bowl. Holds major-college record for passes intercepted, career, with 29, for 356 yds., average of 12.3 yds. Also holds record for consecutive games intercepting pass, with 15, beginning 11/11/50 and ending 10/18/52. Played pro ball only one season, with Chicago Cardinals in 1954.

BROWN, AARON L., JR. Defensive End. B. 11/16/43, Port Arthur, Tex. 6'5", 265. Minnesota, 1963-65. Played tight end and defensive end. Consensus All-America, 1965. Kansas City Chiefs, 1966, 68-72; Green Bay Packers, 1973. Was drafted No. 1 by Chiefs. Missed 1967 season with thigh injury. Had brief trial as pro fullback, before making permanent home at defensive end. Excellent tackler, pass rusher. Not happy in Kansas City area and asked to be traded following 1972 campaign. Chiefs acceded to wishes, sent him to Packers for Francis Peay. Played in Super Bowl, 1967, 70. Owns successful gourmet cookware, glassware and fabric business in Minneapolis.

BROWN, B. STANLEY Running Back. B. 8/4/49, Martinez, Calif. 5'11", 174. Purdue, 1968-70. Was 1969 kickoff return champion with 698 yds. (average of 26.8). Repeated in 1970 with 33.6 average, accumulated on 19 returns for 638 yds. In 1970 tied NCAA record by scoring three TDs on kickoff returns. Career kickoff return average was 28.8, on 49 returns for 1412 yds. Played flanker one season for Cleveland Browns, 1971.

BROWN, C. EDWARD Quarterback. B. 10/26/28, San Luis Obispo, Calif. 6'2", 210. Attended U. of San Francisco. Brown and nine of his college team-mates, including Bob St. Clair, Gino Marchetti, Ollie Matson, became pros. Chicago Bears, 1954-61; Pittsburgh Steelers, 1962-65; Baltimore Colts, 1965. Was serving in marines when drafted by Bears. 1956 NFL passing leader, gaining 1667 yds. (96 of 168 for 11 TDs).

BROWN, GORDON F. (Skim) Guard. B. 9/6/1880, New York, N.Y. D. 5/10/11, Glen Head, N.Y. 6'4", 202. Yale All-America, 1897-1900. One of three men to make All-America four times (others: Frank Hinkey, Truxton Hare). Captained 1900 Bulldogs, one of Yale's best teams, winning all 12 games. All members of starting team named to Camp's All-America, 1900. In 1900 game vs. Columbia, Brown's fine defensive play was major factor in 12-5 victory. George Trevor wrote: "Gordon Brown, scholar and gentleman to the manor born, was the most inspirational of all Yale captains...this sensitive, high-principled youngster never let his nerves get the best of him." Phi Beta Kappa. After graduation became successful banker with J.P. Morgan & Co. Died of diabetes at age 30. Citizens Savings Hall of Fame, National Football Foundation Hall of Fame.

BROWN, HARDY Linebacker. B. 5/8/24, Childress, Tex. 5'11", 180. U. of Tulsa, 1945-47. Brooklyn Dodgers (AAFC), 1948; Chicago Hornets (AAFC), 1949; Baltimore Colts, 1950; Washington Redskins, 1950; San Francisco 49ers, 1951-56; Chicago Cardinals, 1957; Denver Broncos, 1960. Shares distinction with kicker Ben (Automatic) Agajanian of being only players ever to play in AAFC, NFL, AFL.

BROWN, JAMES (Jimmy) Running Back. B. 2/17/36, St. Simons Island, Ga. 6'2", 228. Fullback comparisons begin and end with Jimmy Brown. Had outstanding athletic career at Manhasset (N.Y.) H.S., offered scholarships by 45 colleges. Played for Syracuse U., 1954-56. Consensus All-America, 1956. In senior year, vs. Colgate, scored 43 points for major-college record, on 6 TDs, 7 PATs. Syracuse met TCU in Cotton Bowl where Brown scored 21 points; TCU won, 28-27. During Orange career gained 2091 yds., scored 187 points, including 25 TDs. Played 43 collegiate basketball games, scored 563 points. Also participated in track and lacrosse, placed 5th in national decathlon championships. Played for College All-Stars in 1957 All-Star game. 1st-round draft pick of Cleveland Browns, 1957. Played with Browns, 1957-65. NFL rushing leader in seven years, 1957, 58, 60, 61, 63, 64, 65. Runnerup to Jim Taylor of Green Bay Packers in 1962. Led NFL in scoring, 1958, with 108 points. Scored 21 TDs in 1965, breaking season record. Legged 126 career TDs, decimating former record of 105 by Don Hutson. On 11/24/57, vs. Los Angeles Rams, rushed for 237 yds. on 31 attempts; duplicated that amount, 11/19/61, vs. Philadelphia Eagles; on 9/23/63, vs. Dallas Cowboys, gained 232 yds.; on 10/3/63, vs. Eagles, gained 223 yds. on 28 attempts.

Most feted fullback in football, duals with linebacker Sam Huff were classics. Close friend of Ernie Davis, who broke many of his collegiate records. Instrumental in bringing Davis to Browns, though Davis died of leukemia before playing single pro game. Browns won Eastern Conference championships in 1964, 65. Beat Baltimore Colts, 27-0, in '64 title game; lost to Packers in '65. Retired as greatest ball carrier in NFL history. In nine seasons gained 12,312 yds. rushing, total of 15,459 yds. Became businessman and actor. Outspoken, promotes Black economic causes. Pro Bowl MVP, 1962, 63. All-NFL eight years. Jim Thorpe Trophy, 1958, 63 (shared with Y. A. Tittle), 65. Pro Football Hall of Fame.

BROWN, JOHN H., JR. (Babe) Guard. B. 9/12/1891, Canton, Pa. D. 6/10/63, Wilmington, Del. 6'2", 216. Navy, 1910-13. All-America guard, 1913; 2nd team, 1910; 3rd team, 1912; 3rd team, tackle, 1911. Navy defeated Army three straight years, 1910, 11, 12, without scoring single touchdown. Brown kicked FG to win 1912 game. Served in both world wars. Engaged in submarine operations in South Pacific during World War II. Retired from Navy as Vice Adm. Was president of National Football Foundation and Hall of Fame from 1954 until his death. Inducted into Hall of Fame, 1951.

BROWN, JOHN MACK (Johnny) Running Back. B. 9/1/04, Dothan, Ala. Alabama, 1923-25. All-America, 1925. Primarily ran end-around plays. Member of Wallace Wade's undefeated, untied team of 1925. Squad was first from South to participate in Rose Bowl, 1926. Brown was named outstanding player, scored two of three Tide TDs. Alabama won, 20-19. Hollywood then beckoned, and Brown made film debut in *The Bugle Call*. In 1930, he starred as *Billy the Kid*, also featuring Wallace Beery. Appeared with such popular feminine stars as Greta Garbo, Mary Pickford, Joan Crawford. Concentrated on westerns after 1933, became one of screen's most revered cowboys. Citizens Savings Hall of

Fame, National Football Foundation Hall of Fame.

BROWN, LAWRENCE (Larry) Running Back. B. 9/19/47, Clairton, Pa. 5'11", 195. Kansas State, 1966-68. Transferred there from Dodge City (Kan.) J.C. Good blocker but ran ball very little in college. Developed dislike for Kansas State coach Vince Gibson. Impressed Vince Lombardi and drafted by Washington Redskins on 8th round of 1969 draft. Missed signals in training camp when lined up on left side. Finally admitted to being almost totally deaf in right ear and was given hearing aid. Offensive Rookie of the Year, 1969. Had three 100-yd. games rushing in 1969 season. In 1970, became 22nd NFL player to surpass 1000 yds. in season, led NFL rushers with 1125 yds. Barely beat out New York Giants' Ron Johnson. Six 100-yd. games in 1970. Rushed for 948 yds., 1971; league-leading 1216 yds., 1972; 860 yds., 1973. Has now rushed for more than 5000 yds. One of those gifted runners who seem to smell goal line. Good pass receiver, too. ALL-NFC, 1970, 71, 72. Pro Bowl, 1970, 71, 72, 73. Recipient of Bert Bell Award, Jim Thorpe Trophy, Vince Lombardi Award, Gillette Cavalcade of Champions Award, all in 1972. Author of *I'll Always Get Up*. Played in 1973 Super Bowl.

BROWN, PAUL Coach. B. 9/7/08, Massillon, Ohio. Graduated from Miami (Ohio), 1930. In 1940 received master's degree from Ohio State. Coached Massillon (Ohio) H.S., 1932-40, with phenomenal success. Earned him appointment as Ohio State head coach in 1941. 18-6-1 with Buckeyes, 1941-43. Tutored Great Lakes Naval Training Station, 1944-45. Head coach, Cleveland Browns, 1948-62, and Cincinnati Bengals, 1968-73. At Cleveland won four AAFC titles, six consecutive Eastern Conference (NFL) championships, three world championships. Browns completely dominated four-year history of AAFC, 1946-49. Guided Bengals to AFC Central Division titles, 1970, 73. Pro record: 195-94-9. Currently 3rd winningest pro coach. Made football exact science. Called all plays from sideline by using messenger guards, developed detailed pass patterns. Firm disciplinarian, pioneered use of Black players. Pro Football Hall of Fame.

BROWN, ROBERT S. (Boomer) Tackle. B. 12/8/41, Cleveland, Ohio. 6'4", 280. Graduated from Nebraska. Unanimous All-America guard, 1963. Was voted Lineman of the Year in '63 by Washington, D.C., Touchdown Club. Played in 1963 Gotham Bowl and '64 Orange Bowl. Philadelphia Eagles, 1964-68; Los Angeles Rams, 1970; Oakland Raiders, 1971-73. Giant, menacing figure on field. Has few peers as pass protector. Veteran of six Pro Bowl games. All-NFL, 1964, 65, 68, 69; All-AFC, 1970, 71, 72. Dedicated to off-season weightlifting and conditioning. Owns MEA degree from Pennsylvania.

BROWN, ROGER L. Defensive Tackle. B. 5/1/37, Surry County, Va. 6'5", 285. Played for Maryland State. Drafted on 4th round by Detroit Lions, 1960, and stayed with club thru 1966. Then Los Angeles Rams, 1967-69. Tied NFL record for safeties, season, with two in 1962. Finished career with three, also tying pro record. Replaced Rosey Grier in Ram "Fearsome Foursome." Almost immovable from defensive tackle post. Pro Bowl, 1962, 63, 64, 65, 66, 67.

BROWN, THOMAS A. (Tim) Running Back. B. 5/24/37, Richmond, Ind. 5'll", 198. Graduated from Ball State of Indiana. Drafted on 27th round by Green Bay Packers in 1959. In 1960 released by Packers and signed by Philadelphia Eagles. Helped them to NFL championship. On 9/17/61, vs. Cleveland Browns, returned season-opening kickoff 105 yds. for TD. On 9/16/62, vs. St. Louis Cardinals scored TD on 99-yd. return of FG attempt. On 11/6/66, vs. Dallas Cowboys, netted record 2 TDs on kickoff returns (93 and 90 yds.). Record was tied in 1967 by Travis Williams. Quick halfback, occasionally passed. In 1968, traded to Baltimore Colts for defensive back Alvin Haymond. Played for Baltimore in Super Bowl III, 1969. Launched singing career after football and now plays nightclubs.

BROWN, WILLIAM D. Running Back. B. 6/29/38, Mendota, Ill. 5'11", 221. Illinois, 1958-60. Won All-Big 10 honors as fullback. Won three football letters, three in track (weightman). Chicago Bears, 1961; Minnesota Vikings, 1962-73. Was 2nd-round draft choice of Bears. Holds Viking career records for rushes, rushing yardage, pass receptions. Fine power runner and blocker. Ranks 8th on all-time rushing list with 5797 yds. Serves on Minnesota special teams. Pro Bowl, 1964, 65, 67, 68. Super Bowl, 1970, 74.

BROWN, WILLIAM F. (Willie) Defensive Back. B. 12/2/40, Yazoo City, Miss. 6'2", 190. Attended Grambling, 1960-63. Denver Broncos, 1963-66; Oakland Raiders, 1967-73. Doesn't run back punts or kickoffs as do many defensive players. Signed by Broncos as free agent. In 1964, made nine interceptions for 140 yds., 3rd best in league. On 11/15/64, vs. New York Jets, set AFL game record with four interceptions, leading Broncos to 20-16 win. In 1965, vs. Jets, jarred ball from receiver's hands and ran it back to set up game-winning FG. In 1969, vs. Jets, held George Sauer to one reception, 16 yds. Doesn't make great number of interceptions because opposition stays away from his side. All-AFL cornerback, 1964, 68. AFL All-Star games following 1964, 65, 67, 68 seasons. Named outstanding defensive player in '64 game. AFL championship games, 1967, 68. Super Bowl, 1968. In '73 playoff game intercepted Terry Bradshaw pass and returned it 54 yds. for TD. Pro Bowl, 1971, 72, 73, 74. Off-season works for Shell Oil Co.

BROYLES, FRANK Coach. B. 12/26/24, Decatur, Ga. Graduated from Georgia Tech, 1947. Played QB. Coached Missouri, 1957, with record of 5-4-1. Became head coach at Arkansas, 1958. Still coaching there. Thru 1973 Arkansas record stood at 128-53-1. In 16 years Razorbacks went to Cotton Bowl thrice (1 win, 2 losses), Sugar Bowl four times (1 win, 3 losses), Gator Bowl once (won), Liberty Bowl once (lost). Team sustained 22-game winning streak, 1963-65. Had undefeated season in 1964, Arkansas' first in 55 years; team ranked No. 2 in country. Shared Coach of the Year award in 1964 with Ara Parseghian, first tie for honor. Lost national championship game to Texas, 15-14, in 1969. President

Nixon attended; it was voted "Game of the Century."

BRUMBAUGH, CARL Quarterback. B. 9/22/07, West Milton, Ohio. D. 10/25/69, West Milton, Ohio. 5'10", 165. Florida QB. Chicago Bears, 1930-34, 36, 38. Teammates included Bronko Nagurski, Pug Manders, Red Grange. Cleveland Rams, 1937. First modern T-formation QB. Got trial with Bears thru coach Charlie Bachman, who had played with Chicago coach, George Halas, at Great Lakes Naval Training Station during World War I. Roommate of Nagurski. Assistant coach of Bears under Halas for several seasons after playing career. Later assistant coach for Chicago Cardinals, collegiately at Boston College, Holy Cross, Cincinnati, West Virginia.

BRUMM, DONALD D. (Boomer) Defensive End. B. 10/4/41, Chicago Heights, Ill. 6'4", 250. Purdue, 1960-62. All-America tackle, 1962. Played in East-West, Hula Bowl, College All-Star games. St. Louis Cardinals, 1963-69, 72-73. Philadelphia Eagles, 1970-71. Was 1st-round draft choice of Cardinals. Signed with Eagles as free agent. Returned to St. Louis in 1972 after Eagles placed him on waivers. Returned fumbles for touchdowns in both 1965, 68. Pro Bowl, 1968. Off-season is sales representative for United Van Lines.

BRYANT, BOBBY L. Defensive Back. B. 1/24/44, Macon, Ga. 6'0", 175. Attended South Carolina. Selected by Minnesota Vikings on 7th round of 1967 draft. Member of Minnesota taxi squad, 1967; played that year with Des Moines in Professional Football League of America. In first five years with Vikings made 20 interceptions for 330 yds. and 2 TDs, returned 49 punts for 272 yds., returned 22 kickoffs for 437 yds. Led NFC in interceptions, 1973, with 7 for 105 yds., longest 46 yds., 1 TD. Made two more interceptions vs. Dallas Cowboys in 1973 NFC championship game, one Roger Staubach pass which he ran back 63 yds. for TD. Missed 1970 Super Bowl due to injury, though played regularly during '69 season.

BRYANT, PAUL W. (Bear) Coach. B. 9/11/13, Moro Bottoms, Ark. Played at Alabama, 1933-35. Was teammate of Don Hutson, Dixie Howell. Played in 1935 Rose Bowl. Nicknamed "Bear" because he is supposed to have wrestled one at fair in Fordyce, Ark. Coached Maryland, 1945; Kentucky, 1946-53; Texas A. & M., 1954-57; Alabama, 1958-73. Took Kentucky to 1950 Orange Bowl, losing to Santa Clara, 21-13. Following year defeated Oklahoma, 13-7, in Sugar Bowl. In 1952 Cotton Bowl, Kentucky beat Texas Christian, 20-7. At Kentucky developed Babe Parilli, George Blanda. In 1958 became head coach at Alabama where he coached such luminaries as Joe Namath, Lee Roy Jordan, Ken Stabler. Alabama record is 140-31-7 after 16 seasons. Tide won national championships in 1961, 64, 65 (shared). 1966 team had 11-0 record. Took Alabama to bowl game every year except 1958, inaugural season there. Bowl record: 6-7-1, but 0-6-1 in last seven games.

1973 Alabama team was undefeated, averaging 41 points in 11 games, until it met Notre Dame in 1973 Sugar Bowl. Notre Dame won in clasic battle, 24-23. Coached South in Senior Bowl, 1956, 57, 58, 59, winning every year except '58.

Coach of the Year, 1961. After 29 years, record stands at 231-70-16. Only Alonzo Stagg and Pop Warner have won more games collegiately. In 1963, Bryant and Wally Butts of Georgia, were accused by *Saturday Evening Post* of fixing 1962 Alabama-Georgia game. Both brought suit and Butts awarded large settlement by court. Bryant chose to settle out of court for $300,000. In 1968 received 1/2 vote for President at Democratic National Convention. Also serves Alabama as athletic director.

BUCHANAN, JUNIOUS (Buck) Defensive Tackle. B. 9/10/40, Gainesville, Ala. 6'7", 275. Played for Grambling, 1960-63. Also earned letter in basketball, starring alongside center Willis Reed. Member of College All-Star team that defeated Green Bay Packers in 1963. Drafted by Oakland on 1st round, 1963, but traded to Kansas City Chiefs for two 1st-round draft choices. Voted Chief MVP by teammates in 1965, 67. Knocked down 16 passes in 1967. In 1970, vs. St. Louis Cardinals, blocked FG and knocked down 4th-quarter pass in 6-6 game. Played in 1966 AFL championship game and subsequent Super Bowl. Veteran of seven AFL All-Star games. Enjoys cooking and playing cards. Excellent paddle-ball player. *Pro Football Weekly* All AFL-NFL team, 1969. Pro Bowl, 1971, 72. Also played in Super Bowl IV, 1970. Great speed for size, terrific pass rusher. NAIA Hall of Fame.

BUCHANON, WILLIE J. Defensive Back. B. 11/4/50, Oceanside, Calif. 6', 196. Attended Mira Costa (Calif.) J.C. San Diego State cornerback, 1970-71. All-America, 1971. MVP in East-West Shrine game after intercepting three passes. Starter in 1972 College All-Star game. Green Bay Packers, 1972-73. Was 1st-round draft choice. A.P. Defensive Rookie of the Year. Scored on blocked FG return (57 yds.) against New Orleans Saints in 1972. Has 9.4 speed in 100-yd. dash. Should have great pro career.

BUKICH, RUDOLPH A. (Rifle) Quarterback. B. 12/15/32, St. Louis, Mo. 6'1", 195. Drafted by Los Angeles Rams in 1953 after graduation from Southern California. In military, 1954-55. Played for Rams, 1953, 56; Washington Redskins, 1957-58; Chicago Bears, 1958-59, 62-68; Pittsburgh Steelers, 1960-61. In 1964 tied NFL record (since broken) with 13 consecutive pass completions. Led NFL in TD passes with 20, 1965. That year completed 176 of 312 passes for 2614 yds., 20 TDs.

BULAICH, NORMAN B. Running Back. B. 12/25/46, Galveston, Tex. 6'1", 218. Attended Texas Christian. Won three football letters, two in track. Played in North-South game, 1970. Clocked at 9.6 in 100-yd. dash. Baltimore Colts, 1970-72; Philadelphia Eagles, 1973. Was 1st-round draft choice of Colts. Named AFC Rookie of the Year in 1970 by Minneapolis Sports Club. Greatest year rushing was 1971 when he gained 743 yds. on 152 carries (4.9 average), scored 8 TDs. Scored two TDs in 1970 AFC championship game. Colts then won Super Bowl V over Dallas Cowboys. In pro career has gained 1712 yds. rushing on 424 carries, caught 67 passes for 810 yds., scored 18 TDs. Big season as receiver in 1973, catching 42 passes for 403 yds.

BUNCOM, FRANK J., JR. Linebacker. B. 11/2/39, Shreveport, La. D. 9/14/69, Cincinnati, Ohio. 6'2", 245. Played at Southern California, 1959-61. Last two years under John McKay. College All-Star and East-West Shrine games. San Diego Chargers, 1962-67; Cincinnati Bengals, 1968. Was taken by Bengals in 1968 expansion draft. Played in AFL All-Star games, 1964, 65, 67. Named Outstanding Defensive Player in 1965 game. All-AFL, 1967. San Diego won AFL title game, 1963; lost in 1964, 65. Excellent pass rusher, tackler. In pro career intercepted 5 passes for 60 yds. His death, which resulted from blood clot caused by knee injury, came on opening day of 1969 season.

BUNKER, PAUL D. Tackle-Running Back. B. 5/7/1881, Michigan. D. 3/16/43, Japan. 5'11", 186. Army All-America tackle, 1901; halfback, 1902. While he played Army lost but one game. Had speed and power. Scored two TDs in last game, leading Cadets to 22-8 win over Navy. Defensively gave good bit of punishment to Navy's Ralph Strassberger, whom he met years later in Philippines. "Bunker," Strassberger said upon recognizing old foe, "I hate you. Let's have a drink." National Football Foundation Hall of Fame.

BUONICONTI, NICHOLAS (Skip) Linebacker. B. 12/15/40, Springfield, Mass. 5'11", 220. Notre Dame, 1959-61. All-America, 1961. Drafted on 13th round by Boston Patriots, 1962. Patriots, 1962-68; Miami Dolphins, 1969-73. Strong pass rusher, good tackler. Usually has hand in team's tackles. Holds degree in economics. Traded to Dolphins for QB Kim Hammond, linebacker John Bramlett and draft choice. In 13 years intercepted 30 passes for 283 yds. Has led Dolphins in tackles every year. Is practicing attorney and president of All-Pro Graphics Co. Received law degree from Suffolk Law School, 1968. Played in AFL All-Star games, 1964, 65, 66, 67, 68, 70. All-League four times with Patriots, 1964, 65, 66, 67. Was Miami's first All-League player, 1969. Pro Bowl, 1973, 74. Played in NFL championship games, 1971, 72, 73. Super Bowl, 1972, 73, 74.

BURFORD, CHRISTOPHER W. End. B. 1/31/38, Oakland, Calif. 6'3", 220. Stanford, 1957-59. All-America, 1959. Finished NCAA career 3rd in catches, 14th in receiving yds. Led all receivers in 1959 with 61 catches, also in receiving yds. with 756. Played end for Dallas Texans, 1960-62; Kansas City Chiefs, 1963-67. (Texans moved to Kansas City prior to 1963 season.) Holds team records for passes caught, lifetime, with 391 (5505 yds.); season, 68 (824 yds.) in 1962; game, 11 on two occasions. In seven seasons with K.C. caught 55 TD passes. Also holds K.C. record for TD passes caught, in season, with league-leading 12, 1962. Selected by Cincinnati Bengals in 1968 expansion draft but didn't play. AFL title games, 1962, 66. Super Bowl, 1967. All-AFL, 1962. AFL All-Star game, 1963.

BURK, ADRIAN Quarterback. B. 12/14/27, Mexia, Tex. 6'2", 190. Graduated from Baylor, 1950. 1949 NCAA passing champion with record 110 completions, totaling 191 attempts, 1428 yds., 14 TDs, 57.6 percentage. In 1950, Don Heinrich broke Burk's record. Baltimore Colts, 1950; Philadelphia Eagles, 1951-56. On

10/17/54, vs. Washington Redskins, threw seven TD passes, record shared by four other players. In 1953 teamed with Bobby Thomason to pass for 3089 yds., leading league in team passing. Attorney in Houston, and NFL official.

BURROUGH, KENNETH O. End. B. 7/14/48, Jacksonville, Fla. 6'3", 212. Played for Texas Southern, 1967-69. All-America, 1969. In college career made 138 receptions for 1912 yds. Also star in track. Played in College All-Star game and Senior Bowl. New Orleans Saints, 1970; Houston Oilers, 1971-73. Was 1st-round draft choice of Saints. Traded to Houston with defensive tackle Dave Rowe; Saints received four players and draft choice. In pro career has 150 pass receptions for 1664 yds., 11 TDs.

BURTON, LEON Running Back. B. Flint, Mich. 5'9", 171. Arizona State, 1955-58. In 1955, vs. Hardin-Simmons, made 90- and 80-yd. rushes. Same year, vs. San Diego State, made 77-yd. rush. Made 79-yd. rush, 1957. Was 1957 NCAA rushing champion with 1126 yds. on 117 carries, average of 9.6. Also set season record in scoring with 96 points, on 16 TDs in 10 games. In career scored 256 points on 42 TDs and four PATs. Played with New York Titans, 1960.

BUTKUS, RICHARD J. Linebacker. B. 12/9/42, Chicago, Ill. 6'3", 245. Known by assortment of nicknames: "Animal," "Paddles," "The Enforcer," "Maestro of Mayhem." Played for Illinois, 1962-64, after being schoolboy All-America fullback. Unanimous All-America, 1963; Consensus, 1964. Starred in 1963 Rose Bowl, '65 College All-Star game. Chicago Bears, 1965-73. Intercepted five passes in rookie year. In 1969 game, vs. Pittsburgh Steelers, made 15 unassisted tackles, assisted on 10 more and downed QB Dick Shiner for safety. 1970 poll of NFC coaches voted him "player they would most like to have on team." Called by George Halas "one of the greatest defensive players in the history of the Bears." Premier middle-linebacker of 60s, early 70s, perhaps best of all time. Reported to have received $200,000 rookie year. Has done sports radio shows in Chicago. In 1972 recovered four fumbles, bringing career total to record-tying 23. Pro Bowl, 1965, 66, 67, 68, 69, 70, 71. Plagued by serious knee problems in 1973, leaving future in doubt.

BUTLER, ROBERT P. (Butts) Tackle. B. 4/4/1891, Glen Ridge, N.J. D. 12/17/59. 5'10", 200. Wisconsin All-America, 1912; 2nd team, 1913. Also participated in water polo (captain) and track. Starred for Wisconsin's undefeated Big 10 champs of 1912. Badgers have not won conference title since. Beat Minnesota in '12, 14-10, without substituting. In seven games, they outscored foes 246-29. Played pro ball with Canton Bulldogs. Owned Continental Hatcheries in Memphis. National Football Foundation Hall of Fame.

BUTTERWORTH, FRANK Running Back. B. 9/21/1870, Maineville, Ohio. D. 8/21/50, Mt. Carmel, Conn. 5'11", 158. Yale fullback, 1892-94. All-America, 1893, 94. Yale head coach, 1897-98. Teammate, classmate, life-long intimate of Frank Hinkey. In famous 1892 upset over Harvard, Laurence Bliss scored only TD and Butterworth made conversion. Played in "Slaughter

Game" vs. Harvard, 1894, in which almost everyone was hurt and Butterworth nearly blinded in one eye. Teams of 1892 and '94 undefeated, '93 team lost only one game, to Princeton. Excellent back, strong, fast, determined.

BUTTS, J. WALLACE (Wally) Coach. B. 2/7/05, Milledgeville, Ga. D. 12/17/73, Athens, Ga. Attended Georgia Military College in hometown. Was standout football, basketball and baseball player there. Graduated from Mercer, 1928. Coached preps for nine years, losing only 10 games. Became assistant coach at Georgia, 1938; head coach, 1939. Remained at helm thru 1960. Once said that 1941 and '42 teams were best, with 1946 team next. 1941 record was 8-1-1, 1942 was 10-1-0; 1946 team was undefeated, untied. 1941 team defeated TCU in Orange Bowl, 40-26; in 1942 Bulldogs shut out UCLA, 9-0, in Rose Bowl. Won four SEC championships and played in six bowl games. Other four were: 1947 Sugar Bowl (defeated North Carolina, 20-10); 1948 Gator Bowl (tied Maryland, 20-20); 1949 Orange Bowl (lost to Texas, 41-28); 1960 Orange Bowl (defeated Missouri, 14-0). Posted 138-86-9 record at Georgia. Developed Frank Sinkwich, Charley Trippi, John Rauch, Zeke Bratkowski. Was accused by *Saturday Evening Post* of conspiring with Bear Bryant to fix 1962 Georgia-Alabama game. Both brought suit against Curtis Publishing Co.; Butts was awarded $593,916.75, one of largest judgments in history (Bryant settled out of court). Frank Sinkwich said of Butts: "Coach Butts is the greatest football coach I have ever known. He taught me so much more than football. He made a man of me." Citizens Savings Hall of Fame, National Football Foundation Hall of Fame.

BUTZ, DAVID E. Tackle. B. 6/23/50, Lafayette, Ala. 6'7", 280. Two-time prep All-America at Main South H.S., Park Ridge, Ill. Holds Illinois prep record in discus. Attended Purdue, 1970-72. Consensus All-America defensive tackle, 1972. That year recorded 29 solo tackles, sacked QB seven times, knocked down four passes. Defensive MVP in Senior Bowl and co-captain in East-West Shrine Game, 1972. Also College All-Star Game. St. Louis Cardinals, 1973. Wears size 12½EEEEEEE shoes. Nephew of Dr. Earl L. Butz, U.S. Secretary of Agriculture.

BYRD, GEORGE E. (Butch) Defensive Back. B. 9/20/41, Watervliet, N.Y. 6', 211. Graduated from Boston U., 1964. Buffalo Bills, 1964-70; Denver Broncos, 1971. Intercepted first pass he covered as pro, returned it 72 yds. for TD. On 12/26/65 set AFL playoff game record by intercepting six passes. In same game returned punt for TD, only time feat was ever accomplished in AFL playoffs. All-AFL cornerback, 1965, 66. Appeared in all regular-season games, 1970, 71. Bills won league titles in 1964, 65.

CAFEGO, GEORGE (Bad News) Running Back. B. 8/30/15, Whipple, W. Va. 6', 174. Tennessee, 1937-39. Good blocker, passer, runner, punt returner, kicker; and especially hard to bring down. Tennessee's Bob Neyland called him "only practice bum I ever coached who was genuine All-America." Led Vols to 21 wins in 22 games. SEC Player of the Year, 1938. Consensus All-America, 1939. Pro with Brooklyn Dodgers, 1940, 43; Washington Redskins, 1943; Boston Yanks, 1944-45. Later backfield coach at Furman, Wyoming and Arkansas. In 1955 returned to Tennessee as assistant football coach, head baseball coach. National Football Foundation Hall of Fame.

CAGLE, CHRISTIAN K. (Red) Running Back. B. 5/1/05, De Ridder, La. D. 12/26/42, New York, N.Y. 5'11", 178. Outstanding runner for Army, 1926-29. Unanimous All-America, 1928; consensus All-America, 1927, 29. Swift runner with long stride. Could run just as well to his left as to his right. Fabulous blocker and tackler. Attended Southwestern (La.) Institute, 1925, where he scored 108 points. Made him 5th highest scorer in nation. Led Army to 9-1 record, 1927. Helmet was often knocked off as he wore it with chin-strap hanging in back. Fans were thus often treated to sight of full shock of red hair racing down field at full speed. Forced out of military service when it was discovered that he had broken one of Academy rules by marrying while still a cadet. Coached Mississippi State, played pro ball with New York Giants and wrote newspaper articles. Was co-purchaser of Brooklyn Dodgers (football) in 1932 but sold his interest following year and went into insurance business. Was found at foot of subway stairs in Manhattan, suffering from fractured skull, from which he died in 1942. One of founders of Touchdown Club of New York. 1928 Citizens Savings Player of the Year. Citizens Savings Hall of Fame; National Football Foundation Hall of Fame.

CAHILL, THOMAS B. Coach. B. 10/11/19, Syracuse, N.Y. Attended Fayetteville (N.Y.) H.S. where he played three years of football, basketball and baseball. Then to Niagara, lettering as end in football, guard in basketball, infielder in baseball. Graduated in 1942. Same year became 2nd Lt. in army infantry. Served in South Pacific during World War II and left army with rank of Capt. Spent 13 years as prep coach, 7 as Plebe coach at West Point. Named Cadet head coach in 1966. Coach of the Year that year, his first at helm. Has coached East-West Shrine game in San Francisco, All-America Bowl at Tampa, Football Coaches All-America game in Atlanta. In eight years, 1966-73, compiled 40-39-2 record. Fired in 1973 after 0-10 season, including worst-ever loss to Navy (51-0).

CAIN, JOHN L. (Sugar) Running Back. B. Montgomery, Ala. 183. U. of Alabama, 1930-32. All-America, 1931. Played fullback. Good runner, defender and punter. Member of Alabama's All-Time Team. Called signals for 1930 team under Wallace Wade. In 1931 Coach Frank Thomas decided he was too modest for own good, calling other players to carry ball too much. Switched to Hillson Holley as QB. 1932 game vs. Tennessee was punting dual between Cain and Beattie Feathers. Both men kicked ball 20 times; Cain averaged 45 yds. Played in Rose Bowl game following 1930 season. Head coach at Southwestern Louisiana, 1937-41. Mississippi assistant coach since 1947. Is also assistant athletic director. National Football Foundation Hall of Fame.

CALDWELL, CHARLES W., JR. Coach. B. 8/2/01, Bristol, Va. D. 11/1/57, Princeton, N.J. Coached Williams College, 1928-42; Princeton, 1945-56. 1st Princeton coach to win six "Big 3" championships. Princeton graduate. 1950-51 teams undefeated. From Oct., 1949-Nov., 1952, won 30 of 31 games. Coach-of-the-Year 1950. 1952 N.Y. Touchdown Club Award. As undergraduate, starred in football, baseball. 1945, 1950-51 beat favored Cornell teams. 1946 beat Penn squad favored by 33 pts. 1948 upset Columbia. 1954 scored upsets vs. Colgate, Yale, Dartmouth. Overall, combined football-baseball-basketball coaching record 254-177-6. 1945 Princeton squad won Eastern Intercollegiate Baseball League title. 1925 pitched in major league baseball for N.Y. Yankees and played basketball for Montclair, N.J. AC championship squad. In college earned 3 varsity letters each in football, baseball and 1 in basketball. Excellent golfer, bridge player. Active in American Football Coaches Association; 1949-50 Chairman of its Program Committee. Authored 2 books on football coaching, *Modern Single-Wing Football, Modern Football for the Spectator.* National Football Foundation Hall of Fame. Citizens Savings Hall of Fame.

CAMERON, PAUL Running Back. B. 8/17/32, Burbank, Calif. 6', 190. UCLA, 1951-53. Consensus All-America, 1953; All-America, 1952. 3rd in Heisman

Trophy voting, 1953; 6th in 1952. Produced 68-yd. rush vs. Washington State, 1953; 68-yd. punt vs. USC, 1952. Played little in 1952 due to ankle injury, but in 1953 Rose Bowl limped in to throw winning TD pass vs. Texas Christian. Threw three TD passes vs. Stanford for 24-14 win, 1953. With ankle reinjured played less than four minutes vs. Wisconsin, but broke 7-7 tie by running 12 yds. and then throwing TD pass. In 1954 Rose Bowl game scored 1 TD, passed for 152 yds., had 59- and 52-yd. punts, returned 5 kickoffs for 95 yds. In career gained 3187 yds. total offense (1458 rushing, 1729 passing), scored 18 TDs. Seven school records were broken by Cameron in 1953, to bring three-year total to 12. Made every All-Coast team for three years in succession. Played one year as pro with Pittsburgh Steelers, 1954.

CAMP, WALTER C. Coach. B. 4/17/1859, New Haven, Conn. D. 3/14/25, New York, N.Y. Father of American football. Yale halfback as undergraduate, 1876-79, then attended medical school for two years. Returned to play halfback, 1880-81. Was captain two years. Played in first Yale-Harvard game, 11/17/76, and eight days later Intercollegiate Football Association was formed. Knee injury in midst of '82 season ended playing career. Record while he played was 25-1-6. In 1st half of 1877 Princeton game, Camp caught punt and dashed 80 yds. for TD; in 2nd half rushed 40 yds., shaking off tacklers, and with great strength forced way over goal line for TD. Both conversions were missed and, according to existing rules, no score was made. Game thus ended 0-0. Had several other scores nullified, including FG vs. Harvard because whistle ending half had gone off while ball was in air. During college years was outstanding athlete in other sports: captain of baseball team (early exponent of curve ball), swimming, tennis, gymnastics, track. Was Yale's first head coach (unpaid), 1888-1910.

One of founders of Intercollegiate Football Association, forerunner of today's Ivy League; participating were Yale, Harvard, Princeton and Columbia. Biggest contribution to game was in rules, in which vein, led fight for substitution of scrimmage for Rugby "scrummage", adoption of downs and yards-to-go (originally, 3 downs for 5; later 3 downs for 10, before modern system). Thus created idea of possession, forever separating American form of rugby. Inventor of QB position, player who at first couldn't run with ball. Won adoption of 11-man teams, rather than prevailing 15. Came up with arrangement of players which is still in use, seven on line, four in backfield. Devised method of scoring adopted in 1883 (safety-1, TD-2, PAT-4, FG-5). With modifications, system survives today. Saw greatest victories in 1906 when "neutral zone," which he had advocated since 1885, was adopted, as was forward pass. Served on Rules Committee from 1876 until death, and was chairman until 1911. Succeeded by Edward K. Hall of Dartmouth. Contributed many sports articles and books. Began publishing his All-America selections (which were considered official) in 1889, originally with Caspar Whitney; continued thru 1924. Married daughter of William Graham Sumner, famous sociologist. His son, Walter Jr., was Yale football star in 1913. Death came to Walter Camp, fittingly, during Rules Committee meeting in New York City.

CAMPBELL, DAVID C. End. B. 9/5/1873, Waltham, Mass. D. 6/30/49, Cambridge, Mass. 6', 171. Harvard, 1899-1901. Three-time All-America. Considered greatest defensive end of his time. Captain of Harvard's 1901 national champions. Was fast and mobile, opposing QBs always went to opposite side with play. Worked in mining, took many exploration trips throughout North and South America. Citizens Savings Hall of Fame, National Football Foundation Hall of Fame.

CAMPBELL, HUGH End. B. 5/21/41, Saratoga, La. 6'1", 185. Washington State, 1960-62. In 1960 was NCAA pass-receiving champion with 66 catches for 881 yds. and 10 TDs. At time these totals were all college records. Receiving champion again in 1961 with 53, 725 yds., 5 TDs. In 30-game career caught 176 passes for 2453 yds., 22 TDs, average of 13.9 yds. per catch. Jack Spaulding Trophy, 1962. Did not play pro ball.

CANADEO, ANTHONY (Tony) Tailback. B. 1919. 5'11", 195. Attended Gonzaga, 1938-40. Green Bay Packers, 1941-44, 46-52. All-Pro, 1943, 49. In pro career rushed for 4197 yds., caught 69 passes for 579 yds., scored 31 TDs. Packers were NFL champions in 1944. Named to All-Pro Squad of the 1940s. Used as running back, quarterback, punter and kick returner. Was elusive and opportunistic. No wonder they called him "Gray Ghost of Gonzaga." Pro Football Hall of Fame.

CANNON, JOHN J. (Jack) Guard. B. 1908, Columbus, Ohio. D. 11/12/67. Roving guard for Notre Dame, 1927-29. Consensus All-America, 1929. Made impossible tackles. Occasionally got careless and would be bawled out in front of entire team. Still one of best linemen ever at Notre Dame. Refused to wear helmet. Played brilliantly in Army game of 1929. Kicked off three times and made tackle each time, made key block that sprung winning 96-yd. TD interception. One opposition coach said, "All during the summer, I made up my mind to stop the strong-side play and I did. But, boy, how they went on the weak side." According to Harry Stulhdreher, Cannon's "bare head, bobbing across the gridiron, will long remain in the memory of those who had the pleasure of seeing him play." National Football Foundation Hall of Fame.

CANNON, WILLIAM A. (Billy) Tight End. B. 8/2/37, Philadelphia, Miss. 6'1", 220. Louisiana State halfback, 1957-59. Went there because he was in legal trouble and judge was fanatic LSU fan. Threatened to punish Cannon if he went anywhere but LSU. Suspended sentence. Unanimous All-America, 1958; consensus All-America, 1959. Citizens Savings Player of the Year, 1959. Heisman Trophy, 1959. In 1957 returned kickoff 90 yds. vs. Texas Tech., in 1959 returned punt 89 yds. vs. Mississippi. In Sugar Bowl, 1959, threw 9-yd. TD pass, rushed for 51 yds. Also played in 1960 Sugar Bowl. In college career rushed for 1867 yds., scored 154 points, caught 31 passes for 522 yds., made 7 interceptions for 115 yds., returned 31 punts for 349 yds. and 21 kickoffs for 616, punted 111 times for average of 36.7. First man picked in 1960 NFL draft, by Los Angeles

Rams. Also drafted on 1st round by AFL Houston Oilers. On 12/10/61, vs. New York Titans, rushed for 216 yds. on 25 carries. Same game tied AFL records, TD (5), points (30), total yds. (373). Led league in rushing yds. that year with 948 on 200 attempts, for 6 TDs. Combined net yardage, 1961, was 2043. Traded in 1964 to Oakland Raiders. In 1970 went to Kansas City Chiefs. Established many AFL championship game records. Owns marks for yds. on receptions (357), longest TD pass reception (88 yds.). Retired after 1970 season. In 11-year pro career caught 236 passes for 3656 yds., scored 47 TDs and total of 392 points. Now practices dentistry in Baton Rouge, active as lobbyist for legalizing dog racing. All-AFL, 1961, 67. Played in AFL championship games, 1960, 61, 62, 67, 68, 69. Super Bowl, 1968. Citizens Savings Hall of Fame.

CAPPELLETTI, GINO (Duke, Cappy) End-Kicker. B. 4/26/34, Keewatin, Minn. In high school won 13 letters. Graduated from U. of Minnesota in 1955. In 1956 entered military service; signed with Sarnia of Ontario Rugby Football Association after discharge. Played with Sarnia in 1958. Signed with Boston Patriots, 1960. AFL scoring leader from 1963 thru '66; also led in 1961. Led AFL in FGs, 1961, 63, 64. Holds distinction of scoring first three points in AFL history, on 38-yd. FG. 1964 AFL Player of the Year. Set AFL records for points, season, 155 in 1964; FGs, game, 6, 10/4/64; FG attempts, career, 284; FGs, career, with 156; points, career, 132; years leading league in FGs, 3; seasons scoring 100 or more points, 6; seasons leading league in scoring, 5; consecutive games, 140; total games, 140. Once seen crying in Patriot clubhouse, believing rumor that he'd been traded to New York Titans; however, story proved untrue and Cappy remained with Pats thru 1970.

CAPPELLETTI, JOHN Running Back. B. Upper Darby, Pa. 6'1", 210. Penn. State, 1971-73. Consensus All-America, 1973. Heisman Trophy, 1973, 1st Penn State player to win honor. A.P. All-East Team, 1973. *Football News* Player of the Year. Tough inside, tremendous speed. Follows blockers well and picks holes. Finished 5th nationally in rushing. Coach Joe Paterno says Cappelletti is "best player I've ever been around." Converted from defensive back after sophomore year. Became 2nd-ranking rusher in Penn State history. 1973 totals were 286 carries for 1522 yds., 17 TDs. Left him 45 yds. short of career record of Lydell Mitchell. Also caught 22 passes for 207 yds. and one TD. Missed one game due to injury but averaged 183.4 yds. per game, 5.3 yds. per carry. Two-year totals as tailback are 519 carries for 2639 yds., 29 TDs. Played in winning Orange Bowl effort vs. LSU, 1974.

CARIDEO, FRANK F. Quarterback. B. Mt. Vernon, N.Y. 5'7", 175. Played for Notre Dame, 1928-1930. Unanimous All-America, 1929, 30. Slick quarterback. Bellwether of 1929, 30 teams which Rockne admitted were his best. Played almost every second of every game. Roy Mills, lawyer and kicking specialist, discovered Carideo at Mt. Vernon H.S. and turned him into a punter and excellent corner kicker. Citizens Savings Hall of Fame, National Football Foundation Hall of Fame.

CARMICHAEL, ALBERT R. (Hoagy) Running Back. B. 11/10/29, Boston, Mass. 6'1", 200. Graduated from Southern California. Drafted on 1st round by Green Bay Packers, 1953. In 1955 was league kickoff-return leader with 14 for 418 yds., average 29.9. On 10/7/56, vs. Chicago Bears, returned kickoff 106 yds., setting record. Released by Packers after 1958 season; signed as free agent by Denver Broncos, 1960. Denver, 1960-61. Ended career 3rd in kickoff returns, lifetime, with 191, and yds. returned on kickoffs, lifetime, with 4,798.

CARMICHAEL, L. HAROLD End. B. 9/22/49, Jacksonville, Fla. 6'8", 225. Biggest receiver in football. Attended Southern U. Totaled 86 receptions and 16 TDs as collegian. Starting basketball center, too. Philadelphia Eagles, 1971-73. Caught 20 passes each of first two seasons. Hit stride in 1973 when QB Roman Gabriel acquired by Eagles. Led pro football with 67 receptions and 1116 yds. Scored 9 TDs, giving him 11 for career. Pro Bowl, 1974. He and tight end Charles Young (6'5", 220) gave Gabriel imposing targets.

CARNEY, CHARLES R. (Chuck) End. B. 8/25/1900, Chicago, Ill. 6'1", 190. Graduated from Illinois. Played football, 1918-21. Was Bob Zuppke's All-Time All-America end choice. In 1919, vs. Ohio State, Zuppke ordered QB Lawrence Walquist in last few minutes to throw every pass to Carney. Scheme worked as Illini rallied for 9-7 victory. All-America in both football and basketball, 1920. Won seven letters. In basketball set Big 10 scoring record which stood for 20 years. Later end coach at Northwestern, Wisconsin and Harvard. Investment banker with Dominick and Dominick of New York. Citizens Savings Hall of Fame (basketball). National Football Foundation Hall of Fame.

CAROLINE, JAMES C. (J.C.) Defensive Back. B. 6/17/33, Columbia, S.C. 6'1", 190. Illinois, 1953-54. Consensus All-America, 1953, 1st sophomore so honored since Doak Walker of SMU in 1947. Coach Ray Eliot wrote: "Caroline was one of the greatest prospects as a halfback at Illinois since Red Grange." In 1953 led country in rushing (setting Big 10 record) and all-purpose running. In nine games on 194 plays, he rushed for 1256 yds. and gained total of 1470 yds., average of 163.3 yds. per game. That year Illinois tied Michigan State for Big 10 title, Montreal Alouettes, 1955; Toronto Argonauts, 1955; Chicago Bears, 1956-65. Played in two NFL title games, 1956, 62. Was defensive back during pro career. Obtained his degree from Florida A. & M. in 1967. Now defensive backfield coach at Illinois.

CARPENTER, C. HUNTER Running Back. B. 6/23/1883, Louisa County, Va. D. 2/24/53, Middletown, N.Y. 5'1", 195. Virginia Tech halfback, 1900-03, 05. Played before any Southern players were picked for All-America. Captain of 1905 team that beat Army, Virginia, North Carolina, Washington & Lee, VMI. In 1905 scored 82 points, or 58 more than his opponents combined. Career points: 233. Received more votes on 1st balloting than any other charter member of Virginia Hall of Fame, when it was organized in 1958. National Football Foundation Hall of Fame, only VPI player ever honored.

CARPENTER, WILLIAM S., JR. End. B. 9/30/37, Springfield, Pa. 6'2", 210. Army, 1958-60. Was West Point's "Lonely End." Lined up as flanker 20-30 yds. removed from line, didn't join huddle between plays. Formation caught nation's fancy. It was created by coach Red Blaik in 1958, his last at Point. Millions were left to speculation as to how Carpenter was signaled for plays. Secret was kept entire season — Blaik later revealed that cue was positioning of QB Joe Caldwell's feet. 1958 yielded Army's first unbeaten season in nine years, victories over Navy and Notre Dame, No. 3 national ranking. Blaik considered Carpenter best wingman in Cadet annals. Consensus All-America, 1959. Distinguished himself as Capt. in Vietnam. Ordered napalm bombs dropped on own troops when surrounded by large force of Viet Cong; survived. For act won Silver Star, recommended for Congressional Medal of Honor. Received Distinguished American Award from National Football Foundation, 1966. Now Maj. Carpenter.

CARR, JOSEPH F. Founder. B. 10/22/1880, Columbus, Ohio. D. 5/20/39. Founder and first owner of Columbus Panhandles, featuring Nesser brothers. Also one of founders of NFL in 1919, then known as American Professional Football Association. From 1921-39, president of NFL. Succeeded first president, Jim Thorpe. At his insistence teams adopted rule that barred them from signing college player until class had graduated. Took title from Pottsville Maroons, 1925, after complaint by Frankford Yellowjackets that Pottsville's post-season game vs. Notre Dame All-Stars was invasion of territory. Carr ruled that 2nd-place Chicago Cardinals play supplementary game, vs. Milwaukee Badgers, for title; Cards won and were awarded title. Milwaukee franchise subsequently cancelled and manager Arthur Folz suspended "for life" for using high school players. (Folz is only man in NFL history to draw such sentence.) Overall, very successful commissioner, though during tenure many transfers and experiments were necessary. Pro Football Hall of Fame.

CARROLL, CHARLES O. (Chuck) Running Back. B. 8/13/06, Seattle, Wash. 6', 190. Washington, 1926-28. Consensus All-America, 1928. Led attack that scored 688 points, for three-year record of 24-8. Won 16 athletic letters in high school. Winner of Washington's inspirational award, Flaherty Medal. In 1941 entered army as Capt., discharged in 1946. Appointed King County (Wash.) district attorney in 1948, post he held for 22 years. Active in community affairs. Citizens Savings Hall of Fame, National Football Foundation Hall of Fame.

CARTER, GEORGE R. Guard-Tackle. B. 12/28/1866, Honolulu, Hawaii. D. 2/12/33, Honolulu, Hawaii. Yale, 1885-87. Great tackler. Won job as tackle immediately upon arrival at Yale; final two seasons also played guard. Teammate of Pa Corbin, George Woodruff, Amos Alonzo Stagg. After graduation became well-known banker, civic leader and governor of Hawaii.

CARTER, VIRGIL R. (Virg) Quarterback. B. 11/9/45, Anabella, Utah. 6'1", 185. Attended Brigham Young. Led major colleges in total offense with 2545

63

yds., 1966. Chicago Bears, 1968-69; Cincinnati Bengals, 1970-73. Led Bengals to NFC Central Division championship in 1970. NFL's most accurate passer with 62.2 percent, 1971. Had long gain that year of 90 yds. In 1972 lost starting QB job to Ken Anderson. Intelligent, fine runner and passer. Owns master's degree in mathematics from Northwestern.

CASANOVA, THOMAS R. (Tommy) Defensive Back. B. 7/29/50, New Orleans, La. 6'2", 190. Louisiana State, 1969-71. Consensus All-America, 1970, 71. Played cornerback and some tailback. Considered best all-around athlete on LSU team. Played in 1971 Orange Bowl, '72 Sun Bowl. Played in 1972 College All-Star game. Selected by Cincinnati Bengals on 2nd round of 1972 draft. Team's interception co-leader (tying Lemar Parrish) with 5. Also that year made AFC's longest punt return, 66 yds., vs. Denver Broncos. Was 5th ranked in NFL in punt returns, totaling 30 for 289 yds., 9.6 average. Has 9.7 speed in 100-yd. dash. Planning on career in medicine.

CASARES, RICARDO (Rick) Running Back. B. 7/4/31, Tampa, Fla. 6'2½", 225. Legendary Florida prep, starring in four sports at Jefferson H.S. in Tampa. Played for U. of Florida, 1951-53. Called into service after two games of senior year. Considered best fullback in South. Powerful line-plunger, and fast. Gained 635 yds. in 1952, scored 7 TDs, made 21 of 28 PAT attempts, averaged 41.2 yds. on 24 punts. Chicago Bears, 1955-64. 1956 NFL rushing leader, gaining 1126 yds. and scoring 12 TDs on 234 attempts. Gained 100 yds. or more in seven games in 1956. Played in NFL championship games in 1956 (scored one TD) and '63, both vs. New York Giants. Washington Redskins, 1965; Miami Dolphins, 1966. All-Pro, 1956. Retired in 1967 after 12 years. Retired with 5797 yds. rushing, still among all-time leaders.

CASEY, EDWARD L. (Natick Eddie) Running Back. B. 5/16/1894, Natick, Mass. D. 7/26/66. 5'10", 161. Played for Harvard. All-America, 1919; 2nd team, 1916. Dangerous breakaway runner. Excelled at use of body block to bring his man down. Slim and quick, he sparked Harvard to 7-6 win over Oregon in 1920 Rose Bowl game. Buffalo All-Americans, 1920. Served navy in both world wars. Coached Tufts, 1922-25; Harvard, 1931-34. His Harvard record was 20-11-1. Pro head coach for Boston Redskins, 1935 (2-8-1); Boston Bears of AFL, 1940 (2-8-1).

CASSADY, HOWARD (Hopalong) Running Back. B. 3/2/34, Columbus, Ohio. 5'10", 172. Legendary Ohio State halfback. Played for Buckeyes, 1952-55. Unanimous All-America, 1954, 55. Heisman Trophy, Maxwell Award, Silver Football, Walter Camp Trophy, all 1955. In 1954 made 88-yd. interception return vs. Wisconsin and 68-yd. rush vs. Purdue. In 1955 Rose Bowl rushed for 92 yds. on 21 carries. In four seasons carried 414 times for 2374 yds., average of 5.7; received 42 passes for 608 yds. and intercepted 10 for 230 yds; returned 33 punts for 335 yds. and 40 kickoffs for 958 yds; scored 37 TDs overall. Detroit Lions 1956-61, 63; Cleveland Browns, 1962; Philadelphia Eagles, 1962. In 1957 championship game caught 16-yd. pass from Jerry Reichow to score Detroit's 8th TD.

CAVANAUGH, FRANCIS W. (Frank; Cav) Coach. B. 11/23/1866, Worcester, Mass. D. 8/29/33, Marshfield, Mass. Started as high school end in Worcester. Played three years at Dartmouth, 1895-97. Left to coach at U. of Cincinnati, 1898. Coached at Holy Cross, 1903-05; Dartmouth 1911-16; Boston College, 1919-26; Fordham, 1927-32. Career record: 145-48-17, percentage of .731. At Dartmouth tied for Ivy League championship in 1913, lost only to Carlisle Indians. Developed several All-Americas, including Doc Spears, Milt Ghee. 1920 Boston College team undefeated and placed one man on All-America team. Tough, driving coach. Studied law during early coaching days and admitted to Massachusetts bar. In 1917 went to war, enlisting as private, but gained rank of Maj. War wounds affected sight and in last years at Fordham was practically blind. Nicknamed "Iron Major." Citizens Savings Hall of Fame, National Football Foundation Hall of Fame.

CHAMBERLIN, B. GUY End-Running Back. B. 1/16/1894, Blue Springs, Neb. D. 4/4/67. 6'2", 210. Played for Nebraska, 1913-15. All-America, 1915. "Greatest two-way end of all time," according to George Halas. Missouri Valley Conference MVP, 1914, 15. In eight games scored 96 points, averaged 2 TDs per game, 1915. Played halfback and end in college. Fierce blocker, defender. Decatur Staleys, 1920; Chicago Staleys, 1921; Canton Bulldogs, 1922-23; Cleveland Bulldogs, 1924; Frankford Yellowjackets, 1925-26; Chicago Cardinals, 1927. Was player-coach, 1922-26; coached Cardinals, 1928. Overall record: 66-14-5 (.825 percentage). From high school thru first four pro seasons, didn't play in single losing game. Unique distinction of having been elected to Citizens Savings Hall of Fame, National Football Foundation Hall of Fame, Pro Football Hall of Fame.

CHANDLER, DONALD G. (Babe) End-Kicker. B. 9/9/34, Council Bluffs, Iowa. 6'2", 215. Florida, 1953-55. 1955 NCAA punting champion with 22 punts for 975 yds., average of 44.3. Drafted on 5th round, 1956, by New York Giants. During Giant tenure, roommate of Sam Huff. As rookies they decided to return home one night but were found at airport and brought back by Vince Lombardi, then Giant assistant. In 1957 was NFL punting leader with average of 44.6 yds. on 60 punts. In 1958 led league in number of punts with 65. NFL PAT leader with 52, 1963, and scoring leader with 106 points. Traded to Green Bay Packers in 1965, reunited with Vince Lombardi. That year vs. San Francisco 49ers made 90-yd. punt. Set title-game records for punting average, career, with 42.2 yds., and punts with 38. Played in NFL championship games, 1956, 58, 59, 61, 62, 63, 65, 66, 67, and Super Bowl, 1967, 68. Tied with Lou Groza for most championship games played (9). Owns Super Bowl game marks for PATs (5), FGs (4), points (15). Pro Bowl, 1968.

CHANDNOIS, LYNN E. Running Back. B. 2/24/25, Flint, Mich. 6'2", 195. Played halfback for Michigan State, 1946-49. All-America, 1949. Led 1949 team in scoring with 90 points. Had 20 interceptions during college career for 410 yds. (2nd highest in NCAA), record average of 20.5. In 38 games was involved in 333 plays, gained 2043 yds., responsible for 31 TDs. In 1949 season had 90-yd. rush vs. Arizona and gained 83 yds. on pass reception vs. Notre Dame. Pittsburgh Steelers, 1950-56. Led NFL in kickoff returns in 1951 (12) and 1952 (17), averaging 32.5 and 35.2 yds. Career pro average for kickoff returns was 29.57 yds. (2nd highest).

CHARLES, JOHN C. (J. C.) Defensive Back. B. 5/9/44, Newark, N. J. 6'1", 195. Played three seasons at Purdue where he was All-America in 1966. MVP in 1967 Rose Bowl. (Purdue won over Southern California, 14-13.) Boston Patriots, 1967-69; Minnesota Vikings, 1970; Houston Oilers, 1971-73. Was first defensive back ever chosen on 1st round of NFL draft, by Patriots. Went to Vikings as part of compensation for Joe Kapp, who played out option and signed with Pats. Traded by Vikings to Denver in 1971, but swapped to Houston before season began. Fine one-on-one player. Excellent speed. Has played both cornerback and safety.

CHEYUNSKI, JAMES M. Linebacker. B. 12/29/45, Brockton, Mass. 6'1", 225. Attended Syracuse, but was being scouted by pros long before. Discovered in high school by Boston Patriot scout Ronnie Loudd when he stopped for gas; Cheyunski came out to fill tank. Loudd, impressed with size, asked if he played football. After Syracuse career, 1965-67, drafted by Patriots on 12th round. Played with Pats thru 1972. Once made 37 tackles in three games. In 1973 traded to Buffalo Bills.

CHRISTIANSEN, JACK L. (Chris) Defensive Back. B. 12/20/28, Sublette, Kan. Colorado State, 1948-50. Drafted and signed by Lions, 1951, staying thru 1958. Head coach, San Francisco 49ers, 1963-67. Led NFL in interceptions, 1953, with 12, and tied for lead, 1957, with 10. That year returned one interception for 92 yds. On 10/14/51, vs. Los Angeles Rams, scored two TDs on punt returns (record). Scored two again on punt returns vs. Green Bay Packers, 11/22/51; in that game gained 175 yds. returning punts. Holds record for most TDs returning punts, lifetime, with 8 (1951 — 4; 1952 — 2; 1954 — 1; 1956 — 1). Owns lifetime average of 12.75 yds. on punt returns and holds record for highest average, season, 1952, with 21.5. All-Pro, 1952, 53, 55, 56, 57. Pro Football Hall of Fame 1969. Inauspicious career as coach of 49ers, record of 26-41-3 for five seasons. Stanford head coach, 1972-73.

CHRISTMAN, PAUL C. (Pitchin' Paul) Quarterback. B. 3/5/18, St. Louis, Mo. D. 3/2/70, Lake Forest, Ill. 200. Also called "Merry Magician." Played for Missouri, 1938-40. All-America, all three years. One of great users of forward pass in running era. School records not erased until 1969 (by Terry McMillan). Originally enrolled at Purdue. Missouri coach Don Faurot switched formations for him as he was too slow for double wing. Chicago Cardinals, 1945-49, Green Bay Packers, 1950. 1947 member of Cards' "Dream Backfield." St. Louis won NFL championship in 1947, division title year later. Christman's pro statistics: completed 504 of 1140 passes, 44.2 percent, for 7294 yds. and 58 TDs. In 60s became TV football commentator, known for cogent analysis. "Never insult the intelligence of your viewer," he said. "If you have nothing to say, shut up." Died of heart seizure at age 51. Citizens Savings Hall of Fame, National Football Foundation Hall of Fame.

CHRISTY, RICHARD Running Back. B. 11/24/35, Chester, Pa. D. 8/7/66. 5'10", 190. Attended North Carolina State, 1955-57. Pittsburgh Steelers, 1958; Boston Patriots, 1960. New York Titans, 1961-62; New York Jets, 1963. In four-year AFL career Christy rushed 299 times for 1166 yds., average of 3.9, 10 TDs; returned 125 punts for 1400 yds., average of 11.2, 4 TDs. Led league in punt returns twice, 1961, 62. On 9/24/61 returned two punts for TDs against Denver Broncos, tying Jack Christiansen's pro record. His 21.3-yd. punt-return average is 2nd best in NFL history. (Christiansen's 21.5 is tops.) Christy died in car crash.

CLANCY, JOHN D. (Jack) End. B. 6/18/44, Humboldt, Iowa. 6'1½", 195. Played for Michigan, 1964-66. Consensus All-America, 1966. Drafted by Miami Dolphins on 3rd round, 1967. Dolphins, 1967-69; 72; Green Bay Packers, 1970. Missed 1968 season due to knee injury. In 1967 set AFL rookie record with 67 receptions, gaining 868 yds. AFL All-Star game, 1967.

CLARK, CHARLES (Boobie) Running Back. B. 11/8/50, Jacksonville, Fla. 6'3", 245. Played tight end and running back for Bethune-Cookman. Selected by Cincinnati Bengals on 12th round of 1973 draft. In rookie year gained 988 yds. on 254 carries, 3.9 average, 8 TDs. Gained 188 yds. vs. Pittsburgh Steelers, 106 vs. Kansas City Chiefs. Caught 45 passes for 347 yds., tying him for 5th in AFC. Combines speed and power, can carry tacklers. In 1973 AFC playoff game, vs. Miami Dolphins, held to 40 yds. Acquired nickname from grandmother. Selected by *Football Digest* as Offensive Player of the Year on its 1973 Rookie All-Star team. *Sporting News* named him AFC Rookie of the Year.

CLARK, EARL H. (Dutch) Quarterback. B. 10/11/06, Fowler, Colo, 6', 175. Attended Colorado College where he won 12 letters in four sports. Made baseball, basketball and track teams in addition to football. Was All-Conference in all four. In 1928 scored 108 points. Won first national attention when Alan Gould, A.P. sports editor, selected him for All-America in 1929. In 1930 captained West squad in East-West Shrine game. Joined Portsmouth Spartans, 1931. Led NFL in scoring and FGs in 1932. Moved with Spartans to Detroit (Lions) in 1934, staying with team until 1938. NFL scoring leader again in 1935, 36. Was player-coach, 1937-38. Coached Cleveland Rams, 1939-42. All-Pro, 1931, 32, 34, 35, 36, 37. Fine runner, passer, dropkicker. Extremely intelligent. Redoubtable Clark Shaughnessy said, "If Clark stepped on the field with Grange, Thorpe and Gipp, Dutch would be the general." Citizens Savings Hall of Fame, National Football Foundation Hall of Fame, Pro Football Hall of Fame (charter member). Sales executive for tool and die company in Detroit.

CLARK, GEORGE (Potsy) Coach. D. 11/8/72, La Jolla, Calif. Attended Illinois where he played on 1914 team, called by coach Bob Zuppke his greatest.

Later coached Michigan State, Minnesota and Butler, then turned to professional ranks with Portsmouth Spartans, in 1931. Coached club six years, compiling 53-26-10 record. Spartans moved to Detroit after 1933 season and became Lions. Coached Detroit Lions, team which he also founded. Tutored Brooklyn Dodgers, 1937-39. In 1935 won NFL title which had eluded him in 1934. Athletic director at Nebraska, 1945-53. Pro Football Hall of Fame.

CLARK, MICHAEL V. Kicker. B. 11/7/40, Marshall, Tex. 6'1", 205. Graduated from Texas A. & M. Philadelphia Eagles, 1963; Pittsburgh Steelers, 1964-67; Dallas Cowboys, 1968-71; Buffalo Bills, 1973. Originally signed by Eagles as free agent. Signed by Bills for 1972 season but missed that year due to fractured arm. Played in Pro Bowl, 1967. Led NFL in PATs with 54 (in 54 attempts), 1968. Kicked two FGs and one PAT in 1971 Super Bowl, one FG and three PATs in '72 Super Bowl.

CLEVENGER, ZORA (Clev) Running Back. B. 12/21/1881, Munci, Ind. Played on first Munci H.S. football team, 1897. Indiana, 1900-03. Played baseball and football, was captain of both teams in 1903. Aggressive, elusive runner. Coached baseball, basketball and football at Indiana, 1903-05. Coaching and administrative duties took him to Nebraska Wesleyan, Tennessee, Kansas State, Missouri and back to Indiana. 1914 Tennessee football team was unbeaten. Athletic director at Indiana for 23 years. Brought in Bo McMillin to coach Hoosiers. In 1945, McMillin won first Big 10 football title for Indiana. School gave Clev title of athletic director emeritus. Received Distinguished Alumnus Award. Clevenger Award founded in his honor. Never missed Indiana home game. Member of Basketball Rules Committee, NCAA administrator. One of founders of East-West Shrine game. National Football Foundation Hall of Fame.

COCHRAN, GARRETT B. (Garry) End. B. 8/26/1876, Driftwood, Pa. D. 7/8/18, France. 5'11", 162. Princeton, 1896-98. All-America, 1897. Captain of 1896 team, known as "Cochran's Steamrollers." Overwhelmed Yale to end Bulldogs' 44-game unbeaten streak, and defeated all others except for tie with Lafayette. George Trevor wrote: "Garry Cochran, nonpareil of Tiger wings, was Princeton's counterpart of Tom Shevlin. Cochran could take a bunch of mediocre players and spur them to a berserk frenzy. A bull for strength, his inspirational fervor was infectious." Coached at California, 1899, then at Navy. Became president and general manager of Williamsport Wire Rope Co. Served during World War I with field artillery in France. Achieved rank of Lt. and died aboard ship in 1918. National Football Foundation Hall of Fame.

COCKROFT, DONALD L. Kicker. B. 2/6/45, Cheyenne, Wyo. 6'1", 185. Adams State, 1964-66. Was small-college punting leader with 48-yd. average. Career average per punt was 44.5. Selected by Cleveland Browns on 3rd round of 1967 draft. Member of Cleveland taxi squad, 1967. Kicked 11 consecutive FGs, 1968-69. Led team in scoring with 94 points, 1972, and kicked 81 punts for a record 3498 yds., average of 43.2. His longest was 65 yds., and none were blocked. Had best AFC percentage in FGs, 1972, with .815; kicked longest FG in AFC, 57-yarder vs. Denver Broncos on 10/29/73. Played in NFL championship games 1968, 69. Scored 90 points, averaged 40.5 yds. punting in 1973.

CODY, JOSH C. Tackle. B. 1892, Franklin, Tenn. D. 6/19/61, Mt. Laurel, N.J. 6'4", 220. Vanderbilt, 1914-16, 19. 3rd-team, All-America 1915, 19. Won varsity letters in four sports. Opposing QBs usually took plays other way, avoiding his position. During Cody years Vanderbilt outscored opponents 1099-226, won 23 games and lost 9. Later coached Clemson, Mercer, Vanderbilt, Florida, Temple, retiring in 1961. Early Day All-Time All-America team. Citizens Savings Hall of Fame, National Football Foundation Hall of Fame.

COFFEY, JUNIOR L. Running Back. B. 3/21/42, Kyle, Tex. 6'1", 215. Washington, 1962-64. Drafted by Green Bay Packers on 7th round. Played in NFL championship game, 1965. Chosen by Atlanta Falcons in expansion draft, 1966. Gained 722 yds. combined in 1966, 67; scored four TDs each year. Caught total of 45 passes over those seasons. Missed 1968 due to knee injury. During 1969 season, traded to New York Giants. On kickoff-return squads. Out, 1970, but returned to Giants in 1971 for final season.

COGDILL, GAIL R. (Cougs) End. B. 4/7/37, Worland, Wyo. 6'2", 215. Played 1957-59 at Washington State. Also long-jumped. Drafted by Detroit Lions on 6th round, 1960. Outstanding receiver for Lions, 1960-68. Especially dangerous deep. Rookie of the Year, 1960. Gained 956 yds. on pass receptions in 1961, scored 6 TDs; in 1962 gained 991 yds., scored 7 TDs; in 1963 gained 945 yds., scored 10 TDs. Released by Detroit during 1968 season and signed by Boston Patriots. Atlanta Falcons, 1969-70. Pro Bowl, 1961, 63, 64. All-time Lion leader in receptions (325) and receiving yardage (5220). Overall nabbed 356 passes for 5696 yds., 34 TDs.

COLLINS, GARY J. End. B. 8/20/40, Williamstown, Pa. 6'4", 215. Consensus All-America at Maryland, 1961. "He's in a class all by himself," said Terrapin coach Tom Nugent and few disagreed. Drafted by Cleveland Browns on 1st round, 1962, and played with them thru 1971. Owns championship game records for TD pass receptions, game, three, 1964; TD passes lifetime, five, in four games; shares with Otto Graham mark for TDs, five. Cleveland stunned Baltimore Colts in '64 title game, 27-0. Browns lost title contests in 1965, 68, 69. NFL punting leader with 46.7-yd. average, 1965. Pro Bowl, 1966, 67. All-Pro, 1965.

COLLINS, HARRY W. (Rip) Running Back-Kicker. B. 2/26/1896, Weatherford, Tex. D. 1968. Outstanding football player at Texas A. & M. before big-league baseball career beckoned. Won football letters, 1915, 16, 17; was All-SWC in 1917. Against Texas punted 23 times for 55-yd. average. A. & M. won that game to clinch conference championship. Pitched 315 games in majors, playing for New York Yankees, Boston Red Sox, Detroit Tigers, St. Louis

Browns. Righthander posted 108-82 record. After pro baseball devoted life to law enforcement. Died in Bryan, Tex., where he had been chief of police for 12 years.

CONERLY, CHARLES A. (Charlie) Quarterback. B. 9/19/21, Clarksdale, Miss. 6'1", 185. Played halfback for Mississippi, 1942, 46-47. Consensus All-America, 1947. That year led NCAA in pass attempts with 233, in completions with record 133, in percentage with record 57.1, in TDs with 18. Gained 1367 yds. passing. In 1947, vs. Chattanooga, set game record for most passes without interception, with 32. Also led in total-offense plays that year with 337, TDs-accounted-for with 27. Citizens Savings Player of the Year, 1947. New York Giants, 1948-61. On 12/5/48, vs. Pittsburgh Steelers, completed 36 of 53 passes. Thirty-six completions are 2nd highest to Blanda's record 37. 1959 NFL passing leader with 113 completions in 194 attempts for 1706 yds., scored 14 TDs. That season had only four passes intercepted, fewest in NFL since 1945. Jim Thorpe Trophy (MVP), 1959. Played in NFL championship games 1956, 58, 59, 61. Tremendous competitor. Retired after 1961 season and did radio commercials. National Football Foundation Hall of Fame.

CONCANNON, JOHN J., JR. (Jack) Quarterback. B. 2/25/43, Boston, Mass. 6'3", 200. Attended Boston College. Was fine runner, passer, 1961-63. In 1964 drafted by Philadelphia on 2nd round. Traded to Chicago Bears, 1967, for Mike Ditka (later his teammate in Dallas). On 11/19/67 threw 93-yd. TD pass to Dick Gordon vs. St. Louis Cardinals. That year passed for 1260 yds. and rushed for 279 yds. In 1971 passed for 2130 yds. Traded by Chicago to Dallas Cowboys, 1972, for 2nd-round draft choice.

CONNOR, GEORGE Tackle. B. 1/1/25, Chicago, Ill. 6'3", 240. Holy Cross, 1942-43; Notre Dame, 1946-47. Consensus All-America, 1946-47. Chicago Bears, 1948-55. All-NFL defensive tackle, 1950, 51, 52. Then switched to linebacker and was All-NFL three more seasons. Crushing tackler, excellent blocker. Big, fast, agile, tough enough to break up power play. In 1969 elected to All-Century team, only Notre Dame man to be so designated. Played under Tony Scanlan, Frank Leahy, George Halas. Notre Dame teammate of Johnny Lujack, Terry Brennan, Johnny Lattner. Citizens Savings Hall of Fame, National Football Foundation Hall of Fame.

CONRAD, ROBERT J. (Bobby Joe) End. B. 11/17/35, Clifton, Tex. 6'2", 200. Graduated from Texas A. & M., 1958. Drafted on 5th round by New York Giants. Before '58 season was traded to Chicago Cardinals with defensive back Dick Nolan, for defensive back Lindon Crow and placekicker Pat Summerall. Intercepted 4 passes for 46 yds. in rookie year as he played some defense. In 1960 moved with team to St. Louis. 1963 pass-receiving leader with 73 catches for 967 yds. and 10 TDs. From 1961-68, while with St. Louis, successfully received passes in 94 consecutive games. Performance is 3rd best in NFL history. In 1968 traded to Dallas Cowboys for draft choice in order to close out career in home area. Retired after 12 years, at end of 1969 season.

CONZELMAN, JAMES G. (Jimmy) Quarterback-Coach. B. 3/6/1898, St. Louis, Mo. D. 7/31/70. After freshman year at Washington (St. Louis), assigned to Great Lakes Naval Training Station during World War I. Teammate there of George Halas and Paddy Driscoll. Played Navy for right to go to Rose Bowl and won, 7-6. Defeated Mare Island Marines, 17-0, in 1919 Rose Bowl. Then returned to Washington. All-MVC, 1919. Decatur Staleys, 1920; Rock Island Independents, 1921-22; Milwaukee Badgers, 1923-24; Detroit Panthers, 1925-26; Providence Steamrollers, 1927-29. Coached Rock Island, 1922; Milwaukee, 1923-24; Detroit, 1925-26; Providence, 1928-30; Washington, 1931-39; Chicago Cardinals, 1940-42, 46-48. Detroit owner, 1925-26. Won NFL title and named MVP, 1928. Was pro head coach at age 24. In 1947 guaranteed Cards' owner Charles Bidwill title if team could secure "Dream Backfield": Paul Christman, Pat Harder, Charley Trippi, Marshall Goldberg. This group was acquired, and Cards won title. However, Bidwill died in April of '47 before foursome played together. Once released player named Paul Robeson, who became star of stage and screen. 34-31-3 record with Cardinals gave him overall pro coaching mark of 82-69-14. Extremely versatile, Conzelman was also newspaper publisher, board director with St. Louis baseball Cardinals, song writer, radio commentator, *Saturday Evening Post* writer, middleweight boxing champion of navy, advertising executive. Pro Football Hall of Fame.

COOK, GREGORY L. Quarterback. B. 11/20/46, Chillicothe, Ohio. 6'4", 220. U. of Cincinnati, 1966-68. Led NCAA in total offense, 1968, with 3210 yds., and passing yds. with 3272 (lost 62 rushing). On 11/16/68, vs. Ohio U., completed 35 passes for 554 yds. In 1968 completed 95-yd. pass vs. Louisville, 85-yd. pass vs. Houston, 74-yd. pass vs. Temple. Gained 4760 yds. total offense in career, and was responsible for 40 TDs. 1st-round draft choice of Cincinnati Bengals, 1969. Led AFL in passing that year with 106 completions in 197 attempts for 1854 yds., unprecedented for rookie. College All-Star game MVP, 1969. Sidelined by injuries, 1970-72. Had "bad boy" reputation. Retired 11/73. Without injuries might have been one of game's greatest. Called "Blond Bomber."

CORBIN, WILLIAM H. (Pa) Center. B. 7/20/1864, Union Conn. D. 4/14/43, 6'2", 178. Yale, 1886-88. Captain of 13-0 team, 1888. Called by teammate Pudge Heffelfinger, "one of the best centers I ever played with or against." Wore handlebar mustache, conducted himself in regal manner. Rangy, great fighter and strategist. Strict leader, felt "captain should be the real leader, not the coach." He was inspirational, never swore, but often used epithet, "You big cow." Later secretary of Hartford Chamber of Commerce. Citizens Savings Player of the Year, 1897. Citizens Savings Hall of Fame, National Football Foundation Hall of Fame.

CORBUS, WILLIAM Guard. B. 10/5/11, San Francisco, Calif. 5'11", 195. Stanford, 1931-33. Consensus All-America, 1932, 33. Teammate, Bobby Grayson, called Corbus "one of the most fantastic undergraduates I ever knew." Fine FG kicker, great blocker, strong defensive player. Often led interference from "guards-back" formation. 1933 "Vow Boys" had nine sophs in starting lineup, strongly influenced by Corbus. Honor student, student body president. Currently high-level A. & P. executive. Citizens Savings Hall of Fame, National Football Foundation Hall of Fame.

COSTA, DAVID J. Tackle. B. 10/27/41, Yonkers, N. Y. 6'1", 255. Attended Northeastern (Colo.) J.C. before going to U. of Utah. Played in East-West Shrine, Hula Bowl and Coaches All-America games. Drafted on 7th round by Oakland Raiders, 1963. Was runnerup that season for Rookie of the Year. Began pro career as linebacker, then converted to defensive tackle. Raiders, 1963-65; Buffalo Bills, 1966; Denver Broncos, 1967-72; San Diego Chargers, 1972-73. Leader of front four that led NFL in QB sackings with 44 in 1971. Sacked QB six times himself and accumulated 41 tackles. Defensive captain of Broncos and player representative. AFL All-Star games, 1963, 67, 68, 69. Played in AFL championship game, 1966. Collected 70 tackles as Charger in 1972, 27 unassisted. In season's final game nailed Pittsburgh Steeler QB Terry Bradshaw for safety. Intelligent, team player.

COTHREN, PAIGE Running Back. B. 6/12/35, Natchez, Miss. 5'11", 195. Mississippi fullback and placekicker, 1954-56. All-SEC, 1955, 56. AP National Back of the Week for performance against Arkansas, 1955. Led NCAA in FGs (6) and conference in scoring (74 points). In 1956 Cotton Bowl scored Rebels' opening TD and kicked winning conversion (Mississippi 14, TCU 13). Led NCAA in FGs senior year, again with six. Los Angeles Rams, 1957-58; Philadelphia Eagles, 1959. Kicked 14 FGs to tie Tom Miner for NFL supremacy, 1958.

COULTER, DEWITT E. Tackle. B. Fort Worth, Tex. 6'3", 250. Sophomore on Army's national championship team, 1945. Cadets were superb, winning nine straight games and outscoring foes 412-46. Coulter and seven other cadets won All-America honors. Winning most publicity, of course, was fabled tandem of Doc Blanchard and Glenn Davis. Rose Bowl wanted Army but bid was rejected. Coulter flunked out of West Point after one varsity season, then signed with New York Giants. Developed reputation for fierceness. Ernie Stautner, extremely rugged himself, considered Coulter toughest player he ever faced. Another pro football villain, Don Paul, said of Coulter: "You could never count on him being in the same position. Center, guard, tackle. I think he played end too. Stan West, the old All-America, he and I used to huddle in each other's arms, waiting for the public address announcer to say which one of us had to play in front of Coulter." Played with Giants, 1946-49, 51-52. All-Pro offensive tackle, 1951.

COWAN, CHARLES (Charlie) Tackle. B. 6/19/38, Braeholm, W. Va. 6'4", 265. Attended New Mexico Highlands. Played practically every position but offensive lineman. Led team in rushing, passing, receiving, total offense. Also played basketball. Drafted in 1961 by Los Angeles Rams on 4th round. Switched to offensive tackle at first training camp. Voted Rams' outstanding offensive lineman in 1966. Also on kickoff return squad. Has played offensive guard and tackle in pros. Missed only three games in first 12 years with Rams. Played much of 1971 with injuries. Underwent elbow, knee and foot surgery after season, foot surgery again in 1972. All-NFC, 1971. Pro-Bowl, 1968, 69, 70, 71. All-time L.A. leader from standpoint of service, having played in 179 games in 13 years.

COWAN, HECTOR W. Tackle. B. 7/12/1863, Hobart, N. Y. D. 10/19/41, Stamford, N. Y. 5'11", 181. Princeton, 1887-89. All-America on 1st All-America squad, 1889. Citizens Savings Player of the Year, 1889. According to Pudge Heffelfinger, Cowan "could carry a couple of tacklers on his back, yet he was plenty fast in the open." Played in 10-0 win over Yale, 1889, only loss handed Heffelfinger team. Made All-America in year when three Princeton backs were chosen, only J. S. Black being left off to avoid appearance of partiality. Citizens Savings Hall of Fame, National Football Foundation Hall of Fame.

COX, FREDERICK W. Kicker. B. 12/11/38, Monongahela, Pa. 5'10", 205. Graduated from U. of Pittsburgh, 1962. Drafted by Cleveland Browns as future on 8th round in 1961. Dealt to Minnesota Vikings, 1962. Dropped by Vikings that year but rejoined them in 1963. Spent 1962, part of '63 teaching school. NFL FG leader with 23 in 1965; with 26 in 1969; with 30 in 1970. Led all scorers in 1969 with 121 points; repeated in 1970 with 125. In 1969 championship game scored three PATs and two FGs. In 1972 scored on all 34 PAT attempts and on 21 of 34 FGs. Scoring streak of 151 games (NFL record) broken on 12/2/73 when Vikings were blanked, 27-0, by Cincinnati Bengals. It marked first shutout against Vikes in 161 games. Cox is chiropractor in off-season.

COY, EDWARD H. (Ted) Running Back. B. 5/24/1888, Andover, Mass. D. 1935. 6', 193. Yale, 1907-09. All-America, 1907, 08, 09. Perfectly fit Frank Merriwell image. Brother, Sherman, played end for Yale in 1900. Played in only one losing game and never asked for time out. Good passer when occasion arose, great fullback with speed and power. Considered by many as greatest line player of all time. Magnificent kicker, consistently punting for 60 yds., using his instep instead of toe. In 1907 Princeton game Yale was losing at halftime, 10-0, but rallied to win 12-10. Coy, along with Tad Jones, sparked comeback. Captain of 1909 "Wonder Team" (although just recovered from appendectomy), that defeated all 10 opponents, didn't allow single point, nor any team inside its 25-yd. line. Grantland Rice, in selecting his All-Time All-Americas in 1928, included Coy in backfield along with Heston, Thorpe and Mahan. Coy died suddenly of pneumonia in 1935 at age 47. Selected by Camp to All-Time All-America team, 1910. Citizens Savings Player of the Year, 1909. Citizens Savings Hall of Fame, National Football Foundation Hall of Fame.

CRAWFORD, FRED E. (Freddie) Tackle. B. Waynesville, N.C. D. 3/5/74, Tallahassee, Fla. 6'1", 195. Duke, 1931-33. Consensus All-America, 1933. Played under Wallace Wade. Was first North Carolinian to be honored as All-America by press associations and *Collier's*. Tremendously strong. Doc Newton, former Davidson coach, once said, "If I had a choice of being locked in a cage with

73

Crawford or a bear, I'd take the bear." Due largely to his contributions, Duke won Big 5 championships in 1932, 33. Chicago Bears, 1935. Selected by George Trevor to his All-Time Sectional team. National Football Foundation Hall of Fame. At time of death, Crawford was deputy director in Florida's Motor Vehicles Division.

CRISLER, HERBERT O. (Fritz) Coach. B. 1/12/1899, Earlville, Ill. Father of two-platoon football. Coached Minnesota, 1930-31; Princeton 1932-37, Michigan 1938-47. Michigan was national champion, 1947. Had flashy eye-catching offense. Played at U. of Chicago under Amos Alonzo Stagg, 1919-21. Assistant coach at Chicago, 1922-29. Minnesota athletic director, 1930-31. After coaching career became athletic director at Michigan, also chairman of its athletic board. Served in latter capacity until 1968. Never switched to T formation but used about five T-formation plays. "We called it the alumni-T," he said, "just to show the old grads that we were keeping up with the times." Since 1942, member of NCAA Rules Committee; currently life member, only other one was mentor, Stagg. Arena at Michigan named in his honor. Innovator, night and in the morning, but in the afternoon I toss and turn something awful." Captain of Green Bay East H.S. team that won 1920 Wisconsin state championship. Went to Notre Dame because he liked Rockne's offensive style. In three years gained 1932 yds. Green Bay Packers, 1925; Providence Steamrollers, 1925. Coached Michigan State, 1929-32; Fordham, 1933-41. Composite record: 78-21-10. Ranked with nation's best coaches during span at Fordham. Not only was his record superb (56-13-7), but it was achieved in pressure situations. Developed Fordham's immortal line, "Seven Blocks of Granite." Assistants included Earl Walsh, Hugh Devore, Glen (Judge) Carbarry and Vince Lombardi. Lost 1941 Cotton Bowl, won 1942 Sugar Bowl. Became AAFC commissioner, head coach of AAFC Chicago Rockets, pro official, television company executive. National Football Foundation Hall of Fame.

CROW, JOHN DAVID Running Back. B. 7/8/35, Marion, La. 6'2", 220. Played halfback for Texas A. & M. 1955-57. Unanimous All-America, 1957. Heisman Trophy, Walter Camp Trophy, 1957. In 1956, vs. Southern Methodist, returned punt 56 yds. Played in 1958 Gator Bowl vs. Tennessee. In collegiate career gained 1455 yds. rushing on 296 carries, average of 4.9; completed 7 passes in 16 attempts for 80 yds.; received 13 passes for 280 yds.; intercepted 8 passes for 45 yds., returned 21 punts for 248 yds. and 11 kickoffs for 236 yds.; scored 115 points on 19 TDs and 1 PAT. Drafted on first round by Chicago Cardinals, 1958. Moved with team to St. Louis. That year rushed 1071 yds. on 183 carries, leading league with 5.9 average. Led NFL in fumbles, 1960, with 11, and in 1962 with 14. Scored four TDs on 12/16/62. In 1965 traded to San Francisco 49ers for defensive back Abe Woodson. After 1968 season retired to become Cleveland Brown assistant coach. In 11 pro years rushed for 4963 yds. on 1157 carries and 38 TDs, caught 258 passes for 3699 yds. and 35 TDs, completed 33 of 70 passes for 759 yds. Played in Pro Bowl, 1960, 63, 66. Son, John, footballer at Alabama.

CROW, LINDON Defensive Back. 4/4/33, Denison, Tex. 6'1", 200. Southern California, 1952-54. Chicago Cardinals, 1955-57; New York Giants, 1958-60; Los Angeles Rams, 1961-64. NFL interception leader with 11 in 1956. Longest return was for 42 yds. With Giants established himself as one of league's best defenders. Traded to Los Angeles in 1961 for linebacker John Grizik and defensive back Erich Barnes. Intercepted 38 career passes for 394 yds., 2 TDs. NFL championship games, 1958, 59. Both were losing efforts to Baltimore Colts. Pro Bowl, 1960.

CROWDER, EDWIN B. Coach. B. 8/26/31, Arkansas City, Kan. Oklahoma All-America, 1952. Graduated with B.S. degree in geology. Assistant coach at Army, 1956, and Oklahoma, 1957-62. Head coach, Colorado, 1963-73. Resigned under fire after 5-6 season in '73. Made career record 67-49-2. Despite fine overall showing, teams never seemed to reach full potential under him. Developed outstanding backs in Bob Anderson, Charlie Davis. Twice took Buffaloes to Astro-Bluebonnet Bowl and Liberty Bowl, once to Gator Bowl. Won three, lost two. Remains Colorado athletic director, job held since 1965.

CROWLEY, JAMES H. (Sleepy Jim) Running Back. B. 9/10/02, Chicago, Ill. 158. Notre Dame, 1922-24. One of fabled "Four Horsemen." Played left halfback. Coach Knute Rockne called him "sleepy-looking wit", and "the nerviest back I've ever known." After poor performance in practice one day Rockne yelled, "Crowley, is there anything dumber than a dumb Irishman?" Reply: "No, sir, unless it's a smart Swede." Somnolent appearance earned his nickname. Claimed he was insomnia victim. Told Rockne, "I sleep all right at in California high schools, 1968, 69; in 1969 state title. Citizens Savings Athlete of the Month, 11/73. One of three 1st-round draft picks of New England Patriots, 1973. Rushed for 516 yds. in rookie season.

CSONKA, LAWRENCE R. (Larry; Zonk) Running Back. B. 1/25/26, Stow, Ohio. Syracuse U. halfback, 1965-67. Unanimous All-America, 1967; All-America, 1966. 4th in Heisman Trophy voting, 1967. In 1965 made 56-yd. rush vs. West Virginia. Scored one TD in Gator Bowl, 1967, vs. Tennessee. During collegiate career rushed for 2934 yds. on 594 carries, caught 20 passes for 186 yds., returned 4 kickoffs for 89 yds., scored 128 points on 21 TDs and 2 PATs. MVP in 1968 College All-Star game. 1st-round draft pick of Miami Dolphins, 1968. Wears special helmet to fight migraine headaches. As rookie gained 540 yds. Broke nose in 1969 exhibition game. Gained 566 yds. in regular season. In 1970 gained 874 yds., finishing 2nd in AFC to Denver's Floyd Little, college teammate. In 1971 rushed for 1051 yds. With Mercury Morris, 1972, became only pair of teammates ever to gain 1000 yds. each in one season (Csonka 1117, Morris 1000).

In 1973, despite several ailments, amassed 1003 yds. rushing on 219 carries, many in clutch situations, average of 4.6, 5 TDs. 1973 yardage made him third active player to surpass 3000 yds. in three seasons, others being Larry Brown and John Brockington. Against Oakland Raiders, in 1973 playoffs, scored record 3

TDs and gained 117 yds. on 29 carries. In Super Bowl VIII, 1974, broke Matt Snell's Super Bowl rushing record by carrying 33 times for 145 yds. Also scored two TDs which tied record. Was named game's MVP. AFL All-Star game, 1969. Pro Bowl, 1971, 72, 73, 74. Super Bowls also in 1972, 73. All-AFC, 1971, 72, 73. Teammate Jim Kiick and Csonka are called "Butch Cassady" and "Sundance Kid." Both signed contracts with Toronto (franchise moved to Memphis) for 1975, will play out option year in Miami in 1974. Game's premier power runner beginning '74 season.

CUNNINGHAM, SAM (Bam) Running Back. B. 8/15/50, Santa Barbara, Calif. Southern California, 1970-72. Co-captain of 1972 national champions, with 12-0 record. In 1973 Rose Bowl scored record 4 TDs, leading team to 42-17 win over Ohio State. Attended Santa Barbara H.S. Led USC in rushing in 1971, but switched to blocking back by coach John McKay due to injury. Great on short-yardage plays. Known as "Diving Dervish." Rose Bowl Player of the Game, 1973. Scored 7000 points in first attempt at decathlon. No. 1 shot-putter sponsored two-pt. conversion, widening of crossbars on goalposts. Offered commissionership of both Big 10, AFL but turned down both to remain at Michigan. Citizens Savings Hall of Fame, National Football Foundation Hall of Fame.

CURRIE, DANIEL (Dapper Dan) Linebacker. B. 6/27/35, Detroit, Mich. Consensus All-America at Michigan State, 1958. Collegiate center and linebacker. Drafted No. 1 by Green Bay Packers in 1959. Packers, 1958-64; Los Angeles Rams, 1965-66. Left linebacker for Packers. "I like the feeling you get when you make the good, clean, perfect tackle. With me it's the tackle, instead of just belting the other guy." — Currie. Almost impregnable on running plays. All-NFL, 1961, 62. NFL championship games, 1960, 61, 62.

CURTICE, JACK C. Coach. B. 5/24/07, Glasgow, Ky. Played at Transylvania College, received M.A. from Columbia. From 1930-37 served as high school coach at Elizabethtown and Owensboro high schools in Kentucky. Coached West Texas State, 1940-41; Texas (El Paso), 1946-49; Utah, 1950-57; Stanford, 1958-61; California (Santa Barbara), 1962-69. Composite record: 132-118-8. Was athletic director, 1942-50; 50-57, 63-69. Has served as president, American Football Coaches Association. Member of Rules Committee for 14 years. Citizens Savings Hall of Fame.

CURTIS, ISAAC End. B. 10/20/50, Santa Ana, Calif. 6'1", 193. Attended California and San Diego State. Played two years at California before transferring. Sprinter, passed up chance to make U.S. Olympic team to devote full-time to football. Selected by Cincinnati Bengals on 1st round of 1973 draft. In rookie year, 1973, received 45 catches for 843 yds. and league-leading 9 TDs. Selected for *Football Digest* Rookie All-Star team. In AFC playoff game vs. Miami Dolphins, 1973, held to one reception for nine yds. Pro Bowl, 1974.

CURTIS, J. MICHAEL Linebacker. B. 3/27/43, Rockville, Md. 6'2", 232. Fullback and linebacker at Duke, 1964-66. Led Blue Devils in rushing in 1964 (497 yds. on 121 carries, 4.1 average). Drafted on 1st round by Baltimore Colts, 1965. Broke into pro football as fullback, switched to linebacker after one season. Outside linebacker until 1969, then moved to middle. Intercepted eight passes in both 1969 and '70, three in 1971. Named outstanding defensive player in AFC by Kansas City 101 Club in 1970. Made big play of 1971 when he intercepted Craig Morton's 4th-quarter pass in Super Bowl, setting up Jim O'Brien's 32-yd. FG which won title. Named MVP of 1971 Super Bowl by New York Chapter of Pro Football Writers. Played 1971 season with fractured thumb, missing one game. In 1971 made 14 tackles, 9 unassisted, vs. Miami Dolphins. All-NFL, 1968. Pro Bowl, 1968, 71, 72. Super Bowl, 1969, 71. Real tough customer. Christened "Animal" for rugged play. Wrote book, *Stay off My Turf.*

CUTTER, SLADE D. Tackle. 196. Navy, 1932-34. All-America, 1934. In 1934 Army-Navy game, Navy won first time since 1921. Cutter kicked FG for only points scored in game. Strong on defense, aggressive, great placekicker. Had fine speed, often caught backs going away from his side of line. Columbia's only defeat in 1934 was dealt by Navy. Afterwards Lou Little said of Cutter: "When my backs made a yard through his position, I thought they were running wild. It was like fighting off the surf in a storm. His judgment in diagnosing plays was incredible." National Football Foundation Hall of Fame.

DALE, CARROLL W. End. B. 4/24/38, Wise, Va. 6'2", 200. Graduated from Virginia Tech, 1960. All-America, 1959. Drafted on 8th round by Los Angeles Rams in 1960. In 1965 traded to Green Bay Packers for linebacker Dan Currie. A favorite of coach Vince Lombardi, and favorite receiver of QB Bart Starr. In 1965 NFL title game caught 47-yd. pass from Starr for first score of game. In Super Bowl, 1967, scored TD on 51-yd. pass from Starr. Pro Bowl 1969, 70, 71. Caught winning TD pass in 1970 Pro Bowl game. NFL championship games, 1965, 66, 67. Also Super Bowl II, 1968. Put on waivers by Packers during 1973; claimed by Minnesota Vikings. Dale is avid outdoorsman and hunter.

DALRYMPLE, GERALD (Jerry) End. B. 8/6/07, Arkadelphia, Ark. D. 9/26/62. 6', 178. Played at Tulane under Bernie Bierman, 1929-31. All-America, 1930; consensus All-America, 1931. In three years lost but one regular season game, and in 18 of 29 games opposition was held scoreless. Captain, 1931. Originally, favorite receiver of Bill Banker, later of Don Zimmerman. Zimmerman-to-Dalrymple was noted combination. 1931 squad won 11 straight games until losing Rose Bowl to Southern California, 21-12. Allison Danzig labelled Dalrymple "one of football's most famous players." Called by Bierman "one of the greatest players I ever coached." Citizens Savings Hall of Fame, Football Foundation Hall of Fame.

DALTON, JOHN P. (Jack) Running Back. B. 4/1/1889. D. 3/10/19, Brooklyn, N. Y. Navy halfback, 1910-11. All-America, 1911; 2nd team, 1910. Along with guard Babe Brown, his favorite blocker, among finest players in Navy history.

1910, 11 teams undefeated; one tie in 1910, three in 1911. Excellent punter, dropkicker; in 1910 single-handedly beat Army, 3-0; repeated feat, 1911. Thus nickname, "Three-to-Nothing Jack." Scored 14 career TDs. Suspected at West Point of being descendant of Dalton Boys, gang of bank robbers. Served in World War I as Cmdr. Died of bronchial problems. National Football Foundation Hall of Fame.

DALY, CHARLES D. Quarterback. B. 10/31/1880, Roxbury, Mass. D. 2/12/59. 5'7", 150. Harvard, 1898-1900; Army, 1901-02. All-America, 1898, 99; 2nd team, 1900; 3rd team, 1902. Excellent field general, punt returner, ballhandler. At Harvard played in only one losing game—his last—vs. Yale. Appointed to West Point by Rep. John F. (Honey Fitz) Fitzgerald. Crafty runner, good dropkicker. In 1901 led Army to 16-0 victory, later reported as "Daly 11, Army 5, Navy 0." Deadly tackler. 1907 Harvard backfield coach. Coached Army, 1913-16, 19-22. His 1914, 16, 22 teams were unbeaten. Once called "greatest football player Army has ever seen." Citizens Savings Hall of Fame, National Football Foundation Hall of Fame.

DANIELS, CLEMON (Bo) Running Back. B. 7/9/37, McKinney, Tex. 6'1", 220. Graduated from Prairie View A. & M., 1959. In 1960 signed as free agent by Dallas Texans, released after one season. Signed with Oakland Raiders as free agent, 1961. In 1963 rushed for 1099 yds. on 215 carries to lead AFL. Established AFL career records, 1968, for rushes attempted with 1134, rushing yds. with 5101. Released by Oakland in 1968 and signed with San Francisco 49ers, played one season. Played in 1967 AFL championship game, 1968 Super Bowl. AFL Player of the Year, 1963. All-League, 1963, 66. AFL All-Star games 1964, 65, 66, 67.

DAUGHERTY, HUGH (Duffy) Coach. B. 9/8/15, Emeigh, Pa. Syracuse U. guard, 1937-39. Suffered broken neck, 1938, but came back to play and was captain of 1939 team. Not outstanding player, but made great contribution due to hard work, sense of humor, enthusiasm. In 1940 was part-time freshman coach at Syracuse. Entered Army as Pvt., 1941. Served four years, mostly in South Pacific. Left service as Maj. In 1945 coached at Trinity School in New York. Year later became line coach under Biggie Munn at Syracuse. When Munn moved to Michigan State, Duffy went along as assistant. Munn retired, 1953, and Daugherty became head coach. Under his leadership, Spartans went to Rose Bowl three times, winning in 1954, 56, and losing, 1966. His team was national champion in 1965. Retired in 1972. Finished with 109-69-5 record in 19 seasons. Coach of the Year, 1955. Citizens Savings Hall of Fame. Now football commentator on ABC television.

DAVIS, ANTHONY Running Back. B. 9/8/52, Huntsville, Tex. 5'9", 190. Southern California, 1972-73. All-Pacific 8 both years. Excellent runner, speedy and shifty. In brilliant sophomore season, 1972, carried ball 207 times for 1191 yds., caught 18 passes, returned 12 kickoffs and 7 punts, kicked off 81 times.

Against Notre Dame, 12/2/72, scored 36 points (6 TDs), two scores coming on 97- and 96-yd. kickoff returns. Averaged record 72.7 yds. on returns that day. Performance fell off somewhat in 1973. Off-season automobile injury possible cause. Accomplished baseball player, batted .346 for USC national champs in 1973. Rose Bowl, 1973, 74.

DAVIS, ERNEST Running Back. B. 13/14/39, Uniontown, Pa. D. 5/18/63. 6'2", 210. Achieved fame at Syracuse, 1959-61. Broke records of Jim Brown. Consensus All-America, 1961. Unanimous All-America, 1961. First Black to win Heisman Trophy, 1961. In 1960 Cotton Bowl caught 87-yard pass for major bowl record; Syracuse defeated Texas, 23-14. In career rushed for 2386 yds., scored 35 TDs. First Black ever drafted by Washington Redskins, 1962. Was first player chosen in entire NFL draft that year. Redskins traded him to Cleveland Browns for wide receiver Bobby Mitchell. Set up dream backfield of Davis and Jim Brown, but Ernie destined for tragedy. Stricken with leukemia shortly after trade. Died before playing single down in NFL. Nation saddened. In brief 23½ years had earned respect and adulation reserved for few athletes.

DAVIS, GLENN W. (Mr. Outside) Running Back. B. 12/26/24, Claremont, Calif. 5'9", 172. Formed irrepressible combination with Doc Blanchard, "Mr. Inside." Army halfback, 1943-46. Consensus All-America, 1944. Unanimous All-America, 1945, 46. Walter Camp Trophy, Maxwell Award, 1944. Citizens Savings Player of the Year, 1944, 46. Was 2nd in Heisman Trophy voting, 1944, 45; won it in 1946. In 1944 led NCAA in scoring with 120 points, TDs-accounted-for with 22, in average yds. rushing with 11.5 (667 yds. on 58 carries). In 1945, again led in TDs-accounted-for with 20 and average yds. rushing with 11.5. 11.5-yd. average, accomplished twice, set record as did his 11.7-yd. average per play on total offense (1197 yds. on 102 plays) in 1945. Finished career with six other records, including TDs (59) and points scored (354), highest average gain per play in total offense with 8.53 yds. Completed 57 of 126 passes for 1172 yds., caught 48 passes for 850 yds., made 14 interceptions for 147 yds., 22 punts for average of 33.7 yds., 84 punt returns for 1060 yds., 10 kickoff returns for 278 yds. Also starred in baseball and track. Los Angeles Rams, 1950-51. Played on bad knee suffered in service. Vs. Cleveland Browns, 12/24/50, caught 82-yd. TD pass from Bob Waterfield, 2nd longest in championship game history.

He and Blanchard responsible for sportscaster Bill Stern acquiring nickname, "Lateral Pass." Stern reported Blanchard running with ball, but then realized he had wrong man and said, "Lateral to Davis," continuing as if mistake never made. West Point duo later costarred in football film, *The Spirit of West Point.* Glenn had twin brother, Ralph, nine minutes older. Citizens Savings Hall of Fame, National Football Foundation Hall of Fame. Director of special events for *Los Angeles Times.*

DAVIS, PARKE HILL Coach. B. 7/16/1871, Jamestown, N.Y. D. 6/5/34. Famous football historian. Wrote newspaper articles, discussed game on radio. King of football statisticians. Played for Princeton as regular tackle, 1891-92.

81

Also boxed in college, sparring with John L. Sullivan. After graduation went to U. of Wisconsin to introduce football. In 1894 appointed coach at Amherst. Was football, track and baseball coach at Lafayette, 1895-97. Then decided to continue studies abroad and received M.A. at U. of Leipzig. Studied law and was admitted to bar. Fond of saying he'd studied football with two Presidents: Woodrow Wilson (at Princeton), Calvin Coolidge (at Amherst). Later entered politics, serving as district attorney of Northampton Co., Pa. Appointed to Rules Committee in 1909, serving until 1915. Led call for quarters (rather than halves), uniform numbers, end zones, cessation of interlocking interference. Had "great debate" with Amos Alonzo Stagg when he credited George Woodruff with inventing flying interference in *Collegiate Football Guide*. Stagg credited his former teammate, Pudge Heffelfinger. Davis also listed "push" plays as originating in 1893; Stagg claimed he'd used them as early as 1890. Authored football articles for various encyclopedias and wrote a history of football. Compiled annual *Collegiate Football Guide* until his death in 1934. Lawrence Perry of *New York Sun* wrote of him: "Dreams and memories are fine things to have. We shall not again see Parke Davis' like — but at least we knew him once and will never forget him."

DAVIS, THOMAS R. Kicker. B. 10/13/34, Shreveport, La. 6'0", 225. Attended Louisiana State. Selected as future by San Francisco on 11th round of 1957 NFL draft. Played for 49ers, 1959-1969. Led NFL in FGs with 19, 1960. In 1962 led league in average yds. per punt with 45.6 (48 punts), longest 82 yds. Led in PATs with 52, 1965. Established NFL record for consecutive PATs with 234, 9/27/59 to 12/12/65. Also scored in 87 consecutive games, 1961-67. Lifetime punting average of 44.68 yds. is 2nd highest in league history. Retired in 1970 after 11 years. Pro Bowl, 1963, 64.

DAVIS, WILLIAM D. (Willie) Defensive End. B. 7/24/34, Lisbon, La. 6'3", 245. Played for Grambling, 1954-55; Cleveland Browns, 1958-59; Green Bay Packers, 1960-69. Raised in Texarkana, Ark., and attended Booker T. Washington H.S. there. In sophomore year played on varsity as both defensive tackle and offensive end. Won scholarship to Grambling where he was captain in junior and senior years. Graduated with B.S. degree in 1956. Drafted on 15th round by Cleveland Browns, but before he could report was drafted into army. Made All-Army and All-Service teams, 1957. Reported to Browns, 1958. In 1960 traded to Packers for end A. D. Williams. Became captain of Pack's defensive unit. In career recovered 21 of opponents' fumbles (tied for 2nd highest in NFL history). Earned master's degree in business administration from U. of Chicago, 1968. Pro Bowl following 1963, 64, 65, 66, 67 seasons. All-NFL 1964, 65, 66, 67. Played in NFL championship games 1960, 61, 62, 65, 66, 67; Super Bowl following 1966, 67 seasons. Retired, 1970, after 12 seasons.

DAWKINS, PETER M. Running Back. B. 3/8/38, Royal Oak, Mich. 6'1", 197. Celebrated Army halfback. Suffered polio attack at age 11. Began lifting weights to build himself up. Enrolled at Yale, but as qualified West Point alternate, took

82

special entrance exam and passed. Played three years for Army, 1956-58. Unanimous All-America, 1958. Academic All-America, 1957-58. Won Heisman Trophy and Maxwell Award, 1958. Excellent runner and blocker. Made 80-yd. punt vs. Villanova, 1958. Set NCAA record in average yds. on pass receptions, seasons, with 30.9. Gained career total of 1123 yds. rushing and scored 158 points. Was first captain of cadets (leader of 2491 fellow cadets), class president, one of "star men" (top five percent in class standing), football captain — only man in West Point history to hold all four honors. Attended Oxford on Rhodes Scholarship. Remained in service and didn't play pro football. Man of tremendous drive and dependability. Earned M.A. from Oxford, 1968; MPA from Princeton, 1970.

DAWSON, LEONARD R. Quarterback. B. 6/20/35, Alliance, Ohio. 6', 190. Purdue, 1954-56. Academic All-America, 1956. In 1954 led NCAA in TD passes with 15. Completed 80-yd. pass vs. Iowa, 1954, and 95-yd. pass vs. Northwestern, 1955. Finished career with 243 completions in 452 attempts for 3325 yds. and 29 TDs, 44 points on 1 TD and 38 PATs. Selected by Pittsburgh Steelers in 1st round of 1957 NFL draft. On 1/13/60 traded to Cleveland Browns. Released by Cleveland and signed by Dallas Texans, 1962, who became Kansas City Chiefs. Led AFL in passing, 1962, 64, 66, 68. Completed 61.0 percent of passes in 1961. Set numerous AFL career records. Made it big with Chiefs after long spells on bench at Pittsburgh and Cleveland. AFL Player of the Year, 1962. AFL All-Star games, 1963, 65, 67, 68, 69. Outstanding offensive player in AFL All-Star game, 1969. All-League, 1962, 66. Pro Bowl, 1972. Played in AFL championship games, 1962, 66, 69. Played in Super Bowl, 1967, 70. In Super Bowl IV, 1970, underdog Kansas City upset Minnesota Vikings, 23-7, due to Dawson's varied attack. In 1973 was voted NFL Man of the Year by fans for civic contribution and athletic ability. Has TV sports show on KMBC-TV, Kansas City. Injured much of 1973. One of few men to have thrown for 25,000 yds.

DeGROOT, DUDLEY S. Coach. D. 5/5/70. Played for Stanford under Pop Warner. Member of U.S. rugby team that won Olympic title, 1924. Coached San Jose State, 1933-39. In 1939 was assisted by Pop Warner, team was undefeated and untied. Became physical education department head and football coach of U. of Rochester, 1940. Coached Washington Redskins, 1944-45. Some members of 'Skins then were Angelo Bertelli, Alex Agase, Ben Agajanian. In 1945, Washington won Eastern title but lost NFL championship to Cleveland Browns, 15-14. Coached Los Angeles Dons (AAFC), 1946-47. On roster were Ki Aldrich, Sammy Baugh, Wayne Millner. Also coached at California (Santa Barbara), 1926-28; Menlo College, 1929-31; West Virginia, 1948-49; New Mexico, 1950-52. Collegiate record: 133-74-12. Citizens Savings Hall of Fame.

DeMARCO, ROBERT A. Center. B. 9/16/38, Jersey City, N.J. 6'2", 245. Attended Indiana and Dayton. St. Louis Cardinals, 1961-69; Miami Dolphins, 1970-71; Cleveland Browns, 1972-73. Pro Bowl, 1964, 66. All-NFL, 1967. Played in NFL championship game, 1971. "God knows, I don't have great speed," says

DeMarco. "But I think I have good, real good quickness, and that's the name of the game on the offensive line. Quickness is paramount in a center."

DEMPSEY, THOMAS Kicker. B.1/12/41, Milwaukee, Wis. 6'1", 255. Lost part of right foot in childhood accident. Using same foot, developed into top-notch placekicker. Was All-Conference defensive end and outstanding heavyweight wrestler at Palomar (Calif.) J. C. Went from there to New Orleans Saints in 1969. Played with Saints thru 1970. In 1971 signed as free agent with Philadelphia Eagles, is still with club. Pro Bowl, 1970. On 11/1/70, against Detroit Lions, kicked 63-yd. FG for NFL record. Recipient of Philadelphia Sportswriters Most Courageous Athlete Award in 1971. Best scoring season was 1969 when he kicked 33 PATs and 22 FGs (of league-leading 41 attempts), for 99 points.

DePOYSTER, JERRY D. Kicker. B. 7/6/46, Omaha, Neb. 6'1", 200. Played for Wyoming, 1965-67. All-America, 1967. Was NCAA kick-scoring champion in 1966 with 71 points (32 PATs, 13 FGs). During career scored 182 points on 74 PATs (of 96) and 36 FGs. His FG and point totals were NCAA records. FG mark was broken by fellow Wyoming Cowboy, Bob Jacobs, in 1970. Jacobs booted 38. DePoyster's career feat of six 50-yd. FGs is still unmatched; so is three 50-yd. FG accomplishment vs. Utah in 1966. Those three were from 54, 52, 54 yds. Detroit Lions, 1968; Oakland Raiders, 1971-73.

DESJARDIEN, PAUL (Shorty) Center. B. 8/24/1893, Coffeyville, Kan. D. 3/7/56, Monrovia, Calif. 6'5", 182. U. of Chicago star in four sports: football, basketball, baseball and track. Won 12 varsity letters. All-America, 1913. Helped Chicago win 18 consecutive games. Recruited out of high school by Amos Alonzo Stagg. Kept very strict training habits, at Stagg's insistence. Played season of big-league baseball with Cleveland Indians before entry into business. Citizens Savings Hall of Fame, National Football Foundation Hall of Fame.

DEVANEY, ROBERT Coach. B. 4/13/15, Saginaw, Michigan. Graduated from Alma, 1939. Coached Wyoming, 1957-61. Record: 35-10-5. Nebraska head coach, 1962-72. At Nebraska won seven Big 8 titles, and two national championships: in 1970 with record of 10-0-1, in 1971 with record of 12-0-0. Another strong team in 1965 won Big 8 title for third year in row and had perfect record (10-0-0) until beaten by Alabama in Orange Bowl. Had unbeaten streak of 32 games (31 wins, 1 tie), 1969-71, 5th longest streak in last 50 years. During streak Cornhuskers won 23 straight. Finally beaten by UCLA, 20-17, in 1972. In 11 seasons participated in eight major bowl games: Orange Bowl, 1964, 66, 71, 72, 73; Cotton Bowl, 1965; Sugar Bowl, 1967; Sun Bowl, 1970. Won 5, lost 3. Retired after 1972 season. Nebraska record: 101-20-2. Overall mark of 136-30-7, percentage of .806, placed him 9th among major-college coaches. Citizens Savings Hall of Fame.

DEVINE, AUBREY A. Quarterback. B. 11/21/1897, Des Moines, Iowa. 5'9",

170. Iowa, 1919-21. All-America, 1921. Called by many "the greatest Hawkeye football player of all time." Scored 161 points and ran for nearly 2000 yds. in three varsity seasons. Captained unbeaten 1921 team that ended Notre Dame's 20-game winning streak. Three times won All-Big 10 acclaim. Against Minnesota Gophers in 1921 scored 20 points and passed for 2 TDs, totaling 480 yds. for day. Next week vs. Indiana scored 28 points, accounting for 60 points in eight days. No other college back has equaled that output. Never removed from play because of injuries. Now, at 73, lives in retirement in California. Enjoys golf.

DEVINE, DANIEL J. Coach. B. 12/23/24, Augusta, Wis. Received B.A. degree in social studies from Minnesota (Duluth), 1948, and master's from Michigan State, 1952. Head coach at East Jordan (Mich.) H.S., 1948-49. Assistant coach, Michigan State, 1950-54. Head coach at Arizona State, 1955-57, compiling amazing record of 27-3-1. Became head coach at Missouri, 1958; stayed thru 1970. Had perfect season in 1960, (11-0-0). In 13 seasons had record of 92-38-7. Took team to Orange Bowl three times; once each to Astro-Bluebonnet Bowl, Sugar Bowl and Gator Bowl, winning 4 and losing 2. After 16 years as college coach had record of 119-41-8, percentage of .732. Became coach of Green Bay Packers in 1971, leading them to 1972 NFC Central Division title. Among discoveries for Packers were Chester Marcol, Willie Buchanon.

DEVORE, HUGH J. Coach. 11/25/10, Newark, N.J. Youngest of nine children. Notre Dame end, 1933-34. Captain, 1934. Peripatetic coach. Served assistantships at Notre Dame, Holy Cross, Dayton, Green Bay Packers, Houston Oilers. Head coach, Notre Dame, 1945, 63; Providence, 1938-41; St. Bonaventure, 1946-48; NYU, 1949-51; Philadelphia Eagles, 1956-57. NYU dropped football in 1952. Notre Dame record:9-9-1. Philadelphia record: 7-16-1. In 1964, he was replaced at N.D. by Ara Parseghian. Stayed on two years to serve as assistant athletic director.

DEWITT, JOHN R. Guard. B. 10/29/1881, Phillipsburg, N.J. D. 7/28/30. 6'1", 198. Princeton, 1901-03. All-America, 1902, 03. Led 1903 Tigers to national championship, won 11 games and were undefeated, untied and unscored upon. In 1903, vs. Yale, made 85-yd. TD run with blocked kick, 48-yd. FG from difficult angle, scored all 11 points in season-ending game, only time Yale lost in two years. That year made 80-yd. TD run vs. Dartmouth, FG from 50-yd. line vs. Cornell. Consistently efficient at guard and tackle. Classed with superstars Pudge Heffelfinger, Trux Hare, Gordon Brown, Ned Glass. Versatile. Citizens Savings College Player of the Year, 1903. Citizens Savings Hall of Fame, National Football Foundation Hall of Fame. Named by Walter Camp as tackle on his All-Time All-America team. Also Eastern champ in hammer-throw, 1901-04. Won silver medal in 1904 Olympics.

DEWVEALL, WILLARD L. End. B. Weatherford, Tex. 6'4", 225. Southern Methodist, 1956-58. Drafted in 1959 by Chicago Bears, with whom he played thru 1960. Played out option in 1960. Approached by Houston Oilers and signed with them, 1/14/61, becoming first man ever to jump from NFL to AFL. On 11/25/62, vs. San Diego Chargers, made 98-yd. pass reception for TD, which tied him with four other players for 2nd longest in history. Played with Oilers thru 1964.

DIBBLEE, BENJAMIN H. Halfback. 5'8", 156. Harvard, 1895-98. All-America, 1897, 98. Captain of 1898 team that beat Yale for third time in 24 years and ended Penn's winning streak of 31 games. It was 1st of Harvard's "Big 4" teams, beating Dartmouth, Army, Carlisle, Penn, Brown, and Yale. Dibblee had few equals as broken-field runner. He was fast and shifty. Made runs of 50 and 40 yds. vs. Yale and scored one TD. Coached Harvard, 1899, as Forbes was injured when thrown from horse. Harvard became national champion that year with record of 10-0-1, scoring 210 points and allowing opponents only 10. Citizens Savings College Player of the Year, 1898.

DICKEY, LYNN Quarterback. B. 10/19/49, Paola, Kan. 6'4", 217. One of the greatest QBs in Big 8 history. Played at Kansas State, 1968-70. All Big 8, 1969, 70. In career gained 5779 yds. total offense on 1104 plays, averaging 5.23 yds. In 31 games completed 501 of 994 passes, .504 percent for 6208 yds. and 29 TDs. Selected by Houston Oilers on 3rd round of 1971 NFL draft. Rookie season spent as backup QB. Started one game vs. Oakland Raiders. Completed 19 of 57 attempts for 315 yds. Can throw long ball. Has excellent strength. Only fair runner. Missed entire '72 season due to hip injury. Attended Osawatomie (Kan.) H.S., where he was school's best all-around athlete. School named stadium after him in summer, 1971. Alternated with Dan Pastorini as Oiler QB, 1973.

DIETZ, WILLIAM (Lone Star) Coach. D. 7/20/64. Played at Carlisle under Pop Warner. Was teammate of Jim Thorpe and captained team one season. Head coach at Washington State, 1915-17. Coached Marine Corps team during World War I. Then coached Purdue, 1921; Louisiana Tech, 1922-23; Wyoming, 1924-26; Haskell, 1929-32; Albright, 1937-42. Colorful and astute. His 19-year collegiate record was 97-60-6, percentage of .613. Tutored Boston Redskins, 1933-34 (11-11-2).

DIETZEL, PAUL F. Coach. B. 9/5/24, Mansfield, Ohio. Pilot in World War II. Little All-America center at Miami (Ohio). Cut his coaching teeth under some of greatest: Sid Gillman, Bear Bryant, Red Blaik. Guided Louisiana State, 1955-61, compiling record of 49-43-6. His 1958 LSU team was national champion, with perfect record of 10-0-0. Introduced novel three-platoon system that year. Two-way "White" team was supported by "Go" team and "Chinese Bandits." LSU scored 275 points, its opponents 53. Went to Sugar Bowl following '58 season and triumphed over Clemson, 7-0. Named Coach of the Year, 1958. 1959 team almost equaled previous year with 9-1 record. Coached Army, 1962-65. Record: 21-18-1. Became coach at South Carolina, 1966. Took his team to Peach Bowl, 1968, losing 14-3 to West Virginia. Thru '72 season had lifetime record of 98-44-6. Combines coaching duties with athletic directorship at South Carolina.

86

DILLON, ROBERT (Bobby) Defensive Back. B. 2/23/30, Pendleton, Tex. 6'1", 185. Texas, 1949-51. One of country's leading punt returners. Closed collegiate career with 47 returns for 830 yds., average of 17.7. Played for Green Bay Packers, 1952-59. During pro career made 52 pass interceptions for 976 yds. Chosen defensive halfback on All-League team, 1954, 55, and safety on teams of 1956, 57, 58.

DITKA, MICHAEL K. (Hammer) Tight End. B. 10/18/39, Carnegie, Pa. 6'3", 225. U. of Pittsburgh, 1958-60. Unanimous All-America, 1960. Received 45 passes for 730 yds. in three years. In 1959 caught 56-yd. pass vs. Duke, in 1960 received 59-yd. pass vs. Notre Dame. In 1961 drafted by Chicago Bears on 1st round, playing thru 1966. In 1961, vs. Green Bay Packers, caught 9 passes for 187 yds., 3 TDs. 1961 totals: 56 receptions, 1076 yds., 12 TDs. Was Rookie of the Year. On 10/13/63 made 4 TD receptions. Traded to Philadelphia Eagles for QB Jack Concannon, 1967. In 1969 traded to Dallas Cowboys for end Dave McDaniels. Stayed with Dallas thru 1971. In 1972 became assistant coach for Cowboys. All-NFL 1962, 63, 64. Pro Bowl, 1962, 63, 64, 65, 66. Played in NFL championship game, 1963. Super Bowl, 1971, 72. In 1972 Super Bowl scored one TD. Rugged, fearless competitor.

DIXON, HEWRITT F. (Tank) Running Back. B. 1/8/40, Alachua, Fla. 6'1", 230. Graduated from Florida A. & M., 1963. Chosen by Denver Broncos on 8th round of 1963 AFL draft. Traded to Oakland Raiders for linebacker Archie Matsos, 1966. Set record for longest run from scrimmage, 69 yds., vs. Houston Oilers, 12/31/67. In 1967 AFL title game rushed for 144 yds. Was All-League back, 1968. Played with Raiders thru 1970.

DOBBS, GLENN Running Back. B. Frederick, Okla. 6'3", 195. Tulsa, 1940-42. All-America, 1942, Tulsa's first. Made rugby-type kicks, usually dead run, often making 80-yd. punts. Could not only pass, kick and run, but was also great on defense. In Sun Bowl, vs. Texas Tech in 1941, completed 19 of 24 passes, one for 30-yd. TD and made 86-yd. punt. Led NCAA in passing yds. per attempt, 1942, with average of .626 (107 attempts, 67 completions, 1066 yds.). Also set season record for total offense yds. per play (8.0). Tulsa had undefeated, untied season in 1942 with Dobbs big man in attack. Made 87-yd. punt vs. Oklahoma and 78-yd. punt vs. Drake. In Sugar Bowl following '42 season made 76-yd. punt, had nine consecutive pass completions to set Sugar Bowl records. In service, 1942-45, playing with Randolph Field in Southwest. Brooklyn Dodgers (AAFC), 1946-47; Los Angeles Dons (AAFC), 1948-49. Tied Otto Graham for AFC passing title in 1946, throwing 135 completions in 269 attempts for 1886 yds. Same season led AAFC in punting with average of 47.8 yds. In four AAFC years rushed for 1039 yds. on 262 attempts and scored 12 TDs. Made 934 career passing attempts, had 446 completions, for 5876 yds., 45 TDs, and percentage of 47.8. Became Tulsa athletic director and football coach. Known for wide-open passing game, 1961-68. Citizens Savings Hall of Fame.

DOBIE, GILMOUR (Gloomy Gil) B. 1/21/1879, Hastings, Minn. D. 12/23/48, Hartford, Conn. Terrible pessimist; always predicted worst for teams while coaching at North Dakota State, 1906-07; Washington, 1908-16; Navy, 1917-19; Cornell, 1930-35; Boston College, 1936-38. Had career record of 179-45-15. 1908-16 Washington teams unbeaten. Huskies won 39 straight games from 1908-14, 2nd-longest streak in college history. Undefeated at Cornell, 1921-23. Regarded as miracle man in Ithaca after Cornell's 1920 victory over Penn, team they'd beaten only four times since 1893. Very tough coach; once had team running laps after 72-0 win. Dour personality. Not inventive, but used standard patterns well. Relied primarily on running game, bolstered by power, flawless execution. Never even rated Eddie Haw and George Pflann as anything more than "good," his highest superlative. Hostile to press. Practices always closed, even to alumni; they "have big mouths," he said. Good conversationalist. Held law degree, invested gainfully in stock market. Citizens Savings Hall of Fame, National Football Foundation Hall of Fame.

DODD, ROBERT L. (Bobby) Quarterback. B. 10/11/08, Galax, Va. 6'2", 195. Tennessee QB, 1928-30. All-America, 1930. Tremendous all-round athlete. Vols lost only one game in Dodd era, tied one. Coached Georgia Tech, school which turned him down as student, 1945-66. Compiled 165-64-8 record, percentage of .713. Kept practice sessions down to 90 minutes. Believed football should be fun, but players should study and attend church. Told parents; "We're not miracle workers, but if you send us a good boy to Georgia Tech, we'll send you a good boy home." Won six consecutive bowl games: Orange Bowl twice, Sugar Bowl twice, Cotton Bowl, Oil Bowl. Born leader, salesman. Famous Tech slogan was "In Dodd We Trust." He earned it.

DOMRES, MARTIN F. (Marty) Quarterback. B. 4/14/47, Ithaca, N.Y. 6'4", 215. Played for Columbia, 1966-68. Set 15 school, 12 Ivy League and 3 ECAC records. Gained 5345 yds. total offense on 1133 plays (record since broken by Chuck Hixson). Ranked 3rd nationally in total offense with 2404 yds., 1968. Selected by San Diego Chargers on 1st round of 1969 draft. Played with Chargers thru 1971. Then traded to Baltimore Colts. When John Unitas was dealt by Colts to Chargers following 1972 season, Domres became regular quarterback. In five pro seasons he's completed 290 of 592 passes for 3764 yds.

DONAHUE, MICHAEL J. Coach. B. 6/4/1876, County Kerry, Ireland. After 1904 graduation from Yale, coached at Auburn, 1904-06, 08-22; LSU, 1923-27. At Yale earned varsity letters in football, basketball, track, cross-country. Later coached Spring Hill College. Major college career record: 120-54-7. Not fancy, stuck to basics. Citizens Savings Hall of Fame, National Football Foundation Hall of Fame.

DONCHESS, JOSEPH C. End. B. 3/17/05, Youngstown, Ohio. 6'1", 180. Played at U. of Pittsburgh under Jock Sutherland. Consensus All-America, 1929; All-America, 1928. After graduation stayed on as Sutherland's assistant. During

88

same period studied at Pitt Medical School. In 1934 joined Earl Blaik's staff at Dartmouth. Remained there thru 1937. Chief surgeon, Gary Works, U.S. Steel Corp., 1943-65. Named Letterman of Distinction at Pitt, 1962.

DONELLI, ALDO (Buff) Running Back-Coach. B. 7/22/07, Morgan, Pa. Duquesne, 1927-29. One of Duquesne's "first gridiron immortals." Played center on freshman team, 1926. In 1927, Elmer Layden switched him to backfield. Captain of team, 1928-29; Dukes were 17-1-1 in that span. Fine placekicker, had been soccer star. On graduation became freshman coach, in 1939 became head coach and led Duquesne to undefeated season. In three-year period Duquesne was 23-1-1. Younger brother, Alan, was outstanding player on 1939 and '40 teams. In 1941 replaced Bert Bell as coach of Pittsburgh Steelers, but after seven games was replaced by Walt Kiesling as he was banned by commissioner Layden. Coached Cleveland Rams, 1944; returned to college coaching in 1947 at Boston U. Stayed thru 1956 and compiled record of 40-34-4. Coached Columbia, 1957-67, with record of 30-67-2.

DONOVAN, ARTHUR, JR. Tackle. B. 6/5/25, Bronx, N.Y. 6'3", 265. Son of famous boxing referee. Arthur Sr. handled more championship bouts (14) than any man in history. Grandfather, Mike, was middleweight champion and gave lessons to Teddy Roosevelt. Art Jr. attended Boston College. Drafted in 1950 by Baltimore Colts. In 1951 moved with team to New York (Yanks) and 1952 to Dallas (Texans). In 1953 returned to Baltimore. One of few players on 1950 squad still with Colts in '53. Played thru 1961 with Baltimore. Fierce tackler. All-Pro, 1954, 55, 56, 57. Pro Bowl, 1953, 54, 55, 56, 57. Colts won NFL titles in 1958, 59. Pro Football Hall of Fame.

DORAIS, CHARLES E. (Gus) Coach. B. 7/2/1892, Chippewa Falla, Wis. Passing half of famous combination, with Knute Rockne, which passed Notre Dame to 35-13 upset over Army, 1913. Game taught Army, East how to integrate pass into attack. Coached at Loras, 1914-17; Gonzaga, 1920-24; Detroit, 1925-42. Composite record: 149-70-12. Worked out forward pass with Rockne on beach at Cedar Point, Ohio, on Lake Erie during summer of 1913. Not very big (5'7", 145 QB), fought hard for everything he earned. Taught system much like that of Rockne, his roommate at Notre Dame. Successful both as coach and player. Coached professionally with Detroit Lions, 1943-47 (20-31-2). Citizens Savings Hall of Fame, National Football Foundation Hall of Fame.

DORSET, TONY Running Back. B. Aliquippa, Pa. 5'11", 175. Played as freshman on U. of Pittsburgh varsity, 1973, and was selected All-America. First freshman to receive such honor since Doc Blanchard of Army in 1944. AP All-East team, 1973. Was nation's 2nd-leading rusher with 1586 yds. in 11 games. Probably greatest freshman running back in history. His rushing output smashed previous frosh record of 1291 yds. by Po James in 1968. His 265 yds. vs. Northwestern in third varsity game was best performance ever by freshman. Dorset's 209 yds. were most ever allowed by Notre Dame team.

DOUGHERTY, NATHAN W. Guard B. 3/23/1886, Scott County, Va. 6'2", 185. Tennessee, 1907-09. All-Southern, 1907, 08. Captain senior year. Also basketball and track captain. Known as "Big One." Made Tennessee varsity first day of practice. Played guard and fullback. Returned season-opening kickoff for TD vs. Maryville College, 1908. Scored only TD in last game, against Transylvania in 1909. Good blocker, powerful runner. After graduation worked for master's degree, then taught civil engineering at Cornell. Returned to Tennessee in 1916 as head of civil engineering department. Became chairman of athletic council, 1917, and held post until retirement in 1956. Hired Robert Neyland as head coach in 1925. Served as president of Southern Conference and was one of founders of Southeastern Conference. National Football Foundation Hall of Fame.

DOUGLASS, BOBBY Quarterback. B. 6/22/47, Manhattan, Kan. 6'3", 212. Attended El Dorado (Kan.) H.S. QB at U. of Kansas, 1966-68. All-America, 1968. In 1969 drafted on 2nd round by Chicago Bears, has been club's QB ever since. (Some fans think he should be running back.) Controversial, noted for inconsistency. In 1972 accounted for 17 of Bears' 27 TDs and was team's leading rusher. Ran for 968 yds., most ever by NFL QB; responsible for Bears winning NFC rushing title. Averaged 6.9 yds. per rush, leading league. His 1972 pass completion percentage of 37.9 is record low. Thru 1973 season had passed for 4458 yds. (775 attempts, 329 completions, 28 TDs), rushed for 1682 yds. (332 attempts, 18 TDs). Once threw four TD passes in one game, three after breaking left wrist. Claims he'd prefer not to run but must to compensate for lack of rushing potency by teammates. Blames low completion record also on poor running by team.

DOWLER, BOYD H. End. B. 10/18/37, Rock Springs, Wyo. 6'5", 225. Graduated from Colorado in 1959. Led team in passing, receiving and interceptions thrown as QB. 1957 Orange Bowl was climax of collegiate career. Played in East-West Shrine and College All-Star games. Selected as QB on 3rd round of draft by Green Bay Packers in 1959. Converted to wide receiver in training camp. Led Pack in receiving 1959, 61, 62, 63, 64, 65, 67. In 1968 credited with 45 receptions, 688 yds., 6 TDs. Tied NFL playoff record for TD passes received, career, with four. No. 11 receiver in NFL history with 474 receptions. Retired after 1969 season, becoming assistant coach with Los Angeles Rams under George Allen. Followed Allen to Washington Redskins (as player-coach) in 1971 and played one season. In 1972 retired from play, remaining Redskin assistant coach. Pro Bowl, 1967, 69.

DRAHOS, NICK Tackle. B. Cedarhurst, N. Y. 6'3", 210. Great Cornell tackle. Played in 1938-40. Consensus All-America, 1939-40. Member of 1939 unbeaten and untied team that won Ivy League title, scored stunning upset of Ohio State. Drahos blocked crucial pass attempt by Don Scott and scored final FG as Cornell won 23-14. Played in famous "Fifth Down" game, 1940, vs. Dartmouth. Cornell had apparently won 7-3, Drahos having kicked PAT. Later, officials discovered that Cornell had been allowed 5th down, enabling them to score TD in final six seconds. Cornell forfeited game. New York Americans (AFL), 1941. Citizens Savings Hall of Fame.

DRESSEN, CHARLES W. (Chuck) Quarterback. B. 9/20/1898, Decatur, Ill. D. 8/10/66, Detroit, Mich. 5'5½", 146. Decatur Staleys, 1920, Racine Legions, 1922-23. Primarily known for baseball, playing for Cincinnati Reds, 1925-31; New York Giants, 1932. Managed Reds, 1934-37; Brooklyn Dodgers, 1951-53; Washington Senators, 1953-57; Milwaukee Braves, 1960-61; Detroit Tigers, 1963 until his death. One of smallest QB's of all time. 1920 Staleys featured such notables as George Halas, George Trafton, Guy Chamberlin, Dutch Sternaman.

DRISCOLL, JOHN L. (Paddy) Running Back. B. 1/11/1896, Evanston, Ill. D. 6/29/68, Chicago, Ill. 5'8½", 155. Graduated from Northwestern. Joined 1914 Chicago Cub baseball team. In 1918 entered military service, joining Chicago Cardinals in 1920. Played thru 1925. In 1920 also played one game for Decatur Staleys. Player-coach for Cards in 1921- 22. On 9/28/23 dropkicked record 50-yd. FG vs. Milwaukee Badgers; on 10/11/25 dropkicked record 4 FGs vs. Columbus, including another 50-yarder. Kicked 11 FGs that year. In 1926 joined Chicago Bears, playing thru 1929. In career dropkicked record 49 FGs and scored 377 points. Assistant coach for Bears, 1941; head coach in 1956-57, leading them to Western Conference title in '56 with record of 9-6-1. Lost to New York Giants in championship game. In 1957 finished 5th in Conference with record of 5-7-0. All-Pro squad of the 1920s. Pro Football Hall of Fame.

DRURY, MORLEY E. Quarterback. B. 2/5/03, Midland, Ontario, Canada. 6', 185. Southern California, 1924-27. Consensus All-America, 1927. At graduation from Long Beach Poly (Calif) H.S. in 1924, had earned four letters in football (played center, end, fullback), three letters in basketball, three letters in baseball, four letters in water polo and two letters in swimming. Was captain of football team, 1921, 22. At USC won three varsity letters in football, played water polo for four years, earned one letter in basketball, and played baseball. Was great passer and runner. Led team to 43 first downs in 1925 game vs. Pomona College. 27-5-1 playing record. Also played ice hockey for three years, started local college hockey league. Citizens Savings Player of the Year, 1927. In 1969 was named to All-Time Pacific Coast team. Citizens Savings Hall of Fame, National Football Foundation Hall of Fame.

DUBENION, ELBERT (Duby) End. B. 2/16/33, Griffin, Ga. 5'11", 185. Graduated from Bluffton College, 1959; not drafted. Spotted by Cleveland Brown scout Dick Gallagher, who requested College All-Star coach Otto Graham place Dubenion on squad. Had signed with Saskatchewan of CFL but joined All-Stars, delaying his reporting. Hurt knee in All-Star game. Released by Saskatchewan and signed Brown contract in 1959. Released by Cleveland same year. In 1960, when Gallagher became Buffalo Bill general manager, Duby joined club and remained thru 1968. AFL All-Star game, 1964. AFL

91

championship games, 1964, 65, 66. Bills were champs in 1964 and '65.

DUDLEY, WILLIAM M. (Bullet Bill) Running Back. B. Bluefield, Va. 5'9", 152. Virginia, 1938-42. Only man ever to win MVP awards in college, service and pro football. One of game's last 60-minute men. Consensus All-America, 1941. Called "too small" to play football. Rejected by VPI. Good kicker. 1941 college scoring champion with 135 points, including 18 TDs. Pittsburgh Steelers, 1942, 45-46; Detroit Lions, 1947-49; Washington Redskins, 1950-51, 53. NFL rushing leader, 1942, 46; NFL interception leader, 1946. MVP in NFL, 1946. In 1946 played for $20,000, then highest salary ever, after return from Army Air Corps. Maxwell Award, 1941. Won 1964 Sammy Award from National Sales Executive Club. Citizens Savings Hall of Fame, National Football Foundation Hall of Fame.

DUFFIELD, MARSHALL D. Quarterback. B. 8/5/10, Salt Lake City, Utah. Graduated from Santa Monica (Calif.) H.S., 1927, lettering in football, track, baseball, basketball. Southern California, 1928-30; captain, 1930. All-America, 1930. Fine passer. All-Coast QB, 1929, 30. Graduated from USC in 1931, then attended Southern Western Law School, 1932-34. In consensus of 35 All-America QB selections in 1930 season, Carideo of Notre Dame made most teams, Duffield was second. Citizens Savings Hall of Fame.

DUNAWAY, JAMES E. Tackle. B. 9/31/41, Columbia, Miss. 6'4", 289. Graduated from Mississippi, 1963. Buffalo Bills, 1963-71; Miami Dolphins, 1972-73. Consensus All-America defensive tackle, 1962. Drafted on 2nd round by Buffalo, 1963. Traded with wide receiver Marlin Briscoe to Dolphins, for linebacker Dale Farley and 1st choice in '73 draft. All-AFL tackle, 1966. Played in AFL All-Star games following 1966, 67, 68 seasons. Played in AFL championship games, 1964, 65, 66. Played in Super Bowl, 1973. In 1973 suffered compressed fracture of spinal vertebrae in exhibition game vs. Minnesota Vikings and sidelined for most of the season.

DUNCAN, H. RANDOLPH (Randy) Quarterback. B. Des Moines, Iowa. 6', 180. Iowa, 1956-58. Unanimous All-America, 1958. 2nd in Heisman Trophy voting that season. In 1957, vs. Utah State, completed 80-yd. pass, in '58 vs. Wisconsin completed 68-yd. pass. In 1958 led NCAA in passing percentage with .587, in passing yds. with 1347, TD passes with 11. Played in 1957, 59 Rose Bowls. In '59 Rose Bowl scored TD, threw TD pass, completed 5 of 7 passes. Was injured in 1st half. In 1959 was NFL 1st-round draft pick, by Green Bay Packers. Played only one year of pro ball, however, as QB with AFL Dallas Texans, 1961. Full name: Hearst Randolph Duncan.

DUNCAN, JAMES Defensive Back. B. 8/3/46, Lancaster, S.C. 6'2", 200. QB and safety at Maryland State. Played in 1968 College All-Star game. Selected by Baltimore Colts on 4th round of 1968 draft. Played with Colts thru 1971. Led AFC in kickoff returns, 1970, with average of 35.4 yds., returning 20 for 707 yds.

In 1970 returned kickoff 99 yds. for TD vs. Miami Dolphins. Played in Super Bowl, 1969, 71. In '71 Super Bowl recovered fumble on Baltimore 1-yd. line after own fumble of 2nd-half kickoff set up threat by Dallas Cowboys. Holds several Super Bowl records: shares with Bert Coan and Eugene Morris record of most kickoff returns with 4; shares with Eugene Morris record of yds. gained on kickoff returns with 90; holds record for average on kickoff returns with 22.5 yds.

DUNCAN, LESLIE H. (Speedy) Defensive Back. B. 8/10/42, Tuscaloosa, Ala. 5'10", 180. Signed as free agent by San Diego Chargers, 1964, after graduation from Jackson State. Played with Chargers thru 1970. On 12/26/64 set AFL playoff records for yds. on kickoff returns (147) and longest kickoff return (72 yds.). In 1967 returned interception 100 yds. vs. Kansas City Chiefs. Outstanding Defensive Player, AFL All-Star game, 1967. In 1968 set AFL record for longest punt return (95 yds.). Set record for most seasons leading AFL in punt returns (two). AFL All-Star games, 1965, 66, 67. AFL championship games, 1965, 66. In 1971 dealt to Washington Redskins. Pro Bowl, 1973. 3rd in NFL history in punt-return yardage (1954). His 6493 yds. returning kickoffs and punts are only two shy of all-time leader, Abe Woodson.

DUTTON, JOHN (Lurch) Tackle. B. 2/6/51, Rapid City, S. D. 6'7", 248. Nebraska, 1971-73. Unanimous All-America, 1973. In spite of size is fast and extremely mobile. No one blocker can handle him. Coach Tom Osborne says Dutton has the strongest arms he's ever seen. His span is 84". Cotton Bowl vs. Texas, 1974. Nebraska won, 19-3.

EBER, RICHARD (Rick) Wide Receiver. B. 4/17/45, Torrance, Calif. 6'0", 185. Attended El Camina (Calif.) J.C. where was All-America. Played for Tulsa as receiver, 1966-67. Established NCAA record for most passes caught in single game, 20 for 322 yds. vs. Idaho State, 10/7/67. In college career of 20 games made 119 catches for 1902 yds., 15 TDs, 6.0 catches per game. Selected by Atlanta Falcons on 6th round of 1968 draft. Joined San Diego Chargers as free agent midway through 1969 season and caught 9 passes. Played with San Diego thru 1972.

ECKERSALL, WALTER H. Quarterback. B. 6/17/1886, Chicago, Ill. D. 3/24/30, Chicago, Ill. 5'7", 142. Played high school football at Hyde Park of Chicago, national champions of 1900. From 1903-06 played for U. of Chicago. All-America end, 1904; QB, 1905, 06. Later named to Early Day All-Time All-America team. One of best safeties in football. Twice kicked five FGs in one game: 1905 vs. Illinois and 1906 vs. Nebraska. His coffin-corner punting was major factor in ending Michigan's 56-game unbeaten streak, 1905. Citizens Savings Player of the Year, 1906. Also played baseball and ran track during college career, becoming 10-second sprinter. After graduation signed with Chicago Cubs baseball team as third baseman, but didn't play. Knute Rockne said of him: "With no more than four fundamental plays, he worked so quickly he made his offense bewildering." Citizens Savings Hall of Fame, National Football Foundation Hall of Fame.

EDDY, NICHOLAS M. (Nick) Running Back. B. 8/23/44, Dunsmuir, Calif. 6'1", 205. Notre Dame, 1964-66. Unanimous All-America, 1966. 3rd in Heisman Trophy voting, 1966. Voted MVP on Notre Dame's national championship team of 1966. In 1964 made 91-yd. catch vs. Pitt. and 74-yd. catch vs. Navy. In 1966 made 96-yd. kickoff return vs. Purdue and 85-yd. kickoff return vs. Pitt. Produced 77-yd. rush vs. Duke, 1966. In 30 college games rushed for 1625 yds., gained 708 yds. on pass receptions, and 404 on kickoff returns, scored 140 points. Detroit Lions, 1968-70, 72. Missed 1967 and '71 seasons due to injuries. In 29 pro games gained 523 yds. rushing, 237 more on pass receptions, scored 5 TDs.

EDWARDS, A. GLEN (Turk) Tackle. B. 9/28/07, Mold, Wash. D. 1/10/73, Seattle, Wash. 6'2", 260. Washington State, 1928-30. All-America, 1930. Even with Turk and teammate Mel Hein, State fell to Alabama, 24-0, in 1931 Rose Bowl. Joined Boston Braves, 1932. Played in Boston thru 1936. Name changed to Redskins in 1933. Moved with team to Washington, D.C., and played as Washington Redskin, 1937-40. Strangely, playing career ended with toss of coin. In early part of 1940 season met with same Mel Hein at midfield. After toss of coin Edwards pivoted to return to bench and his knee gave way, ending days as player. Remained with Redskins as assistant coach for five years. Head coach, 1946-48, and later club vice president. All-Pro tackle four times, 1932, 33, 36, 37. Was iron man; in one season of 15 games he played all but 10 minutes of season. Considered by many NFL's all-time great lineman. Spent 18 years in NFL as player and coach. After leaving football operated sporting goods store in Seattle and held political office. Died at age 65. Citizens Savings Hall of Fame, Pro Football Hall of Fame.

EDWARDS, WILLIAM H. (Big Bill) Guard. B. 2/23/1887, Lisle, N.Y. D. 1/4/43, New York, N.Y. 225. Princeton guard, 1896-99. 2nd-team All-America, 1899. Captain of 1899 championship team that beat Yale second successive time. 1898 team kept 11 opponents scoreless and tied Army, 5-5. Worked way thru Princeton, was class orator at graduation. In 1910 won fame for tackling and subjuing would-be assassin who shot New York City Mayor William Gaynor. Gaynor was seriously wounded, and Edwards received flesh wound in arm. Was awarded Carnegie Medal for Heroism. Sometimes served as referee. Authored *Football Days*. Appointed collector of internal revenue for 2nd New York District by President Wilson. President of American Professional Football League, 1926-29. National Football Foundation Hall of Fame.

EISCHEID, MICHAEL D. Kicker. B. 9/29/40, Orange City, Iowa. 5'11", 190. NAIA All-America safety at Upper Iowa, 1962. Earned master's degree from Northern Iowa. Signed by Minnesota Vikings as free agent in 1963, spent following three years on Minnesota and Chicago Bear taxi squads. Oakland Raiders, 1966-70; Kansas City Chief taxi squad, 1971; Minnesota Vikings, 1972-73. Punted 480 times in seven years for 42-yd. average. Best average was 44.3, 1967. Placekicked in 1966, connecting on 37 of 37 PAT attempts and 11 of 37 FGs. Played in AFL championship games, 1967, 68, 69. Super Bowl, 1968, 74.

EISENHOWER, DWIGHT D. Running Back. B. 10/14/1890, Denison, Tex. D. 3/28/69, Washington, D.C. Played at Army, 1912. Moved to Abilene, Kan., at age 2. Fifteen when he started playing football in high school, 1905. Idol was Pudge Heffelfinger. Played at Army under Pot Graves who was impressed with Ike's running and defensive play. New York *Times* suggested the Point had another football hero in making. Teammates called him "Kansas Cyclone." However, played just one season as injured knee in Tufts game and re-injured it vaulting a horse. Was never able to play again. Graduated from West Point, 1915. Won Distinguished Service Medal for work as commander of tank training center at Camp Colt, Gettysburg, Pa., 1918. Became General of Army, Army Chief of Staff, Columbia U. president, NATO Supreme Commander in Europe, 34th President of U.S. In 1958 was first recipient of Gold Medal, award of National Football Foundation. Retired to farm in Gettysburg in 1961. Congress restored his rank as General of Army. Died of heart ailment, is buried in Abilene.

ELIOT, RAY Coach. B. Brighton, Mass. Played at Illinois, 1928-31. Was outstanding lineman and baseball catcher. Worked way thru school and graduated, 1932. Coached Illinois College at Jacksonville, 1933-36. Record of 23-5-1. In 1937 joined U. of Illinois coaching staff. Became head coach, 1942, succeeding Bob Zuppke to whom he was very close as player and assistant. 1951 team was undefeated, Illini's first since 1927. Club was Big 10 champion and ranked 4th nationally in A. P. poll. Won eight and played to scoreless tie vs. Ohio State. Beat Stanford in Rose Bowl, 40-7. In 1953 had another conference championship team, tying State for Big 10 crown. Coached Illinois thru 1959, one of longest tenures in conference history. Placed 5th for Coach of the Year, 1953. In 1955 fellow coaches elected him president of American Football Coaches Association. In 22 years his total record was 102-82-13, percentage of .551.

ELKINS, LAWRENCE C. (Elk) End. B. 7/28/43, Brownwood, Tex. 6'1", 200. Baylor, 1962-64. Consensus All-America, 1963, 64. In 1963 was NCAA receiving champion. In 10 games had 70 catches for 873 yds. and 8 TDs, setting record in catches and yds. Made 92-yd. punt return vs. Texas Christian and 70-yd. catch vs. Oregon State, 1963. Appeared in Astro-Bluebonnet Bowl, 1963. His career catches totaled 144 for 2094 yds., average 14.5, 19 TDs. Houston Oilers, 1966-67. Was Houston's 1st-round draft choice in 1965. Missed '65 season due to knee injury, suffered in pre-season game.

ELLER, CARL (Moose) Defensive End. B. 1/25/42, Winston-Salem, N.C. 6'6", 265. Graduated from Minnesota. Consensus All-America tackle, 1963. Drafted on 1st round by Minnesota Vikings. Minnesota regular, 1964-73. Superb defensive end. Runnerup for Rookie of the Year honors, 1964. All-NFC, 1970, 71, 72, 73. Appeared in all 14 games first 10 years in league. Gives full credit for development to defensive tackle Jim Marshall. In 1967 Western Conference playoff ran 60 yds. to force Willie Richardson (Baltimore Colts) out of bounds. Played tight end for few minutes late in game vs. Green Bay Packers, 1968. Once ran 20 yds. to tackle Gale Sayers. Helped force Detroit Lions into 10 fumbles, league record, 1968. Pro Bowl, 1969, 70, 72, 74. Played in NFL title game, 1969. Super Bowl, 1970, 74.

ELLIOT, CHALMERS W. (Bump) Coach. B. 1/30/25, Detroit, Mich. Attended Purdue and Michigan. All-America halfback at Michigan, 1947. Pete, his younger brother, was Wolverine teammate. They later dueled as head coaches, Bump assisted at Oregon State, 1949-51; Iowa, 1952-56; Michigan, 1957-58. Michigan head coach, 1959-68. Record: 51-42-2. Won 1965 Rose Bowl from Oregon State, 34-7. Developed Rich Volk, Bob Timberlake, Ron Johnson. Iowa athletic director since 1970.

ELLIOT, PETER R. Coach. B. 9/29/26, Bloomington, Ind. Won 12 letters (four each in football, basketball, golf) at Michigan. Quarterbacked 1947 Rose Bowl team which destroyed Southern California, 49-0. 1947 team was national champion as Elliot received All-America mention. Assistant coach at Oregon State, 1949-50; Oklahoma, 1951-55. Head coach at Nebraska, 1956; California, 1957-59; Illinois, 1960-66; Miami (Fla.), 1973. Illinois career featured duels with brother Bump, Michigan head coach. Came out on short end (1-6). Illini defeated Washington, 17-7, in 1964 Rose Bowl. In 1973, Miami upset Texas and gave Oklahoma scare. Both of Elliot's sons also played on Michigan Rose Bowl teams. Also serves as Miami athletic director.

ELLIS, CLARENCE J., JR. Defensive Back. B. 2/11/50, Grand Rapids, Mich. 5'11", 183. Attended Notre Dame, 1969-71. In brilliant Irish career intercepted 14 passes and broke up 32 more. Consensus All-America, 1971. Had 70-yd. interception for TD against Georgia Tech, 1969. Outstanding in Notre Dame's 24-11 Cotton Bowl victory over Texas, 1971. "I've never had a better defensive back play for me," praised Ara Parseghian. Was 1st-round draft pick of Atlanta Falcons. Immediate starter as Falcon safety in 1972, helping secondary become one of best in NFC. Quick, sure tackler.

ELLIS, KENNETH A. Defensive Back. B. 9/27/47, Woodbine, Ga. 6', 195. Attended Southern U. Played flanker and halfback. Led NCAA colleges in punt returns, 1968. Participated in Senior Bowl, 1969. Drafted on 4th round by Green Bay Packers. On opening day, 1971, returned missed FG 100 yds. against New York Giants. Distance tied Al Nelson for 2nd longest in NFL history. NFL's top punt-return artist, 1972, with 15.4 average on 14 returns. Pro Bowl, 1974. Gives Packers tremendous consistency at cornerback. Great acceleration.

ELLISON, WILLIAM H. Running Back. B. 11/1/45, Lockhart, Tex. 6'1½", 205. Attended Texas Southern U. Set school record with 1089 yds. in 186 carries, 1966. Scored 10 TDs and gained 200 yds. vs. Jackson State and 176 yds. vs. Texas A. M. & N. Selected by Los Angeles Rams on 2nd round of 1967 draft. In 1968 led Rams in rushing with 616 yds. On 12/4/71, vs. New Orleans Saints, set NFL record for yds. gained in single game with 247 on 26 attempts, including 80-yd.

TD run. (O. J. Simpson broke record in 1973 with 250 yds.) Gained 1000 yds. rushing, 1971. Named to NFC Pro Bowl team, 1971, but unable to play due to knee injury. Traded to Kansas City Chiefs in 1972 with QB Pete Beathard, for linebacker Bob Stein and two draft choices.

ELMENDORF, DAVID C. Defensive Back. B. 6/20/49, San Antonio, Tex. 6'2", 195. Texas A. & M., 1968-70. Consensus All-America, 1970. That year one of 13 National Football Foundation Scholar-Athletes. Posted grade average of 3.84 out of possible 4.0. Turned down pro baseball offer from Boston Red Sox to sign with Los Angeles Rams, 1971. Named to All-NFL Rookie team. Intercepted six passes first three years at safety, 1071-73. Blessed with fine physical abilities, intelligence.

ENGLE, CHARLES A. (Rip) Coach. B. 3/26/06, Salisbury, Md. Graduated from Western Maryland, 1930. Head coach at Brown, 1944-49, where he introduced winged-T formation. In 1949 Brown won 8 out of 9, losing only to Princeton, 27-14. His six-year record at Brown was 31-27-4. Head coach at Penn State, 1950-65. Overall record there was 101-47-14. National Football Foundation Hall of Fame.

ERDELATZ, EDDIE Coach. B. 1913, San Francisco, Calif. Played end for St. Mary's (Calif.), 1933-35. Line coach at St. Mary's for two years and then went to U. of San Francisco. In 1940 returned to St. Mary's as assistant coach. Entered Navy, 1942, and took indoctrination at Annapolis. Was sent to St. Mary's Pre-Flight School, and in 1945 returned to Naval Academy where he was end coach thru 1948. In 1949 became line coach for San Francisco 49ers. Named head coach at Annapolis, 1950. His 1950 team beat Army to break Cadets' 28-game unbeaten streak (26 wins, 2 ties). It marked first time in eight years Midshipmen had defeated Cadets. 1954 team was called "Desire" and considered best Navy team since 1945, despite losing to Pitt. and Notre Dame. 1954 team defeated Army, 27-20, for fourth time in Erdelatz' five years as coach, record unmatched by any other Navy coach. Played in 1955 Sugar Bowl, ripping Mississippi Rebels 21-0 — 1st bowl game for Navy since 1924 Rose Bowl. Received 4th highest number of votes for Coach of the Year and signed to 5-year contract. Remained coach at Annapolis through 1958. Record: 48-26-8.

EVANS, RAYMOND Running Back. B. 9/22/22, Kansas City, Kan. 6'1", 191. Kansas 1941-42, 46-47. All-America, 1942, 46, 47. Kansas' first All-America. Shattered many Big 6 records. In 10 games, 1942, set records with 200 attempted passes and 101 completions; had only 9 interceptions while throwing for 1117 yds., percentage of .505. As defensive player, same year, led nation in pass interceptions with 10 for 76 yds. Only second player with more than 100 completions for season. In service, 1943-45. Returned to Kansas in 1946 and led team in passing, scoring, rushing, total offense. In 1947 directed Jayhawks to undefeated (8-0-2) season. Also basketball All-America, class president, honor student. Pittsburgh Steelers, 1948. Became bank president in Kansas City.

Citizens Savings Hall of Fame (basketball), National Football Foundation Hall of Fame.

EWBANK, WILBUR (Weeb) Coach. B. 5/6/07, Richmond, Ind. Played QB in high school at Richmond, Va. Attended Miami (Ohio) where he played QB but not 1st string. Graduated in 1930. Immediately became assistant football coach. In 1943 became assistant at Great Lakes Naval Training Station, in 1946 Brown U. assistant. Head coach Washington (St. Louis), 1947-48. In 1949 joined Cleveland Browns as assistant. Named head coach of Baltimore Colts, 1954. Moved Gino Marchetti from offensive lineman to defensive end, and Colts won two NFL championships. Also tutored Johnny Unitas, Alan Ameche, Raymond Berry, Lenny Moore, Art Donovan, Bill Pellington, Jim Parker, Gene (Big Daddy) Lipscomb. In 1963 became head coach for New York Jets. Won Super Bowl IV with Joe Namath starring, 1969. On 12/20/72 announced retirement, effective at end of 1973 season. Son-in-law, Charley Winner, succeeds Ewbank at Jet helm. When in college also played baseball, basketball. One of only two coaches ever to win championships in two different professional football leagues (NFL, 1958, 59; AFL, 1968). Other is his former Cleveland mentor, Paul Brown (AAFC, 1946, 47, 48, 49; NFL, 1950, 54, 55). Twenty-two years as pro head coach, 5th longest tenure. Composite college and pro record: 144-133-7. In pros: 130-129-7. One of only 10 pro coaches to win 100 games.

EXENDINE, ALBERT A. End. B. 1885, D. 1/4/73, Tulsa, Okla. 174. Delaware Indian who played for Carlisle Indian School during Jim Thorpe era, 1905-07. 3rd-team All-America, 1906; 2nd team, 1907. Originally a tackle, was switched to end by Coach Pop Warner who would eventually say he had seen few better ends. Warner described him as "possessed of sheer brilliance." Didn't even know what football was until arrival at Carlisle. Became assistant to Warner and then head coach at Otterbein, 1909-11; Georgetown, 1914-22; Washington State, 1923-25; Occidental, 1926-27; Northwestern Oklahoma, 1928; Oklahoma State, 1934-35. In 20 years as coach compiled record of 93-60-15, percentage of .598. Held law degree from Dickinson College and, after leaving coaching, practiced law in Oklahoma. Later worked for Bureau of Indian Affairs. In 1968 Council of American Indians selected him Indian of the Year. National Football Foundation Hall of Fame (as player). Died at age 88.

FAGAN, JULIAN WALTER, III Kicker. B. 2/21/48, Laurel, Miss. 6'3", 205. Strong punter for Mississippi, 1967-69. Academic All-America and All-SEC, 1969. Led SEC in punting, 1968. Had career 199 punts for 41.6-yd. average. President of Fellowship of Christian Athletes Chapter at Ole Miss. New Orleans Saints, 1970-72; New York Jets, 1973. NFL's leading punter with 42.5-yd. average, 1970. Produced league's longest punt in 1972, for 71 yds. against Los Angeles Rams. Acquired by Jets in trade that also gave them wide receiver Margene Adkins. Saints, in return, received punter Steve O'Neal and QB Bob Davis.

FAIRBANKS, CHARLES L. (Chuck) Coach. B. 6/10/33, Detroit, Mich. Graduated from Michigan State, 1955. Played there under Biggie Munn and Duffy Daugherty. State defeated UCLA, 14-10, in 1954 Rose Bowl. Blue-Gray game, 1954. Assistant at Arizona State, 1958-61; U. of Houston, 1962-65; Oklahoma, 1966. Took Oklahoma head post in 1967. In six-year span compiled 52-15-1 record, including 3-1-1 bowl record. Won two Big 8 championships, shared another. Groomed Heisman Trophy winner Steve Owens, plus 11 other All-Americas. Sooner wishbone-T offense was scourge of nation in 1971, and provided many records. Became head coach-general manager of New England Patriots in 1973. Rookie season won five, lost nine.

FAISON, WILLIAM E. (Tree) Defensive End. B. 1/31/39, Newport News, Va. Attended Indiana. Was 1st-round draft choice of San Diego Chargers in 1961

AFL draft. Played for Chargers until 1966 when traded to Miami Dolphins. Had great season in 1961; was AFL Rookie of the Year, All-League, and Charger MVP. Left pro football in 1966. Physical and mental carelessness shortened career.

FALASCHI, NELLO D. (Flash) Quarterback. B. Oakland, Calif. 6', 195. Santa Clara, 1934-36. All-America, 1936. Great blocking and passing QB. Captain of 1936 team that upset LSU in Sugar Bowl, 21-14. From 1938-41 played for New York Giants. Owns construction company in Oakland, Calif. National Football Foundation Hall of Fame.

FARASOPOULAS, CHRIS V. Defensive Back. B. 7/20/49, Piraeus, Greece. 5'11", 190. Brigham Young, 1968-70. Was 1969 NCAA punt-return leader with 527 yds., returning 35 and scoring 1 TD. Held NCAA record for combined kickoff and punt returns with 2454 yds. Selected by New York Jets on 3rd round of 1971 NFL draft. In 1972 was AFC punt-return leader with average of 10.5 on 17 returns. In 1972, vs. Buffalo Bills, made 65-yd. punt return for TD. Fine free safety, can also handle cornerback slot if necessary. In 1973 returned 14 punts for 111 yds., average of 7.9. Injured and put on waivers by Jets, 12/8/73.

FARLEY, JOHN F. End-Running Back. B. 2/15/1876, Paterson, N.J. D. 1/15/39, Notre Dame, Ind. 160. One of Notre Dame's greatest early-day athletes. Won nine letters in football, basketball, track. Footballer four years, 1897-1900. Captained 1900 team coached by Pat O'Dea. Ordained as priest in 1907. Spent rest of life, except for several years at U. of Portland, as rector at Notre Dame. Was beloved campus figure. Suffered stroke in 1937, had leg amputated year later. Despite adversities, interest in athletic events, school programs never waned, attending many in wheelchair.

FARR, MELVIN Running Back. B. 11/3/44, Beaumont, Tex. 6'2", 208. Played halfback for UCLA, 1964-66. Consensus All-America, 1966. In 1965 made 58-yd. rush vs. Penn State and 58-yd. catch vs. Stanford. In three seasons rushed for 1690 yds., scored 118 points. Against Michigan State rushed for 36 yds. and caught 22-yd. pass in 1966 Rose Bowl. Selected by Detroit Lions on 1st round of 1967 draft. Named NFL Rookie of the Year, 1967 (860 yds. rushing, 317 yds. receiving, 6 TDs.). On 11/12/67, vs. Minnesota Vikings, rushed for 197 yds., one shy of Lion club record. Had two 100-plus days in 1970. Lion co-captain, 1969. In seven years, 1967-73, rushed for 3072 yds., gained 1374 yds. on pass receptions, scored 36 TDs. Voted MVP on offense by teammates, 1967-68. Missed most of 1971 season due to injuries. Pro Bowl, 1968, 71. Brother of Miller, who became Lion teammate in 1973.

FARR, MILLER, JR. Defensive Back. B. 4/8/43, Beaumont, Tex. 6'1", 190. Attended Wichita State. Denver Broncos, 1965; San Diego Chargers, 1965-66; Houston Oilers, 1967-69; St. Louis Cardinals, 1970-72; Detroit Lions, 1973. Excellent cornerback. AFL co-leader in interceptions with 10, 1967. Despite bout with hepatitis, intercepted two passes for TDs in one game, 1968. Those two thefts allowed him to lead AFL in TD interceptions. In 1970 involved in first-ever trade between old NFL and AFL teams. Farr and QB Pete Beathard went to St. Louis, while QB Charley Johnson and defensive back Bob Atkins were shuttled to Houston. All-AFL, 1967, 68, 69. AFL All-Star games, 1968, 69, 70. AFL championship games, 1965, 67. Made 35 interceptions in eight years, 6 for TDs.

FAUROT, DONALD B. Coach. B. 6/23/02, Mt. Grove, Mo. Graduated from Missouri. Coached Northeast Missouri State, 1926-34; Missouri, 1935-42, 46-56. Non-smoker, non-drinker. Did not like high-pressure recruiting. 1948 Missouri Gator Bowl team was composed entirely of native Missourians — 48 of them. Originator of split-T formation. Authored *Science of the Split-T Formation,* accepted bible of system. Known for extracting more from less than just about any other coach. 163-95-13 overall record. Coached teams to five major bowl game appearances. Developed split T from Chicago Bear T formation. 1942 Big 7 championship team led nation in rushing (307 yds. per game), played in Sugar Bowl. Paul Christman, All-America and Hall of Famer, was probably his greatest player. Citizens Savings Hall of Fame, National Football Foundation Hall of Fame.

FEARS, THOMAS JESSE End. B. 12/3/23, Los Angeles, Calif. 6'2", 216. Played end for Santa Clara and UCLA. All-America at UCLA, 1947. College career was interrupted by service in Army Air Force, 1942-45. Received B.A. degree in business from UCLA, 1948. Spectacular pass receiver for Los Angeles Rams, 1948-56. Led NFL receivers in 1948 with 51 catches, for 698 yds. and 4 TDs; in 1949 with 77 catches, for 1015 yds. and 9 TDs; in 1950 when he set season record with 84 catches, for 1116 yds. and 7 TDs. Caught 18 passes, 1950, vs. Green Bay Packers, setting single-game record. One of three men to catch at least 50 passes in each of first three pro seasons (others are Danny Abramowicz and Mike Ditka). Instructed Dick (Night Train) Lane in pass patterns during Lane's rookie year, 1952. In four championship games caught total of 16 passes and in one, 12/24/50, vs. Cleveland Browns, caught 9. All-NFL, 1950. Played in Pro Bowl following 1950 season. Played in NFL championship games, 1949, 50, 51, 55. Assistant coach under Vince Lombardi at Green Bay, 1959, 62-65. Assistant coach for Rams, 1960-61; Atlanta Falcons, 1966. First head coach for New Orleans Saints. Compiled record of 14-40-2, 1967-70. In 1971 became assistant coach for Philadelphia Eagles. Pro Football Hall of Fame. Appeared as himself in movie, *No. 1,* fictional story about New Orleans football player starring Charlton Heston. In 1974 signed to Southern California team in WFL.

FEATHERS, WILLIAM B. (Big Chief) Running Back. B. 8/4/08, Bristol, Va. 5'10", 180. Played halfback at Tennessee, 1931-33. Consensus All-America, 1933. Made 80-, 75- and 60-yd. rushes vs. Mississippi in 1931. Had 70-yd. rush vs. Kentucky that year and 65-yd. rush vs. NYU. In 1933 made 76-yd. punt vs. Florida. In 30 college games rushed for 1888 yds., produced 2014 total offense yds., scored 198 points. Joined Chicago Bears, 1934. All-NFL and rushing leader that season, setting record of 1004 yds. in 117 attempts. Scored eight TDs. Was first pro to gain 1000 yds. in one season. Injured and couldn't play 1934 title game vs. New York Giants. Played with Bears thru 1937, then joined Brooklyn Dodgers. In 1940 closed career with Green Bay Packers. Named by George Trevor to All-Time All-Southern team. Head coach at North Carolina State, 1944-57. Citizens Savings College Player of the Year, 1933. Citizens Savings Hall of Fame, National Football Foundation Hall of Fame.

FELLER, JAMES P. (Happy) Kicker. B. 6/12/49, Fredericksburg, Tex. 6', 195. Texas, 1968-70. Set NCAA record for points scored on PATs, career, with 128. Added 19 FGs for 185 total points (former NCAA record). All-America kicker, 1970. Selected by Philadelphia Eagles on 4th round of 1971 NFL draft. Released by Eagles after one year, signed as free agent by New Orleans Saints. In 1972 attempted 11 FGs, made 6, averaging 30.7 yds. Longest was 46 yds. On inactive list, 1973.

FENIMORE, ROBERT Running Back. B. 10/6/25, Woodward, Okla. 6'2", 188. "Blond Blizzard" played for Oklahoma State, 1943-46. All-America, 1944; consensus, 1945. Terrific triple-threat halfback. Led nation in total offense with 1758 yds., 1944. Repeated, 1945, with 1641 yds. During four years accumulated 4627 total-offense yds., punted for 38.2-yd. average, scored 208 points, accounted for 49 TDs. Injuries plagued him senior season but he did play in five games, chiefly as passer. Led Cowboys to 34-0 victory over Texas Christian in 1945 Cotton Bowl. Year later defeated St. Mary's (Calif.), 33-13, in Sugar Bowl. Chicago Bears, 1947. Built flourishing insurance business in Stillwater. Active in church and community affairs. Citizens Savings Hall of Fame, National Football Foundation Hall of Fame.

FENTON, G. E. (Doc) End-Quarterback. B. 1887, Scranton, Pa. D. 2/8/68, Baton Rouge, La. 165. Louisiana State, 1906-08. During varsity career scored 36 TDs and 36 PATs. As sophomore scored 132 points. Established two FG records which were not broken until 1914 and 1965. In 1908, when he was captain, LSU had perfect record. Coached briefly and was then employed by oil company in Baton Rouge. Lived there until his death. National Football Foundation Hall of Fame.

FERGUSON, ROBERT Running Back. B. 8/29/39, Columbus, Ohio. 6'0", 217. Ohio State, 1959-61. Unanimous All-America fullback, 1960, 61 and in Heisman Trophy voting, 1961. Made 55-yd. rush vs. Michigan State, 1959; 58-yd. rush vs. same team, 1960. In 27 college games rushed for 2162 yds. and scored 158 points. Played for Pittsburgh Steelers, 1962-63; Minnesota Vikings, 1963. Disappointing pro career.

FERNANDEZ, MANUEL J. Tackle. B. 7/3/46, Oakland, Calif. 6'2", 250. Attended San Lorenzo (Calif.) H. S., Chabot (Calif.) J.C. and U. of Utah. Set San Lorenzo bench press record of 305 pounds. Miami Dolphins, 1968-73. One of greatest free agent signees by any team. Has been Dolphins' standout six straight seasons. Played in NFC championship games, 1971, 72, 73; Super Bowl after each of those years. In Super Bowl VII, 1973, was credited with 11 tackles though double-teamed much of time. Quick, mobile, strong. Likes water skiing, body surfing. Hampered by leg injury late in 1973 season. Owns Manny Fernandez Mobile Home Sales in Hallandale, Fla.

FESLER, WESLEY E. End. B. 6/29/08, Youngstown, Ohio. 6', 173. At Youngstown H.S. played football, track, baseball and tennis. Played for Ohio State, 1928-30. Consensus All-America, 1928, 29; unanimous All-America, 1930. Ohio State captain, 1930. Winner of Silver Football, 1930. Was *Phi Beta Kappa* student. Also excelled in basketball (All-America) and baseball. Graduated, 1931; played pro baseball that summer. In fall, 1931, became end coach for Ohio freshman team, and basketball coach. Went to Harvard in 1933 as end coach (assistant to Dick Harlow) and basketball coach. Named head football coach at Wesleyan (Conn.), 1940. Head coach at U. of Pittsburgh, 1946. Returned to his alma mater as head coach in 1947, remaining there four seasons. Record with Buckeyes: 21-13-3. Coached Minnesota, 1951-53, with record of 10-13-4. Retired from coaching after 1953 season to go into business. Now director of sales relations, Investors Diversified Services. Citizens Savings Hall of Fame, National Football Foundation Hall of Fame.

FINCHER, WILLIAM E. Tackle-End. B. Spring Place, Ga. 6', 190. Attended Georgia Tech. All-America, 1920; 2nd team, 1918. Played for John Heisman and Bill Alexander, excelling at two positions. Assistant coach at Tech and William & Mary. "My idea of football is to get across that line of scrimmage and tear the guts right out of them," Fincher told Yale president James Angell during 1929 interview. "Surely, you don't mean that literally?" queried astonished Angell. "Literally, hell!" said Fincher. "I mean it physically." Affiliated with Coca-Cola for many years. National Football Foundation Hall of Fame.

FINKS, JAMES E. Quarterback. B. 8/31/27, St. Louis, Mo. 5'11", 180. Attended U. of Tulsa. Captained both football and basketball teams, 1948. Pittsburgh Steelers, 1949-55. Started pro career as defensive back. When Steelers switched to T-formation from single wing in 1951, Finks assumed quarterbacking role. Made remarkable adjustment. In career completed 661 of 1382 passes for 8622 yds. Played in 1953 Pro Bowl. Minor-league baseball, 1948-49. Backfield coach at Notre Dame, 1956. Star pupil that season was Heisman Trophy winner Paul Hornung. General manager of Minnesota Vikings, 1964-73. Named NFL Executive of the Year by *Sporting News,* 1973.

FISCHER, PATRICK Defensive Back. B. 1/2/40, St. Edward, Neb. 5'9", 170. One of four brothers to play at Nebraska. Pat was quarterback and halfback, 1958-60. St. Louis Cardinals, 1961-68; Washington Redskins, 1969-73. Was 17th-round draft choice of St. Louis. Starting left cornerback all 13 years as pro. Thru 1973 had intercepted 45 passes, returning them for 847 yds., 4 TDs. Played in NFL championship game, 1972, and subsequent Super Bowl VII. All-NFL, 1964. Pro Bowl, 1965, 66, 70. Joined Redskins as free agent. Cardinals were compensated with two draft choices. Real tough little guy. Stockbroker in off-season. Lives in Leesburg, Va.

FISH, HAMILTON, JR. Tackle. B. 12/7/1888, Garrison, N.Y. 6'4", 225. Harvard, 1907-09. All-America, 1908, 09. Captain of 1908 national champions. Last surviving member of Walter Camp's All-Time All-America team. In 1908, vs. Dartmouth, went on long pass route and was nailed by defender on 5-yd. line before ball arrived. But never lost concentration and made catch. Sportswriters called it "miracle" play. Contrary to popular belief, didn't lead play which resulted in death of Ici Byrne of Army; Fish had shifted to other side of line. "He was hurt tackling our low-running fullback, Dodo Monot." said Fish. In 1910 organized Harvard Law School football team, comprised mostly of former Harvard, Yale and Princeton varsity players. In 1912-13 tutored West Point tackles before Yale-Army game. These were first two years that Army defeated Yale. After World War I was offered head coaching at Columbia but turned it down; suggested Percy Haughton. Served in U.S. House of Representatives (R.-N.Y.), 1920-45. Chaired first committee investigating communist and other subversive activities. Responsible for bill to bring back body of Unknown Soldier for burial in Washington. Ranking member of Foreign Affairs Committee. Twice asked to run for Senator but declined nomination. In 1939, while serving as chairman of Congressional Interparliamentary Committee, proposed famous resolution providing for arbitration of Danzig issue. Proposal came only two weeks before World War II began. Grandson, Hamilton Fish III, currently New York congressman. Citizens Savings Hall of Fame, National Football Foundation Hall of Fame.

FISS, GALEN R. Linebacker. B. 7/10/31, Johnson, Kan. 6', 227. Attended Kansas. In military service, 1953-55. Cleveland Browns, 1956-66. Appeared in 139 games, made 13 interceptions for 178 yds. Pro Bowl, 1963, 64. NFL championship games, 1957, 64, 65. Was corner linebacker. At best against running plays. Not flashy but steady. Always gave 100 percent. Sales engineer in Kansas City.

FLATLEY, PAUL R. End. B. 1/30/41, Richmond, Ind. 6'1", 187. Graduated from Northwestern. Selected by Minnesota Vikings on 4th round of 1963 NFL draft. In 1963 appeared in 14 games, caught 51 passes for 867 yds. which earned him Rookie of the Year award. Sold by Minnesota to Atlanta Falcons, 1968, with whom he played thru 1970. With Vikings caught 202 passes for 3132 yds.

FLEMING, MARVIN Tight End. B. 1/2/42, Longview, Tex. 6'4", 232. Attended Utah. All-Skyline Conference, 1962. Appeared in 97 games for Green Bay Packers, 1963-69. With Packers caught 119 passes for 1300 yds., 12 TDs. Played out option with Green Bay and signed to play with Miami Dolphins in 1970. Packers received wide receiver Jack Clancy as compensation. "As good a blocking tight end as there is in football," according to Miami coach Don Shula. Played in NFL championship games, 1965, 66, 67. NFL's wealthiest post-season competitor, seeing action in record five Super Bowls, 1967, 68, 72, 73, 74. Studied acting under Lee Strasberg at Los Angeles Institute of Theatre and Arts. Co-authored book, *The Mind Garden.*

FLORES, THOMAS R. Quarterback. B 3/21/37, Fresno, Calif. 6'1", 200. Attended Fresno J.C. and College of Pacific. At Pacific, 1957-59. Signed as free agent by Oakland Raiders, 1960. In rookie year led AFL in passing efficiency with percentage of 54.0. Attempted 252 passes with 136 completions for 1738 yds. Missed 1962 season due to illness. On 12/22/63 threw six TD passes. Traded by Raiders with end Art Powell and 2nd-round draft choice to Buffalo Bills, for QB Daryle Lamonica, end Glenn Bass and two draft choices in 1967. Went to Kansas City Chiefs, 1969. Ranks 2nd in fewest interceptions thrown, lifetime, with 92 on 1715 attempts. AFL All-Star game following 1966 season.

FLOWERS, ALLEN R. (Buck) Running Back. B. 3/28/1899, Birmingham, Ala. 5'8", 152. Georgia Tech, 1918-20. Punting average of 47 yds. First Georgia Tech man in National Football Foundation Hall of Fame. All-Southern, 1918, 19, 20. W. A. Alexander, long-time Yellowjacket coach, called Flowers "best punter in Georgia Tech history." In 1920 rushed for 819 yds. (80 carries), kicked 14 FGs, one for 44 yds. vs. Vanderbilt, scored 9 TDs. In Auburn game gained 429 yds. on 26 punt returns (not NCAA recognized). 85-yd. punt vs. Davidson. Also baseball, basketball player in 1921. Prominent realty and trust executive. National Football Foundation Hall of Fame.

FLOWERS, CHARLES (Charlie) Running Back. B. Marianna, Ark. 6'0", 198. Mississippi, 1957-59. Consensus All-America fullback and Academic All-America, 1959. Made 70-yd. punt vs. Trinity, 1958. Appeared in Sugar Bowl, 1958, 60; Gator Bowl, 1959 — injured during game. Played for Los Angeles Chargers, 1960; San Diego Chargers, 1961; New York Titans, 1962.

FOLDBERG, JOHN D. (Danny) End. B. 4/22/28, Dallas, Tex. 6'1", 195. Army, 1948-50. All-America, 1949; unanimous All-America 1950. In 27 college career games caught 57 passes for 824 yds., 11 TDs. Fine blocker as well as pass receiver. Captain of 1950 Cadet team. Didn't play pro ball. Not to be confused with Hank Foldberg, Army All-America in 1946. Currently Col. in U.S. Army.

FOLSOM, FREDERICK G. Coach. B. 11/9/1873, Old Town, Minn. D. 11/11/44. Graduated from Dartmouth, 1895. Coached at Colorado, 1895-99, 01-03. Compiled seven-season record of 37-10-1. Returned to Dartmouth as coach, 1903-06. His record there was 29-5-4. Back to Colorado and coached, 1908-15. Eight-year record was 40-13-1. Thus, in 19-year coaching career, compiled ledger of 106-28-6. Percentage of .779 is topped by few coaches.

FORD, JOHN Quarterback. B. Breckenridge, Tex. 5'8", 165. Played for Hardin-

Simmons, 1947-50. Finished career of 39 games 1st nationally in pass completions (291 of 510), 1st in passing yds. (4736), 1st in passing yds. per attempt (9.3), 1st in pass completion percentage (.571), 1st in TD passes (48), 3rd in total-offense yds. (4621), 1st in total-offense yds. per play (7.0). His 26 TD passes set college-division season record, 1949. Appeared in Harbor Bowl, Grape Bowl, Shrine Bowl, Camellia Bowl, 1948. Didn't play pro ball.

FORD, WILLIAM C. Owner. B. 3/14/25, Detroit, Mich. Graduated from Yale, 1949. Played varsity tennis and soccer. Began professional career in sales and advertising, Ford Motor Co. Became general manager of Continental Division of Lincoln-Mercury. Now, vice president of Ford Motor Co., in charge of product planning and design. Grandson of late Henry Ford, and youngest of four children of late Edsel B. Ford. Joined Detroit Lions as board member, 1956. Named Lion president, 1961. Bought out group of stockholders, 1964, who had purchased club in 1948 from Fred Mandel of Chicago. Now, team's sole owner. Has rebuilt club into strong organization.

FOREMAN, WALTER E. (Chuck) Running Back. B. 10/26/50, Frederick, Md. 6',2", 215. Wide receiver and running back for Miami (Fla.), 1970-72. Rushed for 1631 yds. in career, including school-record 951 yds. in 1971. Also caught 56 passes for 732 yds. in three seasons. Was offensive MVP in both Senior Bowl and North-South games. Selected by Minnesota Vikings on 1st round of 1973 draft. Was immediate star. Balance, fine speed, strength made him inside and outside threat. Outstanding receiver, too. In rookie year gained 801 yds. on 182 rushes, average of 4.4 yds. Gained another 362 yds. on 37 pass receptions. Rookie of the Year, 1973. Played in Super Bowl, 1974, and Pro Bowl.

FORTMANN, DANIEL J. Guard. B. 4/11/16, Pearl, River, N. Y. 6'0", 200. Colgate, 1933-35. Drafted by Chicago Bears in 1936, at age 19, and played with them thru 1943. All-NFL, 1938, 39, 40, 41, 42, 43. In 1957 was team physician for Los Angeles Rams. He is now one of nation's top orthopedic surgeons, on staff at St. Joseph's Hospital in Burbank, Calif. Sportswriter Tim Cohane made following tribute: "Although he did not get the credit due him until he later played for the Chicago Bears, guard Danny Fortmann may well have been the equal of any player Kerr (Andy) coached at Colgate. He was a big reason the 1933 and '34 Raiders teams each lost only one game." Tremendous speed and desire. One of the all-time great guards according to his Chicago coach, George Halas. Pro Football Hall of Fame.

FORTUNATO, JOSEPH F. Linebacker. B. 3/28/31, Mingo Junction, Ohio. 6'1", 225. Attended VMI and Mississippi State. Selected as future on 7th round of 1952 NFL draft by Chicago Bears. In military service, 1953-54; reported to Bears for 1955 season. In 12-year career played 155 games, had 16 interceptions for 156 yds., scored 1 TD. Tied NFL record for most opponents' fumbles recovered, career, with 22. Pro Bowl, 1959, 63, 64, 65, 66. Played in NFL title games, 1956, 63. Retired after 1966 season. Entire pro career was spent with Bears.

FOSS, JOSEPH F. Commissioner. B. 4/17/15, near Sioux Falls, S.D. Boxing, track, football participant South Dakota. Entered U.S. Marine Corps as Pvt. and rose to Maj. Won Congressional Medal of Honor by gunning down 26 Japanese planes during World War II. Also served in Korean War as U.S. Air Force Col. Member South Dakota state legislature, 1948-53. In 1954 elected South Dakota governor for first of two terms. Unanimously chosen AFL commissioner, 1959. Served in that capacity during league's nine-year existence. Administrative prowess helped AFL gain national prominence, leading to merger with NFL. Merger meant end of his job though, as Pete Rozelle was named czar over all of pro football. Renowned big-game hunter; some of his safaris have been shown on national television. Uncomplicated by success: "I was born a farmer and the earth has a way of staying in your pores. The farm teaches you early that you either work or you don't eat. I learned it's nice to eat well."

FRANCK, GEORGE Running Back. B. 9/23/18, Davenport, Iowa. 6', 180. Minnesota, 1938-40. Consensus All-America, 1940. 3rd in Heisman Trophy voting, 1940. In 1939 made 78-yd. punt vs. Michigan; 67-yd. interception return vs. Arizona, 1940. In 1940 made 98-yd. kickoff return vs. Washington and 80-yd. kickoff return vs. Purdue. Was MVP in 1941, 45-47. Vs. Chicago Bears, in 1941 title game, caught pass from Tuffy Leemans and ran 27 yds. for TD. Separated shoulder vs. Bears, 12/15/46.

FRANCO, EDMUND Tackle/Guard. B. Jersey City, N.J. 5'8", 196. Played guard and tackle for Fordham, 1935-37. All-America 1936, 37. One of famous "Seven Blocks of Granite." Called "Devil Doll." Short, squat, barrel-chested, with long, gorilla-like arms. Incredibly strong, sometimes called "one-man line." Great blocker and tackler; couldn't be knocked off his feet. Was Fordham ping-pong champion during undergraduate days. Boston Redskins, 1944. Later assistant coach at Fordham.

FRANK, CLINTON E. Quarterback. B. St. Louis, Mo. 5'10", 190. Yale, 1935-37. All-America, 1936, 37. Unanimous choice in '37. Heisman Trophy, Maxwell Award, 1937. Accurate passer. Called by Greasy Neale finest all-around back he'd ever seen, and "a miracle on defense." Combined with Larry Kelley for sensational performance in 20-16 victory over Princeton, 1936. Captain of 1937 team; that year against Princeton scored four TDs, first man to do so for Yale since Bum McClung in 1890. Grantland Rice said of him: "Unquestionably, one of Yale's greatest all-time players. Captained the team, passed, blocked and tackled." Lt. Col. in Army Air Force, aide to Gen. Doolittle during World War II. Father of 10 children. Currently heads advertising agency with offices in New York, Los Angeles, Chicago, Houston, Richmond, Cincinnati. Citizens Savings Hall of Fame, National Football Foundation Hall of Fame.

FRASER, JAMES Linebacker. B. 5/29/36, Philadelphia, Pa. 6'2", 205. Linebacker and kicker for Wisconsin. Played for Denver Broncos, 1962-64, during which time he led AFL in punting three successive seasons. In 1962 made

54 punts for 2400 yds., average of 44.4, longest 75 yds.; in 1963, 78 punts for 3595 yds., average of 45.8, longest 66 yds.; in 1964, 72 punts for 3225 yds., average of 44.6, longest 67 yds. Kansas City Chiefs, 1965; Boston Patriots, 1966; New Orleans Saints, 1968.

FREDERICKSON, IVAN C. (Tucker) Running Back. B. 1/12/43, Ft. Lauderdale, Fla. 6'2", 220. Described by Auburn coach Shag Jordan as "the most complete football player I have seen in the years I have been connected with the game." Played for Auburn, 1962-64. Consensus All-America, 1964. In 30 games gained 1812 yds. Had kickoff-return average of 22.6 yds. Was outstanding on defense in 1964 Orange Bowl vs. Nebraska. Auburn lost, 13-7. Selected 1st in NFL draft (by New York Giants) in 1965 when Dick Butkus, Joe Namath, Gale Sayers, John Huarte were all available. In 1968 led Giants in rushing with 486 yds. on 142 carries (3.4 average). Giants, 1965-71. Pro Bowl, 1966. Knee injuries hampered career, eventually forced retirement.

FRIEDMAN, BENJAMIN (Benny) Quarterback. B. 1905, Cleveland, Ohio. 5'8", 172. Michigan, 1924-26. Consensus All-America, 1925, 26. Considered transferring to Dartmouth after difficult freshman year. Stayed at Michigan. Excellent passer, runner, kicker. Called by coach Fielding Yost, "One of greatest passers, smartest quarterbacks in history." Tremendously competitive, hated to lose. In 1925 made 65-yd. rush vs. Michigan State, 60-yd. punt return vs. Indiana and 60-yd. pass vs. Wisconsin. Combined with end Bennie Oosterbaan to defeat Ohio State Buckeyes, 17-16, in 1926. Red Grange claims Friedman was best QB he ever played against. Played professionally with Cleveland Bulldogs, 1927; Detroit Wolverines, 1928; New York Giants, 1929-31; Brooklyn Dodgers, 1932-34. Is credited with helping to keep pro football alive in New York during lean years due to inventiveness and color. Never injured in all his years of playing, though early squads had only 17-19 men. Citizens Savings Hall of Fame, National Football Foundation Hall of Fame.

FRISCH, FRANK F. (Fordham Flash) Running Back. B. 9/9/1898, New York, N.Y. D. 3/12/73, Wilmington, Del. 5'10", 185. Fordham, 1916-18. Starred in football, basketball and baseball; captain in all three sports. Was skillful halfback. 2nd-team All-America, 1918. Greatest fame came in baseball. Spent total of 40 years as infielder, manager and broadcaster. Member of Baseball Hall of Fame. Died at age 75, five weeks after being injured in auto accident.

FRITSCH, TONI Kicker. B. 7/10/45, Vienna, Austria. 5'7", 185. Starred for Austrian National and Rapid soccer teams for eight years. Didn't attend college. Signed by Dallas Cowboys in Vienna, summer of 1971. That summer kicked in first American football game he ever saw. Set Dallas records for FGs (21) and longest FG (54 yds.), 1972. In 1973 hit 43 of 43 PAT attempts and 18 of 28 on FGs, for 97 points. Makes frequent trips to Europe to buy antiques for importing and auctioning business.

GABRIEL, ROMAN (Gabe) Quarterback. B. 8/5/40, Wilmington, N.C. 6'4", 220. North Carolina State, 1959-61. All-America, 1960, 61. Academic All-America, 1960. Led NCAA in passing percentage, 1959, with 60.4 (81 completions, 134 attempts). Drafted on 1st round by both Oakland Raiders and Los Angeles Rams; signed with L.A. where played thru 1972. Originally such things as "robot quarterback" were used to describe him. Shared QB job, 1962, 65, with Zeke Bratkowski, Terry Baker, Bill Munson. Became full-time starter after Munson's 1965 injury and blossomed under George Allen. In 1962 had only two passes intercepted out of 101 attempts. With Sen. Robert Kennedy when shot in 1968. In 1973 threatened to join Las Vegas Casinos, but on 6/8/73 was traded to Philadelphia Eagles for running back Tony Baker, wide receiver Harold Jackson and three high draft picks. On 12/2/73 completed 28 of 55 passes for 317 yds. Was 4th-ranking passer in NFC, 1973, with 270 completions in 460 attempts for 3219 yds., 23 TDs, 58.7 percentage, 7.3-yd. average per pass. Became 11th QB in NFL history to gain more than 25,000 yds. passing. All-NFL, 1969. Pro Bowl, 1968, 69, 70, 74. Pro Bowl MVP, 1968.

GAECHTER, MICHAEL T. Defensive Back. B. 1/9/40, Santa Monica, Calif. 6'0", 190. Graduated from Oregon, 1962. Signed as free agent, 1962, by Dallas Cowboys and played thru 1969. On 10/14/62 ran 100 yds. for TD with interception. On 11/3/63 tied NFL record for yds. gained on pass interceptions, game, with 121. In 1965 scored TD on FG-attempt return. Played in NFL championship games, 1966, 67.

GAIN, ROBERT Tackle. B. 6/21/29, Akron, Ohio. 6'3", 250. All-America at Kentucky, 1950. Outland Trophy same year. Played in 1950 Orange Bowl (lost to Santa Clara, 21-13), '51 Cotton Bowl (beat Oklahoma, 13-7). Cleveland Browns, 1952, 54-64. Pro Bowl, 1958, 59, 60, 62, 63. Browns were NFL champions in 1954, 55, 64. Originally drafted by Green Bay Packers; Pack dealt him to Browns before rookie season began. Tackle by trade, but also served as defensive end and linebacker. Outstanding against running plays.

GAITERS, ROBERT Running Back. B. 2/26/38, Santa Ana, Calif. 5'11", 200. Played for New Mexico State, 1959-60. Set NCAA record for points per game, career, with 11.9 average (203 points in 17 games) on 32 TDs and 11 PATs. In 17-game collegiate career. 282 plays, gained 1828 yds., average 107.5 per game, and scored 31 TDs. Was 1960 NCAA rushing leader with 1338 yds. on 197 plays in 10 games; also scoring leader with 145 points, on 23 TDs and 7 PATs. Was AFL's 1st draft choice, 1961, by Denver Broncos but signed by New York Giants. Played in N.Y. until 1962, then traded to San Francisco 49ers. Denver Broncos, 1963.

GAITHER, ALONZO S. (Jake) Coach. B. Dayton, Tenn. Had law ambitions; spent many boyhood days hanging around courthouses listening to lawyers plead cases. His dad, who was AME minister, wanted Jake to become minister. Death of father, during senior year at Knoxville College, forced immediate responsibilities — he turned to coaching and teaching. Earned B.S. degree from Knoxville, 1927; M.S. from Ohio State, 1937. Played end for Knoxville Bulldogs. Joined Florida A. & M. staff in 1937, elevated to head coach in 1945. Proceeded to run off string of amazing successes. Guided team to six national Black championships. Retired after 1969 season with 25-year record of 203-36-4. Won conference (SIAC) title every year except 1951, 52, 66. Worst records were 6-4, 1946; 7-3, 1965, 66. Produced at least one Little All-America every year except 1949. Willie Galimore made list three times. Also developed Bob Hayes, Major Hazelton, Ken Riley, Roger Finnie, Al Denson, Hewritt Dixon, Carleton Oates. Gaither and associates wrote *The Split Line T Offense of Florida A. & M. University* for Prentice-Hall, 1963. Active in Fellowship of Christian Athletes. Many awards and honors, including induction into Citizens Savings Hall of Fame. Athletic director, Florida A. & M.

GALIFFA, ARNOLD A. Quarterback. B. 1/29/27, Donora, Pa. 6'2", 190. Army, 1946-49. All-America, 1949. 4th in Heisman voting, 1949. Completed 73-yd. pass vs. Washington & Lee, 1947. In 1948 beat Penn with long pass to Johnny Trent in last 30 seconds. Following season completed 83-yd. pass vs. Columbia. Red Blaik's 1949 team won all nine games, was pressed only by Penn in 14-13 decision. Fine runner, passer and director of T-formation attack. New York Giants, 1953; San Francisco 49ers, 1954.

GARBISCH, EDGAR W. Guard. B. 4/7/1900, Ind. 6', 185. Washington & Jefferson, 1917-20; Army, 1921-24. Played five games vs. Notre Dame with no substitution — "And the only one in history to have survived such an experience," quipped Grantland Rice. Fine kicker, rugged tackler, excellent blocker. All-America, 1922, 1924; 3rd team, 1923. Captain of Army team, 1924. Led Cadets in prayer before each game. In 1922 kicked 47-yd. FG to beat Navy. In 1924 vs. Navy dropkicked four FGs. Also tennis captain. Cadet Capt. 1st Battalion. His father wanted him to be concert pianist until he saw son carried off field on teammates' shoulders after 1924 Navy game — "No matter how magnificent the performance of Paderewski, the audience does not sweep up on the stage and bear the artist off in triumph." Citizens Savings Hall of Fame, National Football Foundation Hall of Fame.

GARRETT, CARL Running Back. B. 8/31/47, Denton, Tex. 5'11", 210. Attended New Mexico Highlands. First three-time Little All-America since Eddie LeBaron. Scored 418 points and gained 3862 yds. rushing during collegiate career. Selected by Boston Patriots on 3rd round of 1969 AFL-NFL draft. Played with Patriots, 1969-72. AFL Rookie of the Year, 1969. In 1972 had 16 kickoff returns for 410 yds., average of 25.6. Also led Patriots (newly renamed New England) in scoring that year with 30 points. In 1971 traded with 1st-round draft choice to Dallas Cowboys, for running back Duane Thomas and two other players. However, deal was voided. Traded to Chicago Bears in 1972 for 1973 1st-round draft choice. Led NFC in kickoff-return average yds. with 30.4, 1973, on 16 returns for 486 yds. Played in AFL All-Star game following 1969 season.

GARRETT, MICHAEL L. Running Back. B. 4/12/44, Los Angeles, Calif. 5'9", 195. Halfback for Southern California, 1963-65. All-America, 1964; unanimous All-America, 1965. Heisman Trophy, 1965. Appeared in 30 games and 612 plays, gained 3221 yds., scored 24 TDs. 1965 NCAA rushing champion with 1440 yds. on 267 carries. Same year returned punts 87 and 74 yds. vs. California, made 77-yd. rush vs. Stanford. Also played college baseball. "Best athlete ever to play at USC," according to coach John McKay. Kansas City Chiefs, 1966-69. In 1967 rushed for 1089 yds. On 1/1/67 tied three AFL playoff career records: 2 TDs, 3 punt returns and 12 points. Also set record for TDs rushing with two. Scored one TD in Super Bowl IV, 1970. Announced retirement after that season to become pro baseball player. Recanted when dealt to San Diego Chargers for future draft choice. In 1972 rushed for 1031 yds. in 272 attempts, leading Chargers. All-AFL, 1967. Played in AFL All-Star games following 1966, 67 season. Played in AFL championship games, 1966, 69; first Super Bowl in 1967. Big heart makes up for small size. Has superior running instincts.

GARRISON, GARY L. (Ghost) End. B. 1/21/44, Amarillo, Tex. 6'2", 190. Attended Millikan H.S. in Long Beach (Calif.), Long Beach City College and San Diego State. Was first State player in East-West Shrine and College All-Star games. Played in 1965 Senior Bowl. Little All-America, All-Coast in '65. Caught 78 passes in 1964, 70 in '65. Selected by San Diego Chargers on 1st round as future in 1965. Played with Chargers, 1966-73. Had over 1000 yds. receiving, 1968 and '70. Charger MVP, 1970. Never caught less than 40 passes in first seven pro

113

seasons. In eight pro years had 334 pass receptions for 6252 yds., 50 TDs. Played in AFL All-Star game following 1968 season. Played in Pro Bowl following 1970, 71, 72 seasons. Hobby is training horses.

GATEWOOD, THOMAS End. B. 3/3/50, Baltimore, Md. 6'2", 205. Played end for Notre Dame, 1969-71. Consensus All-America, 1970; Academic All-America, 1971. Also NCAA Post-Graduate Scholarship and National Football Foundation Scholarship winner. In collegiate career made 157 catches (Notre Dame record) for 2283 yds., scored 19 TDs. Selected by New York Giants on 5th round of 1972 NFL draft. Little action in 1972, 73. Hobbies are painting and writing. Pursuing law degree.

GAUTT, PRENTICE Running Back. B. 2/8/38, Oklahoma City, Okla. 6', 190. Played under Bud Wilkinson at Oklahoma, 1957-59. All-America and Academic All-America, 1959. MVP in 1959 Orange Bowl vs. Syracuse (won 21-6). Also played in 1958 Orange Bowl vs. Duke (won 48-21). First Black to play at Oklahoma. Cleveland Browns, 1960; St. Louis Cardinals, 1961-67. Little playing time as Cleveland rookie fullback-halfback, but went on to have fine career with Cards. Club's leading rusher in 1961 with 523 yds. Missouri assistant coach, 1968-73.

GELBERT, CHARLES S. End. B. 12/24/1871, Hawley, Pa. D. 1/16/36. 5'9", 175. Penn State, 1894-96. All-America, 1894, 95, 96. Ferocious tackler, leader of interference. Sported long blond mustache and full head of tawny hair. Considered "Miracle Man." Coached by George Woodruff, developer of "guards back" play, wherein guards dropped back and drove as massed interference. 1894 team won 12 straight games. Streak stretched over into 1896, was finally broken by Lafayette (6-4). Father of Charley Gelbert, famous major league shortstop and college baseball coach. National Football Foundation Hall of Fame.

GEORGE, WILLIAM Linebacker. B. 10/27/30, Waynesburg, Pa. 6'2", 230. Attended Wake Forest. Played with Chicago Bears, 1952-65; Los Angeles Rams, 1966. Rugged and durable, he gave nothing but consistently fine performances at middle linebacker. Played in 173 league games. In career intercepted 18 passes and recovered 14 opposition fumbles. Owns Chicago record for most seasons as active player. Retired 4th among NFL players in total seasons played (15). All-NFL, 1958, 59, 60, 61, 63. Played in NFL championship games, 1956, 63. Eight-time Pro Bowl participant, 1955, 56, 57, 58, 59, 60, 61, 62. "It's a little embarrassing but I'm thrilled to death," was his reaction after election to Pro Hall of Fame in 1974. George Halas, who coached Bears during George's career, said, "Bill certainly was an excellent choice for the Hall of Fame. He was a great linebacker, a great team man. He was, and still is, a man of character."

GEORGE, WILLIAM J. Center. B. 7/30/1861, Scroggsfield, Ohio. D. 9/15/33, West Palm Beach, Fla. Played for Princeton in the late 1880s. All-America, 1889. Super physique, strength and football knowledge. Was wise counselor, giving sound advice to captains who were then also coaches. Walter Camp chose him as center in 1889 on original All-America team. Became teacher at Lawrenceville School.

GERELA, ROY Kicker. B. 4/2/48, Sarrail, Alta., Canada. 5'10", 185. Attended New Mexico State, 1966-68. Three-year regular as defensive back and punter. Did not placekick until senior year. Also lettered in baseball and soccer. Houston Oilers, 1969-70; Pittsburgh Steelers, 1971-73. Signed with Steelers as free agent. Led AFC FG kickers with 28, 1972. Also scored 119 points. In 1973 AFC stats ranked 1st in scoring (123 points), PATs (36) and FGs (29). String of 106 straight PATs was broken against Minnesota Vikings, 1972. Brother Ted is kicking specialist in CFL. Roy's followers are called "Gerela's gorillas."

GEYER, FOREST P. (Spot) Running Back. B. 12/9/1890, New Haven, Kan. D. 2/7/32, Texas. 6'2", 162. Named for Forest Park Area of Kansas City where he lived as youngster. Played under Bennie Owen at Oklahoma, 1913-15. Captain, 1915. Teammate Hap Johnson recalled: "He (Geyer) never had a dime while he was in school but he was good at anything—dramatics, writing, sign-painting, opera house stage hand or playing in the band. He was a smart lad and a wonderful mixer." In 1914 Bennie Owen converted to air game despite Walter Camp's warning that forward passing "is fraught with wide disaster at times." Result: OU lost only to Texas during period of 1914-15. Owen's bellwether was Geyer who may have been greatest passer of era. Often tossed passes that measured 40-70 yards. Earned moniker by throwing to spots behind enemy safety. Great conversion kicker but almost indifferent at bucking line. Harold Keith wrote in *Oklahoma Kickoff*, 1948: "Probably no fullback in the history of the game at Norman possessed such few mechanical football talents, yet would go so far in spite of his lack of them." At his death was president of Marland Oil Co. of Texas. National Football Foundation Hall of Fame.

GIBBONS, JAMES E. (Gib) Tight End. B. 9/25/36, Chicago, Ill. 6'3", 230. Iowa, 1955-57. All-America, 1957. Drafted by Cleveland Browns in 1958; dealt to Detroit and played entire pro career with Lions. Caught 287 passes for 3561 yds., 1958-68. Scored 20 TDs in 140 games. Consistent performer. Excellent blocker, sure-handed. Played under George Wilson, Harry Gilmer and Joe Schmidt. Pro Bowl, 1961, 62, 65.

GIBBS, JERRY D. (Jake) Quarterback. B. 11/7/38, Grenada, Miss. 6', 180. Played QB for Mississippi, 1958-60. Unanimous All-America, 1960. 3rd in Heisman Trophy voting, 1960. In 1959 made 78-yd. pass vs. Vanderbilt. Played in Gator Bowl, 1959, and Sugar Bowl, 1960, 61. In 1960 Sugar Bowl threw 43-yd. TD pass, in 1961 scored 2 TDs. Career completed 119 of 221 passes for 1850 yds. and 19 TDs. Total offense yds. were 2410. Catcher for New York Yankees, 1963-71. Currently assistant football coach at Ole Miss. Was instructor of All-America QB Archie Manning, currently with New Orleans Saints.

GIBRON, ABRAHAM Guard. B. 9/22/25, Michigan City, Ind. 5'11", 255. Attended Valparaiso before graduating from Purdue. Made career of pro football. Offensive guard with Buffalo Bills (AAFC), 1949; Cleveland Browns, 1950-56; Philadelphia Eagles, 1956-57; Chicago Bears, 1958-59. NFL championship games, 1950, 51, 52, 53, 54, 55. Thrice Pro Bowl participant. All-NFL, 1955. Assistant coach Washington Redskins, 1960-64; Chicago Bears, 1965-71. Blunt, colorful and rotund. Under fire by Chicago press and fans after 1973 season.

GIEL, PAUL R. Running Back. B. 2/29/32, Winona, Minn. 5'11", 185. Attended Winona H.S. and U. of Minnesota. Accounted for 32 TDs during collegiate career, 1951-53. Rushed 2188 yds. and passed for 1922 more. All-America, 1952; unanimous All-America, 1953. Runnerup in Heisman Trophy voting, 1953. Despite Giel heroics Minnesota could do no better than 4-4-1 record, achieved his senior season. After college accepted big bonus to sign with New York baseball Giants. Pitched six years in majors, 1954-55, 58-61, but never lived up to early promise. Later served as Minnesota athletic director.

GIFFORD, FRANCIS (Frank) Running Back. B. 8/16/30, Bakersfield, Calif. 6'1", 200. Began as end and tailback at Bakersfield (Calif.) H.S, 1945-47. Attended Bakersfield J.C. one year before tranferring to Southern California. There was defensive safety, tailback and placekicker, 1949-51. In 1950 played QB vs. Washington State and made 69-yd. TD run, gaining 155 yds. rushing. All-America, 1951. Drafted by New York Giants, 1952; played for them, 1952-60, 62-64. Used as two-way man in 1953 and in '54 became Giants' regular left halfback. Won Jim Thorpe Trophy as league MVP, 1956. Gained 819 yds. running that season and caught 51 passes for additional 603 yds. Giants won league championship in '56. In final game of 1960 season suffered severe brain concussion against Philadelphia Eagles. As result missed all of 1961. Made comeback in 1962, experiencing some early difficulty. On first play from scrimmage at training camp, Gifford ran wrong way. Soon was shifted to flanker. In comeback campaign caught 39 passes for 796 yds., 7 TDs.

Handsome, modest and articulate, Gifford was football glamour-boy. Retired after 1964 season to do color on Giant telecasts, as well as other work for CBS sports. Did so having scored more points than any other Giant (484), caught more passes (387), gained more yds. with catches (5434), scored more TDs (78); also kicked 10 PATs and 2 FGs. Caught 3 TD passes in championship games. In career 840 rushing attempts, gained 3609 yds., average of 4.3. All-AFL, 1955, 56. 57, 59. Eight Pro Bowls, 1954, 55, 56, 57, 58, 59, 60, 64. Appeared in NFL championship games, 1956, 58, 59, 62, 63. Had brief Hollywood career, including movie with Tony Curtis called *All-American*. Currently ABC television sports-caster; play-by-play man on *Monday Night Football*.

GILBERT, CHRIS Running Back. B 10/16/46, Houston, Tex. 5'11", 176. Texas, 1966-68. Consensus All-America, 1968. 20-9-1 playing record. Gained better than 1000 yds. three straight years (record). Figures were 1080, 1019, 1132 for 3231-yd. total. In career had runs of 96, 80, 76, 74 yds. Gained 156 yds. in Astro-Bluebonnet Bowl, 1966. Scored one TD in 1969 Cotton Bowl, winning 36-13 over Tennessee. Now operates Camp Olympia, summer boys camp in Houston.

GILBERT, WALTER Center. B. Fairfield, Ala. 190. Auburn, 1934-36. All-America, 1935, 36. All-SEC, 1934, 35, 36. Atlanta newspaper columnist wrote: "Auburn has in Captain Walter Gilbert a man who can measure ability with any center in the country." Played in era of great centers, like Darrell Lester (TCU), George Shotwell (Pitt) and Alex Wojciechowicz (Fordham). In 1936 game vs. LSU was hounded by two men but still made half of Auburn tackles, two interceptions. After service as artillery Maj. during World War II, became general sales manager, Foreign Sales Department of Texaco, Inc. National Football Foundation Hall of Fame, becoming third Auburn man to achieve distinction. His Auburn roommate, Joel Eaves, is athletic director at Georgia.

GILCHRIST, CARLTON C. (Cookie) Running Back. B. 5/25/35, Breckenridge, Pa. 6'3", 255. Never made it past 11th grade, receiving his education on Canadian and American football fields. After minor-league experience signed with Hamilton Tiger-Cats of CFL, 1956. Played in Canada thru 1961, then signed with Buffalo Bills. In 1962 became second pro rookie to rush for 1000 yds. He had 1096 on 214 trips. Total led AFL. Won second rushing title two years later, amassing 981 yds. on 230 carries. Rushed 243 yds. on 36 carries and scored 5 TDs, 12/8/63. Willie Ellison, with 247 yds., is only player to surpass Gilchrist's 243 one-game figure. Traded by Bills after 1964 season to Denver Broncos. Played with Broncos, 1965, 67. Also with Miami Dolphins, 1967. Career gained 4293 yds. (averaging 4.3 per carry) and scored 37 TDs. All-AFL, 1962, 64, 65. Controversial, rebellious, outspoken during playing career. Now much more diplomatic. Heads group, United Athletes Coalition of America, which hopes to ease athletes' transition into everyday life after careers end. Maybe, Cookie is sugar-coated after all.

GILLIAM, JOHN R. (Tally) End. B. 8/7/45, Greenwood, S.C. 6'1", 195. Played for South Carolina State, 1964-67. Won seven letters (four in football, three in track). Drafted on 2nd round by New Orleans Saints, 1967, and played with club thru 1969. In first 10 seconds of NFL action, Gilliam ran back kickoff 94 yds. for TD against Los Angeles Rams. After 1969 season traded to St. Louis Cardinals. Three years with Cards, then dealt to Minnesota Vikings. With Vikes favorite targer of quarterback Fran Tarkenton. Set personal and Minnesota club records with 1035 yds. receiving, 1973. Caught 47 passes, leading NFL in average yds. with 23.0. Also averaged 26.4 yds. on punt returns. Caught 42 passes, scored 8 TDs, made All-NFC, 1973. Pro Bowl, 1973, 74. Speedy, excellent hands. Operates men's clothing store in Atlanta during off-season.

GILLINGHAM, GALE Guard. B. 2/3/44, Madison, Wis. 6'3", 265. Fullback and tackle at Minnesota. Selected for duty in East-West Shrine, Senior Bowl,

Coaches All-America, College All-Star games. Drafted on 1st round by Green Bay Packers, 1966. Developed into one of game's best offensive guards. Played left side until switched to right in 1969. Packers tried him at defensive tackle in 1972. Costly move. Gillingham injured knee in second game and missed rest of season. NFL championship games, 1966, 67. Packers won both Super Bowl I, 1967, and Super Bowl II, 1968. All-NFC, 1970, 71. Pro Bowl, 1972, 74.

GILLMAN, SIDNEY Coach. B. 10/26/11, Minneapolis, Minn. Star end at Ohio State, 1931-33. Co-captain, 1932. In 1933 Northwestern game recovered fumble and ran 54 yds. for TD. Cleveland Rams, 1936. Assistant coach at Ohio State, 1934, 38-40; Denison, 1935-37, 41; Miami (Ohio), 1942-43; Army, 1948. Head coach at Miami (Ohio), 1944-47. Record of 30-6-1. Defeated Texas Tech in Sun Bowl 13-12, 1948. Head coach U. of Cincinnati, 1949-54. Record: 49-12-1. Defeated Toledo in 1950 Glass Bowl, lost to West Texas State in '51 Sun Bowl. Head coach, Los Angeles Rams, 1955-60. Ram record was 38-35-1. Lost 1955 NFL championship game to Cleveland Browns, 38-14. Lost AFL championship game to Houston Oilers, 24-16, 1960. San Diego Charger head coach, 1961-69, 71. Record: 68-38-6. Won divisional titles in 1961, 63, 64, 65. Defeated Boston Patriots, 51-10, in 1963 title game. Came within five games of coaching Chargers thru entire AFL history.

Duodenal ulcer and hiatal hernia forced premature retirement, 11/10/69. Returned to guide Chargers in 1971 but resigned on 11/22 of that year. In 1973 was hired to rebuild football fortunes of Houston Oilers, as executive vice president-general manager. Midway thru '73 season he replaced head coach Bill Peterson. Oilers finished with dismal 1-13 mark, worst in NFL. Nevertheless, Gillman has high standing. His 115 pro victories are topped by only seven coaches. Two of his former pupils have done well in coaching ranks. They are Paul Dietzel (South Carolina) and Ara Parseghian (Notre Dame).

GILMER, HARRY Running Back. B. 4/14/26, Birmingham, Ala. 6', 175. Played halfback for Alabama, 1944-47. All-America, 1945. 5th in Heisman voting, 1945, 7th in 1946, 5th in 1947. 1944 team was favorite of Coach Frank Thomas. "Oh, how I loved those war babies," he said. "They were just kids, but they gave everything." Kids grew up to perfect season, 1945, culminating with 34-14 demolishing of Southern Cal. Gilmer led NCAA in pass completion percentage with .648, 1945. Also led that year in TD passes (13) and TDs accounted for (22). In 1946 led NCAA in passing attempts with 160. In 1944 returned kickoff 95 yds. vs. Louisiana State. Year later made 95-yd. rush vs. Kentucky. In 1945 Sugar Bowl completed 8 of 8 passes, including one 10-yd. TD. Rose Bowl, 1946, rushed 116 yds. on 16 carries, scored 1 TD and threw 24-yd. TD pass. Also appeared in 1948 Sugar Bowl. Was 1st bonus pick by Washington Redskins, 1948; played with 'Skins, 1948-52, 54; Detroit Lions, 1955-56. Head coach Detroit Lions, 1965-66.

GINN, RALPH Coach. B. 7/23/07, Lenox, Iowa. D. 5/26/72, Brookings, S.D. Attended Tarkio (Mo.) H.S. and U. of Missouri. Coached at high schools in

Tarkio and Brookings; at Tarkio College, Wayne State and South Dakota State. Spent 22 years at latter institution, 1947-68. Twenty-four-year record was 119-98-10. Also coached basketball, track and field; won conference titles in both, as well as football. Produced nine North Central Conference championship teams at South Dakota State. 1950 team was undefeated. Formerly South Dakota commissioner of School and Public Lands. Was active in community affairs in Pierre. Citizens Savings Hall of Fame.

GIPP, GEORGE (Gipper) Running Back. B. 2/18/1895, Laurium, Mich. D. 12/14/20, South Bend, Ind. 6'2", 185. Wore uniform No. 66 for Notre Dame, 1917-20. Notre Dame's 1st-team All-America, 1920. In 1920 recommended for West Point; however, never received offer as parents didn't know where to send application. In 1917 dropkicked 62-yd. FG. Expelled by Notre Dame authorities prior 1920 season because he spent too much free time in pool room. Signed and played with Indianapolis of baseball's American Association, 1920. That summer became interested in religion. At end of baseball season offered job as assistant coach by Rockne and accepted immediately. At Rockne's urging officials agreed to readmit Gipp if he passed test. On 10/20/20, after giving kicking exhibition in which he dropkicked 4 FGs of 50 yds. (2 each way), had greatest game of career. Rushed for 124 yds., passing another 96, returning punts and kickoffs for 112. Same season ran 80 yds. vs. Purdue. Injured left arm later that season against Indiana. Also made two 60-yd. punts vs. Army, 50-yd. pass vs. Northwestern and 42-yd. FG vs. Nebraska. Played 32 consecutive games. Scored 21 TDs. Once ran 100 yds. in 10.2 in full uniform. Called by Pudge Heffelfinger most versatile back of all time.

During 1920 season caught strep throat but insisted on going to Northwestern game where he led Irish to victory. Condition developed into pneumonia, causing hospitalization. Had signed contract with Chicago Cubs baseball team. Three hours before death, baptized as Catholic. Told Rockne, according to legend: "Sometime, when the boys are up against it and the pressure's really on Notre Dame, tell them to win one for the Gipper." Rockne told Irish players eight years later, 1928, and they responded with 12-6 victory over Army. Citizens Savings Player of the Year, 1920. Citizens Savings Hall of Fame, National Football Foundation Hall of Fame.

GIPSON, PAUL Running Back. B. 3/21/46, Jacksonville, Tex. 6'0", 205. Played fullback for Houston, 1966-68. All-America, 1968. In 1968 made 91-yd. kickoff return vs. Cincinnati and 66-yd. rush vs. Texas. Same year gained 1550 yds. rushing, leading NCAA with 6.4 average. Voted Most Outstanding Player in both Blue-Gray and Coaches All-America games. Also played in Hula and Senior Bowl. Selected by Atlanta Falcons on 2nd round of 1969 draft. Played with Falcons thru 1970. Finished NFL career with Detroit Lions, 1972. Saw limited action due to injury in 1971.

GLASS, EDGAR (Ned) Guard. B. 5/24/1879, Syracuse, N.Y. D. 4/9/44. 6'4", 210. Played for Yale, 1900-02. All-America, 1902. Walter Camp called him "the most powerful tackle I ever saw." Tall, raw-boned, Lincolnesque. Blessed with tremendous strength. Could pick up a player and fight his way forward, with tacklers clinging to him. Literally ripped apart enemy lines. George Trevor called him "Heffelfinger's only rival for all-time laurels at New Haven."

GLASS, WILLIAM S. Defensive End. B. 8/16/35, Texarkana, Tex. 6'5", 255. Quality player, quality person. Guard for Baylor Bears, 1954-56. All-America, 1956. Saskatchewan Roughriders, 1957; Detroit Lions, 1958-61; Cleveland Browns, 1962-68. Was pro defensive end. Involved in six-player trade, 1962. Glass, Jim Ninowski, Hopalong Cassady went to Cleveland while Milt Plum, Dave Lloyd, Tom Watkins were shifted to Detroit. Pro Bowl, 1963, 64, 65, 68. NFL championship games, 1964, 65. Browns won 1964 title game, 27-0, over Baltimore Colts. Received D. D. degree from Southwest Baptist Theological Seminary, 1963. Evangelist.

GLICK, FREDERICK C. (Bear) Defensive Back. B. 2/25/37, Aurora, Colo. 6'1", 195. Graduated from Colorado State. Selected by Chicago Cardinals on 23rd round of 1959 NFL draft. Played with Cards thru 1960, then signed by Houston Oilers. In 1963 established AFL record for interceptions, season, with 12, for 180 yds., 15.0 average. Retired after 1966 season with career totals of 30 interceptions for 390 yds., 1 TD; 44 punt returns for 326 yds.; 26 kickoff returns for 584 yds. Played in AFL All-Star games, 1963, 64, 65. AFL championship games, 1961, 62.

GLOVER, RICH Linebacker. B. 2/6/50, Jersey City, N.J. 6'1", 240. Played middle guard for Nebraska, 1970-72. All-America, 1971; unanimous All-America, 1972. Winner of Outland Trophy and Vince Lombardi Trophy as outstanding lineman in college football, 1972. Played on three winning Orange Bowl teams. Nebraska was national champion in 1970, 72. His coach, Bob Devaney, was moved to comment, "Rich Glover is the greatest defensive lineman I've ever seen. We take him for granted some of the time because he never has had a bad game. He always plays from great to super and forces other teams to do things they wouldn't ordinarily do." Selected by New York Giants on "only" 3rd round of 1973 NFL draft; was considered too small to be pro lineman and not quick enough to be linebacker. Put on waivers by Giants, 9/5/73, as ploy to test his weight on NFL market. Giants kept him.

GOEBEL, WILLIAM A. (Dutch) B. 6/24/1887, Cincinnati, Ohio. D. 2/15/60, Cincinnati, Ohio. 6'2", 206. Played right guard for Yale, 1907-09. All-America, 1908; 2nd team, 1909; 3rd team, 1907. Member of great '09 Yale squad captained by Ted Coy. Team shut out all 10 opponents and scored 209 points. John Reed Kilpatrick called Goebel "the strongest man I ever saw." Was Eastern intercollegiate heavyweight wrestling champion.

GOGOLAK, CHARLES P. (Charlie) Kicker. B. 12/29/44, Rabahidveg, Hungary. 5'10", 170. Placekicker for Princeton, 1963-65. Set seven NCAA records, including 50 straight PATs, 81 points in one season, 6 field goals and 20 points in one game. Ranks 5th in career kick-scoring with 170 points; also 5th in points per game with 6.3. Washington Redskins, 1966-68; Boston Patriots, 1970; New England Patriots, 1971-73. Did not play in 1969. Became first kicker ever drafted on 1st round when 'Skins selected him in 1966. Established NFL record for most PATs attempted in one game (10) against New York Giants, 1966. Same game tied record with nine successful conversions. Brother of Pete Gogolak, placekicker for New York Giants.

GOGOLAK, PETER Kicker. B. 4/18/42, Budapest, Hungary. 6'1", 185. Graduated from Cornell. Drafted on 12th round by Buffalo Bills in 1964. As rookie kicked 19 FGs, 45 PATs for 102 points. In 1965 led AFL in FGs with record 28, in record 46 attempts. On 12/5/65 attempted 7 FGs, tying record, and making 5. All-AFL kicker, 1965. After playing out his option in 1966, Gogolak signed with N. Y. Giants. In 1972 led Giants in scoring with 97 points, making 21 of 31 FG attempts, average of 25.3 yds., longest 49 yds. Made 25 of 25 PAT attempts and 17 of 28 FG attempts, scoring 76 points in 1973. Scored 131 consecutive PATs. Played in AFL championship games, 1964, 65. Scored five FGs in championship play (two in 1964, three in 1965). Also scored two PATs in each game. Fled from Hungary with family after Communist takeover. Brother of Charlie, while kicking for Princeton, broke Pete's Ivy League record of 44 consecutive PATs.

GOLDBERG, MARSHALL (Biggie) Running Back. B. 10/24/17, Elkins, W. Va. 5'11", 192. "Mad Marshall" played for U. of Pittsburgh, 1936-38. Consensus All-America halfback, 1937. In 1938 asked to be switched to fullback, made unanimous All-America at that position. One of Pitt's 1938 "Dream Backfield" under Jock Sutherland. 3rd in Heisman voting, 1937; 2nd in 1938. In 1936 made 87-yd. kickoff return vs. Carnegie Tech. and 76-yd. rush vs. Ohio Wesleyan. In 1937 made 77-yd. rush vs. Duquesne and 64-yd. rush vs. Wisconsin. During 29-game Pitt career made 2231 yds. on total offense, scored 18 TDs. Played in Rose Bowl, 1937. Enjoyed writing poetry for campus magazine. Chicago Cardinals, 1939-43, 46-48. During World War II served in navy. In 1941 was NFL interception leader with seven for 54 yds., longest 16 yds. Same year was kickoff return leader with 12 for 290 yds., 24.2 average. In 1942 led in kickoff returns with 15, for 393 yds. and 26.2 average. Currently president of machine tool company. Citizens Savings Hall of Fame, National Football Foundation Hall of Fame.

GONSOULIN, AUSTIN (Goose) Defensive Back. B. 6/7/38, Port Arthur, Tex. 6'4", 213. Cornerback for Baylor. Played in Canada one year before joining Denver Broncos in 1960. Broncos had acquired draft rights for Gonsoulin from Dallas Texans in exchange for draft rights to Jack Spikes. Established AFL record for interceptions, game, with four, 9/18/60; led AFL in interceptions that year with 11. Released by Denver in 1966 after completing six seasons. Signed by San Francisco 49ers and played with them one year. Finished seven-year pro career with 46 interceptions for 551 yds., average of 12.0, 2 TDs. Played in AFL

All-Star games, 1962, 63, 64, 65, 67. All-AFL safety, 1960, 62, 63.

GORDON, RICHARD F. End. B. 1/1/44, Cincinnati, Ohio. 5'11", 190. Michigan State, 1962-64. Didn't earn letter until junior year. As senior 2nd in Big 10 rushing (571 yards on 81 carries), All-Conference. Chicago Bears, 1965-72; Los Angeles Rams, 1973; Green Bay Packers, 1973. Traded following 1973 season to New England Patriots for John Mosier. Led NFL receivers, 1970, with 71 receptions for 1026 yds., 13 TDs. All-Pro, 1970. Pro Bowl, 1971, 72. Squabbled with Chicago management, finally playing out option in 1972.

GOSSETT, D. BRUCE Kicker. B. 11/9/41, Cecil, Pa. 6', 230. Attended Duquesne and U. of Richmond. Signed as free agent by Los Angeles Rams, 1964. With Rams thru 1969. Was then traded to San Francisco 49ers for cornerback Kermit Alexander and draft choice. In 1966 established NFL records for FGs attempted with 49, FGs made with 28. 1966 NFL scoring leader with 113 points, (28 FGs, 29 PATs). In 1970 NFC title game scored one FG and PAT, in 1971 title game made 49-yd. FG. Led 49ers in scoring, 1972, with 95 points. Made 18 of 29 FG attempts, longest being 50 yds. Hit 26 of 26 PAT attempts, 26 of 33 FG attempts for 104 points, 1973. In 10-year pro career booted 349 PATs, 208 FGs for 973 points. All-NFC, 1973. Played in Pro Bowl, 1967, 69.

GOVERNALI, PAUL V. Running Back. B. 1/5/21, Bronx, N.Y. 5'11", 195. Played halfback for Columbia, 1940-42. Consensus All-America, 1942. Maxwell Award winner same year. 2nd in Heisman Trophy voting, 1942. In same year set season record in passing yds. per attempt with 8.7; hit 87 of 165 for NCAA leading 1442 yds. Also had season's highest number of interceptions with 18, TDs with 19. Set game record with 5 TD passes vs. Fort Monmouth that year, and made 76-yd. pass vs. Dartmouth. Finished 26-game career with 175 of 384 for 2513 yds., 25 TDs. Made 3369 total-offense yds. on 690 plays. Played for Boston Yanks, 1946-47; New York Giants, 1947-48.

GRABOWSKI, JAMES S. (Grabo) Running Back. B. 9/9/44, Chicago, Ill. 6'2", 225. Fullback for Illinois, 1963-65. Unanimous All-America, 1965, All-America, 1964. Academic All-America, 1964-65. 3rd in Heisman Trophy voting, 1965. In 1964 led NCAA in average yds. per rush with 5.4 (1004 yds. on 186 carries). Made 58-yd. rush vs. Michigan State and 55-yd. rush vs. SMU, 1964. In '64 Rose Bowl rushed for 125 yds. on 23 carries. Selected by Miami Dolphins on 1st round of 1965 AFL draft, same round by Green Bay Packers of NFL. Chose Packers. He and Texas Tech All-America Donny Anderson joined club same year, 1966. Pair was groomed to replace Paul Hornung and Jim Taylor, touted as great backfield of future. Grabowski disappointing. Exceeded 300 yds. rushing only twice in six-year NFL career. Played final season with Chicago Bears, 1971. Appeared in NFL title game, 1966, and scored TD, recovering Dallas Cowboy fumble. Super Bowl, 1967.

GRADISHAR, RANDY Linebacker. B. 3/3/52, Champion, Ohio. 6'3", 236.

Outstanding for Ohio State, 1971-73. Consensus All-America, 1972, 73. One of best linebackers in Big 10 history. George Hill, State's defensive coordinator, said, "Randy is a great linebacker not only because of his tremendous physical attributes, but also because he is extremely intelligent. He makes plays no other linebacker in the country can make." Finished '73 season with 124 stops for career average of 103 per season. National Football Foundation Hall of Fame Scholar-Athlete, 1973. Rose Bowl, twice vs. Southern Cal., 1973, 74. Ohio State won, 42-21, 1974. Drafted on 1st round of 1974 NFL draft by Denver Broncos, on 3rd round of WFL draft.

GRAHAM, J. KENNETH (Kenny) Defensive Back. B. 11/25/41, Texarkana, Tex. 6'0", 205. Attended Washington State. Selected by San Diego Charges on 13th round of 1964 NFL draft. Played for Chargers thru 1969. Divided 1970 with Cincinnati Bengals and Pittsburgh Steelers. All-AFL, 1966. Played in AFL All-Star games 1966, 68, 69. Played in AFL championship games, 1964, 65.

GRAHAM, OTTO (Automatic Otto) Quarterback. B. 12/6/21, Waukegan, Ill. 6', 205. Northwestern, 1941-43. All-America, 1943 (also in basketball). As Illinois prep made All-State team in basketball and football; also played baseball, ran in track meets and was good swimmer. Known as one of four musical Graham brothers. Played piano, cornet, violin and French horn. Offered scholarships by several colleges, all for basketball, and selected Northwestern. There won eight letters; three in basketball, three in football and two in baseball. In 1942 established Big 10 passing record with 89 of 182 for 1092 yds. In 1943, vs. Wisconsin, scored four TDs and three PATs, passed for one TD, winning 40-0. Ran 97 yds. for TD to lead 1943 College All-Stars to 27-7 victory over Washington Redskins. After graduation entered V-12 program for navy pilots. Navy sent him to Colgate where he played basketball and became All-America for second time. When World War II ended Otto played pro basketball for Rochester Royals.

Reported to AAFC Cleveland Browns in 1946. Was first player signed by Paul Brown. AAFC passing co-leader, 1946, with 95 of 174 for 1834 yds. Led in 1947 with 163 of 269 for 2753 yds.; in 1948 with 173 of 333 for 2713 yds.; in 1949 with 161 of 285 for 2785 yds. In Browns' first NFL game, vs. Philadelphia Eagles in 1950, completed 21 of 38 passes for 346 yds. and 3 TDs. In 1952 led NFL in passing yardage (2816). Led again in 1953 with 167 of 258 for 2722 yds. Against Los Angeles Rams, in 1955 title game, passed for 2 TDs, ran for 2 TDs, hit 14 of 25 for 209 yds. Including AAFC record, Graham completed 1464 of 2614 career passes for 23,614 yds. and 175 TDs. In 10 seasons with Cleveland won divisional title each season and won league championship seven times. Retired as player, 1955. All-NFL, 1951, 52, 53, 54, 55, 57. Became U.S. Coast Guard Academy director of athletics and head football coach. Later, 1966-68, Washington Redskins head coach, preceding Vince Lombardi. Elected to Pro Football Hall of Fame in 1965 when he was 43, youngest member to be elected. Citizens Savings Hall of Fame, National Football Foundation Hall of Fame. Returned to Coast Guard, after leaving Redskins, as athletic director.

123

GRANGE, HAROLD E. (Red) Running Back. B. 6/13/03, Forksville, Pa. 5'10", 170. Hailed as "Galloping Ghost"; "Wheaton Ice Man"; "Old 77." Spectacular career at Illinois, 1923-25. Consensus All-America, 1925; All-America, 1923, 24. At age 15, while in high school, injured leg in ice-wagon accident and told would never play football again; he was ill-advised. Went ahead to win prep letters four years in basketball, baseball, football, track. Scored 75 TDs, 82 PATs for 532 points. In first collegiate game vs. Nebraska, 1923, scored 3 TDs; at end of season had scored 12 TDs and gained 1296 yds. In 1924, vs. Michigan, scored 4 TDs in first 12 minutes, on 95-yd. kickoff return and rushes of 67, 55 and 44 yds.; later scored 5th TD and threw TD pass to finish with 402 total yds. "It was the most spectacular single-handed performance ever delivered in a major game," lauded Alonzo Stagg. In 20 games at Illinois gained 4085 yds. (all categories), scored 31 TDs for 186 points. Grange and Illinois coach Bob Zuppke formed mutual admiration society.

Signed by George Halas in 1925 to play for Chicago Bears; he packed stadiums around country, earning well over $100,000 that year. After money dispute with Halas in 1926, Grange and his manager, C. C. Pyle (called "Cash and Carry"), started own league with New York Yankees. League was financial disaster and folded after one year; New York was then given NFL franchise and retained name Yankees. Played for Yankees, 1927; sat out 1928 due to knee injury; returned to Bears, 1929-34. On 1/27/35, in post-season exhibition game, reinjured knee and left field, never to play again. Assistant coach for Bears, 1936. From high school thru pros played in 247 games, carried ball 4013 times for 33,820 yds. Went into insurance business, then became radio and television announcer for Bears. Retired to Florida where enjoys golf, fishing and boating. Citizens Savings Player of the Year, 1924. Silver Football, 1924. All-Pro, 1931. Citizens Savings Hall of Fame, National Football Foundation Hall of Fame, Pro Football Hall of Fame. Unanimous choice for Modern All-Time All-America team (post-1919); named to Parke Davis' All-Time All-America team (1871-1934).

GRANT, HAROLD P. (Bud) Coach. B. 5/20/27, Superior, Wis. Graduated from Minnesota, 1950. 1st-round draft pick of Philadelphia Eagles that year. Played with Eagles thru 1952. Winnipeg Blue Bombers, 1953-56. In six-year career as player caught 272 passes. Also played pro basketball with world champion Minneapolis Lakers, 1950, 51. In 1957 became Winnipeg coach, winning four Grey Cup titles in 10 years. Left Winnipeg for Minnesota Vikings, 1967. 1968 team finished 1st in Central Division but lost playoff to Dallas Cowboys, 17-13. In 1969 won NFL title but lost Super Bowl to Kansas City Chiefs, 23-7. Won NFC title, 1973, but lost Super Bowl VIII to Miami Dolphins, 24-7. Fined $2500 for criticizing training quarters for Vikings at Super Bowl VIII in Houston. In seven years as Viking coach, 1967-73, has record of 70-25-3. Avid hunter, fisherman, naturalist.

GRANTHAM, J. LARRY Linebacker. B. 9/16/38, Crystal Springs, Miss. 6', 210. Attended Mississippi on baseball scholarship. Played end on football varsity, 1957-59. Sugar Bowl, 1959, 60; Gator Bowl, 1958. Also in Hula Bowl. In 1960 drafted by New York Titans on 1st round. Titans became Jets, 1962. Played with club thru 1972. Had best season in 1971 when elected Jet MVP, playing every game. Suffered broken cheekbone in 3rd quarter of last game of season. Named Pro Athlete of the Year in Mississippi, 1967. Played in AFL All-Star games following 1962, 63, 64, 66, 67 seasons. Played in AFL title game, 1968, and Super Bowl, 1969. All-AFL, 1962, 64. Played in more games (173) than any other Jet.

GRAVES, ERNEST (Pot) Coach. B. 3/27/1880, N.C. D. 6/9/53, Washington, D.C. North Carolina fullback; Army fullback-tackle, 1902-04. Primarily lineman at West Point. Learned basics of line play vs. such Yale stalwarts as Tom Shevlin, Ned Glass, James Hogan. Graduated 2nd in Class of 1905. Borrowed from army duty to coach Harvard, 1908, at intercession of President Theodore Roosevelt who was Crimson football enthusiast. Except in World War I years, Graves was line coach from 1913-22. Developed All-Americas John McEwan, Cowboy Meacham, Babe Weyand, Biff Jones. "Let's see some blood," was common Graves exhortation. Known as "Father of the Engineers." Member Mississippi River Commission, 1927-52. In 1931 named chairman of Interoceanic Canal Board. Brig. Gen. Ernest Graves died at Walter Reed Army Hospital.

GRAYSON, DAVID L. Defensive Back. B. 6/6/39, San Diego, Calif. 5'10", 185. Attended San Diego J.C. and U. of Oregon. Signed as free agent by Dallas Texans, 1961. AFL kickoff-return leader in average yds. with 28.3 (16 for 453 yds.). In 1963 Texans became Kansas City Chiefs. In 1965 traded to Oakland Raiders for defensive back Fred Williamson, played thru 1970. Led AFL in interceptions with 10, 1968, and set AFL career record for yds. on interceptions with 776 (since broken). Gained 933 yds. on interceptions during career. AFL All-Star games, 1963, 64, 65, 66, 67. Played in AFL title games, 1962, 67, 68. Super Bowl, 1968. All-AFL cornerback, 1963, 64, 65, 68, 69.

GRAYSON, ROBERT H. (Bobby) Running Back. B. 12/8/14, Portland, Ore. 5'11", 190. Stanford fullback, 1933-35. Consensus All-America, 1934. Unanimous All-America, 1935. In 1934 Rose Bowl gained 152 yds. rushing. In 1935 Rose Bowl scored one TD, rushed for 59 yds. Also played in 1936 Rose Bowl. Clocked at 9.8 in 100-yd. dash. Superb clutch player. In 1934 led Pacific Coast Conference in scoring. Slippery and strong. In Pop Warner system handled ball on every play. Sixty-minute man. Sure tackler, alert pass defender. In game vs. Washington intercepted four passes, two for TDs. Played on three conference champions, losers of only two games. Called "best back I've ever seen" by Ernie Nevers. Billed as best in nation by Lou Little. In 486-play career gained 2108 total-offense yds. In 1936 drafted on 1st round by Pittsburgh Steelers, but sold to New York Giants for $25,000. Because Giants offered only $5,000 salary, he elected to attend Stanford Law School, serve as backfield coach. Thus never played pro ball. High school baseball teammate of Joe

Gordon; set Oregon prep records in 100- and 200-yd. dashes. Nephew of Harry Grayson, NEA sports editor. Currently Greyhound Corp. executive. Citizens Savings Hall of Fame, National Football Foundation Hall of Fame.

GREEN, BOBBY JOE Kicker. B. 5/7/36, Vernon, Tex. 5'11", 175. Attended Florida. Signed as free agent by Pittsburgh Steelers, 1960. That year led NFL in punts with 64, average of 44.2 yds. Traded to Chicago Bears, 1962. Led again, 1966, in number of punts with 80, average of 42.0 yds. Played in NFL championship game, 1963, and in 1971 Pro Bowl. Holds NFL career records for most punts and most yds. Plays guitar, sings country and western ballads. Operates large cattle ranch in Florida during off-season. Spent 12th season with Bears in 1973.

GREEN, CORNELL Defensive Back. B. 2/10/40, Oklahoma City, Okla. 6'3", 208. Grew up in Richmond, Calif. Attended Utah State, 1960-62. Played no football in college, only basketball. Was All-America as sophomore, thrice All-Skyline Conference. Averaged more than 20 points per game in three varsity seasons. Signed with Dallas Cowboys as free agent, 1963. Within five seasons was All-NFL cornerback. In 1970 switched to strong safety. All-NFL also in 1969, 71. Pro Bowl, 1966, 67, 68, 72. NFL championship games, 1968, 69, 70, 71. Cowboys won Super Bowl VI, 24-3, over Miami Dolphins, 1972. His 32 interceptions are second only to Mel Renfro in Dallas history. Brother, Pumpsie, was American League infielder.

GREEN, JOSEPH (Mean Joe) Tackle. B. 9/24/46, Temple, Tex. 6'4", 270. Played at North Texas State, 1966-68. All-America, 1968. Picked by Pittsburgh Steelers on 1st round of 1969 draft and has been with team since. Very fast, known to have beaten some halfbacks to locker room. Claims "there's no such thing as hitting too hard." Seldom studies films. A.P. NFL Defensive Rookie of the year, 1969. Has been ejected several times for unnecessary roughness. After one ejection was fined $2000 for depriving club of services. Great tackler; by own admission, "liquidator" of quarterbacks. Pro Bowl, 1970, 71, 72, 73, 74. All-Pro, 1970, 71, 72, 73. Generally acclaimed as top defensive lineman in 1972. Won NEA George Halas Trophy as most valuable defensive lineman; named NFL Defensive Player of the Year by A.P., and AFC Lineman of the Year by UPI.

GREEN, WOODROW, JR. (Woody) Running Back. B. 9/20/52, Warren, Ore. 6'1", 202. Played halfback for Arizona State, 1971-73. Consensus All-America, 1972, 73. Finished career 4th on all-time collegiate rushing list. Gained 3754 yds., scored 33 TDs, averaged 6.25 yds. per carry. Fourth collegiate player to pass 1000 yds. rushing three times. Finished last year with 1182 yds. in 184 carries for 6.42 average, 9 TDs. Also made 22 pass receptions for 328 yds. 5 TDs; was 5th in nation in all-purpose running with 158.9 yds. per game. Played on winning Fiesta Bowl teams, 1971, 72, 73. Has 9.5 speed in 100-yd. dash, making him exceptional outside speed threat. Also great power inside. Considered by many scouts finest runner in college football in 1973. Selected on 1st round of 1974 NFL draft by

126

Kansas City Chiefs, 1st round of WFL draft by Florida. Signed with Chiefs.

GREGG, A. FORREST Tackle. B. 10/18/33, Birthright, Tex. 6'4", 250. Attended Southern Methodist. Selected by Green Bay Packers on 2nd round of 1956 NFL draft. Played with Pack, 1956, 58-70. Was player-coach last two years. In military service, 1957. Bulwark of powerful Green Bay offensive line. Played in 188 consecutive games, an NFL record. Played with Dallas Cowboys, 1971. In 1972 became offensive line coach for San Diego Chargers. Pro Bowl, 1962, 63, 64, 65, 66, 67, 71. Super Bowl, 1967, 68, 72. All-NFL, 1960 thru 1967.

GREGORY, JACK, JR. Defensive End. B. 10/3/44, Okolona, Miss. 6'5", 250. Dad, Jack Sr., was guard for 1951 Cleveland Rams. Jack Jr. was collegian at Chattanooga and Delta State. Played with Cleveland Browns, 1967-71. Was starter, 1967-70. Played out option in 1971, joining New York Giants. In 1972 sacked opposing quarterbacks 21 times, three more than entire Giant team of 1971. Big, strong, aggressive. Played in 1969 NFL championship game. Pro Bowl, 1970, 73. All-Pro, 1972.

GRIER, ROOSEVELT (Rosey) Tackle. B. 7/19/32, Linden. N. J. 6'5", 290. Penn State, 1952-54. New York Giants, 1955-56, 58-62; Los Angeles Rams, 1963-66. Missed 1957 due to military service. Outstanding defensive tackle. Was one of Rams' "Fearsome Foursome," along with Lamar Lundy, Merlin Olsen, Deacon Jones. Since retiring from football has sung and acted professionally. Also wrote book entitled *Needlepoint for Men*. Appeared in NFL championship games, 1956, 58, 59, 61, 62. All-NFL, 1956.

GRIESE, ROBERT A. Quarterback. B. 2/3/45, Evansville, Ind. 6'1", 190. Played QB for Purdue, 1964-66. Consensus All-America, 1965; All-America, 1966. 2nd in Heisman Trophy, voting, 1965. In 1965, vs. Notre Dame, completed 19 of 22 passes, percentage of .864. Vs. Indiana, 1966, completed 80-yd. pass. In 1967 Rose Bowl completed 10 of 18 passes for 139 yds., kicked 2 PATs. In collegiate career had .571 passing percentage for 4402 yds., gained 4892 yds. total offense, scored 189 points. Picked on 1st round by Miami Dolphins. On 10/22/67 set AFL record for highest pass completion percentage in one game, 20 or more attempts, going 17 of 21 for 81 percent. Combined with Earl Morrall to lead Dolphins to AFC title in club's sixth season, 1971, earliest title for any expansion club. At age 27, in 1973, was second youngest QB to lead team to Super Bowl win (Joe Namath was 25). AFC passing leader in 1971 with 145 completions in 263 attempts for 2089 yds. AFC Player of the Year and winner of Jim Thorpe Trophy, w1-71. In 1971 AFC title game completed 75-yd TD pass to Paul Warfield. In 1973 completed 116 passes in 218 attempts for 1422 yds., 8 interceptions, 17 TDs. Star of 1973 Super Bowl vs. Washington Redskins. All-AFC, 1970, 71, 73. Pro Bowl, 1971, 72, 74. Played in AFL All-Star games, 1968, 69. Super Bowl, 1972, 73, 74. Models men's fashions, represents National Air Lines, and runs boys camp with Karl Noonan. Does some TV commercials. Cool, articulate, talented.

GRIFFIN, ARCHIE Running Back. B. 8/21/54, Columbus, Ohio. 5'9", 182. Ohio State, 1972-73. In sophomore year, 1973, gained over 100 yds. rushing in every game, totaling 1577. Broke Big 10 single season rushing record. In 1974 Rose Bowl ran 47 yds. for final TD and rolled up total of 149 yds. rushing. "Archie is a remarkable little player," praised Woody Hayes. Powerful, fast tailback. Might eventually rate as greatest runner in Ohio State history.

GRIM, ROBERT L. End. B. 5/8/45, Oakland, Calif. 6', 198. Played three positions in college at Oregon State. MVP in Senior Bowl, 1966. Chosen on 2nd round of 1967 draft by Minnesota Vikings. Against New York Giants, 1967, returned punt 81 yds. for NFL's top seasonal effort. In 1972 dealt to Giants for QB Fran Tarkenton. Played in NFC championship game, 1969, and in Super Bowl, 1970. Pro Bowl, 1971, 72. All-NFC, 1971.

GRISHAM, JIMMIE C. (Jim) Running Back. B. 12/4/42, Houston, Tex. 6'2", 205. Played high school football at Olney, Tex., scoring 21 TDs in 1959 senior year. U. of Oklahoma fullback, 1961-63. Teamed last two years with Joe Don Looney; they gave Bud Wilkinson his greatest fullback-halfback combination. Grisham was tremendous on short-yardage. Often linebacker in crucial situations. Ranked with Sooners' great power backs, joining Leon Heath, Prentice Gautt, Buck McPhail.

GROMAN, WILLIAM F. End. B. 7/17/36, Tiffin, Ohio. 6'0", 194. Graduated from Heidelberg, 1958. Played for Houston Oilers, 1960-63; Buffalo Bills, 1964-65. In 1960 led AFL in yds. on pass receptions with 1473, also led in average yds. per reception with 20.5. In 1961 tied Don Hutson and Elroy Hirsch record for TD passes, season, 17. Led AFL that year in average yds. on pass receptions with 23.5, in TDs with 18. Played in AFL championship games 1960, 61, 62, 64. All-AFL, 1960.

GROSSCUP, CLYDE L. Quarterback. B. 12/27/36, Santa Monica, Calif. 6'1", 185. Utah, 1957-59. As junior, vs. Army, put on one of finest exhibitions of passing ever seen at the Point. Played for New York Giants, 1960-61; New York Titans, 1962. In 1962 exhibition game threw two long TD passes, one of them for 80 yds. Later, in regular season vs. Buffalo Bills, threw two short TD passes. Removed, in Titan '62 home opener, because of torn ligaments. Had reputation as erratic passer. Became sportswriter, announcer. Authored book, *Fourth and One.*

GROZA, LOUIS (The Toe) Tackle-Kicker. B. 1/25/24, Martins Ferry, Ohio. 6'3", 250. Played only freshman football at Ohio State, 1942. Then entered army, served with 96th Infantry in Far East, 1943-45. Joined first Cleveland Brown team when AAFC was formed in 1946. Played thru 1967, spending entire career with Browns. Missed 1961 with back injury. Coach Paul Brown insisted Lou go back to school in off-season, and he eventually received degree in marketing. Was fine offensive tackle, as well as kicker. After back injury served primarily as kicker. Led AAFC in FGs with 13, in scoring with 84 points his rookie year. In four years of AAFC scored 165 PATs, 30 FGs and 259 points, ranking as 2nd highest scorer in league's history. Led NFL in FGs five times: 1950 with 13, '52 with 19, '53 with 23, '54 with 16, '57 with 15. Tied Sam Baker for 1957 scoring lead with 77 points.

Groza retired having scored record 1609 points, despite only single TD. Scored in 107 consecutive games, 1950-59. In NFL career, 1950-60, 62-67, scored 641 PATs, including streak of 138; also booted 234 straight FGs. Played in all four title games in AAFC, 1946, 47, 48, 49; nine in NFL, 1950, 51, 52, 53, 54, 55, 57, 64, 66, for record 13. Scored 55 points in NFL title games (25 PATs, 10 FGs). On 12/26/54, vs. Detroit Lions, scored eight PATs for playoff game record. His longest game FGs were 52 yds. vs. Los Angeles Rams, 1951, and 43 yds. vs. Lions, 1953. Became insurance executive and part owner of dry-cleaning company and boys camp. *Sporting News* Player of the Year, 1954. All Pro, 1951, 52, 53, 54, 55, 57. Pro Bowl, 1950, 51, 52, 53, 54, 55, 57, 58, 59. Pro Football Hall of Fame. Brother of Alex Groza, Kentucky All-America basketball player.

GUGLIELMI, RALPH V. (Goog) Quarterback. B. Columbus, Ohio. 6', 185. Great prep career at Grandview H.S. of Columbus. Wanted by Kentucky (for basketball) and Ohio State but spurned them both for Notre Dame. Played QB Irish, 1951-54. Unanimous All-America, 1954. 4th in Heisman voting, 1954. Led Irish three years in passing and, as defensive player, twice in interceptions. In 1954 completed 68 passes in 127 attempts for 1162 yds., 6 TDs. His four-year passing total of 3117 yds. is Notre Dame record. Also broke Bob Williams' career record with 209 completions in 436 attempts. College All-Star game MVP, 1955. Drafted by Washington Redskins on 1st round of 1954 draft. Played with Redskins, 1955, 58, 60; St. Louis Cardinals, 1961; New York Giants, 1962-63; Philadelphia Eagles, 1963. Led Redskins in passing, 1960, with 125 completions in 223 attempts for 1547 yds., 9 TDs. Also threw 19 interceptions.

GULICK, MERLE A. Quarterback. B. 6/19/06, Jackson, Mich. 6', 180. Called "Hobart Hurricane." Collegiate quarterback at Toledo, 1925, and Hobart, 1927-29. Played high school football, basketball, baseball, track at Maumee, Ohio, starting as 90-pound freshman. Earned 15 high school letters. Played four varsity sports at Toledo, 1925. Lacrosse All-America, 1927, after transferring to Hobart. Basketball captain and baseball player for Statesmen. In 1928 scored 18 TDs, including 99-yd. run from scrimmage, breaking own 1927 record by single yd. All-America mention, 1929. Picked by every opponent as All-Opponent QB. Class president four years; honor society; won Welch Cup for scholastic achievement. Coast Guard Capt. in World War II. Received Legion of Merit. Was vice president of Equitable Life Assurance Society of the U.S. National Football Foundation Hall of Fame.

GUMMERE, WILLIAM S. Founder. B. 6/24/1850, Trenton, N.J. D. 1/26/33, Newark, N.Y. Attended Princeton, 1866-70. Princeton's foremost athlete of era; competing in baseball, track and field; was football leader. In fall of 1869

Gummere and Rutgers' football pioneer, William S. Leggett, scheduled game and set up rules. Each selected and trained players, captained respective teams in match held at New Brunswick, N.J., 11/13/69. Game gave birth to American football. Gummere pioneered in another sport—baseball. Is thought to have invented hook slide. Became chief justice of Supreme Court of New Jersey. Maintained active and intense interest in football all his life.

GUY, RAY Defensive Back-Kicker. B. 12/22/49, Swainsboro, Ga. 6'3", 190. Southern Mississippi, 1970-72. All-America, 1972. Against Mississippi, 1971, punted 93 yds., 4th longest in NCAA history. Holds NCAA record for longest FG, 61 yds., vs. Utah State, 11/18/72. Was 1972 NCAA punting leader, making 58 punts for 2680 yds., 46.2 average. Ranks 2nd in NCAA career punting with 200 punts for 8934 yds., average of 44.7. In career made 51 of 59 PAT attempts, 25 of 59 FG attempts, including seven of 40 yds. or longer. Of his 101 kickoffs, 55 passed goal line. Made eight pass interceptions in 1972 to rank 4th in nation. Excelled as pitcher in baseball, averaging better than one strikeout per inning. 1973 College All-Star game MVP, averaging 44.1 yds. on nine punts vs. Miami Dolphins. Selected by Oakland Raiders on 1st round of 1973 NFL draft. As pro rookie, 1973, averaged 45.3 yds. on 69 punts (3127 yds.). Longest was 72 yds. Pro Bowl, 1974.

GUYON, JOSEPH Tackle-Running Back. B. 11/26/1892, Mohnomen, Minn. D. 11/27/71. 5'11", 190. Tackle and halfback at Carlisle under Pop Warner, 1912-13. Blocked for Jim Thorpe. When Thorpe left school, Guyon replaced him at halfback. Backfield star for Georgia Tech under John Heisman, 1917-18. Consensus All-America, 1918. 1917 team, ranked as one of Tech's finest, scored 491 points and defeated nine opponents. Guyon was big and fast, exceptional blocker and ball carrier, handled punting. Vs. Vanderbilt, 10/27/17, averaged 28.7 yds. per rush (12 for 344 yds.), pre-1937 NCAA record. Heisman rated him as one of three or four greatest players of all time. Canton Bulldogs, 1919-20; Cleveland Indians, 1921, Oorang Indians, 1922-23; Rock Island Independents, 1924; Kansas City Cowboys, 1924-25, New York Giants, 1927. Punted 95 yds., 11/14/20, pro record which stood for 50 years until 98-yd. punt by Steve O'Neal (New York Jets). National Football Foundation Hall of Fame, Pro Football Hall of Fame.

130

HACKBART, DALE L. Defensive Back. B. 7/7/38, Madison, Wis. 6'4", 210. Graduated from Wisconsin, 1960. Won Big 10 Medal of Honor that year. Drafted on 5th round by Green Bay Packers. In 1960 played pro baseball with Grand Forks of Northern League, and with Packers. Traded to Washington Redskins for draft choice, 1961. Played in CFL, 1964-65. Minnesota Viking taxi squad, 1965. Vikings, 1966-70. On 9/13/71 traded to St. Louis Cardinals with linebacker Mike McGill and 4th-round draft pick, for tight end Bob Brown, defensive back Nate Wright. Traded to Denver Broncos, 1973. Punter as well as defensive back. NFL championship game, 1960. Super Bowl, 1969.

HADL, JOHN Quarterback. B. 2/15/40, Lawrence, Kan. 6'1", 214. Kansas, 1959-61. Halfback two years, then switched to QB. All-America, 1960-61. Was NCAA punting leader, 1959, with average of 45.6 yds. on 43 for 1960 yds. That year made 98-yd. interception return vs. Texas Christian, 97-yd. kickoff return vs. Syracuse, 94-yd. punt vs. Oklahoma. Played in Astro-Bluebonnet Bowl, 1961. Only player ever honored MVP in both East-West Shrine, College All-Star games. San Diego Chargers, 1962-72. Los Angeles Rams, 1973. No. 3 draft choice of Chargers. AFL passing leader, 1965, with 174 completions in 348 attempts for 2789 yds. Same season set AFL playoff game record, punting average, with 51.4 yds. In 1967-68 threw TD passes in 19 consecutive games, tying AFL record. Had only six passes intercepted in 1968 tying record for fewest in season. NFL Man of the Year (voted by fans), 1971. In early 1973 traded to Rams for defensive end Coy Bacon and running back Bob Thomas. Guided

Rams that year into NFC playoffs. 1973 passing record: 258 attempts, 135 completions, 15 interceptions, .523 percentage, 2008 yds., 8.49-yd. average, 22 TDs. AFL All-Star games, 1965, 66, 69, 70. AFL championship games, 1963, 65. UPI Player of the Year, 1973, also *Sporting News* Player of the Year. All-AFC, 1973. Pro Bowl, 1974. Called "best passer in the league" by no less authority than Joe Namath. Active in real estate development and charity projects.

HAIK, J. MICHAEL (Mac) End. B. 1/9/46, Meridian, Miss. 6'1", 196. Graduated from Mississippi, 1968. As sophomore played "monster back" before becoming wide receiver. In college, 54 receptions, 755 yds., 6 TDs. Drafted on 2nd round by Houston Oilers. As 1968 rookie accumulated 32 receptions, 584 yds., 8 TDs. Good speed, moves, hands. Retired in 1972 after five seasons, all with Oilers. Currently owns modeling agency, works in real estate.

HALAS, GEORGE S. (Papa Bear) Coach. B. 2/2/95, Chicago, Ill. End for Bob Zuppke at Illinois, 1915-17. Played at 6', 164. Also captained basketball team and played baseball. Suffered broken jaw in college. Entered navy during World War I and led Great Lakes Naval Training Station football team to 1919 Rose Bowl. Played outfield for New York Yankees (baseball), 1919, participating in six games and then suffered leg injury sliding. Returned to minors; was headed back to Yankees when heard of formation of football league. Attended organizational meeting at Canton, Ohio, in 1920, whence NFL was founded, as American Professional Football Association. Represented Staley Starchmakers, Inc., of Decatur, Ill. (for whose baseball team he also played center field and worked in factory). Became player-coach of Staleys in league's first season, 1920. Team moved to Chicago in 1921 and became Bears year later. On 11/23/23, vs. Oorang Indians, Halas recovered fumble and returned it 98 yds., record for many years. Picked up ball on own 2-yd. line, chased length of field by Jim Thorpe. Hit 10 yds. from goal line but managed to slide across for TD. Admitted being scared and said, "If anyone but Thorpe had been chasing me, I doubt if I could have made it."

In 1929 retired as player and "fired" himself as coach. Borrowed money to buy out partner Dutch Sternaman in 1932, becoming sole owner of Bears. Returned to coaching, 1933. In 1934 watched team play in first College All-Star game, brainchild of Arch Ward (Chicago *Tribune* sportswriter who also invented baseball All-Star game); Halas had once recommended Ward for NFL presidency. Final score, 0-0. Led "Monsters of the Midway" to 1940 NFL title, won by largest single-game score in league history, 73-10, over Washington Redskins. Re-entered navy during World War II, 1943, then returned to coach Bears, 1946-55. Left football for three years, returning again to Bears for 1958-67 period. Retired in 1968, having coached total of 40 years, to become club's chairman of the board. Holds records for most years as head coach, most championship games won with seven. Won three other divisional crowns and finished 15 times in 2nd place. Only seven of his 40 teams finished below .500. Coaching record with Bears was 320-147-29.

Was pioneer in many aspects of game. His success with T-formation, man-in-motion attack in 1940 title game set style for modern football. Developed use of two receivers rather than one, flanker as receiver rather than decoy. First coach to hold daily practices, to utilize films of opponents, to barnstorm team, to have games broadcast on radio, to use tarpaulin on field for weather protection. Campaigned for dual Rookie of the Year awards, one for offense and one for defense. Drafted and coached such players as Red Grange, Danny Fortmann, Bronco Nagurski, George McAfee, George Trafton, Sid Luckman, Joe Stry-dahar, Bill George, Bill Hewitt, Gale Sayers. In 1965 brought suit against Chicago assistant coach George Allen to prevent him from joining Los Angeles Rams. Lost suit, and Allen. Named president of NFC, 1970. Only man still in game to have started from pro football's inception in 1920. Pro Football Hall of Fame.

HALL, EDWARD K. Coach. B. 7/9/1870, Granville, Ill. D. 11/10/32, Hanover, N. H. Attended Oberlin College, then transferred to Dartmouth in 1889. End for Dartmouth 1889, 90, 91. Captain his final year. Also won letters in baseball and track. Upon graduation in 1892 received offer from U. of Illinois to organize football and track teams. Along with Alonzo Stagg of Chicago and Parke Davis of Wisconsin, under sponsorship of Chicago Athletic Club, started first annual Western Intercollegiate Championships, 6/94. At Chicago, 19 leading colleges and universities from Midwest competed. In fall of 1894 entered Harvard Law School. Edited *Harvard Law Journal,* and graduated with Bachelor of Law degree, 6/96. Practiced law in Scranton, Pa., and then Boston. Later became vice president of A.T. & T. in New York City. For 15 years was alumni representative on Dartmouth Athletic Council, active alumni member of its board of trustees. Helped organize National Collegiate Athletic Association, (NCAA), 1905. Served on Rules Committee for football, becoming its secretary in 1907 and chairman in 1911. Was opposed to selection of "All" teams and to presentation of awards or trophies, except from player's own school, "Because," he said, "such practices tend to give a boy a false attitude towards life and so interfere with his development, his character, and his career. Sports, no matter how large may be the crowds, after all, are merely minor incidents in a scheme of education."

In 1930 supervised committee which completely recodified the rules. Author of "Football Code." Active as game official, 1906-12. During World War I served on Committee on Education and Special Training of War Department. Retired from business, 1930, returning to Dartmouth as resident lecturer in School of Business Administration. At 25th convention of NCAA presented with inscribed gold football in recognition of service on Rules Committee. Upon news of his death in 1932, news dispatch referred to him as "the savior of American college football." National Football Foundation Hall of Fame.

HALL, L. PARKER Quarterback. B. Tunica, Miss. Played for Mississippi, 1936-38. In senior year was NCAA scoring leader, accounting for 73 points on 11 TDs and 7 PATs. Cleveland Rams, 1939-42. Made 12 punts for Green Bay Packers, 10/26/39. Led league in passing with 106 completions in 208 attempts for 1227 yds. and 9 TDs, 1939. Won Joseph Carr Trophy as rookie, 1939. Played for San Francisco 49ers (AAFC), 1946.

HALL, ROBERT A. Quarterback. B. 9/9/06, Omaha, Neb. 138. Conducted successful fight for TV control plan in 1951, limiting number of games televised. At time, chairman of NCAA TV Committee, Yale Board of Athletic Control. One of best-versed football men in nation. QB for Yale in late 1920s. Was one of lightest players in Elis' history. While studying law served as Yale assistant coach. In 1930s among pioneers in football broadcasting, later TV. Served as film advisor to American Football Coaches All-America Selection Committee.

HAM, JACK Linebacker. B. 12/23/48, Johnstown, Pa. 6'1", 225. Lineman for Penn State, 1968-70. Consensus All-America, 1970. Starred in 1969, 70 Orange Bowls. Drafted on 2nd round by Pittsburgh Steelers, 1971. Led all NFL linebackers in interceptions with seven, 1972. Nick Skorich, Cleveland Brown coach, said of him: "He's so quick, so intuitive, that you just don't get a jump on him. If you can't get him out of position, he's going to hurt you." Fans carry signs saying "dobre shonka," Polish for "good ham." All-AFC, 1973. Pro Bowl, 1974.

HAMILTON, ROBERT A. (Bones) Running Back. Stanford, 1933-35. All-America, 1934, 35. Three teammates, Bobby Reynolds, Bobby Grayson, Monk Moscrip, also made All-America both years. Foursome was backbone of "Vow Boys," so-called because they vowed as freshmen that they'd never lose to Southern California; it was a vow not broken. Overall, during three-year period, Stanford won 25, lost 4, tied 2. In three Rose Bowls Indians lost to Columbia (7-0) and Alabama (29-13), defeated Southern Methodist (7-0). Hamilton captained team against SMU. Considered fine runner but forte was blocking. Also defensive stalwart. Served in navy in World War II. Past director of Stanford Alumni Association. President of Bones Hamilton Buick Co., Inc., Van Nuys, Calif. National Football Foundation Hall of Fame.

HAMILTON, THOMAS J. Running Back. B. 12/26/05, Hoopestown, Ill. 180. Navy, 1924-26. All-America, 1926. Twice Navy coach, 1934-36 and '46-47. One of founders of Naval Pre-Flight Training Program during World War II. One-time skipper of *Enterprise*. Won nine varsity letters, three each in football, baseball, basketball. Class president. Saved Navy season, 1926, kicking FG to tie Army, 21-21. Only 29 when named Navy head coach, had 19-8 record in first session. Athletic director for Navy, 1948. Retired from service in 1949 (as Rear Adm.) to become athletic director at Pitt. Head coach there 1951, 54. Later commissioner of Pacific 8 Conference. Member USOC Board of Directors, NCAA Rules Committee. First chairman, NCAA Football TV Committee. Served on President's Advisory Council on Physical Fitness under Eisenhower and Kennedy. National Football Foundation Hall of Fame. Foundation's 1970 Gold Medal winner; has served as its vice president.

HANBURGER, CHRISTIAN, JR. Linebacker. B. 8/3/41, Fort Bragg, N.C.

6'2", 218. Graduated from North Carolina. Center and linebacker for Tar Heels. Played in Gator Bowl, 1963. Drafted on 18th round by Washington Redskins, 1966. Became one of best linebackers in NFL. Makes numerous "big" plays for 'Skins. Causes many fumbles. Intercepted 2 passes for 30 yds., 1 TD vs. Dallas Cowboys, 1968. Recovered 1 fumble for 19-yd. TD vs. Dallas, 1969. In 1971 scored on 16-yd. fumble recovery vs. St. Louis Cardinals. One of several NFL players who represented league in Vietnam, spring, 1970. Visited frontline troops. All-Pro, 1972. Super Bowl, 1973. Pro Bowl, 1967, 68, 69, 70, 73, 74. Voted NFC Defensive Player of the Year, 1972.

HANRATTY, TERRANCE H. (Terry) Quarterback. B. 1/19/48, Butler, Pa. 6'1", 200. Played QB for Notre Dame, 1966-68. Unanimous All-America, 1968. 3rd in Heisman Trophy voting same year. Completed 84-yd. pass vs. Purdue and 56-yd. pass vs. North Carolina, 1966. Involved in 75 plays (2nd in NCAA history), 9/30/67, for 420 yds. In collegiate career attempted 550 passes, completed 304, for 4152 yds., percentage of .553. All-time Irish passing leader. Ended career with 4738 total-offense yds., 6th in nation. Led Notre Dame to 24-4-2 record. Drafted on 1st round by Pittsburgh Steelers. Played with Steelers, 1969-73. Threw eight TD passes, 1969. Replaced as regular by Terry Bradshaw, 1971. Fine runner when necessary. Hampered by injuries. Lives in Denver during off-season, nurturing love for skiing. Father of three daughters, including twins.

HANSON, VICTOR A. End. B. 7/30/03, Sacramento, Calif. 5'10", 174. Played at Syracuse under Chick Meehan, 1924-26. Line mate of Lynn (Pappy) Waldorf, later famous coach. Superb end. Consensus All-America, 1926. Captained football, basketball (All-America) teams. "He was the best all-around athlete Syracuse ever had," according to Grantland Rice. Played pro baseball (New York Yankee chain) and basketball before returning to Syracuse as head football coach in 1929. In seven years compiled 33-21-5 record. Became prominent insurance counselor. Citizens Savings Hall of Fame (basketball), Naismith Basketball Hall of Fame, National Football Foundation Hall of Fame.

HARDER, MARLIN (Pat) Running Back. B. 5/6/22, Milwaukee, Wis. 5'11", 205. Wisconsin, 1941-43. Coach Harry Stuhldreher called him great fullback, described 1941 team as "an outfit that was close to my heart." College All-Star game MVP, 1943. No. 1 draft pick of Chicago Cardinals, 1944. Played for Cards, 1946-50; member of "Dream Backfield." Led league in scoring three seasons: 1947 with 102 points; 1948 with 110 points; 1949 with 102 (tied). Led in FGs, 1947, with seven. Kicked four PATs in 1947 NFL title game. Set record for most PATs (since tied), game, with nine, 10/17/48. In 1948 scored 53 PATs. Detroit Lions, 1951-53. Scored two PATs and 36-yd. FG to win game in 1952 title game against Cleveland Browns.

HARDWICK, HUNTINGTON R. (Tack) Running Back-End. B. 10/15/1892, Quincy, Mass. D. 6/26/49. 6', 175. Harvard, 1912-14. Played halfback as sophomore, then switched to end. All-America, 1912, 13, 14. Ferocious tackler, runner, receiver, kicker. Once told his coach Percy Haughton that there was nothing he wouldn't do if asked — he'd jump out a window as Haughton would surely figure out way to keep him from getting hurt. Hardwick-Harvard teams won 22 straight games. Early-Day All-Time All-America team. Citizens Savings Player of the Year, 1914. Citizens Savings Hall of Fame, National Football Foundation Hall of Fame.

HARDY, CARROLL End-Running Back. B. 5/8/33, Sturgis, S.D. 6', 185. Colorado, 1952-54. Won school record 10 varsity letters (4 football, 4 baseball, 2 track). San Francisco 49ers, 1955. That year played pro baseball with Cleveland Indians. In U.S. Army, 1956-57. In 1958 left football to concentrate on baseball. Cleveland Indians, 1958-60; Boston Red Sox (where became only man ever to pinch-hit for Ted Williams), 1960-62; Houston Colt 45's (now Astros), 1963-64; Minnesota Twins, 1965. Became Denver Bronco scout, 1965. In 1969 became Bronco ticket manager. Since 1970, director of scouting for Denver.

HARE, TRUXTON Guard. B. 10/12/1878, Philadelphia, Pa. D. 2/2/56. 6'2", 200. Pennsylvania, 1897-1900. One of only three men to be 1st-team All-America four times. Team won all 15 games, 1897; he set Penn scoring record. Played every minute of 55 games during collegiate career. Finished with 48-5-2 record. Captain, 1899, 1900. Named with Pudge Heffelfinger as guard on Early-Day All-Time All-America team. Heffelfinger once wrote that Trux Hare would always stand out in his mind as greatest of Penn linemen. Called by Walter Camp "guard of the year," in 1899. Punter, signal-caller, dropkicker, runner. Devastating on defense. 1900 Olympic hammer-thrower, winning silver medal. Went into law; served in legal division of United Gas Improvement Co. of Radnor, Pa., 1914-42. Also managing director of Bryn Mawr Hospital, 1943-46; its president, 1946-50. Citizens Savings Player of the Year, 1900. Citizens Savings Hall of Fame, National Football Foundation Hall of Fame.

HARGETT, EDWARD E. (Edd) Quarterback. B. 6/26/47, Marietta, Texas. 5'11", 190. Played 1966-68 at Texas A. & M. Set 20 school, 7 conference records. All-SWC and Player of the Year, 1967. 10th nationally in passing yardage with 2321, 1968. That year vs. SMU, 58 attempts, no interceptions, NCAA single-game record. Against Arkansas, same year, made 55 attempts without interception. Passed for two TDs in 1968 Cotton Bowl. Played in Blue-Gray, Coaches All-America games. Live arm, durable. College career: 821 attempts, 403 completions, 40 interceptions, 5379 yds., 6.6 yds. per attempt, 13.4 yds. per completion, .487 percentage, 40 TDs. In 1969 drafted by New Orleans Saints on 16th round. Backed up former All-America Archie Manning. In 1971, after Manning injured, stepped in to lead Saints. 210 attempts, 96 completions, 1191 yds., 6 TDs, 1971. Drove team to surprising wins over San Francisco 49ers and Green Bay Packers. Traded to Houston Oilers prior to 1973 season.

HARLEY, CHARLES W. (Chic) Running Back. B. Columbus, Ohio. D. 4/21/74, Danville, Ill. 5'10", 158. Ohio State, 1916-17, 19. All-America all three years. Army Air Corps, 1918. Called by Walter Camp "one of the greatest players the country has ever seen." Was first Buckeye All-America. Made Ohio State athletics important in Columbus eyes; previously, high school games had drawn larger crowds. Classmate at Columbus East H.S. of George Bellows and James Thurber. Ohio State was Big 10 champion in both 1916 and '17. Always threat to score. In game vs. Wisconsin grabbed ball from arms of Wisconsin runner, and without breaking stride, ran down field to score. Chicago Staleys, 1921. Excellent runner, passer, kicker. Considered in same class with Red Grange. Citizens Savings Hall of Fame, National Football Foundation Hall of Fame.

HARLOW, RICHARD C. Coach. B. 10/19/1889, Philadelphia, Pa. D. 2/19/62. Played tackle at Penn State under Bill Hollenback, 1908-11. Set record for blocking punts in five games, 1911. Assistant coach at State under Hollenback, 1912-14; head coach, 1915-17. Lt. in infantry during World War I, 1917-18. Assistant coach at Penn State under Hugo Bezdek, 1919-21. Head coach at Colgate, 1922-25; Western Maryland, 1926-34; Harvard, 1935-42, 45-47. Brilliant football mind. Known for deceptive offensive plays, usually evolving around single-wing system. Pioneered stunting defensively. Served as professor of ornithology. Often looked sadly at players who did not execute properly and said, "Do it my way, dear boy." Master psychologist, maintained that football was all in mind. Navy Cmdr. in submarine service, 1943-44. Became ill and was not recovered while coaching last three years at Harvard. Retired in 1947 on advice of doctor. Collected birds' eggs and cultivated ferns. Overall record was 150-68-17. Citizens Savings Hall of Fame, National Football Foundation Hall of Fame. Coached two Kennedys, Joe Jr., and Bobby, 10 years apart at Harvard.

HARMON, THOMAS D. (Old 98) Running Back. B. 9/28/19, Gary, Ind. 6'0", 195. Michigan, 1938-40. Unforgettable halfback. Teamed with QB Forest Evashevski. Gained 2338 yds. in 398 carries during collegiate career. Completed 101 passes (233 attempts), for 16 TDs. Scored 237 points (33 TDs, 33 PATs, 2 FGs). Led nation in scoring, 1939, with 102 points; in 1940 with 117. Broke Big 10 records set by Red Grange. Consensus All-America, 1939; unanimous All-America, 1940. Heisman Trophy, AP Athlete of the Year, Maxwell Trophy, 1940. Against both California and Iowa scored 4 TDs. According to Amos Alonzo Stagg, "I'll take Harmon on my team and you can have all the rest." No. 1 draft pick in NFL by (by Philadelphia Eagles), 1941, but played that year with New York Americans (AFL). Served in air force during World War II. Bailed out of destroyed planes twice, once not found for week. Other time hid from Japanese for 32 days before turning up at American base in China. Earned Silver Star, Purple Heart. Los Angeles Rams, 1946-47. Father of Mark Harmon, UCLA QB. Wife, Elyse, former movie actress, met by Tom on Bing Crosby radio program. Currently TV-radio broadcaster, color man on UCLA games and sports director of KTLA in Los Angeles. Citizens Savings Hall of Fame and its college Player of the Year, 1939. Also National Football Foundation Hall of Fame.

HARPER, JESSE C. Coach. B. 12/10/1883, Pawpaw, Ill. D. 7/1/61. Coached Knute Rockne-Gus Dorais Notre Dame team which made forward pass national institution in shattering Army, 1913. That was first Army-Notre Dame game. Coached Alma, 1906-08; Wabash, 1909-12; Notre Dame, 1913-17. 33-5-1 record with Irish. Installed "Notre Dame shift," used by his successor, Rockne, to great success. Had learned it from Amos Alonzo Stagg while playing at Chicago. First used shift in 1914, after Notre Dame was soundly defeated by Yale. Also coached Charlie Bachman, who later became great coach. After Rockne's death served three years, 1931-33, as Notre Dame athletic director. National Football Foundation Hall of Fame. Farming in Kansas when Rockne's plane went down. By quirk of fate, it was Harper who identified body of his successor and former player.

HARPSTER, HOWARD Quarterback. B. 5/14/07, Akron, Ohio. 6', 160. Carnegie Tech, 1926-28. Quarterbacked Tech to 19-7-1 record. Pittsburgh sportswriter stated that Harpster was greatest football player he'd ever seen on any Pittsburgh-area team. Consensus All-America, 1928. East-West Shrine game, 1928; was East captain. Sixty-minute player despite frailness. Also punter, with 65-yd. punts not unusual. Head coach, Carnegie Tech, 1933-36, with record of 12-20-3. Citizens Savings Hall of Fame, National Football Foundation Hall of Fame.

HARRIS, FRANCO Running Back. B. 4/7/50, Mount Holly, N. J. 6'3", 230. Half-Italian, half-Black running star of Pittsburgh Steelers. Attracted loyal fan following, called "Franco's Italian Army." Attended Penn State where was backfield mate of Lydell Mitchell. In 1972 drafted on 1st round by Pittsburgh Steelers, after 12 teams had passed him. That year rushed for 100 yds. or more six consecutive times, tying record of Jim Brown. Became only fifth rookie in football history to gain over 1000 yds., had best average per carry in AFC with 5.6. Other four rookies were: Beattie Feathers (1004, 1934), Cookie Gilchrist (1096, 1962), Paul Robinson (1023, 1968), John Brockington (1105, 1971). Became starter in fourth game of rookie season. Set Steeler record in rushing TDs with 10. In playoffs, 1972, 73. In last 13 seconds of 1972 playoff game vs. Oakland Raiders, Harris caught winning pass from Terry Bradshaw, which ricocheted off Raider Jack Tatum, for 60-yd. TD play. Pro Bowl, 1973, 74. AFC Rookie of the Year, 1972.

HARRIS, TRACY H. Official. B. 7/5/1864; D. 10/27/33, New York, N. Y. Played for Princeton, 1882-86. In early 1880s was one of Princeton's most famous athletes, later one of football's foremost officials. Played four years of baseball, three years of football at guard. In Fall, after his graduation, chosen by

Yale as sole official at its game vs. Princeton. One of earliest volunteer coaches who established college football coaching system. Became well-known lawyer in New York. Familiar figure at every major Princeton game until his death.

HART, EDWARD J. (E. J.) Tackle. B. 5/22/1887, Exeter, N. H. D. 11/28/56, Toronto, Canada. 5'11", 208. Princeton, 1909-11. Member undefeated national co-championship team, 1911. Played three years with broken flange in neck vertebrae. Captain, 1910, 11. All-America, 1911. Playing record of 26-5-6. Extremely fast and strong. Scared even own teammates. Served in both World War I and II in USMC, eventually reaching rank of Lt. Col. Chicago insurance executive for 30 years, then went into mining in Canada. Citizens Savings Hall of Fame, National Football Foundation Hall of Fame.

HART, JAMES W. Quarterback. B. 8/29/44, Evanston, Ill. 6'2", 205. Graduated form Southern Illinois. Collegiate classmate of basketball star Walt Frazier. Signed as free agent by St. Louis Cardinals, 1966. In 1967 gained 3,008 yds. passing. On 12/10/72 tied NFL record for longest nonscoring pass with 98-yarder. Vs. New York Giants, 10/28/73, threw 4 TD passes, 3 to Mel Gray (10 yds., 41 yds., 55 yds.) and 1 to Walker Gillete (48 yds.). That day completed 13 of 18 for 235 yds. 1973 record: 320 attempts, 178 completions, .556 completion percentage, 2223 yds., 15 TDs, 69-yd. longest, 10 interceptions, 6.95-yd average. Holds Cardinal record for most interceptions in one season (30), established in 1967.

HART, LEON J. End. B. 11/2/28, Turtle Creek, Pa. 6'5", 260. Notre Dame, 1946-49. Made varsity in freshman year. Teammate of Terry Brennan and Johnny Lujack. Consensus All-America, 1947, 48; unanimous All-America, 1949. Heisman Trophy, 1949. Co-Captain in 1949, catching 19 passes for 257 yds. and 5 TDs. One of two ends, other being Larry Kelly, to win Heisman. Also received Maxwell Trophy, 1949. In college career had 13 TD receptions. Received 49 passes for 742 yds., average of 15.1 yds. Detroit Lions, 1950-57. All-Pro, 1951. In Hart's career Lions won three NFL titles, 1952, 53, 57. Citizens Savings Hall of Fame, National Football Foundation Hall of Fame.

HAUGHTON, PERCY D. Coach B. 7/11/1876, Staten Island, N.Y. D. 10/27/24, New York, N.Y. Harvard, 1895-98. All-America 2nd team, 1898. After graduation became coach for Cornell, 1899-1900; Harvard, 1908-16; Columbia, 1923-24. 1910, 12, 13 teams won national championship. Regarded as great tactician. Cornell record was 17-5-0, Harvard 71-7-5, Columbia 8-5-1, for overall of 96-17-6, .832 percentage. At Harvard his teams outscored opponents 1427-206. Crimson had streak of 33 consecutive unbeaten games. Pioneered hidden-ball trick, "mouse trap" play. Once asked before Yale game if his men could stop big Yale linemen. Answered, "I'm not going to try." Harvard won, 36-0. Volunteered for army, 1918, becoming Maj. in chemical warfare. Last words were, "Tell the squad I'm proud of them." Died of angina pectoris. Citizens Savings Hall of Fame, National Football Foundation Hall of Fame. National racquets champion, 1906.

HAUSS, LEONARD M. Center. B. 7/11/42, Jesup, Ga. 6'2", 235. Georgia, 1961-63. Was fullback, then moved to center. Made All-SEC sophomore team. Selected by Washington Redskins on 9th round of 1964 NFL draft. Won 1st-string center position midway thru rookie season, started ever since. Considered one of top centers in NFL. All-NFC, 1971. Pro Bowl 1967, 69, 70, 71, 73.

HAWKINS, BENJAMIN C. (Hawk) End. B. 3/22/44, Newark, N. J. 6'1", 180. Attended Arizona State. Played defensive back. Drafted on 3rd round, 1966, by Philadelphia Eagles. In 1967 had 59 receptions, 10 TDs, led league in yardage with 1265 yds. Totaled 42 receptions, 707 yds., 5 TDs, 1968. Also running back. In 1971 led Eagles with five TDs. Accumulated 261 pass receptions in eight seasons. Also on kickoff and punt-return teams. Majored in physical education at Arizona State. All-WAC, 1965. All-America same season. East-West Hula Bowl, College All-Star games. Trademark is dangling chinstrap.

HAWLEY, JESSE B. Coach. B. 3/25/1887, St. Paul, Minn. D. 3/20/46, Orlando, Fla. Won Big 10 gymnastics title as freshman at Minnesota, then transferred to Dartmouth. Big Green football and track letterman, 1908-09. 14-1-2 playing record. New England intercollegiate champion in discus, 100- and 200-yd. dashes, 1909. Coached Iowa, 1910-15; Dartmouth, 1923-28. Overall record: 63-28-4. His Dartmouth elevens compiled 39-10-1 mark and 22-game defeatless string. Tutored Big Green immortals Swede Oberlander and Myles Lane. Advocated scouting opponents and realized advantages of passing game. Might have joined ranks of preeminent coaches but business pressures forced him to give up game. Was president of Hawley Products Co., St. Charles, Ill., manufacturers of molded fiber products. Father of twins; Jesse Jr., graduated from Dartmouth in 1949.

HAXALL, JAMES T. (Jerry) Guard. B. 4/22/1860, Richmond, Va. D. 6/5/39, Baltimore, Md. 158. While playing at Princeton kicked record 65-yd. FG vs. Yale, 11/30/82. It apparently won for Princeton but game bitterly contested; Yale was declared winner, two goals to one. Incident led to adoption of numerical scoring in 1883.

HAYES, ROBERT L. (Bullet Bob) End. B. 12/20/42, Jacksonville, Fla. 5'11", 185. Attended Florida A. & M. Played running back but gained greatest fame with track exploits. Ran 100-yd. dash in 9.1, long-standing record. Won two gold medals in 1964 Olympics at Tokyo. For obvious reasons called "World's Fastest Human." Drafted as future by Dallas Cowboys in 1963. Joined them in 1964. Switched to wide receiver and became one of NFL's most dangerous pass catchers. In 1965 led league in TD pass receptions with 12, and in average yds. per reception with 21.8. Tops again in TD pass receptions, 1966. NFL leader in punt-return yardage (276) and punt-return TDs (1), both in 1967. Punt-return average leader, 1968, with 20.8 yds., same year No. 1 in TD punt returns (2). All-NFL, 1966. Slumped in 1972, catching only 15 passes and scoring no TDs. Came back year later to make 22 receptions, score 3 TDs. NFL championship games, 1966,

67. Super Bowl, 1971, 72. Consistent winner on pro track circuit in 40-yd. dash. Affiliated with Consolidated Wig Corp. in Dallas.

HAYES, W. WOODROW (Woody) Coach. B. 2/13/13, Clifton, Ohio. Tackle at Denison, 1933-35. Majored in English. Also played outfield on baseball team. Achieved primary fame as coach. Assistant at Mingo Junction (Ohio) H.S., 1936. Assistant at New Philadelphia (Ohio) H.S., 1937, and head coach, 1938-40. Served in U.S. Navy, 1941-46, discharged as Lt. Cmdr. Coached Denison, 1946-48. Undefeated, 1947-48. Head coach, Miami (Ohio), 1949-50. Record of 9-1-0 in 1950. That year defeated Arizona State in Salad Bowl. Succeeded at Miami by Ara Parseghian. On 3/11/51 appointed head coach at Ohio State. Led team to Big 10 title, 1954, Buckeyes' first since 1944. They were first unbeaten champs since Alonzo Stagg's 1913 Chicago team. Won O'Donnell Trophy, 1954. Won conference championships again in 1955, 57, 61, 68, 69 (shared), 70, 72, 73 (shared). Won four Rose Bowls, lost two. Shared national championships in 1954 and '57, selected outright champion in 1968. Won Rose Bowl 42-21, 1/1/74, in revenge win over Southern Cal. Outspoken and accused by some, most notably Michigan partisans, of being ill-mannered. In 1973, after tying for Big 10 title with Michigan, Buckeyes were sent to Rose Bowl by hotly-disputed 6-4 vote of conference athletic directors. Much of press sided with Wolverines, but 42-21 win apparently proved Ohio State's claim. Twenty-eight-year record, thru 1973, was 192-60-8. Only Bear Bryant, among active coaches, owns more wins. Extremely competent. Teaches pride, never puts down his players.

HAYMOND, ALVIN H. (Juggie) Defensive Back. B. 8/31/42, New Orleans, La. 6', 193. Attended Southern U. Ran 100-yd. dash in 9.8. Drafted by Baltimore Colts on 18th round, 1964. Colts, 1964-67; Philadelphia Eagles, 1968; Los Angeles Rams, 1969-71; Washington Redskins, 1972; Houston Oilers, 1973. Returned kickoff for 98 yds. against New York Giants, 1968. Best season, 1970, returned 53 punts (NFL record) for 376 yds.; 35 kickoffs for league-leading 1022 yds. Ranks 2nd only to Emlen Tunnell in career punt returns (239) and yardage (2148). NFL championship game, 1964. Super Bowl, 1973.

HAYNES, ABNER (Butch) Running Back. B. 9/19/37, Denton, Tex. 6'1", 198. Played halfback for North Texas State, 1957-59. In 1956, vs. Youngstown, made 60-yd. punt return. Made 82-yd. rush vs. Texas (El Paso) and 65-yd. catch vs. Tulsa, both in 1959. In 1960 Sun Bowl rushed for 72 yds. on 13 carries. Drafted on 1st round by Oakland Raiders, 1960. Draft rights traded to Dallas Texans. Texans, 1960-62. AFL rushing leader, 1960, with 875 yds. On 11/26/61, vs. Oakland, set AFL records for TDs, game, with five. In 1962 set AFL records for TDs rushing, season, with 13; total TDs, season, with 19; TDs, playoff game, with 2. Moved wtih team to Kansas City (Chiefs) in 1963. Chiefs, 1963-64; Denver Broncos, 1965-66; Miami Dolphins, 1967; New York Jets, 1967. Set AFL career record with 46 TDs. Lifetime combined net yardage was 12,065. Rookie of the Year and Player of the Year, 1960. All-League, 1960, 61, 62. AFL All-Star games, 1962, 63, 65. Blundered in 1962 AFL championship game. Texans had won coin flip starting unprecedented sudden-death overtime. They elected to kickoff and captain Haynes, inadvertently, also gave up wind. Nevertheless, Texans won over Houston Oilers, 20-17.

HAZEL, HOMER H. (Pop) End-Running Back. B. 6/2/1895, Pifford, N.Y. D. 2/3/68, Marshall, Mich. 5'11", 226. Played at Rutgers, 1922-24. All-America as end, 1923; as fullback, 1924. Rutgers' record was 14-2-2 during his career. Set several school records, including PATs, longest forward pass. All-round athlete, winning high school letters four years in baseball, basketball, track, as well as football; three letters each in tennis and swimming. Holder of Montclair Academy discus, broad jump, shot-put records. Played baseball, track, basketball, besides football at Rutgers. Later Mississippi athletic director, basketball and football coach. Became golf pro and labor relations manager. Citizens Savings Hall of Fame, National Football Foundation Hall of Fame.

HEADRICK, SHERRILL Linebacker. B. Fort Worth, Tex. 5'11", 220. All-District fullback at North Side H.S. in Forth Worth. North also produced pro football players Yale Lary, Jim Shofner, Tommy Runnels; Olympic shot-putter Darrow Hooper; football coaches Matty Bell and Bo McMillin. Serious only about football, bridge and dancing. Flunked out of Texas Christian. Won trial with Dallas Texans in 1960 and impressed Coach Hank Stram. Became immediate regular, defensive captain. Texans moved to Kansas City (Chiefs) in 1963, Headrick staying with club thru 1967. With Cincinnati Bengals in 1968. All-AFL, 1960, 61, 62. Not big for linebacker but had exceptional instinct at position. Doubtful that any athlete ever had higher pain threshold. He played with compound fractures, shattered ribs, cracked neck vertebrae. Once incapacitated himself by blowing nose so hard that he slipped disc. During one season had hemorrhoid operation on Monday, played following Sunday vs. Oakland Raiders. AFL championship games, 1962, 66. Super Bowl, 1967.

HEALEY, EDWARD Tackle. B. 12/18/1894, Springfield, Mass. 6'1½", 220. Excellent end at Dartmouth, 1918-20. Played in college at 190 pounds. Joined Rock Island Independents, 1921. During 1922 season engaged in on-field battle with George Halas in which his aggressiveness was brought home to "Papa Bear." Said Halas, "I decided I'd much rather have him playing on our side than against us." Thus bought Healey's contract for $100, one of earliest player transactions. Chicago Bears, 1922-27. Watching Bears vs. Chicago Cardinals, 1923, Walter Camp called him "the best I ever saw," wondered why he'd passed Healey over for All-America. Played tackle throughout pro career. Pro Football Hall of Fame.

HEATH, STANLEY Quarterback. B. Milwaukee, Wis. 6'1", 185. Played QB for Wisconsin, 1946; Nevada, 1947-48. All-America, 1948. 5th in Heisman Trophy voting, 1948. Set NCAA records, 1948, for passing yds. with 2005; passing yds. per attempt with 9.0; TD passes with 22. Led nation same year in number of attempts with 222 and number of completions with 126, percentage of .568. Also led in total offense yds. with 1992 and TDs-accounted-for with 23. Set game records with 327 passing yds. vs. Tulsa and .833 completion percentage (20 of 24) vs. St. Mary's (Calif.), 1948. Also had 5 TD passes vs. Oklahoma City. Completed 94-yd. pass vs. North Texas State, 1948. Played in Salad Bowl, 1948; Harbor Bowl, 1949. Green Bay Packers, 1949.

HEFFELFINGER, WILLIAM W. (Pudge; Heff) Guard. B. 12/20/1867, Minneapolis, Minn. D. 4/3/54, Blessing, Tex. 6'2½", 188. Played at Yale, 1888-91. Began playing at age 15. Organized team at Central H.S. in Minneapolis, 1884, and became star back. Played several games for U. of Minnesota while still schoolboy. In freshman football practice at Yale Pa Corbin, Yale varsity captain, saw him catch punt and out-rush all but one tackler. Taken immediately onto varsity by Corbin who told him, "We need linemen more than backs." Played guard for four years. All-America, 1889, first year of selections, as well as 1890, 91. Broke up plays from "flying wedge" by backing away, charging, and landing on man at head of V. Considered by some to be first paid player, receiving $500 for game in Pittsburgh in 1892. Same year became coach at California. Knocked out five Yale players when he suited up to teach by example in 1916 scrimmage; coach Tad Jones had to order 49-year-old Pudge off field. At 53, played over 56 minutes of football on all-star team vs. group of Ohio State graduates. Played last time, at 63, in game for disabled veterans at Minneapolis, 1930. In World War I was draft board commissioner and Red Cross worker. Inventor of "running guards," fore-runner of modern blocking.

Organized Heffelfinger Publications, publisher of *Heffelfinger Football Facts* which became *Original Football Fact Booklet*. Produced first sports quiz show on radio and first espionage show, "Secret Agent K-7." Once urged Henry L. Stimson to run for congressional seat. Often interviewed on radio when visiting New York. Died within few months of his close friend, Grantland Rice. Early-Day All-Time All-America team. Citizens Savings Player of the Year, 1890. Citizens Savings Hall of Fame, National Football Foundation Hall of Fame.

HEIN, MELVIN J. Center. B. 8/22/09, Redding, Calif. 6'3", 198. All-America for Washington State Rose Bowl team, 1930. Played for New York Giants, 1931-45. Grantland Rice said, "Some sort of Oscar ought to go to Hein for stamina." Claimed Alabama, which beat Cougars in 1931 Rose Bowl, was greatest college team he ever saw. Played in seven NFL championship games, 1933, 34, 35, 41, 42, 43, 44. Union College head coach, 1946. Line coach for Los Angeles Dons (AAFC), 1947-48; New York Yankees (AAFC), 1949; Los Angeles Rams, 1950; Southern California, 1959-66. Supervisor, AFL officials, 1966-69. Proudest moment in sports was seeing his son set indoor pole vault record (though later broken). Eight-time All-Pro, 1933, 34, 35, 36, 37, 38, 39, 40. Won Joseph Carr Trophy (NFL MVP), 1938. National Football Foundation Hall of Fame, Pro Football Hall of Fame. Modern All-Time All-America team.

HEINRICH, DONALD Quarterback. B. Bremerton, Wash. 6', 181. Played for Washington, 1949, 51-52. All-America, 1950, 52. In 1950 lost to team by injury before season opener. Led NCAA in pass completions with 134, in completion percentage with .606, yds. passing with 1846, all in 1951. Also led in completions, 1951, with 137 in 270 attempts. In 1952 completed 80-yd. pass vs. Stanford. Passed for 4392 career yds., 33 TDs. New York Giants, 1954-59; Dallas Cowboys, 1960; Oakland Raiders, 1962.

HEISMAN, JOHN W. Coach. B. 10/23/1869, Cleveland, Ohio. D. 10/3/36, New York, N.Y. Played for Brown, 1887-88; Penn, 1889-91. Received letters from both schools. Coached for 36 years: at Oberlin, 1892, 94; Akron, 1893; Auburn, 1895-99; Clemson, 1900-03; Georgia Tech, 1904-19; Penn, 1920-22; Washington & Jefferson, 1923; Rice, 1924-27. Later was athletic director. One of greatest innovators in football history. Originated hidden-ball trick. Played QB as safety when team was on defense, first to do so. Inventor of center snap. Developed modern signals. Began "double pass," interference on end runs; spin buck, Heisman shift. First to list downs, yards on scoreboard. Early exponent of screen pass (which he credited Bob Zuppke with inventing). During off-season was Shakespearean actor, often addressed his players in stage English. Heisman felt "a coach should be masterful and commanding, even dictatorial." 185-68-18 record. Followed certain basic rules of coaching: End runs on 1st, 2nd downs; never two end runs in succession; no end run from inside 25, unless from punt formation; divide work load among players; hammer weak spots; test subs immediately upon their entry into game; never pass inside own 30; best passing down 3rd; pass on 1st down if close to goal; when in doubt, punt; never let punter run immediately before punt play; call signals with pep, cheerfully. Leader in successful fight to legalize forward pass, 1906.

Fond of small players. Coached Joe Guyon, Everett Strupper, Red Barron. Albie Booth of Yale was favorite player. Frequent contributor to Christy Walsh's *Intercollegiate Football.* Lost only one game, 11-10, to Sewanee, 1899. One of greatest exploiters of shift; great exponent of wing-T. Claimed to be first to use double-lateral, 1899. In 1900 unbeaten. His 1916 Yellow Jackets amassed most one-sided victory in history, blistering Cumberland, 222-0. Helped develop Bill Alexander, his successor at Georgia Tech. Credited Stagg with inventing onside kick, Camp with inventing "short-punt" formation. Unveiled Heisman shift while coaching at Tech. In it, according to George Trevor, "the entire team, except the center, dropped behind the scrimmage zone. The four backs took their post in Indian file, at right angles to the rush line, forming the letter T." Heisman Trophy named in his honor. Citizens Savings Hall of Fame, National Football Foundation Hall of Fame.

HENDERSON, ELMER C. (Gloomy Gus) Coach. B. 3/10/1889, Oberlin, Ohio. D. 12/16/65. Graduated from Oberlin College. Head coach at Southern California, 1919-24; Tulsa, 1925-35; Occidental, 1940-42. Prior to 1923 Rose Bowl engaged in first fight with opposing coach, Hugo Bezdek of Penn State, in front of capacity crowd; start of game delayed one hour. In last game at USC,

Henderson beat Chick Meehan of Syracuse, in his last game for Orangemen, 16-0. Overall record was 126-42-7, .740 percentage.

HENDRICKS, TED Linebacker. B. 11/1/47, Guatemala City, Guatemala. 6'7", 215. Prep All-America at Hialeah (Fla.) H.S. Attended U. of Miami (Fla.), 1966-68. Received All-America recognition all three years at defensive end. Unanimous selection, 1967, 68. Won Knute Rockne Trophy as outstanding college lineman in 1968. Baltimore Colts, 1969-73. Drafted on 2nd round in 1969. Converted to linebacker by Colts. Created many problems for opposition with height and mobility. Strong tackler. Ran 31 yds. with fumble recovery to score against Los Angeles Rams, 1971. Same year blocked PAT attempt to save 14-13 win over New York Jets. Super Bowl, 1971. All-AFC, 1971. Pro Bowl, 1972, 73, 74. Likes to hunt, fish, water ski, solve math problems, tinker with cars. Called "Mad Stork."

HENRY, WILBUR F. (Fats) Tackle. B. 10/31/1897, Mansfield, Ohio. D. 2/7/52. 5'10", 230. Washington and Jefferson, 1917-19. Lettered in four sports. Super blocker and punter. All-America, 1919. Twice in college punted 70 yds. On 10/28/23 punted 94 yds. for Canton Bulldogs, recognized as record until 1969 despite 95-yd. punt by Joe Guyon in 1920. (Record broken in '69 by Steve O'Neal, New York Jets, who punted 98 yds.) Canton Bulldogs, 1920-23, 25-26 (1925-26 coach); New York Giants, 1927; Pottsville Maroons, 1927-28 (1928 coach). Sensational tackle, occasionally played in backfield. On 11/13/22, vs. Toledo Maroons, kicked 50-yd. FG. In 1928 scored 49 consecutive dropkicks. Citizens Savings Player of the Year, 1917. Citizens Savings Hall of Fame, National Football Foundation Hall of Fame, Pro Football Hall of Fame. Early-Day All-Time All-America team.

HERBER, ARNOLD (Flash) Quarterback. B. 4/2/10, Green Bay, Wis. D. 10/14/69, Green Bay, Wis. 210. Attended Wisconsin as freshman, then transferred to Regis in Denver. Signed with Green Bay Packers, his hometown team, 1930; remained with team until 1940. Also New York Giants, 1944-45. At Green Bay teamed with Don Hutson, formerly of Alabama, to form Herber-to-Hutson pass combo, one of finest in history. Led league in passing, 1932, 34, 36. Biggest year, 1936, threw for 1239 yds. and 13 TDs. In career accumulated 481 completions for 8033 yds. Played under Curly Lambeau. Pro Football Hall of Fame.

HERSCHBERGER, CLARENCE Running Back. B. 9/9/1876. D. 12/14/36, Chicago, Ill. 5'8", 165. U. of Chicago, 1895-98. All-America, 1898; first non-Ivy Leaguer to make squad as selected by Walter Camp. Played fullback. Fine runner, blocker, punter, placekicker, dropkicker. Pioneer kicker, first to use Statue of Liberty play. Played in 60 games, 48 victories. Gastronomical bout with teammate Walter Kennedy in 1897 cost Chicago its first championship, and piqued coach Alonzo Stagg to no end. Herschberger overate prior to pivotal Wisconsin game and was unable to play. Without him Chicago lost, 23-7. After that episode, Stagg made eating rules more stringent. Otherwise, Herschberger was no problem. Walter Camp wrote, in selecting him for 1898 All-America team: "Against Penn this year, Herschberger exhibited the best kicking of the season . . . he demonstrated in actual combat with first class teams . . . that it is not safe to give him a kick from a fair catch anywhere from 45 to 55 yds. of the opponent's goal." Made All-America with three men each from Penn and Harvard, two each from Yale and Princeton. National Football Foundation Hall of Fame.

HERWIG, ROBERT J. Center. 210. California, 1935-37. All-America, 1936, 37. Won Rose Bowl over Alabama, 1938. Led team to 10 victories and 1 tie, shared All-America honors with Carl Hinkle, Alex Wojciechowicz. Expert tackler and passer, 60-minute man. During World War II served in USMC, winning Navy Cross, Silver Star, Purple Heart. Later junior college baseball and football coach in California. Citizens Savings Hall of Fame, National Football Foundation Hall of Fame.

HESTON, WILLIAM M. (Willie) Running Back. B. 9/9/1878, Galesburg, Ill. 5'8", 185. Halfback for Michigan, 1901-04. Two-time All-America, 1903, 04. 3rd team, 1901, 02. First Wolverine player to be named All-America. Leader of Fielding (Hurry Up) Yost's "point-a-minute" team of 1902. Led Michigan to national championships, 1901, 02. Scored 10 TDs on rushes of 70-90 yds. and 9 TDs on rushes of 50-67 yds. Holds record of most TDs scored in four-year career (72). Never played in losing game. In 1902 Rose Bowl vs. Stanford, which Michigan won 49-0, Heston rushed for 170 yds. on 18 carries. Yardage total set Rose Bowl record, stood for 57 years. Rushed for 2339 yds. in four seasons. Tremendously fast and quick, used devastating stiff arm. Citizens Savings, College Player of the Year, 1904. Early Day All-Time All-America team. Citizens Savings Hall of Fame, National Football Foundation Hall of Fame.

HEWITT, WILLIAM E. End. B. 10/8/09, Bay City, Mich. D. 1/14/47, near Sellersville, Pa. Michigan, 1929-31. Chicago Bears, 1932-36; Philadelphia Eagles, 1937-39; Phil-Pitt (merged), 1943. All-Pro, 1933, 34, 36, 37. Played without helmet. Tremendous pass rusher, so quick he often seemed offside. Killed in auto accident at age 37. Pro Football Hall of Fame.

HIBBS, JESSE J. Tackle. B. 1/11/06, Normal, Ill. 5'11", 185. Southern California, 1926-28. Captained freshman team, 1925. Also played freshman basketball. All-Coast, 1926-28. Consensus All-America, 1927; All-America, 28. Captained 1928 national championship team. Played under Howard Jones. Became assistant freshman coach for Trojans in 1929. Later was assistant motion picture director for Warner Brothers.

HICKMAN, HERMAN M., JR. Guard. B. 10/1/11, Johnson City, Tenn. D. 4/25/58. 225. Played at Tennessee under Bob Neyland, 1929-31. Lost only once during 30-game collegiate career. One of fastest linemen in football history. Awesome blocker, due to power and speed. All-America, 1931, primarily on

146

strength of one-man performance in charity game vs. NUY at Yankee Stadium. Surprisingly nimble. Brooklyn Dodgers, 1932-34. All-Pro, 1933. Also as "Tennessee Terror," professional wrestler; 500 matches. Later coached Wake Forest, North Carolina State, West Point, Yale. At Yale, 1948-51, compiled 15-17-3 record. Also became well-known TV personality, admired for wit and storytelling ability. Considered "Poet Laureate of the Little Smokies." Citizens Savings Hall of Fame, National Football Foundation Hall of Fame.

HICKOK, WILLIAM O. (Wild Bill) Guard. B. 8/23/1874, Harrisburg, Pa. D. 9/4/33. 6'2", 194. All-America at Yale, 1893-94. 1892 Yale squad amassed 435 points. One of Elis' greatest linemen. As freshman broke intercollegiate hammer-throw and shot-put records. AAU shot-put champion, 1895. Captained Yale's first track team. Served unofficially as Carlisle Indian coach, 1896-97. Also coached Yale. Yale posted 13 consecutive shutouts in 1892 eight more in 1893. Streak broken by Princeton. Captained team, 1895. At death, head of machinery manufacturing company. National Football Foundation Hall of Fame.

HICKS, JOHN Offensive Tackle. B. 1951, Cleveland, Ohio. 6'3", 258. Ohio State, 1970, 72-73. Missed 1971 season due to knee injury. Consensus All-America, 1972; unanimous All-America, 1973. Outland Trophy winner, 1973. Runnerup in Heisman Trophy voting same season. The *Sporting News* Player of the Year, 1973, first interior lineman so honored. Woody Hayes called him "best lineman I ever coached." Started every game in three seasons, helping Buckeyes to 27-3-1 record. 4.7 speed in the 40-yd. dash. Hicks opened holes that helped Bucks average 37 points per game in 1973. Faster than some backs who have won Heisman. Has complete respect of opposing teams, teammates and teachers. Sensitive man with concern for other people. Economics major but plans to play pro ball and then teach. First Big 10 player to appear in three Rose Bowls, 1971, 72, 74. One professional observer called him "best offensive lineman I've seen in my seven years of scouting." Drafted on 1st round by New York Giants, 2nd round by WFL Florida Sharks.

HICKS, WILMER K. (W.K.) Defensive Back. B. 7/14/42, Texarkana, Ark. 6'1", 190. After graduation from Texas Southern, signed as free agent by Houston Oilers in 1964. Led AFL in interceptions with nine, 1965, and in yds. on interceptions with 156. Excellent defensive back with good speed. Also punt and kickoff returner. In 1970 traded to New York Jets for draft choice. With Jets thru 1972. Played in AFL All-Star game following 1966 season. AFL championship game, 1967.

HIGGINS, ROBERT A. Coach. B. 11/24/1893, Corning, N. Y. D. 6/6/69, Bellefonte, Pa. Penn State, 1914-16, 19. All-America, 1919; 2nd team, 1915. Played eight games with 89th Division, AEF champions, while he was Capt. in infantry. Returned to Penn State where he played in 1919. Captain of '19 team. In 20-0 victory over Pitt, caught 92-yd. TD pass from Bill Hess which originated from punt formation in end zone. Was 5'10", 181. Coached West Virginia

Wesleyan, 1920. Played for Canton Bulldogs, 1920-21. Returned to Wesleyan, 1922-24. Coached Washington (Mo.), 1925-27. Penn State assistant coach under Hugo Bezdek, 1928-29. Penn State head coach, 1930-48. 1947 team unbeaten, but had 13-13 tie with SMU in Cotton Bowl, only second Penn State bowl appearance. Won Lambert Trophy that year. 1948 team undefeated until 7-0 upset by Pitt. Retired, 1949, because of ill health. Remained in School of Physical Education & Athletics until 11/51. Penn State coaching record: 91-57-9; overall record: 123-80-17. Citizen Savings Hall of Fame, National Football Foundation Hall of Fame.

HILL, CALVIN Running Back. B. 1/2/47, Baltimore, Md. 6'3", 230. Yale halfback, 1966-68. Accounted for more than 2600 yds. total offense. Lost only once his last two seasons. In track had long jump of 25'1¼", triple jump of 51'5¼". Dallas Cowboys, 1969-73. Was Dallas' No. 1 draft choice in '69. Rookie of the Year, scoring eight TDs and gaining 942 yds. on ground. Exceeded 1000 yds. (1036) rushing in 1972 on 245 carries. Also led Cowboys in receiving with 43 catches. Passed 1000 again in '73, picking up career high 1142 yds. Dislocated elbow in 1973 playoffs vs. Los Angeles Rams and missed NFC championship game against Minnesota Vikings. Super Bowl, 1971, 72. All-NFC, 1973. Pro Bowl, 1970, 73, 74. Big and fast but nagged by injuries. 1973 national sports chairman for National Association of Retarded Children. Signed with Hawaii of WFL for 1975 season. Will play out option in Dallas.

HILL, DAN W. (Tiger) Center. 199. Duke, 1936-38. Member of 1938 "Iron Dukes." 1938 squad unbeaten, untied, unscored-upon. Lost Rose Bowl, 7-3, to USC, 1939. Outstanding leader; co-captain, 1938. All-America, 1938. Honor student. In 1939 became assistant athletic director at Duke and served until 1953, except for four years in Navy during World War II. Entered packaging businesses, 1953. Named executive vice president and director of Zapata Industries, Inc., 1969. National Football Foundation Hall of Fame.

HILL, GERALD A. (Jerry) Running Back. B. 10/12/39, Torrington, Wyo. 5'11", 217. Outstanding fullback at Wyoming, 1958-60. Gained 1374 yds. (4.8 average) during collegiate career. All-Skyline Conference, 1960. Drafted on 3rd round by Baltimore Colts and played for them, 1961, 63-70. Relied on basic, tough football. Advocates hitting opponents head first, then with shoulder and forearm. Also kickoff returner; gained 85 yds. on returns, 1964. In 1968 rushed 90 yds. and gained another 31 on pass receptions vs. Los Angeles Rams. Knee problems, 1969-70. Rushed 15 yds. for TD vs. Green Bay Packers, 1970. Knee surgery, 2/71, ended career. Don McCafferty called him "finest blocking fullback in the league." NFL championship games, 1964, 68. Super Bowl, 1968.

HILL, HARLON End. B. 5/4/32, Florence, Ala. 6'3", 198. Attended Florence State. Chicago Bears, 1954-61; Pittsburgh Steelers, 1962; Detroit Lions, 1962. Gained more than 1000 yds. receiving in rookie year. Jim Thorpe Trophy, 1955, only end to ever win award. Exemplary of Hill's play was 1956 game vs. New

York Giants. Bears were behind 17-10, with one minute, 50 seconds left, when QB Ed Brown threw to Hill. Pass appeared overthrown but Hill tipped ball, slid on his stomach, made diving catch in end zone for TD. Conversion then tied score. During career caught 233 passes for 4717 yds., 20.2 average, scored 40 TDs. Retired with highest lifetime average per reception.

HILL, JESSE T. Coach. B. 1/20/07, Yates, Mo. At Corona (Calif.) H.S. won letters in football, baseball, basketball, track, tennis. Riverside (Calif.) J.C., 1925-26. Played fullback at Southern California, 1928-29. Participated in track and baseball, too. Recorded 25'7/8" broad jump. Led USC in 1930 Rose Bowl. Graduated *cum laude*. Played big-league baseball as outfielder, with New York Yankees, 1935; Washington Senators, 1936-37; Philadelphia Phillies, 1937. Coached baseball at Riverside J.C., Corona H.S., Long Beach (Calif.) J.C. Enlisted in navy, 1942. Discharged, 1946, and returned to USC as freshman coach. Trojan track and football head coach, 1951-56. Won two national track and field championships, 1949, 50. Football record: 45-17-1. Two Rose Bowls, 1953, 55. Served as USC athletic director, 1957-71. Currently Pacific Coast Athletic Association commissioner. Citizens Savings Hall of Fame (track).

HILL, MACK LEE Running Back. B. Quincy, Fla. D. 12/14/65, Kansas City, Mo. 5'11", 225. Attended Southern U. Played for Kansas City Chiefs, 1964-65. Signed as free agent. Was powerful runner, popular with Kansas City fans. Led AFL in rushing average, 1964, with 567 yds. on 105 carries for 5.4 average. In two seasons gained 1203 yds. on 230 carries, 5.4 average, and scored 8 TDs. Promising career ended by untimely death — while undergoing knee surgery for ruptured ligament. Exact cause was never ascertained but it's believed that Hill suffered acute heat stroke during operation. Mack Lee Hill Award is given annually by Chiefs to rookie who "best exemplifies the spirit of the late Mack Lee Hill... the man with the giant heart and the quiet way."

HILL, WINSTON C. Tackle. B. 10/23/41, Seguin, Tex. 6'4", 270. Texas Southern, 1960-62. Played both ways. Little All-America, 1962. Selected by Baltimore Colts on 11th round of 1963 draft. Released by Colts and signed by New York Jets same year. Played eight years on left side of line, then moved to right. New York offensive co-captain. Perhaps most proficient pass blocker in game at present. AFL All-Star games, 1965, 68, 69, 70 seasons. AFL championship game, 1968. Super Bowl, 1969. All-AFC, 1973. Pro Bowl, 1971, 72, 73, 74. Was high school tennis champion, still plays regularly. Lives in Englewood, Colo.

HILLEBRAND, A.R.T. (Doc) Tackle. B. Freeport, Ill. D. 1941, S.D. 6', 190. Princeton, 1896-99. Won 43 of 47 games. National champions, 1896. All-America, 1898, 99. Captain, 1899. Baseball coach at Navy, 1901. Princeton football coach, 1903-05, winning 27 of 31 games. Great ability to follow ball. Strong tackler. Stock farmer at time of his death. National Football Foundation Hall of Fame.

HILLENBRAND, WILLIAM Running Back. B. 3/9/02, Armstrong, Ind. 6'0", 195. Indiana, 1941-42. Consensus All-America, 1942. Led NCAA in punt-return yds., 1942, with 481. Had 561 yds., 1941, including 88-yd. return vs. Wisconsin. Made 75-yd. interception return vs. Northwestern, 1941. Finished 18-game college career with 68 pass completions in 161 attempts (.422 percentage) for 1313 yds., 14 TDs, 8.2 yds. per attempt. Chicago Rockets (AAFC), 1946; Baltimore Colts (AAFC), 1947-48. In pro career, 216 rushes for 889 yds., 11 TDs. 7th-ranked in all-time AAFC pass receiving with 110 receptions, 2053 yds., average of 18.7, 18 TDs; also 7th in scoring with 186 points.

HINKEY, FRANK A. (Silent Frank) End. B. 12/23/1871, Tonawanda, N. Y. D. 12/30/25, Southern Pines, N.C. 5'9", 146. Attended Tonawanda H.S. and then Phillips Academy at Andover, Mass. Entered Yale in 1891. All-America, 1891, 92, 93, 94. Strong, intense, resilient despite scrawny and anemic appearance. Carried football around with him, even to class. "Pound for pound, greatest football player of all time," according to Pop Warner. "He drifted through the interference like a disembodied spirit," said Walter Camp. Not fast, but exceptionally quick. Had uncanny knack for getting down field under kicks. Could box a tackle, nail runner with supreme elegance. Shy, introspective, moody. So ferocious that it bothered even most tolerant of men. George F. Sanford said of him: "Hinkey in action was a raving maniac who frothed at the mouth." In 1914 returned to Yale as head football coach but lacked patience to teach inexperienced players techniques. His teams were fine offensively; however, they were totally lacking on fundamentals. Used Canadian team to teach players how to shuttle laterals on dead run, thereby introducing lateral pass to American football. Coached Dayton Triangles, 1921. Suffered many years from lung condition, eventually dying of tuberculosis. Citizens Savings College Player of the Year, 1891. Early-Day All-Time All-America team. Citizens Savings Hall of Fame, National Football Foundation Hall of Fame.

HINKLE, CLARK C., JR. Center. B. 1918, Nashville, Tenn. 6'3", 235. Vanderbilt, 1935-37. Captain of 1937 "Iron Men." Sixty-minute performer. MVP of SEC and All-America, 1937. Led team in tackles that year. Excellent linebacker on defense. In 1938 appointed to West Point and enrolled in hopes of playing football; it was determined that he had used up eligibility and couldn't play. Commissioned as First Captain of Cadets, 1942. B-17 fighter pilot during World War II. Won Distinguished Flying Cross with two Oak Leaf Clusters, Air Medal with three Oak Leaf Clusters, Presidential Unit Citation with one Oak Leaf Cluster, Air Force Commendation Medal, Croix de Guerre. Army assistant coach, 1945. Retired from air force in 1963. Elected to All-Time SEC team in 1969. Vanderbilt Hall of Fame, Tennessee Sports Hall of Fame, National Football Foundation Hall of Fame.

HINKLE, W. CLARKE Running Back. B. 4/10/12, Toronto, Ont., Canada. 5'1", 196. Starred at Bucknell, 1929-31. Led 1931 Bucknell squad to unbeaten season. Saved game vs. Fordham that year with great 4th-quarter running.

Played for Green Bay Packers, 1932-41. Gained 3860 yds. from scrimmage on record 1171 carries during career with Pack. NFL field goal leader, 1940, with nine, in 1941 with six. Scoring leader, 1938, with 58 points. Packers were league champions, 1936, 39. Hinkle was All-Pro, 1936, 37, 38, 41. Tremendously powerful fullback. Green Bay coach Curly Lambeau said of him: "Hinkle runs the middle, runs wide, and blocks and tackles viciously. He punts and placekicks with the best. He can do a job as a pass receiver. And in defense against aerial attack, Hinkle has no superior in professional football." Pro Football Hall of Fame.

HIRSCH, ELROY L. (Crazylegs) End. B. 6/17/23, Wausau, Wis. 6'1", 191. At Wausau H.S. scored 85 points as junior and 110 as senior. At U. of Wisconsin had brief but spectacular career as end and running back. Enlisted in marines and sent to U. of Michigan as V-12 officer candidate. Was able to play football there under Fritz Crisler. Also lettered in basketball, baseball and track. Chicago Cubs (baseball) asked Hirsch to report to training camp, but marines sent him to El Toro, Calif. When war ended, he signed with Chicago Rockets (AAFC), 1946, under Dick Hanley who had coached him at El Toro. Before reporting as pro played on College All-Star team in 1946. Collegians defeated Los Angeles Rams, 16-0, and Hirsch was game's MVP. Rockets did poorly during his three years with them; he suffered many injuries, including fractured skull 10/48. Ten months later signed with Rams.
In 1950 moved to end position from halfback. Developed into premier receiver. Elusiveness in open field inspired nickname, and it fit perfectly. Caught 17 TD passes, to tie Don Hutson's record, 1951. Same year gained 1495 yds., eclipsing Hutson with 66 pass receptions, and led NFL scorers with 102 points. In pro career caught 343 passes for 6249 yds., 53 TDs. All-Pro, 1951. Retired, 1957, and moved to Ram front office. Involved in two movies, *Crazylegs*, 1953, and *Unchained,* 1954. In 1960 became general manager of Rams. Currently athletic director at Wisconsin. In 1973 brought suit against "Crazylegs" panty hose, claiming he owns rights to name. National Football Foundation Hall of Fame, Pro Football Hall of Fame.

HITCHCOCK, JAMES F. Running Back. B. 6/28/11, Inverness, Ala. D. 6/23/59, Montgomery, Ala. 5'11", 170. Played halfback for Auburn, 1930-32. Also served as kicker. Became Auburn's first All-America in 1932. Led Southern Conference in scoring that year, was captain of Tigers' undefeated team. Kicked 232 times without having one blocked. Baseball All-America, 1932. After college played baseball professionally for seven years, including one in majors with Boston Braves, 1938, as shortstop-third baseman. Served as Auburn backfield coach during off-seasons. During World War II was instructor in naval aviation. Elected to Alabama Public Service Commission. Brother of Billy Hitchcock, former major-league baseball player and manager. Citizens Savings Hall of Fame, National Football Foundation Hall of Fame.

HIXSON, CHARLES (Chuck) Quarterback. Southern Methodist, 1966-68.

Fabulous collegiate passer. Holds NCAA record for plays, career, with 1358, on which he gained 6884 yds. and was responsible for 50 TDs. On 9/28/68 set record for passes attempted, game, with 69; completed 37. Holds record for passes completed, career, with 642 of 115; 56 interceptions, 7179 yds., percentage of .576. Also holds record for yds. passing per game, career, with 247.6 (7179 yds. in 29 games) and record 22.1-yd. average per game. In 1968 led NCAA in passing with 265 completions in 468 attempts; 23 interceptions, percentage of .566, 3103 yds., 21 TDs. Shares 2nd spot with Terry Hanratty for most plays, game, with 75. That figure was achieved vs. Ohio State, 9/28/68. He didn't play pro ball.

HOERNSCHEMEYER, ROBERT (Hunch) Running Back. B. 9/24/25, Cincinnati, Ohio. 5'10", 190. Played as freshman, 1943, for Indiana. Collegiate total offense leader that year and one of top passers. In 10 games, 355 plays, gained 1648 yds. Played for U.S. Naval Academy, 1944-45. In 1945, vs. Notre Dame, threw winning TD pass to Skippy Minisi in last minute of play. Chicago Rockets, 1946-47, 49; Brooklyn Dodgers, 1947-48; Detroit Lions, 1950-55. As Lion, tied Jim Spavital for 2nd longest TD run (96 yds.) from scrimmage in NFL history, 11/23/50. Finished pro career 5th in AAFC rushing with 2109 yds. (506 carries); 6th in passing with 4109 yds. (308 of 688). Threw 32 TD passes. Played in NFL championship games, 1953, 54.

HOGAN, JAMES J. (Yale) Tackle. B. 11/1/1876, Glenbane, County Tipperary, Ireland. D. 3/20/10. 5'10", 210. Yale, 1902-04. All-America 1902, 03, 04. Captain, 1904. Called "Yale" by classmates because of great enthusiasm. Strong, aggressive, powerful. Occasionally used as ball carrier. Played with sleeves rolled up and with a smile. Running mate of Ralph Kinney. They were most spectacular pair of tackles in Yale history. Yale lost only two games, to Princeton and Army, in three years. Good student. Member of two debating societies, Skull and Bones, shot-putter on track team, class agent for Alumni Fund. After graduation received degree from Columbia Law School. Practiced law, 1908-10, until death from Bright's disease. Citizens Savings Player of the Year, 1902. National Football Foundation Hall of Fame.

HOLLAND, JEROME H. (Brud) End. B. Auburn, N. Y. 6', 215. Played at Cornell, 1936-38. Consensus All-America, 1938; All-America, 1937. One of the first Blacks ever in Ivy League. One of 13 children. Brud is nickname for "brother," given by brothers and sisters. Worked his way thru Cornell with honors. Holds Ph.D. in sociology. Excelled at end-around; defensive play also superb. Fine all-around skills. Chairman of the Board, Planned Parenthood-World Population. Board of governors, American Red Cross. Director, United Negro College Fund, National Urban League, Boy Scouts of America. Served as president of Hampton Institute and Delaware State before 1970 appointment as U.S. Ambassador to Sweden. National Football Foundation Hall of Fame.

HOLLEDER, DONALD W. End-Quarterback. B. 8/3/34, Rochester, N.Y. D. 10/17/67, Vietnam. 6'2", 187. Played high school football in Rochester; field is now named for him. Army, 1953-55. All-America, 1954. Was outstanding end for Army in 1954. Switched to QB by Earl Blaik in '55. Received much criticism for his passing that season but weathered storm to lead upset of Navy, 14-6. Won Swede Nelson Award for Sportsmanship, 1955. Did not play pro ball. Was killed in Vietnam at age 33.

HOLLENBACK, WILLIAM M. (Big Bill) Running Back. B. 2/22/1886, Blue Ball, Pa. D. 3/12/68. 6'1", 185. Pennsylvania 1906-08. Captain of 1908 national champions. All-America, 1908; 2nd team, 1906, 07. According to great admirer, Pudge Heffelfinger, Hollenback was indestructible. Played with leg fractures, shoulder separations, skin splints, hip bruises. Opened and closed career on undefeated national championship teams. In 1909 became head coach for Penn State; in 1910 went to Missouri, returning to Penn State in 1911. Coached Pennsylvania Military, 1915. In 1916 went to Syracuse, retiring from coaching after that season. Served as Eastern collegiate football official, 1921-36. Later business leader, president of W. M. Hollenback Coal & Coke Co., Inc., of Philadelphia. Citizens Savings Hall of Fame, National Football Foundation Hall of Fame.

HOLLINGBERY, ORIN E. (Babe) Coach. B. 7/15/1893, Hollister, La. D. 1/12/74, Yakima, Wash. Didn't attend college. Coached 17 years at Washington State, 1926-42. Finished career with record of 93-53-14, .625 percentage. Very thorough in teaching fundamentals. Fireball and tireless worker who could instill fighting spirit in his teams. 1930 national championship team included such greats as Turk Edwards, George Hurley and Mel Hein. Invited to Rose Bowl three times, losing all: 1926 to Alabama 20-0; 1931 to Alabama, 24-0; 1937 to Pittsburgh, 21-0. Hein said he always considered Babe outstanding in his field.

HOLOVAK, MICHAEL J. Running Back. B. 9/19/19, Lansford, Pa. 6'2", 214. Boston College fullback, 1940-42. Consensus All-America, 1942 (one of two in B.C. history). 4th in Heisman Trophy voting, 1942. In college career appeared in 25 games, made 393 rushes for 2083 yds., average of 5.3, scored 23 TDs and 140 points. Scored one TD in 1941 Sugar Bowl. In 1943 set Orange Bowl records of 158 yds. rushing, 15.8 yds. per carry and 18 points. Scored on rushes of 65, 35 and 2 yds. Also caught 45-yd. pass. Los Angeles Rams, 1946; Chicago Bears, 1947-48. Coached New England Patriots, 1961-68. Released at end of '68 season. Record: 52-46-9.

HOLT, HENRY C. Center. B. 1/13/1881, New York, N.Y. D. 2/20/55, Putnam, Conn. 6', 210. Played at Yale. Son of federal judge George C. Holt. All-America, 1901, 02. Yale was 22-1-2 during those years. Contemporary of Yale immortals Ned Glass and Jim Hogan. Was banker, retiring at age 46. Died after long illness.

HOPPMANN, DAVID Running Back. B. Madison, Wis. 6'1", 195. Iowa State tailback, 1960-62. All-America, 1962. Vs. Kansas State made 71- and 69-yd. rushes, 1961. NCAA total offense leader that year with 1638 yds. Scored or passed for 13 TDs. Also led in rushing carries with 229, for 920 yds. Finished

153

career 12th in rushing yds. with 2562, 14th in total-offense yds. with 4173. Didn't play in NFL.

HORNUNG, PAUL Running Back. B. 12/23/35, Louisville, Ky. 6'2", 205. Notre Dame, 1954-56. Consensus All-America, 1955; All-America, 1956. Heisman Trophy, 1956. Had 70-yd. interception return vs. North Carolina, 1954. In 42-20 loss to USC, 1955, ran 58 yds. for TD, threw 78-yd. pass, gained 354 yds. total offense. In 1956 made 95-yd. kickoff return vs. USC. Fine all-round skills, excellent at option: Bonus pick by Green Bay Packers, 1957. Played with Pack, 1957-62, 64-66. Ineffective first two pro seasons but was turned around by Vince Lombardi. NFL's leading scorer, 1959, with 94 points; in 1960 with record 176; in 1961 with 146. On 10/8/61, vs. Baltimore Colts, scored 3 TDs, 6 PATs, 3 FGs for 33 points. Packers swamped Giants in 1961 NFL title game, 37-0; Hornung scored 19 points and was selected MVP by *Sport* magazine. Had been called into Army that year but released 10 days before title game. Suffered knee injury, 1962, and lost scoring title to Jim Taylor. On 4/17/63 was suspended, along with Alex Karras, for gambling; Hornung was reinstated in 1964. However, that was off-year for him. Missed five straight FG attempts vs. Baltimore. Asked about it, answered, "I can't kick."

Turned in sensational performance in 1965 title game vs. Cleveland Browns, scoring 13-yd. TD as Pack won 23-12. Retired in 1967 after being selected by New Orleans Saints in expansion draft, replaced by Donny Anderson. Was great triple-threat back. According to Frank Leahy, he ran "like a mower going through grass"; Vince Lombardi's appraisal was, "he smells that goal line." Loved ladies, good times, night life. Favorite of Lombardi, who forgave Paul's playfulness.

HORRELL, EDWIN C. (Babe) Center. B. 9/29/02, Jackson, Mo. 5'11", 185. At Pasadena (Calif.) H.S. played football, basketball, tennis, water polo, ran track, was on swimming team. 1920 football captain, '21 tennis captain. High school football stadium named Horrell Field after Babe and his four brothers. U. of California, 1922-24. Didn't play in losing collegiate football game. Also track, tennis. In 1923, vs. Stanford, Horrell scored eight of team's nine points; ran back blocked punt for TD, scored safety. Captain of California's 1924 "Wonder Team." All-Coast, 1923, 24. All-America same seasons. Consensus choice in '24. Scored first TD in Berkeley's new stadium on blocked Ernie Nevers punt. Class president. UCLA assistant coach, 1926-38; head coach, 1939-44. Guided Bruins to their first Rose Bowl in 1943, although '39 team was undefeated with four ties. Currently land, fruit-packing entrepreneur; holds interest in two golf courses. Citizens Savings Hall of Fame, National Football Foundation Hall of Fame.

HORVATH, LESLIE Running Back-Quarterback. B. South Bend, Ind. 6', 165. Ohio State, 1940-42, 44. Unanimous All-America, 1944. Heisman Trophy, 1944. In first play of collegiate career tackled Tom Harmon to save TD. Led Ohio State to national championship, 1942. In army, 1943. Scored 12 TDs, gained 905 yds. rushing and led Ohio State to Big 10 title in 1944, its first unbeaten season since

1920. Chicago Tribune Trophy, Nile Kinnick Trophy, Christy Walsh Trophy, all in 1944. Exceptional receiver, fine field runner. On active duty with U.S. Navy, 1945-46. Assistant coach, Great Lakes Naval Training Station, 1946, under former college coach Paul Brown. Los Angeles Rams, 1947-48; Cleveland Browns (AAFC), 1949. Ranked 3rd in punt returns, 1948. Currently dentist in Los Angeles. Coaches Jr. Bantam football team there. Citizens Savings Hall of Fame, National Football Foundation Hall of Fame.

HOUSTON, JAMES E. Linebacker. B. 11/3/37, Massillon, Ohio. 6'3", 240. Played end, both ways, for Ohio State, 1957-59. All-America, 1958, 59. Drafted on 1st round by Cleveland Browns. Brown linebacker, 1960-72. Brother of Lin Houston, guard with Browns, 1946-53, and Walt Houston, guard with Washington Redskins, 1955. Returned interception 71 yds. for TD, 1967, vs. New York Giants. Pro Bowl, 1964, 65. NFL championship games, 1964, 65, 68, 69.

HOUSTON, KENNETH R. Defensive Back. B. 11/12/44, Lufkin, Tex. 6'3", 190. Linebacker at Prairie View A. & M., 1964-66. Drafted on 9th round by Houston Oilers, 1967. Rookie year ran back blocked FG 71 yds. for TD. Established records for most TDs on interceptions, season, 1971, with four (tied 1972 by Jim Kearney); most TDs on interceptions, career, 1967-73, with nine. Had 6 interceptions for 32 yds., 1973; longest was 22 yds. All-AFC, 1971. AFL championship game, 1971. AFL All-Star games, 1968, 69. Pro Bowl, 1970, 71, 72. Traded to Washington Redskins in 1973 with draft choice, for tight end Mack Alston, defensive back Jim Severson, defensive end Mike Fanucci, tackle Jim Snowden, wide receiver Clifton McNeil.

HOWARD, FRANK J. Coach. B. 3/25/09, Barlow Bend, Ala. Spent early days on Alabama farm playing cow pasture baseball. Rural background left its imprint, literally. Became foremost country bumpkin, veritable fount of hillbilly lore and legend. Dead serious about football though, and few coaches carried better reputation. Played at Alabama, 1928-30. Wallace Wade's 1930 team defeated Washington State in Rose Bowl, 24-0. Howard was dubbed "Little Giant" of Tide's "Herd of Red Elephants." Clemson line coach, 1931-39. Took head post when Jess Neely went to Rice in 1940. Stayed on job 30 years, retiring after 1969 season. Record: 168-118-12. Athletic director, 1940-71. Used single-wing attack until 1953 when he switched to T formation. Installed I and pro-type set in 1965. Took Clemson to six bowl games: 1949, 52 Gator; 1951, 57 Orange; 1959 Sugar; 1959 Astro-Bluebonnet. In great demand as after-dinner speaker. Retired from Clemson in 1974 after 44-year association. At time was assistant to vice president of student affairs. Citizens Savings Hall of Fame.

HOWE, ARTHUR Quarterback. B. 3/3/1890, South Orange, N.J. D. 3/18/55, Plymouth, N.H. 5'10", 153. Yale, 1909-11. All-America, 1911; 2nd team, 1909-10. On 11/18/11 established two records which still stand: most total kick returns, game, with 18, for 150 yds.; and most punt returns, game, with 17 for 130 yds. (vs. Princeton). Played hockey at Hotchkiss prep school before attending Yale. Entered educational field, taught at Loomis and Taft schools, Dartmouth College before becoming president of Hampton Institute. Also Presbyterian minister. Was chairman of the board of Home for Wayward Boys in Tilton, N.H. National Football Foundation Hall of Fame.

HOWELL, JAMES L. (Jim) Coach. B. 9/14/14, Lonoke, Ark. Jim Lee Howell was big fellow, standing 6'6" and weighing over 200. Played at Arkansas, 1934-36. End for New York Giants, 1937-42, 46-48. Became assistant to Steve Owen in 1948, succeeding him in 1954. Coached Giants, 1954-60, leading some of greatest Giant teams. Won divisional titles, 1956, 58, 59. NFL champions, 1956. Defeated Cleveland Browns, 10-0, to win Eastern Conference title in first sudden-death playoff in NFL history, 1958; then lost "greatest game ever played" to Baltimore Colts, 23-17. Among assistants were Vince Lombardi, Allie Sherman, Norm Hecker, Tom Landry, Harland Svare. Never finished below 3rd in division. Record was 53-27-4. Some of his players were Bill Austin, Rosey Brown, Don Chandler, Charlie Conerly, Lindon Crow, Frank Gifford, Sam Huff, Tom Landry, Don Maynard, Andy Robustelli, Kyle Rote, Pat Summerall.

HOWELL, MILLARD F. (Dixie) Running Back. B. Hartford, Ala. D. 3/2/71, Hollywood, Calif. 5'10", 164. Full name: Millard Filmore Howell. Alabama, 1932-34. Passing end of Howell-to-Hutson combination. Consensus All-America, 1934. Fine triple-threat back vs. Vanderbilt made 80-yd. interception return, 1932. Made 89-, 80- and 83-yd. punts in separate 1933 games. Called "Human Howitzer" by Grantland Rice. Sensational in final regular game, running for two TDs, passing unerringly, leading team to 16-7 win. Played in Rose Bowl last two seasons. In 1935 Rose Bowl completed 9 of 12 passes for 160 yds., one 59-yd. TD; rushed for 79 yds., including 67-yd. TD; returned 4 kicks for 74 yds.; and punted 6 times for 43.8 average beat Stanford, 29-13. Quarterback with Washington Redskins, 1937. Coach for Arizona State, 1938-41, Idaho State, 1942-50. Later was director of public relations for Los Angeles construction company. Citizens Savings College Player of the Year, 1934. National Football Foundation Hall of Fame. Died after two-year fight with cancer.

HOWFIELD, ROBERT Kicker. B. 12/3/36, Bushey, England. 5'9", 180. Pro soccer player in English League for 12 years. Didn't attend college. Originally signed by Kansas City Chiefs, 1968, but released before playing one game. Signed by Denver Broncos, 1968. Traded to New York Jets for kicker Jim Turner, 1971. New Orleans Saints kicked six FGs, 12/3/72. Led AFC in scoring with 121 points, 1972, on 27 FGs and 40 PATs. Converted 27 of 27 PAT attempts, 17 of 24 FG attempts, scoring 78 points in 1973. Pro Bowl, 1972.

HOWLEY, CHARLES L. (Chuck) Linebacker. B. 6/28/36, Wheeling, W. Va. 6'2", 225. After career at West Virginia, 1st-round draft pick by Chicago Bears in 1958. Traded to Dallas Cowboys for two draft choices, 1961. On 10/2/66, vs.

Atlanta Falcons, returned fumble for 97-yd. TD, 2nd longest in pro history. Vs. Baltimore Colts tied record for most passes intercepted in Super Bowl game with two, 1971. In 1972 Super Bowl, vs. Miami Dolphins, intercepted Bob Griese pass to set up TD. Pro Bowl, 1965, 66, 67, 68, 70. All-Pro 1968. Cowboys won 1972 College All-Star game, 20-7.

HOWTON, WILLIAM End. B. 7/3/30, Littlefield, Tex. 6'2", 185. Played end for Rice, 1949-51. All-America, 1951. Set season record in average yds. (22.6) on pass receptions, catching 33 for 747 yds. and 7 TDs. Finished collegiate career with 64 receptions, 1289 yds. and 12 TDs. Made 65-yd. catch vs. Santa Clara, 1950. Made 74-yd. catch vs. Navy, 1951. Green Bay Packers, 1952-58; Cleveland Browns, 1959; Dallas Cowboys, 1960-63. In 1963 broke Don Hutson's career record of 7991 yds. on pass receptions, with 8000. Finished pro career 6th in pass receptions with 503, and 4th in yds. on pass receptions with 8459. All Pro, 1956, 57.

HUARTE, JOHN G. Quarterback. B. 4/6/44, Anaheim, Calif. 6', 185. Played QB for Notre Dame, 1962-64. Consensus All-America, 1964. Heisman Trophy, 1964. 1965 College All-Star game MVP. Set collegiate season records, 1964, in passing yds. per attempt with 10.1; and passing yds. per completion with 18.1. Ranked 2nd nationally that season in total-offense yds. per play with 8.5, on 242 plays for 2069 yds. Completed 91-yd. pass vs. Pittsburgh and 74-yd. pass vs. Navy, 1964. Selected by New York Jets on 2nd round of 1965 AFL draft. Spent that year on taxi squad. Traded to Boston Patriots, 1966. Released by Boston, signed by Philadelphia Eagles, 1967. Philadelphia taxi squad, 1967. Traded to Minnesota Vikings for draft choice, 1969, but released and signed by Kansas City Chiefs. Kansas City placed him on familiar taxi squad. Sold to Chicago Bears, 1972. Disappointing pro career — all downhill after collegiate stardom.

HUBBARD, ROBERT C. (Cal) Tackle-End. B. 10/11/1900, Keytesville, Mo. 6'5", 260. All-America at both Geneva College, where he played tackle, 1922-24; and Centenary College, where he played end, 1926. One of all-time great tackles. Bo McMillin said, "Cal Hubbard was the greatest football player I ever saw or hope to see — back, end, tackle, wherever he played." New York Giants, 1927-28, 36; Green Bay Packers, 1929-33, 35; Pittsburgh Pirates, 1936. All-Pro 1931, 32, 33. American League baseball umpire, 1936-52. Supervisor of A.L. umpires, 1952-70. Elected to both National Football Foundation Hall of Fame and Pro Football Hall of Fame in 1963.

HUBBARD, ROBERT C. (Cal) Tackle-End B. 10/11/00 Keytesville, Mo. 6'5", 260. All-America at both Geneva College, where he played tackle, 1922-24; and Centenary College, where he played end, 1926. One of all-time great tackles. Bo McMillin said, "Cal Hubbard was the greatest football player I ever saw or hope to see — back, end, tackle, wherever he played." New York Giants, 1927-28, 36; Green Bay Packers, 1929-33, 35; Pittsburgh Pirates, 1936. All-Pro 1931, 32, 33. American League baseball umpire, 1936-52. Supervisor of A.L. umpires, 1952-

70. Elected to both National Football Foundation Hall of Fame and Pro Football Hall of Fame in 1963.

HUBERT, ALLISON T. S. (Pooley) Running Back. B. Meridian, Miss. 190. Alabama fullback, 1923-25. Played on teams that won 26 of 29 games. Great team leader. Scored 35 TDs for Alabama. Scored at least three TDs six times. All-Southern, 1924, 25. All America, 1925. Passing combination of Johnny Mack Brown and Pooley Hubert helped Tide reach Rose Bowl in 1926. New York Yankees, AFL, 1926. Teammate of Red Grange. Coached six years at Mississippi State, then went to Virginia Military Institute for 10 more in 1937-46. Named to Alabama All-Time team. Currently owns business in Waynesboro, Ga., serving 'Bama as advisor. National Football Foundation Hall of Fame.

HUFF, ROBERT L. (Sam) Linebacker. B. 10/4/34, Edna Gas, W. Va. 6'1", 230. at Florida State, 1970-72. Set record, 10/2/71 vs. Virginia Tech, for yds. passing per attempt with 15.0 (25 attempts, 374 yds.). 1971 NCAA total offense leader, compiling 241.2-yd. average per game. Finished 30-game career with 436 completions in 796 passing attempts, for 6378 yds., 52 TDs, 42 interceptions. His career total offense was 6086 yds. on 921 plays, 202.9 yds. per game, 6.61 yds. per play and 54 TDs-accounted-for. Selected by Chicago Bears on 2nd round of 1973 draft.

HUFF, ROBERT L. (Sam) Linebacker. B. 10/4/34, Edna Gas. W. Va. 6'1", 230. West Virginia, 1953-55. All-America, 1955. 1956 College All-Star game. Better than average student and football star in high school, and member of dramatic club. Drafted on 3rd round by New York Giants, 1956. During eight-year career with Giants, team won Eastern Conference title six times. Delighted fans with vicious play; they voiced approval by shouting "Huff, Huff, Huff!" Traded with tackle George Seals to Washington Redskins, 3/10/64. Giant coach Allie Sherman said Huff traded because he was slowing down at age 29. Had three-year contract with 'Skins for $100,000, and they promised never to trade him. Entering 1967 season had not missed game since he first became regular with Giants. Retired, 1968, but returned to active ranks year later to play under Vince Lombardi. Assistant coach, Redskins, 1968-71. Currently announcer (with Marv Albert and Chip Cipolla) on N.Y. Giant radio broadcasts. Pro Bowl, 1958, 59, 60, 61, 64 (1960 Pro Bowl Lineman of the Game). Played in NFL title games, 1956, 58, 59, 61, 62, 63. All-Pro, 1958, 59. Named to All-Pro Squad of the 1950s.

HUFFMAN, VERNON Quarterback. B. 11/18/14, Mooreland, Ind. 6'2", 190. Played QB for Indiana, 1934-36. All-Conference basketball player in 1936. Won conference Medal of Honor. Could run and block, was good passer and kicker. According to George Trevor, when Huffman was in game, no one else got chance to pass or punt. Detroit Lions, 1937-38. On 10/17/37, vs. Brooklyn Dodgers, ran 100 yds. for TD on pass interception; now tied with three other players for 3rd longest interception gain in pro history.

HUGHES, CHARLES (Chuck) End. B. 3/24/43, Philadelphia, Pa. D. 10/24/71, Detroit, Mich. 6', 170. Texas (El Paso), 1964-66. On 9/18/65, vs. North Texas State, set NCAA record in receiving yardage with 349 (10 catches). In college career of 30 games made 162 receptions, for 2882 yds., 19 TDs, average of 1.78 yds. per catch and 5.4 catches per game. Selected on 4th round of 1967 AFL-NFL draft by Philadelphia Eagles. Traded, 1970, to Detroit Lions and played with them until death. Collapsed on field, 10/24/71, after attempting to catch pass from Detroit QB Greg Landry. Rushed to hospital after emergency treatment failed to revive him. One hour after game ended, word came that he had died. Heart attack attributable. Hughes was only 28 years old.

HUGHES, HARRY W. Coach. B. 10/9/1887, DeKalb County, Mo. D. 7/26/53, Fort Collins, Colo. Halfback and placekicker at Oklahoma, 1904-06. Loved football so much that coach Bennie Owens often had to chase him off field after practice. In 1910 became Owens' first assistant coach. Year later named head coach at Colorado State, remaining there 31 years. Compiled 125-89-18 record. Was unbeaten twice, 1915, 16. Developed track star Glenn Morris who won 1936 Olympic decathlon championship. Citizens Savings Hall of Fame.

HUMBLE, WELDON G. Guard. B. 4/4/21, Nixon, Texas. 6'1", 210. Full name: Weldon Gaston Humble. Rice star; played under Jess Neely, 1941-42, 46. Fine competitor, genuine leader. All-SWC guard, 1942, 46. All-America, 1946. Won varsity high school letters in football, basketball, swimming, track. Served in World War II and Korea as Marine Capt. Cleveland Browns, 1947-50; Dallas Texans, 1952. Currently Houston bank executive.National Football Foundation Hall of Fame.

HUMPHREY, CLAUDE B. Defensive End. B. 6/29/44, Memphis, Tenn. 6'5", 255. Attended Tennessee State. He and quarterback Eldridge Dickey led Tigers to 35-3-1 three-year record, 1965-67. Won national Black championship, 1967. All-America, 1967. Played in Senior Bowl, Blue-Gray, Coaches All-America, College All-Star games. Selected by Atlanta Falcons on 1st round, 1968. Falcons, 1968-73. Developed rapidly into outstanding pro. Feared pass rusher. Recovered fumble for 24 yds. and TD, 1969. Tackled Charley Johnson, Denver Broncos, for safety, 1972. Pro Bowl, 1971, 72, 73, 74. All-NFC, 1973. Works with underprivileged youth.

HUNT, O. JOEL Quarterback. B. 10/11/05, Texico, N.M. 5'10", 168. Texas A. & M., 1925-27. Halfback, then quarterback; also punter, placekicker, dropkicker. All-Southwest Conference each season. Captain, 1927. Led Aggies to SWC titles, 1925, 27. Scored 128 points in 1927, still conference record. Career: 224 points, 30 TDs. 1927 team unbeaten, one tie (0-0 with TCU). Missed only three minutes during 1927 season. Had rivalry with little Jerry Mann of SMU. Led team to 7-0 win over SMU, 1925, but lost 9-6 following year. In 1927 trouncing of SMU (39-13), Hunt scored three TDs, punted for 44-yd. average, made two TD passes, played both ways, had four interceptions. Led West to 16-6 win in 1927 East-West Shrine game, scoring opening TD. 1927 Aggies, claimed Hunt, introduced "down-the-field pass plus lateral." Coach Dana X. Bible called him "one of the most talented players I ever coached." National Football Foundation Hall of Fame.

HUNTER, ARTHUR Center-Tackle. B. 4/24/33, Fairport, Ohio. 6'4", 245. Notre Dame. Played end, center and tackle under Frank Leahy, 1951-53. Graduated with degree in finance. All-America, 1953. Played on Frank Leahy's last Notre Dame team. One of six players on squad named All-America. Also played baseball, basketball. Drafted by Green Bay Packers in 1954 on 1st round. In military service, 1955. Cleveland Browns, 1956-59; Los Angeles Rams, 1960-65; Pittsburgh Steelers, 1966. NFL championship game, 1957. Pro Bowl, 1960.

HUNTINGTON, ELLERY C., JR. Quarterback. B. 3/11/1893, Nashville, Tenn. 5'9", 160. Colgate, 1910-13. Football, track, basketball letterman. All-America, 1913. Led Red Raiders to overall record of 18-11-2. Walter Camp praised, "Huntington is fast, strong, poised, and an expert passer. He calls his plays well. He is a large factor in Colgate's success." Was Phi Beta Kappa, president of his class. Earned law degree from Harvard. Twice served country in wartime. In World War II headed American Military Mission to Marshall Tito in Yugoslavia, receiving Legion of Merit. Coached Colgate, 1919, 21. Highly regarded as football historian. Prior to retirement, Huntington was chairman of the board of Equity Corp., New York City. Ellery Sr. was Colgate athletic director. Ellery Jr. now lives in Tucson. National Football Foundation Hall of Fame.

HUTSON, DONALD M. End. B. 1/31/13, Pine Bluff, Ark. 6'1", 175. Known as "Alabama Antelope." Played for Crimson Tide, 1932-34. One of most dangerous receivers in history. Moved well, great faker. Invented many patterns. Part of famous Howell-to-Hutson duo. "I just ran like the devil," he once explained, "and Dixie Howell got the ball there." Averaged six-eight receptions per game. Great at catching passes "in traffic." Consensus All-America, 1934. Named to All-Century team. In 1935 Rose Bowl caught 6 passes for 165 yds. Green Bay Packers, 1935-45. NFL receiving leader 1936, 37, 39, 41, 42, 43, 44, 45. NFL scoring leader, 1940, 41, 42, 43, 44, setting record in 1942 (138 pts.) which stood until 1960. Led league in FGs with five, 1943. Caught 99 TD passes and gained 8010 yds. receiving. On 10/7/45, in 2nd quarter, scored 29 points vs. Detroit Lions. At retirement held records for points (825), TDs (105). Nine times All-Pro. Citizens Savings Hall of Fame, National Football Foundation Hall of Fame, Pro Football Hall of Fame. Modern All-Time All-America team.

160

JACKSON, HAROLD End. B. 1/6/46, Hattiesburg, Miss. 5'10", 175. Graduated from Jackson State, 1968. All-Southwest Athletic Conference twice. Timed at 9.5 in 100-yd. dash. Selected by Los Angeles Rams on 12th round, 1968. Caught no passes that year. Rams then traded him to Philadelphia Eagles. Led NFL in receiving yardage, 1969, with 1116 on 65 catches; scored 9 TDs. Eagles' top receiver in 1971 with 47 catches, 716 yds. and 3 TDs. In 1972 again led NFL in receiving yardage with 1048 yds., and in number of receptions with 62. In 1973 traded with RB Tony Baker and three high draft choices to Los Angeles Rams, for QB Roman Gabriel. Caught four TD passes vs. Dallas Cowboys, 1973. Scored 78 points on 13 TDs during '73 season, all on pass receptions, to lead all receivers. All-NFC, 1972, 73. Played in Pro Bowl, 1970, 73, 74. One of quickest, shiftiest receivers in game.

JACKSON, LEVI A. Running Back. B. 8/22/26, New Haven, Conn. 5'10", 190. Youngest of six children. Played for Reggie Root, ex-Yale lineman, at New Haven's Hillhouse High School, 1943-44. Followed Root to Yale, becoming school's first Black football player. Played there, 1946-49. Fine punter, runner, passer. Gained national spotlight when named captain, 1949. Story merited two-column spot on page one of New York *Times;* Jackson received 2000 congratulatory letters and wires. Scored two touchdowns against Harvard in 29-6 victory — first "Big 3" triumph for coach Herman Hickman. Tapped for senior honor society, choosing Berzelius. Presence at Yale brought few repercussions, though problem was feared in 1948 when Hickman became head coach.

161

Hickman, who hailed from Tennessee, promptly dispelled this notion when he told Jackson, "Levi, I sure am glad to see you here."

JACKSON, RICHARD S. (Rich; Tombstone) Defensive End. B. 7/22/41, New Orleans, La. 6'3", 255. Standout end at Southern U., 1961-63, on both offense and defense. Track letterman and NAIA shot-put champion. Signed as free agent by Oakland Raiders, 1965. Suffered broken jaw in training camp and was on taxi squad that year. Played regularly in '66. Traded Denver Broncos, 1967. Had fine career with Denver until knee surgery in 1971. In 1972 traded to Cleveland Browns for 3rd-round draft choice and played 10 games. Released by Browns in summer of '73. Played in AFL All-Star games, 1969, 70. Pro Bowl, 1971, 72. All-AFL, 1968, 69, 70. All-AFC, 1971. Tremendously aggressive player, excelling at pass rush.

JAMES, RICHARD Running Back. B. 5/22/34, Grants Pass, Ore. 5'9", 175. Played for Oregon. Joined Washington Redskins in 1956, played thru 1963. On 12/17/61, vs. Dallas Cowboys, scored four TDs to set Washington game record. Led Redskins in rushing that season with 71 carries for 374 yds., average of 5.3. Also led in 1963 with 104 carries for 384 yds., average of 3.7. Led NFL in punt returns, 1963. In 1964 traded with Andy Stynchula and draft choice to New York Giants, for Sam Huff and George Seals. Traded, 1965, to Minnesota Vikings. Ranks 3rd in NFL in kickoff returns, lifetime, with 189; 4th in yds. gained on kickoff returns, lifetime, with 4676 yds. Also played defensive back.

JAMES, ROBERT Defensive Back. B. 7/7/47, Murfreesboro, Tenn. 6'1", 175. Fisk linebacker and defensive end. First from his college to make good in pro football. Signed as free agent by Buffalo Bills, 1969. Had great year in 1972 and another in 1973 despite painful heel injury which bothered him for five games early in season. Pro Bowl, 1973, 74. All-AFC, 1972, 73. Earned starting cornerback assignment in 1970 after playing mainly on special teams as rookie.

JAMES, RON (Po) Running Back. B. 3/19/49, New Brighton, Pa. 6'1", 202. Received nickname from uncle as youngster. New Mexico State, 1968-71. NCAA record-holder for yds., all-purpose running, four-year career, with 5979. Ranked 2nd in NCAA in career rushing yds. with 3884 on 818 plays, average of 4.75 per carry. Also returned record 172 kickoffs for 1870 yds., 26.0 average. Selected by Philadelphia Eagles on 4th round of 1972 NFL draft; was regular first season, appearing in 14 games. Gained 565 yds. rushing on 182 carries and 156 yds. on 20 pass receptions. In 1973 made 16 kickoff returns for 413 yds., average of 25.8.

JANCIK, ROBERT L., JR. (Bobby) Defensive Back. B. 2/9/40, Houston, Tex. 5'11", 180. Attended Wharton County (Tex.) J.C. and Lamar Tech. Houston Oilers, 1962-67. Selected by Oilers on 19th round in 1962. Established AFL career records for most kickoff returns, 158 (since broken), kickoff return yds., 4185, years leading in kickoff returns, 2 (1963 with 45, 1966 with 34). Holds record for yds., season, 1963, with 1317. Tied for most kickoff returns in title games with nine. Holds record for return yds. in title games with 239. Returned eight kickoffs for 240 yds., 12/22/63. Led league in average yds. per kickoff return in 1962 with 30.3, in 1963 with 29.3. Finished career with 26.5-yd. average.

JANIK, THOMAS A. Defensive Back. B. 9/6/40, Poth, Tex. 6'3", 190. Attended Texas A. & M. and Texas A. & I. Denver Broncos, 1963-64; Buffalo Bills, 1965-68; Boston Patriots, 1969-70; New England Patriots, 1971. Drafted by Broncos on 3rd round in 1963. Traded to Bills in 1965, sold to Patriots in 1969. Tied Miller Farr and Dick Westmoreland for interceptions with 10, 1967. Against New York Jets, 9/29/68, ran back interceptions 100 yds. for TD, tying AFL record. Gained 137 yds. on interceptions that game to give him 2nd highest total in AFL annals. Holds Buffalo record for interception yds., season, with 222 in 1967; career, with 495 yds. Six career TD interceptions placed him 3rd on all-time list. Punted 10 times for 37.4 yd. average in 1964. AFL All-Star games, 1966, 68. Played in AFL championship games, 1965, 66.

JANOWICZ, VICTOR Running Back. B. Elyria, Ohio. 5'9", 189. Ohio State halfback, 1949-51. Unanimous All-America, 1950. Heisman Trophy and Silver Football, 1950. As sophomore was injured and played little. Recovered to play safety in 1950 Rose Bowl vs. California and intercepted 2 passes, returned one 46 yds. (beat California, 17-14). Completed 60-yd. pass vs. Pittsburgh and returned punt 61 yds. vs. Iowa, 1950. Delivered punts of 70 and 68 yds. against Pitt in 1951. In collegiate career gained 802 yds. rushing, 685 passing on 41 completions in 106 attempts. Gained total of 2107 yds. in all categories and scored 103 points. Played pro baseball with Pittsburgh Pirates, 1953-54; batted .214 lifetime. Played pro football with Washington Redskins, 1954-55.

JAYNES, DAVID Quarterback. B. 12/12/52, Bonner Springs, Kan. 6'2", 212. Kansas, 1971-73. Consensus All-America, 1973. Set six Big 8 passing records. Greatest passer in Kansas history. Holds 17 school records, six Big 8 marks. Finished '73 season with 172 completions in 330 attempts for 2131 yds. and 13 TDs, only nine interceptions. Career passing total of 5132 yds. placed him behind only Lynn Dickey in Big 8 history. Passed for more than 200 yds. in 7 of 11 games as junior. Came into '73 season with four consecutive games in which had no pass intercepted, giving him 142 straight passes without interception, 3rd best record in history. Against Tennessee completed first nine attempts, 21 of 27 for 242 yds. and two TDs by halftime, finished with 35 of 53 for 394 yds. and three TDs. Holds every Kansas passing record but one. Excellent at play selection, reading defenses. Intelligent, poised and confident. Liberty Bowl, 1973. Played in East-West Shrine, Hula Bowl, Senior Bowl games following 1973 season. Was first player ever chosen by WFL when selected by Memphis on 1st round of 1974 draft. Selected on 3rd round of '74 NFL draft by K.C. Chiefs. Signed with Chiefs.

JEFFERSON, ROY L. End. B. 11/9/43, Texarkana, Tex. 6'2", 190. Graduated from Utah, 1965. Picked on 2nd round of draft by Pittsburgh Steelers same year.

Caught four TD passes to tie NFL record, 11/3/68. Finished season with 58 receptions for 1074 yds. and 11 TDs, 2nd in league to Clifton McNeil. Only NFL player to gain over 1000 yds. in both 1968 (1074) and 1969 (1079). Led NFL in receptions with 67, 1969. In 1970 traded Baltimore Colts for wide receiver Willie Richardson and draft choice. Following year traded to Washington Redskins for wide receiver Cotton Speyrer and 1st-round draft choice. Collected 41 receptions in 1973 for 595 yds., average of 14.5. Pro Bowl, 1969, 70, 72. Super Bowl, 1971, 73. All-NFL, 1969. All-NFC, 1971.

JENNINGS, JAMES H. (J.J.) Running Back. B. 8/16/52, Holyoke, Mass. Attended Holyoke H.S. and Rutgers. At Rutgers, 1971-73, he set nine records. Included were game and career marks in carries, yardage, TDs. Nation's leading scorer in 1973 with 128 points. Twice won Homer Hazel Trophy as team MVP, 1972, 73. Honored as College Player of the Year by New Jersey Sports Writers Association, 1973. Played halfback. Signed with Toronto of WFL, turning down offer from Kansas City Chiefs.

JENNINGS, MORLEY Coach. B. 1890, Holland, Mich. Played one season in backfield for Albion before attending Mississippi A. & M. (now Mississippi State). Coached Ouachita, 1913-25, where record was 62-14-10; Baylor, 1926-40, where record was 83-60-6. Citizens Savings Hall of Fame, National Football Foundation Hall of Fame.

JENSEN, JACK E. Running Back. B. 3/9/27, San Francisco, Calif. 5'11", 195. California, 1946-48. 21-8-0 playing record. Consensus All-America, 1948. Compiled 60-yd. career rushing average, on 274 carries for 1633 yds. Averaged 7.4 yds. senior year as Golden Bears romped to 10-0 season. They lost 1949 Rose Bowl to Northwestern, 20-14; Jensen scored on 67-yd. rush but was injured in 3rd quarter. Played pro baseball with New York Yankees, 1950-52; Washington Senators, 1952-53; Boston Red Sox, 1954-59, 61. Batted .279 in 1438 games. In 1958 named American League MVP, swatting 35 homers and driving in 122 runs. With Boston played in shadow of Ted Williams. Career hampered by terrible fear of flying. Married Zoe Ann Olsen, Olympic diving star.

JETER, ROBERT D. Defensive Back. B. 5/9/37, Union, S.C. 6'1", 200. Brother of Tony Jeter, Pittsburgh Steeler tight end. Attended Iowa. Drafted on 2nd round by Green Bay Packers, 1960. Vancouver (CFL) flanker, 1960-61. Green Bay Packers, 1962-70. 1963 member of taxi squad. Reserve receiver in 1962. Scored two TDs on interceptions to lead league, 1966. Traded to Chicago Bears for draft choice, 1971. In eight years made 26 interceptions for 333 yds., average of 12.8 yds. Played in Pro Bowl, 1968, 70. Played in NFL championship games 1965, 66, 67. Super Bowl, 1967, 68. All-NFL, 1967.

JOE, WILLIAM (Billy) Running Back. B. 10/14/40, Aynor, S.C. 6'1", 236. Villanova halfback. Selected by Denver Broncos on 11th round of 1963 AFL draft. Broncos, 1963-64. AFL Rookie of the Year. Traded to Buffalo Bills in 1965 for fullback Cookie Gilchrist. Selected by Miami Dolphins in AFL expansion draft, 1966. Released by Miami and signed by New York Jets in 1967. Scored three TDs rushing vs. Boston Patriots, 10/27/68. In six-year career gained 2010 yds. on 539 rushes, 589 yds. on 77 pass receptions; scored 19 TDs. AFL All-Star game, 1966. AFL championship game, 1965.

JOESTING, HERBERT W. Running Back. B. 4/17/05, Little Falls, Minn. D. 10/2/63, St. Paul, Minn. 6'2", 205. Minnesota fullback, 1925-27. All-America, 1926, 27; second Minnesota man in 10 years to achieve honor in two successive years. Workhorse back, good blocker and runner. Played game for all it was worth. Team had winning seasons each year he played. Player-coach for Minneapolis Redjackets, 1929-30; played for Frankfort Yellowjackets, 1930-31; Chicago Bears, 1921-32. Majored in forestry in college. Worked for State of Minnesota Motor Vehicle Division. National Football Foundation Hall of Fame.

JOHNSON, CHARLES L. (Charley) Quarterback. B. 11/22/38, Big Spring, Tex. 6'1", 200. Attended Schreiner Institute as freshman. Transferred to New Mexico State where he played QB, 1958-60. Completed 69-yd. pass vs. Tulane, 1959. In 1960 Sun Bowl threw TD passes of 57 and 15 yds. Year later in Sun Bowl completed 18 of 26 passes for 180 yds. and 2 TDs. Finished collegiate career with 468 yds. rushing on 229 carries, 4144 yds. passing on 311 of 577. Drafted by St. Louis Cardinals (NFL) and San Diego Chargers (AFL). Chose NFL. Played first two seasons with Cards while attending Washington (St. Louis), where he received master's degree in chemical engineering in 1963. Later earned Ph.D. Completed 150 of 308 passes for club record 2440 yds., 1962. Same season set St. Louis passing record by throwing for 386 yds. vs. Philadelphia Eagles. In 1963 threw 28 TD passes and led league in passing attempts with 423. Following year led league in passing attempts with 420, in completions with 223, in yds. with 3045. On 9/26/65 threw six TD passes in one game. Repeated feat four years later against New Orleans Saints; Bill Kilmer of Saints threw six TD passes in same game. On 1/21/70 involved in first trade between old NFL-AFL clubs, going to Houston Oilers with Bob Atkins for Miller Farr and Pete Beathard. Played most of 1970 despite broken left collarbone. Traded to Denver Broncos for draft choice in 1972. In 1973 attempted 346 passes and completed 184 for 2465 yds., 53.2 percentage, 20 TDs. One of top 20 passers in NFL history; threw 3000th pass on 12/16/73. Operates boys camp near Austin during off-season.

JOHNSON, ESSEX L. Running Back. B. 10/15/48, Shreveport, La. 5'10", 201. Attended Grambling. Cincinnati Bengals, 1968-73. Was 5th-round draft choice. In six pro years gained 1260 yds. on 88 pass receptions, scored 9 TDs. Gained additional 303 yds. on 51 punt returns and 749 yds. on 36 kickoff returns. In 1973 rushed for 997 yds., 3rd highest in AFC, on 195 rushes for average of 5.1 yds. Scored 42 points on 7 TDs (4 rushing, 3 receiving), 10th highest in AFC. Injured on opening play of 1973 playoff game against Miami Dolphins. Tremendous speed and acceleration. "Essex has the finest balance of any football player I have coached," said Paul Brown.

JOHNSON, HARVEY Defensive Back-Kicker. B. 6/22/19, Bridgeton, N.J. William & Mary, 1939-43. Played for Bainbridge Naval Station, 1943-45. Drafted by New York Yankees of AAFC and joined them after war, playing 1946-49. Moved with team to NFL, remained thru 1951. Great kicker. In four AAFC years was 6th highest scorer with 213 points, on 147 PATs and 22 FGs. Made 146 consecutive conversions. AAFC FG leader with seven, 1949. Joined coaching staff of Hamilton Tiger-Cats, 1953. Head coach, Kitchener, of Rugby Football Union, 1954-57; won four ORFU championships in as many years. Montreal Alouette assistant, 1958-59. Became defensive back coach of Buffalo Bills, 1960; director of player personnel in 1962, position he still holds. Acted as head coach for 12 games of 1968 season and all of 1971. Raises thoroughbred horses.

JOHNSON, JAMES E. (Jimmy) Defensive Back. B. 3/31/38, Dallas, Tex. 6'2", 187. Santa Monica City College, 1958; UCLA, 1959-60. High school and college letterman in football, basketball, track. First year at UCLA played end. As junior won NCAA high-hurdle championship. As senior played wingback and was team's No. 2 receiver, favorite of QB Bill Kilmer who went with him to 49ers. 1st-round draft pick of San Francisco 49ers. Also drafted by San Diego Chargers. 49ers, 1961-73. Rookie year intercepted five passes for 116 yds. Led team in receiving, 1962, with 34 receptions, 627 yds., before returning to defense to stay. Blcoked only two passes thrown his way against Green Bay Packers, 11/1/70. At end of '73 season had intercepted 38 passes for 532 yds. and 6 TDs. Called Tommy McDonald toughest receiver he faced. All-NFC, 1970, 71, 72. Pro Bowl, 1971, 72, 73. Younger brother of 1960 decathlon gold-medal winner, Rafer Johnson.

JOHNSON, JOHN HENRY (Big John) Running Back. B. 11/24/29, Waterproof, La. 6'2", 225. Attended St. Mary's (Calif.). Drafted on 2nd round by Pittsburgh Steelers in 1953, but signed instead with Canada's Calgary Stampeders. In 1954 signed with San Francisco 49ers, who sent defensive back to Steelers as compensation. Received degree from Arizona State, 1955. In 1957 traded to Detroit Lions. Played three years with Lions, then traded to Steelers for draft choice. As 1962 Steeler rushed for 1141 yds., in 1964 rushed for 1048. Gained 200 yds. rushing on 30 carries vs. Cleveland Browns, 10/10/64. In 1966 signed as free agent with Houston Oilers, finishing career that season. In 13-years gained 6803 yds. rushing on 1571 carries for 48 TDs. Captured 186 passes for 1478 yds., 7 TDs. Scored total of 330 points. Played in Pro Bowl, 1963, 64, 65. NFL championship game, 1957.

JOHNSON, KERMIT Running Back. B. 2/22/52, Los Angeles, Calif. 5'11", 190. UCLA halfback under Pepper Rodgers, 1971-73. All-America, 1973. Ran 100-yd. dash in 9.8. Also has great power. Broke most UCLA running records. Surpassed legendary Kenny Washington's career total of 1945 yds. Johnson had 2495. Rushed for 1129 yds. and scored 16 TDs senior year. Only rarely did individual tacklers handle him alone. Johnson and James McAlister were almost

166

unstoppable combo in Bruins' Wishbone-T offense. "Blair Pair" played together in high school and college. Was 2nd-round draft choice of Southern California (WFL); signed with club along with McAlister, who had been 1st draft choice.

JOHNSON, RANDOLPH K. Quarterback. B. 6/17/44, San Antonio, Tex. 6'3", 205. Attended Texas A. & I. Little All-America, 1965. In collegiate career threw for 4600 yds., 35 TDs, MVP in three post-season games. Selected by Atlanta Falcons on 1st round of 1966 NFL draft. Falcons, 1966-70; New York Giants, 1971-73. Traded to Giants for QB Dick Shiner. In eight pro years completed 585 of 1172 passes for 7524 yds., 7 TDs. Also rushed for 538 yds. on 103 carries and scored 9 TDs. Angered over lack of playing time, Johnson quit football during 1973 season and began working in real estate in Tampa. However, returned to Giants before season ended. Completed 99 of 177 passes in abbreviated year for 1279 yds., percentage of .559, 7 TDs.

JOHNSON, ROBERT D. Center. B. 8/19/46, Cleveland, Tenn. 6'5", 262. Tennessee, 1966-68. Unanimous All-America, 1967. Honor student. Leader in Fellowship of Christian Athletes. Cincinnati Bengals, 1968-73. First player ever drafted by franchise. Appeared in every regular season game since joining club. AFL All-Star game, 1969. Played in AFC playoff game vs. Miami Dolphins, 1973. All-AFC, 1972. Strong blocker, competitor.

JOHNSON, RONALD A. Running Back. B. 10/17/47, Detroit, Mich. 6'1", 205. Michigan halfback, 1966-68. All-America and 6th in Heisman Trophy voting, 1968. Set NCAA record for most yds. in single game with 347, on 31 rushes against Wisconsin, 11/16/68 (broken in 1971 by Eric Allen). In that game gained total of 387 yds., scored five TDs. Played sparingly in 1966. Collegiate totals: 2440 total-offense yds.; 21 receptions for 345 yds.; 40 kickoff returns for 690 yds.; 27 TDs. Cleveland Browns, 1969; New York Giants, 1970-73. Was 1st-round draft pick of Browns. Traded to Giants with linebacker Wayne Meylan, defensive tackle Jim Kanicki, for wide receiver Homer Jones. Didn't believe he'd be traded. Gained 250 yds. first three pro games. In 1970 vs. Philadelphia Eagles had 87-yd. TD run cancelled by penalty, but later ran 68 yds. to score. That year gained 1027 yds., 2nd in league to Larry Brown. Broke team rushing record, became first Giant to gain over 1000 yds. Compiled four 100-yd. games, including 142 vs. Eagles, 140 vs. Dallas Cowboys. Missed almost entire 1972 season due to knee injury. Made remarkable comeback year later. NFL's leading scorer on rushing-passing with 84 points. Giants' top runner with 902 yds. on 260 carries in 1973, average of 3.5 yds.; scored 9 TDs. Brother, Alex, is controversial major-league baseball outfielder. Team chess champion, having defeated tight end Bob Tucker. Pro Bowl 1971, 73.

JONES, BERT Quarterback. B. 2/7/51, Ruston, La. 6'3", 205. Louisiana State, 1970-72. Consensus All-America, 1972. *Sporting News* College Player of the Year, 1972. In senior year vs. Auburn completed 10 of 14 passes for 3 TDs. Same season vs. Ole Miss completed 14 of 21 passes, throwing for winning TD as time ran out. Against Alabama, in another 1972 game, completed 18 of 32 passes for 242 yds. and 2 TDs. '72 team had record of 9-1-1, played in Astro-Bluebonnet Bowl vs. Tennessee. Three times made three TD passes in one game. No other LSU QB accomplished that more than once. In 1972 completed 103 of 199 passes for 1446 yds. and 14 TDs. Collegiate passing totals; 220 completions, 418 attempts, 3255 yds. 28 TDs, only 16 interceptions, .038 interception percentage. Left LSU with 20 passing records (many formerly held by Y. A. Tittle). Selected by Baltimore Colts on 1st round of 1973 draft.

JONES, CLINTON Running Back. B. 5/24/45, Cleveland, Ohio. 6', 206. Michigan State halfback, 1964-66. Consensus All-America, 1966; All-America, 1965. 6th in Heisman Trophy voting, 1966. Rushed for 268 yds. in single game. Teammate of Bubba Smith. During senior year made 80-yd. rush vs. Ohio State, 70-yd. rush vs. Iowa. In 1966 Rose Bowl rushed for 113 yds. on 20 carries. Finished collegiate career with 1921 yds. rushing on 396 carries, 408 yds. on 33 receptions, 162 yds. on 9 kickoff returns. Scored 23 TDs and 2 PATs for 140 points. Minnesota Vikings, 1967-72; San Diego Chargers, 1973. Thrown into starting lineup in 1968 when Dave Osborne was injured; became permanent starter. In seven years rushed for 2178 yds. on 602 carries; received 38 passes for 431 yds.; returned 89 kickoffs for 2209 yds., average of 24.8 yds.; scored 21 TDs for 126 points. Played in NFL championship game, 1969. Super Bowl, 1970.

JONES, DAVID (Deacon) Defensive End. B. 12/9/38, Eatonville, Fla. 6'4", 272. Football, baseball, basketball, track stand-out at Hungerwood H.S. in Eatonville. Attended Mississippi Vocational College in 1957. Transferred to Southern Carolina State where he played tackle both ways and kicked FGs, 1958-60. Nicknamed "Deacon" by teammates because he led squad in prayer. Los Angeles Rams, 1961-71; San Diego Chargers. Originally 14th-round draft choice of Rams. Traded to Chargers in seven-player swap. Member of L.A.'s famous "Fearsome Foursome." Had consecutive game streak of 143 broken in 1971 by leg injury. In prime, game's most feared pass rusher. All-NFL, 1965, 66, 67, 68, 69. All-NFC, 1970. Pro Bowl participant eight years. Hobbies: table tennis, jazz, golf. Appeared in 1972 episode of TV's *Banacek*.

JONES, ED (Too Tall) Tackle. B. Jackson, Tenn. 6'8", 260. Tennessee State, 1971-73. Called "Too Tall" for obvious reasons. Offered 52 basketball scholarships before graduation from high school. Didn't play prep football, only basketball. In three varsity seasons at Tennessee State played in only one losing game. Coach John Merritt rated Jones as best lineman he ever coached. Probably premier defensive tackle in nation, 1973. Little All-America that year. Ran 40-yd. dash in 4.7. No. 1 draft pick of NFL in 1974, by Dallas Cowboys; 3rd-round WFL pick, by Detroit Wheels. Signed with Cowboys.

JONES, HOMER C. (Rhino) End. B. 2/18/41, Pittsburg, Tex. 6'2", 220. Attended Texas Southern. Nickname given by track teammates because of way he moved head while running. Selected by Houston Oilers on 5th round of 1963

AFL draft, New York Giants on 20th round of NFL draft. Released by Houston and signed by New York in 1963. Spent that season on taxi squad. Giants, 1964-69; Cleveland Browns, 1970. Collected 98-yd. pass reception vs. Pittsburgh Steelers, 1966, tying him with four others for 2nd longest. Same season led NFL in average yds. on receptions with 21.8 (1044 yds., 48 receptions). No. 1 again in 1967 with 24.7 (1209 yds., 49 receptions), 1968 with 23.5 (1057 yds., 45 receptions). Also led in TDs on pass receptions with 13, 1967. Played in Pro Bowl, 1968, 69.

JONES, HOWARD H. Coach. B. 8/23/1885, Excello, Ohio. D. 7/27/41, Toluea Lake, N.Y. Yale, 1905-07. Coached Syracuse, 1908; Yale, 1909, 13. Bulldog assistant coach, 1911-12, after one year at Ohio State. 1909, 10 teams undefeated. Became Yale's first paid head coach in 1913. Coached Iowa, 1916-23; Duke, 1924; Southern California, 1925-40. At USC won seven Pacific Coast Conference titles, two national titles, five out of five Rose Bowl games. Brother of Tad, also famous player and coach. Once told his players not to take advantage of ailing Bobby Grayson, Stanford All-American halfback — Grayson was not hit on bad knee all day. Defeating Notre Dame, 10-7, 1921, considered career highlight. Record: 189-64-21. Developed 19 All-Americas, 13 at Southern Cal. Author of two books on football. Citizens Savings Hall of Fame, National Football Foundation Hall of Fame.

JONES, JOHN A. (Spike) Kicker. B. 7/9/47, Louisville, Ga. 6'2", 190. Georgia, 1967-69. Made 194 collegiate punts for 8043 yds., average of 41.5. Holds record for longest punt in Bulldog history at 87 yds. No. 2 punter in nation, 1969, with 43.5-yd. average on 71 punts. Named All-SEC, 1968, 69. Played in Liberty, Sun, Sugar Bowl, College All-Star games. Selected by Houston Oilers in 4th round of 1970 NFL draft. Tied Houston club record that year for most punts in season with 84, 42.4 average. Released by Houston, signed by Buffalo Bills in 1971. In 1970-73 period made 302 punts for 40.7-yd. average.

JONES, LAWRENCE McC. (Biff) Coach. B. 10/8/1895, Washington, D.C. Army, 1914-16. Served in France as Lt. in field artillery, World War I. Returned to West Point after war and served as aide to Charles Daly and John McEwan. Succeeded McEwan after 1925 season; head coach thru 1929 with 30-8-2 record. 1927 brought back Red Blaik as civilian assistant coach, and he worked under Jones three years. Coached at LSU, 1932-34, with record of 20-5-6; at Oklahoma, 1935-36, finishing 9-6-3; at Nebraska, 1937-41, with 28-14-4 record. Took Nebraska to 1941 Rose Bowl, losing to Stanford by 21-13 score. Retired from army as Maj. in 1937. Returned as Col. in 1942, serving as graduate manager of athletics at West Point until 6/48. Citizens Savings Hall of Fame, Football Foundation Hall of Fame.

JONES, STANLEY P. Guard-Tackle. B. 11/24/31, Altoona, Pa. 6', 245. Attended Lemoyne (Pa.) H.S. Maryland tackle, 1951-53. Unanimous All-America, 1953. Teammate of All-Americas Dick Modzelewski, Bob Ward, Jack

169

Scarbath. Played in 1952 Sugar Bowl, 1954 Orange Bowl and College All-Star games. Played with Chicago Bears, 1954-65; Washington Redskins, 1966. Originally 5th-round draft choice of Bears. Played on 1963 world championship team. Played eight years as guard, four as defensive tackle. All-Pro four times, 1955, 56, 59, 60. Played in Pro Bowl, 1956 thru '62. Assistant coach, Denver Broncos, 1966-71; Buffalo Bills, 1972-73.

JONES, THOMAS A. D. (Tad) Coach. B. 2/27/1887, Excello, Ohio. D. 6/19/57. Brother of Howard. Yale halfback. All-America, 1907; 2nd team, 1906. After 1908 graduation coached Syracuse, 1909-10 (9-9-2); Yale, 1916, 20-27 (57-15-4). Molded 1923 squad, regarded by many as Yale's greatest. Included were four transfers: Century Milstead (from Wabash), Mal Stevens (from Washburn), Widdy Neale (Greasy's younger brother, from West Virginia & Marietta), Lyle Richeson (from Tulane). Picked 1916 team as "most courageous." Made one player wear plaster-of-paris cast in 1916 vs. Harvard, after persuading Harvard to abandon leather gloves. Defeated Crimson six out of nine times. Citizens Savings Hall of Fame, National Football Foundation Hall of Fame.

JORDAN, HENRY W. Tackle. B. 1/26/35, Emporia, Va. 6'3", 250. Virginia, 1954-56. Wrestler and football player. Started wrestling in high school. At age 16 won AAU title. Continued in college and won ACC title. In senior year, was runnerup for NCAA wrestling championship. Played in College All-Star game, 1957. Selected by Cleveland Browns on 5th round of 1957 NFL draft. Played two seasons with Browns in various positions, then traded to Green Bay Packers for 4th-round draft choice. Played thru 1969 with Packers. Pro Bowl, 1961, 62, 64, 67. Lineman of the Game in '62 Pro Bowl. All-NFL, 1960, 61, 62, 63, 64. NFL championship games, 1957, 60, 61, 62, 65, 66, 67. Super Bowl, 1967, 68. Exceptional defensive tackle, honoring Packers and profession.

JORDAN, LEE ROY Linebacker. B. 4/27/41, Excel, Ala. 6'1", 221. Center and linebacker for Alabama, 1960-62. Unanimous All-America, 1962. Capped his collegiate career with 31 tackles against Oklahoma in 1963 Orange Bowl. Bear Bryant commented, "If he stays in bounds, Lee Roy will get him." Dallas Cowboys, 1963-73. Drafted No. 1 by Cowboys in '63. In 11 pro years intercepted 24 passes for 369 yds. and 3 TDs. All-NFC, 1973. Pro Bowl, 1968, 69, 70, 74. NFL championship games, 1966, 67. Super Bowl, 1971, 72. Consistently superior linebacker. His philosophy: "I'm not a mean player. I like to think I'm aggressive. If I take a fair shot at a man it reflects my dedication. I try to hit him as hard as I can because he would do the same to me. That's what the game is all about — hitting."

JOSEPHSON, LESTER (Josey) Running Back. B. 7/29/42, Minn. 6'1", 207. Graduated from Augustana (S.D.), 1964. Was football and track star. Contacted all NFL teams but only Dallas Cowboys would offer trial. Dallas wasn't impressed though, and traded him to Los Angeles Rams. Turned out to be super sleeper. Played with Rams, 1965-73. Gained 451 yds. rushing and caught 21 passes rookie year. Had biggest year in 1967. Rushed and caught passes for 1200 yds. Rewarded with Pro Bowl berth. Injured twice, without touching anyone, and missed entire 1968 season. Tore calf muscle when he slipped before player introductions at pre-season game. While recuperating tore Achilles tendon jumping rope. Used unique style of running, called "hesitation hit." Nine-season rushing totals: 786 carries, 3362 yds., 17 TDs. Caught no passes in 1973 but still had 194 career receptions for 1970 yds., 11 TDs.

JUHAN, FRANK A. Center. B. 4/27/1887, Macon, Ga. D. 12/31/67, Sewanee, Tenn. 5'11", 175. West Texas Military Academy halfback, 1905-06. Sewanee, 1908-10. Played every minute of every game in 1909, leading Sewanee to SIAA championship. Strong player both ways. All-Southern, 1909, 1910. Earned additional varsity letters in baseball, track, boxing; earned four degrees. Southern intercollegiate boxing champion, 1909, 10. Later served as Sewanee director of development; Baptist Episcopal bishop of Florida. National Football Foundation Hall of Fame.

JURGENSON, CHRISTIAN A., III (Sonny) Quarterback. B. 8/23/34, Wilmington, N.C. 6', 203. Played QB at Duke. Blue Devils were ground-attack team and Jurgensen threw little; in fact, recorded only six TD passes during 1954-56. Selected by Philadelphia Eagles on 4th round of 1957 NFL draft. Traded to Washington in 1964, along with Jimmy Carr, for Norm Snead and Claude Crabb. In 1961 set record for yds. passing, season, with 3723, on league-leading 235 completions; threw record 32 TDs. Led league in 1962 with 3261 yds. on 196 completions. In 1966 led league in pass attempts with 436, in completions with 254, yds. with 3209. Set NFL passing records in 1967 with 508 attempts, 208 completions, 3747 yds.; threw 31 TD passes. Tied record for longest pass completion, 9/15/68, with 99-yarder. Led league in passing in 1969 with 274 completions in 442 attempts for 3102 yds., 22 TDs. Twice has thrown five TD passes in one game; passed for over 400 yds. on five occasions; exceeded 300 yds. 23 times, three of them in 1969. In 16 years completed 2326 of 4095 yds. for 31,039 yds. Threw 244 TD passes to rank 3rd in NFL history. Happy-go-lucky personality who liked good times. Drove Mercedes Benz with license plate proclaiming SJ-9 — his initials and uniform number. All-Pro, 1961. Played in Pro Bowl, 1965; selected four other times but didn't play. Severed Achilles tendon, suffered in 1972, and requiring immediate surgery, just one of numerous injuries suffered during career.

JUSTICE, CHARLES (Choo Choo) Running Back. B. 5/18/24, Asheville, N.C. 5'10", 165. To Carolinians, Choo Choo Justice was Zeus, Jupiter, Ra on football field. Legend still growing. North Carolina halfback, 1946-49. Consensus All-America, 1948; All-America, 1949. Runnerup in Heisman Trophy voting, 1948, 49. Holds North Carolina total offense record, having gained more than 5000 yds. Holds NCAA punting record of 231 punts for 9839 yds., average of 42.6 yds. 1948 collegiate punting leader, averaging 44.0 yds. on 62 punts for 2728 yds. In 1949 made 63 punts for 2777 yds., 44.1 average. Stunned Wake Forest with 76-yd. punt in 1948. Finished career with 2634 yds. on 536 rushes; completed 159 of 321 passes for 2237 yds.; caught 18 passes for 232 yds.; intercepted 3 passes for 33 yds.; returned 68 punts for 969 yds.; returned 31 kickoffs for 825 yds.; scored 39 TDs for 234 points. Played in Sugar Bowl, 1947, 49; Cotton Bowl, 1950. Feats drew national attention, made him coverboy of several magazines. Inspired song, *All the Way, Choo Choo,* which achieved "hit" ranking. Washington Redskins, 1950, 52-54. Had mastery over tackle named Freddie Stiehl, always running at his position. Stiehl went to Miami (Fla.) as if to escape "Justice", only to discover Miami and North Carolina were to meet. Transferred again, to NYU, where there was no football team. Citizens Savings Hall of Fame, National Football Foundation Hall of Fame.

KAER, MORTON A. (Devil May) Running Back. B. 9/7/02, Omaha, Neb. 5'11", 167. Southern California halfback, 1923-26. Consensus All-America, 1926. Played last two years under Howard Jones. Set career scoring record of 216 points, not surpassed at USC until 40 years later by O. J. Simpson. Won bronze medal in pentathlon at Paris Olympics, 1924. QB for Frankfort Yellowjackets, 1931. Performed miracles with little Weed (Calif.) H.S. Compiled 187-47-7 record over 28-year period. Under Kaer, Weed had five unbeaten seasons, nine with only one loss, won or shared 17 championships. National Football Foundation Hall of Fame.

KAPP, JOSEPH Quarterback. B. 3/19/38, Santa Fe, N.M. 6'2", 215. Played QB for California, 1956-58. All-America, 1958. 5th in Heisman Trophy voting, 1958. That year made 92-yd. rush vs. Oregon. Played in Rose Bowl, 1959, and threw 17-yd. TD pass. Finished collegiate career with 146 completions (286 attempts) for 1897 yds., 28 interceptions, 7 TDs, passing percentage of 51.0, average of 13.0 yds. per completion. Also rushed for 931 yds. on 274 carries, scored 8 TDs and 4 PATs for 52 points. Drafted by Washington Redskins on 11th round of 1959 draft. Signed instead with Calgary Stampeders of CFL. After 1960 season traded to British Columbia Lions. With Lions became two-time CFL All-Star, 1963, 64. League MVP, 1963. Also punted in CFL. NFL draft rights waived by Washington in 1966. Signed with Minnesota Vikings, 1967. In 1969 vs. Baltimore Colts, Kapp threw record-typing seven TD passes as Vikes rolled, to 52-14 win. Led Vikings to NFL title that year but lost Super Bowl IV to Kansas City Chiefs. In 1971 filed anti-trust suit against all 26 NFL teams for exclusion, after his demand to be traded by Boston Patriots (who had acquired him in 1970) received no takers. Announced retirement early in 1971 exhibition season; he had lost starting job to Jim Plunkett, fellow Chicano-Indian, and wasn't able to renegotiate contract.

KARRAS, ALEXANDER G. Tackle. B. 7/15/35, Gary, Ind. 6'2", 255. Graduated from Iowa. Consensus All-America and Outland Trophy winner, 1957. Selected by Detroit Lions on 1st round of 1958 NFL draft. Lions, 1958-62, 64-70. On 4/17/63 suspended indefinitely, along with Green Bay's Paul Hornung, for betting on NFL games. Reinstated on 3/16/64. Brother of Ted Karras, guard for Pittsburgh Steelers, and Lou Karras, tackle for Washington Redskins. Retired in 1971 after 12 years with Lions. Currently sportswriter for Detroit newspaper, *Free Press.* Color man on Pro Football from Canada. All-Pro defensive tackle, 1960, 61, 62, 65. Pro Bowl, 1961, 62, 63, 66. Wore out many foes with strength and quickness. Loved to sack QB. Unique character, witty and irreverent. Acquired moniker "Tippy Toes." Made impressive film debut in *Paper Lion.* Has other acting credits.

KATCAVAGE, JAMES R. (Kat) Defensive End. B. 10/28/34, Wilkes-Barre, Pa. 6'3", 240. Attended Dayton, graduated in 1956. Selected by New York Giants on 4th round of 1956 NFL draft and played with them thru 1968. Tied NFL record for most safeties, lifetime, three. Joined Dick Modzelewski, Rosey Grier, Andy Robustelli as rookie to help form famed "Fearsome Foursome." That frontline carried Giants to NFL title in '56, via 47-7 trouncing of Chicago Bears. Premier defensive end. All-NFL, 1961, 62, 63. Pro Bowl, 1962, 63, 64. Played in five other championship games, 1958, 59, 61, 62, 63. Alex Webster, who was close friend, released Katcavage in first official act as head coach in 1969. However, rewarded for long service and named team's defensive line coach. Remained in that capacity five years.

KAVANAUGH, KENNETH W. End. B. 11/23/16, Little Rock, Ark. 6'3", 204. Louisiana State, 1937-39. Consensus All-America, 1939. Half of Bird-to-Kavanaugh combo of 1939. Played in 1938 Sugar Bowl. Often compared to Don Hutson for receiving "in traffic." Returned fumble 100 yds. in 1937 game vs. Rice. Made 62-yd. reception against Texas, 1938. Senior year returned interception 80 yds. to stun Holy Cross. Led NCAA in several categories during career. Three times All-SEC. Played in two Sugar Bowls, 1937, 38, making Sugar Bowl All-Star team both times. SEC MVP, 1939. Played in Blue-Gray, College All-Star games. Received Knute Rockne Trophy in 1939, first lineman ever to win honor. After graduation from LSU signed to baseball contract by Branch Rickey for St. Louis Cardinals, football contract by George Halas for Chicago Bears. Played for Bears, 1940-41, 45-50. Career interrupted by service in World War II as bomber pilot. Won Distinguished Flying Cross, Air Medal with 4 Oak Leaf Clusters. Scored on 30-yd. TD pass from Sid Luckman in 1940 title game. Year later in title game vs. New York Giants, recovered fumbled lateral pass and

174

ran 42 yds. for TD. Scored on another TD pass from Luckman in '46 championship contest. Formerly Giant assistant. Coached for six Eastern Conference champions, world championship team of 1956. All-NFL, 1946, 47. Chicago Bears Hall of Fame, Arkansas Hall of Fame, Louisiana Hall of Fame, Citizens Savings Hall of Fame, National Football Foundation Hall of Fame.

KAW, EDGAR L. Running Back. 6'0", 185. Cornell, 1920-22. All-America fullback, 1921; halfback, 1922. Fine offensive and defensive player. In 1921 scored five of team's six TDs vs. Penn at Franklin Field. Was NCAA leader in TDs with 15 in 1921. Also excellent punter. Won three varsity letters in baseball. Played on unbeaten teams, 1921, 22. Buffalo Bisons, 1924. Joined Fox studios as executive, 1925; later served in front office of dog-food manufacturer. Citizens Savings Hall of Fame, National Football Foundation Hall of Fame.

KAZMAIER, RICHARD W., JR. (Kaz) Running Back. B. 11/23/30, Toledo, Ohio. 5'11", 165. Played tailback for Princeton,1949-51. All-America, 1950; unanimous, 1951. Heisman Trophy and Maxwell Trophy, 1951. Inspired two consecutive undefeated teams. Played on 1950, 51 Ivy League, "Big 3" champs. Triple-threat; great kicker, runner, passer. In 1949 game vs. Brown made 67-yd. punt. Completed 65-yd. pass against Harvard in 1950. Completed two 61-yd. passes, 1951, one vs. Brown, one vs. Harvard. Set game record in pass completion percentage with .882 (15 of 17) vs. Cornell, 1951; same season in rushing yds. with 262 vs. Brown. In 1951 led NCAA in passing percentage with .626, total offense with 1827 yds. and TDs-accounted-for with 22. Finished collegiate career with .595 completion percentage, gained 4354 yds. in total offense. Went to Princeton for "a good education." Once, when asked to pick All-America team, chose entire Princeton lineup. Played in East-West Shrine game. No wonder they called him "Mr. Everything" and "Nassau Nugget." Citizens Savings Hall of Fame, National Football Foundation Hall of Fame. Named president of National Football Foundation Hall of Fame in 1974.

KEANE, THOMAS Defensive Back. B. 9/7/26, Bellaire, Ohio. 6'1", 190. Attended Ohio State and West Virginia. Drafted on 2nd round by Los Angeles Rams, 1948. Spent four years with Rams. Involved in whopping 11-for-1 trade on 6/12/52. Keane, Dick Hoerner, Gabby Sims, Joe Reid, Red Phillips, Jack Holliday, Vic Vasicek, Dick Wilkins, Dick McKissak, Billy Baggett, Dave Anderson were sent to Dallas Texans for draft rights to Les Richter and cash. 1953 team became Baltimore Colts. Traded to Chicago Cardinals for running back Dick Youns, 1955. All-NFL, 1953. Pro Bowl, 1954. Played in NFL championship games, 1949, 50, 51. Brother of Jim Keane, who played end for Chicago Bears and Green Bay Packers.

KEARNEY, JAMES L. Defensive Back. B. 1/21/43, Wharton, Tex. 6'2", 206. Graduated from Prairie View A.M., 1965. All-Conference and NAIA All-America. Selected by Detroit Lions on 11th round of 1965 NFL draft. Lions thru 1966, then sold to Philadelphia Eagles. Released by Eagles, signed by Kansas

City in '67. Played on Chief taxi squad before becoming regular safety in 1968. Made 60-yd. TD interception vs. Denver Broncos, 1969, and four other interceptions that season. Led NFL in interception yds. with 192, average yds. with 38.4, both in 1972. Same season tied record for TDs on interceptions with four. Played in Super Bowl, 1970. Likes to play saxophone.

KEATING, THOMAS A. Defensive Tackle. B. 9/2/42, Chicago, Ill. 6'2", 247. Graduated from Michigan. Three-year letterman, 1962-64. Played in North-South, Coaches All-America, College All-Star games. Buffalo Bills, 1964-65; Oakland Raiders, 1966-72. Was dealt to Pittsburgh Steelers in 1973 but placed on inactive list due to knee injury. Originally 5th-round draft choice of Bills. Missed 1968 season due to surgery on Achilles tendon. Strong, quick-reacting. All-AFC defensive tackle, 1967, 70. AFL All-Star games, 1967, 68. AFL championship games, 1967, 68, 69. Super Bowl, 1968.

KECK, J. STANTON (Stan) Tackle. B. 9/11/07, Greensburg, Pa. D. 1/20/51, Pittsburgh, Pa. 5'11", 206. Played for Bellefonte Prep School under Carl Snavely, then for Princeton in 1919-21. All-America, 1920; 2nd team, 1921. After graduation coached football at Norwich College, Princeton and Waynesburg, Pa., where he was also director of athletics. National Football Foundation Hall of Fame.

KELLEY, LAWRENCE M. (Larry) End. B. 5/30/15, Conneaut, Ohio. 6'1½", 185. Yale, 1934-36. Unanimous All-America, 1936. Heisman Trophy, 1936. Scored at least one TD vs. Harvard, Princeton in each of varsity seasons. In 1934 upset of Princeton caught 43-yd. pass to score only TD of game. Scored 91 points, 1936. Voted MVP in East-West Shrine game, 1936. Often cunning, radical innovator. 1936 captain. Played with Clint Frank; they were two of most unbeatable players ever paired. Against Princeton in 1936, duo forged come-from-behind victory, 23-20. Allison Danzig wrote in the New York *Times*: "What will linger on, etched indelibly in the minds of all who have followed the progress of his amazing career, is the almost phenomenal genius of Larry Kelley of Yale as a headlined hunter who always got his ball and touchdown regardless of the odds." Well-liked, known for his sense of humor. Boston (AFL), 1937. National Football Foundation Hall of Fame.

KELLY, LEROY Running Back. B. 5/20/42, Philadelphia, Pa. 6', 205. Attended Morgan State. Cleveland Browns, 1964-73. Real steal as 8th-round draft choice. Led league in average yds. on punt returns with 15.6 (17 for 265 yds.), 1965, and in punt return TDs with two. NFL leader following year in average yds. gained rushing with 5.5 (1141 yds. on 209 carries), rushing TDs with 15, total TDs with 16. No. 1 in rushing with 1205 yds., in carries with 235, in average yds. with 5.1, in TDs with 11, all in 1967. Led again in 1968 with 1239 yds. rushing, 248 carries, 16 rushing TDs. That year became third three-time 1000-yd. gainer in NFL history; also led in scoring with 120 points on 20 TDs. Brother of Pat Kelly, Chicago White Sox outfielder. All-NFL, 1966, 67, 68. Pro Bowl, 1967 thru 72. NFL championship games, 1964, 65, 68, 69. Hails from big family, most of whose members live around Philadelphia. Named by *Esquire* magazine one of best-dressed athletes in America. Active with Base Enterprises, television producing company out of Los Angeles. After 10 years of service thru 1973, ranked 4th on all-time rushing list with 7274 yds. "Truly a super star," according to Cleveland coach Nick Skorich, and many others.

KELLY, MICHAEL Tight End. B. 1/14/48, Davidson, N. C. 6'3", 222. Played for Davidson, 1967-69. In nine games, 1968, received 63 passes for 936 yds. and 11 TDs; in 1969 caught 70 passes for 891 yds. and 6 TDs. In collegiate career of 23 games made 156 catches for 2114 yds., average of 13.6, and 17 TDs. Signed as free agent by Cincinnati Bengals in 1970. Traded to New Orleans Saints for future draft choice on 4/11/73.

KELLY, WILLIAM (Wild Bill) Quarterback. B. Denver, Colo. D. Syracuse, N.Y. 185. U. of Montana, 1924, 26. Born in Denver but raised in Missoula, Mont. Led Missoula H.S. to its first state title. In sophomore year at Montana, scored 9 TDs on rushes of over 40 yds. Returned five kickoffs for TDs, including two over 90 yds. All-America, 1926. Played in East-West Shrine game in 1927, throwing winning pass to defeat East. Died at age 27 while watching football game in Syracuse. New York Yankees, 1927-28. Frankford Yellowjackets, 1929; Brooklyn Dodgers, 1929-30. National Football Foundation Hall of Fame.

KEMP, JOHN F. (Jackie) Quarterback. B. 7/13/35, Los Angeles, Calif. 6'0", 205. Attended Occidental College. 17th-round draft choice of Detroit Lions, 1957, but traded to Pittsburgh Steelers for two draft choices. In 1958 released by Pittsburgh and joined New York Giants (taxi squad). On taxi squads of Calgary Stampeders and San Francisco 49ers, 1959. Year later signed with AFL Los Angeles Chargers as free agent. Led AFL in passing, 1960, with 211 completions in 407 attempts for 3018 yds. In 1961 moved with Chargers to San Diego, then 1962 sold to Buffalo Bills for remainder of career. Missed entire 1968 season due to injury. Set three AFL career playoff records: pass attempts with 139; completions with 68; yds. passing with 993. Played in five AFL title games, 1960, 61, 64, 65, 66 (two with Chargers, three with Buffalo). Retired in 1970. Elected to U.S. House of Representatives (New York's 38th C.D.), 1970, highest elective office ever achieved by pro football player. All-AFL QB, 1960, 65. Played in AFL All-Star games, 1962, 63, 65, 67.

KENNEDY, ALBERT R. (Doc) Coach. B. 10/24/1876, Douglas County, Kan. D. 9/3/69. Attended Kansas and Pennsylvania. Kansas captain, 1897. Combined dentistry with coaching. Tutored Kansas, 1904-10; Haskell, 1911-16. Record: 85-31-7 (.720). 53-9-4 at Kansas, winning 19 straight games in 1907-09. Respected for ability to analyze defenses.

KERN, REX W. Defensive Back. B. 5/28/49, Lancaster, Ohio. 6'1", 190. Attended Lancaster H.S. and Ohio State. Great prep athlete, winning honors in football, basketball, baseball. Quarterbacked Ohio State to 27-2 record, 1968-70. Voted MVP in 1969 Rose Bowl as Buckeyes defeated Southern Cal, 27-16. Career total offense was 3990 yds. (1586 rushing, 2604 passing). Scored 27 TDs and passed for 19 more. Won NCAA post-graduate scholarship. Received Ernie Davis Memorial Award for leadership at Coaches All-America game, 1971. Baltimore Colts, 1971-73. Not big, and lacking natural passing ability, he was shifted to defensive back by Colts. Missed much of '72 season with dislocated hand. Capable of playing cornerback or safety. Comparable to Baltimore teammate Jack Mildren, another defensive back converted from QB. Both are rugged, pressure players. Kern is excellent public speaker. Married Rose Bowl queen.

KERR, ANDREW Coach. B. 10/7/1878, Cheyenne, Wyo. D. 3/1/69, Tucson, Ariz. Attended Dickinson College where he was QB, baseball outfielder and high jumper. Studied law and taught at business college in Johnstown, Pa.; coached football at Johnstown H.S. In 1914 became track coach at U. of Pittsburgh and then assistant football coach there, under Pop Warner, 1915-21. Went to Stanford as "substitute" head coach for Warner in 1922-23, until Warner's contract at Pittsburgh was finished. Was Warner's assistant at Stanford, 1924-25. Head coach Washington & Jefferson, 1926-28; his first team suffered only one defeat, 1927 team undefeated. Three-year record was 16-6-5. Became head coach at Colgate, 1929, stayed 18 years thru 1946. Team was famous for use of lateral pass. Colgate's 1929-34 record was 47-5-1. In last 12 years record slipped to 48-45-6. 1929 team gave up only 19 points and lost only one game. 1932 undefeated team considered his best. When Pittsburgh was asked to Rose Bowl that year Kerr made famous remark, "We were unbeaten, untied, unscored upon and uninvited." Coached at Lebanon Valley, 1947-49. Record, 1922-46, 137-71-14. Lebanon scores are not available. Helped organize East-West Shrine game. Citizens Savings Hall of Fame, National Football Foundation Hall of Fame.

KETCHAM, HENRY M. (Hank) Center-Guard. B. 6/17/1892, Englewood, N.J. 6', 175. Played at Yale, 1911-13. All-America center, 1911, 12; 2nd team guard, 1913. Captain of 1913 team. During his collegiate career, Yale won 19, lost 5 and tied 5, scored 376 points to its opponents 81. Played every varsity game for three years, taken out only once for slight injury. Never wore helmet. Generally credited with inventing term, "roving center." Became prominent lumberman and banker in Seattle. National Football Foundation Hall of Fame.

KEYES, LEROY Defensive Back. B. 2/18/47, Newport News, Va. 6'3", 210. Halfback and defensive back for Purdue, 1966-68. Unanimous All-America, 1967-68. Runnerup in Heisman Trophy voting, 1968; 3rd in 1967. Returned interception 95 yds. for TD, 1966. In 1967 made 81-yd. rush vs. Iowa and 78-yd. pass reception vs. Northwestern. Played in 1967 Rose Bowl. Led NCAA in TDs with 19, scoring with 114 points in 1967. Finished collegiate career with total offense of 2271 yds. on 376 plays. Selected by Philadelphia Eagles on 1st round of 1969 draft. In four years with Eagles, 1969-72, gained 368 yds. rushing on 123 carries, 276 yds. on 29 pass receptions, 200 yds. on nine kickoff returns and 31 yds. on eight interceptions. Traded with Ernie Calloway to Kansas City Chiefs for Gerry Philbin and draft choice, 1973. Played only sparingly that year.

KHAYAT, EDDIE Tackle. B. 9/14/35, Moss Point, Miss. 6'4", 248. Attended Tulane. Signed by Washington Redskins in 1957. Traded to Philadelphia Eagles, 1958. With great defensive play helped win world championship for Eagles, 1960. Played again with Redskins, 1962-63; returned to Eagles for 1964, 65 seasons. Closed out 10-year career in 1966 with Boston Patriots. Became defensive line coach for New Orleans Saints, 1967. Joined Philadelphia staff in 1971 and was named head coach on 10/6 of that year. Led Eagles to 6-7-1 record for balance of season and finished in 3rd place in NFC Eastern Division. 1972 Eagles finished in last place with 2-11-1 record. Replaced by Mike McCormack, 1973. Brother of Bob Khayat, Washington kicker, 1960-63. Now defensive line coach for Detroit Lions.

KIESLING, WALTER Guard. B. 5/27/03, St. Paul, Minn. D. 3/2/62. Attended St. Thomas College. Played for Duluth Eskimos, 1926-27; Pottsville Maroons, 1928; Boston Braves, 1929; Chicago Cardinals, 1929-33; Chicago Bears, 1934; Green Bay Packers, 1935-36; Pittsburgh Steelers, 1937-38. All-Pro, 1932. Replaced John McNally as head coach of Pittsburgh Steelers after first three games of 1939 season. Coached Steelers thru 1942. Philadelphia and Pittsburgh merged for '43 season and Kiesling and Greasy Neale were co-coaches. In 1944 Pittsburgh merged with Chicago Cardinals, co-coaches were Kiesling and Phil Handler. In 1945 replaced by Jim Leonard as Steeler head coach, but returned nine years later, 1954, replacing Joe Burk, remaining thru 1956. Overall record was 35-61-4. Died at age 58. Pro Football Hall of Fame.

KIICK, JAMES F. Running Back. B. 8/9/46, Lincoln Park, N.J. 5'11", 215. Wyoming, 1965-67. Selected by Miami Dolphins on 5th round of 1968 draft. As rookie was 7th in AFL in rushing with 621 yds. In 1969 led league in rushing TDs with nine. In six pro years, 1968-73, rushed for 3370 yds. on 931 carries, and 27 TDs; caught 203 passes for 2055 yds., 2 TDs. Played in AFL All-Star games, 1969, 70. Played in Super Bowl, 1972, 73, 74. Upset in recent years over lack of playing time. Alternated in Miami backfield with Mercury Morris. Hailed as "Butch Cassady" while teammate Larry Csonka is "Sundance Kid." Signed with Toronto of WFL for 1975. Franchise was later shifted to Memphis. To play out option in Miami, 1974.

KILLINGER, W. GLENN Running Back. B. 9/13/1898, Harrisburg, Pa. 5'9", 163. Played halfback for Penn State, 1918-21. All-America, 1921. Drove Nittany Lions to two undefeated seasons, 1920 and '21. Was early exponent of "spinner" play, by which he pulled off many long runs. Coach Hugo Bezdek named him, along with John Beckett and Steve Creekmore, as greatest college athletes he ever coached. Earned master's degree at Columbia, then coached at West Chester State. Was also dean of men there. Gettysburg gave him honorary D.S. degree. Is now retired and living in West Chester. National Football Foundation Hall of Fame.

KILMER, WILLIAM O. (Billy) Quarterback. B. 9/5/39, Topeka, Kan. 6', 204. Attended Citrus H.S. in Azusa, Calif. Played halfback for UCLA, 1958-60. All-America, 1960. 5th in Heisman Trophy voting, 1960. In 1960 made 88-yd. rush vs. Air Force. Same season led NCAA in total offense yards with 1889 on 562 plays. In collegiate career gained 1386 yds. rushing on 307 carries, 1881 more passing on 109 of 255 passes for 15 TDs. Also gained 3123 yds. on 75 punts, average of 41.6 yds. Scored 78 points on 12 TDs and 6 PATs. College All-Star game MVP, 1961. Drafted (1st round) and signed by San Francisco 49ers. For two years triggered club's "shotgun" offense, 1961-62. Had auto accident in 1963; as result missed all of '63, part of '64, all '65. Only sporadic service with 49ers in 1966. Drafted from 49ers by New Orleans Saints in expansion draft, 1967. Hit Walt Perry for 96-yd. TD pass against Philadelphia Eagles, 11/19/67. Threw six TD passes vs. St. Louis Cardinals in 1969; St. Louis QB Charley Johnson also threw six TD passes in same game. Traded to Washington Redskins for linebacker Tom Roussel and two draft choices, 1971. In 1972 led NFL in TD passes with 19 and percentage of TD passes thrown with 8.4. Was 5th in NFL passing percentage in 1973 with 53.7; completed 122 of 227 passes for 1656 yds., 14 TDs, with nine interceptions. All-NFC, 1972. Pro Bowl, 1973. Played in Super Bowl, 1973. Gutsy player who simply won't quit against any odds. Passes often wobble, but usually find right hands. Won award as Most Courageous Athlete of the Year in 1971, given by Philadelphia sportswriters.

KILPATRICK, JOHN R. End. B. 6/15/1889, New York, N.Y. D. 5/7/60. 5'11", 190. Played for Yale, 1908-10. All-America, 1909, 10. Part of famous 1909 team captained by Ted Coy, under head field coach Howard Jones. Tough defensively, fine blocker and runner. In 1910 caught long TD pass from Art Howe to defeat Princeton, which had been unbeaten and unscored upon. Claimed to be first (probably incorrect) to use overhand forward pass. President of Madison Square Garden from 1939 until death. Was Gen. Kilpatrick. Citizens Savings College Player of the Year, 1910. National Football Foundation Hall of Fame.

KIMBROUGH, JOHN (Jarrin' Jawn) Running Back. B. Haskell, Tex. 6'2", 221. Played fullback for Texas A. & M., 1938-40. Unanimous All-America, 1940. Consensus All-America, 1940. Runnerup in Heisman voting, 1940; 5th in 1939. Played 60 minutes of football both ways. Ran 100-yd. dash in 9.8. Caught UCLA speedster Jackie Robinson from behind in 1940 game and forced him out of action with jolting tackle. In 1940 Sugar Bowl rushed for 152 yds. on 26 carries, scored 2 TDs, one on 10-yd. run ending 18-yd. pass-lateral play. Scored one TD, rushed for 58 yds. in 1941 Cotton Bowl. Collegiate totals: 1357 yds. rushing on 375 carries. 24 receptions for 197 yds., 12 interceptions for 198 yds., 21 TDs for 126 points. Played for New York Americans (AFL), 1941; Los Angeles Dons (AAFC), 1946-48. With Dons gained 1224 yds. rushing on 329 carries, 17 TDs. Scored 23 TDs overall for 138 points. Citizens Savings Hall of Fame, National Football Foundation Hall of Fame.

KINARD, FRANK M. (Bruiser) Tackle. B. 10/23/14, Pelahatchie, Miss. 6'1", 212. Mississippi, 1935-37. All-America, 1936, 37, first from his state named. Also first from Ole Miss selected All-SEC, to play in College All-Star game at Chicago; first Mississippian to make All-Pro. Named to All-Time All-SEC team and Modern All-Time All-America team. Named to Pop Warner's All-Time team, 1925-50 era. Charter member of Orange Bowl Hall of Fame. One of four brothers to play football at Ole Miss. Averaged 55 minutes per game for 34 varsity games. In 1936 employed for 708 of possible 720 minutes. Clocked 10.4 in full uniform for 100 yds. Also played basketball and track. During World War II served in navy. Played pro ball with Brooklyn Dodgers, 1935-44; New York Yankees, 1946-47. All-Pro, 1940, 41, 42, 44. Ole Miss line coach for many years, joining staff in 1948. Citizens Savings Hall of Fame, National Football Foundation Hall of Fame, Pro Football Hall of Fame.

KING, HENRY Defensive Back. B. 1/25/45, San Francisco, Calif. 6'4", 205. Utah State, 1965-66. All-America, 1966. Was NCAA interception leader, 1966, with 11 for 180 yds. Tied for most TDs scored on interceptions, with two, on 11/5/66 vs. Pacific. Had 18 career interceptions for 373 yds., average of 20.7. Selected by New York Jets on 3rd round of 1967 draft. Released by Jets in 1968 and played that year with Sacramento of Continental Football League. Signed by Buffalo Bills in 1969 but didn't play.

KING, PHILLIP Quarterback. D. 1938. 5'6", 154. QB and halfback at Princeton, 1890-93. All-America QB, 1891, 93; halfback, 1892. Scored 11 TDs rushing in 85-0 rout of Columbia, 11/4/90, record shared by Jeff Fletcher and Henry Beecher. With King in control, Tigers compiled 46-4-1 composite record and were undefeated in 11 games in 1893. Many believe him to be greatest quarterback in Princeton history. Great tackler and could take punts on dead run. In four years scored 50 TDs and kicked 56 PATs. In senior year did most of coaching. He revived open play, double and triple passes and long lateral pass. Initiated new formation which today is known as double wingback. In 1893 Princeton rated national championship. In last three years held 31 of 38 opponents scoreless. Coached Princeton, 1894-96, and was equally brilliant as coach. Coached Wisconsin, 1897-1903. Won 9, lost 1 in both 1897, 98. Won Western Conference (Big 10) title three times and finished with 63-11-2 record. Coached Georgetown to 7-3 season, 1904. Graduated from New York Law School, practiced in Madison and Washington, D.C. Citizens Savings Player of the Year, 1893. National Football Foundation Hall of Fame.

KINNICK, NILE Quarterback-Running Back. B. Omaha, Neb. D. 6/2/43, Gulf of Paria. 5'8", 167. Iowa, 1937-39. Consensus All-America, 1939. Heisman Trophy, Maxwell Trophy, Silver Football, 1939. In 1937 returned kickoff 74 yds. vs. Michigan and made 69-yd. pass vs. Minnesota. In 1938 punted 65 yds. vs. Minnesota. Completed 63-yd. pass vs. South Dakota and 71-yd. pass vs. Michigan, 1939. Was NCAA leader in yardage on kickoff returns, 1939, with 377 yds. on 15 returns. In collegiate career gained 724 yds. rushing on 254 carries, passed for 1445 yds. on 88 completions in 229 attempts. Made 18 pass interceptions for 111 yds., 6.2 average. Killed in World War II when his Navy fighter plane crashed into Gulf of Paria. Citizens Savings Hall of Fame, National Football Foundation Hall of Fame.

KIPKE, HARRY G. Running Back. D. 9/14/72, Port Huron, Mich. 5'10½", 155. Michigan halfback, 1921-23. All-America, 1922. Captain, 1923. Great back and considered finest punter in country. Earned nine varsity letters, three each in football, basketball and baseball. Became assistant coach at Missouri, 1924, at Michigan State in 1928. Head coach at Michigan, 1929-37. Shared Big 10 title with Northwestern, 1930, and with Purdue and Northwestern, 1931. Won it outright, 1932 and '33. Won all games in 1932, but tied once in 1933. Believed in powerful defensive line, anchored by exceptional center and good passing and kicking. Believed best offense was good defense. Said, "If they can't score, they can't beat you." During stretch of 30 games, Michigan beaten just once. Had overall record of 46-26-5. Was president of American Football Coaches Association. At death was vice president of Coca-Cola Co. in Chicago. Citizens Savings Player of the Year, 1922. Citizens Savings Hall of Fame, National Football Foundation Hall of Fame.

KISER, NOBLE E. Coach. B. 3/11/01, Plymouth, Ind. D. 1940. Notre Dame, 1922-24. One of famed "Seven Mules," who blocked for "Four Horsemen." Irish were national champions in 1924. Also played basketball (guard) three years. Coached Purdue, 1930-36. Logged 42-13-3 mark, for .764 percentage, highest in Purdue history. Achievements included two Western Conference (Big 10) co-championships, 1931, 32. Ill health forced retirement in 1937 and led to untimely death three years later. Noble E. Kiser Award given at Purdue since 1958. It honors football letterman of highest academic excellence.

KITZMILLER, JOHN Running Back. B. 11/25/04, Harrisburg, Pa. 6', 170. Played halfback for Oregon, 1927-29. After high school went to New York Military Academy with eye on West Point. But when John McEwan, Army coach, moved to U. of Oregon, Kitzmiller followed. Was great ball carrier, triple-threat. Led Ducks to national prominence. Playing record of 23-7-0. Called "Flying Dutchman." Played for New York Giants one season, 1931, then returned to Oregon as backfield coach for four years. In World War II served as Capt. in Army Air Force. Now heads manufacturing company in Willamette Valley of Oregon. National Football Foundation Hall of Fame.

KLOSTERMAN, DONALD Quarterback. B. Le Mars, Iowa. 5'11", 180. "Duke of Del Rey" in playing days at Loyola (Calif.), 1949-51. Broke national one-game records in 1951 with 372 yds. passing, 33 completions, 63 attempts vs. Florida. Year before had 355 yds., 26 completions against Pacific. Set season record, 1951, in completions with 159; led NCAA in passing attempts that year with 315 and yds. with 1843, for 9 TDs. In collegiate career completed 268 of 729 passes for 4481 yds., 33 TDs, 44 interceptions, percentage of 50.5, average of 6.1 yds. per attempt. Gained 4392 yds. on total offense and scored 97 points. Loyola retired his number (10) following brilliant career. No. 1 draft choice of Cleveland Browns, 1952, but played that season with Los Angeles Rams. Calgary Stampeders, 1953-57. For many years held CFL record with 106-yd. pass completion. In 1957 paralyzed by skiing accident; however, walked out of hospital after eight operations, 18 months later. Now golfs, swims, dances. Loyola Alumnus of the Year, 1970. Chief talent scout, San Diego Chargers, 1960-62; Kansas City Chiefs, 1963-65. General manager, Houston Oilers, 1966-69; Baltimore Colts, 1970-71; Los Angeles Rams, 1972-73.

KNIGHT, CURT Kicker. B. 4/14/43, Gulfport, Miss. 6'2", 190. Played split end, safety and placekicked for U.S. Coast Guard Academy, 1965-67. Signed as free agent by Washington Redskins, 1968; on taxi squad that year. Leading placekicker in NFC in 1970, making 20 of 27 FG attempts. Kicked four FGs in 2nd quarter vs. New York Giants., 11/15/70, to tie NFL records. In 1971 won NFC scoring title with 114 points, on 29 of 49 FGs and 27 PATs (no misses). Forty-nine FG attempts tied NFL record. In five years, 1969-73, attempted 172 PATs, making 169, attempted 175 FGs and made 101, for 372 points. In 1973 playoff game vs. Minnesota Vikings made 2 FGs, 1 for NFC playoff record of 52 yds. All-NFL, 1971. Pro Bowl, 1972. Played in Super Bowl, 1973.

KNOX, CHARLES R. (Chuck) Coach. B. 4/27/32, Sewickley, Pa. 6', 212. Played tackle for Juniata College of Huntingdon, Pa., 1951-53. Assistant coach, Juniata, 1954; Tyrone (Pa.) H.S., 1955; Ellwood City (Pa.) H.S., 1956-58; Wake Forest, 1959-60; U. of Kentucky, 1961-62; New York Jets, 1963-66; Detroit Lions, 1967-72. Became head coach for Los Angeles Rams in 1973 and won 12 games, while losing 2, for most victories in history of franchise. Won first six games, then lost two, then won six. Put Rams in playoffs first time since George Allen in 1970; came within three points of undefeated season as lost to Minnesota Vikings, 10-9, and to Atlanta Falcons, 15-13. Led Rams to No. 1 finish in defense and points scored. Made wholesale changes in Ram lineup; aided by acquisition of QB John Hadl from San Diego Chargers. Known as man of poise, warmth and dignity. Named Coach of the Year as rookie, feat not accomplished by Vince Lombardi, Don Shula, George Allen, or anybody else.

KOCH, BARTON (Botchey) Guard. B. 8/13/06, Temple, Tex. D. 4/28/64. 6', 195. All-America at Baylor, 1930. Named Most Outstanding Player in East-West Shrine game of 1930. Noted for quick, aggressive line play. Later served as line coach at George Washington, Tulsa and Baylor. Contracted fatal illness in South America during World War II. National Football Foundation Hall of Fame.

KOCH, DESMOND Running Back. B. Shelton, Wash. 6'0", 207. Played halfback for Southern California, 1951-53. Made 72-yd. punt vs. Texas Christian, 1951. Collegiate punting leader, 1952, with average of 43.7 yds. on 47 punts for 2043 yds.; in 1953 with 44.6-yd. average on 22 punts for 981 yds. Boomed two 64-yd. punts vs. Oregon State and one vs. Notre Dame, 1953. Set record in punting average, career, with 43.7 yds. on 102 punts for 4453 yds. Set Rose Bowl records with 72-yd. punt and 50.9 punting average on 7 punts. Might have become great tailback if he hadn't injured knee just before 1951 season opener. Was NCAA discus champ his final year. Didn't play pro ball.

KOCOUREK, DAVID A. Tight End. B. 8/20/37, Chicago, Ill. 6'5", 235. Played for Wisconsin. Signed as free agent by Los Angeles Chargers in 1960 and moved with team to San Diego following year. Played with Chargers thru 1965. Selected from S.D. by Miami Dolphins in AFL expansion draft, 1966. Traded by Miami to Oakland Raiders for draft choice in 1967, retired after 1968 season. Established AFL championship game career records for games played, seven, 1960, 61, 63, 64, 65, 67, 68; TD receptions with two. Established AFL championship game record for receptions with seven, 12/21/61. Played in AFL All-Star games, 1962, 63, 64, 65. Played in Super Bowl, 1968. All-AFL, 1962.

KRAMER, GERALD L. (Jerry) Guard. B. 1/23/36, Jordan, Mont. 6'3", 245. Played at U. of Idaho. Selected by Green Bay Packers on 4th round of 1958 NFL draft. In 1962 NFL title game kicked one PAT and record-tying three TDs. Retired after 1968 season with 11-year pro record of 136 games, 90 of 94 PATs, 29 of 54 FGs, 177 points. All-NFL guard, 1960, 66, 67; tackle, 1962, 63. Played in Pro Bowl, 1963, 64, 68. NFL championship games, 1960, 61, 62, 65, 66, 67. Super Bowl, 1967, 68. Overcame unbelievable number of injuries. Authored critically acclaimed book, *Instant Replay; The Green Bay Packer Diary of Jerry Kramer.* Edited *Lombardi: Winning Is the Only Thing.* Spent entire career with Packers.

KRAMER, RONALD Tight End. B. 6/24/35, Girard, Kan. 6'3", 235. Played end for Michigan, 1954-56. Unanimous All-America, 1956; consensus All-America, 1955. 6th in Heisman voting, 1955, 8th in 1956. Made 65-yd. catch vs. Iowa and 70-yd. catch vs. UCLA, 1956. Finished collegiate career with 54 pass receptions, 888 yds., average of 16.4, 8 TDs. Kicked 42 PATs, scoring total of 102 points. Also played basketball, threw shot-put and discus, high-jumped. Played for Green Bay Packers, 1957, 59-64. Benched, and nearly traded, by Vince Lombardi in 1960 for bad attitude. Bounced back in '61 to become regular. Big, intelligent, pulverizing blocker, fine receiver — ideal tight end. As much as any man, made his position powerful force in football. Favorite target of Bart Starr. Caught two TD passes against New York Giants in 1961 title game. Finished career with Detroit Lions, 1965-67. All-NFL, 1962. Also played in 1962 championship game.

KRAUSE, PAUL J. Defensive Back. B. 2/19/42, Flint, Mich. 6'3", 200. Played for Iowa State, 1961-63. Baseball player before shoulder injury curtailed career. Selected by Washington Redskins on 2nd round of 1964 NFL draft. As rookie led NFL in interceptions with 12 for 140 yds., average of 11.7, 1 TD. Established NFL record for consecutive games intercepting pass (seven). Traded to Minnesota Vikings for Marlin McKeever and draft choice, 7/4/68. In 10 pro years, 1964-73, made 62 interceptions for 836 yds. and 3 TDs. Pilfered seven passes in 1968, setting Viking record. Has fine range, great hands. Enjoys instructing younger players. All-Pro, 1964, 65; only safety ever to be consensus All-Pro first two years in league. All-NFC, 1971, 72, 73. Pro Bowl, 1965, 66, 70, 72, 73, 74. NFL championship game, 1969. Played in Super Bowl, 1970, 74.

KRISHER, WILLIAM Guard. B. 9/18/35, Perry, Okla. 6'1", 230. All-State and All-America prep at Midwest City, Okla. U. of Oklahoma, 1955-57. Three-year regular. Consensus All-America, 1957; All-America, 1956. Played in 1956 and '58 Orange Bowl games. Senior Bowl, Hula Bowl and College All-Star games. Started for All-Stars against Detroit Lions, 1958. Pittsburgh Steelers, 1958; Dallas Texans, 1960-61. All-AFL offensive guard, 1960. Now Southwest regional director for Fellowship of Christian Athletes.

KROLL, ALEX Center. B. Leechburg, Pa. 6'2", 228. Played center and called defensive signals at Rutgers, 1959-61. Consensus All-America and National Football Foundation Scholar-Athlete, 1961. Coached by John Bateman. Outstanding academically. Captained 9-0 team of 1961. Record was almost blemished in season's last game against Columbia. Rutgers trailed, 19-7, starting 4th quarter. Then, with Kroll, halfback Pierce Frauenheim, reserve QB Bill Speranza providing inspiration, Scarlet Knights put on frenzied rally. They eventually won, 32-19. Gave school first unbeaten season in 93 years — since initiating intercollegiate football with Princeton way back in 1869. Kroll chose AFL New York Titans over NFL Los Angeles Rams for pro career. Played only one season, 1962. Became creative director of Young & Rubicam, one of nation's leading advertising agencies.

KRUEGER, CHARLES A. (Charlie) Tackle. B. 1/28/37, Caldwell, Tex. 6'4", 255. Played defensive tackle for Texas A. & M., 1955-57. Selected by San Francisco 49ers on 1st round of 1958 NFL draft. Missed '58 season after suffering broken arm. Tied NFL record in 1961 for most safeties, lifetime, with three. Played in Pro Bowl, 1961, 62, 63, 64, 65. Brother of Rolf Krueger, San Francisco teammate in 1972, 73. Charlie was defensive starter 15 years, 1959-73. Seemingly unaffected by pain. Considered technically faultless. "I've never been a star, but I've always done my job." — Krueger. Retired after 1973 season.

KUHARICH, JOSEPH L. Coach. B. South Bend, Ind. As grade school kid hung around Notre Dame practice field. Once held hands with Knute Rockne. Grew up to play guard for Irish. Entered college in 1935 weighing around 150. Later played pro ball at 225. Graduated from Notre Dame in 1938. Chicago Cardinals, 1940-41, 45. Was All-NFL right guard, 1941. Coached U. of San Francisco, 1948-51. Ollie Matson, Joe Scudero, Gino Marchetti starred on 1951 team that won all nine of its games. School then abandoned football. Head coach for Cards, 1952; record of 4-8-0. Head coach of Washington Redskins, 1954 thru '58, with 26-32-2 record. In 1958 replaced Terry Brennan as Notre Dame head coach. Quit after '62 season and Hugh Devore took over. Notre Dame record: 17-23-0. Went to Philadelphia Eagles as general manager and coach on 15-year contract, 1964. In 1966 tied with Cleveland Browns for 2nd place in Eastern Division of NFL. Replaced after '68 season when team sold to Leonard Tose. Pete Retzlaff became general manager, Jerry Williams field boss. Overall record with Eagles was 28-41-1. In 17 years of coaching compiled 84-104-3 mark.

KUNZ, GEORGE J. Tackle. B. 7/5/47, Ft. Sheridan, Ill. 6'5", 257. Played for Notre Dame, 1966-68. Consensus and Academic All-America, 1968. Dean's List student, *cum laude* graduate. Majored in philosophy and communication. Received Scholar-Athlete Award from National Football Foundation. Played in Hula Bowl, East-West Shrine, Coaches All-America, College All-Star games. Atlanta Falcons, 1969-73. Was 1st-round draft choice of Falcons. Pro Bowl, 1972, 73, 74. Punishing blocker, expert at delivering "first lick." Fast off ball, tremendous lateral movement.

KUSH, FRANK Coach. B. 1/20/29, Windber, Pa. Conquered adversity. One of 15 children. Only apparent future was to follow his dad into Pennsylvania coal mines. Found outlet in football. Won scholarship to Washington & Lee, but transferred to Michigan State after freshman year. Although only 5'9", 170, won starting berth as sophomore guard in 1950. That year, Michigan State fell to Maryland, 34-7, Kush's only loss as collegian. In summer of 1952 was struck in eye by piece of steel while working with construction crew. Doctors thought he might not play again but came back that fall to win All-America honors. After two years in service, Kush joined Dan Devine's staff at Arizona State, in 1955. Was line coach three years, then took head job at age 28 when Devine went to Missouri. Sixteen years later, thru 1973, Kush ranked as 2nd winningest (percentage) major college coach. Record: 132-34-1. Was 11-0 in 1970, 11-1 in '71, 10-2 in '72, 11-1 in '73 for 43-4 mark last four years. Earned consecutive Fiesta Bowl victories over Florida State (45-38, 1971); Missouri (49-35, 1972), Pittsburgh (28-7, 1973). His teams are annually among national leaders in most offensive departments. Developed such speedsters as Charley Taylor, Travis Williams, Henry Carr, Larry Walton, Fair Hooker, J.D. Hill, Steve Holden, Woody Green, plus numerous other pro players.

KUTNER, MALCOLM J. (Mal) End. B. 3/27/21, Dallas, Tex. 6'2", 197. Played for Dana X. Bible at Texas, 1939-41. All-America, 1941. Selected by Pittsburgh Steelers on 26th round of 1942 draft but went into military service, 1942-45. Draft rights traded to Chicago Cardinals in 1946, playing with club thru 1950. Led NFL in pass receiving yardage in 1947 with 944, average yds. with 23.0 (on 41 receptions), TD pass receptions with 14, total TDs with 15. In pro career gained 59 yds. rushing; caught 145 passes for 3060 yds., average of 21.1; made 31 TD catches. Scored 198 points overall on 33 TDs. Intercepted 13 passes for 151 yds. All-NFL end. 1947, 48. Played in NFL title games same seasons. National Football Foundation Hall of Fame.

KWALICK, THADDEUS J. (Ted) Tight End. B. 4/15/47, McKees Rocks, Pa. 6'4", 226. Penn State, 1966-68. Unanimous All-America, 1968; All-America,

1967. 4th in Heisman Trophy voting, 1968. Made 60-yd. reception vs. Syracuse, 1967; 63-yd. catch vs. Pittsburgh, 1968. Started at wingback in 1968 Gator Bowl and caught 12-yd. TD pass. Orange Bowl, 1969, against Kansas, caught six passes for 74 yds. Penn State edged Jayhawks, 15-14. Caught 86 career passes for 1343 yds., average of 15.6. Also scored 12 TDs, kicked 8 PATs, for 80 points. Selected by San Francisco 49ers on 1st round of 1969 draft. Seized 151 passes for 1595 yds. and 16 TDs during 1969-73 period. All-NFC, 1973. Played in Pro Bowl, 1972, 73, 74.

LADD, ERNEST Tackle. B. 1938, Orange, Tex. Starred at Grambling. San Diego Chargers, 1961-65; Houston Oilers, 1966-67; Kansas City Chiefs, 1967-68. AFL championship games, 1963, 64, 65. All-AFL, 1964, 65. Stormy career. Man of tremendous strength, surprising agility, terrible temper. Fought management over salary, league office over right to wear beard. Formed with Buck Buchanan, of Kansas City, what was probably biggest defensive tackle combination in history. Buchanan, 6'7", 275, was also Grambling teammate. Ladd combined wrestling with football career.

LAHR, WARREN Defensive Back. B. 9/5/23, Wyoming, Pa. D. 1/19/69. Attended Western Reserve. Played with Cleveland Browns, 1949-59. All-Pro, 1951. Intercepted 40 passes in NFL career, returned 5 for touchdowns. Played in six straight NFL championship games, 1950-55. Browns won 3 and lost 3.

LAMBEAU, EARL L. (Curly) Running Back-Coach. B. 4/9/1898, Green Bay, Wis. D. 6/1/65. Dark, wavy hair won nickname. Played one season at Notre Dame, 1918. Started career as sub for fullback George Gipp, then was shifted to quarterback. Left school to have tonsils removed and never returned. Persuaded his boss at Indian Packing Co., Green Bay, to sponsor football team, 1919. This was genesis of Green Bay Packers. Team joined NFL, 1921, with Lambeau as player-coach. Played halfback for Packers thru 1929, coached them thru 1949. His 29-year Green Bay coaching career is longest uninterrupted tenure in pro history. One of first coaches to realize usefulness of passing game. Won seven divisional, six NFL titles, including three straight, 1929-31. Green Bay record:

213-104-22. Tutored such greats as Cal Hubbard, Mike Michalske, Johnny McNally (Blood), Arnie Herber, Clarke Hinkle, Cecil Isbell, Don Huston. Resigned Packers when he was no longer able to maintain one-man rule over club. Also coached St. Louis Cardinals, 1950-51 (8-16); Washington Redskins, 1952-53 (10-13-1). Pro Football Hall of Fame.

LAMMONS, PETER S., JR. Tight End. B. 10/20/43, Crockett, Tex. 6'3", 228. Linebacker and tight end at Texas, 1963-65. Team won 1963 national championship. In 1964 Orange Bowl, Lammons intercepted two passes thrown by Alabama's Joe Namath (future teammate). Drafted by New York Jets, 1966. In rookie year caught 41 passes for 565 yds. Following season led all AFL tight ends with 45 receptions, 515 yds. Played in AFL All-Star game, 1967. Caught one TD pass from Namath in 1968 AFL title game. Jets were Super Bowl champions in 1969. Played with New York thru 1971. Finished career with Green Bay Packers, 1972.

LAMONICA, DARYLE P. Quarterback. B. 7/17/41, Fresno, Calif. 6'3", 215. Graduated from Notre Dame, 1963. Buffalo Bills, 1963-66. Drafted on 24th round. In 1963 punted 52 times for 40.1-yd. average. Traded to Oakland Raiders in 1967 with Glen Bass and two draft choices, for Tom Flores, Art Powell and draft choice. Played with Raiders, 1967-73. AFL passing leader with 220 completions in 425 attempts for 3228 yds. and record 30 TDs. Established AFL record for fewest passes had intercepted on 1000 or more attempts, with 58. 1970 AFC passing leader with 179 completions in 356 attempts for 2516 yds. Tied league record for most times on championship team, three, 1967. Pro Bowl, 1971, 73. AFL Player of the Year, 1967, 69. Played in AFL title games, 1964, 65, 66, 67, 68, 69. All-AFL, 1967, 69. AFL All-Star games, 1966, 68. Super Bowl, 1968 (two TD passes). Had string of 25 straight games throwing TD pass, 1969-70, 2nd longest in pro history.

LANDRY, THOMAS Coach. B. 9/11/24, Mission, Tex. Methodical man, builder of champions. Fashioned NFL Dallas Cowboys, from lowly expansion team, into consistent winner. Landry and Cowboys struggled thru 0-11-1 season in 1960 after Dallas received NFL franchise. Five years later reached .500 first time (7-7). In 1971 Cowboys won Super Bowl VI, climaxing long struggle for supremacy. In 1973 made playoffs eighth straight year. Landry-football love affair blossomed during Texas boyhood days. Developed into All-Region fullback at Mission H.S. Played QB for U. of Texas until relinquishing post to guy named Bobby Layne; went back to fullback. Junior year was All-SWC; senior year, co-captain. Played on winning Sugar Bowl, 1948, and Orange Bowl, 1949, teams. Signed by AAFC New York Yankees for punting-defensive duties. Played one year with Yankees, 1949, and then moved over to New York Giants for six years at cornerback, 1950-55. Last two as player-coach. Was All-Pro, 1954. Remained Giant assistant thru 1959, earning "best defensive coach in the business" tribute from head coach Jim Lee Howell. Then to Cowboys and slow rise to top. Became tenth pro coach in history to win 100 games, 1973. Ranks 9th on all-time list with 110-80-6 record.

Quiet, introspective, religious. Was national president of Fellowship of Christian Athletes in 1973. Style has encountered criticism. Some thought it hypocritical to mix religion and football violence. Others found Landry incapable of winning "big one" (theory dispelled in 1971); aloof, uncommunicative and unfeeling. But, from most, has earned respect. Billy Truax gave him notable panegyric after coming to Cowboys in 1971 trade: "Coach Landry will never be a loser, simply because he refuses to lose. He's a solid individual, like the Rock of Gibraltar."

LANE, MacARTHUR Running Back. 6'1", 220. B. 3/16/42, Oakland, Calif. Attended Merritt (Calif.) Junior College, Oakland, before matriculating at Utah State. Linebacker there first two years, then switched to fullback. 1st-round draft choice of St. Louis Cardinals, 1968. 3rd-leading NFC rusher, picking up 977 yards (2nd highest in Cardinal history). Played in 1971 Pro Bowl. Obtained by Green Bay Packers after arguing publicly with St. Louis officials, 1972. Lane and John Brockington proceeded to give Pack NFC's best one-two punch. Club's top receiver, most valuable offensive player, 1972. Powerful runner and blocker. 4.6 speed in 40-yd. dash. Loves clothes, collects and restores antique cars — "I hate to see anything of the past destroyed."

LANE, MYLES J. Running Back. B. 11/2/03, Melrose, Mass. 6'1", 185. Dartmouth halfback, 1925-27. Holds Dartmouth single-game records for TDs with 5, points with 33. Also holds school records for TDs, season, with 18; points, season, with 125; TDs, three seasons, with 48; points, three seasons, with 308. National scoring leader with 125 points, 1927. Also played defenseman on Dartmouth hockey team; later played in NHL with New York Rangers, 1928-29; Boston Bruins, 1929-33. East-West Shrine game, 1927. Head coach at Boston U., 1932; Harvard backfield coach, 1936. Cmdr. in Navy during World War II. Later served as U.S. attorney for Southern New York, 1951-53. Chairman of New York State Commission of Investigation, 1958-68. Justice of New York State Supreme Court, serving since 1968. National Football Foundation Hall of Fame.

LANE, RICHARD (Night Train) Defensive Back. B. 4/16/28, Austin, Tex. 5'11", 180. Football star at Anderson H.S. in Austin. Offensive end at Scottsbluff (Neb.) J.C., 1947. Served three years in army and played service ball at Ft. Ord, Calif. After 1952 discharge, Lane walked into office of Los Angeles Rams and got conditional contract. At first had difficulty learning plays. Often studied late at night, using flashlight, and went to end Tom Fears' room for help. Fears had record of "Night Train" which always seemed to be playing when Lane arrived. Teammates started saying, "Here's Night Train visiting us again," and nickname stuck. Converted to defensive halfback. In rookie year, 1952, led NFL in interceptions with record-setting 14, amassing 298 yds., longest 80 yds. Traded to Chicago Cardinals in 1954, and again topped league in interceptions with 10 for 181 yds., longest 64 yds. Caught 98-yd. TD pass from Ogden Compton 11/13/55.

In 1960 traded to Detroit Lions. Vince Lombardi called Lane best cornerback he'd ever seen. Opposing coaches usually ordered QBs never to throw pass near his area. Played in 1962 Pro Bowl with great stomach pain; nevertheless, he intercepted pass and ran 42 yds. for West's first TD. Operated on two days later for appendicitis. Retired after 1964 season and later worked in Lion front office. All-Pro, 1956, 60, 61, 62, 63. Pro Bowl, 1961, 62, 63.

LANGFORD, WILLIAM S. Official. B. Yonkers, N.Y. D. 3/2/42, Yonkers, N.Y. Graduated from Trinity College of Hartford. Son of minister. Prominent football official, 1904-19. Army-Navy battle of 1919 was last game he officiated. Secretary of Rules Committee, 1925-39. Illness forced resignation. Received Touchdown Club of New York Award in 1940 for outstanding contributions. Called "the demand for victory" worst feature of football. Kept in background but dedicated to sports.

LANIER, WILLIE E. (Contact) Linebacker. B. 8/21/45, Clover, Va. 6'1", 245. There are few, if any, better linebackers playing pro football today than Willie Lanier of Kansas City Chiefs. Strong, fleet, rarely fooled — that's Lanier in nutshell. Loves to "hit," hence nickname "Contact." Came to Chiefs from Morgan State. Was 2nd-round draft choice. Played in four straight Pro Bowls, following 1970, 71, 72, 73 seasons. Each of those years named AFC Linebacker of the Year by Players Association. Defensive MVP in 1971 Pro Bowl. Selected NFL Man of the Year, 1972, in national Vitalis poll. Is partner in Kansas City beer distributorship. Devotes considerable time to Drug Abuse Campaign. His resume would also include movie credit and television sports announcing.

LaROCHE, CHESTER J. Administrator. B. Boston, Mass. Graduated from Dorchester (Mass.) H.S., Tilton (N.H.) School, Phillips Exeter Academy and Yale. In 1916 called weak-side tackle play that yielded Yale's first TD against Harvard since 1907. It stood up for 6-3 victory. Served as Lt. aboard USS *Arkansas* during World War I. Returned to play at Yale in 1919. Coached Yale freshmen, 1920. Reporter for Boston *Post,* then turned to sales promotion and advertising work. Graduated to president and chairman of board at Young & Rubicam. Left to form own advertising agency, which became LaRoche, McCaffney and McCall. Initiated Advertising Council and American Round Table. Leading role in development of National Football Foundation. Served as its chairman, created Center for Leadership. Received Foundation's Gold Medal Award in 1968. Same year he retired from business life.

LARSON, PAUL L. Quarterback. B. 3/19/32, Turlock, Calif. 5'11", 180. Attended Turlock H.S. and U. of California. Played under Pappy Waldorf, 1951-54. All-America, 1954. Entered college with formidable reputation as single-wing tailback. Ran 72 yards first time he carried ball as freshman, vs. Minnesota. Averaged 6.4 yds. per carry as sophomore halfback. Junior year was switched to quarterback when regular QB, Sam Williams, was injured. Results were startling. National total-offense leader with 1572 yds., 1953. Led in completions (125), passing percentage (.641) and passing yardage (1537), 1954. His .641 percentage set NCAA record but has since been broken. Backfield coach Wes Fry called Larson "the greatest passer I've ever seen from the standpoint of passing quickness." Previous to Larson, Fry coached Otto Graham at Northwestern. Chicago Cardinals, 1957; Oakland Raiders, 1960. Now manages western wear store in Modesto, Calif.

LARY, R. YALE Defensive Back. B. Fort Worth, Tex. 5'11", 190. Texas A. & M., 1949-51. All-SWC. Signed both pro baseball and football contracts. Gave up baseball to concentrate on career with Detroit Lions. Played 11 years, 1952-53, 56-64, with service interruption. Handled ball inordinate number of times since he punted and returned punts, besides defensive back chores. Totals of 503 punts, 126 punt returns and 50 interceptions are Detroit club records. Thrice led league in punting average, 1959, 61, 63. 48.9-yd. average, 1963, is still 2nd-best average, season. Stands 3rd, lifetime, with 44.3-yd. average. Booted 72-yarder vs. Cleveland Browns, 12/27/53, setting championship game record. NFL championship games, 1952, 53, 54, 57; Lions lost only in '54. All-Pro safety, 1956, 57, 58, 61. Nine Pro Bowls. Was member of Texas legislature. Now partner in Ford dealership near Fort Worth. All-Pro Squad of the 1950s.

LATOURETTE, CHARLES P. (Chuck) Defensive Back. B. 7/21/46, San Antonio, Tex. 6', 190. Received pre-med degree from Rice, 1966. Signed with St. Louis Cardinals in 1967 and played for them thru 1971, excepting '69 when he didn't play. In 1968 broke two Abe Woodson records by running back 46 kickoffs for 1237 yds. On punts gained another 345 yds. for 1582 total on kick returns. Returned three punts for single-game record 143 yds., 9/29/68. Also handled punting chores for St. Louis, finishing 3rd in '68 with 41.6 average. Completed career with 248 punts, 40.5 average. Owns many Cardinal punt- and kickoff-return standards.

LATTNER, JOHN J. (Johnny) Running Back. B. 10/24/32, Chicago, Ill. 6'1", 190. Notre Dame, 1951-53. 23-4-3 playing record. Unanimous All-America, 1952-53. Heisman Trophy, Walter Camp Trophy, 1953. Punted, played both ways. Rushed for 1724 yds., recorded 13 interceptions. Had 92-yd. kickoff return vs. Pennsylvania, 1953. Played with Pittsburgh Steelers, 1954, making Pro Bowl. Ruined knee in service game and was forced to give up pro football after one year. Requested and received new Heisman Trophy when his melted during restaurant fire. It's now on display in Johnny Lattner's Steak House, Marina Towers, Chicago. Citizens Savings Hall of Fame.

LAVELLI, DANTE End. B. Hudson, Ohio. Set on attending Notre Dame. Even made deposit on school fees. Changed mind when Ohio State hired Paul Brown to be head coach in 1941. Played only one varsity season with Buckeyes, as sophomore in 1942, and was often injured. Following season army ruled its officer trainees on college teams wouldn't be eligible for sports. Lavelli and 37 other Buckeyes were thus faced with immediate service commitments. Lived thru

Battle of the Bulge and returned home — broke. Found Paul Brown coaching Cleveland Browns in fledgling AAFC. Asked for tryout, impressed, and was signed. Other one-time Buckeyes also signed with Browns, among them Lin Houston, Lou Groza, Gene Fekete, George Cheroke, Bill Willis. These developments enraged Ohio State officials. Former colleague Paul Brown stealing players, it seemed, but actually wasn't acting illegally. Signees' college classes had graduated. Lavelli, like Houston, Groza, and Willis, went on to become outstanding pro. Formed tremendous pass-catching tandem with Mac Speedie. In four-year history of AAFC, Lavelli caught 142 passes for 2580 yds. 29 TDs. His 142 receptions rank 4th on all-time AAFC list. AAFC-NFL career combined, 1946-56, 386 receptions, 6488 yds., 62 TDs. All-Pro, 1951, 53. Set championship game career record with 24 catches, for 340 yds. Cleveland won titles in 1950, 54, 55. Paul Brown commented: "Lavelli had one of the strongest pair of hands I've ever seen. Nobody could take it away from him once he had it in his hands." Now owns furniture and appliance store in Cleveland.

LAYDEN, ELMER F. Running Back. B. 1903, Davenport, Iowa. D. 6/30/73, Chicago, Ill. 6', 162. Played fullback at Notre Dame, 1922-24. One of "Four Horsemen." Consensus All-America, 1924. Hero in 1925 Rose Bowl vs. Pop Warner's Stanford Indians. Scored three TDs, had 78- and 70-yd. interception returns, punted 54 and 53 yds. High school injury made Knute Rockne, Irish coach, skeptical about ability to play. However, he later said, "Elmer made a believer out of me. I was never too sure about that knee, but it never bothered him. He was always using an exceptionally quick start with the maximum amount of speed. He has a right to ride with the gridiron great." Played one year of pro ball with Brooklyn Horsemen (AFL), 1925. Coached at Columbia College (now Loras) in Dubuque, Iowa, 1925-26; record was 8-5-2. Duquesne coach in 1927 thru 1933, with 48-16-6 record. Went to Notre Dame as head coach in 1934 and remained thru 1940. Led Irish to 47-13-3 record. Probably most exciting game was 1935 upset victory over Ohio State, 18-13. Total coaching record was 103-34-11, .733 percentage. Named commissioner of NFL in 1941, replacing Carl Storck. In 1946, Layden was replaced by Bert Bell.

LAYNE, ROBERT Quarterback. B. 12/19/26, Santa Anna, Tex. 6', 191. Attended Highland Park H.S. (Dallas). Played at U. of Texas, 1944-47, against his high school teammate, Doak Walker of SMU. First T-formation QB in Southwest, gaining distinction when Blair Cherry replaced Dana X. Bible (retired) as coach. Consensus All-America, 1947. Set numerous Texas records, including career marks for TD passes (25), passes attempted (410), completions (200), yds. passing (3145), total offense (3990), average per play (6.2 yds); season record for TD passes (9); game records for TD passes (3), longest pass completions (80 yds.), points (24), TDs (4). Led NCAA in pass completions with 77 in 1946, attempting 140 (.55) and gaining 1122 yds. Chicago Bears, 1948; New York Bulldogs, 1949; Detroit Lions, 1950-58; Pittsburgh Steelers, 1958-62. Scored one TD in 1952 title game vs. Cleveland Browns, won 17-7 by Lions. On 11/26/53 passed to Cloyce Box for 97-yd. TD pass vs. Green Bay Packers. Hit 4 of 6 passes in last 2½ minutes of '53 title game, closing with 33-yarder that tied game. PAT gave Detroit winning margin over Browns. Led NFL in scoring, 1956, with 5 TDs, 33 PATs, 12 FGs for 99 points. Lions walloped Browns, 59-14, for another NFL crown, 1957. Lost title game in 1954.

Layne, who thrived on competition, had no peer as field engineer. He was tough and demanding, and though no picture player, always seemed to get job done. Played with only one object in mind: to win. It's been said that he never lost game — only time ran out on him few times. Gained notoriety for free wheeling antics off field. All-Pro, 1952, 56. Finished career as most productive passer in pro history. Pitched 3700 times, completed 1814, for 49.0 percentage, 26,768 yds., 196 TDs. Also threw 243 interceptions. Currently business consultant in Lubbock, Tex. First player from U. of Texas named to National Football Foundation Hall of Fame, in 1968. Pro Football Hall of Fame.

LEA, LANGDON (Biffy) Tackle. 6'1", 187. B. 5/11/1874, Germantown, Pa. D. 10/4/37. 41-5-1 Princeton playing record, 1892-95. All-America, 1893, 94, 95. Captain, 1895. Caspar Whitney observed of Lea, 1893: "In the Yale game he was one of the cleverest linemen ever seen in New York. Better even than the great Ma Newell of Harvard. Biffy's all-around tackle play — his blocking and tackling — were unsurpassed." Princeton shut out opposition 35 times during Lea's 47-game career. Citizens Savings Hall of Fame, National Football Foundation Hall of Fame.

LEAHY, FRANK Coach. B. 8/27/08, O'Neill, Neb. D. 6/21/73, Portland, Ore. Raised in South Dakota, near Winner, appropriate name for future coaching immortal. Graduated from Notre Dame, 1931. Was lineman under Knute Rockne, 1929. In senior year ripped cartilage in knee and never played again, but hung around practice sessions and learned about football. Became line coach at Fordham under Jim Crowley in 1933. Got first head coaching job in 1939, at Boston College. First season his team won 9, lost 2, including win in Cotton Bowl at Dallas. 1940 team was undefeated, untied, winning 11, including 19-13 win over Tennessee in Sugar Bowl. In 1941 succeeded Elmer Layden at Notre Dame, compiling 8-0-1 record that year. Voted Coach of the Year, 1941. 1942 record was 7-2-2. National championship team of 1943 rated among best teams of all time. It won nine straight before losing to Great Lakes in final minutes of last game, 14-19. Served in U.S. Navy, 1944-45. Had three more national championship teams, 1946, 47, 49. Beginning in 1946, and carrying thru opening game of '50 season, Notre Dame was unbeaten in 39 straight games. In 1946 Irish played to 0-0 tie with Army; in 1948 tied USC, 14-14, in season's final game. Streak was ended by Purdue in second game of 1950 campaign. In 1953 collapsed in dressing room during halftime of game with Georgia Tech, which was beaten first time in 32 games. Leahy's problem was diagnosed as pancreatitis, and it signaled end of one of most successful coaching careers in history. Record during nine Notre Dame years was 80-5-5, percentage of .941; overall record for 13 years was 107-13-9, percentage of .864. Overall percentage trails only Knute Rockne. Named to Knights of Malta by Pope Pius XII. Died after long illness. Citizens Savings Hall of Fame, National Football Foundation Hall of Fame.

LEAKS, ROOSEVELT Running Back. B. 1/31/53, Chappell Hill, Tex. 5'11", 220. Outstanding runner for Texas. Totaled 1099 yds. rushing in sophomore season, 1972. All-America junior year, 1973. Broke Southwest Conference record by gaining 342 yds. vs. SMU, 11/3/73. Previous record of 297 yds. set by Bob Smith of Texas A. & M. in 1950. Leaks fell just eight yds. short of all-time NCAA record of 350 set by Eric Allen of Michigan State, 1971. Finished 4th nationally in rushing and led Texas to sixth consecutive conference title. Amassed league record 1415 yds. for season. Coach Darrell Royal said Leaks makes many long plays that fans admire, but it is consistent 4-, 5-, and 6-yd. runs that impress him. Rambles like bull, straight up middle, with head down. Played offensive guard in 9th grade, starting defensive tackle in 10th grade. Played in only three losing games, was twice all-state fullback. Prep grades were good, had excellent attitude. Very powerful, can take out two players with one block. Appeared in Cotton Bowl, 1973, 74. In losing 19-3 to Nebraska in '74 classic, Leaks injured knee and required surgery. Will miss 1974 season as result.

LeBARON, EDWARD W., JR. Quarterback. B. 1/7/30, San Rafael, Calif. 5'7", 165. Pint-sized package of dynamite. College of Pacific QB at age 16, youngest college football player in nation. Played four years under Alonzo Stagg, 1946-49. Passed for more than 1000 yds. each of last three seasons. Little All-America, 1946, 47, 48. Quarterbacked 1950 College All-Star team to 17-7 upset of Philadelphia Eagles, 17-7. No. 10 draft choice of Washington Redskins, 1950. Played two exhibition games with 'Skins, then went into marines. Served two years, spending nine months in Korea and received letter of commendation for heroism. Was wounded twice, acquiring shrapnel in right shoulder and leg. During first year with Washington, 1952, divided QB chores with Sammy Baugh. Threw four TD passes vs. New York Giants and was subsequently named Rookie of the Year. Played in CFL, 1954; returned to Washington, 1955-59. Played in Pro Bowl, 1956. Threw 5 TD passes vs. Chicago Cardinals in 1958, leading NFL in passing that year with 79 completions in 145 attempts for 1365 yds., percentage of 54.3. Was Redskin MVP, 1958. Actually, his 1957 percentage of 59.3 was better (99 completions, 167 attempts, 1508 yds.). Attended Georgetown Law School, 1956-58; received degree. Joined law firm in Midland, Tex., after being admitted to California Bar.

Announced retirement from football in 1960. Changed his mind and was traded to Dallas Cowboys that year. Threw shortest TD pass ever (two inches), to Dick Bielski, 10/9/60, vs. Washington (former team). In 1962, vs. Steelers, again threw five TD passes. Was alternated with Don Meredith at QB, 1962, and dropped to role of backup in 1963. At end of '63 season retired and joined cement company in Reno, Nev., as executive vice president. Later became TV announcer. Was smallest QB in pro football and once said, "Maybe being smaller actually helped me. It might have made me work harder to concentrate on making up for my size. I might not have gone so far if I had been big."

LeBEAU, C. RICHARD (Dick) Defensive Back. 6'1", 185. B. 9/9/37, London, Ohio. Two-way back at Ohio State. Drafted on 5th round by Cleveland Browns but released, 1959. Picked up by Detroit Lions who engaged him for 14 seasons, 1959-72. Played in 171 straight games. Intercepted 62 passes for 3rd place on all-time list behind Emlen Tunnell and Dick Lane. Intercepted nine passes, 1970. Played in three Pro Bowls. Loves golf; once won NFL Players Association tournament. Assistant coach Philadelphia Eagles, 1973.

LEE, DAVID A. Kicker. B. 11/8/43, Shreveport, La. 6'4", 230. Football, baseball, track letterman at Louisiana Tech. Signed as free agent by Cleveland Browns in 1965, played that year on taxi squad. Traded to Baltimore Colts in 1966. Proceeded to lead NFL in punting, averaging 45.6 yds. Led again, 1969, with 45.3-yd. average. NFL championship game, 1968. Super Bowl, 1969, 71. All-AFC punter, 1969. Longest punt of career was 76-yarder vs. New York Giants, 1971. Slumped to 38.7-yd. average in 1973, lowest of career.

LEECH, JAMES C. (Jimmy) Running Back. B. 4/13/1897, Lexington, Va. D. 8/18/51, Hamden, Conn. 5'8", 155. Attended VMI. 3rd-team All-America, 1920. Rare honor for Southerner to be selected by Walter Camp. Nation's leading scorer with 210 points in 1920. Unbeaten, untied Keydets outscored foes, 431-20. Biggest victory was 136-0 walloping of Hampden-Sydney. Exceptional passer, defensive back, tackler, blocker. Vice president of his 1921 VMI class. Became assistant secretary of Security Insurance Co. of New Haven, Conn. Citizens Savings Hall of Fame, National Football Foundation Hall of Fame (first collegian elected from state of Virginia).

LEEMANS, ALPHONSE E. (Tuffy) Running Back. B. Superior, Wis. 6', 185. Son of Belgian miner who immigrated to Wisconsin. Juggled iron ore as youngster to build himself up. Dumped two bigger, older boys one day playing football, and kids started calling him "Tuffy." Played at George Washington U. Won MVP honors in 1936 College All-Star game, racing 75 yds. for touchdown first time he handled football. Convinced by 19-year-old Wellington Mara, representing father-owner Tim, to play for New York Giants. Had been their No. 2 draft choice. Signed for $3000. Started eight years at halfback for Steve Owen-coached Giants, 1936-43. Called signals from his right-half position. Rookie season led NFL rushers with 830 yds. In career rushed 3117 yds., scored 19 TDs. All-Pro twice, 1936, 39. Suffered severe blow to head during game against Chicago Bears, 1942, resulting in loss of hearing in one ear. Injury kept him out of service. Settled in Washington, D.C., area after football retirement; now lives in Silver Spring, Md.

LEGGETT, EARL Tackle. B. 3/5/35, Jacksonville, Fla. 6'3", 250. All-City prep in Jacksonville. Attended Hinds (Fla.) J.C. before enrolling at Louisiana State. Played in Junior Rose Bowl, 1954. All-SEC, 1955. College teammate of Jimmy Taylor. Blue-Gray, Senior Bowl and College All-Star games. Chicago Bears, 1957-65; Los Angeles Rams, 1966; New Orleans Saints, 1967-68. Drafted on 1st round by Bears in 1957. Missed 1962 season due to knee injury. Excellent defensive tackle. Member world championship, 1963. Now TCU freshman coach.

LEGGETT, WILLIAM J. B. 10/12/1848, Ghent, N.Y. D. 10/28/25. Rutgers captain in first intercollegiate football game, 11/6/69. It was played at Rutgers (New Brunswick, N.J.); home team won, 6-4, over Princeton. In rematch one week later, Princeton won by 8-0 score. Leggett and William Gummere, Old Nassau's first captain, were reunited on 10/14/25 at New Brunswick. Occasion was inauguration of Dr. John M. Thomas as president of Rutgers. Leggett typified ideal college man of his period. Received number of oratorical prizes as student; president of first *Targum* Association (student newspaper), member of boat crew, 1869-71; football captain in 1869, 70; *Phi Beta Kappa*. Attended New Brunswick Theological Seminary, 1872-75. Rose to prominence in ranks of Dutch Reformed Church. Authored numerous religious articles. Father of eight children. Died after suffering stroke.

LeVIAS, JERRY End. B. 9/5/46, Beaumont, Tex. 5'9", 177. Attended Beaumont's Herbert H.S. Three-time All-SWC at Southern Methodist, 1966-68. Playing, academic All-America, 1968. Broke numerous SMU records, including receptions (155), reception yds. (2275) and TDs (22). Marketing major. Member Houston Oilers, 1969-70, and San Diego Chargers, 1971-73. Drafted on 2nd round by Oilers. Set AFL record for most combined kickoff-punt returns (73). Led Oiler receivers in both 1969, 70. Exceptionally fast, good balance.

LEWIS, ART (Pappy) Coach. B. 2/8/11, near Middleport, Ohio. D. 6/13/62, Pittsburgh, Pa. Oldest of nine children, born on farm along Ohio River. Worked coal mines two years before attending Middleport H.S. Acquired nickname "Pappy" because he was 21-year-old freshman at Ohio U., 1932. In senior year, top defensive player in East-West Shrine game. New York Giants, 1936. Became line coach of Cleveland Rams, 1937. Promoted to head coach after three games into '38 season. At age 27, thus became youngest head coach in pro history. Tenure lasted eight games, winning four and losing four. Spent four more years with Rams (two as player-coach, 1938, 39) before assistantships at Washington & Lee, St. Mary's Pre-Flight, Mississippi State. Head coach Washington & Lee, 1946-48; West Virginia, 1950-60. With Mountaineers compiled 58-38-2 record. Southern Conference Coach of the Year twice, won 30 straight league games. Lost 1954 Sugar Bowl to Georgia Tech, 42-19. Lewis, admittedly superstitious, wore same clothes in all Pitt-West Virginia games after 1952. That was year Mountaineers upset Panthers, 16-0. On Pittsburgh Steeler staff when he died of heart attack in 1962.

LEWIS, DAVID R. Quarterback-Kicker. B. 10/16/45, Clovis, Calif. 6'2", 215. Full-blooded Chukchansi Indian. Played QB, kicked for Stanford, 1964-66. Primarily running QB. No. 2 collegiate punter, 1965, 44.9-yd. average, just one-tenth of yd. behind Mississippi's Frank Lambert. Moved to running back in 1966 to make room for Gene Washington (now of San Francisco 49ers); however, moved back three games later, Washington becoming receiver. In 1967 drafted by New York Giants, but lost out in training camp to several punters, including Frank Lambert. Joined CFL's Montreal Alouettes. Functioned as all-round player for Alouettes, playing QB, running back, receiving and kicking. Backup punter for Giants, 1969. Brought to Cincinnati Bengals in 1970 (after release from N.Y.) on recommendation of Bill Walsh, Bengal assistant coach, formerly of Stanford. Slated for QB duty, but job turned into battle between Virgil Carter and Ken Anderson. AFC punting leader in 1970 with 46.2-yd. average, best in football since 1965. Included was 63-yd. punt, 10/18/70, vs. Kansas City Chiefs. Punted six times for 323 yds. vs. San Diego Chargers, prompting S.D. sportswriter to say that if any reader could name punter better than Lewis, "I will walk naked down the widest street in Germany." 1971 AFC punting leader with 44.8-yd. average on 72 punts. In 1973 made 68 punts for 2790 yds., 41.0 average, longest 60 yds.

LEWIS, SHERMAN (Tank) Running Back. B. 6/29/42, Louisville, Ky. 5'8", 154. Attended Dupont Manual H.S., Louisville, and Michigan State. 18-8-1 playing record with Spartans, 1961-63. All-America and 3rd in Heisman Trophy voting, 1963. Consistently made big play. During senior year made 88- and 87-yd. pass receptions, 87-yard rush. Now assistant coach at his alma mater.

LEWIS, WILLIAM H. Center. B. 11/30/1868, Berkeley, Va. D. 1/1/49. 5'11", 177. Attended Amherst and Harvard. Son of former slaves. Moved to New England at early age. Harvard All-America, 1893. Was first Black to reap such honor. In 1893 was captain vs. Princeton (probably first Black captain). Fast, excellent student of football. In 1911 became first Black admitted to American Football Association. First of his race to coach at major-college level, handling Harvard line. Wrote one of earliest books on game — *How to Play Football.*

LILLY, ROBERT L. Tackle. B. 7/26/39, Olney, Tex. 6'5", 260. Played tackle for Texas Christian, 1958-60. Unanimous All-America, 1960. Feats at TCU were well charted by Dallas Cowboys, and he was their 1st-round draft pick in 1961. In fact, first player ever drafted by Cowboys. First two seasons was disappointment at defensive end, so was switched to tackle and became instant star. Most important talent is quickness in getting past blocker. Tom Landry said, "...Lilly *always* broke through his first block. *Always.* And sometimes through second and third blocks. There is no one man in football who can contain Lilly." Landry added, "There won't be another Bob Lilly in my time. You're observing a man who will become a legend." All-NFL, 1966, 67, 68, 69. All-NFC, 1971, 72. Missed Pro Bowl selection only in 1962 and '64. Missed NFC championship game due to injury, 1973. Active in several businesses, including Bob Lilly's Other Place, near Dallas' Love Field.

LINCOLN, KEITH Running Back. B. Pullman, Wash. 6'1", 213. Attended Washington State. San Diego Chargers, 1961-66, 68; Buffalo Bills, 1966, 67.

Foursome of fullback Lincoln, QB Tobin Rote, halfback Paul Lowe, flanker Lance Alworth. Sparked AFL championship for Chargers in 1963. San Diego bombed Boston Patriots, 51-10, in title game; Lincoln scored two TDs. Also played in 1964, 65 title games, losing both to Buffalo Bills. All-AFL, 1963, 64. Led league in rushing attempts (222) and total yardage (1121), 1965. In eight-year career scored 19 TDs on ground, gained 3383 yds.

LIPSCOMB, EUGENE (Big Daddy) Tackle. B. 11/9/31, Detroit, Mich. D. 5/ 10/63, Pittsburgh, Pa. 6'6", 285. Tragic football figure. Lost his mother at age 11 — she was viciously stabbed to death at Detroit bus stop on way to work. Took variety of odd jobs growing up, drifting finally into service. Developed game at Camp Pendleton, Calif. Upon discharge signed with Los Angeles Rams for $4800 & beef steak breakfast, 1953. Played three years with Rams and then with Baltimore Colts, 1956-60, and Pittsburgh Steelers, 1961-62. Spent greatest years in Baltimore, twice winning All-Pro honors as defensive tackle and helping Colts to two world titles. Quick and agile for size, had great lateral speed. Pro wrestler also in later years. Was haunted by troubled youth, lack of education (no college), self-conscious about size and unsure of role as Black man. "Life has been one long scare for me," he acknowledged in 1962. One year later he was dead of apparent heroin overdose, stirring considerable controversy. Teammates maintained that Lipscomb was afraid of needles, wouldn't even take pain-killer shots.

LITTLE, FLOYD D. Running Back. B. 7/4/42, New Haven, Conn. 5'10", 196. Born to be explosive football player. Was July 4th baby and grew up in shadow of Yale Bowl. Attended Hillhouse H.S. in New Haven and Bordentown (N.J.) Military Academy. Influenced to attend Syracuse by Ernie Davis. Played left halfback, in tradition of Davis and Jim Brown, and wore same No. 44. Three-time All-America, 1964, 65, 66. Scored unbelievable five TDs in 1964 collegiate debut vs. Kansas. Scored 46 career TDs, including 19 to lead nation in 1965. Responsible for 5529 yards at Syracuse: 2704 rushing, 582 pass receiving, 845 on punt returns, 797 on kickoffs, 19 passing. 1964 Orange backfield featured Little and Jim Nance. They led Syracuse to Sugar Bowl, losing 13-10 to LSU. In 1967 Little set Gator Bowl rushing record with 216 yds. vs. Tennessee. Denver Broncos, 1967-73. Was first No. 1 draft choice ever signed by club. Broke Denver TD season mark with 13, 1972. Pro Bowl, 1971, 72, 74. All-AFL, 1969. All-AFC, 1970, 71. In 1970, 71 led AFC in rushing. Voted outstanding pro back by Pro Football Writers Association, 1971, after rushing for 1133 yds. and catching 26 passes for 255 more. Injured knee in 1972 and underwent post-season surgery. Scored 12 TDs in 1973 to tie for AFC leadership. Same year gained 979 yds. rushing, giving him 5566 for career. Possesses tremendous speed and balance. Clocked 9.7 for 100-yd. dash. Participant in NFL Drug Abuse program. Works closely with Denver youth groups. 1973 Brian Piccolo Award winner.

LITTLE, LARRY C. Guard. B. 11/2/45, Grovetown, Ga. 6'1", 265. Grew up in Miami. Returned there to play with NFL Dolphins. Bethune-Cookman MVP and captain, 1966. Same season was All-Southern Intercollegiate Conference. College tackle both ways. Signed as free agent by San Diego Chargers, 1967. Traded, 1969, to Dolphins for cornerback Mack Lamb — one of greatest steals of all time. Lamb was dropped by Chargers, while Little developed into premier pulling guard. Leads way for Larry Csonka, Jim Kiick, Mercury Morris. All-Pro, Forrest Gregg and Fuzzy Thurston Trophies recipient (both as NFL's best offensive lineman), 1972. Pro Bowl following 1971, 72, 73 seasons. Directs Miami Dolphins-Larry Little Gold Coast Camp for underprivileged children. It accommodates up to 600 kids. Received honorary D.S. and Human Relations degree from Biscayne College.

LITTLE, LAWRENCE (Lou) B. 12/6/1893, Boston, Mass. Famous as Columbia coach, following career as tackle at Pennsylvania, 1916-19. Massillon Tigers, 1919; Buffalo All-Americans, 1920-21. Coached Georgetown, 1924-29. In 1930 succeeded Charlie Crowley at Columbia. Retired after 1956 season. Currently on Executive Committee, National Football Foundation and Hall of Fame. "Some of the best teaching at Columbia," one of his colleagues said, "is done down at the football field by Lou Little." One year, former Columbia player fell ill. Little sent out mailing asking for funds, with stipulation that only he could contribute more than $5.00. Described his coaching philosophy by saying, "I want players who will knock the other fellow's brains out, then help him up and brush him off." Sartorially splendid, owning vast wardrobe. Pronounced proboscis gave him look of eagle. Compiled 148-138-12 record overall and was only 110-116-10 at Columbia; despite lackluster record, he did more for football than most. Top products were Bill Swiacki, Paul Governali, Sid Luckman, Gene Rossides. Citizens Savings Hall of Fame, National Football Foundation Hall of Fame.

LOCKE, GORDON C. Quarterback. B. 8/3/1898, Denison, Iowa. D. 11/9/69, Washington, D.C. 5'10", 180. 19-2 playing record at Iowa, 1920-22. All-America, 1922. 1921, 22 Iowa teams were unbeaten, untied. In 1921, coach Howard Jones introduced his two-runner, two-blocker backfield system. Locke, Aubrey Devine handled rushing while Glenn Devine, Aubrey Shuttleworth provided blocking. Locke was triple threat from tailback position. Assistant coach at Iowa and Western Reserve before devoting full time to law practice. Citizens Savings Hall of Fame, National Football Foundation Hall of Fame.

LOCKHART, CARL (Spider) Defensive Back. B. 4/6/43, Dallas, Tex. 6'2", 175. North Texas State flanker, defensive back. Caught 32 passes, intercepted 10, punted 95 times for near 40-yard average while in college. Also track hurdler, baseball player. Drafted on 13th round by New York Giants, 1965. Was part of Giant bumper rookie crop—others were Tucker Frederickson, Ernie Koy, Willie Williams, Chuck Mercein. Developed into team leader and outstanding free safety. Ranks only behind Emlen Tunnell and Jimmy Patton in club interceptions. Tunnell (then defensive backfield coach) bestowed Lockhart with nickname in 1965: "... he was all over those guys, like a spider." Off-season works for Bache & Co.

LOGAN, JERRY Defensive Back. B. 8/27/41, Graham, Tex. 6'1", 190. NCAA's leading scorer with 110 points at West Texas State, 1962. Scored winning touchdown in Sun Bowl as West Texas edged Ohio U., 15-14. 10-year fixture at safety for Baltimore Colts, 1963-72. Intercepted 34 passes during that period for 397 yards and five TDs. Latter is Colt record. Participant three Pro Bowls. Traded to Los Angeles Rams prior to 1973 season.

LOMBARDI, VINCENT T. Coach. B. 6/11/13, Brooklyn, N.Y. D. 9/3/70, Washington, D.C. Played college football at Fordham, where he was guard for 1936 "Seven Blocks of Granite." Head coach at St. Cecilia's H.S., Englewood, N.J., 1939-46. Suspended two days for fighting in 1936. Four years later played vs. New York Giants on semipro team, losing 35-7. Served 1947 as Fordham freshman coach, and was varsity assistant next year. Joined Red Blaik at Army, 1949, staying until he took job as assistant with the New York Giants owned by Fordham classmate, Wellington Mara, in 1954. Named head coach of Green Bay Packers, 1959. Stayed with Pack until 1968 (last year was strictly general manager), during which time his team appeared in eight championship games, tied record of five championships won, appeared in first two Super Bowls. Expressed his philosophy on football in famous quote, "Winning isn't everything; its the only thing." Coach of the Year, 1961. Street on which Packer offices are located named Lombardi Ave. after him. Trophy given to Super Bowl winner named for him. Instrumental in forging merger of NFL and AFL, at meeting on 6/8/66. Went back to coaching in 1969 with Washington Redskins and took them to first winning season in 14 years. Wellington Mara, on hearing that Lombardi was incurably ill, said, "It's like hearing that the Rock of Gibraltar has a crack in it." NFL record for 10 years was 141-39-4. Pro Football Hall of Fame.

LOMBARDO, THOMAS A. (Lombo) Quarterback-Running Back. B. 4/17/22, Missouri. D. 9/24/50, Korea. Army, 1942-44. Captained 1944 team that won national championship. Fifteen players from squad were mentioned on All-America teams, including Doc Blanchard and Glenn Davis. Lombardo was Korean War victim.

LOONEY, JOE DON Running Back. B. 10/10/42, San Angelo, Tex. 6'1", 225. "Never was a man more aptly named," adjudged George Sauer (New York Jets) of Joe Don Looney. Enormous potential never realized due to poor attitude and eccentricities. After stops at U. of Texas, TCU and Cameron (Okla.) J.C., arrived at U. of Oklahoma in 1962. Spent 1962-63 under Bud Wilkinson. All-America, 1962. Rushed for 852 yds. (5th nationally) that year and led NCAA punters with 43.4-yd. average. Between junior and senior years spent summer in Baton Rouge, La., health studio. Boosted weight 15 pounds to 222, expanded muscles tremendously; ran 100-yd. dash in 9.8, lifted 200 pounds in military squat, drank gallon of milk per day, swallowed 20 kinds of protein pills.

202

Four pro teams gave him shot: Baltimore Colts, 1964; Detroit Lions, 1965-66; Washington Redskins, 1966-67; New Orleans Saints, 1969. All were awed by potential but failed in efforts to rehabilitate. Stayed with Giants 28 days. Wouldn't throw socks and jock in carefully marked bin — "No damn sign is going to tell me what to do," he said. Bored by practice, he preferred playing catch with youngsters on sidelines. Ran wrong holes — "Anyone can run where the holes are. A good football player makes his own holes." With Colts asked someone to "watch my cheeseburger for me" so he could attend team meeting. In one practice got off booming punt, then asked, "How'd you like that one, God?" Told to carry message into Detroit QB Milt Plum in 1966. "If you want a messenger," Joe Don told coach Harry Gilmer, "call Western Union." Occasional bursts of greatness only false alarm, always reverted to undisciplined, nonsensical style. Looney, who served army hitch in 1968, retired to farming near San Angelo, Tex. Father, J. Donald, also played pro ball.

LOTHRIDGE, BILLY L. Quarterback-Kicker. B. 1/1/42, Cleveland, Ga. 6'1", 200. Attended Georgia Tech. All-SEC, 1962, 63. All-America and 2nd in Heisman Trophy voting, 1963. Played in Gator and Astro-Bluebonnet Bowls, both 1962. Scored 204 collegiate points: 15 TDs, 15 PATs, 21 FGs. Holds seven Tech offensive and scoring records. "The best quarterback I ever coached," said Bobby Dodd. Dallas Cowboys, 1964; Los Angeles Rams, 1965; Atlanta Falcons, 1966-71; Miami Dolphins, 1972. Led NFL in punting with 43.7-yd. average on 87 punts, 1967; again following year with 44.3-yd. average on 75 punts. NFL championship game, 1972. Super Bowl, 1973.

LOURIE, DONALD B. Quarterback. B. 8/22/1899, Decatur, Ala. 5'11", 160. Ranked among Princeton's greatest field generals. All-America, 1920. Won twice, 1919, 20, over Yale. 1919 game featured Callahan brothers, Tim of Yale and H. G. (Mike) of Princeton, as rival centers. Lourie received both Arthur Wheeler and Poe Cups for proficiency in scholarship, leadership and athletics. President of senior class. Following graduation became Princeton backfield coach and scout, prominent referee in Midwest. Spent entire business career with Quaker Oats Co.; served as president and chairman of board. Under-secretary of state during President Eisenhower's first administration. Received honorary degrees from Cornell College and Lincoln College. Princeton dormitory, Lourie-Love Hall, named for him and friend, Cupe Love. Received Gold Medal Award from National Football Foundation, 1964. In 1974 named to Foundation's Hall of Fame.

LOWE, PAUL E. Running Back. B. 9/27/36, Homer, La. 6', 205. Attended Compton (Calif.) J.C. and Oregon State. Tried out with San Francisco 49ers and was cut. Signed as free agent by Los Angeles Chargers, 1960. San Diego Chargers, 1961-68. Kansas City Chiefs, 1968-69. Set two AFL career records: games gaining 100 or more yards rushing (15); highest average, 700 or more rushes (4.88 yds.). AFL rushing leader with record 1121 yds., 1965. Set AFL career playoff records for rushes (57), yds. rushing (380), TDs rushing (2). AFL

Player of the Year, 1965. AFL All-Star games, 1963, 64, 65. AFL title games, 1960, 61, 63, 64, 65. All-AFL, 1960, 65. Great balance, quick.

LUCAS, RICHARD Quarterback. B. Glassport, Pa. 6'1", 185. 20-8-1 playing record at Penn State, 1957-59. Maxwell Award, Consensus All-America, 1959. Accumulated 1238 yds. total offense during senior season. Penn State defeated Navy, 7-0, in Liberty Bowl, 1959 — Lucas was injured in 2nd quarter. During career rushed 203 times for 609 yds., completed 121 of 256 passes for 1822 yds., intercepted 7 passes for 143 yds., 69 punts for 36.2 average, 8 punt returns for 63 yds., 3 kickoff returns for 38 yds.

LUCCI, MICHAEL G. Linebacker. B. 12/29/40, Ambridge, Pa. 6'2", 230. Attended U. of Pittsburgh & Tennessee. All-SEC, 1960, 61. Played with Cleveland Browns, 1962-64; Detroit Lions, 1965-73. Replaced Joe Schmidt in 1966 as Lion middle linebacker. All-Pro, 1971; Pro Bowl following same season, 1971. Fierce competitor. Acted in movie, *Paper Lion*. Retired, 1973, claiming Detroit coach Don McCafferty couldn't control team. Is vice president and national fitness director for chain of health clubs.

LUCKMAN, SIDNEY Quarterback. B. 11/21/16, Brooklyn, N.Y. 5'11", 197. Attended Erasmus H.S. and was most publicized schoolboy player in New York City. Offered many scholarships, but elected to work way thru Columbia and play tailback. Three-year regular, 1936-38. All-America, 1938. Under coach Lou Little became one of best triple-threats in country. In 1937 made 82-yd. kickoff return vs. Army, 72-yd. punt vs. Syracuse, 60-yd. pass vs. Penn. Connected on 65-yd. pass vs. Brown, 1938. Career passing record was 180 completions, 376 attempts, 2413 yds., percentage of .479. Drafted by Pittsburgh Steelers, but traded to Chicago Bears and introduced to T formation by George Halas. Grew to symbolize excellence as T quarterback. Played for Bears, 1939-50. Scored 2nd TD of title game in Chicago's 73-0 rout of Washington Redskins. 11/14/43 was Sid Luckman Day at Polo Grounds. In that game, vs. New York Giants, he threw seven TD passes to break Sammy Baugh's record of six. Won Joseph Carr Trophy as league MVP, 1943. Tied Baugh for passing championship in 1945. While Luckman quarterbacked, Bears won five Western Conference titles, and four NFL championships, 1940, 41, 43, 46. During career completed 904 of 1744 passes (51.8 percent) for 14,683 yds., 139 TDs, average gain of 8.42 (2nd all-time best). Later executive with Chicago cellophane company, but took time to tutor Bear QBs. Also scouted. 1956 Bears voted him share of playoff money; he returned it to player pool. All-Pro, 1941, 42, 43, 44, 47. Citizens Savings Hall of Fame, National Football Foundation Hall of Fame, Pro Hall of Fame.

LUJACK, JOHN Quarterback. B. 1/4/25, Connellsville, Pa. 6', 180. Notre Dame, 1943, 46-47. Unanimous All-America, 1946, 47. In military service, 1944-45. Heisman Trophy winner, 1947. Chicago Bears, 1948-51. Chicago coach George Halas once said that when stripped of his many skills as player, Lujack still possessed indispensable quality — poise. In 1943 replaced Angelo Bertelli (drafted into marines), and was outstanding vs. Army, engineering 26-9 win. Three years later, single-handedly tackled Doc Blanchard, preventing TD, becoming first ever to do so. Sixty-minute player. Chicago Bears, 1948-51. Gained 468 yds. passing against Chicago Cardinals, 12/11/49. Chosen as best collegiate QB of quarter-century by *All America Review* in 1949, beating out Sammy Baugh, Frankie Albert, Frank Carideo, Benny Friedman. Citizens Savings Hall of Fame, National Football Foundation Hall of Fame.

LUND, FRANCIS L. (Pug) Running Back. B. 4/18/13, Rice Lake, Wis. 5'11", 185. Minnesota, 1932-34. Consensus All-America, 1934; All-America, 1933. Captain of 1934 national champions. Great competitor, according to coach Bernie Bierman. Excellent runner, passer, kicker. Gained 637 yds. in eight games in 1934, winning Silver Football that year. Threw TD passes vs. Michigan despite thumb injury. Scored two TDs in first six minutes vs. Wisconsin, threw for winning TD vs. Pitt. In career of 17 games and 595 plays, gained 2854 yds. Currently insurance executive in Minneapolis. National Football Foundation Hall of Fame.

LUNDY, LAMAR Defensive End. B. 4/17/35, Richmond, Ind. 6'7", 235. Honor student, football and basketball player at Purdue. Los Angeles Rams, 1957-69. Member of Ram first-generation "Fearsome Foursome." Others were Rosey Grier, Merlin Olsen, Deacon Jones. They played together first time in 1961. Roger Brown replaced Grier when latter was forced into retirement by ruptured Achilles tendon, 1967. Lundy began pro career as offensive end but shifted to defense in 1959.

LUPPINO, ARTHUR E. Running Back. B. 10/24/34, La Jolla, Calif. 5'9", 178. Attended La Jolla H.S. and U. of Arizona. Was four-year college player, 1953-56. Performed magnificently as sophomore, leading nation in six departments: rushing yds. (1359) and carries (179); kickoff returns (20) and yds. (632); TDs (24); total points (166). That season had 92- and 88-yd. kickoff returns. Year later again led NCAA in rushing yds. (1313) and carries (209). In career scored 337 points on 24 TDs and 22 PATs. After graduating from Arizona went back to California and began high school teaching career.

LYMAN, WILLIAM R. (Link) Tackle. B. 1898, Table Rock, Neb. 6'2", 246. Didn't play football at McDonald Rural Federated (Neb.) H.S. since only seven boys attended there. Took up sport at U. of Nebraska and quickly overcame lack of experience. Starred for powerful 1921 Cornhusker team which lost only to Notre Dame in eight games and outscored its opposition 283-27. Pro fixture for 11 seasons, playing with Canton Bulldogs, 1922, 23, 25; Cleveland Bulldogs, 1924; Frankford Yellowjackets, 1925; Chicago Bears, 1926-28, 30-31, 33-34. Helped Bears win NFL championship in 1933 and division title one year later. Was outstanding at diagnosing plays, and exceptionally agile. One of first linemen to shift positions at snap of ball. Pro Football Hall of Fame. After retiring from active competition returned to his alma mater as line coach, and later owned insurance agency in San Marino, Calif.

LYNCH, JAMES E. Linebacker. B. 8/28/45, Lima, Ohio. 6'1", 235. Captain, All-America, Maxwell Trophy winner for Notre Dame's national champions, 1966. Participated in East-West Shrine, Coaches All-America, College All-Star games. No. 2 draft choice, Kansas City Chiefs, 1967. Intercepted 11 passes first five seasons with Chiefs. AFL All-Star game, 1969. Fine competitor, underrated. Starting K.C. right linebacker since 1968, giving team great trio with Willie Lanier (middle) and Bobby Bell. Has announced sports on television. Off-season, New York City stockbroker.

LYNCH, RICHARD Defensive Back. B. Oceanside, N.Y. 6'2", 205. Two-way halfback at Notre Dame, 1955-57. Scored "biggest" TD of career against Oklahoma, 1957. It dealt Sooners 7-0 defeat, thereby ending longest collegiate win streak at 47 games. Washington Redskins, 1958; New York Giants, 1959-66. All-Pro, 1963. No. 1 in interceptions, 1961; co-leader (tied with Rosey Taylor), 1963. Played in superb Giant secondary with Jimmy Patton and Erich Barnes. Missed carrying football and fan adulation from Notre Dame days, thus became frustrated defensive halfback. Wrote "I Want to Play Offense" for *Sport* magazine in 1963. Never got that chance.

McAFEE, GEORGE A. (One Play) Running Back. 6', 175. Duke, 1937-39. All-America, 1939. Teamed with fullback Eric Tipton for outstanding combination. Played on varsity teams with 24-5 record, 17 shutouts. 1938 team was 9-0 before losing to USC in Rose Bowl. 1938 teammate of Tommy Prothro, later coach for UCLA, Los Angeles Rams. Extremely swift halfback, equally excellent going wide or up middle. Fine receiver, punt returner. Chicago Bears, 1940-41, 45-50. Intercepted pass and returned it 34 yds. for TD in 1940 title game vs. Washington Redskins. Appeared in 1941 championship game vs. New York Giants, scoring one TD. All-Pro, 1941. Sensational safety in addition to offensive work. Dangerous as left-handed passer. Also served as emergency punter. Retired due to injured bone in heel. National Football Foundation Hall of Fame, Pro Football Hall of Fame.

McALISTER, JAMES E. Running Back. B. 9/5/51, Pasadena, Calif. 5'11", 202. Prep All-America in football and track. During 1967-69 career at Blair H.S. in Pasadena, McAlister rushed for 4380 yds. on 533 carries, 8.2 average, and scored 54 TDs. Tied national prep long jump record with 25'7" leap. Matriculated at UCLA. Suspended for 1971 season, NCAA ruling he had taken entrance exam illegally. Played halfback in 1972, fullback in '73. All-Pac 8 both years. He and Kermit Johnson were standouts in Pepper Rodgers' version of wishbone T. In 1973, UCLA was national leader in rushing offense (400.3 yds. per game) and runner up in scoring (42.7 points per game). Summer of '73, McAlister recorded 27'½" long jump for all-time collegiate mark. Best 100-yd. dash time is 9.6. McAlister, Johnson and guard Booker Brown (USC) were first players signed by

WFL — by Southern California Sun. Planned to continue track career at UCLA after signing under new NCAA policy. However, organization ruled he used agent in negotiations with Sun; thus was no longer eligible to compete.

McBRIDE, ARTHUR (Mickey) Owner. B. 1887. D. 11/10/72, Cleveland, Ohio. Founder of Cleveland Browns (AAFC), 1946. Got into football when All American Football Conference was formed. Hired Paul Brown as his coach, and retained team until 1953 when he sold it to syndicate for $600,000. Responsible for term "taxi squad", as among many business interests were several taxicab companies. In McBride's day pro football didn't have reserve list as it does now, so he kept ready reserve by having fringe players drive cabs until their services were needed. Died at age 85.

McCLENDON, CHARLES Y. (Cholly Mac) Coach. B. 10/17/23, Lewisville, Ark. One of nine children. Earned bachelor's and master's degrees at Kentucky where supervised by Paul (Bear) Bryant. Started coaching career at Kentucky as graduate assistant. Then took assistantship at Vanderbilt, followed by one at LSU. Named LSU head coach in 1962 and has been there ever since. 96-32-5 record, thru 1973, ranking him with best collegiate mentors. Experienced no losing seasons. Bowl record is now 6-4 following 16-9 Orange Bowl setback to Penn State, 1974. Coached numerous post-season All-Star teams.

McCLINTON, CURTIS R. Running Back. B. 7/25/39, Muskogee, Okla. Attended Wichita (Kan.) North H.S. and U. of Kansas. Played in superb 1961 Kansas backfield, with John Hadl, Bert Coan, Hugh Smith. Dallas Texans, 1962; Kansas City Chiefs, 1963-69. AFL championship games, 1962, 66. Super Bowl, 1967. Scored Chiefs only TD in Super Bowl I on seven-yd. pass from Len Dawson. Against Denver Broncos caught five passes for K.C. record 213 yds., 1965. Gained 3124 yds. on 762 carries, 4.1-yd. average, and scored 18 TDs in eight-year career. Powerful runner and blocker. Accomplished singer, has done concert work. Now bank vice president in Kansas City.

McCLUNG, THOMAS L. (Bum) Running Back. B. 3/26/1870, Knoxville, Tenn. D. 12/19/14, London, England. 5'10", 167. Yale, 1889-91. All-America, 1890, 91. Coached by Walter Camp. Scored 500 points in Yale career. Good runner, used scissors step. Rated by Pudge Heffelfinger (teammate) with Red Grange, George Gipp. Used one play which called for him to veer suddenly off-tackle after fake end run. Scored four TDs in 1890 vs. Princeton, unmatched by Tiger foe until 1937 by Clint Frank. Captain in 1891. Later Yale treasurer and Treasurer of United States. National Football Foundation Hall of Fame.

McCOLL, WILLIAM End. B. 4/2/30, San Diego, Calif. 6'4", 230. Attended Hoover H.S., San Diego, and Stanford. 21-7-3 Stanford playing record, 1949-51. Consensus All-America, 1950; unanimous All-America, 1951. 4th in Heisman Trophy voting in 1951. Played in 1952 Rose Bowl; Stanford lost to Illinois, 40-7. Chicago Bears, 1952-59. Was ideal for Bears' slot halfback position — great on short passes, as blocker. Combined pro football and medicine. While with Bears finished medical education at U. of Chicago. "Some years it wasn't certain whether I could continue to play ball and do my work at the same time. But Coach Halas always told me that when football and medicine conflict, medicine takes precedence." When retired from game Dr. McColl ran missionary hospital in Korea. Citizens Savings Hall of Fame, National Football Foundation Hall of Fame.

McCORD, DARRIS Defensive Tackle-End. B. 1/4/33, Detroit, Mich. 6'3", 250. All-America tackle at Tennessee, 1954. Played in Blue-Gray, Senior Bowl and Coaches All-America games. Spent entire pro career in hometown with Lions, 1955-67. Lions walloped Cleveland Browns, 1957, to win world championship. Played offense occasionally. Pro Bowl, 1958. Fine balance, lateral speed. Became executive with photography company in Detroit.

McCORMACK, MIKE Tackle. B. 6/21/30, Chicago, Ill. 6'4", 250. Moved to Kansas City, Kan., as youngster. All-Big 7, for Kansas Jayhawks, 1950. Played in East-West Shrine, College All-Star games. Member New York Yanks (No. 1 draft choice), 1951; Cleveland Browns, 1954-62. Acquired by Cleveland in 15-player deal. Mainstay in Brown offensive line. Great blocker. Starter, right tackle, in Cleveland's 38-14 NFL championship victory, 1955. Offensive line coach for Washington Redskins under Otto Graham, Vince Lombardi, George Allen, 1966-72. Head coach Philadelphia Eagles, 1973.

McCORMICK, JAMES B. Running Back. B. 3/21/1884, Boston, Mass. 6', 185. D. 1/7/59. Princeton 1905-07. 24-4-1 playing record. All-America, 1905-07; 2nd team, 1906. Princeton head coach, 1909. Record: 6-2-1. National Football Foundation Hall of Fame.

McCORMICK, VANCE C. Quarterback. B. 6/19/1872, Harrisburg, Pa. D. 6/16/46, Harrisburg, Pa. 5'7", 152. Attended Harrisburg schools and Andover Academy. Yale varsity, 1891-93. Captain, All-America, 1892. Only game lost in 37-game career was his last — 6-0 to Princeton. Was senior class president. First coach of Carlisle Indians. Publisher of Harrisburg *Evening News* and Harrisburg *Patriot*. Active in mining, steel and iron manufacturing. Harrisburg mayor, 1902-05. Led campaign, as chairman of Democratic National Committee, which re-elected President Woodrow Wilson to second term, 1916.

McCRACKEN, G. HERBERT (Herb) Coach. B. 1899, Pittsburgh, Pa. Attended U. Pittsburgh. Teammate of Jock Sutherland. Coach Pop Warner called McCracken, "My finest all-around undergraduate player at Pitt." Coached Allegheny and Lafayette colleges, 1921-35. Spent 12 years at Lafayette, 1924-35, compiling 59-40-6 record. In process brought Leopards national prominence. Defeated his alma mater (coached by Sutherland) three times. Developed All-America lineman Charlie Berry, later pro baseball umpire. Pioneered lateral pass behind scrimmage line. Left coaching for publishing. Has held many of highest management positions at Scholastic Magazines, Inc. National Football Foundation Hall of Fame.

McCULLOCH, EARL (Pearl) End. B. 1/10/36, Clarksville, Tex. 5'11", 182. Track and football star at Southern California. Led 1967 national championship team with 30 catches for 540 yds. and 5 TDs. Held NCAA hurdle records both indoor and out. Co-holder of national prep low hurdle record (8.1 seconds) at Long Beach Polytechnical H.S. Passed up chance at Olympics to sign with Detroit Lions in 1968. Scored three times in first two games as pro. Caught 40 passes in '68 for 680 yds., 5 TDs. Names Rookie of the Year. Scored 19 TDs and caught 70 passes thru 1973.

McCUTCHEON, LAWRENCE (Larry) Running Back. B. 6/2/50, Plainview, Tex. 6'1", 205. Carried football 649 times for 2917 yards, 22 touchdowns at Colorado State, 1969-71. Bettered 1000 yards rushing each of last two seasons. 3rd-round draft pick Los Angeles Rams, 1972. Spent most of that season on ready reserve list, rushing nary once in league game. Blossomed as pro in 1973, reaching exclusive 1000-yd. plateau. His 1097 yds. on 210 carries set Ram rushing record. Rewarded with NFC starting berth in 1974 Pro Bowl.

McDANIEL, E. WAHOO Linebacker. B. 6/19/38, Bernice, Okla. 6'2", 248. Son of Choctaw Indian father. Colorful player. New York Jets' original hero, ushering in Joe Namath era. Began career as fullback at Midland (Tex.) H.S. Sifted through 60 scholarship offers and chose U. of Oklahoma. Played end and defensive halfback under Bud Wilkinson. Houston Oilers, 1960; Denver Broncos, 1961-63; New York Jets, 1964-65; Miami Dolphins. Signed out of college with Dallas Cowboys, but released when he dislocated shoulder. Fiery temper, flair for dramatic and ferocious tackling style made him big favorite of New Yorkers. Wrestled in off-season as "Chief Wahoo." Wore Indian feathers at award presentations, catering to image.

McDONALD, THOMAS (Tommy) End. B. 7/26/34, Roy, N.M. 5'9½", 170. Played halfback for Oklahoma, 1954-56. Consensus All-America, 1956; All-America, 1955. 3rd in Heisman Trophy voting, 1956. Maxwell Award, 1956. In 1954 completed 62-yd. pass vs. Iowa State, in 1955 made 91-yd. punt return vs. same opponent. Played in Orange Bowl, 1956, and scored one TD. Became close friend of coach Bud Wilkinson while playing at Oklahoma. Wilkinson had great influence over Tommy. College All-Star game, 1957. No. 3 draft pick by Philadelphia Eagles, 1956. One of smallest regulars in NFL. Great pass catcher, even though had lost tip of left thumb in motorbike accident in 8th grade. In 1959, despite broken jaw, had 47 catches and 10 TDs, finishing behind Ray Berry. 1961 was best year. Caught 64 passes, including 13 TDs and led receivers in yardage with 1114. In 1962 caught 56 passes, 41 in 1963. Traded to Dallas Cowboys, 1963. Los Angeles Rams, 1965-66; Atlanta Falcons, 1967; Cleveland Browns, 1968. Scored one TD in 1960 NFL title game. Zany, comedic. Sometimes referred to as the Jim Piersall of football.

McELHENNY, HUGH (King) Running Back. B. 12/31/28, Los Angeles, Calif. 6'1", 198. Attended George Washington H.S., Los Angeles, and Compton (Calif.) J.C. Scored 23 TDs for Compton, 1948. Gained 2499 yds. at Washington, 1949-51. Scored on 100-yd. punt return, 1951; totaled 125 points to rank 2nd nationally. Washington ran afoul of NCAA regulations; some said McElhenny took pay cut to turn pro. San Francisco 49ers, 1952-60; Minnesota Vikings, 1961-62; New York Giants, 1963; Detroit Lions, 1964. Six Pro Bowls. Twice All-Pro halfback, 1952, 53. Y.A. Tittle maintained, "There was never an open-field runner like McElhenny." Totaled 11,375 career yds. (rushing, pass catching and kick returns). Gained 5281 yds. rushing, had 4.6 average. Scored 59 pro TDs, 39 rushing and 20 as pass receiver. Artistic runner, with uncanny knack for avoiding tacklers. Utilized high knee action owing to scholastic hurdling experience. McElhenny and Joe Perry (fullback) gave 49ers tremendous offensive combination. Suffered numerous injuries. Great self-confidence, fierce competitor. 1952 Rookie of the Year, averaging 10.69 yds. per carry. Figure is 2nd highest by non-qualifier in NFL history. Pro Football Hall of Fame.

McEVER, EUGENE T. (Wild Bull) Running Back. B. 9/15/08, Birmingham, Ala. 5'11", 190. Tennessee All-America, 1928, 29 (consensus), 31. Suffered knee injury and didn't play in 1930. Vols were unbeaten in McEver years. Half of famous "Hack and Mack" backfield combo with Buddy Hackman. Led NCAA in scoring, 1929, with 130 points, all-time school record. Same year scored 21 TDs to share national leadership with Clark Hinkle of Bucknell. In 1929, vs. Centre, made 90-yd. TD run. Against Ole Miss scored on runs of 50 and 30 yds. Unleashed 100-yd. TD run vs. Alabama, deciding 15-13 game. Davidson assistant coach, 1932; head coach, 1936-43. Interim head coach, North Carolina, 1944. VMI assistant, 1945. Coached North Carolina Clippers pro team, 1946-49. Returned to Davidson as frosh coach in 1968. National Football Foundation Hall of Fame.

McEWAN, JOHN J. (Cap) B. 6/18/1893, Alexandria, Minn. D. 8/9/70, New York, N.Y. 6'2", 220. Army, 1914-16. Probably greatest center in West Point history. Frequent knee injuries, but he played with them. Fastest man on team. Often kicked off, then tackled the returner. Usually, after snap, would take out at least one player with block. Tabbed "Rover Center" and "Giant from Minnesota." Team captain, 1916. All-America, 1914; 2nd team, 1916; 3rd team, 1915. Army head coach, 1923-25 with 18-5-3 record. Coached Oregon, 1926-29; Holy Cross, 1930-32. Brooklyn Dodgers, 1933-34. Taught English at West Point. National Football Foundation Hall of Fame.

McFADDEN, J. BANKS Quarterback. B. 2/7/17, Fort Lawn, S.C. 6'3", 180. Clemson, 1937-39. Consensus All-America, 1939. Basketball All-America, 1938-39, as center. Also track star. Called greatest all-round track man in history of S.C. Great runner, passer, punter, defender. 1939 totals: 72 carries for 436 yds.; 29 of 67 passes for 546 yds., 1 TD; 42-yd. punt average; three pass interceptions. In 1940 led Clemson to upset win (6-3) over Boston College, previously undefeated, in Cotton Bowl. College All-Star game, 1940. Same year with Brooklyn Dodgers; 2nd among NFL rushers. During World War II served in U.S. Army Air Force Special Services as Maj. Later Clemson football assistant (backfield coach), head basketball coach. National Football Foundation Hall of Fame.

McFADIN, LEWIS B. (Bud) Tackle. B. 8/21/28, Iraan, Tex. 6'4", 275. Country boy. Almost left U. of Texas freshman year because he was homesick for horse. Unanimous All-America, 1950. No. 1 draft choice Los Angeles Rams, MVP College All-Star game, 1951. Played with Rams, 1952-56; Denver Broncos, 1960-63; Houston Oilers, 1964-65. Lost most of stomach when he was accidentally shot on hunting trip following 1956 season. As result, retired for three years and entered cattle business. Made remarkable comeback with Broncos, twice earning All-AFL honors. Abner Haynes, AFL's 1960 MVP, once called McFadin best defensive player he'd faced. Fierce competitor, pass rusher.

McGEE, MICHAEL Guard. B. 12/1/38, Washington, D.C. 6'1", 230. All-America at Duke, 1959. Won Outland Trophy same year. Was prep trackster and wrestler. Brilliant offensively and defensively for Blue Devils. Once provoked Georgia Tech QB to ask, "No. 68, why don't you give me a chance sometimes?" St. Louis Cardinals, 1960-62. Duke head coach, 1970-73.

McGEE, WILLIAM M. (Max) End. B. 7/16/32, Saxton City, Nev. 6'3", 205. Maybe football's all-time fun-loving free spirit. Neither top defenders nor Green Bay Packer coach Vince Lombardi could stay dedication to swinging life. Lombardi and McGee did have several memorable confrontations when Max was caught breaking curfew. These left Max short of money but rarely short of breath. In 1957 struck up friendship with Paul Hornung. Two became constant companions, roommates and night-life associates. "I adopted him right away," McGee recalled their first meeting. "It was an unbeatable combination, his charm and my looks." Was winner on field. Football saga began in Waco, Tex., where one of McGee boys (there were four) dominated high school's backfield during period of 1936-50. Two brothers attended Notre Dame with Coy playing briefly in AAFC. Max was Tulane halfback before switching to end in pros. Led nation in kickoff returns with 21.8-yd. average. Spent entire NFL career with Packers, 1954, 57-67. Was interrupted by air force duty, serving as pilot and flight instructor. Played on five NFL and two Super Bowl championship teams. At age 34, slowing up and stamina failing, Max caught seven passes for 138 yds. — more than gathered entire regular season. Career stats read 345 receptions for 6346 yds. (18.1-yd. average) and 50 TDs. Not bad for guy who stayed out too late.

McGOVERN, JOHN F. Quarterback. B. 9/15/1887, Arlington, Minn. D. 12/14/63, Le Seur, Minn. 5'9", 155. Minnesota, 1908-10. Captain, 1909, 10. All-America, 1909; first Minnesota player to achieve honor. Western Conference (Big 10) champions, 1909. That year vs. Chicago dropkicked three FGs. 1910 team tied Chicago for conference title. Missed only one game in three varsity seasons. Won Outstanding Achievement award, 1910; in 1911 Most Outstanding Alumnus. After graduation became sports editor of Minneapolis newspaper. Later attorney. National Football Foundation Hall of Fame.

McGUGIN, DANIEL E. Coach. B. 7/29/1879, Tingley, Iowa. D. 1/19/36, Memphis, Tenn. Brother-in-law of Fielding (Hurry Up) Yost. Both men were football coaches and lawyers. McGugin played for Yost at Michigan, 1902-03. Dan spent entire coaching life at one school — Vanderbilt — doubling as athletic director, 1904-17, 19-34. Psychological master, revered for ability to motivate. Red Sanders, Vanderbilt quarterback and later UCLA coach, maintained: "It was from McGugin that I learned psychology, particularly the art of handling men." Vanderbilt dedicated its new stadium, 1922, against Yost's Michigan team. In pre-game huddle McGugin pointed to nearby military cemetery and then to Michigan team before counseling his players: "In that cemetery sleep your grandfathers, and down on that field are the grandsons of the Damn Yankees who put them there." Vanderbilt tied Michigan that day and went on to unbeaten season. McGugin's record: 197-55-19 (.762). Citizens Savings Hall of Fame, National Football Foundation Hall of Fame.

McKAY, JOHN H. Coach. B. 7/5/23, Everettsville, W. Va. College teammate of Norm Van Brocklin. Scored eight touchdowns as running back, 1948, helping Oregon gain Cotton Bowl berth against SMU. Ducks lost to Mustangs, 21-13. Drafted by New York Yankees (AAFC) but turned to coaching. Oregon assistant 10 years, 1950-59. In 1960 named 16th head coach at Southern California. Produced four national championship teams there, 1962, 67, 68, 69. Only coach to qualify team for four straight trips to Rose Bowl, 1966-69. Rose Bowl appearances also in 1973, 74. Won seven Pacific-8 championships. Coached son, J. J., wide receiver, 1971-73. Also Southern Cal athletic director. Developed such players as Mike Garrett, Ron Yary, O. J. Simpson, Charles Young, Anthony Davis, Lynn Swann, Hal Bedsole. Overall record: 110-34-7.

McKEEVER, MARLIN Tight End-Linebacker. B. 1/1/40, Cheyenne, Wyo. 6'1", 230. Born on New Year's Day, 1940, 10 minutes earlier than brother Mike. At Southern Cal they became most famous twin combination in college football history. Marlin was two-time All-America end, 1959, 60. Played two seasons as linebacker with Los Angeles Rams and then switched to tight end. Enjoyed banner year, 1965, catching 44 passes for 542 yds., 4 TDs. Reverted to linebacker when he joined Washington Redskins under Vince Lombardi, 1968. Has been permanent 'backer ever since. Dealt back to Rams in unique 1971 trade. Rams gave up six players and one draft choice, Redskins countered with seven choices and one player (McKeever). Also cavorted for Minnesota Vikings, 1967. Played in 1967 Pro Bowl. Public relations consultant during off-season.

McKEEVER, MIKE Guard. B. 1/1/40, Cheyenne, Wyo. D. 8/24/67, Montebello, Calif. 6'1", 230. Twin brother of Marlin. Equally talented but always seemed to get bad breaks. Played with Marlin at Mt. Carmel H.S., Los

Angeles, and Southern California. Mike's USC career was controversial. Inflicted fractured cheekbone and broken nose on California's Steve Bates in 1959 game. Mike had fallen atop Bates out of bounds, creating outrage among Cal fans and officials. Cal coach, Pete Elliott, called it "the most flagrant violation I've ever seen in football." Berkeley threatened to break off athletic relations but USC president, Dr. Norman Topping, cooled matters by publicly apologizing for incident. McKeever received hundreds of angry letters, nonetheless, including two death threats. Midway thru senior year was kicked in head in Stanford game. Brain injury resulted, forcing operation for blood clot and retirement from football. Plans for pro career thus snuffed out. Brothers had announced that they would play pro only if drafted by same team. Mike was defensive terror, harassed QBs, routed blockers. Also ran 10.2 for 100 yds., slightly faster than Marlin who was pass-catching end at USC. On 12/3/65, Mike entered hospital for another brain injury, suffered in car accident. Marlin, truly brother's keeper, kept constant vigil. Mike remained hospitalized for over 21 months, until death came.

McLAREN, GEORGE W. (Tank) Running Back. D. 11/13/67. 185. Played for Pitt, 1916-18, never in losing game. Stationed at halfback-fullback. Played with 1916 national champions, called by Pop Warner his greatest. All-America 2nd team, 1917, 18. In 1917 ran 91 yds. from scrimmage for TD, long-time Pitt record. Scored 13 TDs that season, also long-standing record. Captain in 1918. Class president. Later earned dental degree and worked in industrial relations in Baltimore. National Football Foundation Hall of Fame.

McLAUGHRY, DeORMOND (Tuss) Coach. B. 5/19/1893, Chicago, Ill. Raised in Sharon, Pa. Spent freshman year at Michigan State. Then transferred to Westminster (Pa.) College where he played three sports. Associated with football as player, coach, administrator for 55 years. Coached Westminster, 1916-17, 20-21; Amherst, 1922-25; Brown, 1926-40; Dartmouth, 1941-42, 45-54. Record: 140-155-15. Best years were spent at Brown (76-58-5). Brown's 1928 "Iron Men" won nine straight games, before they were tied by Colgate (10-10). Coached his sons, John and Bob, at Dartmouth. John was later Brown head coach for eight years. Tuss coached East squad four times in East-West Shrine game. Served many years as secretary-treasurer of American Football Coaches Association. Citizens Savings Hall of Fame, National Football Foundation Hall of Fame.

MacLEOD, ROBERT F. Running-Back. B. 10/15/17, Glen Ellyn, Ill. 6', 190. Red Blaik's greatest player at Dartmouth, 1936-38. Inspired defeatless string of 22 straight games. Captain and consensus All-America, 1938. Scored on 85-yd. interception return in matchup with Clint Frank (Yale), 1937. Game ended 9-9. Complete player, overcoming early deficiencies defensively. Chicago Bears, 1939. Became prominent publishing executive. Now editor and publisher of *Teen* magazine, Los Angeles.

McMILLAN, ERNEST C. Tackle. B. 2/21/38, Chicago Heights, Ill. 6'6", 265. Earned B.S. degree in education from Illinois, 1961. Played end. St. Louis Cardinals, 1961-73. Only 13th-round draft choice by Cards, McMillan was immediate starter in 1961 though Army call forced him to miss half of season. Returned in 1962, never missing game since. Holds Card record of 174 consecutive games. Tied with Larry Wilson for most seasons (13) by St. Louis player. Last survivor of club's great offensive line of 1960s. Group included Bob DeMarco, Ken Gary, Bob Reynolds, Irv Goode. Pro Bowl, 1966, 68, 70. Active in St. Louis community affairs. Affiliated with *Pride* magazine.

McMILLIN, ALVIN N. (Bo) Quarterback. B. 1/12/1895, Prairie Hill, Texas. D. 3/31/52, Bloomington, Ind. 5'9", 165. Centre (U. of the South), 1919-21. All-America, 1919; 2nd team, 1920, 21. Milwaukee Badgers, 1922-23; Cleveland Indians, 1923. Rugged, quick. In 1921 led "Praying Colonels" to stunning 6-0 win over Harvard. McMillin provided only TD with 32-yd. run. Afterwards, Edwin P. Morrow said, "I'd rather be Bo McMillin at this moment than the governor of Kentucky," which he was. Had been star schoolboy QB in Fort Worth. Played tailback at Centre, called signals. Specialty was flanking short-side end on reverse. Oft-imitated, he threw bullet passes. Completed remarkable 119 of 170 tosses in 1921. During first season kicked FG to give Centre 3-0 win over Kentucky, team they'd lost to, 68-0, year before. It was only FG attempt he ever made. Stern, tough, spiritual leader. Indiana coach, 1934-47. Coach of the Year in 1945 via undefeated season and Western Conference (Big 10) championship. Complained of team's "po little fellas", most of whom weighed 225-240 lbs. 63-48-11 at Indiana. Also coached collegiately at Centenary, Geneva, Kansas State. In 1948 became head coach of Detroit Lions. Best record with Lions was 6-6, 1950, but he did good job of promoting pro football. Replaced by Buddy Parker in 1951 and became coach of Philadelphia Eagles. Resigned that post after losing first two games. Citizens Savings Player of the Year, 1919. Citizens Savings Hall of Fame, National Football Foundation Hall of Fame.

McNALLY (BLOOD), JOHN V. (Johnny) Running Back. B. 11/27/04, New Richmond, Wis. 6'1", 190. Flamboyant character. Four-sport letterman at St. John's (Minn.). Attended Notre Dame but declined football competition when freshman coach George Koegan tried converting him to tackle. Milwaukee Badgers, 1925-26; Duluth Eskimos, 1926-27; Pottsville Maroons, 1928; Green Bay Packers, 1929-33, 35-36; Pittsburgh Pirates 1937-38; Pittsburgh Steelers, 1939. Player-coach with Pittsburgh (6-19). All-Pro, 1931. Member four world championship teams as Packer, 1929, 30, 31, 36. Scored 37 TDs for Green Bay, including 13 in 1931. Extremely fast, self-confident. Known as Johnny Blood throughout pro career, adopting name from movie, *Blood and Sand.* Engineered many off-field capers. Had no tolerance for curfews and training rules. Often borrowed money to maintain swinging lifestyle. Once engaged in Shakespeare-quoting contest with John Barrymore in Pittsburgh bar. Was, at various times, bartender, stenotyper, air force sergeant, cryptographer in China. Now operating two employment agencies around Minnesota's Twin Cities. Named to All-Pro Squad of the 1930s. Pro Football Hall of Fame.

McNEIL, CLIFTON A. (Spider) Wide Receiver. B. 5/25/40, Mobile, Ala. 6'1½", 186. Graduated from Grambling. Drafted on 11th round of 1963 draft by Cleveland Browns. After year on taxi squad made Brown roster in 1964. Played four years with Cleveland. Traded to San Francisco 49ers, 1968. League's leading receiver that year with 71 receptions for 794 yds. and 7 TDs. In 1970 dealt to New York Giants, then traded to Washington Redskins midway thru 1971 for three draft picks. In 1973 traded to Houston Oilers in seven-player deal. Placed on waivers by Houston, 11/73. Pro Bowl, 1969. Played in NFL championship game, 1964. Super Bowl, 1973.

McPEAK, WILLIAM End. B. 7/24/26, New Castle, Pa. Attended U. of Pittsburgh. Played with Pittsburgh Steelers, 1949-57. Coached in pros by John Michelosen, Joe Bach, Walt Kiesling, Buddy Parker. Tied NFL record for safeties, lifetime, with three. Head coach Washington Redskins, 1961-65. Record: 21-46-3. Assistant coach Steelers, Detroit Lions, Miami Dolphins. Currently with Dolphins (offensive coach). Although failed to win as head coach, he's still highly regarded for fine football mind, patient ways.

McPHEE, FRANK R. End. B. 3/19/31, Youngstown, Ohio. 6'3", 203. Graduated from Princeton, 1953. Consensus All-America, 1952; All-America, 1951. Princeton lost only once in 1952, to Penn, and it snapped 24-game winning streak. Skein largely attributable to play of McPhee, Heisman winner Dick Kazmaier. Affiliated with Prudential Life Insurance Co. in Houston. Citizens Savings Hall of Fame.

McRAE, BENJAMIN P. (Bennie) Defensive Back. B. 12/8/39, Newport News, Va. 6', 182. Led Michigan rushers with 4.4-yd. average, 1960. Graduated in 1962. Chicago Bears, 1962-70; New York Giants, 1971. Drafted on 2nd round by Bears. Member world championship team, 1963. As Bear intercepted 27 passes, returning them for 485 yds. and four TDs. Gave sole concentration to defense in pros.

McVEA, WARREN D. Running Back. B. 7/30/46, San Antonio, Tex. 5'9", 182. Legend in Texas schoolboy football. Scored almost 600 points in three years at San Antonio's Breckenridge H.S., 1962-64. In 1963 scored six TDs in playoff epic against crosstown rival Robert E. Lee — Breckenridge still lost, 55-48. In 1964 became first Negro athlete at U. of Houston. Scores of offers were thus rejected, including letter from Harry Truman in behalf of U. of Missouri. Houston, 1965-67. All-America, 1967. Cincinnati Bengals, 1968; Kansas City Chiefs, 1969-73. Shared Chief club record with 80-yard TD run, 1969. Missed 1972 due to knee injury. Released by Chiefs midway thru 1973. Signed by Detroit Wheels (WFL) for 1974.

McWHORTER, ROBERT L. Running Back. B. 6/4/1891, Athens, Ga. D. 6/29/60, Athens, Ga. 5'10", 180. Georgia, 1910-13. In four games vs. Georgia Tech, McWhorter-led teams allowed but one TD. All-America, 1913. Also played baseball. Good runner, blocker. Excellent defensive player. After graduation went to U. of Virginia Law School. Served in World War I, practiced law in Athens, served as law professor at Georgia. Mayor of Athens, 1940-48. Citizens Savings Hall of Fame, National Football Foundation Hall of Fame.

MACK, THOMAS L. Guard. B. 11/1/43, Cleveland, Ohio. 6'3", 250. Swimmer, football and baseball player at Cleveland Heights H.S. Junior starter on Michigan's 1964 Rose Bowl team which mastered Oregon State, 34-7. All-Big 10, All-America, 1965. Participated in East-West, Hula Bowl, College All-Star games. 1st-round draft choice of Los Angeles Rams, 1966. Only Ram named All-NFC, both 1971, 72, at offensive guard. Has made six Pro Bowl appearances. Father, late Ray Mack, played major league baseball with Cleveland Indians.

MACKEY, JOHN Tight End. B. 9/9/41, Queens, N.Y. 6'2", 224. Attended Hempstead (N.Y.) H.S. and Syracuse U. Lettered in football, lacrosse and basketball at Syracuse. Drafted No. 2 by Baltimore Colts in 1963. Played with Colts thru 1971. Finished career with San Diego Chargers in 1972. Caught 331 passes as pro for 5236 yds., 38 TDs. Might be said that Mackey refined tight end play after Ron Kramer gave position its definition. Fast, extremely powerful. Like runaway tank once he caught football. All-Pro, 1966, 67, 68. Pro Bowl, 1964, 66, 67, 68, 69. NFL championship games, 1964, 68. Super Bowl, 1969. Voted greatest tight end of NFL's first 50 years in 1969. Also named to All-Pro Squad of the 1960s. Articulate and popular; former president of NFL Players Association. Now represents players for William Morris Agency in New York City.

MADDEN, JOHN E. Coach. B. 4/10/36, Austin, Minn. Football tackle and baseball catcher at California Poly. Spent one year with Philadelphia Eagles, 1960, knee injury cutting short career. Head coach, Hancock J.C., Santa Maria, Calif., 1962-63; Oakland Raiders, 1969-73. Was assistant at San Diego State, 1964-66. In four of five years Raiders won AFC Western Division title. They were 2nd in 1971. 47-16-7 record thru 1973. Lost AFL championship game to Kansas City Chiefs, 17-7, in 1969. Coached AFC All-Stars in 1974 Pro Bowl. Shirtsleeved, 6'4", 260-pound redhead unmistakable on sidelines. AFL Coach of the Year, 1969.

MADIGAN, EDWARD P. (Slip) Coach. B. 1896. D. 10/10/66. Notre Dame, 1916, 17, 19. Coached Portland, 1920; St. Mary's (Calif.), 1921-39; Iowa, 1943-44. 125-59-14 record. When hired to build St. Mary's fortunes, school had only 71 students. Gaels had lost to California, 127-0, one year before Madigan took job. Developed two unbeaten teams, 1926, 29. Latter team was scored upon only by Oregon (31-6), season's last game. Handsomely paid for his era, receiving (at St. Mary's) salary plus share of gate receipts. Scouted Stanford for alma mater prior to 1925 Rose Bowl. His report led to touchdown return by Elmer Layden which helped Notre Dame win, 27-10. Citizens Savings Hall of Fame, National Football Foundation Hall of Fame.

MAGUIRE, PAUL L. Linebacker. B. 8/22/33, Youngstown, Ohio. 6', 225. Drafted on 1st round by Los Angeles Chargers from The Citadel, 1960. AFL punting leader with 40.5-yd. average. Team moved to San Diego in 1961. Maguire was sold to Buffalo Bills in 1964. Set AFL record for lifetime punts, 634. Set AFL career playoff record with 25 punts. Set AFL record, most times on championship team, three. AFL All-Star game, 1962, 65. Played seven years with Bills and then retired after 1970 campaign.

MAHAN, EDWARD W. (Natick Eddie) Running Back. B. 1/19/1882, Natick, Mass. 5'11", 171. Harvard fullback, 1913-15. Named by Grantland Rice to all-time college backfield. All-America, 1913, 14, 15. Great runner, passer, blocker, tackler, kicker. Didn't want anyone to run interference for him, preferring to clear own path. Very fast. Citizens Savings Hall of Fame, National Football Foundation Hall of Fame.

MAHER, BRUCE D. (Beaver) Defensive Back. B. 7/25/37, Detroit, Mich. 5'11", 190. Attended U. of Detroit. In 1959 drafted on 15th round by Detroit Lions. Detroit, 1959-67. In 1968 dealt to New York Giants, for whom he played thru 1969. Played minor-league baseball with Durham, 1961. Tied NFL record for safeties, career, three.

MAJORS, JOHN Running Back. B. 1935, Huntland, Tenn. 5'10", 162. Played for Dad at Huntland H.S. Triple-threat tailback at U. of Tennessee, 1954-56. Unanimous All-America and runnerup for Heisman Trophy, 1956. Sportswriter tabbed him "player without a weakness." In 1955 led SEC in total offense with 1133 yds. Handled ball more times (313) that year than any college player. After 10-0 regular season, 1956, Tennessee lost 13-7 verdict to Baylor in Sugar Bowl. Career statistics: 2757 yds. total offense (1622 rushing, 1135 passing), 83 punts (39.1-yd. average), 36 punt returns (12.2-yd. average), 27 TDs-accounted-for (16 TDs rushing). Coached Iowa State, 1968-72; Pittsburgh, 1973. Took Iowa State to Liberty Bowl in 1972, marking school's first bowl appearance. Cyclones lost to Georgia Tech, 30-28. Moved to Pitt for reported $35,000. Revived Panther fortunes initial season. From 0-10 in 1972, team finished 7-5-1 in '73 and earned trip to Fiesta Bowl. Big 8 Coach of the Year, 1972; national Coach of the Year by Football Writers Association of America, 1973.

MAJORS, SHIRLEY I. Coach. B. 5/27/13, Beechgrove, Tenn. Head of Tennessee's foremost football family. Attended Murfreesboro College and Memphis State. Detested farming (inherited 104 acres from father) and turned to coaching in 1942. Without college degree started career at Lynchburg (Tenn.) H.S. Then to Franklin County (Tenn.) H.S., Huntland (Tenn.) H.S. and Sewanee (U. of the South). In eight years at Huntland, 1949-56, compiled 76-6 record. Forty-seven wins came consecutively. Sewanee record: 73-51-5, 1957-72.

218

His 1958 club was perfect, becoming first Tiger team since 1899 to finish unbeaten, untied. Success is remarkable considering school offers no athletic aid and has lofty academic standards. Four sons — Johnny, Joe, Bill, Larry — starred for their father at Huntland. Larry also played for Dad at Sewanee. Bobby came along too late for Dad's tutoring, but distinguished himself at Tennessee before turning pro. Johnny, all-time great Vol tailback, is now head coach at Pittsburgh. Joe (Florida State, '59) is lawyer; Larry is high school coach. Bill, former Tennessee player and assistant, lost life in car-train accident. Shirley Ann, only daughter of elder Majors, was cheerleader. Not surprisingly, she married football player.

MALLORY, WILLIAM N. (Memphis Bill) Running Back. B. 1/20/01, Memphis, Tenn. D. 2/19/45. 5'10", 173. Yale fullback, 1921-23. Captained 1923 squad; regarded by many as Yale's greatest. Aggressive, modest player. Hockey star and member of Skull and Bones. All-America, 1923. Outstanding citizen. Joined Army Air Force as captain in 1942, becoming Maj. in 1943. Won Legion of Merit for "Operation Mallory," destroying 22 bridges across Italy's Po River. Killed in 1945 plane crash on first leg of return trip home. National Football Foundation Hall of Fame.

MALONE, ARTHUR L. Running Back. B. 3/20/48, Tyler, Tex. 5'11", 200. Attended Santa Cruz Valley H.S., Eloy, Ariz., and Arizona State. Scored 37 TDs and led Santa Cruz to state championship, 1965. Was Arizona State 120-yd. high and 180-yd. low hurdles champion. All-WAC, 1967-69. Gained 2549 yds. rushing, scored 30 TDs and scored 184 points. In junior year alone rushed for 1431 yds. Played in East-West Shrine and College All-Star games. Drafted No. 2 by Atlanta Falcons in 1970. In four years, 1970-73, rushed for 1708 yds. and caught 112 passes for 1180 more. Banner season was 1972. That year gained 798 yds. rushing, caught 50 passes for 585 yds., scored 10 TDs. Owns number of Atlanta offensive records.

MANCHA, VAUGHN Center. B. 10/7/21, Sugar Valley, Ga. 6', 238. Alabama, 1945-47. Consensus All-America as sophomore. Member of All-Time Sugar Bowl team. Won 1946 Sugar Bowl over Southern Cal, 34-14, but lost to Texas in 1948, 27-7. Assistant coach at Florida State, 1952-56, and Columbia, 1956-58. Became Florida State athletic director in 1959 and didn't relinquish post until 1973. Now full professor in Florida State's College of Education. Contributes research articles to athletic magazines and journals.

MANDERS, JOHN (Automatic Jack) Running Back. B. 1910, Milbank, S.D. Football, basketball, track letterman at Milbank H.S. All-Conference fullback three years at U. of Minnesota, 1929-31. Chicago Bears, 1933-40. Exceptional placekicker. Scoring leader twice, 1934, 37; FG leader four times, 1933, 34, 36, 37. In 1933-37 period kicked 72 consecutive PATs. Member two world championship teams, 1933, 40. Brother Pug, Drake alumnus, was also fine fullback and pro player.

MANDICH, JIM Tight End. B. 7/30/48, Cleveland, Ohio. 6'2", 224. Michigan, 1967-68. School's No. 2 all-time receiver with 111 catches, 1415 yards. Consensus All-America, Academic All-America, team captain, 1969. Caught 42 passes senior year plus 8 in Rose Bowl against Southern Cal. 2nd-round draft choice of Miami Dolphins, 1970. Played behind Marv Fleming first three pro seasons, in 1973 gained starting berth. Played on 1972, 73 Super Bowl championship teams.

MANNING, ARCHIE Quarterback. B. 5/19/49, Cleveland, Miss. 6'3", 210. Attended Drew (Miss.) H.S. Set SEC record with 5576 yards total offense at U. of Mississippi, 1968-70. In career completed 412 of 761 passes for 4753 yards, 31 TDs — all Ole Miss records. Accounted for 540 yards total offense vs. Alabama, 1969. Consensus All-America, 1969. MVP in Sugar Bowl, 1970; Gator Bowl, 1971. Drafted by Chicago White Sox as shortstop, 1st round by New Orleans Saints, 1971. Threw 18 TD passes and rushed for 5.6-yd. average with Saints, 1972. Scrambling QB trying to learn dropback style. Swift, with 4.6 speed in 40-yd. dash.

MARA, TIMOTHY J. Owner. B. 7/29/1887, New York, N.Y. D. 2/16/59, New York, N.Y. Quit school at 13 to support himself and widowed mother. Sold newspapers, worked as theater usher and runner for bookmakers. Latter job led him to full-time bookie status. Bought pro football franchise for New York, 1925. It cost him $500. He said, "Any New York franchise is worth $500." Lacked technical knowledge of football (often quipped he founded club on "brute strength and ignorance") but molded New York Giants into solid organization. Also made it family enterprise. Sons Jack and Wellington ran club for many years. Wellington is still president. Grandson, also named Timothy J., is now Giants vice president-treasurer. Senior Mara was man who kept his word. Retained coach Steve Owen for 22 years on nothing more than verbal agreement and handshake. Pro Football Hall of Fame. Died in his beloved New York.

MARA, WELLINGTON T. Owner. B. 8/14/16, New York, N.Y. Nine years old when his dad, Tim, bought New York Giants in 1925. Affiliated with club ever since. Started as ball boy, became secretary in 1936 and president in 1965. As youngster dubbed "Duke of Mara"; official NFL football later named "The Duke." Fordham classmate of Vince Lombardi. Giants gave Lombardi first pro coaching job in 1951; Mara later tried to lure him back to New York from Green Bay as head coach, but contracts stood in way. Unique talent for scouting and finding players. Made first major discovery at age 19, bringing Tuffy Leemans to Giants. Completely dedicated to football. Father of 10 children. Resident of Westchester County, N.Y. Related family story: "My son, John, told me the other day: 'Don't leave me the business, Dad. I want to be a player.' "

MARCHETTI, GINO Defensive End. B. 1/2/27, Antioch, Calif. 6'4", 253. Son of Italian immigrant tavern owner. In 1942, shortly after 14th birthday, U.S. government sent Gino and his parents to detention farm in California. Morning of 18th birthday, Gino enlisted in army. After completing service, family released and he went to work in father's bar. Soon Brad Lynn, assistant coach for U. of San Francisco, drove to Antioch to invite Gino to USF practice. He then enrolled. Eleven men he played with there went on to NFL, including running back Ollie Matson, QB Ed Brown and offensive tackle Bob St. Clair. 2nd-round draft choice of New York football Yankees in 1952; shortly thereafter franchise moved to Dallas, and following Marchetti's rookie year team moved to Baltimore and became Colts. First played defensive tackle without much success, then moved to offensive tackle. Weeb Ewbank became head coach for Colts in 1954 and made Marchetti defensive end. In 1958 NFL title game vs. New York Giants, Colts trailed with two minutes to play, 17-14. Marchetti stopped New York's effort for 1st down, allowing Colts to regain ball and score tying FG. It led to sudden-death period. Broke his leg in overtime session and missed only Pro Bowl in 1955-64 span. Announced retirement after 1963 season but urged by management to return and did. Played two more seasons, 1965, 66. In 12 seasons with Colts, Marchetti played prominent role in two NFL championships and three Western Conference titles. Voted best defensive end in history of NFL. All-Pro Squad of the 1950s. All-League, 1956, 57, 59, 60, 61, 62, 63, 64. Elected to Pro Football Hall of Fame in 1972, his first year eligible.

MARCHIBRODA, THEODORE Quarterback. B. 3/15/31, Franklin, Pa. 5'10", 180. Played with St. Bonaventure, 1950-51; U. of Detroit, 1952. Transferred to Detroit when St. Bonaventure dropped football. Drafted on 1st round by Pittsburgh Steelers. Played with Steelers, 1953, 55-56; Chicago Cardinals, 1957. NFL's 2nd leading passer, hitting 124 of 275 for 1585 yds. and 12 TDs. Assistant coach, Washington Redskins, 1961-65, 71-73; Los Angeles Rams, 1966-70. Currently Redskin offensive coordinator.

MARCOL, CZELSLAW C. (Chester) B. 10/24/49, Opole, Poland. Called "Polish Messiah", was soccer goalie, immigrated to America with family at age 15. Attended Hillsdale College of Michigan; drafted on 2nd round by Green Bay Packers, 1972. Roommate Jerry Tagge (former Nebraska QB) said, "The only reason Chester wasn't chosen on the 1st-round is that by the time they found Hillsdale, the first round was over." At Hillsdale kicked 104 consecutive extra points and 8 FGs of 50 yards or more. Set NAIA record by kicking 62-yard FG, 1971. Little All-America, 1971. Kicked four FGs, 12/3/72, vs. Detroit Lions. NFL FG leader with 33, 1972. Also scoring leader with 128 points. Broke team record of 19 FGs. Became first player ever to lead NFL in scoring on kicking alone. All-NFC, 1972. Pro Bowl, 1973. Scored 82 points in 1973.

MARINARO, ED Running Back. B. 3/3/50, New York, N.Y. 6'2½", 210. Most productive rusher in college football history. Gained 4715 yds. on 918 carries (5.1 average) at Cornell, 1969-71. First major collegian to rush 4000 yds. in three seasons. Set 17 NCAA records. 1971 won national scoring and all-purpose running crowns, led Cornell to Ivy League co-title, was unanimous All-America. Biggest game, against Harvard in 1969, gained 281 yds., scored 5 TDs. Once missed ball trying to quick-kick. Biggest disappointment though was not winning

1971 Heisman Trophy, finishing runnerup to Pat Sullivan. Later commented, "I was a couple of years ahead of my time. The world wasn't ready for an Italian Heisman Trophy winner. I just blazed a trail for John Cappelletti (1973 winner)." Cute, but not accurate. Angelo Bertelli (Notre Dame) won in 1943, Alan Ameche (Wisconsin) likewise 11 years later. Played with Minnesota Vikings, 1972-73. Was 2nd-round draft choice. Fine runner, pass receiver.

MARSHALL, GEORGE P. Owner. B. 10/11/1896, Grafton, W. Va. D. 8/9/69, Washington, D. C. Attended Randolph-Macon. Made fortune in laundry. Had 57 branches when he sold Washington business, 1945. Company's slogan was "Long Live Linen." Owner of Washington Redskins, 1932-63. Team was stationed in Boston first five years. Inspired many changes in pro game: split into two divisions, championship playoff, Pro Bowl, return of goalposts from end zone to goal line, passing permitted anywhere behind line of scrimmage. Great promoter and showman. Famous for halftime entertainment, featuring pro game's first marching band. He said; "Football without a band is like a musical without an orchestra." Criticized many years for not signing Black players. In 1962, Bobby Mitchell became first Black Redskin. Pro Football Hall of Fame.

MARSHALL, JAMES L. Defensive End. B. 12/20/37, Danville, Ky. 6'4", 252. Ohio State tackle, 1957-58. All-America, 1958. Member of 1957 Rose Bowl team. 1958 Buckeyes didn't win conference but boasted outstanding personnel, such as Bob White, Dick LeBeau, Jim Houston, Dick Schafrath, Jim Tyrer, besides Marshall. Houston, Schafrath, Tyrer, Marshall manned one of greatest lines in collegiate history. Passed up senior season to turn pro with Saskatchewan Roughriders, 1959. Then Cleveland Browns, 1960-61; Minnesota Vikings, 1962-73. Pro Bowl, 1970. Thru 1973 played in 182 consecutive league games; proof enough of his durability. Member of Viking "Purple Gang" or "Purple People Eaters," at one time considered classiest defensive front four in pros. Tied most fumble recoveries, lifetime, with three. 1968 brought most embarrassing moment. Picked up loose ball during regular season game and ran wrong way, eventually being hauled down for safety. Incident was out of character. He's articulate, man of many passions: fencing, snow skiing, water skiing, scuba diving, oil painting, poetry writing, hunting, fishing. As sky diver jumped more than 200 times. NFL championship game, 1969. Super Bowl, 1970, 74.

MARTIN, BEN Coach. B. 6/28/21, Prospect Park, Pa. Attended Princeton, 1940-42. Earned B.S. degree from Navy, 1946. Assistant coach, Navy, 1946-55. Head coach at Virginia, 1956-57, and Air Force, 1958-73. First season at Air Force produced unbeaten Cotton Bowl team. Produced All-Americas Brock Strom and Rich Mayo. Author of *Flexible T Offense* and *Football End Play.* Overall record of 92-85-8. Avid golfer. Excellent after-dinner speaker known for quick wit.

MARTIN, JAMES R. (Jungle Jim) Linebacker-Kicker. B. 2/14/19, Concord, N.H. 6'2", 225. Notre Dame, 1946-49. All-America, 1949. Partook in one of school's great eras — 37 wins, no losses, 2 ties. Irish were national champions, 1946, 47, 49. Matriculated at Notre Dame after two and one-half years with marines, including stop at Okinawa. Defensive end for Frank Leahy. Cleveland Browns, 1950; Detroit Lions, 1951-61; Baltimore Colts, 1963; Washington Redskins, 1964. Was pro linebacker. NFL FG leader with 24, 1963. NFL championship games, 1951, 52, 53, 54, 57. On 12/29/57 tied Lou Groza's record of eight PATs in championship game. Kicked 31-yd. FG same game. In 14-year career drilled 158 PATs, 92 FGs for 434 points. Booted part of '64 campaign with broken leg. Assistant coach, Detroit Lions, 1967-72.

MARTIN, OTHOL H. (Honest Abe) Coach. B. 10/18/08, Jacksboro, Tex. Texas Christian letterman, 1928-30. Played on school's first SWC championship team, 1929. Coached alma mater 13 years, 1953-65. 64-48-4 record. Took Horned Frogs to three Cotton Bowls and single appearances in Astro-Bluebonnet and Sun Bowls. Including stints at three high schools, overall mark reads 169-77-8. In 1968 received Amos Alonzo Stagg Award. Past president, American Football Coaches Association. Recipient of Distinguished American Award from North Texas Chapter of the NCAA Hall of Fame, and TCU Distinguished Alumni Award. Currently TCU athletic director.

MARX, GREGORY A. Tackle. B. 7/18/50, Detroit, Mich. 6'4", 260. Notre Dame defensive tackle, 1970-72. Unanimous All-America, 1972. During career made 263 unassisted tackles, throwing enemy backs for minus 142 yds. Academic All-America twice, 1971, 72. Played in Cotton Bowl, 1971; Orange Bowl, 1973. Graduated with B.A. degree in psychology. Played with Atlanta Falcons in 1973 after being their No. 1 draft choice. Enrolled in law school at Notre Dame.

MASON, THOMAS C. (Tommy) Running Back. B. 7/8/39, Lake Charles, La. 6'1", 195.Southern gentleman. Charmed way through Lake Charles H.S., Tulane and 11-year pro career. To support expensive lifestyle had to play mighty good football, and did! In heyday Coach Norm Van Brocklin of Minnesota Vikings called him "best football player in the National League." Romanced by all SWC and SEC schools after outstanding prep showing. Chose to follow in brother Boo's footsteps and attended Tulane. There, 1958-60 under Andy Pilney, gained 2224 yds. on rushes, passes, and kicks. Senior year led SEC in rushing. Played six years for Vikings, 1961-66, after being No. 1 draft choice. Also played for Los Angeles Rams, 1967-70; Washington Redskins, 1971. In career gained 4203 yds. on 1040 carries for 4.0 average, scoring 32 TDs. Picked up 146 yds. vs. Baltimore Colts on only 12 carries, 1963. Was All-Pro that season. Bachelor Tommy Mason, once regarded by peers as game's "greatest lover," has met Waterloo. Is now married to gymnast Kathy Rigby. Professionally, Mason provides color for NFL telecasts on CBS.

MASTERSON, BERNARD E. (Bat) Quarterback. B. 8/10/11, Shenandoah, Iowa, D. 5/16/63. Attended Nebraska. Chicago Bears, 1934-40. Completed 155 of 408 passes for 3372 yds. and 33 TDs. Member of Chicago's 1940 world championship team. Started NFL title game, 1937, losing 28-21 to Washington Redskins at Polo Grounds in New York. It was only championship game ever played on neutral field. Coached Nebraska, 1946-47 (5-13).

MATSON, OLIVER G. Running Back. B. 5/1/30, Trinity, Tex. 6'2", 220. U. of San Francisco, 1949-51. All-America, 1951. 1951 NCAA rushing champion, gaining 1566 yds. on 245 rushes in nine games; also was scoring leader with 126 points. Tied record of two kickoff-return TDs in game vs. Fordham. Set season record average of 174.0 yds. rushing per game. Finished with career all-time rushing record of 3166 yds. on 547 plays in 30 games; averaged 105.5 yds. per game, scored 35 TDs. Won silver (1600-meter relay) and bronze (400-meter run) medals at Helsinki Olympics, 1952. Blinding speed in football uniform made him pure dynamite halfback. Had penchant for long sideline runs. Drafted on 1st round by Chicago Cardinals, 1952. Three years later led league in punt-return yardage with 245 on 13 attempts, in average yds. with 18.8, in TD punt returns with two. Pro Bowl Player of the Game, 1955. On 10/14/56 returned kickoff 105 yds. for TD vs. Washington Redskins. In 1959 traded to Los Angeles Rams for 9 players: Frank Fuller, Ken Panfil, Glenn Holtzmann, Art Hauser, John Tracey, Don Brown, two unnamed players and draft choice. Remained with Rams four years, then traded to Detroit Lions for guard Harley Sewell. In 1964 traded to Philadelphia Eagles, along with Floyd Peters, for J. D. Smith. Retired after 14 years in 1967, holding 2nd-best record in combined yardage with 12,844 yds. All-Pro, 1954, 55, 56, 57. Pro Football Hall of Fame.

MATTE, THOMAS R. (Kid) Running Back. B. 6/14/39, Pittsburgh, Pa. 6'1", 215. Ohio State, 1958-60. Son of pro hockey player. In 1960 accounted for 48 percent (1419 yds.) of Ohio State's total yardage. Named, as result, to All-Big 10 team. Baltimore Colts, 1961-72. Scored 57 TDs and rushed for 4619 yds. Played in two Pro Bowls, 1969, 70. Excellent competitor. Spent most of pro career as running back. In 1965 played quarterback three games when John Unitas and Gary Cuozzo were injured. In those games Matte engineered victory over Los Angeles Rams, lost Western Conference title match to Green Bay Packers, and then defeated Dallas Cowboys in Playoff Bowl. NFL championship games, 1964, 68. Super Bowl, 1969. Scored three TDs against Cleveland Browns to tie championship game record. During career rushed 1200 times for 4646 yds., 3.9 average, 45 TDs.

MATTHEWS, RAYMOND (Rags) End. B. 8/17/05, Ft. Worth, Tex. 180. Attended Texas Christian. All-SWC, 1926, 27. Was also All-Conference in basketball (guard) twice. One of first four Texans to play in East-West Shrine game at San Francisco, 1927. Tremendous defensive end, helping Southwest achieve its first national football recognition. Is now partner, Christensen-Matthews Production Co., Houston. National Football Foundation Hall of Fame.

MATUSZAK, JOHN Tackle. B. 10/25/50, Oak Creek, Wis. 6'8", 282. Began college career at Fort Dodge (Iowa) J.C. Sophomore tight end for Missouri's Dan Devine, 1969. Left Missouri after pleading guilty to common assault charge, stemming from fraternity party fight. Tampa defensive tackle and end, 1971-72. All-America, 1972. Pro football's No. 1 draft choice in 1973, taken by Houston Oilers. Magnificent physical specimen. Has 52-inch chest, wears size 50 suits. Cystic fibrosis claimed lives of brother and sister, currently afflicts another sister.

MAULBETSCH, JOHN F. (Johnny) Running Back. B. 6/20/1890, Ann Arbor, Mich. D. 9/14/50. 5'9", 165. Attended Adrian College before going to U. of Michigan. Wolverine halfback, 1914-16. All-America, 1914; captain, 1916. 1914 team was 6-3, which included heartbreaking 7-0 loss to Harvard despite Maulbetsch's 133 yds. from scrimmage. Coached Phillips U., 1917-20; Oklahoma State, 1921-28; Marshall, 1929-30. Quit coaching, 1930, to purchase drug store in Huntington, W.Va. Later owned auto dealership in Adrian, Mich. Died of cancer. John F. Maulbetsch Award is given annually to Michigan outstanding freshman player. National Football Foundation Hall of Fame.

MAUTHE, J. L. (Pete) Running Back. B. 7/8/1890, DuBois, Pa. D. 1/1/67. Penn State tailback, 1910-12. Captain in 1912. Nittany Lions outscored foes 484-12, 1911-12. Dropkicked 51-yd. FG, 1912. National Football Foundation Hall of Fame.

MAXWELL, ROBERT W. (Tiny) Tackle. B. 1884, Chicago, Ill. D. 6/30/22, Norristown, Pa. Gained football prominence at U. of Chicago, 1902; Swarthmore, 1904-05. Weight thrower, too. Photograph of Tiny, being pummeled by Penn players in 1905, changed face of football. President Theodore Roosevelt saw picture and was enraged. Ordered elder statesmen to legislate some order into game or face possibility of ban. Far-reaching reforms resulted in 1906, forward pass was introduced at same time. Maxwell, who stammered and ate voraciously, was often target of good-natured fun. Became noted official and sportswriter, winning admiration of Walter Camp. At time of his death, in car accident, Maxwell was sports editor of Philadelphia *Evening Public Ledger*. Maxwell Club formed to honor him, gives award annually to outstanding collegian. National Football Foundation Hall of Fame.

MAYNARD, DONALD (Sunshine) End. B. 1/25/37, Crosbyton, Tex. 6'1", 185. Attended Rice, then Texas (El Paso) where he was three-year star player. Appeared in Blue-Gray and Sun Bowl games. Holds two master's degrees. Selected as future on 9th round of 1957 draft. Signed with New York Giants, 1958. In 1959 signed with Hamilton Tiger-Cats of CFL. Year later became first player ever signed, as free agent, by AFL New York Titans (later Jets). Set AFL record, pass reception yds., career, with 10, 373. Also AFL championship game record for TD passes, game, with 2. Led league in TD pass receptions with 14,

1965. Two years later led league in yds. on pass receptions with 1436, in average yds. on pass receptions with 22.8. Caught 10 passes for record 228 yds., 1968 vs. Oakland Raiders. Caught 632nd pass of career in 1972, breaking Ray Berry's all-time record by one. On 9/10/73 traded by Jets to St. Louis Cardinals for draft choice. Made but one reception that season. Also all-time yardage receiving leader, having accumulated 11,834 yds. or about 6 2/3 miles' worth. AFL All-Star games following 1965, 67, 68 seasons. Co-MVP of 1968 game. NFL championship game, 1958; AFL championship game, 1968. Super Bowl, 1969. Pro Bowl, 1970. Holds distinction of being only man to play with Giants and Titans-Jets. In marketing and sales promotion for Farah Slacks.

MAYS, JERRY Defensive End. B. 11/24/39, Dallas, Tex. 6'4", 250. Southern Methodist tackle, 1958-60. Teammate of Don Meredith. Straight-A student in engineering despite fact he was married and father of three children. Dallas Texans, 1961-63; Kansas City Chiefs, 1964-69. Texans moved to Kansas City before 1964 season. Drafted on 5th round by Dallas. Started pro career at defensive tackle, made all-AFL there in 1962. Later converted to defensive end, becoming premier player. Was All-AFL at that position twice, 1967, 68. Played in Super Bowls I and III, 1967, 70. Texans-Chiefs won three AFL titles with Mays in lineup. Maneuverable, resourceful player. Now in construction business with his father, provides color on Chief radio broadcasts.

MEADOR, EDWARD Defensive Back. B. 8/10/37, Dallas, Tex. 5'11", 185. Graduated from Arkansas Tech, 1959. Los Angeles Rams, 1959-70. Rams considered him their best all-around player. Club's all-time leader in interceptions with 44, returned them 525 yds. Scored five career TDs on interceptions. Returned punts in 1967, 68. Pro Bowl, 1961, 65, 66, 68. All-Pro safety, 1967, 68.

MEADOWS, EDWARD (Country) Defensive End. B. 1932. Oxford, N.C. 6'2", 224. Played tackle at Duke. All-America, 1952, 53. Chicago Bears, 1954, 56-57; Pittsburgh Steelers, 1955; Philadelphia Eagles, 1958; Washington Redskins, 1959. Converted to end by George Halas. Remembered for controversial pummeling of Bobby Layne, Detroit Lion QB, in 1956 NFL title game. Layne was knocked senseless, leaving game with concussion. Detroit owner Edwin J. Anderson accused Meadows of "deliberately slugging" Layne and demanded immediate explusion from football. Films later vindicated Meadows, but Detroit's outrage was never quieted. Curiously, officials later banished Meadows from title game after he slugged Lion tackle Lou Creekmur.

MEEHAN, JOHN F. (Chick) Coach. B. 9/5/1893, Shelburne Falls, Mass. D. 1/9/72. Syracuse U. graduate, 1918. Coached Syracuse, 1920-24; NYU, 1925-31; Manhattan, 1932-34. Record: 115-44-14 (.705). At age 27 succeeded Orangemen's Buck O'Neill. Had excellent rivalry, close relationship with Pop Warner. "Pop Warner was like a father to me," said Meehan. Devoted to off-tackle play. Teams were always sound defensively, superiorly conditioned.

226

Handed Notre Dame its only setbacks of 1922 (14-6), 1923 (14-7). Latter game was only time "Four Horsemen," used as unit, ever tasted defeat. Coached NYU against Fordham in "Battle of the Bronx," 1928-31. Games were played before 55,000-to-70,000 at Polo Grounds and Yankee Stadium. At NYU developed "military shift" in which players used military cadence coming out of huddle. Notable products include Pappy Waldorf, Vic Hanson, Joe Alexander, Ken Strong. Citizens Savings Hall of Fame.

MERCER, E. LEROY Running Back. B. 10/30/1888, Kennett Square, Pa. D. 7/3/57. 6′, 175. Pennsylvania, 1910-12. 1910 team was Ivy League champion. All-America fullback, 1910, 12; 3rd-team halfback, 1911. Captain, 1911, 12. Playing record: 23-10-1. Member of U.S. Olympic track team, 1912. Won IC4A broad-jump title in 1912, 13. Graduated with M.D. degree. Physical education professor, Swarthmore; also athletic director, 1914-31. Served 22 years at Penn as dean of physical education department. Citizens Savings Hall of Fame, National Football Foundation Hall of Fame.

MERCER, MICHAEL Kicker. B. 11/21/35, Algona, Iowa. 6′, 200. Well-traveled college player, making stops at Minnesota, Florida State, Hardin-Simmons, Arizona State. Gypsy pro also — Minnesota Vikings, 1961-62; Oakland Raiders, 1963-66; Buffalo Bills, 1967-68; Green Bay Packers, 1968-69; San Diego Chargers, 1970. AFL FG leader with 21, 1966. Also did some punting. Averaged 55.3 yds. on four punts vs. San Diego Chargers, 1965. In 10-year career scored 594 points, on 288 PATs (223 attempts) and 112 FGs (219 attempts). AFL championship game, 1966. In subsequent Super Bowl I booted one FG, one PAT. Also did some punting. Father, Kenneth, played QB for Frankford Yellowjackets, 1927-29.

MEREDITH, JOE DON (Dandy Don) Quarterback. B. 1938, Mt. Vernon, Tex. 6′3″, 205. Played at Southern Methodist, 1957-59. All-America, 1959. Dallas Cowboys, 1960-68. Growing up, considered ministry and law for careers. Older brother B. J., played for TCU. Started pro career as rookie quarterback in rookie NFL city. Alternated with Eddie LeBaron until 1963, then took over as regular Dallas Cowboy. Suffered torturous times in early years and was often target of booing fans. Dallas failed to win single game in 1960, didn't reach .500 until 1965. Folksy and gregarious, Meredith also had difficult time winning over teammates who thought him lackadaisical. While playing would sing *I Didn't Know God Made Honky Tonk Angels*. Worked on self-discipline and really asserted leadership qualities in 1964. During that season suffered torn knee cartilage (gift from Ray Nitschke), separated shoulder, sprained ankle, bruised thigh, ruptured stomach muscle. Still managed to play all but two games and, in one stretch, to direct Cowboys to three straight victories. Coach Tom Landry said, "I have never seen such a display of courage. He did the job for us when no other quarterback in football would have walked on the field."

In last three seasons under Meredith, Cowboys compiled records of 10-3-1, 9-5, 12-2. Dallas lost to Green Bay in both 1966 and '67 championship games. 1967 contest, decided on quarterback sneak by Bart Starr, is remembered for weather elements. "I've been a few places in my life, pardner," Meredith said years later. "I've seen most of the country fairs, but I've never seen anything like that day." Temperature was 13 degrees below zero and 15-mile-per-hour wind made chill factor even lower. In career, Meredith completed 1170 of 2308 passes (50.7 percent) for 17,199 yds., 135 TDs. Also threw 111 interceptions. Cowboy leader in almost every all-time passing department. Twice passed for over 400 yds. in one game, including 460-yd. day against San Francisco 49ers, 1963. Pro Bowl, 1967, 69. Football's reigning poet-clown-philosopher retired in 1969. Year later he joined ABC-TV on *Monday Night Football* and won instant acclaim. Repartee with Howard Cosell entertained nation. Won Emmy for performance in 1972. Left ABC, 1974, to act in movies for NBC. Don Meredith no longer performs one-act plays and judges shrubs for FFA, like he did back in Mt. Vernon.

MERILLAT, LOUIS A., JR. End. B. Illinois. D. 4/26/48, Chicago, Ill. 5'9", 165. Army All-America, 1913. That was pivotal year in West Point football fortunes. On 11/1/13, Notre Dame and Army met for first time. Irish won, 35-13, behind aerial circus of Gus Dorais (QB) and Knute Rockne (end). Eastern football was thus exposed to passing attack successfully integrated into offense. Army was good pupil. In ensuing Navy clash Cadets used similar passing principles. Results were impressive: Army won 22-9, teams meeting in New York — at Polo Grounds — for first time. President Wilson and 40,000 fans attended. Merillat scored two TDs and set up another with 60-yd. run. Became famous pass combination with QB Vernon Prichard. Called "Forward Pass King." After graduating stayed on to coach Army ends. Canton Bulldogs, 1925. Served with AEF in World War I. Col., World War II.

MERRITT, JOHN A. Coach. B. 1/26/26, Kentucky. Attended Central H.S. of Louisville and Kentucky State College. Earned M.S. from U. of Kentucky. Coached Jackson State, 1953-62; Tennessee State, 1963-73. Lifetime record: 165-39-5. Tremendous success at Tennessee State. In 11 years Tigers won 93, lost 11, tied 2. In 1970-73 period, won 43 of 45 games. Named Black college Coach of the Year in 1973 as Tigers were ranked No. 1, won 10 straight games. Declined offer after that season to become first Black coach of major-college team — at Wichita State. Cited loyalty to Tennessee State coaching staff. Developed such players as Joe Gilliam, Eldridge Dickey, Verlon Biggs, Claude Humphrey, Ed (Too Tall) Jones. Jones was No. 1 draft choice of entire NFL, signing with Dallas Cowboys. Overall, 117 of Merritt's players drafted by pros.

MERZ, CURTIS Guard. B. 4/17/38, Newark, N.J. 6'4", 267. Defensive end at Iowa, 1957-59. Played in glory years of Forest Evashevski. All-America, 1958. Injured knee vs. Ohio State that year and had to undergo surgery at conclusion of season. Hawkeyes crushed Iowa, 38-12, in 1959 Rose Bowl. Dallas Texans, 1962; Kansas City Chiefs, 1963-68. AFL championship games, 1962, 66. Super Bowl. Now radio sportscaster with WDAF, Kansas City.

METCALF, TERRANCE R. (Terry) Running Back. B. 9/24/51, Seattle, Wash. 5'10", 185. Attended Everett (Wash.) J.C. and Long Beach State. Twice college-division All-America, 1971, 72. In 1971 gained 1673 yds. on 267 carries (6.0-yd. average). Also scored 29 TDs that year, establishing college-division record. Broke number of rushing marks held by Leon Burns. Suffered stretched Achilles tendon during 1972 but came back to score five TDs in final game. Won conference long-jump and triple-jump titles. Played in East-West Shrine, Coaches All-America (MVP), College All-Star games. St. Louis Cardinals, 1973.

MEYER, LEO R. (Dutch) Coach. B. 1/15/1898, Waco, Tex. Born of German parents, spoke no English until grade school. Texas Christian football letterman, 1916-17, 20-21. Accurate basketball set-shooter. Best sport was baseball. Might have been big-league pitcher except for ligament injury to pitching (right) arm. 30-4 record as TCU sophomore; played in minors. In 1934 replaced Francis Schmidt, who shifted to Ohio State, as TCU coach. Coached Frogs 19 years; 109-79-13 record. Developed 10 All-Americas. Best known were quarterbacks Sammy Baugh and Davey O'Brien, center Ki Aldrich. Used two split ends, two and later three wingbacks, to utilize Baugh and O'Brien. Nephew, Lambert, scored all TCU Cotton Bowl points in 1937 — 16 to Marquette's 7. 1938 club won national championship, was unbeaten in 11 games and defeated Carnegie Tech in Sugar Bowl (15-7). Became full-time athletic director, retiring 10 years later. Famous Meyer line to his troops: "Fight 'em until hell freezes over, and then fight 'em on the ice." Citizens Savings Hall of Fame, National Football Foundation Hall of Fame. Tabbed "Saturday Fox" and "Old Iron Pants."

MEYLAN, WAYNE A. Linebacker. B. 3/2/46, Bay City, Mich. 6'2", 225. Nebraska middle guard, 1965-67. Twice consensus All-America, 1966, 67. Played in Cotton Bowl, 1965, and Orange Bowl, 1966. Cornhuskers lost both games, to Arkansas (10-7) and Alabama (39-28) respectively. Linebacker in pros with Cleveland Browns, 1968-70, and Minnesota Vikings, 1971. Traded to New York Giants in 1970 but released to Vikings.

MICHAELS, LOUIS A. Defensive End-Kicker. B. Swoyersville, Pa. 6'2", 235. Kentucky tackle. Consensus All-America twice, 1956, 57. Later named to All-Time SEC team. Los Angeles Rams, 1958-60; Pittsburgh Steelers, 1961-63; Baltimore Colts, 1964-69; Green Bay Packers, 1971. Led NFL in FGs with 26, 1962. In 13-year career scored 386 PATs, 187 FGs, 1 safety for 977 points. Was 4th greatest scorer at retirement. NFL championship games, 1964, 68. Super Bowl, 1969. Pro defensive end. Brother of Walt, 12-year pro guard.

MICHAELS, WALTER Linebacker. B. 10/16/29, Swoyersville, Pa. 6', 230. Washington & Lee fullback and linebacker. Played with Green Bay Packers, 1951; Cleveland Browns, 1952-61; New York Jets, 1963. Was pro linebacker. Played on two NFL championship teams, 1954, 55. Brother, Lou, was defensive end and kicking specialist. Defensive coach, Oakland Raiders, 1962; New York Jets, 1963-72. Joined former Brown teammates, Mike McCormack and John

Sandusky, on Philadelphia Eagle coaching staff in 1973.

MICHALSKE, AUGUST (Mike) Guard. B. 4/24/03, Cleveland, Ohio, 210. Penn State. All-America, 1925. Joined AFL New York Yankees, 1926, team launched by promoter C. C. Pyle. League folded after one season, and New York joined NFL. Played with Yankees, 1926-28; Green Bay Packers, 1929-35, 37. Signed with Packers after Yankees folded, joining club same year with Johnny (Blood) McNally and Cal Hubbard. Packers were world champions Michalske's first three seasons. One of first to use blitz; he and Hubbard pioneered stunting. Played almost sixty minutes of every game. All-NFL, 1931, 35. Head coach, Iowa State, 1942-47. Assistant coach, Lafayette, St. Norbert, Baylor, Texas A. & M., Texas, Baltimore Colts. Pro Hall of Fame.

MICHIE, DENNIS M. Running Back. B. 4/10/1870, West Point, N.Y. D. 7/1/1898, San Juan, Cuba. 142. Prepped at Lawrenceville (Mass.) School. Army captain-coach in first Army-Navy game, 1890. Navy won, 24-0. Army won 1891 rematch, 32-16, as Henry L. Williams coached Cadets without remuneration. Michie and 1891 Navy foe, Worth Bagley, were killed in Spanish-American War. Army's Michie Stadium named in his honor.

MICKAL, ABE Running Back. B. 7/9/12, Talia, Syria. 5'10", 170. Louisiana State, 1933-35. Deadly passer, legend he could hit fly with pass at 100 paces. Excelled at long bomb. In 1933 hurled TD passes of 57, 48 yds. Part of Mickal-to-Tinsley aerial combination. Excellent runner, too. Threw 65-yd. TD pass to tie SMU, 14-14. During his three years, team compiled 20-6-5 record. Became surgeon. National Football Foundation Hall of Fame.

MIKE-MAYER, NICHOLAS Kicker. B. 3/1/50, Bologna, Italy. 5'8", 186. Father was famous Hungarian soccer player. Nick played little soccer, turning to American football as youngster. Went to Temple. Hit on 13 of 20 FGs, 24 of 26 PATs in 1972. Recorded 48-yd. FG against Villanova, 1971. Drafted No. 10 by Atlanta Falcons in 1973. Brilliant rookie year — made 26 of 38 FGs, 34 of 34 PATs. His 112 points were 4th best in NFL. Kicked five FGs to beat Los Angeles Rams, 15-13. Pro Bowl, 1974.

MILLER, CREIGHTON E. Running Back. B. 9/26/22, Cleveland, Ohio. 6', 188. One of eight in Miller family to play at Notre Dame. Millers, and Poes of Princeton, rate as football's most famous families. Creighton's father, M. Harry (Red) Miller, was star halfback and first of five brothers to matriculate at Notre Dame. Others were Ray, Walter, Donald, Jerold. Ray became mayor of Cleveland, while Donald, of "Four Horsemen" fame, rose to U.S. attorneyship. Creighton was independent and self-assured, refused football scholarship because dad (legal counsel for DuPont de Nemours Co.) could afford to pay tuition. Rebelled against Frank Leahy's strict discipline, but still made consensus All-America in 1943. Later, would be picked to Notre Dame's All-Time team. Some of campus escapades are legendary. He placed empty beer bottle in hand of

Father Sorin's statue. Once apologized to baldheaded priest (called "The Skull" by students) for "getting in your hair." After assisting both Notre Dame and Yale coaching staffs, joined Cleveland Browns in 1946. With Cleveland served as assistant coach, scout and legal counsel until 1953. Ohio assistant attorney general, 1949-50. Organized National Football League Players Association, 1956; was its legal counsel 13 years. Received L.L.B. degree from Yale, 1947; today practices law in Cleveland.

MILLER, DONALD Running Back. B. Defiance, Ohio. Notre Dame, 1922-24. One of five brothers, at least one of whom was at South Bend continuously for 20 years. Brother, Walter, teammate of George Gipp. One of "Four Horsemen," nickname coined by Grantland Rice for Notre Dame backfield of 1923-24. Probably most dangerous Horseman in open field. Averaged 6.8 yds. per carry, 1923. Senior class president. Won varsity letter in basketball. Providence Steamrollers, 1925. Father of seven, grandfather of 21. Currently judge in Cleveland, formerly U.S. attorney for Ohio, Northern District. Citizens Savings Hall of Fame, National Football Foundation Hall of Fame.

MILLER, EDGAR E. (Rip) Tackle. B. Canton, Ohio. Notre Dame, 1922-24. One of "Seven Mules" line which played in front of "Four Horsemen." 1924 Notre Dame regulars were polled to determine whether Mules or Horsemen were more important to national championship. Mules won, 7-4. First Mule in Hall of Fame. Strong both offensively and defensively. Opened many holes for Horsemen. Played high school football in Canton, Ohio, during greatest days of Canton Bulldogs. Bulldogs would practice on high school field, then stay and teach school's players. Miller's high school teams unscored upon for three years, outscoring opponents 268-0. After receiving Brian Kanaley Award at graduation from Notre Dame, became assistant coach at Indiana. Switched to Navy in 1926. Navy head coach, 1931-33. In 1933 led Navy to first victory Notre Dame. Developed six All-Americans. Currently Navy assistant athletic director. Not related to Notre Dame's famous Miller family. National Football Foundation Hall of Fame.

MILLER, FRED D. Tackle. B. 10/8/40, Homer, La. 6'3", 245. Louisiana State, 1960-62. Captained Charlie McClendon's first LSU team, 1962. Bengals finished 9-1-1, tripped Texas in Cotton Bowl. Baltimore Colts, 1963-72. Starter every year. Intelligent, always aggressive defensive tackle. NFL championship games, 1964, 68. Super Bowl, 1968, 71. Pro Bowl, 1968, 69, 70.

MILLER, WILLIAM End. B. 4/17/40, McKeesport, Pa. 6', 190. Quarterback and end at McKeesport H.S. Became permanent pass receiver in college at Miami (Fla.). In three seasons caught 93 aerials for 1456 yds. and 8 TDs, 1959-61. Consensus All-America, 1961; All-America, 1960. First Miami junior to win All-America football honors. As senior, favorite target of QB George Mira. Dallas Texans, 1962; Buffalo Bills, 1963; Oakland Raiders, 1964, 66-68. AFL championship games, 1967, 68. Super Bowl, 1968. Now owns Flanker Lounge in Miami.

MILLNER, WAYNE End. B. 1/13/13, Roxbury, Mass. 6'1", 190. Notre Dame, 1933-35. Consensus All-America, 1935. In 1935, vs. Ohio State, caught long pass from Bill Shakespeare for TD, inside last minute, to pull out 18-13 victory. Boston Redskins, 1936; Washington Redskins, 1937-41, 45. Roomed with Sammy Baugh. 1936 team was "Homeless Redskins." Played title game at Polo Grounds after owner George P. Marshall had spat with press. It attracted 58,285 who saw Packers beat Washington, 21-7. In 1937 championship game vs. Chicago Bears, Millner made 11 receptions, two for TDs. Asked how he ran so fast on TD receptions, he answered, "That's easy. You'd run fast, too, if you had those big devils chasing you." On 73-0 victory over Bears in 1940 title clash: "We beat them a few weeks before that game 7-3. They just took out the dash and made it 73." Served in U.S. Navy, 1942-44. Intended receiver on Baugh pass in 1945 title game against Cleveland Rams. Ball hit crossbar of goalpost and rebounded into end zone becoming safety for Rams. Rams won, 15-14; rules were changed following year to disallow such safeties. Played some exhibitions in 1946, but ordered by Marshall to become full-time assistant coach. Later assistant at Catholic U., Maryland, Baltimore Colts, Philadelphia Eagles. Briefly Eagle head coach in 1951. Now public relations director for auto dealer and part-time scout for Redskins. Citizens Savings Hall of Fame, Pro Football Hall of Fame.

MILSTEAD, CENTURY A. Tackle. B. 1/1/1900, Rock Island, Ill. D. 6/1/63. 6'4", 220. Named by father who maintained birth coincided with new century. His mother argued correctly, but to no avail, that 20th century wouldn't begin until 1/1/01. Transferred to Yale from Wabash in 1922. He and three other transfers, Mal Stevens, Lyle Richeson, Widdy Neale, figured prominently in Yale's 8-0 season, 1923. Team is considered Yale's greatest. Milstead and Ted Blair formed school's finest tackle combination. Played with New York Giants, 1925, 27-28; Philadelphia Quakers (AFL), 1926.

MINDS, JOHN H. (Jack) Running Back. B. 1871, Clearfield County, Pa. D. 12/31/63. 5'11", 180. Pennsylvania, 1894-97. All-America, 1897; 2nd team, 1895, 96. Captain, 1897. Credited with having made first placekick; kick was good. Played guard on "guards back" play. Great winning attitude. Specialty was coffin-corner kicking. Often used punt from running formation. Also excellent in delayed-pass plays, forerunner of "hidden ball." After graduation became Philadelphia lawyer. National Football Foundation Hall of Fame.

MINGO, EUGENE Running Back-Kicker. B. Denver, Colo. 6'1", 200. Didn't attend college. Denver Broncos, 1960-64; Oakland Raiders, 1964-65; Miami Dolphins, 1966-67; Washington Redskins, 1967; New Orleans Saints, 1967; Pittsburgh Steelers, 1969-70. AFL scoring leader in 1960 with 123 points. Repeated in 1962 with 137 points. FG leader with 18, 1960; in 1962 with 27. In 11-year career toed 215 PATs, 112 FGs for 629 points.

MIRA, GEORGE Quarterback. B. 1/11/42, Key West, Fla. 6', 190. Miami (Fla.), 1961-63. Olive-skinned passing wizard. Compiled 5125 yds. total offense at Miami, including 4623 rushing. All-America, 1962. Led major colleges with 2318 yds., 1963. Participated in 1961 Liberty, 1962 Gotham Bowls. In Gotham threw for 321 yds., two TDs against Nebraska. Played with San Francisco 49ers, 1964-68; Philadelphia Eagles, 1969; Miami Dolphins, 1971. After '71 season joined CFL.

MITCHELL, LYDELL Running Back. B. 5/30/49, Salem, N.J. 5'11", 204. Played basketball and football at Salem H.S. Junior, senior class president. Unanimous All-America at Penn State, 1971. Holds three NCAA records: points, season (174), TDs, season (29), TDs rushing, season (26). In 1972 Cotton Bowl carried 27 times for 146 yds. against Texas. Penn State won, 30-6. Penn State teammate of Franco Harris. Played with Baltimore Colts, 1972-73. Was 2nd-round draft choice.

MITCHELL, ROBERT C. (Bobby) End. B. 6/6/35, Hot Springs, Ark. 6', 195. Graduated from Illinois, 1958. Caught two TD passes as College All-Stars upset Detroit Lions, 35-19. Co-MVP with Jim Ninowski. Cleveland Browns, 1958-61; Washington Redskins, 1962-68. Rushed for 232 yds. vs. Redskins, 11/15/59. Traded to Washington for draft rights to Ernie Davis; thus became first Black Redskin. Led NFL receivers, 1962, with 72 catches for 1384 yds. and 11 TDs. Tied NFL mark with 99-yd. pass reception, 9-15-63. Led all flankers in yardage that season with 1436. Premier rusher-receiver. Extremely shifty with 9.5 speed. Pro totals: rushing — 513 attempts, 2735 yds., 5.3 average, 18 TDs; receiving — 521 receptions, 7953 yds., 15.3 average, 65 TDs; kickoff returns — 102, 2690 yds., 26.4 average, 5 TDs; punt returns — 69, 689 yds., 10.2 average, 3 TDs. Amassed 14,077 total yds., placing him 2nd only to Jim Brown. Pro Bowl, 1962, 63, 64, 65. Assistant director of scouting, Redskins.

MIX, RONALD J. Tackle. B. 3/10/38, Los Angeles, Calif. 6'4", 250. Mixed violence with acumen, which is why he was called "Intellectual Assassin." Southern California, 1957-59. Los Angeles Chargers, 1960; San Diego Chargers, 1961-69; Oakland Raiders, 1971-72. Originally drafted by Boston Patriots; who traded rights to Chargers. Great blocker; forte was extraordinary speed and explosiveness from stance. During one Charger game announcer reported, "I think I just saw Ron Mix take out three men! Is that possible?" It was; he did. Planned to play only two years, then retire to teach. Earned law degree from U. of San Diego. Authored articles for several sports magazines. All-AFL from 1960 thru '68. AFL All-Star games, 1962, 63, 64, 65, 67, 68, 69 seasons. AFL championship games, 1960, 61, 63, 64, 65. Now executive counsel with Chargers. Member All-Time AFL team.

MODELL, ARTHUR B. Owner. B. 6/23/25, Brooklyn, N.Y. Achieved boyhood dream of owning pro football team when he acquired Cleveland Browns in 1960. Put together syndicate which purchased franchise for

$3,925,000. Twenty years earlier had gone to work as electrician's helper at Bethlehem Steel Co. Was paid 47 cents per hour. Father, wine dealer, went broke during Depression. He died when Art was 14, leaving family penniless. After air force duty in World War II made mark in television and advertising. Sold ABC idea of installing custom-made TV sets in 200 large supermarkets in New York City area. Sold production company and partnership in ad agency to raise $500,000 down payment for Browns. Highly respected for personal involvement in NFL affairs. League president, 1967-70. Broke deadlock in merger meeting, 1969, by agreeing to switch Browns to AFC side. Married to Patricia Breslin, of television and film fame. Long way to top for Modell, but he made it.

MODZELEWSKI, RICHARD (Little Mo) Tackle. B. 2/16/31, West Natrona, Pa. 6'1", 260. Member of Maryland's 1951 club which defeated Tennessee, 28-13, in Sugar Bowl. All-America and winner Knute Rockne Trophy, 1952. Played with Washington Redskins, 1953-54; Pittsburgh Steelers, 1955; New York Giants, 1956-63; Cleveland Browns, 1964-66. Played on NFL championship teams, 1956, 64. At retirement had played 180 consecutive games. Brother Ed (Big Mo) was six-year NFL performer. Presently defensive line coach for Browns.

MOEGLE, RICHARD L. (Dicky) Running Back. B. Taylor, Tex. 6', 175. Star swimmer-diver, basketball, track, football performer at Taylor H.S. Wanted to attend SMU or TCU but they frowned on 150-pound frame. Rice was interested, and Moegle finally accepted school's scholarship bid. Played for Owls in 1952-54. Added poundage (25 pounds) and became 1954 consensus All-America. Prior to 1952 campaign stuck hand thru window while trying to open it in English class. Injury required 30 stitches and forced him to miss most of season. Averaged 7.3-yds. per carry to lead nation, 1953. Rushed for 905 yds. and scored 12 TDs, 1954. In 1955 Cotton Bowl victory (28-6) over Alabama, Moegle scored 3 TDs and made rushes of 79, 34, and 95 yds. Actually, Moegle never completed his 95-yd. run. Alabama fullback Tommy Lewis, frustrated at sight of Moegle running with clear field, jumped from bench and tackled flying Owl at Crimson Tide 41. Officials were not bemused and awarded Rice TD. Play is unsurpassed for uniqueness, excepting Roy Riegels' wrong-way run (1931 Rose Bowl), in major bowl history. Moegle's 95-yd. rush, 265 rushing yds. and 24.1-yds. per carry (11 carries) established major bowl records. Switched to defensive back in pros. Played with San Francisco 49ers, 1955-59; Pittsburgh Steelers, 1960; Dallas Cowboys, 1961.

MOFFAT, ALEXANDER Running Back-Kicker. B. 9/27/1862, Princeton, N.J. D. 2/23/14, New York, N.Y. Played halfback at Princeton, 1881-83. Captain, 1883. First of great kickers. "Here was a youth with wings on his heels," said John Heisman. "He could stop dead from a hard run and in that same moment boot the ball, frequently 65 yds." Alonzo Stagg wrote of him: "Moffat invented the spiral punt in 1881 and changed thereby the whole science of punting. He was the first of the great gridiron heroes of the Tiger." In 1883 kicked 16 FGs, 7 PATs,

234

scored 7 TDs. Against Harvard, in '83, Moffat kicked four FGs — two with his right foot and two with left. Successful in contracting-building business until death. National Football Foundation Hall of Fame.

MOLESWORTH, KEITH F. Quarterback. B. 10/20/06, Washington, D.C. D. 3/12/66. Monmouth College QB. Chicago Bears, 1931-37. In pro career rushed for 1705 yds. and scored 9 TDs, completed 83 of 213 passes for 1591 yds., 11 TDs. Returned eight punts in championship games, 2nd only to Willie Wood; tied NFL record with four in one game. 1931 Bears won playoff vs. Portsmouth, 9-0, for NFL title. Game was played indoors at Chicago Stadium because of bitter weather. Played in 1934 "Sneakers Game" at Polo Grounds, won 30-13 by New York Giants. New York trailed at halftime, 10-3 then wore basketball shoes 2nd half to overcome ice-caked playing field. Good idea as Giants easily made up halftime deficit for NFL crown. Coached Baltimore Colts, 1953 (3-9).

MONTGOMERY, CLIFFORD Quarterback. B. Natrona Heights, Pa. 167. Played at Natrona Heights H.S., later to produce George Barclay, brothers Modzelewski, Cookie Gilchrist. After year at Kiski Prep, went to Columbia to play under Lou Little in 1930. Columbia earned Rose Bowl invitation in 1934; Lions were rated "a bunch of high-school kids" against Stanford, but won 7-0. Captain and All-America, 1933. College All-Star game, 1934. Signed with Brooklyn Dodgers in 1934; had no-cut, no-trade contract. Endorsed line of helmets, also did advertisements. Teammate of Chris Cagle, Ralph Kercheval, Herman Hickman. Played with Dodgers only one year. Retired after injury to knee. National Football Foundation Hall of Fame.

MOOMAW, DONN D. Center. B. 10/15/31, Santa Ana, Calif. 6'4", 220. College: UCLA. Rev. Donn Moomaw has affected a lot of people — both on the field and in the pulpit he now occupies at Bel Air Presbyterian Church in Los Angeles. Was three-time All-America at UCLA, 1950, 51, 52. Consensus choice in 1952. Went thru entire collegiate career without being penalized. Named one of world's 10 greatest athletes by Stanley Woodward in "Who's Who in Sports," 1953. Although played only seven of 14-game schedule, was All-Pro Canada for Toronto Argonauts, 1954. Named one of state's five outstanding young men by California Junior Chamber of Commerce. Received B.S. degree from UCLA; B.D. from Princeton Theological Seminary; D.D. from Sterling College in Kansas. Is youngest member of National Football Foundation Hall of Fame. Also has niche in Citizens Savings Hall of Fame. Popular, dynamic minister.

MOORE, ANDREW C., JR. (Scrappy) Coach. B. 9/25/02. D. 5/3/71, Chattanooga, Tenn. Georgia, 1923-25. Played under George (Kid) Woodruff. Coached Tennessee (Chattanooga) 35 years, 1931-42; 45-67. Record: 172-146-13. Made moccasins power among small colleges. College-division Coach of the Year, 1967. Retired as Chattanooga athletic director in 1970. Citizens Savings Hall of Fame.

MOORE, BERNICE H. Coach. B. 4/30/1894, Jonesboro, Tenn. D. 11/6/67, Winchester, Tenn. Graduated from Carson-Newman, 1917. Son of Baptist minister. Saw front-line combat in World War I. Coached Mercer, 1925-27, and Louisiana State, 1935-47. Co-National champion, 1936. Record: 95-51-8, including 83-39-6 at LSU. Developed such players as Phoney Smith and Wally Butts of Mercer; Gaynell Tinsley, Steve Van Buren and Ken Kavanaugh of LSU. Sent five Bengal teams to bowls: three Sugar, 1936-38; Orange, 1944; Cotton, 1947. 1-3-1 bowl record, winning only Orange, 19-14 over Texas A. &. M. Won 12 SEC track titles in 15 years. In 1933 captured NCAA championship with five-man team. While not coaching was avid bird hunter, enjoyed farming and raising stock. Was czar of SEC sports; served as league commissioner, 1948-66. National Football Foundation Hall of Fame.

MOORE, DERLAND Defensive End. B. 10/7/51, Malden, Mo. 6'4", 250. Oklahoma, 1970-72. Played in three bowl games (two Sugar, one Astro-Bluebonnet). All-Big 8, All-America, winner Oklahoma's Gomer Jones Award as best lineman, 1972. Went to college on track (shot-put) scholarship. Business education major. Mobile, good speed. Drafted on 1st round by New Orleans Saints, 1973.

MOORE, LEONARD (Lenny) Running Back. B. 11/25/33, Reading Pa. 6'0", 190. Penn State, 1953-55. Led NCAA in average yds. gained per rush with 8.0, 1954. In 18 collegiate games rushed for 2380 yds., average of 6.2 per carry. Drafted by Baltimore Colts in 1956, and immediate star. Suffered head injury in 1961, broken kneecap in '62, damaged ribs in '63. Emergency appendectomy and dizzy spells kept him out of last five games of 1963 season. Nearly traded; however, in 1964 was switched from wide flanker to tight halfback and made stirring comeback. Set NFL record with 20 TDs that season and led league with those 120 points. Carried 157 times and gained 584 yds. Caught 21 passes for 472 yds., totaling 1046 yds. overall. Won Jim Thorpe Trophy. Holds many Colt scoring records: points, game, with 24 thrice; points, season, with 120; points, lifetime, with 678; TDs, game, with 4 thrice; TDs, season, with 20; TDs, lifetime, with 113. Retired after 1967 season. Spent all 11 years with Colts. Pro Bowl, 1959, 60, 61, 62, 64. All-NFL, 1958, 59, 60, 61, 64. NFL championship games, 1958, 59.

MORAN, CHARLES B. (Uncle Charley) Coach. B. 2/22/1879, Nashville, Tenn. D. 6/13/49. Attended Tennessee. Head coach, Texas A.& M., 1909-14; Centre, 1919-23; Bucknell, 1924-26; Catawba, 1930-33. Co-coach Frankford Yellowjackets, 1927. College record: 122-33-12. His A. & M. teams were 38-8-4, outscoring foes 1091-190. Won national acclaim at Centre where "Praying Colonels" compiled 42-6-1 record. Included was stunning 6-0 upset of Harvard, 1921. Pitcher and catcher for National League St. Louis Browns, 1903, 08. N. L. umpire, 1916-39. Citizens Savings Hall of Fame.

MORIN, MILT Tight End. B. 10/15/42, Leominster, Mass. 6'4", 236.

Graduated from Massachusetts, 1966. Played with Cleveland Browns, 1966-73. Aggressive blocker, pass catcher. Recorded longest catch in Brown history with 87-yarder, 1968. Suffered herniated disc but made speedy recovery following surgery, 1969. Pro Bowl, 1969, 72. Cleveland coach Nick Skorich labels Morin "a devastating man in the secondary, like a wild bull on the rampage."

MORLEY, WILLIAM R. Running Back. B. 1877, New Mexico. D. 5/27/32, Pasadena, Calif. 5'10", 166. Columbia, 1900-02. All-America, 1900; 3rd team, 1901. Tremendously effective on short gains, as defender and for running interference. Member of Columbia's "chain-lightning backfield" of 1899, with Harold Weekes, that defeated Yale for first time. Weekes became noted for line hurdling, only briefly due to danger involved. Morley succeeded George F. Sanford as Columbia coach.

MORRALL, EARL E. Quarterback. B. 5/17/34, Muskegon, Mich 6'2", 210. Attended Muskegon H.S. and Michigan State. 19-8 Michigan State playing record, 1953-55. Passed for 2016 yds. punted 56 times for 39.2 yd. average. Played in two Rose Bowls, 1954, 56. Michigan State won both over UCLA. Played with San Francisco 49ers (1st-round draft choice), 1956; Pittsburgh Steelers, 1957; Detroit Lions, 1959-64; New York Giants, 1965-67; Baltimore Colts, 1968-71; Miami Dolphins, 1972-73. Stepped in for injured John Unitas, 1968, leading Colts to Super Bowl engagement while winning Jim Thorpe Trophy. In 1972 gave repeat performance at Miami — stepped in for injured Bob Griese and led Dolphins into Super Bowl. 1968 was best year as he passed for 2909 yds. and 26 TDs. Father of five: Matthew Earl, Mardi Jane, Mindi Rae, Mitchell, Meghan.

MORRIS, EUGENE (Mercury) Running Back. B. 1/5/47, Pittsburgh, Pa. 5'10", 190. At Pittsburgh's Avonworth H.S., lettered in football, baseball, basketball. Gained 3338 yds. for West Texas State, 1966-68. Total was all-time NCAA best until surpassed by Steve Owens. Ranked 2nd nationally in rushing junior and senior seasons. Scored 252 collegiate points. Played in same West Texas State backfield with Duane Thomas. Rushed for even 1000 yds., scored club record 12 TDs for world champion Miami Dolphins, 1972. Tremendous outside threat, giving Miami great combination with powerful Larry Csonka. Also capable running inside. Relinquishes pass-catching duties to Jim Kiick. Selected for Pro Bowl, following 1971, 72, 73 seasons.

MORRIS, LAWRENCE C. (Larry) Linebacker. B. 12/10/33, Decatur, Ga. 6'2", 230. Georgia Tech, 1952-54. Played in 1952 Orange Bowl, '53 and '54 Sugar Bowl, '55 Cotton Bowl. All-SEC center, 1952, 53, 54. Consensus All-America, 1954. All-SEC in baseball, 1954. Pro linebacker with Los Angeles Rams, 1955-57; Chicago Bears, 1959-65; Atlanta Falcons, 1966. Bears had tremendous linebacking trio of Bill George, Joe Fortunato, Morris. Chicago won NFL title in 1963, defeating New York Giants, 14-10. In title game Morris intercepted two passes for 83 yds., including 61-yarder. Now owns land development company in Atlanta.

MORTON, CRAIG L. Quarterback. B. 2/5/43, Flint, Mich. 6'4", 214. Raised in Campbell, Calif. All-State football, basketball, baseball player. Passed for 4501 yds., 36 touchdowns at U. of California, 1962-64. Threw 5 TD passes against San Jose State, 1963. All-America, 1964. Drafted on 1st round by Dallas Cowboys, 1965. Passed for 2619 yds., 21 TDs, 1969. Broke Don Meredith's Cowboy completion record with 185, 1972. Had surgery on passing (right) arm following 1969, 70 seasons. Morton and Roger Staubach gave Cowboys excellent QB tandem. Bachelor. Partner in Wellington's, Dallas restaurant-lounge.

MORTON, WILLIAM H. (Air Mail) Quarterback. B. 9/17/09, New Rochelle, N.Y. 5'11", 178. Top runner, punter, passer, placekicker. 19/6/2 playing record at Dartmouth, 1929-31. All-America, 1931. Same season engineered rally to tie Yale, 33-33. Dartmouth trailed 33-10 when Morton told teammates, "Come on fellers, we only need three touchdowns and a field goal to beat 'em." Morton accounted for one TD pass, two FGs and three conversions, but missed on one PAT that would have won game. Pop Warner gave following praise: "Bill never knows when he's down, and his hard-running, twisting and pivoting causes an opponent plenty of anxiety." National Football Foundation Hall of Fame. President, American Express Co., 1968-73.

MOSES, HAVEN End. B. 7/27/46, Los Angeles, Calif. 6'3", 208. Little All-America, at San Diego State 1967. Played in East-West Shrine, Coaches All-America, College All-Star, Senior Bowl games. Buffalo Bills (No. 1 draft choice), 1968-72; Denver Broncos, 1972-73. Traded to Denver for wide receiver Dwight Harrison. Pro Bowl, 1974. Likes motorbikes, horseback riding.

MOTLEY, MARION Running Back. B. 6/5/20, Leesburg, Ga. 6'2", 235. Attended McKinley H.S. in Canton, Ohio. Lost only three games in three years. Defeats were all to Massillon, coached by Paul Brown. Motley impressed Brown and subsequently played for him with Great Lakes Naval Training Station and Cleveland Browns. In 1945, Motley starred in Great Lakes' 39-7 upset of Notre Dame. Previously had attended U. of Nevada. Gained 4712 yds. rushing and scored 31 TDs for Brown and Cleveland Browns, 1946-53. Unable to play due to knee injury, 1954. Following season failed in comeback bid with Pittsburgh Steelers. Browns won four AAFC and two NFL titles with Motley at fullback. All-time AAFC rusher with 3024 yds. on 489 carries; scored 31 TDs. AAFC rushing leader, 1947; NFL leader, 1950. Tremendously strong, possessed sprinter's speed. Devastating on trap play, which became known as "Motley trap." Effectiveness limited somewhat by fact that Brown ran him only inside, failing to capitalize on great outside speed. Often compared with Jim Brown. All-Pro fullback, 1950. Pro Football Hall of Fame.

MUDD, HOWARD E. Guard. B. 2/10/42, Midland, Mich. 6'2", 254. Attended Michigan State and Hillsdale College. Drafted by San Francisco 49ers, 1964. 49ers, 1964-69; Chicago Bears, 1969-70. All-Pro, 1968. Pro Bowl, 1969, 70. Knee injury forced retirement. Assistant coach at California, 1973.

MUL-KEY, HERBERT Running Back. B. 11/15/49, Atlanta, Ga. 6', 190. Great success story. Had no collegiate experience but attended Washington Redskins free agent tryout camp in 1972. Impressed Redskins, and was signed. Made phenomenal debut, subbing for Larry Brown, vs. Dallas Cowboys in next-to-last game of '72. Rushed for 60 yds. on 8 carries, caught 2 passes for 38 yds., returned 6 kickoffs for 173 yds. Total production: 271 yds. NFC's 2nd-leading kickoff returner in 1973, averaging 28.1 yds. on 36 chances. One went for 97 yds. Extremely fast, dangerous. Named to Pro Bowl, 1974.

MULLER, HAROLD P. (Brick) End. B. 6/12/01, Dunsmuir, Calif. D. 5/17/62. 6'1", 190. California, 1920-22. Major role in success of "Wonder Teams." All-America, 1921, 22; 3rd team, 1920. Could throw football 60 yds. on line. Swift end. Brought West Coast football into national limelight. Threw 55-yd. TD pass against Ohio State in 1921 Rose Bowl. Also played in 1922 Rose Bowl. Scored winning TD in 1925 East-West Shrine game. Never played losing collegiate game, winning 27 and tying one. Los Angeles Buccaneers, 1926. Later was orthopedic surgeon in Berkeley. During World War II served in Army Medical Service as Maj. Team physician for U.S. Olympic team, 1956. Citizens Savings Hall of Fame, National Football Foundation Hall of Fame.

MUNN, CLARENCE L. Coach. B. 9/11/08, near Minneapolis, Minn. Graduated from Minnesota, 1932. Consensus All-America guard, 1931. Twice Minnesota MVP, 1930, 31. Was punishing lineman. Had sprinter's speed — in 10-flat 100 range — belying size. Played at 5'11", 217. Sometimes ran and sometimes kicked from punting position, both with great skill, which made him extremely dangerous. Assistant coach at Minnesota, 1932-35; Syracuse, 1936; Michigan, 1938-45. Head coach at Albright, 1936-37, Syracuse, 1946; Michigan State, 1947-53. Compiled 54-9 record with Spartans. 1951, 52 teams were unbeaten. Named Coach of the Year, 1952. Michigan State athletic director since 1954. In 1956 received *Sports Illustrated* Silver Anniversary All-America Award. Voted Minnesota Outstanding Achievement Alumni Award, 1957. Also Honorary Alumnus of Michigan State. Member of both Minnesota and Michigan sports halls of fame. Director, past president of Fellowship of Christian Athletes. National Football Foundation Hall of Fame.

MUNSON, WILLIAM A. Quarterback. B. 8/11/41, Sacramento, Calif. 6'2", 210. Attended Foothill (Calif.) J.C. and Utah State. Rewrote USU record book, threw fewest interceptions (three) nationally in 1964. Played in East-West Shrine and Senior Bowl games. Los Angeles, Rams, 1964-67, and Detroit Lions, 1968-73. Best season, 1968, set Lion record of 181 completions while throwing for 2311 yds., 15 TDs. Traded to Detroit for Milt Plum, Tommy Watkins, Pat Studstill. In 10 seasons hit 772 of 1454 passes, compiling 1454 yds. and 65 TDs. Due to knee injury saw action in only two games in 1972.

MURPHY, BILLY J. (Spook) Coach. B. 1/13/21, Lorenzo, Tex. Mississippi State tailback, 1941, 42, 46. Assistant coach Memphis State, 1947-51; Mississippi

State, 1952-53; Minnesota, 1954-57. Worked under Murray Warmath at both Mississippi State and Minnesota. Memphis State head coach, 1958-71. Record: 91-44-1. Won three MVC titles and 28-9 decision in 1971. Pasadena Bowl. Established Tigers as Southern football power. MVC Coach of the Year thrice. Memphis State athletic director, 1966-73. Served with USMC, 1943-46. Recommended for Bronze Star.

MURPHY, GEORGE L. Administrator. B. 7/4/02, Donora, Pa. Former President of National Football Foundation. U.S. senator from California, 1965-71. Played freshman football at Yale. Shares same hometown, Donora, with Stan Musial. Son of Mike Murphy, first U.S. Olympic track coach of Yale and Penn fame. In 1934, after working as coal miner, toolmaker and Wall Street runner, embarked upon Broadway-movie career, appearing in six Broadway shows, including *Of Thee I Sing,* lampoon of politics. Countless films. Head of Screen Actors Guild two terms. Served as first vice president of Academy of Motion Arts and Sciences. Also studio executive. Won one Oscar. During Eisenhower administration headed USIA.

MURRAY, FRANCIS J. (Frank) Coach. B. 2/12/1885, Maynard, Mass. D. 9-12/51, Milwaukee, Wis. Attended Tufts College. Never played organized football, yet recognized as one of game's outstanding students. Served two stints at Marquette, 1922-36; 46-49. Sandwiched was nine-year sojourn at Virginia, 1937-45, where he developed William (Bullet Bill) Dudley. Marquette unbeaten three seasons under Murray, and 1936 Warriors went to Cotton Bowl. They lost to Texas Christian, 14-7, but it was still school's greatest moment. Murray's early Marquette teams were labeled "Singing Hilltoppers" because he led players in song before games. Exponent of flanker and spread formations, always emphasizing passing. Overall record: 145-89-11. As far back as 1930 directed team by remote control — via telephone from press box. Marquette, thanks to Murray, was once football proud — but no more. Warriors don't even field intercollegiate team. Citizens Savings Hall of Fame.

MURRAY, WILLIAM D. Coach. B. 9/9/08, Rocky Mount, N.C. Won All-Southern acclaim as Duke halfback. School's MVP, 1931. Was student president; held membership in ODK, national leadership fraternity, and Red Friars, Duke's highest honorary society for men. Received Robert E. Lee Award as outstanding member of '31 graduating class. Coached Delaware, 1940-42, 46-50. Record: 51-17-3. Performance earned him invitation to return to Duke. Coached Blue Devils, 1951-65. Despite difficult schedule compiled 93-51-9 record. Highlights were Orange Bowl and Sugar Bowl wins, seven conference championships. Eight of last 13 Duke teams finished in top 20 in wire service polls. For 15 years Murray was guiding force behind AFCA Ethics Committee. Recipient of coveted Amos Alonzo Stagg Award. Citizens Savings Hall of Fame, National Football Foundation Hall of Fame.

MUSSO, GEORGE F. (Moose) Tackle-Guard. B. Edwardsville, Ill. 6'2", 225.

Participated in football, basketball, baseball, track at Millikin. Played left tackle, 1929-32. Captain, 1932. Chicago Bears, 1933-44. In 1933, number of players besides Musso began fine careers with Bears. Among them: Jack Manders (Minnesota), Bill Karr (West Virginia), Gene Ronzani (Marquette). Musso was All-Pro, 1935. Played on four world championship teams and three other divisional winners. Tackle until 1937, when he moved to guard. Coach George Halas was so pleased with adjustment that he called Musso "the greatest guard in professional football ranks." NAIA Hall of Fame. In 1958 elected sheriff of Madison County, Ill.

MUSSO, JOHNNY Running Back. B. Birmingham, Ala. 5'11", 194. Alabama, 1969-71. Consensus All-America, 1971. All-SEC tailback, 1970, 71. Played in Coaches All-America and Senior Bowl games. Received National Football Foundation Scholar-Athlete Award, 1971. Rushed more times (2741), scored more points (232), scored more TDs (38), scored more TDs rushing (34), gained more yardage rushing (2741) than any Alabama player in history. Rushed 42 times for 221 yds. vs. Auburn, 1970. Put some Italian *pzazz* into 'Bama's offense in 1971. After 6-5 years in 1969, 70, Musso spearheaded '71 record of 11-1. Only setback, to Nebraska, occurred in Orange Bowl. After graduation Musso elected to play Canadian football.

MYHRA, STEVEN Guard-Kicker. B. 4/2/34, Wahpeton, N.D. Attended U. of North Dakota. Baltimore Colts, 1957-61. Led NFL in FGs with 21, 1961. NFL championship games, 1958, 59. In '58 game booted 20-yd. FG with seven seconds left to tie New York Giants, 17-17, and force sudden-death overtime. Colts eventually won on Alan Ameche's TD. Kicked eight PATs vs. Green Bay Packers, 1958. Scored in 55 straight games. In career toed 180 PATs.

MYLIN, EDWARD E. (Hooks) Coach. B. 10/23/1894, Leaman Place, Pa. Graduated from Franklin & Marshall. Coached Lebanon Valley, 1923-33; Bucknell, 1934-36; Lafayette, 1937-42, 46; NYU, 1947-49. Lafayette undefeated in 1937 (8-0), 1940 (9-0). Coach of the Year, 1937. Citizens Savings Hall of Fame, National Football Foundation Hall of Fame.

MYSLINSKI, CASIMIR J. Center. B. 3/6/20, Steubenville, Ohio. 5'11", 186. Army letterman, 1942-43. Unanimous All-America, Knute Rockne Trophy, Army captain, 1943. Earned B.S. degree (engineering education) from Columbia. Headed physical education departments at Army and Air Force Academy. Named athletic director at U. of Pittsburgh, 1968. He said, "Pitt athletics belong on top. We intend to be major league, and we intend to win." His first year Pitt athletic teams compiled 81-63-2 record (.563), school's best in 11 years.

NAGURSKI, BRONISLAW (Bronko) Running Back. B. 11/30/08, Rainy River, Ont., Canada. 6'3", 238. Football's Paul Bunyan. "He's the only man I've ever seen who runs his own interference," commented serious George Halas. Tackle and fullback at Minnesota, 1927-29. Lost only four times in 24-game career, by total of five points. Consensus All-America, 1929. As pro, 1930-37, 43 with Chicago Bears, used almost exclusively at fullback. Bears won NFL titles in 1932, 33, 43. Nagurski certainly made no big money. When he hinted retirement in 1937, at height of fame, Chicago boosted pay to $5000. Quit when club refused his $6000 demand for 1938. Nearing 35, he was coaxed out of retirement in 1943 for one final fling. In prime inspired player, powerful, numb to pain. Beneath good-natured and undemonstrative exterior lurched smouldering volcano ready to erupt. Advisable not to arouse him. Tremendously storied athlete. In 1936, two members of Pittsburgh Pirates tried to stop Nagurski from reaching end zone. One suffered broken shoulder and other knocked cold. In game vs. Portsmouth Spartans went 45 yds. for winning TD, play ending as Nagurski collided with goalpost and caromed into brick wall at Chicago's Wrigley Field. "The last guy hit me awful hard," said Bronko after he was revived. Claimed plowing produced his well-developed muscles. "But plowing is commonplace among country boys," it was pointed out by teammate. "Every farmer's boy has done plowing." "Yes," Bronko answered, "but not without horses?"

Elected to Pro Football Hall of Fame in 1963 but didn't receive official ring until year later. Reason for delay was that L. G. Balfour Co. had never made size 19½ ring. Balfour officials maintain it is largest ring ever made in America. Most of life spent in frigid clime of International Falls, Minn. Son, Bronko Jr., played for Notre Dame and then in CFL. All-Pro, 1932, 33, 34. Tackle on Modern All-Time All-America team. Citizens Savings Hall of Fame, National Football Foundation Hall of Fame, Pro Football Hall of Fame.

NALLEY, LEE Running Back. B. 1925, Nashville, Tenn. 5'9", 163. Attended Vanderbilt, 1947-49. Playing record of 19-11-1. Specialized as punt returner. In career returned 109 punts for 1695 yds., averaging 15.5. National leader in 1948, 49. His 791 yds. in 1949 and career total of 1695 are still NCAA records. Formerly held national mark for punt-return yds., game, with 203 vs. Kentucky in 1948. Rushed only twice during career, gaining eight yds.

NAMATH, JOSEPH W. (Broadway Joe) Quarterback. B. 5/31/43, Beaver Falls, Pa. 6'2", 200. Joe Namath made trip to football immortality via Beaver Falls H.S., U. of Alabama and New York Jets. En route he earned some critics, mainly for lifestyle reasons, but even they couldn't deny Joe's ability to throw football. Bad knees, beautiful women, big cars, bright lights, strong beverage, were all part of Namath legend and he promoted it with flair. "If you've got it, flaunt it," said Namath in television commercial. 27-3-0 playing record at Alabama, 1962-64. Completed 203 of 373 passes (54.4 percent) for 2714 yds. and 25 TDs. Bear Bryant, Alabama coach, called him "the greatest athlete I've ever coached." Bryant gave no quarter though, suspending Namath for final regular season game of 1963 and subsequent Sugar Bowl for breaking training rules. Did play in Orange Bowl twice, 1963, 65. MVP of '65 Orange Bowl on eve of signing with New York Jets. Was drafted on 1st round by Jets and NFL St. Louis Cardinals. Signed for $427,000 package. His joining AFL helped hasten merger between two pro leagues. Rookie of the Year, 1965. Led AFL in four passing categories in 1966: attempts (471); completions (232); yds. (3379); interceptions (27). Four more in 1967: attempts (491); completions (258); yds. (4007, all-time record); average gain (8.16). Directed Jets to 16-7 upset victory over Baltimore Colts in Super Bowl III, 1969. Win had been brazenly predicted by Namath.

After 1968 campaign received almost every conceivable award, including Hickok Belt, AFL MVP, Super Bowl MVP, George Halas Award as most courageous player. In spring of 1969 ordered by commissioner Pete Rozelle to sell interest in Bachelors III, bistro on Manhattan's East Side, because it was frequented by gamblers. Namath refused, and in tears, announced retirement. It was renounced six weeks later as he consented to Rozelle's demand. Tossed for 496 yds. vs. Baltimore, 9/24/72. Holder of Super Bowl game record for pass completions (17). Thru 1973 completed 1374 of 2738 passes for 21,065 yds. and 131 TDs; was intercepted 149 times. MVP of 1965 AFL All-Star game; co-MVP, 1967. Pro Bowl, 1973. All-AFL, 1968. All-AFC, 1972. Three movie credits: *Norwood, C.C. and Company, The Last Rebel.* Had TV show syndicated in 1969, and '70. Autobiography — *"I Can't Wait Until Tomorrow Cause I Get Better Looking Every Day —* not well received. Had four major knee operations. Joe's football future rests on those fragile limbs.

NANCE, JAMES S. (Bo) Running Back. B. 12/30/42, Indiana, Pa. 6', 235.

Graduate of Indiana H.S. and Syracuse U. Twice NCAA wrestling champion, losing only once in 92 matches during three-year career, 1962-64. 20-11 playing record for football Orangemen. Pro with Boston Patriots, 1965-70; New England Patriots, 1971; New York Jets, 1973. Signed with Jets after sitting out 1972 season. Set seven AFL records, including most rushing yds. (1458) and carries (299). Gained over 100 yds. rushing eight times in one season, 1966. League's leading rusher twice, 1966, 67. AFL Player of the Year, 1966. High on all-time pro rushing list with 6001 yds. AFL All-Star game, 1968. All-AFL, 1966, 67.

NAUMOFF, PAUL P. Linebacker. B. 7/3/45, Columbus, Ohio. 6'1", 215. Attended Eastmoor H.S. in Columbus. Played three positions in three seasons at U. of Tennessee, 1964-66. Wide receiver as sophomore, defensive end as junior, linebacker as senior. Consensus All-America, 1966. Detroit Lions, 1967-73. Although one of NFL's smallest linebackers, Naumoff has been Detroit regular since late in rookie season.

NEALE, EARLE (Greasy) Coach. B. 11/5/1891, Parkersburg, W. Va. D. 11/2/73, Lake Worth, Fla. Acquired nickname from boyhood friend who caught Earle eating bread with butter oozing over his face. Liked games of all types. Worthy competitor in football, basketball, baseball, golf, bridge. Played three sports at West Virginia Wesleyan, 1912-14. End in football. Led Wesleyan to three straight wins over West Virginia. As sophomore against Mountaineers, he caught 14 straight passes. Played outfield seven years for Cincinnati Reds. Batted .357 in infamous 1919 World Series. "I never realized Chicago [White Sox] was throwing the Series," Greasy said. Saw last football action at age 39, with Irontown (Ohio) team that became Detroit Lions. Coached college football at alma mater, Washington & Jefferson, Marietta, Muskingum, Virginia, West Virginia and Yale (assistant). His W. & J. club surprised California "Wonder Team" with 0-0 tie, 1922. Head coach, Philadelphia Eagles, 1941-50; in '43 he was co-coach with Walter Kiesling of merged Eagles-Pittsburgh Steelers wartime team. 63-43-5 pro record. Won Eastern Division title, 1947, and two world championships, 1948, 49. Tutored two superstar backs: Clint Frank (Yale) and Steve Van Buren (Eagles). Responsible for many innovations — five-man defensive line, man-to-man pass defense, fake and triple reverse. National Football Foundation Hall of Fame, Pro Football Hall of Fame.

NEELY, JESS C. Coach. B. 1/4/1898, Smyrna, Tenn. End and halfback for Vanderbilt's Dan McGugin, 1920-22. Lost one game in playing career — to Iowa in 1921. Captained 1922 team that was tied only by Michigan. Head coach at Southwestern College (Tenn.), 1924-27; Clemson, 1931-39; Rice, 1940-66. Participated in seven bowl games (six at Rice), winning four. His last Clemson eleven, starring Banks McFadden, edged Frank Leahy-coached Boston College, 6-3, in Cotton Bowl. Ten years later his Rice Owls romped over North Carolina in Cotton Bowl, 27-13. That 10-1 team starred Tobin Rote and Froggie Williams, and is rated with best in Southwest history. Neely's last Cotton victory was 28-6 verdict over Alabama in 1954; Dicky Moegle stunned Crimson Tide with 265-yd.

effort. Overall record was 207-176-19. Could have been much better except for some lean years his final decade at Rice. One of most respected men in coaching profession. Was voted Amos Alonzo Stagg Award for long and distinguished service. Returned to Vanderbilt as athletic director after retiring from coaching. Resigned to life of leisure in 1971. Citizens Savings Hall of Fame, National Football Foundation Hall of Fame.

NEELY, RALPH E. Tackle. B. 9/12/43, Little Rock, Ark. 6'6", 265. Attended Farmington (N.M.) H.S. Played football and basketball as prep. 22-7-1 playing record at U. of Oklahoma, 1962-64. Consensus All-America, 1964. Dallas Cowboys, 1965-73. Pro Bowl, 1967, 69. Moved from right to left offensive tackle, making room for Rayfield Wright in Cowboy line in 1970. Started 13 games despite broken hand, 1972.

NELSEN, WILLIAM K. Quarterback. B. 1/29/41, Los Angeles, Calif. Attended El Rancho H.S. in Pico Rivera, Calif., and Cerritos J.C. in Norwalk, Calif. With Nelsen at quarterback Cerritos averaged 46 points per game, 1958. Southern California, 1960-62. Earned starting job as sophomore after beating Fran Tarkenton and Georgia, 10-7. Shared duties last two seasons with Pete Beathard. Both Nelsen and Beathard became starting pro quarterbacks. Member of Trojans' national championship team, 1962. Played for Pittsburgh Steelers, 1963-67, and Cleveland Browns, 1968-72. At Cleveland overcame bad knees and reputation for erratic play. Led Browns to Eastern Conference titles first two years. In pro career completed 963 of 1905 passes for 14,164 yds. and 98 TDs. Pro Bowl, 1970. Completed 13 straight passes, 12/18/66, and again, 9/17/67, to tie NFL record. Threw only one interception in 1966 season, setting NFL mark. Season interception percentage, 0.89 in 1966, also pro record.

NELSON, ALBERT Defensive Back. B. 10/27/43, Cincinnati, Ohio. 5'11", 190. Attended Robert A. Taft H.S. of Cincinnati. Running back at U. of Cincinnati. Bearcat captain and All-MVC, 1964. Played in College All-Star and East West Shrine games. Defensive starter first nine seasons with Philadelphia Eagles, 1965-73. Selected to All-Rookie team. Holds NFL record for 101-yd. return of missed FG, 1971. Had 100-yarder in 1966. Has intercepted 13 passes, career, for 148 yds. NFC runnerup in kickoff returns, 1972, returning 25 for 29.1-yd. average. Cornerback with speed and savvy.

NEVERS, ERNEST A. Running Back. 6', 205. B. 6/11/03, Willow Grove, Minn. "America's all-time one-man team." 21-4-1 playing record at Stanford, 1923-25. Consensus All-America, 1925. Eleven-letter man. Relentless, hard-driving fullback. Also passed, punted, played defense. In 1925 Rose Bowl, recovering from two broken ankles, ran for 114 yds. Stanford coach was Pop Warner, who also developed Jim Thorpe at Carlisle. Warner argued Nevers was superior — "He could do everything Thorpe could do and he tried harder. No man ever gave more of himself than Ernie Nevers." Played pro football, baseball and basketball. As footballer with Duluth Eskimos, 1926-28; Chicago Cardinals,

1929-31. Missed only 27 minutes of 29-game, 5-month, 17,000-mile season, 1926. Eskimos won 19, lost 7, tied 3. Scored NFL record 40 points (6 TDs, 4 PATs) vs. Chicago Bears on 11/28/29; achievement is still unsurpassed. Pitched 45 games for St. Louis Browns, 1925-27. In 1927 allowed two long balls to Ruth in Babe's 60-homer season. Modern All-Time All-America team. Citizens Savings Hall of Fame, National Football Foundation Hall of Fame, Pro Football Hall of Fame.

NEWELL, MARSHALL (Ma) Tackle. B. 4/21/1871, Clifton, N.J. D. 12/24/97. 5'7", 170. Harvard, 1890-93. All-America thrice, 1891-93. Extremely strong in legs and shoulders. Known for powerful tackling, blocking ability. Respected by both friend and foe. Also rowed for Harvard crew. Took care of lonely freshmen, hence his nickname. Cornell's first paid coach, 1893, 94. Coached Joe (later Col. Joe) and Clint Wyckoff at Cornell. Clint was Big Red's first All-America. Killed by locomotive while in employ of Boston & Maine Railroad. Citizens Savings Hall of Fame, National Football Foundation Hall of Fame.

NEWHOUSE, ROBERT Running Back. B. 1/9/50, Hallsville, Tex. 5'10", 202. Twice captain of Galilee H.S. team in Hallsville. U. of Houston, 1969-71. Rushed for 2961 yds. in his collegiate career, averaging 6.4 yds. and scoring 19 TDs. Suffered near fatal car accident prior to junior season. Averaged 159.7 yds. rushing for 4th best total in NCAA history, 1971. Dallas Cowboys, 1972-73. No. 2 draft choice. Became regular for Cowboys in 1972. According to Dallas teammate Dave Edwards, "Tackling him (Newhouse) is like tackling a shot-put."

NEWMAN, HARRY L. Quarterback. B. 9/5/09, Detroit, Mich. 5'7", 175. Attended Detroit's Northern H.S., lettering in three sports. U. of Michigan, 1930-32. Played under Harry Kipke. Injured much of junior season. Unanimous All-America as senior. His FG, in snow against Minnesota at Minneapolis, gave Michigan 3-0 victory; perfect season (8-0-0); national championship, 1932. Played on three straight Western Conference (Big 10) championship teams. East-West Shrine and East-West Chicago *Tribune* games, 1933. New York Giants, 1933-36. NFL title games, 1933, 34, 35. All-Pro quarterback, 1933. In game against Green Bay played offense (rushing 38 times) and defense, returned kickoffs and kicked field goals (three). Record of 38 rushes surpassed by O.J. Simpson in 1973. Formerly car dealer in Detroit and Denver. Now retired and living in Pompano Beach, Fla.

NEYLAND, ROBERT R. Coach. B. 2/17/1892, Greenville, Tex. D. 3/28/62, New Orleans, La. Attended Texas A. & M. one year while awaiting appointment to West Point. Attended Army, 1914-16. As Cadet was 35-5 baseball pitcher, football end, heavyweight boxing champion three years. Co-winner of Gold Sabre with Walt Britton, who later assisted Neyland at Tennessee. Neyland turned down pro baseball offers from New York Giants and Philadelphia Athletics. Coached Tennessee for 21 years, 1926-34; 36-40; 46-52. Posted 173-31-12 record (.829 percentage) for 5th place on all-time coaching list. Won or shared five SEC titles. Volunteers were undefeated eight times in regular season play. In one seven-season period Neyland teams had 56-1-5 mark, held opponents scoreless in 42 games. Trademarks were defense, kicking game and single-wing attack. Took Vols to all four major bowls. Fostered numerous coaches, such as Bobby Dodd, Murray Warmath and Bowden Wyatt. Worked with Army Corps of Engineers much of life and rose to rank of Brig. Gen. Earned engineering degree from MIT. Knute Rockne considered Neyland football's greatest coach. Citizens Savings Hall of Fame, National Football Foundation Hall of Fame.

NICHOLS, DWIGHT E. Running Back. B. 10/21/36, Knoxville, Iowa. 5'10", 164. Virtual one-man show three years at Iowa State, 1957-59. Ran and passed for 3946 yards, and scored 17 TDs. Was small but shifty tailback. Nichols also played defensive back, punted and returned kicks. Went out winner, after two losing seasons, as Iowa State finished 7-3 in 1959. Same year Nichols was given All-America recognition.

NILAND, JOHN H. (Big John) Guard. B. 2/29/44, Quincy, Mass. 6'3", 245. Iowa. Attended Amityville Memorial (N.Y.) H.S. and U. of Iowa. After playing fullback as college sophomore, Niland moved to guard where he found permanent home. Won university weightlifting championship. Played in East-West, Hula Bowl and College All-Star games following 1965 senior year. Dallas Cowboys, 1966-73. Played in six straight Pro Bowls, 1969, 70, 71, 72, 73, 74. He and Blaine Nye give Cowboys one of best offensive guard combinations in NFL. Scored TD against Philadelphia Eagles, 1972 recovering fumble in end zone. "My job is to hit the guy across the line on every play and drive him back as far as I can. It's that simple" — Niland. Music and flying buff. Drafted No. 1 by Cowboys in 1966. All-NFL, 1969. All-NFC, 1971, 72, 73. NFL championship game, 1966. Super Bowl, 1971, 72.

NITSCHKE, RAYMOND E. Linebacker. B. 12/29/36, Elmwood Park, Ill. 6'3", 240. Struck fear into many hearts during days as Green Bay Packer middle linebacker, 1958-72. Attended Proviso H.S. in Maywood, Ill. Played fullback at U. of Illinois. Intercepted 25 passes during pro career for 385 yds. and 2 TDs. Named All-First 50 Year NFL Middle Linebacker and to All-Pro Squad of the 1960s by Pro Football Hall of Fame. Accumulated nine tackles against Oakland in Super Bowl II, 1968. Voted outstanding player at his position, 1967. Noted for ferocious hitting and tackling ability. Civic-minded. Has served as chairman of Wisconsin Cerebral Palsy Telethon and on Green Bay Boys Club board of directors. Pro Bowl, 1965, All-NFL, 1964-65, 66. NFL championship games, 1960, 61, 62, 65, 66, 67. Also played in Super Bowl I, 1967.

NOBIS, THOMAS H., JR. (Tommy) Linebacker. B. 9/20/43, San Antonio, Tex. 6'2", 237. Graduated from Jefferson H.S., San Antonio, and U. of Texas. One of most honored college linemen. Consensus All-America, 1965; All-America, 1964. Recipient of Maxwell Award and Outland Trophy, 1965. Texas won Cotton Bowl, 1965, and Orange Bowl, 1966, Runnerup to USC's O. J. Simpson in news media survey to pick greatest college player of 1960s. Named to

Sports Illustrated All-Century team. No. 1 draft choice of Atlanta Falcons, 1966. In response, Nobis won Rookie of the Year honors. Played in five Pro Bowls, 1967, 68, 69, 71, 73. Intercepted three passes for Falcons in 1972, one for TD. Known for great tackling ability. Has had surgery on both knees. All-NFL, 1967.

NOLAN, RICHARD C. Defensive Back. B. 3/26/32, Pittsburgh, Pa. 6'1", 185. Raised in White Plains, N.Y. Played offense and defense as Maryland won national championship, 1953. Defensive back with New York Giants, 1954-57, 59-61; Chicago Cardinals, 1958; Dallas Cowboys, 1962. Intercepted 23 passes during pro career. NFL championship games, 1956, 59. Defensive assistant with Cowboys, 1962-67. Head coach, San Francisco 49ers, 1968-73. Won three NFC Western Division titles 1970, 71, 72. 43-36-5 record thru 1973.

NOLL, CHARLES H. (Chuck) Coach. B. 1/5/32, Cleveland, Ohio. Graduated from Dayton. Cleveland Browns, 1953-59. NFL championship games, 1953, 54, 55. Offensive guard early part of career, then switched to linebacker. Eight lifetime interceptions. Assistant coach, San Diego Chargers, 1960-65; and Baltimore Colts, 1966-68. Head coach of Pittsburgh Steelers, 1969-73. Suffered 1-13 year in 1969. Reversed fortunes and won 11 of 14 games in 1972. Lost AFC championship game that year to Miami Dolphins, 21-17. 33-37 record thru 1973. Enjoys excellent communication with players.

NOMELLENI, LEO Tackle. B. 6/19/24, Lucca, Italy. 6'3", 262. Grew up in Chicago. As marine participated in Pacific invasion of Saipan and Okinawa, 1944-45. Consensus All-America twice at Minnesota, 1948, 49. Ferocious and intimidating defensive tackle. San Francisco 49ers, 1950-63. Never injured, he retired with NFL record for consecutive regular-season games played (174). Appeared in 10 Pro Bowl games. Named one of 16 all-time great pros and to All-Pro Squad of the 1950s by Pro Football Hall of Fame. All-Pro, 1951, 52, 53, 54, 57, 59. Named twice offensively to prove versatility. Stayed in shape as pro wrestler during off-season. Pro Football Hall of Fame.

NOONAN, KARL P. End. B. 2/17/44, Dubuque, Iowa. 6'2", 198. Played football and basketball at Assumption H.S. in Davenport, Iowa. Then on to U. of Iowa. Set Big 10 reception record as junior with 40 catches, 1964. Played in East-West Shrine game. Miami Dolphins, 1966-71. One of team's original members. Signed with Dolphins as free agent. In best pro season caught 58 passes for 760 yds. and 11 TDs, 1968. Established club record for catches in consecutive games (17). First six years with Dolphins played in every regular season game (84). Runs summer boys camp with Bob Griese. Super Bowl, 1972. Nabbed 136 passes as pro, lugging ball 1798 yds. and scoring 17 TDs.

NORTHCROFT, PERCY W. Tackle. B. 8/31/1886, LaVernia, Tex. D. 12/20/67, Piedmont, Calif. Son of actor Wilfred North. Wilfred wanted his boy "to be classy," decided naval officer represented *beau ideal*. Percy was thus destined for U.S. Naval Academy. Developed into outstanding lineman. Was strong, bull-like. Kicked 46-yd. FG vs. Army as Middies won 10-0, 1906. Following year was suspended when he fell behind in studies. During suspension worked out in New York City with Jack Chesbro and John Clarkson, of major-league pitching fame. They were impressed with Percy's arm, induced him to try baseball career. Refused — "I owe it to my father to go back to Annapolis, and I am going to do so. He wants me to be classy, as he says, and I am going to show him I can be." Returned to earn Navy captaincy and 3rd-team All-America honors, 1908. Became captain in U.S. Navy, fulfilling Dad's dream. Retired in 1937, but returned to active duty in 1940 and served until 1946.

NORTON, DONALD End. B. 3/13/38, Anamosa, Iowa. 6'2", 185. Halfback and safety at Anamosa H.S. Switched to end at U. of Iowa, playing both ways. Caught 30 passes for 428 yds., 4 TDs, 1959. Was co-captain and All-America that year. In 1960 chose Los Angeles Chargers, soon to become San Diego, over Philadelphia Eagles and Winnipeg Blue Bombers. Played with Chargers, 1960-66. AFL championship games, 1961, 63, 64, 65. Took job as circulation manager of Des Moines *Register,* 1969.

NORTON, GERALD (Jerry) Defensive Back. B. Midland, Tex. 5'11", 195. Attended Southern Methodist. Philadelphia Eagles, 1954-58; Chicago Cardinals, 1959; St. Louis Cardinals, 1960-61; Dallas Cowboys, 1962; Green Bay Packers, 1963-64. Classy defensive player, punter. All-Pro, 1960. Intercepted 10 passes, 1960, to tie Dave Baker for NFL interception title. Same year won punting crown by averaging 45.6 yds. on 39 punts. Missed half of '56 season with broken arm.

NORTON, HOMER H. Coach. B. 6/15/1891. D. 1965. Son of Methodist minister. Four-sport star at Birmingham Southern — football, basketball, baseball and track. Head coach at Centenary, 1920-21, 26-33; Texas A. & M., 1934-47. Was Centenary assistant from 1922-25 when Bo McMillin, nationally known Centre quarterback, was hired as head coach to get school into Southwest Conference. McMillin failed and Norton, as result, got his old job back. In 14 years at A. & M. he lifted $210,000 mortgage which bank held on Kyle Field, leaving school's athletic association with better than $250,000 surplus. His Aggie successes included three straight SWC titles, four major bowl appearances, national championship in 1939. '39 team outscored opponents 198-18 and defeated Tulane in Sugar Bowl. Norton developed such A. & M. standouts as John Kimbrough, Marshall Robnett, Joe Routt, Jim Thomason. Correctly predicted that Routt would be A. & M. 1st All-America. Overall record: 142-73-18. After he stopped coaching, Norton was in motel-restaurant business. Citizens Savings Hall of Fame, National Football Foundation Hall of Fame.

NOWATZKE, THOMAS M. Running Back. B. 9/30/42, La Porte, Ind. 6'2", 235. Indiana, 1962-64. Scored 136 points and rushed for 1438 yds. All-Big 10 twice. Played in East-West Shrine, College All-Star and Senior Bowl games. No. 1 draft choice of Detroit Lions. Lions, 1965-69; Baltimore Colts, 1970-72; Houston Oilers, 1973. Super Bowl, 1971; scored two-yd. TD run vs. Dallas

Cowboys. Best pro season picked up 512 yds. rushing, scored six TDs, 1966. Running back most of career with Lions and Colts, but switched to linebacker at Houston.

NUGENT, THOMAS N. Coach. B. Lawrence, Mass. Graduated from Ithaca College, 1936. Coached VMI, 1949-52; Florida State, 1953-58; Maryland, 1959-65. Record: 89-80-3. Respected for original football mind. Developed I formation, typewriter huddle and V huddle. Brought VMI and Florida State out of doldrums. Tied Maryland for Southern Conference title in 1951. Developed Garv Collins, Maryland consensus All-America. Father of nine children. Resident of Tallahassee.

NUSSBAUMER, ROBERT End-Defensive Back. B. 4/23/24, Oak Park, Ill. Played three sports at Michigan. Member, Green Bay Packers, 1946; Washington Redskins, 1947-48; Chicago Cardinals, 1949-50. Caught 47 passes, 1947. Led league in interceptions with 12, 1949. Scout, assistant coach for Detroit Lions, 1953-64. With Cleveland Browns since 1965. Currently player personnel director. Wife, Marie, is columnist for Ravenna (Ohio) *Record.*

NYDAHL, MALVIN J. (Mally) Running Back. B. 11/24/06, Minneapolis, Minn. Minnesota, 1926-28. Three-sport standout, Nydahl (halfback) and Herb Joesting (fullback) provided tremendous one-two punch. Mally was baseball and basketball captain, conference Medal of Honor winner — all in 1928. Tried minor league baseball five years, 1929-33. Was Western League batting champion runnerup (.368) while playing with Omaha, 1933. Played with Frankford Yellow Jackets, 1930-31. Turned to prep and collegiate officiating when retired from active competition. Primary field was medicine, gaining prominence as Minneapolis physician and surgeon.

OBERLANDER, ANDREW J. (Swede) Running Back. B. 2/17/05, Chelsea, Mass. D. 1/1/68, New Vernon, N.Y. 6', 198. Dartmouth, 1923-25. Tackle as sophomore and junior. Switched to backfield in time for senior year by coach Jesse Hawley. Proceeded to throw 12 TD passes and was unanimous All-America. Led Dartmouth to 1925 national championship. Lost only one game in three years. Graduate of Yale Medical School. At death was medical director of Eastern home office of Prudential Insurance Co., Newark, N.J. Citizens Savings Hall of Fame, National Football Foundation Hall of Fame.

O'BRIEN, JAMES E. End-Kicker. B. 2/2/47, El Paso, Tex. 6', 195. U. of Cincinnati, 1966-68. Set NCAA record with 22 catches in 1968. Led nation in scoring that season with 142 points (12 TDs, 31 PATs, 13 FGs). Kicked three FGs in North-South game. Holds nearly all Cincinnati kicking and receiving records. Baltimore Colts, 1970-72, and Detroit Lions, 1973. After scoring 263 points first three seasons as pro, failed to score in 1973. As rookie kicked 19 of 34 FGs, including three of 45, 44, 47 yds. in same game. Biggest moment of career came in 1971 when he booted 32-yd. FG to win Super Bowl V. Excellent tennis player.

O'BRIEN, ROBERT D. (Davey) Quarterback. B. 6/22/17, Dallas, Tex. 5'7", 150. Attended Woodrow Wilson H.S., Dallas, and Texas Christian. Succeeded Sammy Baugh as TCU quarterback. Accounted for 245 points and 3481 yds. total offense during collegiate career, 1936-38. Counting interceptions, kickoff and punt returns, he amassed 5462 total yds. Won Heisman Trophy and Maxwell Award, 1938. Unanimous All-America same season. Played on winning Sugar

Bowl (16-6 over Marquette, 1937) and Cotton Bowl (15-7 over Carnegie Tech, 1939) teams. Played only with Philadelphia Eagles in brief NFL career, 1939-40. All-NFL, 1939. In last pro game completed 33 of 60 passes, setting record of completions. Quit football to join FBI. Citizens Savings Hall of Fame, National Football Hall of Fame. Now with Dresser Atlas Oil of Fort Worth.

O'DEA, PATRICK J. Running Back-Kicker. B. 3/17/1872, Melbourne, Australia. D. 4/4/62. 6', 169. Rugby star in Australia before coming to America. Enrolled at Wisconsin because brother was track coach there. Played football three years, 1897-99. 2nd-team All-America, 1898; 3rd team, 1899. In his day goals were dropkicked, skill abetted by rounded-end football. Recorded goals of 62, 60 and two of 57 yds. Sixty-two yarder is 2nd longest in college history. Punts were also eye-catching, reaching 87 yds. In 1899 kicked four FGs and returned kickoff 90 yds. against Beloit. Same season forced to sidelines vs. Michigan because of broken bone in right hand — only time he failed to go 60 minutes. Coached Notre Dame, 1900-01; Missouri, 1902. Taught Notre Dame's Red Salmon art of punting. Without informing family joined Anzacs (Australian army), 1917. Mysteriously dropped out of sight, for 17 years, and was feared missing in action. In 1934 was located in Westwood, Calif., using name "Charles J. Mitchell." He explained to San Francisco sportswriter: "Probably I was wrong, changing my name and all. Mrs. Mitchell, that is, Mrs. O'Dea, always thought I was. But I wanted to get away from what seemed to me to be all in the past. As Pat O'Dea, I seemed very much an ex-Wisconsin football player." Citizens Savings Hall of Fame, National Football Foundation Hall of Fame.

ODSON, URBAN L. Tackle. B. 11/17/18, Clark, S.D. 6'3", 247. Won 10 letters at Clark H.S. U. of Minnesota tackle, 1939-41. Consensus All-America, 1940, Member two straight national championship teams, 1940, 41. Bernie Bierman's 1941 team is considered one of all-time best. Played with All-Americas George Franck, Bruce Smith, Dick Wildung. Green Bay Packers, 1946-49.

O'HEARN, JOHN E. (Jack) End. B. 7/28/1893, Brookline, Mass. 5'8", 186. Member of Brookline's greatest athletic family. Jack and four brothers, Bill, Frank, Ed, Charlie, grew up on Davis Avenue — adjacent to Cypress Street playground, first in America, and directly across from site of nation's first indoor swimming pool. Ed played pro ball with Canton Bulldogs; Charlie quarterbacked Yale, then served alma mater as assistant to president; Bill was three-sport high school star; Frank was freestyle swimming champion; Jack played four years at end for Cornell, 1912-15. All-America, 1914; team captain, 1915. Sportswriter Allison Danzig said, ". . . Holy Cross put three men on him [Jack] to block him on sweeps. Michigan gave up early to get around his flank. He was called the fiercest interference-buster in Cornell history." O'Hearn worked with Army Engineer Corps in World War I and then became civilian engineer in Brookline. National Football Foundation Hall of Fame.

OKESON, WALTER R. Official. B. Port Royal, Pa. D. 11/4/43, Bethlehem,

Pa. Prepped at Shortridge Academy, Media, Pa. Lehigh end and fullback, 1893-95. Studied engineering. Became prominent football official. Coached at Hobart and Lehigh. Elected chairman of Football Rules Committee and rulebook in 1933. Served both posts until death. Often referred to as "czar" of gridiron officials. Maintained athletics were taken too seriously. Vice president of Lehigh, 1939-43. Received Touchdown Club of New York Award, 1941. Succeeded by Walter J. Bingham, Harvard, as Rules Committee chairman.

OLCOTT, HERMAN P. Center. B. 1/1/1879, New York, N.Y. D. 1/4/29, Wallingford, Conn. 5'11", 197. Attended Middletown (Conn.) H.S; Betts Academy, Stamford, Conn; and Yale. All-America, 1900, year that Yale students first sang *Boola, Boola.* Member Yale basketball, track, water polo (school's first squads as well. Head football coach at North Carolins, NYU, Kansas. Long-time coach, athletic director at Choate School, Wallingford. Enjoyed golf, crossword puzzles, tennis.

OLIPHANT, ELMER Q. (Ollie) Running Back. B. 7/9/1893, Bloomfield, Ind. 5'7", 174. Likable egotist. One of America's most versatile athletes. Starred in four sports at Purdue; won letters in four major sports at Army, competed in three others. Life-size pictures of him, dressed out for football, basketball, baseball and track, hang on one wall of Purdue's trophy room. Best remembered for football. Played seven consecutive years, 1911-17, first three at Purdue and last four at Army. During that span scored 468 points, 333 of them for Black Knights. Consensus All-America twice, 1916, 17. Earned spot on Early-Day All-Time All-America team. Name has been linked with Jim Thorpe and Charley Brickley as greatest dropkickers. Suffered broken ankle against Illinois in 1913, but still kicked FG to win 3-0 for Purdue. Built like bull, combined good speed with excellent moves ("I show the tackler the hip and then pull it away"). Dangerous outside, uncompromisingly tough inside. Still holds Army records for points scored, game (45, 1916); most TDs, game (6, 1916); most points scored, season (125, 1917). Athletic scholarship has been named for him at Purdue. Buffalo All Americans, 1920-21; Rochester Jeffersons, 1920-21. Citizens Savings Hall of Fame, National Football Foundation Hall of Fame. Lives in New Canaan, Conn.

OLIVAR, JORDAN Coach. B. 1/30/15, Brooklyn, N.Y. Attended Curtis H.S., Staten Island, N.Y., but played no football. Played for Harry Stuhldreher, 1935, and Clipper Smith, 1936-37, at Villanova. Co-Captain, 1937. Gained fame for calling signals from tackle post. Graduated with honors, majoring in romance languages. At age 28, 1943, succeeded Smith as Villanova head coach. Coached Villanova, 1943-48; Loyola (Calif.), 1949-51; Yale, 1952-60. Record: 105-53-6. In 1960 produced Yale's first unbeaten, untied team (9-0-0) in 37 years. Now associate manager with Mutual of New York; lives in Beverly Hills, Calif.

OLSEN, MERLIN J. Tackle. B. 9/15/40, Logan, Utah. 6'5", 270. One of nine children. Utah State, 1959-61. Consensus All-America, 1961. Hula Bowl, East-

West, All-America and College All-Star games. Hula Lineman of the Game. Los Angeles Rams, 1962-73. Named to Pro Bowl each of first 12 seasons. Recipient of numerous honors. Thru 1973 Olsen had played in 156 straight games. In '72 sacked QBs 14 times, deflected 6 passes, recovered 1 fumble, forced passers out of pocket 47 times. He and Romas Gabriel are partners in Southern California Porsche and Volkswagen dealerships. Olsen has acted in movies and co-hosted own TV show. Last of original "Fearsome Foursome." Other three members were Deacon Jones, Rosey Grier, Lamar Lundy. Brother of Phil.

OLSEN, PHILLIP V. Tackle. B. 9/15/40, Logan, Utah. 6'5", 265. Attended Logan H.S. and Utah State. Youngest of football-playing Olsen brothers. All-America defensive end, 1969. Played in East-West and Hula Bowl games. Drafted on 1st round by Boston Patriots in 1970. Suffered knee injury during practice with College All-Stars, 1970, and underwent knee surgery. Consequently became free agent, signing with Los Angeles Rams in 1971. Los Angeles, 1971-73. Joined brother, Merlin, on Ram defensive line. Switched to tackle.

OLSON, HARVEY S. Center. B. 2/28/08, Chicago, Ill. Attended Highland Park (Ill.) H.S. Won three football letters at Purdue, 1926-28. Captained 1928 team. Golf letterman, 1929. Majored in civil engineering. Abandoned engineering career after falling "deeply, passionately and irrevocably in love with Europe" when on 1929 journey there. Became professional traveler, one of noted men in field. Wrote *Aboard and Abroad,* complete guide to Europe, 1953. Was regularly updated thru 13 editions, 23 printings. Author numerous other guidebooks. In 1963 named to *Sports Illustrated* Silver Anniversary All-America team. Now director of three travel companies in Chicago.

OLSZEWSKI, HARRY G. Guard. B. 10/11/46, Baltimore, Md. 5'11", 237. Clemson, 1965-67. School's only consensus All-America, selected in 1967. All-ACC, 1966, 67. Quick and fast with good lateral movement. Grabbed fumbled center snap in mid-air against South Carolina and rambled 12 yds. for TD, 1966. Majored in recreation and parks administration. Drafted and signed by Cleveland Browns in 1968; was cut before season began.

OLSZEWSKI, JOHN Running Back. B. 12/21/29, Washington, D.C. 5'11", 200. California, 1950-52. School's career rushing leader with 2504 yds., 1950-52. Co-captained 7-3 team his senior year under Pappy Waldorf. All-America, 1952. Played in East-West Shrine and College All-Star games. Member, Chicago Cardinals, 1953-57; Washington Redskins, 1958-60; Detroit Lions, 1961; Denver Broncos, 1962. Rather small, yet rugged fullback. Director of Long Beach City (Calif.) lifeguard service.

O'NEILL, FRANK J. (Buck) Coach. B. 1875. D. 4/21/58, Hamilton, N.Y. Williams fullback. Nickname derived from ability to crash enemy lines. Won eight letters in football and track. Coached at Colgate, 1902, 04-05; Syracuse,

1906-07; 13-15, 17-19; Columbia, 1920-22. Enjoyed best years at Syracuse with records of 9-1-2, 1915, and 8-1-1, 1917. Latter team featured Chick Meehan and Ty Cobb, who were finishing their careers, and Joe Alexander, who was just starting his. On retirement from business world, O'Neill was president of Royal Indemnity Co. and affiliate, Eagle Indemnity Co., insurance companies. National Football Foundation Hall of Fame.

OOSTERBAAN, BENJAMIN G. (Bennie) End. B. 2/24/06, Muskegon, Mich. 6', 198. Almost forced to give up sports because of family tragedy. Bennie's older brother died from infected foot blister while playing for Muskegon H.S. Oosterbaan parents then vowed their 2nd son could not participate in athletics. Took delegation of Muskegon students and town's leading citizens to dissuade them of ban. Bennie proceeded to star in four sports at Muskegon, and at U. of Michigan, where he won nine letters. He and Benny Friedman formed one of college football's classiest passing duos. Friedman commented on their collaboration: "It was the confidence we had in each other that made us so successful. Bennie would tell me exactly where he'd go and I knew he'd be there, and he knew I'd deliver the ball to that point." Three-time All-America for Fielding Yost: consensus in 1925, 26; unanimous in 1927. Yost called '25 team his greatest as it outscored opponents 227-3. Oosterbaan was also All-America in basketball, Olympic calibre discus thrower, conference batting champion in baseball. As Michigan head football coach compiled 63-33-4 record, 1948-58. During rookie season, after succeeding Fritz Crisler, led troops to perfect 9-0-0 season and national championship. Wolverines defeated California, 14-6, in 1951 Rose Bowl. Member Modern All-Time All-America team. Citizens Savings Hall of Fame, National Football Foundation Hall of Fame.

O'ROURKE, CHARLES C. (Chuckin' Charley) Quarterback. B. 5/10/17, Montreal, Que., Canada. 5'10½", 150. Attended Malden (Mass.) H.S., Boston College. Considered one of East's all-time triple-threat performers. Scored winning TD as Boston College defeated Tennessee, 19-13, in 1941 Sugar Bowl. Played at B.C. under Gil Dobie and Frank Leahy, 1938-40. Stalled for 23 seconds to preserve B.C.'s 19-18 decision over rival Georgetown, 1940. Chicago Bears, 1942; Los Angeles Dons (AAFC), 1946-47; Baltimore Colts (AAFC), 1948-49. Backfield coach, Holy Cross; head coach, Massachusetts, 1952-59. Served as commissioner of Pop Warner Football League. National Football Foundation Hall of Fame.

ORR, JAMES E., JR. (Jimmy) End. B. 10/4/35, Seneca, S.C. 5'11", 180. Football and basketball standout at Seneca H.S. Enrolled at Clemson College but transferred to Georgia. Went out for Bulldog football team without scholarship, impressed, and soon had one. Playing halfback, twice won SEC pass-receiving title, 1955, 57. Played in Blue-Gray game. Pittsburgh Steelers, 1958-60; Baltimore Colts, 1961-70. Originally drafted by Los Angeles Rams but traded to Steelers before 1958 season began. Was NFL Rookie of the Year, catching 33 passes for 910 yds., 7 TDs. Career: 400 receptions for 7914 yds., 66

TDs. Average per reception of 19.8 yds. is among 10 best in pro history. All-NFL, 1965. Played in Super Bowl, 1969, 71. Colts defeated Dallas Cowboys, 16-13, in Super Bowl V. Now color analyst on Atlanta Falcon radio network.

ORTMANN, CHARLES H. (Chuck) Running Back. B. Milwaukee, Wis. 6'1", 190. Last in long line of triple-threat tailbacks at U. of Michigan. Successor to All-America Bob Chappuis, who graduated in 1947. Played under Bennie Oosterbaan, 1948-50. Passed with great accuracy and ran with considerable power. Also caught passes, punted. Seldom has player given better exhibition of punting than Ortmann in "Snow Bowl" of 1950 against Ohio State. Game, played at Columbus, was nearly cancelled. Weather conditions were following: 10-degree temperature, 30-mile-an-hour wind, 24-inch snowfall. Still, over 50,000 Buckeye fans braved elements. They saw Ortmann punt 24 times (Big 10 record) and Michigan score only TD on fumble recovery in end zone. Wolverines won, 9-3, although they gained nary one 1st down. Gave Michigan fourth straight conference title and bid to Rose Bowl where California was victimized, 14-6. In career Ortmann gained 2199 yds. rushing, passed for 676 more. Pittsburgh Steelers, 1951; Dallas Texans, 1952. Now self-employed, he lives in Glen Ellyn, Ill.

ORVIS, HERB Defensive Tackle-End. B. 10/17/46, Petoskey, Mich. 6'5", 250. Attended Beecher H.S., Flint, Mich., and U. of Colorado. Played on service teams during two-year army stint in Germany. All-America, 1970, 71. Totaled 189 tackles in collegiate career, including 39 QB sacks for 237 yds. in losses. Detroit Lions, 1972-73. Lions' No. 1 draft choice in 1972. Fine speed and agility for size.

OSBORN, DAVID V. Running Back. B. 3/18/43, Cando, N.D. 6', 205. Played football and ran track at North Dakota. Minnesota Vikings, 1965-73. 13th-round draft choice in 1965. Returned 18 kickoffs for 422 yds., 1965. Gained 972 yds. rushing, 1967. Scored eight TDs in 1969, helping Minnesota to Super Bowl IV appearance. Thru 1973 had gained 3712 yds. rushing and scored 24 TDs. Hard, slashing runner. Another Super Bowl appearance in 1974.

OSGOOD, WINCHESTER D. (Win) Running Back. B. 4/12/1870, Port Bananas, Fla. D. Cuba. 5'9", 180. Brilliant athlete — accomplished rower, intercollegiate wrestling and boxing champion, bicycle record-holder (two-mile), outstanding football player. "He loved any kind of a contest. The smell of powder was almost incense to him" — New York *Sun.* Played two years each at Cornell, 1891-92, and Pennsylvania, 1893-94. Carried Penn to 24-3 record, including 1894 national championship. "The nearest thing to Red Grange as a broken-field runner I've seen," according to Pudge Heffelfinger. Lost life in Cuban Insurrection. National Football Foundation Hall of Fame.

OSMANSKI, WILLIAM T. Running Back. B. 12/29/15, Providence, R.I. 6'1", 205. Holy Cross fullback, 1936-38. All-America, 1937, 38. Playing record: 23-3-

3. "Osmanski was a good defensive player and a good pass receiver," commented coach Eddie Anderson. "He was not a passer or a kicker, but he was, I think, one of the finest ball carriers I've ever seen. In college ranks the other man I would compare him with would be Tom Harmon, of Michigan." Chicago Bears, 1939-43, 46-47. Led NFL rushers rookie season, amassing 699 yds. on 121 carries. All-Pro same season. Scored 68-yd. TD run, on 2nd play of game, starting Bears '73-rout of Washington Redskins in 1940 title game. Gained 1752 yds. during pro career on 382 attempts, 4.69 average; scored 20 TDs. Member three other world championship teams, 1941, 43, 46. While playing for Bears earned dental degree at Northwestern. Now practicing dentist in Evanston, Ill. Named to *Sports Illustrated* Silver Anniversary All-America team. National Football Foundation Hall of Fame.

OSS, ARNOLD C. Running Back. B. 8/23/1899, Lidgerwood, N.D. 5'11", 178. Won eight letters at Minnesota: three in football and basketball, two in track. 3rd-team All-America, 1919. Basketball All-America, 1921. Hampered by injuries last two seasons, 1920, 21. In 1919 led Gophers to their first victory over Michigan since 1893, 34-7. Oss' 67-yd. run highlighted game which returned Little Brown Jug to Minneapolis. Coach, Dr. Henry Williams, believed healthy Oss would have ranked with Red Grange as ball carrier. Was flashy, extremely fast. Received Minnesota Alumni Service Award, 1961. Spent many years in insurance business. Citizens Savings Hall of Fame (basketball).

OTIS, JAMES E. Running Back. B. 4/29/48, Celina, Ohio. 6', 220. Ohio State fullback. Consensus All-America, 1969. All-Big 10, 1968, 69. Big 10 MVP, 1969. Ohio State defeated USC, 27-16, in '69 Rose Bowl. MVP in Coaches All-America game, rushing for 145 yds. on 27 carries. Powerful runner, blocker. New Orleans Saints, 1970; Kansas City Chiefs, 1971-72; St. Louis Cardinals, 1973. Mainly backup runner in pros. Gained 234 yds. on ground in '73.

OTTO, AUGUST J. (Gus) Linebacker. B. 12/8/43, St. Louis, Mo. 6'1", 220. Attended McBride H. S. of St. Louis, participating in four sports. Set school records in discus and shot-put. Played fullback and linebacker at U. of Missouri. Captain and All-Big 8, 1964. Played in Blue-Gray, Coaches All-America and Senior Bowl games. Nine-year starter for Oakland Raiders, 1965-73. Intercepted two passes for TDs, 1965. Played in AFL All-Star game, 1970. Owns B.S. degree in physical education and master's in counseling, both from Missouri. AFL championship games, 1967, 68, 69. Super Bowl, 1968.

OTTO, JAMES E. Center. B. 1/5/38, Wausau, Wis. 6'2", 255. Attended Wausau H. S. where he won All-State honors as linebacker and center. Graduated from U. of Miami (Fla.). Set school career record for most tackles. Selected to Iron Arrow, university's highest honorary fraternity. Entire pro career with Oakland Raiders, 1959-73. Never missed starting assignment with Raiders, covering 182 straight league games in first 14 seasons. Adding 63 pre-season, nine post-season and 12 All-Star contests, Otto has played in 266 overall as pro. Named to Pro

Football Hall of Fame's All-Time AFL team. Twice winner of Gorman Award as "Player Who Best Exemplifies the Pride and Spirit of the Oakland Raiders." Familiar for No. 00 jersey. Entering 1973 season Otto was only original Raider still active and one of five AFL players who remain in competition. AFL championship games, 1967, 68, 69. Super Bowl, 1968.

OUTLAND, JOHN H. Tackle-Running Back. B. 3/17/1871, Hesper, Kan. D. 3/24/47, Laguna Beach, Calif. 5'11", 192. Attended Friends U., Kansas and Pennsylvania. Played football and baseball at Kansas. Penn All-America, 1897-98, winning honors first year at tackle and second at halfback. Coached for Franklin & Marshall, Kansas, Haskell and Washburn. Known as "Father of Kansas Relays." Also Jayhawk athletic director. Outland Trophy, named in his honor, given to outstanding collegiate lineman (guard or tackle) each year. First winner was George Connor of Notre Dame, 1946. Outland earned M.D. degree at Penn and was surgeon for many years.

OWEN, BENJAMIN G. (Bennie) Coach. B. 7/24/1875, Chicago, Ill. D. 2/26/70, Houston, Tex. Starting quarterback for Kansas Jayhawks under Fielding Yost, 1899. Coached Washburn, 1900; Bethany (Kan.), 1901-04; Oklahoma, 1905-26. Owen became Sooner coach before Oklahoma Territory achieved statehood. Offensive-minded Oklahoma teams amassed 122-54-16 record, finished four seasons unbeaten. They outscored opposition 282-15, 1911, and 278-7, 1918. One of first coaches to experiment with direct pass from center, and use forward pass. Firm believer in fair play and sportsmanship. Lost arm in hunting accident. Served as Oklahoma athletic director, 1927-34. Overall record: 155-60-19. Oklahoma's Owen Field, seating 61,826, named for him. Citizens Savings Hall of Fame, National Football Foundation Hall of Fame.

OWENS, JAMES D. Coach. B. 3/6/27, Oklahoma City, Okla. Played under Jim Tatum and Bud Wilkinson at Oklahoma. Co-captain of unbeaten 1949 team that blanked LSU in Sugar Bowl, 35-0. Received All-America mention that year at end. Assisted Bear Bryant at Texas A. & M., 1951-56. Named Washington head coach, 1957. Thru 1973 had 92-67-6 record. 1960, 61 teams broke Big 10's domination of Rose Bowl. Huskies defeated Wisconsin, 44-8, in 1960; following year clipped Minnesota, 17-7. West Coast Coach of the Year, 1960. Believes "you have to teach men to come up with the second and the third effort." Music buff. Washington athletic director since 1960.

OWENS, RALEIGH C. (R. C.) End. B. 11/12/33, Shreveport, La. 6'3", 190. Attended College of Idaho. Top college-division receiver in 1954, catching 40 passes for 905 yds., 7 TDs. San Francisco 49ers, 1957-61; Baltimore Colts, 1962-63; New York Giants, 1964. Developed "alley-oop" pass at San Francisco with QB Y. A. Tittle. Ball was thrown almost straight up into air by Tittle; Owens, using basketball rebounding skills learned in college, would then leap high to make catch. Play was treated derisively at first by foes, but they came to respect it. Tittle and Owens combined for two alley-oop scores vs. Los Angeles Rams in

1957. Now resides in Belmont, Calif.

OWENS, STEVE E. Running Back. B. 12/9/47, Gore, Okla. 6'2", 218. 5th of nine children. State hurdles champion from Miami (Okla.) H. S. Set 7 NCAA, 9 Big 8 and 13 U. of Oklahoma records, 1967-69. Carried football 905 times during collegiate career, amassing 3867 yds. Also scored 56 TDs. Gained over 100 yds. in 17 straight games. Rushed 55 times (NCAA record) for 261 yds. in game against Oklahoma State, 1967. Heisman Trophy winner and unanimous All-America senior year. Detroit Lions, 1970-73. Missed most of rookie season due to shoulder injury. Became first Lion player to join 1000-yd. club, 1971, gaining 1035 on 246 carries. Remains folk hero to many in Sooner State. Main street of hometown Miami has been renamed Steve Owens Boulevard. Quepaw Indians have made Owens honorary chief, tabbing him *Ki He Gha* (Leader). Pro Bowl, 1972.

PAGE, ALAN C. Tackle. B. 8/7/45, Canton, Ohio. 6'4", 247. Attended Central Catholic H. S. in Canton. Member national co-championship team at Notre Dame, 1966. One of four Irish All-Americas that season with Tom Regner, Nick Eddy and Jim Lynch. Majored in political science. Minnesota Vikings, 1967-73. Recovered 16 fumbles, including seven in '70, in first six pro seasons. First defensive player to be named NFL MVP, 1971. Has played in Pro Bowl each year except rookie campaign. Forms Viking "Purple Gang," also "Purple People Eaters," with tackle Gary Larsen and ends Jim Marshall, Carl Eller. Simply sensational performer; quick, strong, aggressive. NFL championship game, 1969. Super Bowl, 1970. Pro Bowl, 1969, 70, 71, 72, 74.

PAPIT, JOHN Running Back. B. Philadelphia, Pa. 6', 195. Attended Northeast H.S., Philadelphia, and U. of Virginia. 27-10-1 playing record at Virginia. Finished college career 1st in rushing yards (3237), 3rd in rushing yds. per carry (6.0) and 7th in total-offense yards per play (6.0). Scored 26 TDs and returned 30 kickoffs for 651 yds. All-American fullback, 1949. Longest play of career was 68-yd. rush vs. North Carolina.

PARDEE, JOHN P. (Jack) Linebacker. B. 4/19/36, Exira, La. 6'2", 225. Attended Christoval (Tex.) H.S. and Texas A. & M. Honor student in college. All-SWC, 1956, 57. Named outstanding player in both Blue-Gray and North-South All-Star games, 1957. Played for Los Angeles Rams, 1957-64, 66-70; Washington Redskins, 1971-72. Retired briefly to coach at Texas A. & M., 1965. All-NFL, 1963. All-NFC, 1971. Intercepted three passes against St. Louis, one

263

for TD in 1972. Produced 22 career interceptions. Active in American Cancer Society programs. Enjoys basketball and softball. Linebacker coach for Redskins, 1973. Super Bowl, 1973. Played in 196 pro games to rank near top 10 for service.

PARILLI, VITO (Babe) Quarterback. B. 1930, Rochester, Pa. 6'1", 188. Kentucky, 1949-51. Consensus All-America twice, 1950, 51. Led Wildcats to three straight bowls: Orange, 1950; Sugar, 1951; Cotton, 1952. Wildcats won Sugar, 13-7 over Oklahoma; and Cotton, 20-7 over Texas Christian. No. 1 nationally in TD passes, 1950, 51. Threw for 4351 yds. as collegian, and 50 TDs. MVP in College All-Star game, 1952. Green Bay Packers, 1952-53, 57-58; Cleveland Browns, 1956; Ottawa Roughriders, 1959; Oakland Raiders, 1960; Boston Patriots, 1961-67; New York Jets, 1968. Still holds many Patriot passing records. AFL MVP, 1964. Super Bowl, 1969. Retired from pro football with 1522 completions on 3330 attempts for 22,681 yds. and 178 TDs. Citizens Savings Hall of Fame. Quarterback coach of Pittsburgh Steelers, 1971-73. Joined WFL as coach in 1974.

PARKER, CLARENCE (Ace) Quarterback. B. 5/17/13, Portsmouth, Va. 5'11", 175. Duke consensus All-America, 1936. Starred as single-wing passer and runner. Brooklyn Dodgers, 1937-41; Boston Yanks, 1945; New York Yankees AAFC, 1946. League MVP and All-Pro QB in 1940, overcoming broken leg suffered in summer months preceding season. All-Pro also in 1938. For many years Duke baseball and assistant football coach. Doubled in baseball as undergraduate. National Football Foundation Hall of Fame, Pro Football Hall of Fame. Now NFL scout, Parker lives in hometown of Portsmouth.

PARKER, JAMES Guard. B. 4/3/34, Macon, Ga. 6'2", 251. One of six children of poor Southern family. Jim's dad was track laborer for Central of Georgia Railroad. Suffered appendicitis attack when he was 15 but didn't know it— "I thought it was a bellyache and would go away." Appendix finally burst and peritonitis set in; lost weight drastically but finally recovered. Moved north, spent senior year at Toledo's Scott H.S. Then enrolled in Woody Hayes' school of Ohio State football. Winner 23 times in 28 games, 1954-56. Buckeyes won Rose Bowl during Parker's sophomore season, 20-7 over Southern Cal, and were co-national champions. Consensus All-America and Outland Trophy winner, 1956. Linebacker on defense, guard on offense. Hayes praised: "...he was great on blocking, pulling or trapping. And he gave us great protection for our passer. He would lead the sweeps when Howard (Hopalong) Cassady was carrying the ball." One of biggest moments defensively occurred against Northwestern when he grabbed fumble and ran 42 yds. for TD. Concentrated on offense in 11 remarkable years with Baltimore Colts, 1957-67. All-Pro seven straight times, 1958-64. NFL championship games, 1958, 59, 64. Gave Johnny Unitas outstanding pass protection. Named to All-Pro Squad of the 1950s. Pro Football Hall of Fame, also Modern All-Time All-America team. Lives in Baltimore.

PARKER, RAYMOND (Buddy) Coach. B. 12/16/13. Halfback at Centenary. Quarterback and defensive end with Detroit Lions, 1935-36; Chicago Bears, 1937-43. Head coach for St. Louis Cardinals, 1949; Lions, 1951-56; Pittsburgh Steelers, 1957-64. One of 10 pro coaches to win 100 games (102-72-0). Won consecutive NFL championships, 1952, 53. Lost title game in 1954. Coached Lion stars Bobby Layne and Joe Schmidt. Surprised pro football world when he resigned at Meet the Lions banquet two days before first pre-season game in 1965. Respected for patience and ability to get maximum effort from all players.

PARKS, DAVID W. Tight End. B. 12/25/41, Muenster, Tex. 6'2", 220. All-State end at Abilene (Tex.) H.S. before enrolling at Texas Tech. All-SWC, 1962-63. All-America, 1963. Played in East-West, Coaches All-America and College All-Star games. No. 1 draft choice of San Francisco 49ers, 1964. 49ers, 1964-67; New Orleans Saints, 1968-72; Houston Oilers, 1973. Led NFL pass receivers with 80 receptions in 1965, for 1344 yds. and 12 TDs. Three Pro Bowl games, 1965, 66, 67. Played out option to sign with Saints. Traded to Oilers with Edd Hargett and Tom Stincic, for Kent Nix and Ron Billingsley. Began career as split end, then switched to tight end in 1969. Formidable blocker and receiver with excellent speed. Thru 1973 took even 400 aerials, gained 6179 yds., scored 47 TDs.

PARRINGTON, VERNON L. Coach. B. 8/3/1871, Aurora, Ill. D. 6/16/29, Winchcomb, England. Coaching career obscured by contributions as historian and educator. Was first football coach at Oklahoma. Pioneered for such successors as Bennie Owen, Bud Wilkinson, Biff Jones, Jim Tatum, Chuck Fairbanks, Barry Switzer. 9-2-1 record in four years, 1897-1900. According to Sooner historian John Keith, "The vicious cross-blocking Parrington taught the varsity forwards was probably his outstanding tactical achievement at Norman." Graduated from Harvard, 1893. English professor at Oklahoma, 1898-1908. Left Oklahoma to teach at U. of Washington, remaining there until death. Authored three-volume *Main Currents in American Thought,* 1927-30. First two volumes merited Pulitzer Prize for history in 1928.

PARRISH, BERNARD J. (Bernie) Defensive Back. B. Gainesville, Fla. 5'11", 195. Played baseball and football at Florida. Was baseball All-America, batted .438 and led SEC in RBI. Signed $130,000 bonus with Cincinnati Reds, forgoing senior football season. Grew disenchanted while playing with Topeka of Three I-league. Manager was Johnny Vander Meer. Quit to try out with Cleveland Browns. Had been their 9th-round draft choice. Browns, 1959-66; Houston Oilers, 1966. Played all but 11 games with Cleveland. Was cornerback. Led revolt to fire Cleveland coach Paul Brown. Indicted pro football establishment in *They Call It a Game.* Accused owners of "blackballing" him. Played on Browns' 1964 championship team.

PARSEGHIAN, ARA Coach. B. 5/21/33, Akron, Ohio. Three-sport letterman at Miami (Ohio). Halfback in Sun Bowl, 1947. Played at Great Lakes Naval Station and briefly with Cleveland Browns, 1948-49, both under Paul Brown.

Assisted Woody Hayes one year at alma mater, 1950, then took head job there. 39-6-1 record at Miami, 1951-55; 36-35-1 at Northwestern, 1956-63; 85-15-4, at Notre Dame, 1964-73. His 100th win, 51-0 over USC, clinched national title for Irish, 1966. Won 24-11 over Texas in 1971 Cotton Bowl, ending Longhorns' 30-game victory streak, longest in nation. Notre Dame has finished in top 10 in both wire service polls during each of Parseghian's seasons at South Bend. Produced All-Americas John Huarte (Heisman Trophy winner), Jack Snow, Jim Lynch, Alan Page, Kevin Hardy, Terry Hanratty, Jim Seymour, Joe Thiesmann, Walt Patulski, Greg Marx, Clarence Ellis. 160-56-6 overall record. Capped perfect season, 1973, with victory over Alabama in Sugar Bowl. Performance earned Parseghian's Irish another national championship.

PASTORINI, DAN Quarterback-Kicker. B. 12/25/41, Sonora, Calif. 6'3", 200. Played at Bellarmine Prep, San Jose, Calif., and Santa Clara. Outstanding high school baseball player, drafted by New York Mets. Rated best QB in Santa Clara history. Following senior year, 1970, played in East-West Shrine game (MVP), Senior Bowl (MVP) and College All-Star games. 1st-round draft pick of Houston Oilers. Threw 14 TD passes and punted for 40.9-yd. average in first two seasons with Oilers, 1971-72. Alternated with Lynn Dickey in 1973. Fierce competitor. Married actress June Wilkinson, 1973.

PATERNO, JOSEPH V. Coach. B. 12/21/26, Brooklyn, N.Y. Attended Brooklyn Preparatory School. Played in backfield with brother, George, now football coach at Kings Point. Only loss in 8-1 senior year, 1945, was to Vince Lombardi-coached St. Cecilia's of Englewood, N.J. Took degree in English literature at Brown. Accepted by Boston U. Law School, but never enrolled as he turned to coaching. Offensive backfield coach 16 years under Rip Engle (Penn State), 1950-65. Developed quarterbacks Richie Lucas, Milt Plum, Al Jacks, Tony Rados, Dick Hoak, Galen Hall, Pete Liske. Penn State head coach, 1966-73. 74-13-1 record in first eight years. Won Orange Bowl in successive years, 1968, 69. Routed Texas, 30-6, in Cotton Bowl, 1971. Produced winning streaks of 23, 31 and 15 games. Winning percentage of .825 best nationally among major-college coaches with at least five years experience. Coach of the Year, 1968; Walter Camp Foundation Coach of the Year, 1972. Paterno rejected several lucrative pro football offers to stay at Penn State in 1973. Lost 1973 Sugar Bowl to Oklahoma but won Orange Bowl, 1974, to cap perfect season.

PATTON, JAMES R., JR. (Jimmy) Defensive Back. B. 9/29/33, Greenville, Miss. D. 12/72, Villa Rica, Ga. 5'11", 175. Mississippi, 1952-54. Co-captain, 1954. New York Giants, 1955-66. All-Pro, 1958, 59, 60, 61, 62. Little Jimmy Patton constantly worried parents that he would get hurt playing football. Dad made him quit playing as 140-pound high school sophomore. Loved football too much, however, to give it up for good. Played two ways for Johnny Vaught at Mississippi. Scored 26 points against Tulane, 1953. Member 1952 and '54 Sugar Bowl teams. Used guile and instinct to become one of pro's best defensive backs. During Giant career intercepted 52 passes for 712 yds., 2 TDs. Led NFL in interceptions with 11, 1958. Returned punts and kickoffs until 1960. In rookie year brought back kickoff 98 yds. for TD, punt 78 yds. for another. Could not sleep after games, so he roamed streets of Manhattan with fellow safety Dick Nolan. "Coaches talk about playing with abandon — he played with abandon!" assessed New York coach Jim Lee Howell. Wore no hip pads to increase speed. Died in car accident.

PATULSKI, WALTER G. Defensive End. B. 2/3/50, Fulton, N.Y. 6'6", 265. Attended Christian Brothers Academy of Syracuse, N.Y. Consensus All-American for Notre Dame, 1971. Started every game during 1969-71 collegiate career. Played in Hula Bowl and Cotton Bowl. First player chosen in entire pro football draft, 1972. Signed three-year contract with Buffalo Bills for reported $150,000 per year. Admits "I'm placid in a game. I don't loaf but I play too easy, too unemotional." Likes golf and bike riding.

PAUL, DONALD Linebacker. B. 3/18/25, Los Angeles, Calif. 6'11", 230. Attended UCLA. All-Coast center, 1946, 47. Played in 1947 Rose Bowl (UCLA lost to Illinois, 45-14). Los Angeles Rams, 1948-55. Durable, hard-hitting linebacker. Detroit tight end Leon Hart called him "dirtiest player in the league" in 1954. Paul considered it compliment. Played in four world championship games 1949, 50, 51, 55. 1951 Rams won title over Cleveland Browns, 24-17. Selected thrice to Pro Bowl 1952, 53, 54. Assistant coach with Rams, 1959. Now Southern California restaurant owner; also provides color on taped telecasts of Ram home games.

PAZZETTI, VINCENT J. (Pat) Quarterback. B. 1/2/1890, Wellesley, Mass. D. 8/3/72, Bethlehem, Pa. 5'11", 160. Excelled in baseball, football and hockey at Wellesley (Mass.) H.S. Performed football, baseball wizardry at Wesleyan (Conn.), 1908-09; Lehigh, 1911-12. Pitcher in baseball. As captain, 1912, guided Lehigh to 9-2 football record. Same season named 2nd-team All-America. His game featured broken-field running and spot punting. Earned degree in mining engineering. Assistant football coach at Lehigh for 13 years. Worked nearly 50 years with Bethlehem Steel Corp., retiring as general manager of parent plant. Received Boys' Clubs of America Silver Keystone Award and Lehigh University Alumni Award. National Football Foundation Hall of Fame.

PEABODY, ENDICOTT (Chub) Guard. B. 2/15/20, Lawrence, Mass. 6, 185. Attended William Penn Charter School, Philadelphia, and Groton School in Massachusetts. Latter was founded by his grandfather. Groton also produced Huntington (Tack) Hardwick, who, like Peabody, would be selected to National Football Foundation Hall of Fame. Matriculated at Harvard. All-America left guard and Knute Rockne Trophy winner, 1941. Recognized as Harvard's finest lineman, Peabody's defensive tactics earned him title "Baby-faced Assassin." Offensively, he was outstanding running guard for coach Dick Harlow. Also played hockey and tennis. As naval officer decorated with Silver Star for gallantry in action in World War II. His ship, *Tirante*, sank Japanese ammunition ship and two destroyers in mined Korean harbor. Governor of Massachusetts, 1963-64. Democratic candidate for U.S. Senate, 1966. Founder and present partner in law firm, Peabody, Rivlin and Lambert, Washington D.C. National Football Foundation Hall of Fame.

PEAKS, CLARENCE E. Running Back. B. 9/23/35, Greenville, Miss. 6'1", 220. Grew up in Flint, Mich. Michigan State letterman under Duffy Daugherty, 1954-56. Scored one TD and passed for another in Spartans' 17-14 Rose Bowl win over UCLA, 1956. Suffered knee injury during senior year which thwarted bid for All-America honors. Scored 13 TDs in Michigan State career. Philadelphia Eagles, 1957-63; Pittsburgh Steelers, 1964-65. Member of Eagles' NFL championship team, 1960. Pro rushing totals: 951 carries, 3660 yds., 3.8-yd. average, 21 TDs.

PEARSON, CHARLES M. (Stubby) Tackle. B. 5/7/20, Madison, Wis. D. 3/30/44, Palau Islands. 6'4", 220. Brilliant high school career at Madison, starring in three sports. Dartmouth captain, 1941. Class president three years. Also called "Abe Lincoln" and "Senator" because of sense of humor and farm-boy sincerity. Played in 1940 "Fifth Down" game that Cornell "won" 7-3, then conceded to Big Green. Fond of poetry, Keats especially. Girlfriend was *Life* cover girl prior to Pearl Harbor. Became navy dive-bomber pilot, losing his life diving on Japanese destroyer in Palau campaign. *Sports Illustrated* Silver Anniversary All-America team. 1966.

PECK, ROBERT D. Center. B. 5/30/1891, Lock Haven, Pa. D. 6/14/32. 5'8", 180. U. of Pittsburgh, 1914-16. Known primarily as center, he was also cagey defensively. Twice All-America, 1915-16. Aggressive player with fine speed. Pop Warner considered 1916 Pitt team, named national champion, as greatest club he ever coached. Peck was teammate of Jock Sutherland. In three-year period played in only one losing game. Citizens Savings Hall of Fame, National Football Foundation Hall of Fame.

PEDEN, DONALD C. Coach. B. 1899, Kewanee, Ill. D. 2/23/70, Oxford, Ohio. Played halfback at Illinois. Fast, wiry, shifty. Threw TD pass to Laurie Walquist vs. Ohio State, 1921, providing 7-0 victory. Marked only time that season Buckeyes were scored on by conference foe. Coached Ohio U., 1924-42; 45-46. Record: 121-46-11. Unbeaten three seasons, 1929, 30, 35. Also coached baseball 25 years, producing 261-42 record. Ohio's Peden Stadium named in his honor. Citizens Savings Hall of Fame.

PELLINGTON, WILLIAM A. Linebacker. B. 9/25/27, Ramsey, N.J. 6'2", 238. Physical education major at Rutgers. Baltimore Colts, 1953-64, saw action at both corner and middle linebacker. At best against running plays. In his last eight seasons Baltimore never finished below .500, winning NFL titles in 1957, 58. Also played in '63 title game. Before joining Colts had brief trial with Cleveland Browns. Now owns The Iron Horse restaurant in Baltimore.

PENDLETON, TALBOT T. Running Back. B. 2/14/1891, Berkeley Springs, W. Va. D. 6/4/73. 5'10", 165. Princeton captain, All-America, 1910. Was Texas oilman before buying Baca Float Ranch at Tubac, Ariz. There he raised vegetables and cattle, not necessarily in that order.

PENNOCK, STANLEY B. Guard. B. 6/15/1892, Syracuse, N.Y. D. 11/27/16. 5'8", 185. Harvard, 1912-14. Sixty-minute guard for Percy Haughton. One of school's five three-time All-Americas. Harvard was national co-champion each season and won 27 straight games — Crimson was tied by Penn (13-13) and Brown (0-0). Citizens Savings Hall of Fame, National Football Foundation Hall of Fame.

PEOPLES, WOODROW (Woody) Guard. B. 8/16/43, Birmingham, Ala. 6'2", 252. Graduate of Grambling. Spent 1966-67 in military service. San Francisco 49ers, 1968-73. Pro Bowl, 1973, 74. Started 56 straight games, 1970-73. Signed originally as free agent. Strong, talented blocker.

PERDONI, RENSO (Rock) Tackle. B. 12/10/41, near Milan, Italy. 5'11", 230. Moved to U.S. with parents when he was 7. Attended Wellesley (Mass.) H.S. and Ferrum (Va.) J.C. Named All-America and nation's outstanding junior college lineman by NJCAA, 1968. Georgia Tech, 1969-70. Georgia Amateur Athlete of the Year, Consensus All-America, Tech co-captain, finalist for Vince Lombardi Award, 1970. Won many plaudits for speed and strength. "Perdoni may well be Georgia Tech's best defensive tackle ever...I know he's the best that I've ever seen," said Tech athletic director Bobby Dodd. Rock is now playing with Saskatchewan Roughriders.

PERKINS, DONALD A. Running Back. B. Waterloo, Iowa. 5'11", 200. Attended West Waterloo H.S. Rushed for even 2000 yds. at U. of New Mexico, 1957-59. Set 12 school records. Had 90-yd. kickoff return vs. Wyoming, 1959. National kickoff-return champion that season with 34.7-yd. average. Dallas Cowboys, 1961-68. Missed what would have been rookie year with broken foot, 1960, thereby avoiding Dallas' 0-11-1 season. Consistency was trademark. Led Cowboys in rushing each of his eight seasons. Retired as 5th greatest rusher in NFL history, amassing 6217 yds. on 1500 carries. Scored 42 career TDs. Six Pro Bowls, 1962, 63, 64, 67, 68, 69. All-NFL, 1962. Played halfback and fullback. Suffered many injuries and lacked great speed, size, but always gave 100 percent. Buddy Dial praised: "Perkins is the most amazing football player I've ever known. Except for Bobby Layne (until Perkins) I've never known a player who got everything out of his ability on every down." NFL championship game, 1967.

PERRY, DOYT L. Coach. B. Croton, Ohio. Attended Bowling Green. Spent 18 years coaching all sports at Ohio high schools. In 1951 became backfield coach for Woody Hayes' first Ohio State team. At Columbus tutored All-America backs Vic Janowicz and Hopalong Cassady. In 1955 named Bowling Green head coach, remaining there 10 years. Compiled excellent 77-10-5 record. Sent numerous B. G. players to pro ranks, including Bob Reynolds, Bernie Casey,

Jamie Rivers. Many of his pupils are now coaching. Bo Schembechler, current Michigan mentor, was first assistant he hired at Bowling Green. B. G. athletic director, 1965-71; golf coach, assistant A.D. at Miami International, 1971-73. Heart attack and open heart surgery forced retirement in 1973.

PERRY, FLETCHER (Joe) Running Back. B. 1/27/27, Stephens, Ark. 6', 185. Ranks with greatest pro backs. Prep track star at Jordan H.S. in Los Angeles. Attended Compton (Calif.) J.C., scoring 22 TDs in one season. While playing for Alameda Naval Air Station, Perry impressed nearby San Francisco 49ers. They signed him out of service; he proceeded to play 14 years for 49ers, 1948-60, 63. First two seasons San Francisco was AAFC team. Also played with Baltimore Colts, 1961-62. Leading AAFC, 1949, and NFL, 1953, 54 rusher. His 1018 yds. in '53 made him 4th pro player to pass 1000-yd. figure. Colts' Lenny Moore called Perry "the best conditioned athlete I ever saw. He was first class in everything..." During pro career Perry rushed for 9723 yds. and 5.0 average; also scored 71 TDs. Retired with more rushing yardage than any back in NFL history; amassed 10,346 yds. overall. All-Pro fullback, 1953, 54. Pro Football Hall of Fame.

PETERS, RICHARD L. Coach. B. 4/10/20, Valley Falls, Kan. D. 5/26/73, Manhattan, Kan. All-Big 6 end at Kansas State. Coached Ottawa U. (Kan.), 1949-53, 57-71. Record: 129-42-3. Made Ottawa powerhouse in small-college circles. Won seven Kansas Conference titles. Assisted at SMU, colleague of Hank Stram in 1956. Stram was SMU backfield coach. On team were Ray Berry, Forrest Gregg, Lamar Hunt. At Ottawa, Peters developed fine defensive clubs, excellent passing attacks. One QB, Ed Buzzell, threw 73 TD passes for career NAIA record. Assisted Vince Gibson at Kansas State, 1972. Died suddenly of heart attack. NAIA Hall of Fame.

PETERSON, WILLIAM E. Coach. B. 5/14/23, Toronto, Ohio. Captained Ohio Northern, 1948. Assistant coach at LSU, 1955-59; head coach at Mansfield (Ohio) H.S., 1951-54; Florida State, 1960-70; Rice, 1971; Houston Oilers, 1972-73. Got start in college as offensive line coach under LSU's Paul Dietzel. Compiled 62-42-11 record at Florida State. Took Seminoles to four bowls: Gator twice, 1965, 68; Sun, 1967; Peach, 1969. 2-1-1 record. Also athletic director at Rice when he left to join pros. Won only one of 14 games with Oilers in 1972. When losing skid reached 17 straight in 1973, Peterson was fired and replaced by Houston general manager Sid Gillman. Rice career depicted in book, *Saturday's Children,* by Giles Tippette.

PETTIBON, RICHARD A. (Richie) Defensive Back. B. 4/18/38, New Orleans, La. 6'3", 208. Graduate of Jesuit H.S., New Orleans, and Tulane. All-SEC quarterback, 1958. 2nd-round draft choice of Chicago Bears. Played 10 years for Bears, 1959-68; then Los Angeles Rams, 1969-70; Washington Redskins, 1971-72. Intercepted eight passes and helped Bears to NFL championship, 1963. All-Pro same season. Pro Bowl, 1963, 64, 67, 68. Missed most of '72 season due to knee injury. Ranked with game's best safeties. Returned interception 101 yds. for

TD vs. Los Angeles Rams, 12/9/62, 2nd longest in NFL annals. Career interception totals: 48 thefts, 801 yds., 16.7-yd. average, 3 TDs. Super Bowl, 1973.

PFANN, GEORGE R. Quarterback. B. Marion, Ohio. 5'10", 190. Never defeated or tied as Cornell quarterback, 1921-23. In 24-game career Cornell outscored its foes 1022 to 81. Big Red amassed such scores as 110-0 over Western Reserve, 84-0 over Susquehanna and 59-7 over Dartmouth. All-America, 1923. Earned law degree at Oxford where he lettered in rugby and lacrosse. Head coach five years at Swarthmore. Lt. Col. in World War II, serving as Secretary of 7th and 3rd U.S. Armies under Gen. Patton. Pfann was awarded seven Battle Stars and one Arrowhead. Before and after war practiced law in New York City. Citizens Savings Hall of Fame, National Football Foundation Hall of Fame.

PHELAN, JAMES M. (Jimmy) Coach. B. 12/5/1891, California. Notre Dame, 1915-17. One of numerous Knute Rockne proteges. Coached Missouri, 1920-21; Purdue, 1922-29; Washington, 1930-41; St. Mary's (Calif.), 1942-47. Record: 136-87-14. Developed All-Americas Elmer Sleight and Ralph Welch (Purdue); Max Starcevich, Rudy Mucha, Ray Frankowski (Washington); Herman Wedemeyer (St. Mary's). Citizens Savings Hall of Fame, National Football Foundation Hall of Fame. Lives in Sacramento.

PHILBIN, GERALD J. (Gerry) Defensive End. B. 7/31/41, Pawtucket, R.I. 6'2", 245. All-East and Academic All-America at SUNY (Buffalo), 1963. 3rd-round draft choice of New York Jets, 1964. Played with Jets thru 1972. Named All-AFL twice, 1968, 69. Played with numerous injuries. Traded to Kansas City Chiefs after 1972 season but balked at playing in K.C. Chiefs then dealt him to Philadelphia Eagles for Leroy Keyes and Ernie Calloway. Selected to All-Time AFL team by Pro Football Hall of Fame. Owner of Gerry Philbin Goal Post restaurants in East Massapequa, N.Y., and Pawtucket. Invited to White House in recognition of work against drug abuse.

PHILBIN, STEPHEN H. (Silent Steve) Running Back. B. 6/7/1888, New York, N.Y. D. 11/13/73, Old Lyme, Conn. 5'10½", 177. Yale, 1907-09. All-America for unbeaten, untied, unscored-upon team captained by Ted Coy, 1909. Baseball captain and *Phi Beta Kappa* graduate, 1910. Took Harvard law degree, 1913. 2nd Lt. Army Signal Corps, World War I. President, Harvard Law School Association of New York City, 1941. President, New York Patent Law Association, 1942. Specialized in patent law litigation. Was senior partner of Fish & Neave law firm, NYC.

PHILLIPS, JAMES (Red) End. B. 2/5/36, Alexander City, Ala. 6'1", 198. Averaged 19.5-yds. per catch at Auburn, 1955-57. All-SEC, 1955, 57. Unanimous All-America, 1957. One of two Los Angeles Ram 1st-round draft choices, 1958; other was Lou Michaels. Played with Rams, 1958-64; Minnesota Vikings, 1965-67. Caught passes in 68 consecutive games, 1958-63. All-NFL and

Ram MVP, 1961. Played in three Pro Bowls. During career caught 401 passes for 6044 yds. Complete end whose specialty was long pass patterns. Excellent blocker. Assistant coach, San Diego Chargers, 1969-71; Florida State, 1972-73.

PHILLIPS, LLOYD Defensive End. B. 5/2/45, Fort Worth, Tex. 6'3", 230. Named Texas All-Star game MVP and to Texas Super Team at Longview H.S., 1962. First U. of Arkansas player selected All-SWC three times, 1964, 65, 66. Also Razorbacks' first two-time All-America, 1965, 66. Unanimous choice in '66, consensus in 65. Credited with 22 tackles against Tulsa, 1965. Outland Trophy winner, 1966. Arkansas won national championship his sophomore season, defeating Nebraska in Cotton Bowl. Tackle in college, Phillips moved to defensive end as pro. Chicago Bears, 1967-69. Now lives in Springdale, Ark.

PHIPPS, MICHAEL E. Quarterback. B. 11/19/47, Shelbyville, Ind. 6'2", 205. Prep All-America in football, twice All-State in baseball at Anderson (Ind.) H.S. Purdue, 1967-69. Tri-captain, MVP, All-America and runnerup in Heisman Trophy voting, 1969. Set 24 Purdue and Big 10 records. First Boilermaker to gain 5000 yds. in career (5883 total offense). 22-5 record as Purdue starter. Completed 24 of 39 passes for 424 yds. in game against Stanford. No. 1 draft choice of Cleveland Browns, 1970. Browns, 1970-73. Blossomed as pro quarterback, leading Browns to divisional playoffs in 1972. That season completed 144 passes for 1994 yds. and 13 TDs. Threw for 1719 yds. and 9 TDs, 1973.

PICCOLO, L. BRIAN (Pic) Running Back. B. 10/21/43, Pittsfield, Mass. D. 6/16/70, New York, N.Y. 6', 195. Attended Central Catholic H.S. in Fort Lauderdale, Fla., and Wake Forest. Received only two college offers — from Wichita State and Wake Forest. Led NCAA scorers (111 points) and rushers (1044 yds) in 1964. Played five seasons with Chicago Bears, 1965-69. Gained 927 yds. on 157 carries (3.5 average), caught 58 passes for 537 yds. and scored 5 touchdowns in NFL. Victim of cancer. Subject of book, *Brian Piccolo: A Short Season* and award-winning television movie, *Brian's Song*. Inspiration to millions with courageous fight for life.

PIERCE, PALMER E. Administrator. B. 10/23/1865, Savanna, Ill. D. 1/17/40, New York, N.Y. Manager of first Army football team, 1890. Graduate manager of West Point football, 1902-07. Athletic officer with AEF in China, 1912-14. Served as president of both NCAA and AAU. Member, General Munitions and War Industries Boards, 1917-18. Commanded 54th Infantry Brigade in France, 1918. Edited *Who's Who in American Sports*. Achieved rank of Brig. Gen. Hobbies were tennis and golf.

PIETROSANTE, NICHOLAS V. Running Back. B. 9/10/37, Ansonia, Conn. 6', 221. Powerful fullback and candid personality. Notre Dame, 1956-58. Spent much of 1956 season on bench. Told coach Terry Brennan to play him or would go elsewhere. Persuaded to stay, Nick received All-America mention last two seasons. Most rewarding game occurred vs. Army in 1957. Before hometown

Ansonia folks at Yankee Stadium, scored two touchdowns, one on 65-yd. run. Played with Detroit Lions, 1959-65; Cleveland Browns, 1966-67. Established Lion career records for rushing attempts (938) and yds. (3933). Selected twice to Pro Bowl, 1961, 62. Hard-nosed, aggressive runner. Dependable on 3rd-down situations. In career rushed for 4026 yds. on 955 carries, 4.2 average, and 28 TDs.

PIHOS, PETER L. (Big Dog) End. B. 10/22/23, Orlando, Ill. 6'2", 220. Indiana, 1942-43, 45-46. Career interrupted by army service. Played first two years at end, latter two at fullback. Broke all Indiana career records for pass receiving, total points and TDs. Led Hoosiers to conference title, 1945. Called plays while stationed at fullback. Played nine years as two-way end for Philadelphia Eagles, 1947-55. NFL title games, 1947, 48, 49. All-Pro five times, 1947, 48, 53, 54, 55. Thrice led league in pass receiving, 1953, 54, 55 (shared). Retired from NFL with 373 receptions for 5619 yds., 61 TDs. Citizens Savings Hall of Fame, National Football Foundation Hall of Fame, Pro Football Hall of Fame. Now in insurance business in Fort Wayne, Ind.

PILOT, JAMES (Preacher) Running Back. B. Kingsville, Tex. 5'11", 205. Grew up in Kingsville, near Corpus Christi. Played on runnerup state championship team. Besieged by college offers, finally choosing Kansas. Played freshman year there. Was fraternity brother of Wilt Chamberlain. Ran afoul of grade problems, though, and transferred to New Mexico State. There played final three seasons under Warren Woodson, 1961-63. Sensational as sophomore and junior, rushing for 1278 and 1247 yds. National leader in rushing average (6.7 yds.) and points (138: 21 TDs, 12 PATs), 1961. Led in TDs with 15, 1962. Slumped senior year or would have had considerably more than 2971 career yds. rushing.

PITTMAN, CHARLES V. Running Back. B. 1/22/48, Baltimore, Md. 6'1", 208. Rushed for 2236 yds. and scored 32 TDs at Penn State, 1967-69. All-America, 1969. Played on two winning Orange Bowl teams, 1969, 70. Also played in Senior Bowl. St. Louis Cardinals, 1970; Baltimore Colts, 1971; New England Patriots, 1973. Drafted on 3rd round by Cardinals, 1970. Kickoff return specialist in pros, averaging 23.6 yds. on 24 attempts, 1970-71. Didn't play in 1972.

PITTS, FRANK (Riddler) End. B. 11/12/43, Atlanta, Ga. 6'2", 195. Attended Archer H.S., Atlanta, and Southern U. Little All-America, 1963. Kansas City Chiefs, 1965-70; Cleveland Browns, 1971-73. Played in two Super Bowls with Chiefs, 1967, 70. In '70 Super Bowl, vs. Minnesota Vikings, gained 37 yds. on end-around plays. Chiefs traded Pitts to Browns for draft choice following 1970 season. Enjoyed best year with 36 catches for 620 yds. and 8 TDs, 1972. Same season caught winning 38-yd. TD pass against San Diego. Antique car buff. Drives 1936 Pontiac and has turned down offers for it up to $7,000; originally bought car for $85.

PLUM, MILTON R. Quarterback. B. 1/20/35, Westville, N.J. 6'2", 205. 18-8 playing record at Penn State, 1954-56. Cleveland Browns, 1957-61; Detroit Lions, 1962-67; Los Angeles Rams, 1968; New York Giants, 1969. Completed 54.0 percent of career passes for 17,536 yds. and 122 TDs. NFL passing leader twice consecutively, 1960, 61, record he shares with Cecil Isbell. Plum threw 208 passes in one stretch without being intercepted. NFL championship game, 1957. Now sales manager in Raleigh.

PLUNKETT, JIM Quarterback. B. 12/5/47, San Jose, Calif. 6'2", 210. Son of blind parents. Thyroid tumor (non-malignant) ruined freshman year at Stanford, 1967. Coach John Ralston suggested move to defensive end but Plunkett insisted, "I'm a quarterback." Lettered, 1968-70. Unanimous All-America, Heisman Trophy, Maxwell Trophy, 1970. During career accounted for 7887 yds. total offense, more than any player in history. Scored and passed for 62 TDs. Led Stanford to 27-17 Rose Bowl victory over favored Ohio State, 1971. First player chosen in 1971 NFL draft, by New England Patriots. Threw 19 TD passes rookie season to win AFC's Rookie of the Year honors. Only Charlie Conerly threw more TD passes as NFL rookie. With Patriots, 1971-73. Aggressive, strong-armed quarterback.

PODOLAK, EDWARD J. Running Back. B. 9/1/47, Atlantic, Iowa. 6'1", 204. Quarterback first two years at Iowa, then switched to tailback in fourth game of senior season in 1969. Finished 2nd in Big 10 rushing that year and set Iowa one-season record with 937 yds. Performed in East-West Shrine and Hula Bowl games. No. 2 draft choice of Kansas City Chiefs in 1970. Chiefs, 1970-73. Versatile back in pros; handles passes and kickoff-punt returns, besides rushing duties. Gave greatest performance against Miami in 1972 AFC championship game, accounting for 350-yds. Chiefs' leading rusher four straight years. Owns national insurance, real estate and banking business. Also sports director for radio station, KUDL, Kansas City.

POE, ARTHUR End. B. 3/22/1879, Baltimore, Md. D. 4/15/51. 5'7", 146. Probably best of John Prentiss Poe's football playing sons, all six of whom went to Princeton. All-America, 1899; 2nd team, 1898. His brothers, Edgar Allen and John, were also All-Americas. Their father was nephew of famous poet. Arthur beat Yale with 95-yd. run after recovering fumble, 1898; again on dropkick, first he ever attempted, in 11-10 win, in 1899. National Football Foundation Hall of Fame.

POLLARD, FREDERICK D. (Fritz) Running Back. B. 1/27/1894, Chicago, Ill. 5'8", 150. Product of Chicago's Lane Technical H.S. where he starred in three sports. Brown, 1914-16. First Black to make Walter Camp's 1st-team. All-America, 1916. Scored two TDs against both Yale and Harvard in 1916, leading Brown to upset victories on successive Saturdays. Intercollegiate hurdles champion, 1916, 17. Played in first modern Rose Bowl game, 1916, and first pro football league; was first Black pro coach in America. After college played for Akron Indians, 1919-21, 25-26; Milwaukee Badgers, 1922; Hammond Pros,

1923-25; Providence Steamrollers, 1925. Player-coach at Akron, 1920-21, and Hammond, 1923-25. Fritz rose high in business circles. Served as president of Pollard Investment Co. and Pollard Coal Co. Former firm represents first Black investment company in America. Not to be overshadowed brother, Leslie, played football at Dartmouth, 1908; sister, Naomi, was first Black woman to graduate from Northwestern, 1905; and son, Frederick Jr., won bronze medal in Berlin Olympics, 1936. Citizens Savings Hall of Fame, National Football Foundation Hall of Fame.

PONDELIK, JOSEPH, JR. Guard. B. 5/8/02, Chicago, Ill. D. 1/21/65. 5'11", 215. U. of Chicago, 1922-24. All-Conference each year. All-America 2nd team, 1924. Was last of Amos Alonzo Stagg players so honored. Played in memorable Chicago-Princeton game of 1922, won 21-18 by Tigers. Also wrestled at Chicago. Line coach under Stagg, 1925. At death was owner of Pondelik Construction Co., Cicero, Ill.

PONT, JOHN Coach. B. 11/13/27, Canton, Ohio. Born in city where Pro Football Hall of Fame is located. Attended Miami (Ohio). All-Mid-American Conference halfback, 1949-51. Played first two years under Woody Hayes, final season for Ara Parseghian. Still holds eight Miami records, including TDs (27) and rushing yardage (2390). Head coach at Miami, 1956-62; Yale, 1963-64; Indiana, 1965-72; Northwestern, 1973. Composite record: 88-87-4. Won two Mid-American titles, one Big 10 co-championship. Lost to Southern California, 14-3, in 1968 Rose Bowl. One of large number of Miami graduates who have distinguished themselves in coaching. Among them are Earl (Red) Blaik, Paul Brown, Parseghian, Weeb Ewbank, Paul Dietzel, Jack Faulkner. Non-alumni who have coached at Miami include Hayes, Sid Gillman, Stu Holcomb.

POOLE, G. BARNEY End. B. 10/29/23, Gloster, Miss. 6'3", 225. Youngest of Mississippi Poole brothers. Played at Ole Miss, 1942, 47-48; Army, 1944-46. All-America, 1944, 47, 48. Earned 23 varsity letters in football, basketball, baseball. Made two key tackles in Army's famed goal-line stand against Navy, 1946. They preserved 20-18 Army victory, giving Black Knights third straight unbeaten campaign. Teamed with Charlie Conerly in 1947 to give Ole Miss its first SEC title. Set NCAA one-game record that year with 13 receptions vs. Chattanooga. Captained College All-Star team, 1949. New York Yankees (AAFC), 49; New York Yanks, 1950-51; Dallas Texans, 1952; Baltimore Colts, 1953; New York Giants, 1954. Coached at Alabama, LSU, Southern Mississippi. Now manager, Mississippi Memorial Stadium, Jackson. National Football Foundation Hall of Fame.

POOLE, JAMES E. (Buster) Defensive End. B. 9/9/15, Gloster, Miss. Mississippi, 1934-36. Three-year regular in football, baseball, basketball. Won Norris Trophy senior year, presented to outstanding Ole Miss scholar-athlete. New York Giants, 1937-41, 45-46; Chicago Cardinals, 1945. Pro career interrupted by naval service. Became regular in rookie year with Giants. All-Pro,

1939. In 1954, Sammy Baugh voted Poole one of two best defensive ends in pro history. Played baseball in minors, 1937-38, 41. James, Jr. was Ole Miss tight end, 1969-71. Now retired, Buster was long-time defensive line coach at Mississippi. Was first addition to Rebel staff after Johnny Vaught was named head coach in 1947. Brother of Ray and Barney.

POST, RICHARD M. (Dickie) Running Back. B. 9/27/45, San Pedro, Calif. 5'9", 190. U. of Houston, 1964-66. Captain, 1966. Gained 2219 yds. rushing during career, led Houston runners all three seasons. San Diego Chargers, 1967-70; Denver Broncos, 1971; Houston Oilers, 1971. Hit peak in 1969, then ineffective final two years. AFL's leading rusher with 873 yds., 1969. In pro career made 608 carries for 2605 yds., caught 96 passes for 903 yds., scored 19 TDs. Also returned 29 kickoffs for 21.2 average. AFL All-Star games, 1968, 70.

POTTIOS, MYRON J. (Mike) Linebacker. B. 1/18/39, Van Voorhis, Pa. 6'2", 232. Attended Charleroi (Pa.) H.S. Notre Dame, 1958-60. Center and linebacker in college, winning three letters. East-West Shrine and College All-Star games. Drafted by Pittsburgh Steelers on 2nd round in 1961. Steelers, 1961-65; Los Angeles Rams, 1966-70; Washington Redskins, 1971-73. Missed entire '62 season due to injuries. Three Pro Bowls, 1962, 64, 65. In 13 seasons intercepted 12 passes for 224 yds. Super Bowl, 1973.

POWELL, ARTHUR End. B. San Diego, Calif. 6'2", 212. Attended San Diego State. Left school in 1957 to sign with Toronto Argonauts. After playing two seasons in CFL, he joined Philadelphia Eagles for 1959. Then New York Titans, 1960-62; Oakland Raiders, 1963-66; Buffalo Bills, 1967; Minnesota Vikings, 1968. Caught 479 passes during career for 8046 yds., 81 TDs. In 1963 handled 73 passes for 1300 yds., 16 TDs. Disappointed that he didn't win league MVP award that year — recipient was Oakland roommate, Clem Daniels. "I was happy for Clem," said Powell, "but the award belonged to me." Had problems with management, usually concerning his worth as player. Labeled "troublemaker" and "clubhouse lawyer."

POWELL, WALTER D. Center B. 7/15/1891, Reedsburg, Wis. D. 9/15/67, Gastonia, N.C. All-Conference center for Wisconsin's Big 10 champions, 1912. Head coach at three colleges: Western Reserve, 1914-17; Montana State, 1919; Stanford, 1920-21. Also athletic director at Stanford, 1921. Was member of Football Rules Committee. Originated movement to build Walter Camp Memorial on national basis at Yale. Leading football official. For many years affiliated with John Hancock Life Insurance Co.

PRESNELL, GLENN E. Running Back. B. 7/28/05, Gilead, Neb. 5'10", 190. All-America halfback at Nebraska, 1927. Played in East-West Shrine game. Portsmouth Spartans, 1931-33; Detroit Lions, 34-36. All-NFL, 1933. That season tied Jack Manders (Chicago Bears) for league FG leadership with six. Coached Nebraska, 1942; Eastern Kentucky, 1954-63. Composite record: 45-56-

3, including 42-49-3 at Eastern. Best year was first as Maroons went unbeaten in regular season play, losing only to Omaha, in Tangerine Bowl. Eastern's first full-time athletic director, school's golf coach since 1956.

PRICE, EDWARD J. (Eddie) Running Back. B. 9/2/25, New Orleans, La. 5'11", 190. Tulane fullback, 1946-49. All-America, 1949. Finished career 1st in rushing yds. (3095) and 3rd in rushing yds. per carry (6.0). Led nation with 6.6-yd. average rushing in 1949. In four years totaled 31 TDs. New York Giants, 1950-56. Largely to Price's efforts, Giants compiled 9-2-1 record in 1951. Gained 971 yds., leading league, on 271 carries which established NFL record. Eleven times during career rushed for 100 yds. or more. Was All-Pro twice, 1951, 52. Now in real estate business in New Orleans.

PRUITT, GREGORY D. Running Back. B. 8/18/51, Houston, Tex. 5'9", 185. Graduate of B.C. Elmore H.S. in Houston. U. of Oklahoma, 1968-70. Sooners' No. 2 career rusher with 2844 yds. on 385 carries. Originally recruited as split end. Shifted to halfback when Oklahoma adopted wishbone-T system. Helped make wishbone one of the most popular offenses in country. In 1971 averaged 151.4 yds. per game (3rd best nationally), 9.41 yds. per carry and rushed for 294 yds. against Kansas State. Unanimous All-America, 1971, 72. Played in three bowl games: Astro-Bluebonnet, 1970; Sugar, 1972-73. Blessed with great speed. Signed by Cleveland Browns in 1973 after being drafted on 2nd round. Ranked 3rd that season in AFC kickoff returns (28.3-yd. average), 4th in punt returns (11.3-yd. average). For efforts named to Pro Bowl.

PUGH, JETHRO, JR. Tackle. B. 7/3/44, Windsor, N.C. 6'6", 220. Attended Southwestern H.S. in Windsor. Matriculated at Elizabeth City State without scholarship. Developed into two-time All-Conference tackle and team's Most Valuable Lineman. Dallas Cowboys, 1965-73. From 11th-round draft choice became one of most feared defensive tackles in pro football. Stationed on left side. Dallas coach Tom Landry complimented: "Pugh is just a great athlete who can do everything." Toured Far East military bases and hospitals with Cowboy teammates Rayfield Wright and Pat Toomay, 1973. NFL championship games, 1966, 67. Super Bowl, 1971, 72.

PUND, HENRY R. (Peter) Tackle. B. 1/27/07, Augusta, Ga. 6', 200. Georgia Tech, 1926-28. Nicknamed "Peter the Great." Captain and unanimous All-America, 1928. During senior year Georgia Tech crushed nine straight opponents and then, in Rose Bowl, edged California, 8-7. Rose game featured "wrong way" run of Cal's Roy Riegels, which set up margin of victory for Tech. Named center on Best Eleven of 1920s by national board of experts, 1969. National Football Foundation Hall of Fame. Retired as executive with Shipbuilding Department of Bethlehem Steel Corp. Lives in Darien, Conn.

PURVIS, DUANE Running Back. B. 11/13/12, Decatur, Ill. 6'1", 190. Followed brother, Jim, to Purdue. In Duane's first varsity game, 1932, scored season's inaugural touchdown for Purdue, catching pass and crossing south goal line. Feat matched brother's earlier performance exactly — Jim caught pass and scored season's opening TD in 1929 by crossing south goal line. Believe it or not both men, three years apart, wore same number (88), played same position (right halfback) and scored against same foe (Kansas State). Duane broke open close game with 85-yd. touchdown run against NYU as Boilermakers won 34-9, 1932. He and Jim Carter were known as "Touchdown Twins." They scored nine of Purdue's 16 TDs. in 1933. Purvis was All-America, 1933, 34. Consensus choice in '34. Now assistant professor of physical education, Purdue.

PUTNAM, DUANE Guard. B. 9/5/28, Pollock, S.D. 6', 231. Attended College of Pacific. Played football and threw shot-put. Regarded as "the last of the great small pro guards." Outstanding talent at pulling out and leading play. Played for Los Angeles Rams, 1952-59, 62; Dallas Cowboys, 1960; Cleveland Browns, 1961. NFL championship game, 1955. Pro Bowl, 1955, 56, 58, 59. All-Pro three times, 1955, 57, 58. Originally reported to Rams at 195 pounds; via weightlifting added 40, retained quickness. Offensive line coach with San Diego Chargers, 1970-73. Formerly assistant coach at Los Angeles Valley College.

PYLE, MIKE Center. B. 7/18/39, Keokuk, Iowa. 6'3", 235. Captained Yale's first unbeaten, untied team in 37 years, 1960. That season Bulldogs shared Lambert Trophy with Navy. Gave Chicago Bears nine solid seasons, 1961-69, earning starting berth as rookie and maintaining it throughout career. Fine straight-ahead blocker.

QUINLAN, WILLIAM D. Defensive End. B. 6/19/32, Lawrence, Mass. 6'3",
250. Only sophomore starter for Michigan State, 1953. Spartans defeated
UCLA, 28-20, in '54 Rose Bowl. Quinlan played both ways at end. Left school
before junior year. Stationed at defensive end in pros where he was known as
gambler, hard rusher. Spent best years with Green Bay Packers, 1959-62. Also
played with Cleveland Browns, 1957-58; Philadelphia Eagles, 1963; Detroit
Lions, 1964; Washington Redskins, 1965. Packers were NFL champions, 1961,
62; lost title game in 1960.

RALSTON, JOHN Coach. B. 4/26/27, Oakland, Calif. Attended Norway (Mich.) H.S. and U. of California. Assistant coach at California, 1956-58; head coach at Utah State, 1959-62; Stanford, 1963-71. Took teams to Gotham Bowl, 1961, and two Rose Bowls, 1971, 72. Defeated Ohio State, 27-12, and Michigan 13-12, in those games at Pasadena. Coached West team three times in East-West Shrine game. Developed Merlin Olsen (Utah State), Jim Plunkett and Randy Vataha (Stanford). 31-11-1 record at Utah State; 54-36-3 at Stanford. Took command of Denver Broncos in 1972. Finished 5-9 first season, then improved to 7-5-2 in 1973. Known for enthusiasm, positive approach.

RAMSAY, STEVEN W. Quarterback. B. 4/22/47, Dallas, Tex. 6'2", 210. Graduate of W. W. Samuell H.S., Dallas; and North Texas State. Finished collegiate career 1st in following NCAA categories: pass completions (491), passing yds. (7076), TD passes (69) and total-offense yds. (6568). Recorded 93- and 87-yard passes in separate games against Cincinnati, 1968, 69. 37.2-yd. career punting average at North Texas State. 22-6-1 playing record, 1967-69. Twice All-MVC, 1968, 69. Selected on 5th round by New Orleans Saints in 1970. Saints, 1970; Denver Broncos, 1971-73.

RANDLE, ULMO (Sonny) End. B. 1/6/36, Washington, D.C. 6'2", 187. Graduated from Virginia. Led nation in kickoff returns with 24.1-yd. average. Ten-year pro standout with St. Louis Cardinals, 1959-66; San Francisco 49ers, 1967; Dallas Cowboys, 1968. All-NFL, 1960. Owns Cardinal records for career touchdowns (60), one-game receptions (16) and one-game reception yardage

281

(256). Caught 365 passes during career for 5996 yds., 65 TDs. Won two Southern Conference titles while compiling 22-10 record as head coach at East Carolina, 1971-73. Returned to alma mater, 1974, becoming seventh Virginia coach in 21 years. Randle said, "I'm home, I'm delighted to be home — and I don't plan to leave anytime soon."

RANKIN, DAVID W. End. B. 2/2/19, Tarkio, Mo. 6'1", 190. Although native Missourian, Warsaw, Ind., considered hometown. Attended Warsaw H.S. and Purdue. Three-year Purdue letterman, 1938-40; consensus All-America, 1939. Captained 1940 Boilermakers and '41 College All-Star team. Inducted into Marine Corps, along with three teammates, during intermission of All-Star contest. In track, formerly shared world record for 60-yd. low hurdles. Twice toured South Pacific as fighter pilot in marines. Flew 150 missions, received four Air Medals. Purdue track coach, 1946-73. Involved with special research in muscular physiology and track construction. Designed Purdue's self-contained track and field facility, originally used in 1953. School thus became first to use all-weather surfaces for all field events. Service duty, 1941-45, marked Rankin's only departure from Purdue during adult life since enrolling in 1937. *Sports Illustrated* Silver Anniversary All-America team, 1965.

RASHAD, AHMAD End. B. 11/19/49, Portland, Ore. 6'2", 200. Formerly Robert E. (Bobby) Moore. Prep All-America in Tacoma, Wash. Receiver as U. of Oregon sophomore, tailback last two years, 1969-71. Set 14 school records, including 36 TDs, 226 points. Ran for 1211 yds. as senior. All-America, 1971. Caught 59 passes for 909 yds. 6 TDs with St. Louis Cardinals, 1972-73. Was St. Louis' 1st-round draft choice. Teamed with Jim Hart for longest non-scoring scrimmage play in NFL history (98 yards), 1972. Wears glasses on field. Traded to Buffalo Bills for QB Dennis Shaw following 1973 season.

RATTERMAN, GEORGE Quarterback. B. 11/12/26, Cincinnati, Ohio. Notre Dame, 1945-46. Was back-up QB to All-America Johnny Lujack. Could have started at most other colleges. Majored in engineering and economics. Buffalo Bills (AAFC), 1947-49; New York Yanks, 1950-51; Cleveland Browns, 1952-56. Completed 438 of 831 passes during AAFC career, for 6194 yds. 52 TDs. With Browns, again in understudy role, this time to Otto Graham. When Graham retired after 1955 season, was finally afforded chance to prove himself in NFL. Browns slumped, however, to 5-7 record under Ratterman, after easily winning NFL titles in 1954, 55. He then called it quits. In 1956 completed 11 straight passes vs. Pittsburgh Steelers for Cleveland record (now shared with Milt Plum). Took law degree while playing pro ball. Extremely versatile. Has been author, telecaster, tax counsel, sheriff (Newport, Ky.). Was counsel for American Football League Players Association. Talented pianist.

RAUCH, JOHN Quarterback. B. 8/20/27, Philadelphia, Pa. 6', 185. As youngster with heart defect, told by doctor to give up sports. Switched doctors and finally given green light to play. Was all-round star at Little Yeadon (Pa.)

H.S. Coach Wally Butts watched Rauch perform in touch football game and offered scholarship to U. of Georgia. Butts made him quarterback (from prep fullback), gave speedy indoctrination of Georgia's four types of T-formation passes: drop-back, angle-back, roll-out, play pass. Rauch learned well. Started every game at quarterback, 1945-48. Steered Bulldogs to two SEC titles, four post-season bowl games. In 1940 Georgia enjoyed perfect season (11-0), climaxing with 20-10 Super Bowl victory over North Carolina. In four seasons Rauch passed for 4004 yds., accounted for 48 TDs. When awarded consensus All-America honors in 1948, gave all credit to coach: "They should have named Coach Butts to this thing. He did it, not me." New York Yanks, 1949; New York Bulldogs, 1950-51; Philadelphia Eagles, 1951. Assistant coach at Florida, 1952-53; Tulane, 1954, 62; Georgia, 1955-58; Army, 1959-61. Head coach, Oakland Raiders, 1966-68 (33-8-1); Buffalo Bills, 1969-70 (7-20-1).

RAY, BUFORD (Baby) Tackle. B. 1916, Una, Tenn. 6'6", 260. Attended Nashville Central (Tenn.) H.S. and Vanderbilt. Collegian, 1935-37. Green Bay Packers, 1938-48. NFL championship games, 1938, 39, 44. Packers were champs in '39 and '44. Member All-Pro Squad of the 1940s. Called "Baby" because of his "smallness." Assistant coach at Vanderbilt, 1949-66. Served under three coaches: Bill Edwards, Jack Green, Art Guepe. Presently, scout for Packers in Southeast. Lives in Nashville, where he's civic leader.

RAY, CARL P. Center. B. 11/9/14, New York, N.Y. 5'10", 190. Dartmouth, 1934-36. Son of prominent New York physician. Attended Deerfield Academy before Dartmouth. Reported one September 30 pounds overweight to coach Red Blaik. Trainer Rollie Bevan prescribed lettuce diet, and Ray quickly lost excess poundage. Remembered primarily for eight-yard TD interception that meant 14-6 defeat for Yale, 1935 — Dartmouth's first-ever win over Elis covering 52-year period. In 1961 named to *Sports Illustrated* Silver Anniversary All-America team. Member of board of directors, National Football Foundation Hall of Fame. Office equipment manufacturing executive.

RAY, HUGH (Shorty) Official. B. 9/21/1884, Highland Park, Ill. D. 9/16/56. NFL technical advisor and supervisor of officials, 1938-56. Absolute authority on rule-interpretation problems. Visited pro training camps each season to explain rule changes to players and coaches. Gave officials stringent written tests, making them completely knowledgeable of rulebook information. As league's technical advisor took more than 300,000 stopwatch observations. Although only 5'6", 136, Ray was first basketball captain at U. of Illinois, 1906. Devoted to sports safety. His motto: "Football is great as long as you don't get hurt." Pro Football Hall of Fame.

RAYMOND, HAROLD R. (Tubby) Coach. B. 11/14/25, Flint, Mich. Guard and QB at Michigan. Captained Michigan baseball team, 1949. Head coach at Delaware, 1966-73. 54-18 record in seven seasons, building powerful offensive machine. Two teams led college division in rushing, another was champ in total offense. Delaware crushed C. W. Post, 72-22, for its 4th-straight Boardwalk Bowl title, 1971. Raymond was named Kodak college-division Coach of the Year twice in succession, 1971, 72. Hens won A.P. & UPI national college titles both seasons. Served nine years as Delaware baseball coach and compiled 141-56 record.

REAVES, T. JOHNSON (John) Quarterback. B. 3/2/50, Anniston, Ala. 6'3", 210. Four-sport standout at T. R. Robinson H.S. in Tampa. Majored in marketing at U. of Florida. Set NCAA career passing record with 7594 yds. 1969-71. Attempted 1128 passes for another record. Established 19 Southeastern Conference records. Logged 54 TD tosses. Co-captain, All-Conference and All-America as senior. Played in East-West Shrine and Senior Bowl games. No. 1 draft choice of NFL (Philadelphia Eagles), 1972. Named to NFL All-Rookie team, throwing seven TD passes in 11 games for Eagles. Gave up starting job in favor of Roman Gabriel, 1973.

RECHICHAR, ALBERT Defensive Back-Kicker. B. Belle Vernon, Pa. 6'2", 210. Offensive wingback and defensive safety at Tennessee. As junior, 1950, led SEC in pass interceptions and punt returns. Same season returned punt 100 yds. for TD against Washington & Lee, feat duplicated by only six other players. Rushed 15 times, caught 4 passes and intercepted 2, returned 20 punts and 2 kickoffs, scored 2 touchdowns and kicked 26 PATs en route to All-SEC honors, 1951. Cleveland Browns, 1952; Baltimore Colts, 1953-59; Pittsburgh Steelers, 1960; New York Titans, 1961. Pro Bowl 1956, 57, 58. NFL title games, 1952, 58, 59. Intercepted 30 passes for 375 yds., one TD during pro career. Kicked record 56-yd. FG vs. Chicago Bears, 9/27/53, in first attempt in league game. Associated with Russell Industries of Bridgeville, Pa.

REDMAN, RICK C. Linebacker. B. 3/7/43, Portland, Ore. 6'0", 220. Attended Blanchett H.S. of Seattle. Consensus All-America guard at U. of Washington, 1963, 64. Most Valuable Lineman in East-West Shrine Game, 1964. 5th-round draft choice of San Diego Chargers. Chargers, 1965-73. Punter first three seasons, averaging 37.5 yds. on 153 kicks. Scored only pro TD on fumble recovery, 1966. As player-coach Redman totaled 66 tackles from weak side linebacker position in 1972. Played middle linebacker most of pro career. AFL All-Star game, 1968.

REED, OSCAR L. Running Back. B. 3/24/44, Memphis, Tenn. 6', 222. Had sensational game at Booker T. Washington H.S. in Memphis, and his shoes were bronzed. Attended Colorado State. Scored five TDs and picked up over 200 yds. rushing vs. Air Force Academy, 1967. Minnesota Vikings, 1968-73. Minnesota's leading rusher with 639 yds., No. 2 receiver with 205 yds., 1972. "His biggest asset is his quickness," said coach Bud Grant. "He runs very low, has a very distinctive style. He's low and sneaky. He squirts through the line. Once in a while there's a bubble and out comes Oscar." NFL championship game, 1969. Super Bowl, 1970, 74.

REEVES, DANIEL E. (Deacon Dan) Running Back. B. 1/19/44, Rome, Ga. 6'1", 205. South Carolina QB, 1962-64. Called Dallas Cowboys for tryout, earned invitation to training camp and was signed as free agent in 1965. Spent seven years with Cowboys, 1965-71. Enjoyed sensational year in 1967. Rushed for 757 yds., caught 41 passes for 557 more, scored league-leading 16 TDs. Not particulary fast, nor overpowering but had talent for finding hole and stretching for extra yardage. Was never again same runner after 1968 knee injury. Carried ball only 52 times during last two years. Scored 42 career TDs. Offensive backfield coach, Cowboys, 1972.

REEVES, DANIEL F. Owner. B. 6/30/12, New York, N.Y. D. 4/15/71, Los Angeles, Calif. Began sportdom's occupation of California by moving Cleveland Rams to Los Angeles, 1946. Ram owner for 31 years, 1941-71. First became captivated with California when he saw USC play in Coliseum in 1935. Reeves, heir to grocery chain fortune, failed in attempts to buy interest in Pittsburgh Steelers and Philadelphia Eagles before landing Rams. Was stubborn and petulant personality. Threatened to pull Rams out of NFL when owners turned down request of moving to Los Angeles. They relented, of course, and Reeves moved west. Helped integrate sport, signing Black halfback Kenny Washington of UCLA, and pioneered "road TV." His recommendations led to development of NFL "blackout" policy. Graduate of Georgetown. Pro Football Hall of Fame. Suffered from Hodgkin's disease.

REGNER, THOMAS E. Guard. B. 4/19/44, Kenosha, Wis. 6'1", 255. Attended St. Joseph's H.S., Kenosha, and Notre Dame. 25-3-2 playing record under Ara Parseghian, 1964-66. Consensus All-America, 1966. Houston Oilers, 1967-72; Baltimore Colts, 1973. Drafted on 1st round by Oilers. Traded to Colts with 3rd-round draft choice for center Bill Curry.

REID, MICHAEL B. Tackle. B. 5/24/48, Altoona, Pa. 6'3½", 258. Graduated from Altoona H.S. and Penn State. Unanimous All-America, winner of Outland Trophy, Maxwell Award and Knute Rockne Trophy, 1969. 28-2 playing record at Penn State, 1967-69. Played in Gator Bowl, 1967; two Orange Bowls, 1969, 70. All-AFC defensive tackle, 1972. Named NFL defensive player of the week during 1972 season after he sacked Kansas City Chief QBs five times. Considered one of quickest and most intelligent players. Plays piano and writes music. Has made guest appearances with Cincinnati Symphony Orchestra and others. Pro Bowl, 1973, 74.

REID, STEPHEN E. Guard. B. 12/16/14, Chicago, Ill. 5'9", 192. 7th son of Chicago fireman. Overshadowed early years by brother John, who captained Loyola (Chicago) and became noted criminologist. Steve was captain and consensus All-America for Northwestern's Big 10 champions, 1936. *Sports Illustrated* Silver Anniversary All-America team, 1961. Now noted, in own right, as surgeon. Has been team physician for Northwestern since 1951. Engaged, since 1961, in research study on football head injuries using radio telemetry.

REID, WILLIAM T. Running Back. B. 10/25/1878, San Francisco, Calif. Associated with three unbeaten Harvard teams, 1898-1900, twice as player and once as coach. Crimson was 11-0 in 1898 and 10-0-1 in 1899. Both clubs featured hard-driving Reid at fullback. Unable to play in 1900 due to tendon injury. '98 team shut out Yale, 17-0, for Harvard's greatest victory to that time over Elis. First Crimson man to score two TDs in one game against Yale. Secretary of Football Rules Committee which is credited with saving football, 1906. Group authored far-reaching reforms at behest of President Theodore Roosevelt, who responded to mass of public protest against football cruelty. Eighteen deaths and 149 serious injuries were reported in 1905 season. Eight major changes were instituted, most revolutionary being forward pass (Reid credited Walter Camp with its origination). Reid persuaded Harvard administration not to abolish football during crisis period. Celebrated 95th birthday at home in Brookline, Mass., in 1973. National Football Foundation Hall of Fame.

REINHARD, ROBERT R. Tackle. B. 10/17/20, Hollywood, Calif. 6'3", 220. Suffered thru 14-18 varsity career at California, 1939-41. Still made All-America twice, 1940, 41. Senior season won team's Andy Smith Memorial Trophy — for most playing time. Los Angeles Dons (AAFC), 1946-49; Los Angeles Rams, 1950. Named to All-Time All-Pacific Coast team, 1969. Citizens Savings Hall of Fame.

REIFSNYDER, ROBERT H. (Reef) Tackle. B. 6/18/37, Brooklyn, N.Y. 6'1", 230. Fullback for Baldwin H.S. in Rockville Center, N.Y. Actively recruited by Iowa, Maryland, Navy and Army. Navy, 1955-57. Almost chose Army because of Felix (Doc) Blanchard, at time member of Cadet coaching staff. Transferred to tackle (owing to size) by coach Eddie Erdelatz. Played one of finest games against Army in 1957, thwarting All-America Pete Dawkins repeatedly in 14-0 victory. Maxwell Trophy winner as college Player of the Year, 1957. All-America same season. Defeated Rice, 20-7, in 1958 Cotton Bowl. Suffered broken nose 14 times during athletic career. New York Titans, 1960-61.

REMINGTON, FREDERIC End. B. 10/21/1861, Canton, N.Y. D. 12/26/09, Ridgefield, Conn. Attended Yale. Excelled in all sports, including boxing, horsemanship and football. Loved to knock heads in football combat. "To make it look more businesslike," dipped jersey in blood at local slaughterhouse before Yale's 1879 game with Princeton. Never graduated, leaving school due to illness of his father. While at Yale published first illustration. It depicted wounded football lineman sitting in his room with right foot elevated. Liniment bottles adorned desk top. Caption read: "A fellow must get used to the Rugby rules, you know — the doctor says I'll be all right by Thanksgiving, and that's all I care for now." Remington went on to gain universal fame as artist, specializing in American frontier scenes. Produced about 2800 paintings and drawings, hundreds of other magazine illustrations, 25 statues. Also authored and illustrated 13 books.

RENFRO, MELVIN L. Defensive Back. B. 12/30/41, Houston, Tex. 6', 190. Grew up in Portland where he attended Jefferson H.S. All-America halfback at Oregon, 1962. Played in College All-Star game, 1964. As collegiate trackster ran 100-yd. dash in 9.6, high hurdles in 13.8 and broad-jumped 25' 11¾". Dallas Cowboys, 1964-73. Started pro career at free safety, switched to cornerback in 1970. Named to Pro Bowl each of first 10 seasons. MVP in Pro Bowl, 1971. Holds Cowboy career records for interceptions (42) and kickoff returns (85 for 26.4-yd. average). His 10 interceptions, 1969, are also team standard; they led NFL that year. All-NFC, 1971. NFL championship games, 1966, 67. Super Bowl, 1971, 72. Lives in Wood Village, Ore., in off-season. Operates Mel Renfro's Bicycle City in Portland. Hobby is golf.

RENFRO, RAYMOND End. B. 11/7/30, Whitesboro, Tex. 6'1", 192. Attended North Texas State. Played 12 years with Cleveland Browns, 1952-63. Browns were NFL champs in 1954, 55. Caught 281 passes for 5508 yds., averaging 19.6 per reception. Averaged 29.0 yds. on 21 receptions, 1957. Biggest game, 11/26/61, caught seven passes for 166 yds. vs. New York Giants. Played in three Pro Bowls. Pass offense coach, Dallas Cowboys, 1968-72. Prior to Cowboys assisted Washington Redskins, Detroit Lions.

RENTZEL, T. LANCE End. B. 10/14/43, Flushing, N.Y. 6'2", 202. All-America at Casady H.S., Oklahoma City. Caught two passes in first collegiate game for Oklahoma, against Texas at Cotton Bowl in 1962. Hitchhiked to get there. Had been left home on injury list but was determined to play. All-Big 8 halfback, 1964. Minnesota Vikings, 1965-66; Dallas Cowboys, 1968-70; Los Angeles Rams, 1971-73. Played on special teams with Vikings. Developed into outstanding wide receiver after being traded to Cowboys. Named to Eastern Conference All-Star team, 1968. Led NFL receivers with 22.3-yd. average and 12 TDs, 1969. Author of *When All the Laughter Died in Sorrow*. Accomplished organist and pianist. Formerly married to singer-dancer Joey Heatherton. Suspended for 1973 season by NFL commissioner Pete Rozelle for conduct detrimental to football. NFL championship game, 1967. In 11 seasons caught 250 passes for 4430 yds. and 37 TDs. Returned punts and kickoffs in early stages of pro career.

RESSLER, GLENN E. Guard. B. 5/21/43, Dornsife, Pa. 6'3", 250. Attended Mahanoy (Pa.) H.S. Agriculture education major at Penn State. Played for Rip Engle, 1962-64. Consensus All-America and Maxwell Award winner senior year. Selected on 3rd round by Baltimore Colts in 1965. Colts, 1965-73. Utility player first two pro seasons before becoming regular. Played in Super Bowl, 1968.

RETZLAFF, PALMER (Pete) End. B. 8/21/31, Ellendale, N.D. 6'1", 212. Attended South Dakota State. Drafted by Detroit Lions but never played for them. Philadelphia Eagles, 1956-66. Tried defensive and offensive back before finding home at end. Shared reception championship (56 catches) with Raymond Berry, 1958. Excellent blocker, receiver. Capable of playing tight end and flanker. Favored down-and-out pattern. Retired as fifth greatest NFL receiver, making 447 catches, 7412 yds. 1960 Eagles won world championship — Retzlaff and Tommy McDonald formed league's finest pass-catching duo. NFL analyst for CBS-TV. Formerly was Philadelphia general manager.

REYNOLDS, ROBERT (Bobby) Running Back. B. Grand Island, Neb. 5'11", 180. Enjoyed sensational sophomore season at U. of Nebraska, 1950, scoring 22 touchdowns and rushing for 1342 yds. (7.0 average). Was All-America and 5th in Heisman Trophy voting. His TD run against Missouri at Lincoln remains one of college football's most spectacular plays. Taking wide pitchout, Reynolds was trapped behind line of scrimmage and retreated — 30-yds. He then reversed field, cut to sidelines, faked out three would-be tacklers, picked up key block and scampered to daylight, turning apparent 30-yd loss into 60-yd TD run. Last two Cornhusker seasons were disappointing as he managed only 854 rushing yds. combined in 1951, 52. Now insurance executive in Lincoln.

RHOME, GERALD B. (Jerry) Quarterback. B. 3/6/42, Dallas, Tex. 6', 181. Attended Sunset H.S. in Dallas where he played for his father, Byron. MVP in North-South prep game at Baton Rouge, 1960. Played collegiately at Southern Methodist, 1962, then closed career at Tulsa, 1963-64. Setting 16 NCAA records, Rhome was All-America and Heisman Trophy runnerup, 1964. Threw 98-yd. TD pass against Wichita State and compiled 488 yds. thru air vs. Oklahoma State, 1964. Same year led nation in total offense and passing. One of most impressive records is lowest percentage (.012) of passes intercepted in one season. Dallas Cowboys, 1965-68; Cleveland Browns, 1969; Houston Oilers, 1970; Los Angeles Rams, 1971. Now assistant coach at Tulsa.

RICE, HOMER C. Coach. B. Ft. Thomas, Ky. Son of Methodist minister. Little All-America quarterback at Centre College. Earned A.B. degree from Centre, B.S. and M.E. from Eastern Kentucky. Played three years of minor league baseball. In 1961 received award as Winningest Football Coach in America for 101-9-7 high school record. Head coach, U. of Cincinnati, 1967-68. In 1968 team led nation in passing offense. Author of *How to Organize Football Practice, The Explosive Short T* and *Homer Rice on the Triple Option Offense.* Athletic director at North Carolina.

RICHARDS, EUGENE L. B. 6/14/1863, New Haven, Conn. D. 9/17/27. Played at Yale, 1881-84. Dropkicked 72 goals without miss, 1883. Goals were then valued at four points. 1883 team had its closest contest against Princeton, winning 6-0. Rev. Henry W. Beecher viewed game and commented next day from pulpit: "I stood yesterday afternoon to see Yale and Princeton at football. I always did hate Princeton, but I took notice there was not a coward on either side, although I thank God that Yale beat." Attended Columbia Law School, 1885-87. Coached Williams College, 1892. Helped Walter Camp reconstruct rules, 1895. Counsel to New York State insurance department, 1896-98. Participated, during that period, in campaign against fraudulent insurance companies, forcing over 100 companies out of business. Was lawyer and banker. Victim of tuberculosis.

RICHTER, LESLIE A. Linebacker. B. 10/6/30, Fresno, Calif. 6'1", 242. Played three positions and placekicked for California Golden Bears. Excelled in both football and rugby. Consensus All-America guard twice, 1950, 51. Played in two Rose Bowls. Taken on 1st round of NFL draft by old Dallas Texans, but never played for them. Was called into service for two years and, upon discharge, Los Angeles Rams gave up all of 11 players for him. Did not disappoint Rams, finding permanence and greatness at middle linebacker. Twice voted their most valuable player and seven times played in Pro Bowl during his nine-year career, 1954-62. During that time became football's most hated player. Many opponents considered him hatchet man; Norm Van Brocklin called him "an overrated oaf." But others thought Richter simply aggressive, all-out player. Alex Webster, New York Giant running back of the '50s and '60s, voiced such testimony: "Les simply goes hard all the time. He gives 200% on every play, but he's not a dirty player. I'd say he just gets wound up, like everybody else." NFL championship game, 1955. Richter, placed on Pacific Coast All-Time team, is now president of Riverside (Calif.) Raceway.

RIGGINS, JOHN Running Back. B. 8/4/49, Centralia, Kan. 6'2", 230. Twice Kansas 100-yd. dash champ as prep, both times at 9.8. Set state record with 6.4 60-yd. dash. Never missed game or practice at U. of Kansas, 1968-70. Played for Pepper Rodgers. Broke many of Gale Sayers' records, including yds. career (2706) and season (1131). All-Big 8, 1969, 70. Played in Orange Bowl against Penn State, 1969. College All-Star and North-South games participant. No. 1 draft choice of New York Jets. As rookie first Jet to lead team in both receiving and rushing, 1971. Rushed for 944 yds., 7th best in AFC in 1972. Compiled 168 yds. same season on 32 carries against New England Patriots. Claims biggest thrill was seeing himself on bubble gum card. Possibly fastest "big" back in game. Reported late to Jets in 1973 after long holdout. Consequently slumped to season total of 482 yds. on 134 carries.

RINGO, JAMES Center. B. 11/21/32, Orange, N.J. 6'1", 220. Attended Phillipsburg (N.J.) H.S. and Syracuse U. Played center and linebacker in college. Orange Bowl, 1953. 7th-round draft choice of Green Bay Packers. Packers, 1953-63; Philadelphia Eagles, 1964-67. All-Pro, 1957, 59, 60, 61, 62, 63. Named to 10 Pro Bowls. Packer captain eight years. NFL championship games, 1960, 61, 62. Played in 182 straight games, pro record at retirement. Offensive line coach for Buffalo Bills, 1972-73. Formerly coached for Chicago Bears, 1969-71.

ROBB, A. JOE Defensive End. B. 3/15/37, Lufkin, Tex. 6'3", 245. Texas Christian, 1956-58. Tri-captain, 1958. Played in 1959 Cotton Bowl vs. Air Force, ending in 0-0 tie. Drafted on 14th round by Chicago Bears but traded to Philadelphia Eagles before 1959 season began. Eagles, 1959-60; St. Louis Cardinals, 1961-67; Detroit Lions, 1968-71. Philadelphia was NFL champion in 1960; during season Robb played more than any other Eagle save Chuck

Bednarik. Demanded "too" much money for efforts and was dealt to Cards prior to '61 campaign. Pro Bowl, 1967.

ROBBIE, JOSEPH Owner. B. 7/7/16, Sisseton, S.D. Managing general partner, Miami Dolphins. Received A.B. and LL.B. degrees from South Dakota. Was national debate champion. Also attended Northern State (N.D.). Served navy in World War II, taking part in five South Pacific theater invasions. Earned Bronze Star. Then took up law practice. Active in numerous governmental, political, and civic programs. Democratic candidate for governor of South Dakota, 1950. Awarded AFL franchise for Miami, 8/15/65. AFL commissioner Joe Foss and Robbie had been classmates at South Dakota. Fortunes of Miami Dolphins, struggling in 1966-69, took turn when Don Shula was hired as head coach in 1970. Shula came from Baltimore Colts, and switch was controversial. WFL commissioner Peter Rozelle, as compensation, gave Colts 1st-round draft pick of Dolphins. Rozelle ruled Dolphins had approached Shula without Baltimore's permission. At any rate, Robbie-Shula combination clicked. Dolphins appeared in 1972, 73, 74 Super Bowls, winning titles last two years. Success was not all sweet. Robbie alienated players with acid manner, and what they considered inequitable salaries. Following '73 season three Dolphins, Larry Csonka, Jim Kiick, Paul Warfield, signed with WFL Toronto franchise (relocated to Memphis). Robbie also feuded with Shula. Miami future unsettled.

ROBERTS, ARTHUR J. (Archie) Quarterback. B. Holyoke, Mass. 6'2", 195. Played for dad, Art, at Holyoke H.S. Art was NYU quarterback. At Columbia Archie did everything asked of him, and more. Played QB and defensive safety, handled punting chores, did post-game interview show for campus station. Specializing as passer, though there was nothing ordinary about any of his football skills. Gave outstanding performance vs. Rutgers, 1964, completing 25 of 39 passes for 320 yds., 3 TDs. Set many Ivy League marks, most since broken by Marty Domres. One — 1962-64 career completion average of .571 — still stands. Off football field was excellent pre-med student. Took assorted jobs to help pay school expenses such as delivering New York *Times* (for three years) to Columbia dormitories. Spent two years on Cleveland Brown taxi squad after drafted on 1st round in 1965. During period studied medicine at Western Reserve. Miami Dolphins acquired him in 1967. First game was nightmare; Dolphins lost to Kansas City Chiefs, 41-0. When season concluded, Roberts got out stethoscope and packed football away for good.

ROBERTS, JAMES M. (Red) Running Back. B. 1900, Somerset, Ky. D. 6/27/45, Middlesboro, Ky. Played on famous Centre College teams of 1918-21. Centre shocked nation with 6-0 upset of Harvard in 1921, touchdown coming on Bo McMillin's 32-yd. run. Against Crimson, Roberts played fullback, end and tackle. End with Toledo Maroons, 1922; Akron Pros, 1923; Cleveland Panthers (AFL), 1926. Coached at Waynesburg College. Died when fire swept through his Cumberland Hotel in Middlesboro.

ROBERTS, JOHN D. (J. D.) Guard. B. 10/24/32, Oklahoma City, Okla. 5'10", 210. Attended Jesuit H.S., Dallas, and U. of Oklahoma. Played so well against Notre Dame in 1953 that Irish coach Frank Leahy wrote Roberts personal letter of congratulation. Consensus All-America, 1953. Member of winning Orange Bowl team (7-0 over Maryland, 1954). Played for Hamilton Tiger-Cats, 1954, and Quantico Marines, 1955, 56. Assistant coach U. of Denver, 1957; Oklahoma, 1958-59; Navy, 1960; Auburn, 1961; U. of Houston, 1962-64; New York Jets, 1966; New Orleans Saints, 1967-68. Head coach for Richmond Roadrunners, 1969-70, and New Orleans Saints, 1970-72. Joined Saints midway thru 1970. Fired prior to 1973 campaign. New Orleans records 7-25-3.

ROBESON, PAUL L. End. B. 4/9/1898, Princeton, N.J. 6'2½", 210. One of 10 Rutgers undergraduates to win letters in four sports. Besides football, he participated in baseball (catcher), basketball (center) and track (discus). All-America twice under George Sanford, 1917, 18. Captained Rutgers debating team, and was school's extemporaneous speaking champion four times. Named to *Phi Beta Kappa* and senior honor society, Cap and Gown. Played with Hammond Pros, 1920; Akron Pros, 1921; Milwaukee Badgers, 1922. Graduate of Columbia Law School, 1923. Deciding against law career he turned to stage, quickly becoming internationally acclaimed actor and singer. *Showboat, Othello* and *The Emperor Jones* are just sampling of numerous stage and film successes. Because he was Black and deeply committed to support of communist cause, Robeson became figure of great controversy. Denied U.S. passport, 1950-58; when ban was lifted went to live in Soviet Union. Returned to America in 1963; now lives in Philadelphia. Robeson, *in absentia,* was given "cultural celebration" on 75th birthday at Carnegie Hall, 1973. Many leading Black spokesmen came to pay him tribute, including entertainers Dizzy Gillespie, Odetta, Leon Bibb, Sidney Poitier and Harry Belafonte.

ROBINSON, EDDIE G. Coach. B. 2/13/19, Jackson, La. Black football's Knute Rockne. Attended Leland College (now defunct) at Baker, La. Once completed 59 straight passes over six-game period. Hired to coach Grambling at age 22, by R. W. E. Jones in 1941. Took him only two years to produce unbeaten, untied, unscored-upon team. Kept winning and winning . . . and winning. Thru 1973, Robinson ledger read 225-77-11. His gospel salvaged Southern Black youths, provided chance for education and pro football career. Sent staggering number of 108 players to pros. Following '73 season, 10 more signed pro pacts. Outstanding pupils: Paul (Tank) Younger, Ernie Ladd, Buck Buchanan, Essex Johnson, Willie Davis, Rosey Taylor, Willie Brown, Clifton McNeil, Nemiah Wilson, James Harris, John Mendenhall, many others. In 1966 cited by FWAA as "the man who made the biggest contribution to college-division football during the last 25 years." Past president of NAIA. Widely respected humorist, public speaker. Only three men — Bear Bryant, Alonzo Stagg, Pop Warner — have won more games than Eddie Robinson.

ROBINSON, EDWARD N. (Robbie) Coach. B. 1873. D. 1945. Won nine letters as Brown athlete, (four football, three baseball, two track). Head coach at Nebraska, 1896-97; Brown, 1898-1901, 04-07, 10-25; Maine, 1902. Known as "Walter Camp of Brown Football." Brown teams were 140-82-12. Overall record: 156-88-13. Lost to Washington State, 14-0, in second (first modern) Rose Bowl game, 1916. Washington State was coached by William (Lone Star) Dietz who, after 19-year coaching career, became drama critic in Pittsburgh. Robinson beloved by players for his kind and gentle ways. Running back Fritz Pollard was greatest of his five Brown All-Americas. Citizens Savings Hall of Fame, National Football Foundation Hall of Fame.

ROBINSON, JOHNNY N. Defensive Back. B. 9/9/38, Baton Rouge, La. 6', 205. One-third of LSU's home-grown backfield which sparked Tigers to national championship, 1958. Uniquely, trio of Billy Cannon, Warren Rabb and Robinson, played at different high schools in Baton Rouge. Rabb attended Baton Rouge, Cannon Istrouma, and Robinson University. "I'll never forget how Cannon, Robinson and Rabb worked on their own during the summer (1958)," said LSU coach Paul Dietzel. "They were out practically every day tossing the ball around and polishing their ball-handling. When they reported in the fall, they formed a classic backfield." During collegiate career, 1957-59, Robinson rushed for 893 yds., caught 36 passes for 447 more and scored 14 TDs. Kansas City Chiefs, 1960-71. Adjusted easily to defensive secondary when moved there in 1962. Won All-AFL recognition five times at safety, 1965, 66, 67, 68, 69. All-AFC, 1970. AFL championship games, 1962, 66, 69. Super Bowl, 1967, 70. Robinson, playing with three broken ribs, stalled Minnesota with 4th-quarter interception as Chiefs conquered Vikings, 23-7, in Super Bowl IV. Led AFL twice in interceptions, totaled 57 for career. Still holds championship game records for interception yardage, career (122) and longest return, game (72 yds.). Operated health studio in Kansas City before joining Birmingham (WFL) as assistant coach. Named to All-Time AFL team.

ROBINSON, RICHARD D. (Dave) Linebacker. B. 5/3/41, Mt. Holly, N.J. 6'3", 245. College: Penn State. Graduate of Mooretown (N.J.) H.S. and Penn State. Majored in civil engineering at Penn State. Played in Hula Bowl, Gator Bowl, Coaches All-America and College All-Star games. With Green Bay Packers, 1963-72; Washington Redskins, 1973. Packers drafted Robinson on 1st round. Redskins acquired him in 1973 for future draft choice. Starting outside linebacker in all of 10 seasons with Green Bay, helping team reach greatest heights under coach Vince Lombardi. Played on two winning Super Bowl teams, 1967, 68. Named outstanding player in Pro Bowl, 1968. Two other Pro Bowls, 1967, 70. Likes to play bridge and chess. All-NFL, 1967, 68, 69. In 11 seasons intercepted 25 passes for 420 yds. Pilfered four passes in 1973 and scored first pro TD.

ROBNETT, MARSHALL F. (Foxey) Guard. B. Klondike, Tex. D. 11/28/67, Lisbon, Tex. Marshall Foch Robnett never gave up — not on football field nor in battle for life against lung cancer. Began career as high school fullback at

Cooper, Tex. Entered East Texas State but stayed only briefly, transferring to Texas A. & M. There assigned Joe Routt's No. 43 and converted to guard. Developed into one of all-time great Aggies under Homer Norton. All-SWC, 1939, 40. Consensus All-America, 1940. A. & M. won two bowl thrillers with Robnett-John Kimbrough duo providing heroics. Aggies stopped Tulane in 1940 Sugar Bowl, 14-13; one year later nipped Fordham, 13-12, in Cotton Bowl. Fordham game was disastrous though for Robnett who suffered serious knee injury. Chicago Cardinals, 1943, 45; Card-Pitt, 1944. Made comeback effort with Cardinals in 1947 but reinjured knee and forced to retire. Put up valiant struggle against lung cancer. Underwent surgery in 1965 and never regained health. Cheerful and uncomplaining to end, death came at age 49.

ROBUSTELLI, ANDREW End. B. 12/6/30, Stamford, Conn. 6'1", 230. Andy Robustelli came out of tiny Arnold College (now part of Bridgeport U.) to make big name for himself. Went all the way, in fact, to enshrinement in Pro Football Hall of Fame. Was twice All-Pro with Los Angeles Rams before they blundered into trading him to New York Giants. Robustelli had asked permission to report two weeks late to camp so he could be with expectant wife. When Rams refused, angry Andy said he might just sit out season. Enter Well Mara. Year was 1956, pivotal one for Giant fortunes. Mara acquired Robustelli and Dick (Little Mo) Modzelewski, drafted Sam Huff, Don Chandler, Jim Katcavage and moved team into Yankee Stadium. Giants then rolled to NFL championship, overwhelming Chicago Bears by 47-7 score. They also made finals two of next three years. Robustelli and tackle Modzelewski played alongside each other in Giant' "Fearsome Foursome." Other members were tackle Rosey Grier and alternating ends Walt Yowarsky and Jim Katcavage. Andy was All-Pro five straight years in New York, 1956-60, made seven Pro Bowl appearances overall. Spent five years with Rams, 1951-55; nine with Giants, 1956-64. NAIA Hall of Fame. Following 1973 season named director of operations for Giants.

ROCKNE, KNUTE K. Coach. B. 3/4/1888, Voss, Norway. D. 3/31/31, near Cottonwood Falls, Kan. Came to America at age 5. Grew up in Chicago, becoming standout amateur pole-vaulter and half-miler. Arrived at Notre Dame as overage (22), balding freshman in 1910. Called himself, in autobiography, "a lone Norse Protestant in a stronghold of Irish Catholics." Fifteen years later joined Catholic church, after death of devout Lutheran mother. Played end at Notre Dame, 1910-13. Was 5'8", 145. He and QB Gus Dorais revolutionized football in 1913. In summer prior to season, they worked on passing game while lifeguarding at Cedar Point, Ohio. On 11/1/13, at West Point, N.Y., Dorais-Rockne team humbled Army 35-13, with marvelous exhibition. Game was pivotal because it showed East, and nation, how to utilize passing game. Dorais completed 14 of 17 passes for 243 yds. Rockne was 3rd-team All-America, 1913. After graduation taught chemistry and assisted Jess Harper with football team. Also played with Massillon Tigers, 1919.

In 1918 succeeded Harper as N.D. head coach and athletic director, beginning storied career. In next 13 years won 105 games, lost 12 and tied 5. Percentage of

.881 is still unsurpassed. Never had losing season, was undefeated in 1919, 20, 24, 29, 30. Developed national champions in 1924, 29, 30. 1924 team immortal, featured "Four Horsemen" and "Seven Mules." Earlier developed George Gipp, fabled halfback. Considered 1930 team, his last, masterpiece. It starred backfield of Frank Carideo (QB), Marchy Schwartz and Marty Brill (halfbacks), Joe Savoldi (fullback).

Not known as innovator. Did pioneer use of "stunting" or "looping," "shock troops" and all-major-league schedule. Marvelous, spellbinding speaker. At one time suffered from stammer and lacked confidence. Practiced by belting out orations in woods near Notre Dame campus. Many of his Irish pupils became successful coaches: Frank Thomas, Frank Leahy, Slip Madigan, Jim Crowley, Charlie Bachman, Buck Shaw, Eddie Anderson, Adam Walsh, Jim Phelan. Rockne's untimely death, in plane crash, sent shock waves throughout nation. Another pupil, Harry Mehre, spoke of Rockne's contribution to football: "Rockne sold football to the men on the trolley, the elevated, the subway . . . the baker, the butcher, the pipe fitter who never went to college. He made it an American mania. He took it out of the thousand-dollar class and made it a million-dollar business." Named greatest all-time coach in football's centennial year, 1969. Citizens Savings Hall of Fame, National Football Foundation Hall of Fame. Knute Rockne Memorial Trophy presented annually to nation's outstanding collegiate back.

RODGERS, FRANKLIN C. (Pepper) Coach. B. 10/8/31, Atlanta, Ga. His birth coincided with 1931 World Series that starred Pepper Martin. Infant's grandfather took cue and nicknamed new arrival. Graduated from Brown H.S. in Atlanta where he earned All-State honors in football, basketball and baseball. QB under Bobby Dodd at Georgia Tech, 1951-53. 30-2-1 playing record, helping Tech land three major bowl berths and extend winning streak to 32 games. Booted winning FG in 1952 Orange Bowl. Kicked 4 PATs and 1 FG, threw 3 TD passes as Yellow Jackets routed West Virginia, 42-19, in 1954 Sugar Bowl. Named game's outstanding player. Assistant coach at Georgia Tech, 1954; Air Force Academy, 1958-59; Florida, 1960-64; UCLA, 1965-66. Head coach at Kansas, 1967-70; UCLA, 1971-73. Instrumental in developing six All-America backs: Rich Mayo, Air Force; Steve Spurrier and Larry DuPree, Florida; Gary Beban and Mel Farr, UCLA; and Bobby Douglass, Kansas. Won Big 8 co-championship at Kansas, 1968. Jayhawks lost subsequent Orange Bowl to Penn State, 15-14. Began using wishbone T offense in 1972. UCLA won 9 of 11 games in 1973; when season ended he took head job at Georgia Tech.

RODGERS, IRA E. (Rat) Running Back. B. 5/26/1895, Bethany, W. Va. D. 2/15/63. 5'10" 203. West Virginia fullback. All-America, 1919. Led nation in scoring with 147 points as West Virginia won 8 of 10 games. Threw 51-yd. scoring pass, 2nd longest of collegiate season in 1917. Head coach at alma mater, 1943-45. 14-10-1 record. National Football Foundation Hall of Fame.

RODGERS, JOHN Running Back. B. 7/5/51, Omaha, Neb. 5'9", 173. As runner, pass receiver and kick-return artist, Rodgers had few equals in football history. Set 28 Nebraska records, eight Big 8 and broke or tied 4 NCAA marks during 1970-72 career. Consensus All-America twice, 1971, 72. Senior year won Heisman Trophy, Walter Camp Trophy and ABC-Chevrolet Offensive Player of the Year Scholarship. Led Nebraska to three straight Orange Bowl victories: 17-12 over LSU, 38-6 over Alabama, 40-7 over Notre Dame. Rodgers set Orange Bowl record in last game with four TDs, adding TD pass in process. Amassed 5691 all-purpose yds. — NCAA career record. CFL Rookie of the Year in 1973. Rushed 55 times for 303 yds., caught 41 passes for 841 yds. and 7 TDs. Played with Montreal Alouettes.

ROGERS, EDWARD L. End. B. 4/14/1876, Libby, Minn. Son of Minnesota lumberman and Chippewa Indian mother named Song-gwa-nay-be-quay. Attended Carlisle, 1896-1900, and Minnesota, 1901-03. Captained 1900 Carlisle team under Pop Warner. Left end for Minnesota; captain of Henry Williams' 1903 club which tied Michigan, 6-6. That game was genesis of Little Brown Jug Trophy tradition. Coached Carlisle, 1904, and St. Thomas, 1905-07. Named to Pop Warner's all-time Carlisle team. Practiced law for 66 years, retiring at age 90 in 1966. National Football Foundation Hall of Fame.

ROLAND, JOHNNY E. Running Back. B. 5/21/43, Corpus Christi, Tex. 6'2", 220. Attended Roy Miller H.S. in Corpus Christi. All-America defensive back at U. of Missouri, 1965. Played both defensive and running back in college, concentrating on latter in pros. St. Louis Cardinals, 1966-72, and New York Giants, 1973. Named to two Pro Bowls, 1967, 68. NFL Player of the Week in first pro game. League's 4th-leading rusher with 876 yds., 1967. Holds Cardinal all-time records for rushes (962) and yds. (3608). In eight years rushed 1015 times for 3756 yds.; scored 35 TDs overall. Retired after 1973 season, joined Green Bay Packers as assistant coach.

ROMIG, JOSEPH Linebacker. B. 4/11/41, Salt Lake City, Utah. 5'10", 196. 21-10 playing record at Colorado, 1959-61. Consensus All-America, Knute Rockne Trophy recipient for Big 8 champs, 1961. Consensus All-America also in 1960. Lost 25-7 to LSU in Orange Bowl, 1962. Speed one of his greatest assets — he was timed at 10.2 in 100-yd. dash — mighty fast for linebacker. Majored in physics, minored in mathematics. After graduating from Colorado, he attended Oxford on Rhodes Scholarship. Took Ph.D. degree from Colorado. Currently research physicist for Martin-Marietta in Denver.

ROMNEY, ERNEST L. (Dick) Coach. B. 2/12/1895, Salt Lake City, Utah. D. 2/5/69, Salt Lake City, Utah. Four-sport standout at Utah. Played on school's national championship AAU basketball team, 1916. Utah State's first football coach, compiling 132-91-16 record over 30-year period, 1919-48. Won or shared four conference titles. Won 225 games as 22-year basketball coach. Commissioner 10 years of Mountain States Conference. Served on both NCAA football and basketball rules committees. His brother, G. Ott Romney, was basketball coach at Montana State and Brigham Young. Dick Romney is member of Citizens Savings Hall of Fame and National Football Foundation Hall of Fame.

ROONEY, ARTHUR J. Owner. B. 1/22/01, Coulterville, Pa. Attended Georgetown and Duquesne. Became millionaire, owner of Pittsburgh Steelers. Franchise originally cost him $2500 in 1933; team was named Pirates after baseball club which shared same city. Club renamed Steelers, 1940. Son of saloonkeeper, Rooney was all-round athlete. Boxed professionally, played semi-pro football (occasionally against Jim Thorpe) and minor league baseball. Batted .372 and stole 55 bases for Wheeling, W.Va., of Middle Atlantic League, 1925. As Pittsburgh club president signed Colorado's Whizzer White for $15,800 salary, 1938. At time it was highest salary ever paid in pro football. Legendary horseplayer, Rooney is reported to have won $250,000 in two-day period at Saratoga. He and five sons control 10 different corporations. Pro Football Hall of Fame. Senior Rooney still lives in Pittsburgh neighborhood where he grew up. It's within walking distance of Steelers' home field — Three Rivers Stadium.

ROSENBERG, AARON Guard. B. 1912, Brooklyn, N.Y. 6'2", 225. Southern California, 1931-33. 27-2 playing record. Only losses were to St. Mary's (Calif.) in 1931, Stanford in 1933. Consensus All-America, 1933; All-America, 1932. Tremendous competitor. Talked constantly on field. National Football Foundation Hall of Fame. Became leading movie producer. *Mutiny on the Bounty* (remake), *To Hell and Back, The Detective* are three of many film credits.

ROSENBLOOM, CARROLL D. Owner. B. 3/5/07, Baltimore, Md. Attended Pennsylvania's Wharton School of Finance. Halfback on Penn football team and pitcher for baseball nine. Revived pro football in Baltimore (Colts) in 1953. Previous franchise there had dissolved after 1950 season. Bought club at urging of Bert Bell, old friend and NFL commissioner. In 19 years at Baltimore won four NFL titles, including one Super Bowl. Colts suffered no losing seasons in 1957-71 period. Took unprecedented move in 1972 by trading Colts to air-conditioning magnate, Robert Irsay, in exchange for Los Angeles Rams. Irsay had purchased Los Angeles franchise from estate of late Dan Reeves. Original suggestion that Rosenbloom acquire Rams came from Reeves in 1968. At time Reeves was in failing health; he died three years later. Rosenbloom took command of Rams on 7/3/72, as owner and president. In 1973 hired Chuck Knox as head coach and traded for QB John Hadl. Pair was instrumental in L.A.'s 12-2 season, NFC Western Division title. Known for fairness to players and outstanding knowledge of game.

ROSENFELDER, CHARLES H. (Rosey) Tackle. B. 11/7/47, Milan, Tenn. 6'1", 220. All-State lineman at Humboldt (Tenn.) H.S. Also participated in basketball, baseball and track as prep. Started 33 straight games for U. of Tennessee, 1966-68, playing in Gator, Orange and Cotton Bowl games.

296

Unanimous All-American, 1968. While at Knoxville Johnson was lauded by offensive line coach Ray Trail: "He is intelligent, furnishes leadership, always gives us a full day's work and, most important of all, he's a winner." Was active in Tennessee's Fellowship of Christian Athletes chapter. Affiliated with Humble Oil and Refining Co., Asheville, N.C.

ROSSOVICH, TIMOTHY J. Defensive End-Linebacker. B. 3/14/46, Palo Alto, Calif. 6'4", 245. Maybe football's all-time eccentric, overshadowing fine playing career. "A big boy, an intelligent boy, but above all, a mean boy," recalled coach John McKay about collegiate days. Was 1967 All-America and co-captain for USC national championship team. Trojans defeated Indiana, 14-3, in Rose Bowl to climax 10-1 season. Played in College All-Star, Coaches All-America, East-West Shrine games. Defensive end for Trojans, and first two years with Philadelphia Eagles, 1968-69. Converted to middle linebacker in 1970. Traded to San Diego Chargers for No. 1 draft choice in 1972. Pro Bowl, 1969. Off-field stunts are legendary. They would include eating light bulbs, standing on head in hotel lobbies (sometimes head in bucket of water), setting himself on fire, wearing Dracula capes and frontier buckskins, driving motorbike off piers, opening bottles with teeth. Once bored at birthday party, he leap-frogged naked into birthday cake. *Au naturel* was way he met USC dean of men — Rossovich wandered onto dormitory ledge in broad daylight, to dry off after showering.

ROTE, KYLE W. Running Back. B. San Antonio, Tex. 6', 190. Attended Thomas Jefferson H.S. in San Antonio. Scored 32 TDs and amassed 2686 yds. total offense at Southern Methodist, 1948-50. Played 1948-49 with Doak Walker, and they formed nation's finest offensive combination. Walker was injured much of '49, and it afforded Rote opportunity to assert himself. He did, in remarkable fashion, during season's last game against powerful and unbeaten Notre Dame. Favored by 28 points, Irish were pushed to wire by Rote and co. before claiming 27-20 decision — their 36th straight victory. Rote ran for 115 yds. and passed for 148 more. He scored all three SMU TDs and averaged 48 yds. on punts. It was probably his finest hour, though he was to know many big days as pass receiver for New York Giants. Played with Giants, 1951-61. NFL championship games, 1956, 58, 59, 61. Consensus All-America, 1950. National Football Foundation Hall of Fame. Became football analyst for NBC-TV. Applied same coolness in broadcasting booth as he did in gridiron.

ROTE, TOBIN C. Quarterback. B. San Antonio, Tex. 6'3", 220. Rice, 1946-49. Played on two SWC co-championship teams, 1946, 49. Orange Bowl, 1947, and Cotton Bowl, 1950. Green Bay Packers, 1950-56; Detroit Lions, 1957-59; Toronto Argonauts, 1960-62; San Diego Chargers, 1963-64; Denver Broncos, 1966. First and only QB to direct championship teams in both NFL and AFL. In 1957 commanded NFL title-game victory (59-14) over Cleveland Browns. Had taken over late in season for Detroit superstar Bobby Layne, who suffered broken leg. With Rote at quarterback, San Diego won AFL title in 1963, overwhelming Boston Patriots by 51-10 score. Same season, at age 35, was All-

League and AFL passing leader — completed 170 passes for 2510 yds. Contradiction that QB should run "only from sheer fright." In 10 NFL seasons gained 3078 yds., averaging 5-yds. per carry. Tremendous competitor. In AFL-NFL career compiled 1329 completions, 148 TD passes, 18,850 yds.

ROUTT, JOSEPH E. Guard. B. Chappell Hill, Tex. D. 12/10/44, Holland. 6', 193. Things didn't go smoothly for Joe Routt after arriving at Texas A. & M. (had been All-District back at Brenham, Tex.). Failed to win freshman numerals in 1933 and was academically ineligible in 1934. But as converted lineman, was destined for greatness. Under coach Homer Norton became first A. & M. All-America, 1936. Repeated year later, this time as consensus choice. Twenty-five years later would be named to National Football Foundation Hall of Fame. Had unstoppable defensive charge despite being doubled and triple-teamed. "He was a glutton for hard all-afternoon play and was at his best when the going was toughest," Grantland Rice observed. Named outstanding lineman in East-West Shrine game at San Francisco, 1937. Became infantry Capt. in World War II, losing life leading troops in Battle of the Bulge. A. & M. and entire state of Texas are proud of Joe Routt. And that's a lot of pride!

ROYAL, DARRELL K. Coach. B. 7/6/24, Hollis, Okla. Quarterback, halfback, punter, defensive back, 1946-49. All-America, 1949. Played on two winning Sugar Bowl teams, 1949-50. Holds Sooner career record for interceptions (17). Returned punt 95 yds. vs. Kansas State, 1948. Head coach at Mississippi State, 1954-55; Washington, 1956; Texas, 1957-73. Gave Texas perennially powerful teams. Took over Longhorns after they experienced 1-9 season in 1956; club has never finished worse than 6-4 since. Guided Texas to 30 straight victories, 1968-70; and six straight Cotton Bowl appearances, 1969, 70, 71, 72, 73, 74. His teams feature outstanding rushing offenses. Perfected wishbone-T formation. Coach of the Year twice, 1963, 70 (shared). 161-49-4 record after 20 seasons. Longhorns under Royal have twice been national champions, 1969, 70 (shared).

ROZELLE, ALVIN R. (Pete) Commissioner. B. 3/1/26, South Gate, Calif. Pete Rozelle made meteoric rise to commissionership of pro football. In 1946 became part-time publicity assistant for Los Angeles Rams. Thirteen years later, age 34, was named NFL czar. Prepared for job as athletic news director-assistant athletic director at U. of San Francisco, 1948-50; public relations director of Rams, 1952-55; public relations consultant, 1955-57; general manager of Rams, 1957-60. Named NFL commissioner, 1/26/60. Took refuge that day in men's room before learning of announcement; later said he must have washed his hands seven times in nervous anticipation. Learned of appointment from reporters after emerging and he was moved to comment, "I am taking this job with clean hands." Called "Boy Commissioner," but there was nothing juvenile about executive ability. Became czar in fullest sense, controlling football in ironclad fashion. Named commissioner of major pro football, 6/66, with merger agreement between NFL and AFL. "Rozelle Rule," whereby team is given compensation for loss of player who has fulfilled option year, was under fire after 1973 season. NFL Players

Association wanted policy abolished, issued other demands and threatened to strike for '74 season. Rozelle attended Compton (Calif.) J.C. and U. of San Francisco.

RUSSELI, C. ANDREW (Andy) Linebacker. B. 10/29/41, Detroit, Mich. 6'2", 225. Attended LaDue (Mo.) H.S. and U. of Missouri. Fullback and linebacker at Missouri. Participated in Orange, Astro-Bluebonnet and Southwest Challenge Bowls. Economics major. Owns master's degree in business administration. Pittsburgh Steelers, 1963, 66-73. Regular as linebacker since rookie season. Has never missed pro game except to spend two seasons, 1964, 65, in army. Made NFL Vietnam tour, 1968. Played in four Pro Bowls, 1969, 71, 72, 73. Received Whizzer White Humanitarian Award for outstanding contributions to team, community and country, 1973. All-AFC, 1970, 72. Intercepted 16 passes in nine seasons.

RYUN, FRANK B. Quarterback. B. 7/12/36, Fort Worth, Tex. 6'1", 190. Mathematical and football star. Any correlation? — "It's absolutely false to pursue any notion that football and mathematics are related." — Dr. Frank B. Ryun. He was, in fact, too much of diagnostician at one time. Learned to be pragmatic and stardom ensued. "I'm not a natural athlete," he admitted. "I pick up a dart and people start running." Attended Paschall H.S. in Fort Worth before going to Rice. Spent most of college career as understudy to King Hill. Played with Los Angeles Rams, 1958-61; Cleveland Browns, 1962-68; Washington Redskins, 1969-70. Peaked with Browns, leading club to world championship in 1964. Holds Cleveland records for most pass completions, career, with 907; season, 1966, with 200. Thrice selected for Pro Bowl, 1965, 66, 67. During career completed 1093 of 2133 passes for 16,042 yds., 149 TDs. Had completion percentage of 51.2. Owns B.A. (physics), M.A. (math), Ph.D. (math) degrees, all from Rice. Spent one year, during Ph.D. studies, trying to solve unsolvable problem. Finished dissertation in 1965. Title: "A Characterization of the Set of Asymptotic Values of a Function Homomorphic in the Unit Disc." Is director of House Information Systems Committee on House Administration, U.S. House of Representatives. Has taught at Rice and Case Western Reserve. Wife, Joan, is newspaper columnist.

SABAN, LOUIS H. Coach. B. 10/13/21, Brookfield, Ill. Indiana QB and captain, 1942. World War II interrupted education. Commissioned 1st Lt. in U.S. Army. Assigned to China-Burma theater. Student of Chinese language (Mandarin). Cleveland Browns (AAFC), 1946-49. Browns won league championship each season. All-AAFC, 1948, 49. Head coach, Case Institute, 1950-52; Northwestern, 1953; Western Illinois, 1957-59; Boston Patriots, 1960-61; Buffalo Bills, 1962-65; Maryland, 1966; Denver Broncos, 1967-71; Buffalo Bills, 1972-73. Won nine straight games at Western Illinois, 1959. Guided Buffalo to AFL championships in 1964 and '65. 9-5 season in 1973 gave him 76-85-7 career pro record.

SAIMES, GEORGE Defensive Back. B. 9/1/41, Canton, Ohio. 5'10", 186. Attended Lincoln H.S. in Canton, played three sports. Set city records for pole vault and low hurdles. Running back at Michigan State, 1960-62. Spartan captain and consensus All-America, 1962. Played for Buffalo Bills, 1963-69, and Denver Broncos, 1970-72. Safety in pros. Bills won AFL championships in 1964, 65; lost title game in 1966. All-AFL, 1964, 65, 67. Seemed to have Joe Namath's number, as always in right place for interception or deflection. Great interest in sociology and philosophy. Called "Existentialist Pass Defender" and "Camus in Shoulder Pads."

ST. CLAIR, ROBERT B. (Geek) Tackle. B. 2/18/31, San Francisco, Calif. 6'9", 260. Played on 1951 U. of San Francisco squad (9-0) coached by Joe Kuharich.

Teammates included Ollie Matson, Joe (Scooter) Scudero, Gino Marchetti. USF dropped football after '51 season, and St. Clair transferred to Tulsa to finish collegiate career. San Francisco 49ers, 1955-63. Was NFL's tallest player, fast afoot, loved to hit. "His pass-blocking is invincible," determined 49er teammate Monty Stickles. Had penchant for raw meat, liver not excepted. Fortunately, appetite never problem on field. While playing elected mayor of Daly City, Calif., suburb of San Francisco. Blocked 10 FG attempts in 1956. All-Pro, 1955. Four Pro Bowls. Tabbed "Geek" by Bruno Banducci.

SAMPLE, JOHN B. Defensive Back. B. 6/15/37, Cape Charles, Va. 6'1", 200. Attended Maryland State. Deserves place on All-Time Controversial team. Accused of all sorts of roughhouse tactics. Talked constantly on field, in flippant style, often angering and unnerving foes. Great competitor — loved to play against best receivers. Wasn't all mouth. Could play, as All-Pro Safety status in 1961 testifies. Played for four pro teams: Baltimore Colts, 1958-60; Pittsburgh Steelers, 1961-62; Washington Redskins, 1963-65; New York Jets, 1966-68. Apparently, Sample didn't endear himself much to management either. Played, nevertheless, on three championship teams. Colts won NFL crowns in 1958, 59, and Jets won Super Bowl (over Colts) following 1968 season. Authored *Confessions of a Dirty Ballplayer* in 1970.

SANDERS, CHARLES A. (Charlie) Tight End. B. 8/25/46, Greensboro, N.C. 6'4", 235. Football, basketball standout at James B. Dudley H.S. in Greensboro. Outstanding blocker-receiver at U. of Minnesota. Caught 21 passes, 1967. Detroit Lions, 1968-73. Was 3rd-round draft choice. All-NFL, 1969. All-NFC, 1970, 71. Pro Bowl each of first four seasons. Specializes in "impossible" catches. Scored six TDs, 1970. Co-chairman, 1973 Detroit March of Dimes drive. Great competitor with speed and agility. In five pro seasons caught 208 passes for 3084 yds., 19 TDs.

SANDUSKY, ALEXANDER B. Guard. B. 8/17/32, McKees Rocks, Pa. 6'3", 242. Attended Clarion State, 1950-53. Was two-way end. NAIA All-America in 1952, helping Clarion to 13-6 win over East Carolina in Lion's Bowl. Virtually unknown when drafted by Colts on 16th round, 1954. Moved to offensive guard. Became starter in rookie season and remained one throughout 13-year career. He, Art Donovan, Jim Parker, Art Spinney, formed nucleus of great offensive line during Colt glory years. Played on two world championship teams, 1958, 59. Missed only one regular season game. Retired after 1966 campaign. NAIA Hall of Fame. Now director of Waterways Improvement Department of Natural Resources for State of Maryland. Lives in Annapolis.

SANFORD, GEORGE F. (Sandy) Center-Coach. B. 6/4/1870, Ashland, N.Y. D. 5/23/38, New York, N.Y. Chalked lines on Yale field as youngster. Ballroom dancing enthusiast while growing up. Played on Yale's 1891, 92 teams, both of which were unbeaten and unscored upon. In 1927, New Haven *Courier-Journal* picked Sanford as Yale's all-time center. Tutored clubs at Columbia, 1899-1901, and Rutgers, 1913-23. Columbia's 5-0 victory over Elis in 1899 doomed his dream of returning to New Haven as head coach. Old Blues considered it sinful for Yale man to beat Yale, and Walter Camp didn't approve of Sanford personally though he acknowledged Sandy's ability to teach line play. At Rutgers Sanford won 56, lost 32 and tied 5. Biggest win there was 14-0 verdict over heavily favored Newport Naval Reserve All-Stars, 1917. Produced All-Americas Bill Morley, Harold Weekes (Columbia); Homer Hazel, Paul Robeson (Rutgers). Another Rutgers product, not so well-known for football, was Ozwalt G. (Ozzie) Nelson. Bellicose, demanding and often profane, Sanford was nevertheless admired by his players. They paid for and dedicated bronze plaque in his honor at entrance to Rutgers Stadium. National Football Foundation Hall of Fame.

SAUER, GEORGE H. Running Back. B. 12/11/10, Stratton, Neb. 6'2", 195. Played four sports — football, baseball, basketball and track — at Nebraska, 1931-33. All-America fullback, 1933. Co-captain of College All-Stars against Chicago Bears, outstanding player in East-West Shrine game, 1934. All-Stars tied Bears, 0-0; Sauer scored both TDs as West won 12-0. Green Bay Packers, 1935-37. Packers were world champs, 1936. Head coach at New Hampshire, 1938-42; Kansas, 1946-47; Navy, 1948-49; Baylor, 1950-56. Took Kansas to Orange Bowl, 1948; Baylor to Orange Bowl, 1952, and Gator Bowl, 1955. Lt. Cmdr. on USS *Enterprise* during World War II. Baylor athletic director, 1950-60; general manager, New York Titans, 1961-62; director of player personnel, New York Jets, 1969-71; pro scout, New England Patriots, 1971-73. Son, George Jr., was standout receiver for New York Jets. George Sr., received Distinguished Service Award from Nebraska, 1971. National Football Foundation Hall of Fame. Now chairman of Recreation Supervision Program, Texas State Technical Institute, James Connally Campus, Waco, Tex.

SAUER, GEORGE H., JR. End. B. Waco, Tex. 6'1", 200. Not to be overshadowed by Hall of Fame father, George Jr. was sensational in abbreviated career. Played under Darrell Royal at Texas. New York Jets, 1965-70. Caught 309 pro passes for 4965 yds. and 28 TDs. Led all of pro football with 75 receptions for 1189 yds., 1967. Caught eight passes vs. Baltimore Colts in 1969, setting Super Bowl record. Over disillusionment with game, retired after 1970 season. Falling out had begun in collegiate days. "I really didn't like football that much," George recalled. "I didn't like to block and tackle and all that crap. I just like to catch the football." Talked of returning when WFL formed in 1974, but Jets maintained that he owed them option year.

SAVOLDI, JOSEPH A. (Jumpin' Joe) Running Back. B. Italy, 1909. D. 1/25/74, Cumberland Shores, Ky. Notre Dame, 1928-30. Played two national championship teams, 1928, 29. Was powerful, pile-driving runner. Massive torso, heavy black beard intimidated foes. Grew up in Three Oaks, Mich., in household where only Italian was spoken. This posed problem when he got to Notre Dame — consequently, quarterback Frank Carideo would issue signals to Savoldi in Neopolitan dialect. In 1930 Savoldi broke rules when he married and was expelled from school. Played with Chicago Bears, 1930, starting in same backfield with Red Grange and Bronko Nagurski. In 1931 began pro wrestling career which lasted 20 years. Earned his degree from Evansville U. in 1962, 30 years after leaving Notre Dame. Was science teacher thereafter until ill health forced retirement.

SAXTON, JAMES E. (Jimmy) Running Back. B. 5/21/40, Bryan, Tex. 5'11", 165. Texas, 1959-61. Unanimous All-America, 1961. Real scatback. "He's like one of those toy balloons you blow up and turn loose. Lord knows where he's going." — Darrell Royal. During Saxton's career under Royal, Texas won 25 of 30 games and played in three bowl games (Astro-Bluebonnet, two Cotton). Longhorns were 9-1 in 1959, 61. Saxton was 3rd-string freshman quarterback in 1958. Moved to halfback in sophomore year to capitalize on speed, shiftiness. Career average of 6.4 yds. per carry. In 1961, led NCAA with 7.9-yd. average. Occasionally surprised with option pass, twice recording TD tosses. Unable to pinpoint running success but offered theory: "I used to run through the woods (as youngster), dodging pine trees. Maybe that helped." Now bank vice president in Austin.

SAYERS, GALE E. Running Back. B. 5/30/43, Wichita, Kan. 6', 198. As good as any halfback who ever lived. Complemented 9.5 speed with tremendous running instincts. Growing up lived for time on farm near Speed (how appropriate!), Kan. Moved to Omaha and attended high school there, at Central. Surprised folks when he chose U. of Kansas from scholarship offers. Many believed he would stay near home and attend Nebraska. Rushed for 2675 yds., in K.U. career, 1962-64. Had sensational sophomore year, gaining 1125 yds. on 158 carries. That 7.1-yd. average led nation. Gained 286 yds. rushing vs. Oklahoma State, 1962. Against Nebraska, 1963, had 99-yd. run from scrimmage. In three seasons rushed for 6.5-yd. average. Consensus All-America, 1963, 64. Drafted by Chicago Bears and Kansas City Chiefs. Bears, 1965-71. Set NFL record by scoring 22 TDs in rookie season. Scored six TDs, 12/12/65 vs. San Francisco 49ers, to tie mark of Dub Jones and Ernie Nevers. Added four more TDs, 324 yds. rushing vs. Minnesota Vikings. Was landslide choice for Rookie of the Year. Won league rushing title with 1231 yds., 1966; gained 339 total yds. vs. Vikings. After nine games in 1968, on way to best season, injured right knee requiring surgery. Staged remarkable comeback in '69 and won second rushing title, picking up 1032 yds. In 1970 injured other knee. Surgery failed to correct problem and he spent two agonizing seasons, 1970, 71, mainly on Chicago bench. Was able to play briefly in only four games during that span. Retired with impressive statistics. Had rushed for 4956 yds. on 991 carries (5-yd. average), and scored 39 TDs. As kickoff returner left 30.6-yd. average in record book, still unsurpassed. Overall held eight NFL and 15 Chicago records. All-NFL, 1965, 66, 67, 68, 69. Pro Bowl, 1966, 67, 68, 70. Named Pro Back of the Game in '66, Offensive Player of the Game in '67. In 1970 accepted George Halas Award as most courageous player in pro football. Accepted award and paid tribute to teammate Brian Piccolo, at time dying of cancer: "I tell you here and now I accept this award for Brian Piccolo, a man of courage who should receive it. It is mine tonight but Brian Piccolo will have it tomorrow.... When you hit your knees tonight, please ask God to let him live." Wrote autobiography, *I Am Third*. Now assistant athletic director at Kansas.

SCARBATH, JOHN C. (Jack) Quarterback. B. Baltimore, Md. 6'1", 190. Attended Baltimore's Polytechnic H.S. 23-4-1 playing record at U. of Maryland, 1950-52. Unanimous All-America and 2nd in Heisman Trophy voting, 1952. Amassed 2822 yds. and 13 TDs during college career, finishing 7th nationally in passing yds. per attempt. Scored one TD as Maryland won 1952 Sugar Bowl, 28-13, defeating Tennessee. Pro experience with Washington Redskins, 1953-54, and Pittsburgh Steelers, 1956. Resident of Rising Sun, Md.

SCARPITTO, ROBERT End-Kicker. B. Rahway, N.J. 5'11", 196. Notre Dame, 1958-60. Caught 15 passes for 297 yds., 4 TDs. San Diego Chargers, 1961; Denver Broncos, 1962-67; Boston Patriots, 1968. Led AFL punters with 45.8-yd. average, 1966; again in '67 with 44.9 average. Produced 87-yd. punt vs. Denver Broncos, 9/29/68. Caught three TD passes vs. Buffalo Bills, 1966. Caught 90-yd. pass from John McCormick, 1965. Flanker with Broncos and Patriots, defensive back with Chargers.

SCHAFF, DAVID S. Contributor. B. 10/17/1852, Mercersburg, Pa. D. 3/2/41. Son of Rev. Philip S. Schaff, who was president of American Committee for revision of authorized version of Bible. David's biography of his father was published in 1931. Steered Yale into intercollegiate football. In 1872 his efforts led to formation of Yale Football Association, school's first formal body governing game. Was elected president of association and captain of Yale team. Despite Schaff's rugby experience (he attended Rugby School in England), Yale adopted soccer rules. Scheduled Yale's first football game for 11/16/72 against Columbia. Yale won, 3-0, at New Haven; Schaff was unable to play because of knee injury. Later became distinguished minister; also educator, lecturer and author.

SCHEMBECHLER, GLENN E. (Bo) Coach. B. 4/1/29, Barberton, Ohio. All-State at Barberton H.S. Offensive tackle at Miami (Ohio), 1949-51. Played under George Blackburn and Woody Hayes. Teammate and roommate of John Pont, 1950. Both Schembechler and Pont were destined to coach alma mater, and in Big 10. Schembechler was assistant at Presbyterian College, 1954; Bowling Green, 1955; Northwestern, 1956-57; Ohio State, 1958-62. Head coach at Miami, 1963-68, and Michigan, 1969-73. He was fourth straight Miami head coach to take over Big 10 team — others were Woody Hayes (Ohio State), Ara Parseghian (Northwestern), Pont (Indiana). Shared two MAC championships. Won one and shared two other Big 10 titles. Lost twice in Rose Bowl: 10-3 to USC, 1970, and 13-12 to Stanford, 1972. Suffered mild heart attack on eve of first Rose game. To keep fit he now combines steady diet of running and walking. Tied Ohio State for Big 10 crown in 1973; Schembechler was incensed when conference voted Buckeyes, instead of Wolverines, into Rose Bowl.

SCHLOREDT, ROBERT Quarterback. B. Deadwood, S.D. 6', 190. Played at Washington, 1958-60. Grew up in Gresham, Ore. As tyke threw passes to 75-year-old grandfather. In boyhood accident with firecrackers, lost 90 percent of vision in left eye. Managed to develop remarkable depth perception. Had to learn about 260 plays in Jim Owens' Washington offense. Did just about everything — skirted ends, rammed line like fullback, passed, punted, defended. Guided Huskies to 44-8 win over Wisconsin in 1960 Rose Bowl.

SCHMIDT, FRANCIS Coach. B. 12/3/1885, Downs, Kan. D. 9/19/44. Graduated from Nebraska. Head coach at Tulsa, 1919-21; Arkansas, 1922-28; Texas Christian, 1929-33; Ohio State, 1934-40; Idaho, 1941-42. Attained rank of Capt. during World War I. Coaching record: 158-57-11. He was 46-6-5 at TCU, winning two Southwest Conference titles. Developed Johnny Vaught, TCU guard and later well-known coach. Won one Big 10 crown and tied for another at Ohio State. Buckeyes lost to Notre Dame, 1935; duel voted century's most outstanding game. Citizens Savings Hall of Fame, National Football Foundation Hall of Fame. Varied and powerful offensive attack earned nickname, "Close the Gates of Mercy."

SCHMIDT, JOSEPH Linebacker. B. 1/18/32, Pittsburgh, Pa. 6', 220. Learned football basics on sandlots of Western Pennsylvania. At age 14 was playing against full-grown men. U. of Pittsburgh, 1950-52. Converted to guard from high school fullback. Before 1952 game with Notre Dame, Pitt coach Red Dawson placed Schmidt in charge of team in dressing room. "You guys better whip Notre Dame," he warned mates, "or so help me, I'll whip you." Pitt defeated Irish, 14-point favorites, 22-14. Middle linebacker with Detroit Lions, 1953-65. Brilliant career. He was, according to Vince Lombardi, "a great diagnostician, a great tackler, and a strong defensive leader." Kept complete "book" on every player in league. Astonishingly thin-legged for man having 48-inch chest. Teammate Dave Middleton called him "Thorax." Nine times All-Pro middle linebacker, played in 10 Pro Bowls. NFL championship games, 1953, 54, 57. Named to All-Pro Squad of the 1950s. Detroit linebacker coach, 1966; head coach, 1967-72. Record: 43-34-7. Quit to spend more time with family, also cited loss of enthusiasm. Pro Football Hall of Fame. Lions originally picked Schmidt on 7th round, signed him for $5700. Some bargain!

SCHNELKER, ROBERT Tight End. B. 10/17/28, Galion, Ohio. 6'4", 215. Attended Bowling Green. Drafted on 17th round by Cleveland Browns in 1953. Played with Philadelphia Eagles, 1953; New York Giants, 1954-60; Minnesota Vikings, 1961; Pittsburgh Steelers, 1961. Three NFL title games with Giants, 1956, 58, 59. Giants routed Chicago Bears, 47-7, for world championship in 1956. Made 9 receptions for 175 yds. in 1959 title game vs. Baltimore Colts. Assistant coach for Los Angeles Rams, 1963; Green Bay Packers, 1964-71; San Diego Chargers, 1972-73.

SCHNELLBACHER, OTTO O. (Claw) Defensive Back. B. 4/15/23, Sublette, Kan. 6'5", 185. Kansas football and basketball star, 1943, 46, 47, 48. All-Big 7 cager, 1948. New York Yankees (AAFC), 1948-49; New York Giants, 1950-51. Nicknamed "Claw" because of powerful hands. Part of "umbrella" defense (it resembled open umbrella) that Giants unveiled against Cleveland Browns in 1950. N.Y. lined up in 6-1-4, with Tom Landry, Emlen Tunnell, Harmon Rowe joining Schnellbacher in defensive backfield. They switched to 4-1-6 with ends James Duncan and Barney Poole dropping back. Browns were befuddled, especially QB Otto Graham who didn't complete single pass. Schnellbacher led NFL in interceptions with 11 in 1951, returning them 194 yds., including one for 46. All-Pro that year. Stunned Giants when he retired, at peak of game, after '51 season. Also played pro basketball. Now managing insurance agency in Topeka.

SCHOONOVER, WEAR K. End. B. 3/18/10. 6'2", 190. Arkansas, 1927-29. First SWC player to earn official All-America honors, 1929. During that season played every minute of nine-game schedule, caught 14 passes against Baylor, scored 54 points overall, intercepted 5 passes against Centenary including one for 92-yd. TD. Played under Francis Schmidt and Fred Thomsen. Standout also in basketball and track. National Football Foundation Hall of Fame. Retired after 38 years with civil service. Lives in Arlington, Va.

SCHRAMM, TEXAS E. Administrator. B. 6/20/20, Los Angeles, Calif. Earned B.A. degree (journalism) from Texas, 1947. Achieved rank of captain in Air Transport Command. Sports editor of Austin *American-Statesman.* Joined Los Angeles Rams as publicity director in 1947; in 10-year career rose to general manager. Left Rams in 1957 to join CBS as assistant director of sports. In 1960 named general manager of Dallas Cowboys by board chairman Clint W. Murchison, Jr. Driving force, with Lamar Hunt of Kansas City Chiefs, in AFL-NFL merger. Named Dallas president, 1966, retaining title of general manager. Introduced new era of sports to Dallas area, culminating in Super Bowl VI victory in 1972. While with Rams hired Pete Rozelle to front office job, thus bringing future commissioner into pro football.

SCHREINER, DAVID N. End. B. 3/5/21, Lancaster, Wis. D. 1944, Okinawa. 6'2", 198. Wisconsin, 1940-42. All-Big 10, 1941, 42. Unanimous All-America and co-captain of Wisconsin's 3rd-ranked team, 1942. Badgers were 8-1-1, losing only 6-0 to Iowa. Wisconsin coach Harry Stuhldreher said Schreiner "had no peer" at his position. Played in East-West Shrine game, 1943. Killed during World War II in Okinawa campaign against Japanese. He was marine Lt. In his honor Wisconsin established David N. Schreiner Memorial Scholarship and retired jersey, No. 80. Citizens Savings Hall of Fame, National Football Foundation Hall of Fame.

SCHUH, HARRY F. Tackle. B. 9/25/42, Philadelphia, Pa. 6'3", 260. Graduate of Neshaminy H.S., Feasterville, Pa., and Memphis State. One of all-time great Memphis State linemen. All-America, 1964. Selected to play in Blue-Gray, Senior Bowl, College All-Star and Coaches All-America games. Oakland Raiders, 1965-70; Los Angeles Rams, 1971-73. Raiders' 1st-round draft pick.

307

AFL championship games, 1967, 68, 69. Super Bowl, 1968. AFL All-Star games, 1968, 70. Pro Bowl, 1971. All-AFC, 1967, 69. Superior offensive tackle.

SCHULZ, ADOLPH (Germany) Center. B. 4/9/1883, Ft. Wayne, Ind. D. 4/14/51, Detroit, Mich. 6'4", 245. Michigan, 1904-05, 07-08. 32-4-1 playing record. All-America, 1907; captain, 1908. As freshman Schulz was teammate of Willie Heston; pair is regarded best of Fielding Yost's super players in early century. Schulz, on defense, played more like linebacker as he backed up line and cavorted sideline to sideline. Offensively he was one of first to use one-hand spiral snap. Head coach at U. of Detroit, 1923. Early-Day All-Time All-America team. Citizens Savings Hall of Fame, National Football Foundation Hall of Fame.

SCHWAB, FRANK J. (Dutch) Guard. B. 1895, Madera, Pa. D. 12/12/65, Spangler, Pa. 5'11", 195. Worked in Pennsylvania mines much of childhood, receiving as little as 90 cents per day. Played four years at Kiski (Pa.) Academy after scout spotted him as 12-year-old sandlotter. Met Lafayette coach Jock Sutherland in service, and he persuaded Schwab to play for Leopards. All-America, 1921, 22. Leopard captain as sophomore, 1921. Later operated hardware store in Spangler. Citizens Savings Hall of Fame. He and Charles (Babe) Rinehart are only Lafayette players in National Football Foundation Hall of Fame.

SCHWARTZ, MARCHMONT (Marchy) Running Back. B. 1909, New Orleans, La. 5'11", 178. Attended St. Stanislaus H.S. of Bay St. Louis, Miss. 25-2-1 Notre Dame playing record, 1929-31. National champions, 1929, 30. Consensus All-America, 1930, 31. 1930 Irish team was Knute Rockne's last, and considered his masterpiece. It featured backfield of QB Frank Carideo, halfbacks Marv Brill and Schwartz, fullback Joe Savoldi. They averaged 186 pounds, 22 more than famed "Four Horsemen," and were every bit as effective. During collegiate career Schwartz scored 17 TDs and provided 2501 yds. total offense, 1945 by rushing. Coached Stanford, 1942-50. Record: 28-28-4.

SCHWARTZWALDER, FLOYD B. (Ben) Coach. B. 6/2/09, Pt. Pleasant, W. Va. West Virginia, 1930-32. Coached in home state at Sistersville, Weston and Parkersburg high schools, and McKinley H.S. of Columbus, Ohio, prior to World War II. Won Silver Star, Purple Heart, Bronze Star and several battle stars during military career. Head coach at Muhlenberg, 1946-48, Syracuse, 1949-73. Record of 153-71-3 at Syracuse. Overall: 178-96-3. His Orangemen won 1952 Lambert Trophy but then lost to Alabama, 61-6, in Orange Bowl. 2-3 bowl record overall. Won 1960 Cotton Bowl, '61 Liberty Bowl. Developed such power running backs as Larry Csonka, Jim Brown, Jim Nance, Floyd Little. Retired after 2-9 record in 1973, his worst won-loss year at Syracuse.

SCHWEGLER, PAUL (Schweg) Tackle. B. 5/22/11, Raymond, Wash. 6'4", 205. Played football, basketball and baseball in high school. Named to 43 all-star teams during his U. of Washington career, 1929-31. All-America, 1931. Same season was team captain and won inspirational award (Flaherty Medal). Coach Jim Phelan considered Schwegler best lineman he ever coached. Played in East-West Shrine game at San Francisco, 1932. Citizens Savings Hall of Fame, National Football Foundation Hall of Fame.

SCOTT, CLARENCE Defensive Back. 4/9/49, Atlanta, Ga. 6', 180. Wide receiver at Trinity H.S. in Decatur, Ga. Compiled 12 interceptions, 105 unassisted tackles and 80 assists in Kansas State career, 1968-70. All-America and All-Big 8, 1970. Played in College All-Star game, 1971. Cleveland Browns, 1971-73. Instant hit with Browns after being their No. 1 draft choice. Returned blocked FG 55 yds. for 1st pro TD, against Green Bay Packers, 1972. Intercepted four passes in 1971, five in '73. Pro Bowl, 1974.

SCOTT, CLYDE (Smackover) Running Back. B. 8/29/24, Dixie, La. 6', 175. Attended Smackover (Ark.) H.S., which explains nickname. Played four sports as prep. Halfback at Navy, 1945, and Arkansas, 1946-48. First player in Razorback history to win All-Conference recognition three straight years. Consensus All-America, 1948. Scored 15 TDs in Arkansas career and rushed for 1463 yds. Averaged 5.2-yds. per carry. Played in Cotton Bowl, 1947. Track sprinter and hurdler. Won silver medal in high hurdles in Olympic games at London, 1948. Philadelphia Eagles, 1949-52; Detroit Lions, 1952. National Football Foundation Hall of Fame. Vice president of Union Life Insurance Co., Little Rock.

SCOTT, JACOB E., III (Jake) Defensive Back. B. 7/20/45, Greenwood, S.C. 6', 188. Attended Washington & Lee High School, Arlington, Va., and Bullis Prep, Silver Spring, Md. All-SEC at U. of Georgia, 1967-68. Nation's 2nd-leading punt returner, consensus All-America, SEC's Outstanding Player, 1968. Same season set conference interception record with 10. Gave up senior year to play with Vancouver of CFL, 1969. Safety for Miami Dolphins, 1970-73. Won numerous honors in 1972, climaxed by being named Super Bowl MVP by *Sport* magazine. Holds 11 Miami punt-return records. Georgia immortal Charley Trippi predicted Scott's pro success while latter was collegian. "Scott will make a great safetyman in the pros," said Trippi. "Jake has tremendous range and great football instinct." Super Bowl, 1972, 73, 74. Pro Bowl, 1972, 73, 74. Had 21 interceptions thru 1973.

SEARS, VICTOR W. Tackle. B. 3/4/18, Ashwood, Ore. 6'4", 230. Oregon State, 1938-40. All-America, 1940. Philadelphia Eagles, 1941-53. Philadelphia and Pittsburgh Steelers merged for '43 season. Played both ways first 10 years, offense only 11th, defense only 12th and 13th. Averaged over 50 minutes nine years. Only player chosen to Philadelphia's All-Time team both offensively and defensively. World championship teams, 1948, 49. Lost 1947 title game. All-Pro, 1943, 49. Hobbies include fishing, gardening, making Early American furniture, Little League baseball and football coaching. Manufacturers representative, resident of Bucks County, Pa. Member All-Pro Squad of the 1940s.

SEIBELS, HENRY G. Running Back. B. 8/22/1876, Montgomery, Ala. D. 1967. From distinguished family which included one U.S. senator, Confederate Army colonel and Belgian minister. Played right halfback at Sewanee, 1896-99. Captain, 1899. Senior season Sewanee won all 12 games, outscoring foes 322-10. Five of games were played in six-day period and covered 3000 miles. Also baseball pitcher, active in student affairs. Naval aviator in World War I. Founder and president of Birmingham Fire Insurance Co. Outstanding civic and business leader. Granted Doctor of Civil Laws degree. National Football Foundation Hall of Fame.

SEIDEL, GLENN E. Quarterback. B. 7/27/14, Minneapolis, Minn. Minnesota QB. Member of 1934 national championship team. Captain in 1935. Teammate of Hall of Famers Pug Lund and Bud Wilkinson. Earned BME degree with distinction. Assistant football coach at Tulane, 1936-40. President of Marquette Computer Corp., 1963-67; now director.

SELLERS, RON End. B. 2/5/47, Jacksonville, Fla. 6'4", 195. Attended Paxton H.S., Jacksonville, Fla., and Florida State. Led NCAA receivers with 86 catches for 1496 yds., 1968. Finished 1967-69 career 2nd in catches (212), 1st in receiving yds. (3598), 3rd in TD catches (23) and 4th in yds.-per-catch (17.0). Led Florida State to three bowl games. Consensus All-America, 1967; All-America, 1968. Drafted on 1st round by Boston Patriots, 1969. Played with Boston, 1969-70; New England Patriots, 1971; Dallas Cowboys, 1972; Miami Dolphins, 1973. Participated in AFL All-Star game, 1970. Super Bowl, 1973, 74. In six seasons caught 112 passes for 2178 yds., 18 TDs. Called "Jingle Joints."

SELMON, LUCIOUS Linebacker. B. 3/15/51, Muskogee, Okla. 5'11", 236. Oklahoma, 1971-73. Oldest and possibly strongest of three football-playing brothers. There were nine children overall in family of Mr. & Mrs. Jesse Selmon. LeRoy and Dewey followed Lucious to Oklahoma. Lucious grew up on sharecropper's farm where he ploughed with mules (Selmons owned no tractor) and retrieved hogs when they broke loose. Fullback in high school at Eufaula, Okla. (pop. 2500), switching to defense in college. Made 13 tackles, including two for 19 yds. in losses, during 17-6 victory over Missouri in 1972. All-Big 8, 1972, 73. Consensus All-America, 1973. Ran 40-yd. dash in 4.7 Bench pressed 585 pounds. Kansas State coach Vince Gibson said Selmon boys are "close to being the three best defensive players I ever saw on one team, let alone the three best brothers." Dewey and LeRoy were Sooner sophomores when Lucious was senior in 1973. Played in Sugar Bowl, 1972, 73.

SESTAK, THOMAS Tackle. B. Gonzales, Tex. 6'1", 255. Texas born and bred. Grew up in Gonzales, "chicken capital of the world." Bear Bryant plucked him for Texas A. & M., but Aggies were soon on probation and Sestak transferred to Baylor. Brief stay there was followed by two-year army hitch. Upon discharge enrolled at McNeese State, where he was found in 1961 by scout Harvey Johnson (Buffalo Bills). Joined Bills in 1962. Developed into premier defensive tackle.

Chosen thrice All-AFL, 1963, 64, 65. Later was named to All-Time AFL Team. Rival coach Mac Speedie once offered following praise: "God gave everybody a certain amount of ability. To Tom Sestak, he gave too much." Bothered by painful knee injuries which curtailed career. Wore about 15 pounds of pads and bandages. Retired after 1968 season.

SEWELL, HARLEY Guard. B. 4/18/31, Arlington, Tex. 6'1", 230. Texas All-America, 1952. Detroit Lions, 1953-62; Los Angeles Rams, 1963. Drafted No. 1 by Lions in 1953. Detroit coach Buddy Parker considered him NFL's best at pulling out and leading interference. Never made All-Pro but earned high respect from teammates and foes alike. Liked to play guitar, sing country music. NFL championship games, 1953, 54. Lions were champs Sewell's rookie year, defeating Cleveland Browns by 17-16 score. Pro Bowl, 1958, 59, 60, 63. Now scouting for Rams.

SEYMOUR, PAUL Tackle. B. 2/6/50, Detroit, Mich. 6'5", 252. Michigan, 1970-72. Began Wolverine career as tight end, moved to offensive tackle senior year. All-Big 10 and consensus All-America, 1972. Lost 1972 Rose Bowl, 13-12, to Stanford. Played in East-West Shrine and Hula Bowl games. Majored in physical education. Likes to play guitar. Brother of Jim, pro wide receiver. No. 1 draft choice of Buffalo Bills, 1973. Extremely strong, fine speed.

SHAKESPEARE, WILLIAM V. Running Back. B. 9/27/12, Staten Island, N.Y. D. 1/17/74, Kenwood, Ohio. Triple-threat halfback at Notre Dame, 1933-35. Remembered for 19-yd. touchdown pass that vanquished Ohio State 18-13, 1935. Game, played at Columbus, is considered one of greatest in collegiate history. Irish overcame 13-0 halftime deficit; Shakespeare's winner was unleashed inside last 30 seconds. Tabbed "Bard of Staten Island." Infantry captain during World War II, earning Bronze Star for Battle of the Bulge gallantry. President of Cincinnati Rubber Manufacturing Co., 1960 until death.

SHAUGHNESSY, CLARK D. Coach. B. 3/6/1892, St. Cloud, Minn. D. 5/15/70, Santa Monica, Calif. Father of modern T formation. End, fullback and two-way tackle at Minnesota, 1911-13. His coach, Dr. Henry Williams, called him "the finest foward passer Minnesota ever had, and, in my opinion, the best ever developed in the Midwest." Head coach at Tulane, 1915-20, 22-26; Loyola (New Orleans), 1927-32; Chicago, 1933-39; Stanford, 1940-41; Maryland, 1942, 46; Pittsburgh, 1943-45; Los Angeles Rams, 1948-49; Hawaii, 1965. Technical advisor for Chicago Bears, 1951-62. Lost NFL title game in 1949. Became Tulane head coach at age 23. School president turned down Rose Bowl invitation, 1925, without even consulting Shaughnessy. Learned T from George Halas (Bears) and Ralph Jones (Lake Forest College) while coaching at Chicago. Halas put man in motion (primary difference with old T), spreading defense and allowing for long gainers. Shaughnessy took new T to Stanford. His first team there, led by Frankie Albert, went unbeaten and defeated Nebraska in Rose Bowl before 88,447. That bowl appearance caused modern T to be adopted throughout country. Offense evolved into split T, slot T, wing T and other variations. 149-116-17 collegiate record. Citizens Savings Hall of Fame, National Football Foundation Hall of Fame.

SHAVER, GAIUS (Gus) Running Back. B. 8/14/10, Covina, Calif. 5'11", 188. Southern California, 1929-31. Consensus All-America, 1931. Triple-threat back, also played defense. Passing heroics spurred 16-14 victory over Notre Dame, 1931, ending N.D. undefeated string at 26 games. Trojans won 1932 Rose Bowl over Tulane, 21-12. Citizens Savings Hall of Fame.

SHAW, LAWRENCE T. (Buck) Coach. B. 3/28/1899, Mitchellville, Iowa. Called "Silver Fox" because of striking silver hair. Notre Dame tackle under Knute Rockne, 1919-21. Playing weight was 178. College coach at North Carolina State, 1924; Nevada, 1925-28; Santa Clara, 1936-42; California, 1945; Air Force Academy, 1956-57. Was Air Force's first head coach, helping to organize its athletic program. 46-10-2 record at Santa Clara — two wins over LSU in consecutive Sugar Bowls, 1937-38. Coach, San Francisco 49ers, 1946-54; Philadelphia Eagles, 1958-60. Retired after beating Green Bay Packers for NFL championship, 1960. 90-55-5 pro record. National Football Foundation Hall of Fame.

SHAW, WILLIAM L. (Billy) Guard. B. 12/15/38, Natchez, Miss. 6'3", 237. Georgia Tech, 1958-60. All-SEC, 1960. Buffalo Bills, 1961-69. All-AFL, 1963, 64, 65, 66. Tremendous pulling guard. Member All-Time AFL team. Now division manager for Southeastern Precast Concrete Co., Tucker, Ga.

SHELTON, MURRAY N. End. B. 4/20/1893, Dunkirk, N.Y. 6'1", 170. Attended Dunkirk H.S. and Phillips Academy in Andover, Mass. Played at Cornell under A. H. Sharpe, 1913-15. All-America, 1915. Recovered fumble on Harvard's 25 that resulted in Cornell TD, 1915. Big Red won, 10-0, handing Harvard first defeat in four years. Buffalo All Americans, 1920-22. Served in both world wars. National Football Foundation Hall of Fame. Retired from civil engineering practice. Lives in Black Mountain, N.C.

SHERMAN, ALEX (Allie) Coach. B. 2/10/23, Brooklyn, N.Y. Born in Brownsville section of Brooklyn. Grew up to coach New York Giants, team he cheered from bleachers as youngster. At 125 pounds was too small to make Boys H.S. team. Played at Brooklyn College when coach Lou Oskins switched to T formation. Was left-handed quarterback. Graduated *cum laude*, majoring in three subjects: psychology, sociology, economics. Played with Philadelphia Eagles under Greasy Neale, 1943-47. Giant assistant coach, 1949-53, 59-60; head coach, 1961-69. Coached Winnipeg Blue Bombers, 1954-56. Went to New York originally on recommendation of Greasy Neale, who claimed Sherman had "one of sharpest minds in our business." Expert on modern T-formation football. Helped Steve Owen install T in New York system before becoming head coach. Guided Giants to three Eastern Conference titles, 57-51-4 record.

Fired in 1969 after team lost five straight exhibition games. Still had five years to go on $50,00-per-year contract and drew thru 1974. Now member of Sanford C. Bernstein & Co., money management firm in NYC. Avid platform tennis player. Admits, "I miss football a lot."

SHEVLIN, THOMAS L. End. B. 3/1/1883, Muskegon, Mich. D. 12/29/15, Minneapolis, Minn. 5'10", 195. Son of Thomas H. Shevlin, whose lumber empire made him one of nation's leading industrialists. Younger Shevlin attended Hill School in Pottstown, Pa., starring in three sports before enrolling at Yale. Regarded as one of Blue's greatest football performers. Playing record of 42-2-1, 1902-05. All-America, 1902, 04-05; 2nd team, 1903. Played end primarily, but as sophomore, appeared in several games at fullback. Also returned two kickoffs for TDs. Known for intelligence, speed, strength. While at Yale had 60-horsepower Mercedes, own chauffeur, resplendent wardrobe of suits, overcoats, hats and haberdashery. When returned to coach Yale in 1915, he cut sporting figure on sidelines with cane, bowler and boutonniere. Also assisted Dr. Henry Williams at Minnesota. Died of pneumonia. Citizens Savings Hall of Fame, National Football Foundation Hall of Fame.

SHINNICK, DONALD Linebacker. B. 5/15/35, Kansas City, Mo. 6', 235. Attended San Pedro (Calif.) H.S. and UCLA. Baltimore Colts, 1957-69. Was 2nd-round draft choice. Intercepted 37 passes, NFL record for linebackers. NFL championship games, 1958, 59, 64, 68. Super Bowl, 1969. Tournament handball player. Linebacker coach with Oakland Raiders, 1973. Formerly coached for St. Louis Cardinals, 1972, and Chicago Bears, 1970-71.

SHIVELY, BERNIE A. Guard. B. 5/26/02, Oliver, Ill. D. 12/10/67, Lexington, Ky. 6'4", 215. All-America at Illinois, 1926. Was conference heavyweight wrestling champion twice, 1926, 27. Also participated in track (javelin, hammerthrow). Long, productive association with U. of Kentucky athletics. Assistant football coach, 1927-45; head coach, 1945. Head track coach, 1927-34; athletic director, 1938-67. Many years was president of SEC athletic directors. Chairman of NCAA Basketball Tournament Committee, 1958-65. President of National Association of Athletic Directors, member of organization's hall of fame. Earned M.S. degree from Kentucky in 1935.

SHOFNER, DELBERT M. (Del) End. B. 12/11/34, Center, Tex. 6'3", 185. Led Baylor in every offensive department except passing, 1956. MVP Sugar Bowl basketball tournament, 1957. Chose Baylor because it was only school offering him basketball scholarship. Ran leg on Bears' 440-yd. relay team that tied world record. Spurned pro cage career for NFL. Distinguished himself as pass receiver with Los Angeles Rams, 1958-60, and New York Giants, 1961-67. Started pro career as defensive back but was switched to end because of his 9.8 speed. Master of down-and-out patterns, unstoppable on "fly." Five times All-Pro, 1958, 59, 61, 62, 63. Member of All-Pro Squad of the 1960s. Target of numerous anemia and ulcer attacks. Close friend and favorite receiver (with Giants) of fellow Texan, Y. A. Tittle.

SHOFNER, JAMES Defensive Back. B. 12/18/35, Grapevine, Tex. 6'1", 190. Played three years for Abe Martin at Texas Christian, 1955-57. Twice participated in Cotton Bowl. Cornerback and punt returner for Cleveland Browns, 1958-63. Used outstanding speed to intercept eight passes, 1960. San Francisco 49er assistant coach, 1967-73. "This is the one college job I would go to," commented Shofner after he was named head coach at his alma mater, beginning in 1974. Martin, now TCU athletic director, praised former pupil: "We were looking for a real man first and a football coach second, but we got both."

SHULA, DONALD F. Coach. B. 1/4/30, Painesville, Ohio. "This is the greatest moment in my coaching life . . . we can let the record speak for itself. We have gone unbeaten and won the big one, and nobody else has done that." Don Shula was speaking about his Miami Dolphins' 14-7 Super Bowl VII victory in 1973. Miami thus became first NFL team ever to go through regular and post-season play without defeat (17-0). Dolphins became first team to play in three straight Super Bowls, winning over Minnesota Vikings in 1974. Shula, John Carroll graduate, prepared for coaching ranks with seven years of NFL playing service. Defensive back, Cleveland Browns, 1951-52; Baltimore Colts, 1953-56; Washington Redskins, 1957. Spent three seasons as Detroit Lion assistant before joining Colts as head coach in 1963. In seven years with Baltimore Shula guided Colts to two divisional titles while compiling 71-23-4 record. Colts lost Super Bowl III, 16-7 in 1969, stunning decision to New York Jets that ended NFL superiority over AFL. Shula left Baltimore for Miami in 1970, creating storm of controversy. Made mortal enemy of Colts (now Los Angeles Rams) owner Carroll Rosenbloom. Commissioner Pete Rozelle compensated Baltimore with Miami's No. 1 draft choice. Rozelle ruled Dolphins had approached Shula without notifying Colts in advance. 1971 Dolphins lost Super Bowl VI to Dallas Cowboys after edging Kansas City, 27-24, for AFC title in longest pro game ever played. Shula owns 117-32-5 overall record after 11 seasons. With good reason, many consider him premier NFL coach.

SIANI, MICHAEL J. End. B. 5/27/50, Staten Island, N.Y. 6'2", 195. Prep All-American at New Dorp H.S. on Staten Island. Drafted while schoolboy by New York baseball Yankees and, at Villanova, by Los Angeles Dodgers. Turned them down. One of all-time leaders among NCAA pass receivers. Finished 5th in yds. receiving with 2776, 1969-71. Owns all Villanova game, season and career reception records. Scored 33 TDs. East-West Shrine and Hula Bowl games. Caught 28 passes in first pro season with Oakland Raiders, 1972. Siani is cousin of Mike Strofolino, who was Villanova and NFL linebacker. Caught 45 passes for 742 yds., 1973, finishing season in 5th-place tie among AFC receivers. Drafted No. 1 by Raiders in '72.

SIEMON, JEFFREY G. Linebacker. B. 6/2/50, Bakersfield, Calif. 6'2½", 230. Stanford tri-captain and All-America, 1971. Key figure in Stanford's Rose Bowl upsets of Ohio State, 1971, and Michigan, 1972. No. 1 draft choice of Minnesota Vikings, 1972. Vikings, 1972-73. Coach Bud Grant predicted great future as middle linebacker. Worked with Campus Crusade for Christ and Fellowship of Christian Athletes.

SIMMONS, OZZIE E. Running Back. B. 6/6/14, Gainesville, Tex. Iowa halfback. Made spectacular debut in 1934. Rushed 166 yds. and returned punts for 124 more. Following year scored five TD runs of 51-71 yds. against major opponents. Also became outstanding defensive player. Closed career in 1936, having rushed for 1544 yds. and scored 14 TDs. Longest TD jaunt was 85-yds. with intercepted pass vs. Ohio State, 1934. Injuries kept him from fully realizing potential. In 1934 knocked out three times vs. Indiana. He was never again same player, but still mighty good. Resident of Chicago.

SIMONS, CLAUDE, JR. (Monk) Running Back. B. 1/16/14, New Orleans, La. 190. Grew up on Tulane campus where his father was school's athletic trainer. Attended Newman H.S. in New Orleans. Tulane halfback, 1932-34. All-America, 1933. Scored Tulane's first touchdown, on record 86-yd. run, against Pop Warner-coached Temple in first Sugar Bowl, 1935. Green Wave won, 20-14. Record was broken in 1974 Sugar Bowl. Simons later became Sugar Bowl president. Football authority H. J. Stegeman wrote: "... Simons is regarded as one of the South's outstanding backs of all times." Monk coached at Transylvania, 1935-38, and Tulane, 1938-47. National Football Foundation Hall of Fame. Now vice president, D. H. Holmes Ltd., New Orleans.

SIMPSON, ORENTHAL J. (O. J.) Running Back. B. 7/9/47, San Francisco, Calif. 6'1", 214. Irrepressible runner. Product of Gailileo H.S. in San Francisco. Before Simpson, school produced such sports immortals as Lawson Little, Hank Luisetti, Joe DiMaggio. Scored 54 TDs, rushed for more than 2500 yds. at San Francisco City College, 1965-66. Southern California, 1967-68. Unanimous All-America both years. Won Heisman Trophy, Maxwell Award, Walter Camp Trophy, numerous other honors in 1968. Was Heisman runnerup, 1967, to crosstown rival, Gary Beban of USC. Complemented 9.3 speed with power, great quickness. National rushing champ in '67 with record 1415 yds. Repeated in '68, surpassing old mark with 1709. Record fell to Ed Marinaro (Cornell) in 1971. Finished career 1st in running yds. per game with 164.4. That standard was also eclipsed by Marinaro. Scored 33 collegiate TDs. Brilliant in two Rose Bowl appearances, gaining 299 yds. on ground and scoring three TDs. Buffalo Bills, 1969-73. Was drafted No. 1. As heralded rookie gained 697 yds. rushing. Didn't really blossom with Bills until 1972. Led NFL rushers with 1251 yds., had 94-yarder vs. Pittsburgh Steelers. Was named All-AFC, AFC Player of the Year, Pro Bowl MVP.

Surpassed all expectations in 1973. Became only player to gain 2000 (2003) yds. rushing in one season. Also set records for season carries (332), game carries (39), games of 100 or more yds. rushing (11), games rushing for 200 or more yds. (3), game yds. (250). Won every conceivable honor. Setting season rushing mark was big thrill. It pushed aside Jim Brown's standard of 1863 yds. Simpson, as nervy youngster in San Francisco, had told Brown he'd someday break record.

Movie and TV actor in off-season. Also works for ABC-TV sports. Voted College Athlete of the Decade for 1960s. Modern All-Time All-America team. Citizens Savings Hall of Fame.

SINGTON, FREDERICK W. Tackle. B. 2/24/10, Birmingham, Ala. 6'2", 215. Alabama, 1928-30. *Phi Beta Kappa,* unanimous All-America and student body vice president in 1930. That year starred on one of South's greatest teams, culminating with 14-0 victory over Washington State in Rose Bowl. Tide thus finished season 10-0. Played pro baseball with Washington Senators, 1934-37, and Brooklyn Dodgers, 1938-39. Lt. Cmdr. in U.S. Naval Reserves during World War II. Southeastern Conference official for 20 years. Citizens Savings Hall of Fame, National Football Foundation Hall of Fame. Still lives in Birmingham and is president of four sporting goods stores throughout state.

SINKWICH, FRANK (Fireball Frankie) Running Back. B. 10/10/20, McKees Rocks, Pa. 5'8", 180. Georgia, 1940-42. Previously attended Chaney H.S. in Youngstown, Ohio. Was triple-threat tailback. Led nation in rushing with 1103 yds., 1941, and total offense with 2187 in 1942. Played with fractured jaw most of 1942. Established all-time major bowl record, compiling 382 yds. total offense as Georgia whipped Texas Christian, 40-26, in Orange Bowl, 1942. During game threw three TD passes and scored on 43-yd. run. Scored one TD in 1943 Rose Bowl, Georgia winning over UCLA, 9-0. Threw 90- and 80-yd. passes vs. Cincinnati, 1942. Completed career with 4602 yds. (2271 rushing, 2331 passing) total offense. Scored 28 TDs and accounted for 27 more. Twenty-six TDs, scored or passed for, led nation in 1942. Teammate that year of Charley Trippi. Achieved, thru hard work and dedication, "the ability to pick the open man better than anybody I ever saw" — Wally Butts. Unanimous All-America, 1942; consensus, 1941. Heisman Trophy, 1942. Detroit Lions, 1943-44; New York Yankees (AAFC), 1946-47; Baltimore Colts (AAFC), 1947. League MVP, All-Pro and punting leader, 1944. Citizens Savings Hall of Fame, National Football Foundation Hall of Fame. Now in private business in Athens, Ga.

SISEMORE, JERRY Tackle. B. 7/16/51, Olton, Tex. 6'4", 260. Attended Plainview (Tex.) H.S. where he played football and basketball, threw shot-put. U. of Texas, 1970-72. Unanimous All-America twice, 1971, 72. Played in Cotton Bowl three years. Senior Bowl and College All-Star games. No. 1 draft choice of Philadelphia Eagles, 1973. Was No. 3 pick overall. Extremely skillful blocker, seemed almost scientific.

SITKO, EMIL M. (Six Yards) Running Back. B. 9/7/23, Fort Wayne, Ind. D. 12/15/73, Fort Wayne, Ind. 5'8", 180. Played in 39 games involving Notre Dame, and was on other side in Irish's only losing effort during that span, to Great Lakes Naval Training Station in 1943. Halfback on three unbeaten Irish teams, 1946, 47, 48. All-America, 1948. Switched to fullback his last season, 1949, leading team to 10-0 record as he won unanimous All-America rating. Earned nickname because he averaged six yds. per carry. Classmate Joe Doyle, who became South

Bend *Tribune* sports editor, recalled: "Emil was about 5 feet 8 with virtually no neck and short legs. He was especially quick in getting through holes. Because of those short legs he had a tendency to run out of gas after going 70 or 80 yds." Still Notre Dame one-game rushing record-holder (186 yds.). San Francisco 49ers, 1950; Chicago Cardinals, 1950-51.

SIXKILLER, ALEX (Sonny) Quarterback. B. 9/6/51, Tahlequah, Okla. 5'11", 190. Full-blooded Cherokee Indian. Attended Ashland (Ore.) H.S. and U. of Washington. Only 3rd-string quarterback in spring practice, 1970, Sixkiller developed rapidly. Led major-college passers that year with 2303 yds. In Washington career completed 385 of 811 passes for 5496 yds. and 35 touchdowns, 1970-72. Holds 15 school records. Helped Huskies to 8-3 seasons in 1971, 72. Signed as free agent by Los Angeles Rams, 1973, but released before season began.

SKORICH, NICHOLAS L. Coach. B. 6/26/21, Bellaire, Ohio. 195-pound guard at U. of Cincinnati. Graduated in 1943. Later earned master's degree from Michigan State. Played with Pittsburgh Steelers, 1946-48. Served assistantships with Steelers, Green Bay Packers, Philadelphia Eagles, Cleveland Browns. Head coach, Rensselaer Poly, 1953; Philadelphia Eagles, 1961-63; Cleveland Browns, 1971-73. Eagles won NFL title in 1960 when Skorich was offensive coach. Guided Browns to AFC Central Division title, 1971. 41-38-6 pro record thru 1973.

SKORONSKI, ROBERT F. Tackle. B. Chicago, Ill. 6'3", 245. Captained Indiana Hoosiers, 1954. Three-year starter, 1953-55; team's MVP his senior year. Played in College All-Star game, 1956. Eleven-year offensive tackle for Green Bay Packers, 1956, 59-68. Skoronski played left side and Forrest Gregg right — they formed Green Bay's tackle combination at zenith of club's success in 1960s. Planned to retire before '68 season but stayed on to help Phil Bengston begin his regime as Vince Lombardi's successor. Lives in Menasha, Wis., and is jewelry salesman.

SKORUPAN, JOHN Linebacker. B. 5/17/51, Beaver, Pa. 6'2", 214. Penn State, 1970-72. Named thrice to All-ECAC team. Cotton Bowl, 1972; Sugar Bowl, 1973. Consensus All-America, 1972. Excelled at open-field tackling and pass coverage. Signed with Buffalo Bills, 1973, after being their No. 6 draft choice.

SLOAN, BONNIE R. Tackle. B. 6/1/48, Lebanon, Tenn. 6'5", 260. Attended Isaac Litton H.S. in Nashville where he was football and track star. Overcame handicap of total deafness. Twice All-Conference at Austin Peay, 1971, 72. Exceptionally quick defensive lineman. St. Louis Cardinals, 1973. Drafted on 10th round. Selected Better Hearing honorary chairman by St. Louis Hearing and Speech Center, 1973.

SLOAN, STEPHEN C. Quarterback. B. 8/19/44, Austin, Tex. Led Cleveland

(Tenn.) H.S. to football and basketball state championships. Then to U. of Alabama. Played three years under Bear Bryant, 1963-65. Came to prominence after Joe Namath was suspended prior to final regular season game of 1963. Sloan stepped in and guided Tide to 17-12 win over Miami (Fla.). Ensuing Sugar Bowl, he engineered 12-7 decision over Mississippi. Next two years, with Sloan at quarterback, Alabama won back-to-back SEC and national championships. Orange Bowl victories climaxed both seasons. Atlanta Falcons, 1966-67. Assistant coach at Alabama, 1968-70; Florida State, 1971; Georgia Tech, 1972. In 1973 named Vanderbilt head coach.

SMITH, ANDREW L. Coach. B. 9/10/1883, DuBois, Pa. D. 1/8/26, Philadelphia, Pa. All-America fullback for Pennsylvania's 12-0 national champions, 1904. Penn outscored foes 222-4. Smith was 6', 185. Head coach at Penn, 1909-12; Purdue, 1913-15; California, 1916-25. Best known for California "Wonder Teams." In five-year period Bears were unbeaten, winning 44 and tying four, 1920-24. Defeatless string reached 50 games, ended with 15-0 loss to Olympic Club of San Francisco in 1925. Compiled 74-16-5 record at California and was 116-32-3 overall. Most famous Cal All-America was end Harold (Brick) Muller. Developed Elmer (Ollie) Oliphant at Purdue. Citizens Savings Hall of Fame, National Football Foundation Hall of Fame.

SMITH, BILLY RAY (Black Rabbit) Tackle. B. 1/27/35, Augusta, Ark. 6'4", 235. Won heavyweight Golden Gloves championship six times in Arkansas. Lost only seven of 54 fights, including one to former Olympic champ Pete Rademacher. Never considered pro boxing career, though, which turned out to be football's blessing. Originally enrolled at Auburn. Lured back to home state by Arkansas coach Bowden Wyatt. One of "24 Little Pigs." Played in 1955 Cotton Bowl game, losing to Georgia Tech, 14-6. All-SWC tackle, 1956. Los Angeles Rams, 1957; Pittsburgh Steelers, 1958-60; Baltimore Colts, 1961-62, 64-70. Started pro career at defensive end. Hit stride with Colts, playing defensive tackle. Compensated for lack of heft with quickness and agility. NFL championship games, 1964, 68, 70. Colts defeated Dallas Cowboys, 16-13, in Super Bowl IV, 1971. Smith's motto: "Money, marbles or chocolate — I play to win."

SMITH, BRUCE P. (Boo) Running Back. B. 2/8/20, Faribault, Minn. D. 8/28/67. 6', 193. Minnesota halfback. Although injured much of season, Smith played enough to win All-America honors and Heisman Trophy in 1941. He was also team captain for Gophers who extended their win streak to 17 games. Minnesota was national champion two straight years with Smith in lineup, 1940-41. Captained East in East-West Shrine game and MVP for College All-Stars against Chicago Bears following his Minnesota career. All-Service for Great Lakes Naval Air Station and St. Mary's Pre-Flight School, 1942, 43. Played collegiately for Bernie Bierman. Green Bay Packers, 1945-48, and Los Angeles Rams, 1948. Victim of cancer. National Football Foundation Hall of Fame.

SMITH, CARNIE H. Coach. B. 1/19/11, Weir, Kan. Compiled 116-52-6 record at alma mater, 1949-66. Included were NAIA championships in 1957 and 1961. Both seasons finished 11-0. 1957 club won Holiday Bowl at St. Petersburg, Fla; in 1961 captured Camelia Bowl at Sacramento. Latter squad outscored its 11 foes 299-25. Now Pittsburg State athletic director. NAIA Hall of Fame.

SMITH, CHARLES A. (Bubba) Defensive End. B. 2/28/45, Orange, Tex. 6'7", 265. Attended Charlton-Pollard H.S., Beaumont, Tex., where he played for father, Willie Ray. Michigan State, 1964-66. Became legend there. Unanimous All-America, 1966; consensus, 1965. Baltimore Colts, 1967-72, and Oakland Raiders, 1973. Was No. 1 draft choice of Colts. Pro Bowl, 1971, 72. All-AFC, 1970, 71. Blocked four FG attempts and sacked nine QBs in finest season, 1971. Missed entire season due to knee surgery, 1972. Traded to Raiders for Raymond Chester, 1973. Outspoken, has had numerous feuds with coaches throughout career. NFL championship game, 1968. Super Bowl, 1969, 71.

SMITH, CLYDE W. Center. B. 7/17/04, Steelville, Mo. All-MVC center, 1922, 23, 24. First Missouri graduate to enter pro ball. Played with Kansas Cowboys, 1926; Cleveland Bulldogs, 1927; Providence Steamrollers, 1928-29. Steamrollers won NFL title, 1928; Smith was All-Pro. Coached Oklahoma and Illinois high schools and College of Emporia (now defunct). Retired in 1970 after 35 years as florist. Has been active in numerous civic affairs around Lawrenceville, Ill.

SMITH, ERNEST F. (Ernie) Tackle. B. 11/26/09, Spearfish, S.D. 6'2", 215. Played at Gardena (Calif.) H.S. and Southern California. 28-3 playing record at USC, 1930-32. Unanimous All-America, 1932. Trojans won Rose Bowl victories over Tulane, 1932 (21-12); Pittsburgh, 1933 (35-0). Won 20 straight games, 1931-32. Green Bay Packers, 1935-39. All-Pro, 1936. Packer coach Curly Lambeau praised Smith: "He is one of the greatest tackles . . . truly an all-time college and pro player." Citizens Savings Hall of Fame, National Football Foundation Hall of Fame. Active in many musical and USC alumni organizations. Member Tournament of Roses Committee. Insurance executive.

SMITH, GIDEON E. Running Back. B. 7/13/1889, Norfolk County, Va. D. 5/6/68, Salem, Va. Attended Hampton Institute and Michigan State. First Black to play at Michigan State. Standout on 1913 team. Member Class of 1916. Pioneer Black pro player — with Canton Bulldogs. Competed against such greats as Knute Rockne and Jim Thorpe. Was Hampton Institute coach for more than 30 years; also physical education professor. Charter member of National Football Foundation Hall of Fame. Died after long illness.

SMITH, HARRY E. (Blackjack) Guard. B. 8/26/18, Russellville, Mo. 5'11", 218. Played for Howard Jones at Southern California, 1937-39. Started 28 straight games for USC, finishing with 21-3-4 playing record. All-America, 1939.

Member of two Rose Bowl championship teams, 1939, 40. USC whipped Duke, 7-3, and Tennessee, 14-0, respectively. Detroit Lions, 1940. Assistant coach, Missouri, 1941-43; frosh coach at Southern Cal, 1949-50; head coach of Saskatchewan Roughriders, 1951. Citizens Savings Hall of Fame, National Football Foundation Hall of Fame.

SMITH, J.D. Running Back. B. 7/19/32, Plainville, S.C. 6'1", 201. Attended North Carolina A. & T. Drafted by Chicago Bears as defensive back in 1956. Dropped after six games, whereupon he was picked up by San Francisco 49ers. Played defense thru 1957 and then shifted to halfback. In 1959 hit highwater mark, rushing for 1036 yds. All-Pro that year. Teamed in 49er backfield with Hugh McElhenny. Roomed with R. C. Owens. Following 1964 season traded to Dallas Cowboys. Remained with Dallas thru 1966. During career rushed for 4672 yds. on 1100 carries (4.2 average), scored 40 TDs. Essentially straight-ahead runner but could maneuver for yardage if necessary. One of those players who seem to "smell" goal line. J. D. always claimed he had no given name.

SMITH, JACKIE L. Tight End. B. 2/23/40, Columbia, Miss. 6'4", 235. Played tailback at Kentwood (La.) H.S. Football and track standout at Northwestern Louisiana. St. Louis Cardinals, 1963-73. Holds Cardinal all-time receiving yardage record with 7188. Pro Bowl, 1967, 68, 69, 70, 71. Punishing blocker and all-out competitor. Served as St. Louis punter for three seasons, 1964, 65, 66. Regarded as one of NFL's finest tight ends. Thru 1973 caught 434 passes, scored 40 TDs.

SMITH, JERRY T. (Shane) Tight End. B. 7/19/43, Oakland, Calif. 6'3", 208. Arizona State, 1962-64. Transferred to Arizona State from Eastern Arizona J.C. Caught 82 passes for 1040 yds., making Juco All-America team in 1961. Hauled in 42 passes for 618 yds. senior year for Sun Devils. Played in Senior Bowl and All-America Bowl games. Washington Redskins, 1965-73. Started pro career as flanker, moved to tight end sophomore season. Produced 67 receptions, 1967, representing all-time NFL season record for tight end. His 52 career TDs are also NFL record at position. All-NFL, 1969. One of six NFL players to visit front-line troops in Vietnam, 1971. Pro Bowl, 1968, 70. Super Bowl, 1973. In nine seasons captured 329 aerials for 4470 yds., 52 TDs.

SMITH, LARRY Running Back. B. 9/2/47, Tampa, Fla. 6'3", 220. Attended Robinson H.S. in Tampa, participating in track and football. Three-year starter at U. of Florida, 1966-68. All-America, 1968. Gained 2186 yds. and scored 21 TDs during college career. Compiled 187 yds., including 94-yd. TD run, in Florida's 27-12 Orange Bowl victory over Georgia Tech in 1967. One of three first-round draft choices of Los Angeles Rams, 1969. Plagued by numerous injuries: broken foot, hamstring pulls, sprained ankles, broken nose, etc. Rams, 1969-73. Solid runner, blocker and pass receiver.

SMITH, LAWRENCE E. (Tody) Defensive End. B. 12/24/48, Orange, Tex.

6'5", 250. Attended Michigan State and Southern California. Acquired nickname in junior high school Spanish class. Tody comes from *toro* (bull) — he was largest in class. Played for dad, Willie Ray, at Charlton-Pollard H.S. of Beaumont, Tex. USC All-America, 1969. No. 1 draft choice of Dallas Cowboys in 1971. Played in Super Bowl, 1972. Traded to Houston Oilers with wide receiver Billy Parks, 1973, in exchange for two draft choices. Brother, Bubba, starred in college and pros.

SMITH, NOLAND (Super Gnat) End. B. 1943, Jackson, Miss. 5'6", 154. Exciting little man. Attended Tennessee State, 1963-66. Won four football letters and four in track. Ran 100-yd. dash in 9.4. Kansas City Chiefs, 1967-69; San Francisco 49ers, 1969. Instant sensation with Chiefs, delighting Kansas City fans with his kickoff and punt returns. Against Denver Broncos, 12/17/67, returned kickoff 106 yds. for TD. Runback set AFL record and tied pro mark held by Al Carmichael of Green Bay Packers. Owns K.C. record for longest punt return (80 yds.). Established pro mark with nine kickoff returns vs. Oakland Raiders, 11/23/67. Career declined after 1968. One of 14 children. His twin brother, Norland, was five inches taller and 35 pounds heavier. Appropriately, "Super Gnat" collected insects as hobby.

SMITH, ROGER D. (Zeke) Guard. B. 9/29/36, Walker Springs, Ala. 6'2", 220. Grew up in Uniontown, Ala., where he attended high school. There, as full-back, acquired moniker "Zeke" from coach who thought running style resembled Georgia's Zeke Bratkowski. Moved to center as Auburn freshman, then permanently to guard. Became two-time All-America, 1958, 59. Was consensus choice and Outland Trophy winner in 1958. Auburn was national champion in Smith's sophomore season, 1957. Never lost game collegiately until senior campaign when Tigers "slumped" to 7-3. Baltimore Colts, 1960; New York Giants, 1961.

SMITH, RONALD Defensive Back. B. 5/3/43, Chicago, Ill. 6'1", 195. Wisconsin, 1962-64. Lettered in track and football. As sprinter ran 100-yd. dash in 9.4, 60 in 6.1. Chicago Bears, 1965, 70-72; Atlanta Falcons, 1966-67; Los Angeles Rams, 1968-69; San Diego Chargers, 1973. Signed originally by Bears as free agent. Taken by Falcons in 1966 expansion draft. Was traded to L.A. in '68, then back to Bears in 1970. All-time NFL leader in number of kickoff returns (256) and yardage returning kicks (6522). Also owns standards for combined punt returns (450) and yardage (7794). Led NFL in kickoff returns with 30-yd. average. No. 1, AFC punt returns, 13.0-yd. average, 1973. Seems to be getting better with age.

SMITH, ROYCE Guard. B. 6/7/49, Savannah, Ga. 6'3", 245. All-City fullback at Groves H.S. in Savannah. U. of Georgia, 1969-71. Started college career at defensive end. Unanimous All-America, 1971, leading Georgia to 7-3 victory over North Carolina in Gator Bowl. Same season named South's outstanding lineman by Atlanta Touchdown Club, received Jacobs Trophy as best blocker in

SEC. Started in rookie season at right guard with New Orleans Saints, 1972. Was drafted by New Orleans on 1st round. With Saints again in 1973.

SNAVELY, CARL G. (King Carl) Coach. B. 7/31/1894, Omaha, Neb. Football and baseball captain at Lebanon Valley, 1915. Head coach, Bucknell, 1927-33; North Carolina, 1934-35, 1945-52; Cornell, 1936-44; Washington (Mo.), 1953-58. 180-96-16 record overall. May have been first coach to study football films, and he did so religiously. Used single-wing offense throughout career. Favorite play was quick-kick .— he developed master at trade in North Carolina All-America Charlie Justice, often using it as offensive weapon. Developed Clarke Hinkle (Bucknell) and Jerome (Brud) Holland (Cornell). Snavely was aloof, introverted person who shunned reporters and strangers. Citizens Savings Hall of Fame, National Football Foundation Hall of Fame.

SNEAD, NORMAN B. Quarterback. B. 7/31/39, Halifax County, Va. 6'4", 215. Attended Warwick H.S. in Newport News, Va. Three-year regular for Wake Forest, 1958-60. Also played freshman basketball in college. Senior Bowl, Blue-Gray, College All-Star and Coaches All-America games. MVP in Senior Bowl. 1st-round draft choice of Washington Redskins in 1961. Redskins, 1961-63; Philadelphia Eagles, 1964-70; Minnesota Vikings, 1971; New York Giants, 1972-73. Went to New York in trade that sent Fran Tarkenton to Minnesota. Won NFL passing championship with 2307 yds. on 60.3 percentage, 1972. Latter is Giant club record. Interested in Civil War history. Pro Bowl, 1964, 66, 73. In 13 seasons completed 2049 of 3963 passes, accumulating 28,238 yds., 182 TDs. Bothered by interceptions, threw 22 in 1973 to increase lifetime total to 235. Led league twice, 1963, 68. Pro Bowl, 1964, 66, 73.

SNELL, MATHEWS (Matt) Running Back. B. 8/18/41, Garfield, Ga. 6'2", 219. Ohio State, 1961-63. Prize catch in AFL-NFL bidding war. Signed with New York Jets, who won out over crosstown rival Giants, 1964. He was first No. 1 draft choice to sign with Jets. Played with New York, 1964-72. AFL Rookie of the Year as he gained 948 yds., still club record. Same season picked up one-game record of 180 yds. on 31 carries. Rushed for 121 yds. and scored game's only TD in Jets' 16-7 Super Bowl win, 1969. Plagued by injuries in nine-year career. Last three seasons was able to play only 12 games. Suffered from torn knee ligaments, torn Achilles tendon and ruptured spleen at various times. Retired, 1973, commenting: "Because of the years, injuries and the general wear and tear of pro sports, I feel it is time to move on to other endeavors. I've had a great career and I don't want anything to detract from it." Held Super Bowl game records for rushing attempts (30) and yds. (121). AFL All-Star games, 1965, 67, 70. Gained 4285 yds. on ground during career, scored 31 TDs.

SNOW, JACK T. End. B. 1/25/43, Rock Springs, Wyo. 6'2", 190. Graduated from St. Anthony H.S. in Long Beach, Calif.; was city's Lineman of the Year, 1960. Formed outstanding pass combination at Notre Dame with QB John Huarte. Played for Irish, 1962-64. Consensus All-America, catching 60 passes for 1114 yds. and 9 TDs in 1964. Produced 312 receptions and 41 touchdowns in first eight seasons with Los Angeles Rams, 1965-73. Ram leader in receiving four straight years, 1969-72. Hobby is golf.

SOLEM, OSCAR M. (Ossie) Coach. B. 12/13/1891, Minneapolis, Minn. D. 10/26/70, Minneapolis, Minn. Began coaching career while still student at Minnesota. Tutored Normal School of River Falls, Wis., in afternoon, pro team in Minneapolis at night. Played end for Minnesota, graduating in 1915. Head coach of Luther College, 1920; Drake, 1921-31; Iowa, 1932-36; Syracuse, 1937-45; Springfield, 1946-57. Thirty-seven year record: 162-117-20. Created controversy when he introduced Y formation in 1941. It featured center who faced backfield, making direct passes and pitchouts. Formation was used in 1941 but banned by Rules Committee prior to '42 season. Bud Wilkinson and Biggie Munn were Solem assistants who achieved prominence as head coaches. Duffy Daugherty, who played under Solem at Syracuse, became Michigan State mentor. Citizens Savings Hall of Fame.

SONNENBERG, GUSTAVE (Dynamite Gus) Tackle. B. 3/6/1898, Ewen, Mich. D. 9/12/44. Attended Dartmouth and U. of Detroit. Played tackle in memorable 7-7 game, Dartmouth vs. Colgate, that featured returning war veterans and All-American in 1919. Sonnenberg, Cuddy Murphy, Adolph Youngstrom and Norm Crisp were heart of Dartmouth's powerful line. Indians handed Penn State its only loss (19-13) in three years, 1921. Moved to guard in pros, playing with Columbus Tigers, 1921; Detroit Panthers, 1925-26; Providence Steamrollers, 1927-28, 30. Turned to wrestling when he gave up football; took heavyweight championship from Strangler Lewis, 1929, and won rematch, 1930. Introduced "flying tackle" to pro wrestling.

SPALDING, JESSE Running Back. B. 1/18/1889, Chicago, Ill. D. 7/18/34, New York, N.Y. Captain of once-beaten Yale, 1912. Harvard dealt only defeat, 20-0. 1912 spawned last major rule revisions: touchdown value increased from 5 points to 6; field length reduced from 110 yards to 100, as end zones established (touchdowns therein allowed); 4th down added. Director of athletics, Service of Supplies, World War I, Tours, France. Won Maidstone Golf Club championship, East Hampton, N.Y., 1925. Investment banker and broker most of professional life.

SPAULDING, WILLIAM H. Coach. B. 5/4/1880, Melrose, Wis. D. 10/13/66, Los Angeles, Calif. Wabash halfback and track sprinter. Claimed he ran match races with horses at 50 yds. and that he always lost. Head coach, Western Michigan, 1907-21; Minnesota, 1922-24; UCLA, 1925-38. Record: 144-83-16. Coached Frank Thomas at Western Michigan. Thomas subsequently attended Notre Dame and won fame as Alabama coach. Of Spaulding's many UCLA stars, Kenny Washington is most well-known. Spaulding's arrival at UCLA coincided with move of Howard Jones from Iowa to Southern California. They pioneered one of nation's most heated rivalries. After retiring from coaching served as Bruin athletic director for 10 years, then went into business. Citizens Savings Hall of Fame.

SPEARS, CLARENCE W. (Doc) Guard. B. 7/24/1894, DeWitt, Ark. D. 2/1/ 64. 5′9″, 230. Dartmouth, 1914-15. Was transfer from Knox College. All-America, 1915; 3rd team, 1914. Dartmouth lost only two of 18 games with Spears in lineup. Head coach at Dartmouth 1917, 19-20; West Virginia, 1921-24; Minnesota, 1925-29; Oregon, 1930-31; Wisconsin, 1932-35. Compiled 7-2 record and won Ivy League title, 1920. Developed Bronko Nagurski at Minnesota. Composite record: 135-78-13. Studied medicine at Chicago and Rush Medical School and eventually left coaching for full-time medical practice. Citizens Savings Hall of Fame (as coach), National Football Foundation Hall of Fame (as player). Also called "Fat" and "Cupid."

SPEARS, WILLIAM D. Quarterback. B. 8/31/06, Jasper, Tenn. 155. 22-5-2 playing record at Vanderbilt, 1925-27. All-America, 1927. Coach Dan McGugin commented, "Spears was a classic example of the result a boy can gain if he works hard enough and has a fighting heart. Bill was as skillful as any man who ever played football. A great student of the game, our boys had implicit confidence in his judgment. His spirited leadership gave us a tremendous lift." Admitted to Tennessee bar, 1932. National Football Foundation Hall of Fame. Now member of firm Spears, Moore, Redman & Williams, Chattanooga, Tenn. Also Vanderbilt trustee.

SPEEDIE, MAC End. B. 1/12/20, Odell, Ill. Overcame early physical handicap. Due to bone deficiency left leg, at age 8, was shorter than right by two inches. Had to wear steel brace from hip to ankle next four years. Each week, during period, orthopedist adjusted screw that stretched leg. Developed into fine football player and track man at Utah. All-Rocky Mountain Conference twice. Consistently ran under 10 seconds in 100-yd. dash; fine hurdler. According to Paul Brown, "His track experience taught him a wonderful sense of how to run, how to change speed, and no one quite knew how to play against him. . . ." Played seven years for Brown and Cleveland Browns, 1946-49, 50-52. All-time AAFC pass catcher with 211, for 3554 yds. and 24 TDs. All-Pro, 1952. Coached Denver Broncos, 1964-66 (6-19-1). Now affiliated with Wilson Sporting Goods Co.

SPEYRER, CHARLES W. (Cotton) End. B. 4/29/49, Port Arthur, Tex. 6′, 175. Texas All-America, 1969, 70. Given nickname by parents because he was born with white hair. Made many clutch catches as Texas wide receiver. Member of Longhorns' national championship teams, 1969, 70 (shared). Played in two Cotton Bowls, 1970, 71. Drafted on 2nd round by Washington Redskins, 1971, who traded him to Baltimore Colts. Has played only for Colts in pros. Missed entire season due to broken arm, 1971, and nine games, 1972, due to severe muscle pull. Caught 17 passes for 311 yds., 4 TDs. in 1973.

SPIEGEL, JOHN E. Running Back. B. 11/18/1891, Detroit, Mich. D. 8/14/51,

Detroit, Mich. 145. Attended Detroit University School, Lafayette and Washington & Jefferson. Graduated from W. & J. in 1915. Played halfback. Led nation in scoring with 127 points, 1913; W. & J. finished unbeaten. 2nd team All-America, 1914. Coached Chattanooga, 1915-16, and Muhlenberg, 1920-21. Worked many years in real estate and lumber-builder supplies in Detroit.

SPIKES, JACK E. Running Back. B. 2/5/36, Big Spring, Tex. 6′2″, 220. Attended Texas Christian. All-SWC fullback, 1958-59. TCU was league champ, 1958, and co-champ, 1959. Spikes led team in rushing both years, averaging 4.7 yds. per rush each season. Played in East-West Shrine game, 1960. Dallas Texans, 1960-62; Kansas City Chiefs, 1063-64; Houston Oilers, 1965; Buffalo Bills, 1966. AFL championship games, 1962, 66. Named game's outstanding player, 1962. Now with Lehman Bros., Inc., of Dallas.

SPRACKLING, WILLIAM E. (Sprack) Quarterback. B. 9/6/1890, Cleveland, Ohio. 5′9″, 150. Attributed much of success to fundamentals learned under Jo Fogg, ex-Wisconsin quarterback, at East H.S. in Cleveland. Brown, 1908-11. Except for opener Sprackling played every minute of every game during four-year college career. Although wore no padding, he played entire span without single injury. Returned kickoff 110 yds. for TD against Carlisle; Brown won, 21-8, 1909. Following year same teams met again in showdown between Sprackling and Jim Thorpe. Brown won again, 15-6. Sprackling accounted for 456 of Brown's 608 yds. in 21-0 victory over Yale in 1910, first win for Bruins over Bulldogs in 30 years. Sprackling kicked three FGs (4th was nullified by holding penalty) and tossed one TD pass during game. Threw 11 TD passes during career. Still holds six career records at Brown. All-America, 1910; 2nd team, 1911; 3rd team, 1909. Away from football was Brown freshman class president, served on Student Governing Board. National Football Foundation Hall of Fame. Retired as president of Anaconda Wire and Cable Co., Los Angeles. Lives in Beverly Hills.

SPRAGUE, MORTIMER E. (Bud) Tackle. B. 9/8/04, Dallas, Tex. 6′2″, 210. Best of football-playing family. Bud Sprague and brothers, Howard, John and Charlie, all captained college teams. Bud was Army captain, 1928; others were SMU captains. Consensus All-America, 1928. Bud played six years of varsity football, three at Texas, 1922-24, and three at Army, 1926-28. Playing record of 44-9-3. As Cadet cleared path for such runners as Harry Wilson, Chris Cagle. During World War II served as executive, Planning Division, Office of Chief of Transportation. Present at both Malta and Yalta conferences. Retired as vice president of Home Insurance Co., New York City. Citizens Savings Hall of Fame, National Football Foundation Hall of Fame.

SPRINKLE, EDWARD A. Defensive End. B. 9/3/23, Abilene, Texas. 6′1″, 207. Ed Sprinkle wasn't real big, but he was real tough. Fans hated him, players feared him. Heyday was 1944-55 with Chicago Bears. Coach George Halas called him "the greatest pass-rusher I've ever seen." Tuscola (Tex.) H.S. furnished his football cradle. Played there first, as senior, on six-man team. Matriculated at Hardin-Simmons, where he was All-Border Conference twice. In 1943 enrolled at Annapolis and helped Navy beat Army, 13-0. Then to Bears. 1946 club won world championship, defeating New York Giants, 24-14, in title game. Played in six Pro Bowls. Was effective on offense, as well as defense. Once accused by St. Louis Cardinal coach Buddy Parker of deliberately stomping on running back Elmer Angsman. Latter gave corroboration, revealing chest emblazoned with five cleat marks. Ed Sprinkle meant business!

SPURRIER, STEVE O. Quarterback. B. 4/20/45, Miami Beach, Fla. 6'2", 203. Attended Science Hill H.S. in Johnson City, Tenn. U. of Florida quarterback, 1964-66. Became sixth QB to win Heisman Trophy, 1966. Unanimous All-America, 1966; All-America, 1965. 22-8 playing record. In three years completed 392 of 692 passes for 4848 yds., 36 TDs; compiled 5290 yds. total offense. Had career punting average of 40.3 yds. (130 punts). Finished high nationally in many career categories. Set Sugar Bowl records of 27 completions (in 45 attempts), 352 yds. passing, 344 total offense; threw 2 TD passes as Florida lost to Missouri, 20-18. Completed 14 passes for 160 yds. in 1967 Orange Bowl, winning 27-12 over Georgia Tech. Taken on 1st round by San Francisco 49ers in AFL-NFL draft, 1967. 49ers, 1967-73. Mainly backup QB for John Brodie with San Francisco, finally got starting shot in 1972. That year threw for 1983 yds. and 18 TDs. Back to irregular basis in 1973. Regular punter three of first four years. Didn't throw single pass in 1968.

STABLER, KEN M. Quarterback. B. 12/25/45, Foley, Ala. 6'3", 215. 28-3-2 playing record at Alabama, 1965-67. Set Tide one-season passing percentage record with 64.9. Played in Orange, Sugar and Cotton Bowls. MVP in Sugar, 1967. Alabama was AP national champion, 1966. Also played baseball in college. Oakland Raiders, 1970-73. Was on Raider taxi squad, 1968, and didn't play in 1969. Made significant progress as pro. Completed 10 of 11 passes against Bears, 1972, and 25 of 29 against Colts, 1973. Scored Oakland's only TD vs. Steelers during 13-7 AFC playoff game defeat, 1972. Southpaw. Had banner year in '73. Completed 62.7 percent (163 of 260) for 1997 yds., 14 TDs. Was leading AFC passer, gained berth in Pro Bowl. Created stir by signing with Birmingham of WFL, 1974. Still had one year on contract to complete, plus option year.

STAGG, AMOS ALONZO Coach. B. 8/16/1862, West Orange, N.J. D. 3/17/65, Stockton, Calif. Horatio Alger prototype. "I subscribe to his creed," Stagg admitted and "there is something of Alger in my story." Born to extreme poverty during Civil War, seven years before emergence of American football. Won first fame as baseball pitcher. Led Yale to five consecutive championships, 1886-90. Success prompted offers from six National League teams. Disdaining professionalism, Stagg turned them down. Began to take football seriously in 1888, and in '89 was end on first All-America team ever chosen. Entered Yale Divinity School, 1889. Took notion that he was poor public speaker, so abandoned ministry. Turned to coaching. Remarkable career unfolded! Was head coach for 57 years: at Springfield, 1890-91; Chicago, 1892-1932; College of Pacific, 1933-46. When he reached mandatory retirement age — 70 — at Chicago, was offered several advisory jobs. Not interested — "I refuse to be idle and a nuisance." Pacific considered Stagg no nuisance, hired him and was head coach there until age 84. At 81 named NCAA Coach of the Year in 1943. Helped his son five years at Susquehanna after leaving Pacific. Thus, at 89, he was still down on field coaching.

Won 314 games, more than any other college coach (one more than Pop Warner). At Chicago won seven Western Conference (Big 10) titles. 1905 team, starring Walter Eckersall, was greatest. It outscored foes 212-5; won 10 straight games, including 2-0 cardiac thriller over Michigan; was designated national champion. Acknowledged as game's foremost innovator. Developed end-round, hidden-ball trick, double reverse, huddle, handoff from fake kick, quick-kick, charging sled, padded goal posts, man-in-motion, backfield shift, quarterback keeper, wind sprints, cross-blocking, *ad infinitum*. His teams were first to practice under lights; Springfield played first night game against squad of former Yale players in 1891. No wonder Knute Rockne said, "All football comes from Stagg." Inventive in other sports, too. Pioneered headlong slide and batting cage in baseball. Also conducted inaugural tour of Japan by American baseball players. Introduced troughs for overflows in swimming pools. Held national schoolboy basketball tournament in Chicago, 1917-30, helping to standardize play. Paragon of clean living and sportsmanship. Foe of smoking, drinking, profanity and hot dog. "Jackass" was closest he came to cursing. "Grand Old Man of the Midway" was 103 when he died, outliving his Yale coach, Walter Camp, by 40 years. It had been full life. Citizens Savings Hall of Fame, National Football Foundation Hall of Fame.

STANFILL, WILLIAM T. Defensive End. B. 1/13/47, Cairo, Ga. 6'5", 250. Georgia, 1966-68. Abandoned promising basketball and track careers to concentrate on football. At Cairo H.S. Stanfill won 11 letters and set state discus record. Starter in 33 straight games for Georgia Bulldogs, including Cotton Bowl, Liberty Bowl, Sugar Bowl. Consensus All-America tackle and Outland Trophy recipient, 1968. Miami Dolphins' No. 1 draft choice in 1969. Dolphins, 1969-73. Ranked with pro's finest defensive ends. Made 69 stops, including 10 sacks, 1972. Super Bowl, 1972, 73, 74. Pro Bowl, 1972, 73, 74. All-AFC, 1972, 73. Owns Hoagie's restaurant in Athens, Ga., where he lives in off-season.

STARR, BYRAN B. (Bart) Quarterback. B. 1/9/34, Montgomery, Ala. 6'1", 195. Attended Sidney Lanier H.S., Montgomery, and U. of Alabama. At Alabama, 1952-55. Completed 8 of 12 passes for 93 yds. as Alabama defeated Syracuse 61-6 in Orange Bowl, 1953. Lost to Rice, 28-6, in Cotton Bowl, 1954. Recorded 63-yd. punt return against Southern Mississippi, 1953. Not drafted by pros until 17th round (Green Bay Packers), but developed into one of football's greatest quarterbacks. NFL passing leader, 1962, 64, 66. Player of the Year, 1966; Super Bowl MVP, 1967, 68. Set NFL records for highest career passing percentage (57.5) and most consecutive passes thrown without interception (294, 1964-65). Also set four championship game records. Pro Bowl, 1961, 62, 63, 67. Packers won five league championships and two Super Bowls with Starr in command. Played entire pro career with Green Bay, 1956-71. Extremely modest, highly regarded for ability to lead and motivate. NFL passing totals: 3149 attempts, 1808 completions, 57.4 percent, 24718 yds., 1952 TD passes, 138 interceptions, 7.85-yd. average. Green Bay assistant coach, 1972. Now car dealer, pro analyst for CBS-TV.

STAUBACH, ROGER. Quarterback. B. 2/5/42, Cincinnati, Ohio. 6'3", 197. Attended Purcell H.S. in Cincinnati. At one time considered going to Notre Dame to study for priesthood. Before enrolling at Navy spent one year at New Mexico Military Institute. Produced 4253 yds. total offense for Middies, 1962-64. Threw for 3571 yds. and 18 TDs. Completed .631 percent of passes to establish NCAA record which still stands. Unanimous All-America, Heisman Trophy and Maxwell Award winner as junior. Completed 21 of 31 passes as Navy lost to Texas in Cotton Bowl, 1964. Also lettered in basketball and baseball. Spent four years in service, one year as port officer in Vietnam after graduating. Dallas Cowboys, 1969-73. Became regular Cowboy quarterback, 1971, and led team to 24-3 victory over Miami in Super Bowl VI. Passed for two TDs and was named game MVP. NFC Player of the Year same season. Suffered shoulder separation during pre-season game and saw limited action 1972. Admired for leadership qualities. Active in Fellowship of Christian Athletes. Known as great scrambling QB; in fact rushed for 343 yds. on 8.4 average in 1972, besides throwing for 15 TDs. Pro Bowl, 1972.

STAUTNER, ERNEST Tackle. B. 4/2/25, Calm, Bavaria. 6', 230. Served in Marine Corps, 1943-46, then attended Boston College. Played under Dennis Myers, 1947-49. Pittsburgh Steelers, 1950-63. All Pro, 1958. Named one of 16 greatest pros and to All-Pro Squad of the 1950s by Pro Football Hall of Fame. Tied NFL career record for safeties, three in 1962. Played in nine Pro Bowl games. Recovered 21 fumbles lifetime. Tremendously strong, aggressive, durable defensive tackle. Had huge, punishing hands. "As tough as any man who ever played," decreed Steeler Coach Buddy Parker. Pro Football Hall of Fame. Defensive coordinator, Dallas Cowboys, 1966-73. Developed Dallas' "Doomsday Defense."

STEGEMAN, HERMAN J. (H. J.) Coach. B. 1/21/1891, Holland, Mich. D. 10/22/39, Athens, Ga. Graduated from U. of Chicago, 1915. All-round athlete under Amos Alonzo Stagg. Participated in football (guard), basketball and track. Ran leg on one-mile relay team that won national AAU title at San Francisco, 1915. Coached Beloit College before going to Georgia in 1919. Bulldog head coach three years, 1920-22. Record: 20-6-3. Gave Georgia its first unbeaten (8-0-1) season, 1920. Georgia athletic director, 1919-36. Stegeman and coaching predecessor, W. A. Cunningham, established winning tradition at Athens.

STEIN, HERBERT A. Center. B. 3/27/1898, Warren, Ohio. 6', 185. Pittsburgh, 1918-21. All-America, 1920. Captain, 1920, 21. Outstanding center-linebacker. Converted fullback with excellent speed. One Pitt spokesman called him "a combination of the blast furnace, the open hearth and the Bessemer converter." Named center on Parke Davis' All-Time team. National Football Foundation Hall of Fame. Became one of Cleveland's leading business executives. President of H. A. Stein Co., and Herb Stein Inc., 1954-73.

STEIN, RUSSELL F. Tackle. B. 4/21/1896, Warren, Ohio. D. 6/1/70. 6'2", 210. Attended Washington and Jefferson. Captain and All-America under Earle (Greasy) Neale, 1921. Presidents played California to 0-0 tie in Rose Bowl, 1922. Stein was chosen game MVP. Played for Toledo Maroons, 1922; Frankford Yellowjackets, 1924; Pottsville Maroons, 1925; Canton Bulldogs, 1926.

STEINMARK, FREDDIE J. Defensive Back. B. 1/27/49, Wheatridge, Colo. D. 6/6/71. 6'0", 165. Played on state championship team at Wheatridge H.S., 1966. Wanted to attend Notre Dame but received no offer. Did from Texas, accepted and became fine defensive player under Darrell Royal. On 12/6/69 played in national championship game vs. Arkansas. Texas won in classic battle, 15-14. Six days later lost his left leg to cancer, 19 months later died. Battle against cancer earned him national respect as symbol of courage and inspiration. During illness wrote book, *I Play to Win,* which aptly sums up his life.

STENERUD, JAN Kicker. B. 11/26/42. Festund, Norway. 6'2", 187. Saw his first American football game after matriculating at Montana State. Born and raised in Norway. Outstanding college ski jumper, developed into standout placekicker as well. Kicked 59-yd. FG vs. Montana, 1965. Kansas City Chiefs, 1967-73. Set AFL career record for FG percentage (70.3). Kicked 16 consecutive FGs to break Lou Groza's pro record of 12, 1969. AFC scoring leader, 1970. AFL All-Star games, 1969, 70. MVP in Pro Bowl, 1971. Also 1972 Pro Bowl. Owns career best three-pointer (pros) of 55 yds. Is Chiefs' all-time leading scorer, having averaged better than 100 points per season. Major disappointment was missing 31-yd. FG attempt against Miami that would have given K.C. AFC championship, 1971. While out of uniform Stenerud is vice president of Kansas City bank and does radio sports show. Missed only three of 236 PAT attempts in seven seasons, two of them in 1973. In that span booted 179 FGs for 770 total points.

STEPHENS, SANFORD (Sandy) Quarterback. B. Uniontown, Pa. 6', 215. One of few, and most successful Black quarterbacks. 17-10 playing record at Minnesota, 1959-61. Consensus All-America, 1961. All-round skills. Extremely effective in Murray Warmath's "possession and position" football. Liked to roll out and run, pass or pitch out to halfback Bill Munsey. During career passed for 1475 yds., ran for 791, accounted for 31 TDs, intercepted 9 passes, punted 97 times, returned 42 punts and 19 kickoffs. Most productive as senior, gaining 1281 yds. via air and 487 on ground. Teammate of Bobby Bell and Carl Eller. Stephens directed Gophers in 1961 (lost to Washington, 17-7) and '62 (beat UCLA, 21-3) Rose Bowls. Against UCLA scored 2 TDs and hit 7 of 11 passes for 75 yds.

STEPHENSON, DONALD P. Center. B. 7/10/35, Bessemer, Ala. Two-time All-America at Georgia Tech, 1956, 57. All-SEC same years. Captain, 1957. 1956 Tech team was 9-1-0 and ranked 4th in both wire service polls. Operates Shalimar Plaza Motel in Panama City, Fla. Citizens Savings Hall of Fame.

STERNAMAN, EDWARD D. (Dutch) Running Back. D. 1/1/73, Chicago, Ill. Co-founder with George Halas of Chicago Bears. Team was originally stationed in Decatur, Ill., and known as Staleys. Sternaman met Halas when they were teammates at U. of Illinois. Their franchise in 1920s was hardly sophisticated. Both men were forced to supplement their incomes — Sternaman by working at gas station, Halas by selling cars. Gas station site was often used to sign players. George Trafton, Guy Chamberlin and Red Grange are only sampling of many pro greats who were employed by Bears during club's first decade. Charley Dressen, major league baseball manager, was member of original 1920 team. Sternaman played eight seasons for Bears, 1920-27. Sold his interest to Halas in 1932 for $38,000. Associated with Chicago Black Hawks for several years upon leaving football, and then operated oil products company.

STEUBER, ROBERT J. Running Back. B. 10/25/21, Wenonah, N.J. 190. Attended Christian Brothers H.S., St. Louis, and U. of Missouri. All-Conference and All-America under Don Faurot, 1941, 42. 1941 Missouri team lost to Fordham, 2-0, in Sugar Bowl. Played service ball at DePauw, leading nation with 129 points in only five games in 1942. Scored opening touchdown for College All-Stars vs. Washington Redskins, 1943. All-Stars won, 27-7. Chicago Bears, 1943; Cleveland Browns (AAFC), 1946; Los Angeles Dons (AAFC), 1947; Buffalo Bills (AAFC), 1948. Broken back led to playing retirement. Since then he's been in sales and sports radio work in St. Louis. National Football Foundation Hall of Fame.

STEVENS, BILLY Quarterback. B. 8/27/45, Galveston, Tex. 6'3", 195. Texas (El Paso), 1965-67. Had attended Galveston's Ball H.S. 19-9-1 college playing record. Finished career 1st in passing yards (6495), 2nd in pass completions (426). In 1965 threw for 3042 yds. 21 TDs. Member two winning Sun Bowl teams, 1966, 68. Assistant coach at alma mater, 1972-73.

STEVENS, HOWARD Running Back. B. 2/9/50, Harrisonburg, Va. 5'5", 165. Attended Harrisonburg H.S. In two years at Randolph-Macon, 1968-69, and two at Louisville, 1971-72, Stevens rushed for 5297 yds. Figure represents all-time collegiate record. Also owns career collegiate marks for TDs (69), points (418) and rushing TDs (58). Set NCAA standard with 193.7-yd. per-game average as all-purpose runner. All-Conference in all four seasons of college play. Regarded by his Louisville coach, Lee Corso, as "the greatest running back in the country, bar none." Stevens compensated for lack of size with tremendous

330

balance and quickness. New Orleans Saints, 1973. NFC's 2nd-leading punt returner, averaging 10.1 yds. on 17 attempts.

STEVENS, MARVIN A. (Mal) Running Back. B. 4/14/01, Stockton, Kan. Attended Washburn (Kan.) and Yale. Grew up in athletic family. Father, Calvin, was track performer at Syracuse U.; once struck and killed horse while throwing hammer. Calvin became inventor, but turned down chance to enter three-way business partnership with college friend Harry Marvin (for whom Mal is named) and Thomas A. Edison. At Washburn Mal played QB and defensive end for three years, 1919-21. One of two celebrated Yale transfers (other was Century Milstead who first played at Wabash). In only varsity season Mal helped Blue to 8-0 record, 1923. Triple-threat back was at best against Maryland, scoring Yale's 2nd TD in team's narrowest victory of perfect season (16-14). Played in one of tremendous rainstorms vs. Harvard. Weather forced 25 fumbles and 54 punts. Coached Yale, 1928-32; NYU, 1934-41; Brooklyn Dodgers. At Yale developed Albie Booth, one of most heralded college players of all time. Overall record: 54-45-10. Stevens became leading bone specialist and expended much time in fight against polio. National Football Foundation Hall of Fame.

STEVENSON, VINCENT M. (Steve) Quarterback. B. 1884, Livingston, Ky. D. 8/7/62. 5'10", 148. Attended Pennsylvania. All-America, 1904. Played under Carl Williams. Quakers won all 12 of their games. Stevenson was regarded as outstanding open-field runner. Used straight arm and flying hurdle to perfection. May have been first to employ latter in open field. National Football Foundation Hall of Fame.

STICKLES, MONTFORD (Monty) End. B. 8/16/38, Poughkeepsie, N.Y. 6'4", 225. Notre Dame 1957-59. Offered 70 college football scholarships, 40 basketball. Wanted to attend Army but was turned down when he failed eye examination. In 1957 Notre Dame defeated Army, 23-21, on Stickles' first FG ever — same season Irish broke Oklahoma's 47-game winning streak. Supplied many other clutch kicks during college career. All-America, 1959. Played with San Francisco 49ers, 1960-66. Caught eight passes in first NFL game. Was 49ers' 1st draft choice.

STIEHM, EWALD O. (Jumbo) Coach. B. 4/9/1885, Johnson Creek, Wis. D. 8/18/23. 6'4", 230. Wisconsin, 1906-08. Coached Ripon, 1910; Nebraska, 1911-15; Indiana, 1916-21. Record: 59-23-4 (.709). 35-2-3 at Nebraska, losing no games last three years. 1915 team, featuring end Guy Chamberlin and halfback Dick Rutherford, counted Notre Dame (20-19) among its eight victims.

STILLWAGON, JIM Linebacker. B. 2/11/49, Mt. Vernon, Ohio. 6', 220. Ohio State middle guard. Unanimous All-America, 1970; consensus All-America, 1969. Played on powerhouse Buckeye teams. Teammates included Rex Kern. Jack Tatum, Jim Otis. Spurned NFL for CFL Toronto Argonauts.

STINCHCOMB, GAYLORD R. (Pete) Running Back. B. 1896, Fostoria, Ohio. 5'10", 165. Ohio State, 1918-1920. Attended Naval Ensign School in Cleveland and played on its Naval Reserve team. Football, track and basketball performer at Ohio State. Spent two years in shadow of Chic Harley. Stinchcomb was left halfback, Harley right half. As senior Stinchcomb held center stage. Named All-America as he led Buckeyes to unbeaten (7-0) regular season, 1920. They lost only to California "Wonder Team" in Rose Bowl. Collegiate broad jump champion, 1921. Chicago Staleys, 1921; Chicago Bears, 1922; Columbus Tigers, 1923; Cleveland Indians, 1923; Louisville Colonels, 1926. Was in construction business much of life. National Football Foundation Hall of Fame. He lived in Findlay, Ohio.

STOVALL, JERRY L. Defensive Back. B. 4/30/41, West Monroe, La. 6'2", 195. Rushed 219 times, caught 30 passes and intercepted 7, returned 19 punts and 15 kickoffs, punted 165 times, scored 15 TDs for Louisiana State, 1960-62. Consensus All-America under Charlie McClendon, 1962. Louisiana State won Sugar Bowl that season by defeating Texas, 13-0. Defensive back with St. Louis Cardinals, 1963-71. Pro Bowl, 1967, 68, 70. Abandoned dentistry career to become assistant coach for Paul Dietzel at South Carolina.

STOWE, OTTO. End. B. 2/25/49, Chicago, Ill. 6'2", 188. Lettered in football, basketball and track at Fetishens H.S., in Springfield, Ill. Holds Iowa State and Big 8 record of 132 career receptions. Catches were good for 1751 yds. and 10 TDs. Played in North-South and Coaches All-America games. Miami Dolphins, 1971-72; Dallas Cowboys, 1973. No. 2 draft choice of Dolphins. Caught 6 passes for 2 TDs and 140 yds. against St. Louis, 1972. Traded to Cowboys, 1973, for No. 2 draft choice and Ron Sellers. Caught 23 passes for 6 TDs in '73.

STRAM, HENRY L. (Hank) Coach. B. 1/3/24, Chicago, Ill. All-State halfback at Lew Wallace H.S. in Gary, Ind. Won seven letters at Purdue, four in baseball and three in football. Assistant coach at Purdue, SMU, Notre Dame and Miami (Fla.). Joined pro ranks in 1960 as head coach of AFL Dallas Texans. Regarded as imaginative offensive teacher in college, leading to development of four All-America quarterbacks — Dale Samuels and Len Dawson (Purdue), George Izo (Notre Dame) and Fran Curci (Miami). In pros enjoyed substantial success. Kansas City Chiefs (Texans moved to Kansas City in 1963) played in Super Bowl I, 1967, and won Super Bowl IV, 1970. One of only nine pro coaches to win more than 100 games (119). Lost 67 games, tied 10. Overall captured five divisional titles. Also enlarged upon collegiate record as offensive tactician and innovator. Helped bring to prominence moving quarterback pocket and developed tight-end I. Defensively, he introduced "stack", 1962, which other NFL teams adopted. Dapper and portly figure. Has won numerous coaching awards. Given 10-year contract as Chief head coach and vice president, 1972.

STROCK, DON Quarterback. B. 11/27/50, Pottstown, Pa. 6'5", 205. Attended Pottstown H.S. Amassed 5871 yds. total offense at Virginia Tech, 1970-72. Led nation's major colleges in total offense and passing as senior — compiled 3170 yds. on 480 plays, threw for 3243 yds. and 16 TDs. Overall, as Gobbler, Strock completed 440 of 829 passes (.531) for 6009 yds. Played in Hula Bowl and Blue-Gray (MVP) games. Majored in distributive direction. Signed with Miami Dolphins, 1973.

STROM, BROCK T. Tackle. B. 9/21/34, Munising, Mich. 6', 217. First consensus All-America at Air Force Academy, 1958. Led Falcons to 9-0-1 regular season and into 1959 Cotton Bowl against TCU. Result was 0-0 tie, one of only three scoreless games in major bowl history. Served as senior navigator aboard C-130, FC-47 aircraft. Won following decorations: two Distinguished Flying Crosses, two Bronze Star Medals, three Air Medals, two Air Force Commendation Medals. Presently director of Aerospace-Mechanics Sciences, Seiler Research Lab., USAF Academy. Holds rank of Maj.

STRONG, KENNETH E. Running Back. B. 8/6/06, West Haven, Conn. 6'1", 210. Extraordinary runner and kicker. All-State twice at West Haven H.S. Scored 285 points for Chick Meehan at NYU, 1926-28. Meehan employed "military shift" which baffled opponents but delighted fans. During senior year Strong led nation's scorers with 160 points (22 TDs, 28 PATs) and gained 2100 yds. rushing. He destroyed unbeaten Carnegie Tech in 1928 (NYU won 27-13), scoring two TDs and throwing for two more. Tech coach Walter Steffen was very much impressed: "I've seen Willie Heston. I've seen Walter Eckersall. But Ken Strong is the greatest football player I ever saw." Staten Island Stapletons, 1929-32; New York Yanks (AFL), 1936-37; and New York Giants, 1933-35, 39, 44, 47. League co-scoring leader, 1933; FG leader, 1944. Giants were world champions in 1934 and division title-holders three other times. "Sneakers" game decided '34 NFL championship, won 30-13 at expense of Chicago Bears. Played at New York's Polo Grounds on sheet of ice in nine-degree weather, Giants scored 27 points in 2nd half after they switched to basketball sneakers at intermission. Strong scored 17 points himself.

Retired in 1939, but was lured back by Giants to serve as kicking specialist. In nine seasons with them Strong scored 351 points. Retired with club records for longest FG (47 yds.), extra points (147), consecutive extra points (67) and season points (72). Promising baseball career ended in minors. He crashed into fence chasing fly ball, and subsequent botched operation made it impossible to bend his throwing hand backwards. Hit 450-foot homer at NYU and batted .342 for one minor-league season. Citizens Savings Hall of Fame, National Football Hall of Fame, Pro Football Hall of Fame. After assisting Giant coaching staff, became sales representative in New York City.

STUBER, EMMETT R. (Abe) Coach. B. 10/12/04, St. Joseph, Mo. Missouri quarterback, 1924-26. Coached Westminster (Mo.), 1929-31; Southeast Missouri State, 1932-46; Iowa State, 1947-53. Record: 145-69-15. Was 23-3-1 at Westminster, 98-28-11 at SEMS. Assisted Philadelphia Eagles, 1955. Personnel director, St. Louis Cardinals, 1960-72; now personnel consultant. Citizens Savings Hall of Fame.

STUDSTILL, PATRICK L. End-Kicker. B. 6/4/38, Shreveport, La. 6', 180. Played mostly defensive back at U. of Houston. Saw only 10 minutes of action senior season, 1960. Detroit Lions, 1961-62; 64-67; Los Angeles Rams, 1968-71; New England Patriots, 1972-73. Signed originally as free agent with Lions. Missed 1963 due to injury. On special teams, 1961-65, returning 75 kickoffs for 1924 yds. In 1966 took over for retired Terry Barr, wide receiver, and enjoyed banner season. Caught 67 passes for 1266 yds., was named All-Pro. Played in two Pro Bowls, 1966, 67. Exceptional moves. Led NFL two straight seasons in total punts, 1968, 69.

STUHLDREHER, HARRY Quarterback. B. 10/14/01, Massillon, Ohio. D. 1/22/65. 5'7", 151. Notre Dame, 1922-24. Member of immortal "Four Horsemen." Stuhldreher's first contact with Knute Rockne was as youth in hometown of Massillon. Carried helmet into stadium (for free admission) for Rockne when he was player-coach for Massillon Tigers. Stuhldreher subsequently played three years under Rockne. Shifty back and fearless blocker. All-America in senior year along with two other Horsemen, Jim Crowley and Elmer Layden. After college played for Brooklyn Lions and Brooklyn Horsemen (AFL), both 1926. Head coach, Villanova, 1925-36, and Wisconsin, 1937-47. At Fordham developed "Seven Blocks of Granite." Overall record: 110-87-15. At death was executive with U.S. Steel Corp. Citizens Savings Hall of Fame, National Football Foundation Hall of Fame.

STYDAHAR, JOSEPH L. (Jumbo Joe) Tackle. B. 3/17/12, Kaylor, Pa. 6'4", 230. Lived most of early life in Shinnston, W. Va. Recruited by Jock Sutherland for Pittsburgh, but left school after one month due to homesickness, and enrolled at West Virginia. Left tackle for Mountaineers, 1933-35, specializing in blocking punts. Blocked one on Duquesne's 15-yd. line, retrieved ball and ran it in for TD to give West Virginia 7-0 win, 1934. Twice All-Eastern Conference in basketball. Chicago Bears, 1936-42, 45-46. Won All-Pro honors four times, 1937, 38, 39, 40. Leading role in Bears' back-to-back world championship seasons, 1940, 41. Often would throw up at game time, but tension passed when hitting started. Coached Los Angeles Rams, to NFL title, 1951. While coaching Rams he moved Elroy (Crazylegs) Hirsch from halfback to end, adding years and greater fame to Hirsch's career. Stydahar was fired in early part of third season with Los Angeles, 1952, as owner Dan Reeves was not man who allowed coaches longevity. Jumbo Joe left coaching for good after two years with Chicago Cardinals, 1953-54. *Sports Illustrated* Silver Anniversary All-America team, 1960. National Football Foundation Hall of Fame, Pro Football Hall of Fame. All-Pro Squad of the 1930s. Now president of Big Bear Container Corp., Chicago.

SUFFRIDGE, ROBERT L. Guard. B. 3/17/16, Fountain City, Tenn. D. 2/4/73, Knoxville, Tenn. Tennessee, 1938-40. Instrumental figure in Tennessee's 31-2 record over three-year period. Vols played in Orange, Rose and Sugar Bowl games consecutively as Suffridge won way into each bowl's hall of fame. Coach

Robert Neyland said of him: "Suff had the quickest and most powerful defensive charge of any lineman I've ever seen. I have never seen a lineman play his position so well. He never made a bad play." Once blocked same PAT attempt three times in-a-row, twice being called offside though he actually wasn't. Neyland was not appreciative of Bob's high-spiritedness. Pair had misunderstanding prior to '39 Orange Bowl and Suffridge was never again in coach's good graces. In fact, he was forced to report following season and practice with freshmen after Neyland announced plans (some thought it disciplinary measure) of converting his star lineman to running back. Not long, however, before Suffridge was back at familiar guard slot. 1938 club was Tennessee's greatest. It finished 11-0, won 17-0 over Oklahoma in Orange Bowl, showcased one of game's all-time guard combinations in Suffridge and Edward Molinski and produced four National Football Hall of Famers: Suffridge, Neyland, George Cafego, Bowden Wyatt. Bob was unanimous All-America, 1940. Philadelphia Eagles, 1941-45. Citizens Savings Hall of Fame, National Football Foundation Hall of Fame. Named to Modern All-Time All-America team. After retiring from football Suffridge entered insurance business.

SUGAR, LEO T. (Shug) Defensive End. B. 4/6/29, Flint, Mich. 6'1", 230. Purdue, 1949-51. Co-captain and All-America, 1951. Played in 1952 College All-Star game. Chicago Cardinals, 1954-59; St. Louis Cardinals, 1960; Philadelphia Eagles, 1961; Detroit Lions, 1962. Great agility and lateral pursuit. Pro Bowl, 1961. Knee injury and operation in 1962 hastened end to career. Shares NFL record for fumble recovery TDs, lifetime, with three. Owner of golf club and flower shop in Grand Blanc, Mich.

SULLIVAN, WILLIAM H., JR. Owner. B. 9/13/15, Lowell, Mass. Owner and president of New England Patriots. Earned A.B. degree at Boston College, 1937. Did postgraduate work at B.C. and Harvard. Publicist for baseball's Boston Braves, 1946-52. Owner of All-Star Sports, Inc., 1952-55. Awarded AFL's 8th franchise, for Boston, on 11/16/59. Lou Saban was later hired as club's original head coach. Team played as Boston Patriots until 1971. Then renamed New England. Served on three-man AFL committee that effected pro football merger in 1966. President of AFL, 1963-69. Son, Charles W., is on Pats' board of directors.

SUMMERALL, GEORGE (Pat) End-kicker. B. Lake City, Fla. 6'3", 220. Caught 43 passes for 670 yds. and 7 TDs at Arkansas, 1949-51. Co-captain, 1951. Originally recruited for basketball and football. Earned master's degree in Russian history. Detroit Lions, 1952; Chicago Cardinals, 1953-57; New York Giants, 1958-61. NFL FG leader with 20, 1959. Kicked one FG and two PATs in NFL championship game, 1958. Giants lost sudden-death thriller and title, 23-17, to Baltimore Colts at Yankee Stadium. Played in three other title games, 1952, 59, 61. Three members of Giants' 1958 team, Summerall, Kyle Rote and Frank Gifford, became successful sports announcers. Summerall started on CBS radio, out-auditioning two other Giants, Charlie Conerly and Alex Webster, and quickly moved to television side. Now CBS-TV's top NFL analyst. Also NBA basketball, golf, tennis and bowling assignments. Resident, with wife and three children, of Saddle River, N.J.

SUTHERLAND, JOHN B. (Jock) Coach. B. 3/21/1889, Coupar-Angus, Scotland. D. 4/11/48, Pittsburgh, Pa. U. of Pittsburgh graduate. Porter and baggage clerk, "loon" (light farmhand) and caddy during Scottish boyhood. Arrived in Pittsburgh at age 18. Prepped for Pitt at Oberlin (Ohio) Academy. Won scholarship to Pittsburgh Dental School. Guard in three football seasons, 1915-17, after being moved from tackle by coach Pop Warner. Never played with loser during those years, winning 25 times. Became American citizen, 1917. Head coach at Lafayette, 1919-23; Pitt, 1924-38. His Panthers gave some of game's most powerful rushing (single-wing) exhibitions. Under Sutherland Pitt compiled 111-20-12 record, won two national championships and played in four Rose Bowls. He taught 24 All-Americas. Declined another Rose Bowl invitation, 1937. Notre Dame dropped Pitt from schedule after Irish lost five of six games and were blanked four times, 1932-37. "Dream Backfield" unfolded in his last season: Dick Cassiano and Curly Stebbins (halfbacks), Marshall Goldberg (fullback) and Johnny Chickerneo (quarterback). Fellow of American Dental Society. 144-28-14 overall college record. 28-16-1 with Pittsburgh Steelers and Brooklyn Dodgers, two seasons each. Dour and unshakable. Left estate of $500,000. Came to America penniless. Friend, Grantland Rice, wrote following tribute upon Jock's death: "There's a fog now over Scotland, and a mist on Pittsburgh's field;/No valiant hand to flash the sword or hold the guiding shield./There's a big, braw fellow missing from the golden land of fame,/For Jock Sutherland has left us — and the game is not the same."

SVARE, HARLAND Linebacker. B. 11/15/30, Clarksville, Minn. 6', 215. Offensive and defensive end at Washington State. Drafted 17th by Los Angeles Rams. Played with Rams, 1953-54, and New York Giants, 1955-60. Linebacker in pros. NFL championship games, 1956, 58, 59. Assistant coach with Giants, 1960-61, 67-68; Rams, 1962; Washington Redskins, 1969-70. Head coach of Rams, 1962-65, and San Diego Chargers, 1971-73. With Rams developed "Fearsome Foursome" defensive line of Merlin Olsen, Roosevelt Grier, Lamar Lundy, David (Deacon) Jones. Originally joined Chargers as general manager — took over as head coach with four games left in 1971 season. Fired as coach before 1973 season completed.

SWANN, LYNN Wide Receiver. B. 1952, Foster City, Calif. 6', 180. Attended Southern California. "He is as valuable to us as Johnny Rodgers was to Nebraska," complimented USC coach John McKay. "In our offense, Swann is called on to run, block and catch passes and he is excellent in all three." Also used as punt returner and ball carrier. All-America, 1973. Totaled 6 receptions for 108 yds. and 1 TD in '73 Rose Bowl. Has 9.8 speed in 100. Recorded 24'10" long jump in track. Also played in 1974 Rose Bowl.

SWANSON, CLARENCE E. End. B. 1898, Wakefield, Neb. D. 12/3/70, Lincoln, Neb. 5'10", 167. Played at Nebraska, 1919-21. All-America 2nd team, 1921. Captain same year, leading Cornhuskers to 7-1 record. Only defeat was to Notre Dame. Held Nebraska record for TD passes, season, with nine, for 50 years. Owned seasonal scoring mark of 61 points until broken by Bobby Reynolds in 1950. Served in navy before entering college. Upon graduation entered retail business. Was active in alumni and Lincoln community affairs. National Football Foundation Hall of Fame.

SWEENEY, WALTER F. Guard. B. 4/18/41, Cohasset, Mass. 6'4", 256. Attended Cohasset H.S. and U. of Syracuse. Played in Coaches All-America, Senior Bowl, College All-Star, North-South games. Missed no games first ten seasons in pros, 1963-72. Drafted No. 1 by San Diego Chargers and played with them throughout career. AFL championship games, 1963, 64, 65. AFL All-Star games, 1965, 66, 67, 68, 69, 70. All-AFL, 1967. "There is no better guard in pro football," according to Oakland's Tom Keating. Sweeney was named Blocker of the Year by 1000-yard Club of Wisconsin, 1971.

SWEETLAND, EDWIN R. Coach. B. 1/10/1875, Dryden, N.Y. D. 10/21/50. Played football and ran track at Union College (N.Y.); football, basketball and crew participant at Cornell. Coached collegiately 11 years with seven stops; Syracuse, 1900-02; Ohio State, 1904-05; Colgate, 1908; Kentucky, 1909-10; Miami (Ohio), 1912; West Virginia, 1913; Tulane, 1914. 68-31-9 record (.671). When he left coaching Sweetland turned to farming, and spent rest of his life tilling soil in native New York.

SWIACKI, WILLIAM End. B.10/2/25, Southbridge, Mass. 6'2", 198. Attended Holy Cross and Columbia. Consensus All-America, 1947. Claimed such status with remarkable performance vs. Army. Made eight diving catches on passes from QB Lou Rossides, spearheading comeback that led to 21-20 Columbia victory. Army had taken 20-7 advantage into 4th quarter. Rossides' PAT eventually provided winning margin. Loss ended Cadets' defeatless string at 32 games. Fullback Ventan Yablonski and halfback Lou Kusserow also starred for 1947 Morningside Heights club. It was one of Lou Little's best, finishing with 7-2 record.

SWIFT, DOUG Linebacker. B. 10/24/48, Syracuse, N.Y. 6'3", 226. Attended Nottingham H.S. in Syracuse where he played football and basketball. Amherst linebacker and offensive tackle, 1968-70. Helped team win 13 of 16 games last two seasons. In career intercepted eight passes. Signed by Miami Dolphins as free agent in 1971, becoming Amherst's first pro player. Developed into one of game's outstanding outside linebackers, making 92 total stops in 1972. Super Bowl, 1972, 73, 74.

SWINK, JAMES E. Running Back. B. 3/14/36, Sacul, Tex. 6'1", 180. Attended Rusk (Tex.) H.S. and Texas Christian. Unanimous All-America and runnerup for Heisman Trophy, 1955. Academic All-America, 1955, 56. Led nation that year with 8.2 yds. per rush, 20 TDs and 125 total points. 20-10 playing record, 1954-56. Lost 14-13 to Mississippi, 1956, and won 28-27 over Syracuse, 1957, in Cotton Bowl games, Scored three TDs combined in both games. Dallas Texans, 1960. Now orthopedic surgeon in Fort Worth.

SWITZER, BARRY Coach. B. 10/5/37, Crossett, Ark. Arkansas center-linebacker, 1957-59. Played under Jack Mitchell and Frank Broyles. Captained Razorbacks' SWC and Gator Bowl champions, 1959. Assistant coach at Arkansas, 1960-65, and Oklahoma, 1966-72. Oklahoma head coach, 1973. Offensive coordinator for Sooners when they set NCAA records, 1971, in rushing (472.4 yds. per game) and total offense (566.5). 1971 team averaged 44.9 points. Helped popularize wishbone-T offense. At Oklahoma developed Steve Owens, Jack Mildren, Greg Pruitt, Joe Washington. Has coached in 11 bowl games. Likes hunting, fishing and golf for hobbies. Named Coach of the Year in '73 after Sooners won Big 8 title, compiled 10-0-1 overall mark. Banned from bowl competition, however, due to recruiting infraction.

SYZMANSKI, RICHARD Linebacker. B. 11/7/32, Toledo, Ohio. 6'3", 235. Played at Notre Dame, as did brother Frank. Spent 13 years with Baltimore Colts, 1955, 57-68. In service, 1956. Frank played five years of pro ball. Dick started as rookie center, then shifted to defense in 1958. Became permanent center in 1961. Suffered ruptured spleen in '55. Exceptional blocker. Colts defeated Cleveland Browns for NFL title, 1968, but then lost Super Bowl III to New York Jets. Colts also won NFL titles in 1958, 59.

TAGGE, JERRY L. (Tags) Quarterback. B. 4/12/50, Green Bay, Wis. 6'2", 220. Attended Green Bay West H.S. Guided U. of Nebraska to two straight national championships, 1970, 71. 33-2-1 playing record, 1969-71. Cornhuskers won 23 straight games and two Orange Bowls with Tagge at QB. Suffered only 4 interceptions senior year in 258 attempts. MVP in Hula Bowl. Starting QB for College All-Stars against Dallas Cowboys, 1972. Holds Big 8 record for pass completion percentage (.592), number of Nebraska marks. Realized lifetime ambition when he signed with Green Bay Packers in 1972 — he was their No. 1 draft choice. Sold popcorn at Lambeau Field, Green Bay home of Packers. Used infrequently, 1972-73.

TALAMINI, ROBERT Guard. B. Louisville, Ky. 6'1", 250. Graduated from Kentucky. Weighed only 195 pounds when drafted on 24th round by Houston Oilers in 1960. Added considerable poundage and became top-notch pro guard. Played with Oilers, 1960-67, and New York Jets. All-AFL six of first eight years. Houston won AFL titles in 1960, 61; lost crown in '62. In lone season with Jets, club won Super Bowl.

TALBOOM, EDWARD Running Back. B. 5/5/21, Delphos, Ohio. 5'10", 157. Attended Washington H.S. of South Bend, Ind., and U. of Wyoming. Skyline Conference scoring leader and All-League tailback, 1948-50. All-America, 1950. Scored 303 points and compiled 3137 yds. total offense in Cowboy career. Graduated 1st nationally in points-responsible-for (429). Accounted for

Wyoming's entire 20-point output as Cowboys sacked Washington & Lee, 20-7, in 1951 Gator Bowl. Win was 10th of season without defeat for coach Bowden Wyatt. Talboom now lives in Niles, Mich.

TALIAFERRO, GEORGE (Scoop) Running Back. B. 1/8/27, Halls, Tenn. Indiana tailback. As sophomore, 1945, helped Indiana win nine straight games, first Big 10 title. Team coached by Bo McMillin, also starred Pete Pihos. Los Angeles Dons (AAFC), 1949; New York Yanks, 1950-51; Dallas Texans, 1952; Baltimore Colts, 1953-54; Philadelphia Eagles, 1955. In lone AAFC season passed for 790 yds., scored four TDs. Returned eight kickoffs vs. New York Giants, 12/3/50. Now assistant to president, U. of Indiana. Citizens Savings Hall of Fame.

TALIAFERRO, MYRON E. (Mike) Quarterback. B. 7/26/41, Houston, Tex. 6'2", 202. Illinois, 1960, 62, 63. Passed for 1589 yds. Captain in 1963. Led Fighting Illini to '63 Big 10 title and 17-7 win over Washington in Rose Bowl. New York Jets, 1964-67; Boston Patriots, 1968-70; Buffalo Bills, 1972. Originally drafted as future on 28th round by New York, 1963. Traded to Boston for QB Babe Parilli, 1968. Tied Joe Namath for most TD passes (17) in AFL, 1969. AFL Comeback Player of the Year, 1969. AFL All-Star game, 1970. Released after five games with Buffalo in 1972, then picked up by Washington Redskins and spent remainder of year on taxi squad.

TAMBURO, RICHARD P. Linebacker. B. 2/6/30, New Kensington, Pa. 6', 180. Michigan State, 1950-52. All-America for Biggie Munn's national championship team, 1952. Majored in police administration. Assistant coach, Arizona State, 1958-66; Iowa, 1967-70. Now associate athletic director at Illinois.

TARKENTON, FRANCIS A. (Fran) Quarterback. B. 2/3/40, Richmond, Va. 6', 190. Son of Methodist minister. Named for missionary of Revolutionary War period. Attended Athens (Ga.) H.S. 19-11 playing record at Georgia, 1958-60. Threw two TD passes in Orange Bowl as Georgia defeated Missouri, 14-0, 1960. Nation's passing percentage leader (.584, 1960). Finished career 4th in pass completion percentage (.585). Minnesota Vikings, 1961-66, 72-73; New York Giants, 1967-71. Traded by Vikings to Giants for four draft choices; returned to Vikings for Norm Snead, Bob Grim, Vance Clements and two draft choices. Set NFL record for consecutive passes completed (13, 1961). Pro Bowl, 1965, 66, 68, 68, 70, 71. Intelligent, poised leader. Epitome of scrambling quarterback. Accounted life in *Better Scramble Than Lose*. Differences with coach Norm Van Brocklin caused him to quit Vikings after 1966 season. After receiving Fran's letter of resignation, Van Brocklin also resigned. Tarkenton then traded to New York. In 13 pro seasons completed 2459 of 4410 passes for 33,248 yds., 249 TDs. Super Bowl, 1974. Involved in numerous business ventures.

TATUM, JACK Defensive Back. B. 11/18/48, Cherryville, N.C. 5'11", 200. All-

State fullback, gaining 1421 yds. as senior at Passaic (N.J.) H.S. Also ran track. All-Bid 10 thrice at Ohio State, 1968-70. Unanimous All-America, 1970; consensus All-America, 1969. Rose Bowl, 1969, 71. No. 1 draft choice of Oakland Raiders in 1971. Started 42 straight games at safety during first three pro seasons, 1971-73. All-Rookie NFL team, 1971. Recovered fumble and returned it 104 yds. for TD to set pro record. Noted for strong, aggressive, almost exterminating tackling. Has injured or kayoed number of opposing players. In 1972 AFC championship game, ball caromed off Tatum into hands of Franco Harris (Pittsburgh Steelers). Harris then ran, on 63-yd. play, for winning TD as time expired. Pro Bowl, 1974.

TATUM, JAMES M. Coach. B. 7/22/13, McColl, S.C. D. 7/23/59, Chapel Hill, N.C. Youngest of five brothers, all of whom played tackle in college — two at Clemson, two at Wofford, Jim at North Carolina. Head coach for Tar Heels, 1942, 56-58; Oklahoma, 1946; Maryland, 1947-55. 100-35-7 overall record, including 73-15-4 with Maryland. Tatum was Coach of the Year as Terrapins won national championship, 1953. Learned split-T attack, which he used throughout career, from Don Faurot of Iowa Pre-Flight team. Criticized for zealousness in recruiting high school players. Citizens Savings Hall of Fame.

TAYLOR, ALTIE Running Back. B. 9/29/47, Pittsburgh, Calif. 5'10", 205. Attended Pittsburgh H.S. and Diablo (Calif.) J.C. Gained 3925 yds., 1959 rushing, in three seasons at Utah State, 1966-68. Was halfback and kickoff-return specialist. Gained 168 yds. vs. Utah, 1968. Participated in North-South game, 1968. No. 2 draft choice of Detroit Lions, 1969. Lions, 1969-73. Rushed for 3127 yds. and caught 122 passes for 1119 yds. in first five seasons with Lions.

TAYLOR, BRUCE L. Defensive Back. B. 5/28/48, Perth Amboy, N.J. 6', 193. Boston U. graduate. Drafted No. 1 by San Francisco 49ers in 1970. 49ers, 1970-73. Was NFC Rookie of the Year. Pro Bowl, 1972. Returned missed FG 92 yds. for TD, 1970. In 1972 returned missed FG 55 yds. to score. Outstanding cornerback. Made six interceptions in 1973, giving him 14 lifetime. As rookie returned 15 kickoffs for 15.8-yd. average. Brother of Brian, star cager with Princeton and New York Nets.

TAYLOR, CHARLES A. (Chuck) Coach. B. 1/24/20, Portland, Ore. Stanford, 1940-42. Attended San Jose (Calif.) H.S. Won three letters as Stanford guard, 1940-42. Indian teams were known in that period as "Wow Boys." Served in U.S. Navy, 1943-45. Miami Seahawks, 1946. Stanford freshman coach, 1947-49. Line coach with San Francisco 49ers, 1950. Head coach at Stanford, 1951-57, succeeding Marchy Schwartz. Won first nine games of rookie Stanford season before losing to California (20-7), then Illinois (40-7) in Rose Bowl. Coached Bob Mathias, Olympic decathlon champion and standout running back.

TAYLOR, JAMES (Jimmy) Running Back. B. 9/20/35, Baton Rouge, La. 6', 215. Louisiana State fullback, 1956-57. All-America, 1957. Green Bay Packers,

1958-66, and New Orleans Saints, 1967. Punishing runner and blocker, fierce competitor. Gave Packers tremendous tandem with halfback Paul Hornung. NFL scoring (19 TDs) and ground-gaining leader (1474 yds.) in 1962. Rushed for over 1000 yds. five straight years. In Taylor era Pack won four NFL championships, 1961, 62, 65, 66, and 1967 Super Bowl. Never intimidated and rarely injured. "Jimmy is tougher than Japanese arithmetic," appraised Norm Van Brocklin. Unsophisticated, preferred to run over players rather than around them. Had muscles on muscles, was weightlifting addict. Overshadowed somewhat during playing days by another fullback, Jim Brown. Ranks 2nd to Brown as all-time rusher with 8597 yds. Averaged 4.4 yds. per carry. Scored 93 career TDs. Had greatest year in 1963, considering circumstances. Recovering from infectious hepatitis and playing without suspended Hornung, rushed for 1018 yds. on 248 carries. Played out option with Packers in 1966, failing to agree on salary terms with Vince Lombardi. All-NFL, 1962. Pro Bowl, 1962, 63, 64, 65, 66.

TAYLOR, LIONEL End. B. 1936, Kansas City, Mo. Attended New Mexico Highlands. AllFrontier Conference flanker. Also lettered in basketball and track. Chicago Bears, 1959; Denver Broncos, 1960-66; Houston Oilers, 1967-68. AFL championship game, 1967. Led AFL in receiving four of his first five years. First pro to catch 100 passes in one season, 1961. His 567 receptions rank 3rd on all-time pro receiving list. Owns AFL records for most passes caught, game, 13, years leading league in receiving, 5. Now receiver coach for Pittsburgh Steelers.

TAYLOR, OTIS End. B. 8/11/42, Houston, Tex. 6'3", 215. Attended Prairie View A. & M. on basketball scholarship. Kansas City Chiefs, 1965-73. Caught 26 passes rookie year, then catapulted into premier receiver ranks in 1967. Caught 58 passes for 1297 yds., 8 TDs. Led AFL that year with 22.4-yd. average. Topped league in TD receptions with 11, 1967. Accumulated 1110 yds. receiving to lead NFL in 1971. AFL championship games, 1966, 69. Super Bowl, 1967, 70. Scored on 46-yd. pass-run play in Super Bowl IV. Pro Bowl, 1972, 73. All-AFL, 1966. All-AFC, 1971. Sensational catch specialist, of circus and diving variety. In nine seasons made 386 grabs for 6931 yds., 58 TDs. Has been bothered by leg injuries. Coach Hank Stram commented: "Before we got Otis, we traveled by bus. With Otis we travel by jet. I think when he's able to play and express his ability, there's not a better flanker, there's not a better athlete in professional football."

TAYLOR, ROOSEVELT (Rosey) Defensive Back. B. 7/4/37, New Orleans, La. Wide receiver and defensive back at Grambling. Set school record for pass interceptions (12) in one season. Signed by Chicago Bears as free agent in 1961. Bears, 1961-68; San Francisco 49ers, 1969-71; Washington Redskins, 1972. Set Bear season record with nine interceptions as he earned All-Pro honors, 1963. Selected 49er MVP by teammates and given Len Eshmont Award, 1970. Pro Bowl, 1964, 69. NFL championship game, 1963. Super Bowl, 1973. In 12-year career intercepted 32 passes for 486 yds., 3 TDs. Returned kicks first three seasons.

THEISMANN, JOSEPH R. Quarterback. B. 9/9/49, South River, N.J. Notre Dame, 1968-70. Playing and Academic All-America, 1970. Another in superior line of Notre Dame QBs. Look at list: Harry Stuhldreher, Frank Carideo, Paul Hornung, Bob Williams, John Lujack, Frank Tripucka, John Huarte, George Izo, Daryle Lamonica, Terry Hanratty, Angelo Bertelli. Theismann near top in most Irish passing departments. One of his marks, 526 yds. passing vs. Southern Cal in 1970, will be hard to beat. It's also 2nd-best mark ever by collegian. Set N.D. career record with 57.8 passing percentage (290 of 509). Cotton Bowl, 1970, 71; won one, lost one vs. Texas. Played in CFL, 1971-73. Signed with Washington Redskins for 1974.

THISTLETHWAITE, GLENN F. Coach. B. 3/18/1885, Sheridan, Ind. D. 10/6/56, Richmond, Va. Earlham college graduate. Started coaching career at Oak Park (Ill.) H.S., replacing Bob Zuppke who went to Illinois. Head coach at Earlham, 1912; Northwestern, 1922-26; Wisconsin, 1927-32; Carroll (Wis.), 1933-34; Richmond, 1934-41. 24-year record of 114-71-14 (.608). His Northwestern teams tied Michigan for Big 10 title, 1925, 26. Before taking Richmond post was seriously considered for North Carolina head job, but lost bid to Carl Snavely. During career served as athletic director 24 years. After leaving football was real estate agent in Richmond.

THOMAS, B. CLENDON Defensive Back. B. 12/28/35, Oklahoma City, Okla. 6'2", 188. Graduate of Oklahoma City Southeast H.S. and U. of Oklahoma. Averaged 6.9 yds. per rush during college, 1955-57. Played behind All-America Tommy McDonald as sophomore. Led nation with 18 TDs, 1956. All-America, 1957. Versatile player. Intercepted five passes and averaged 37.6 yds. punting, 21.8 on punt returns, 24.7 on kickoff returns during Oklahoma career. Mechanical engineering major. Played on two winning Orange Bowl teams, 1956, 58. Defensive back with Los Angeles Rams, 1958-61; Pittsburgh Steelers, 1962-68. Operates Clendon Thomas Construction, Inc., Oklahoma City.

THOMAS, DUANE Running Back. B. 6/21/47, Dallas, Tex. 6'1", 205. Football's most puzzling personality. Great talent but has never made complete commitment to game. Vegetarian, likes to be left alone. Unresponsive to press, management and almost everything. Has had several altercations with law. Attended West Texas State, 1967-69. Rushed for 2378 yds. and 6.0 average. Played in same backfield with Mercury Morris. Drafted No. 1 by Dallas Cowboys in 1970. Netted league's best rushing average (5.3 yds.) as rookie running back. Scored 11 TDs, 1971. Scored one TD in both Super Bowl V and VI. Following '71 season was traded to San Diego Chargers for Billy Parks and Mike Montgomery. Failed to reach contract agreement with Chargers and sat out 1972. Was then dealt to Washington Redskins whose coach, George Allen, was hailed as Thomas' salvation. However, Duane carried football only 32 times in 1973, getting most work on special teams.

THOMAS, FRANK W. Coach. B. 11/15/1898, Muncie, Ind. D. 5/10/59. Notre Dame, 1920-22. Coached at two schools during 20-year career: Chattanooga, 1925-28, Alabama, 1931-46. First Notre Dame graduate to coach at major Southern school. 108-20-7 at Alabama for .841 percentage. Overall record: 141-33-9 (.785). Steered Crimson Tide to six bowl games, three Rose, one Cotton, one Orange, one Sugar. 4-2 record. Used basic offensive style which offered little more than 20 running plays. Citizens Savings Hall of Fame, National Football Foundation Hall of Fame.

THOMAS, JOSEPH H. Administrator. B. Warren, Ohio. Ohio Northern end. Earned master's degree and doctorate credits at Indiana. Assistant coach, with DePauw, Indiana, Baltimore Colts, Toronto Argonauts. Player personnel director of Minnesota Vikings, 1960-64, and Miami Dolphins, 1965-71. Vice president and general manager, Baltimore Colts, 1972-73. Known for ability to evaluate talent. Built expansion Dolphins into Super Bowl champion. Controversial with Colts. Dealt away many experienced players in youth movement. Dealt such stalwarts as John Unitas and Bubba Smith. Booted two coaches in one season: Don McCafferty and John Sandusky, 1972. Finally arrived at present Baltimore coach, Howard Schnellenberger. Blunt, never vacillates.

THORNE, SAMUEL B. (Brinck) Running Back. B. New York, N.Y. D. 1930, New York, N.Y. 6'1½", 168. 39-1-2 playing record at Yale 1893-95. Scored two TDs, set up another and kicked two conversions final college game, 20-10 victory over Princeton in 1895. All-America, 1895. Played two years with Frank Hinkey. Won 13 of 14 games as Yale field coach, 1896. Only loss was to Princeton, 24-6, at Manhattan Field in New York. It snapped Yale winning streak of 44 games. Served as president of various oil companies. National Football Foundation Hall of Fame.

THORNHILL, CLAUDE E. (Tiny) Coach. B. 4/19/1893, Richmond, Va. D. 6/29/56. U. of Pittsburgh graduate. Played with Jock Sutherland and Red Carlson. Massillon Tigers, 1919; Buffalo All Americans and Cleveland Panthers, 1920. Coached Stanford, 1933-39. Succeeded Pop Warner who would later claim, "Leaving Stanford was the worst mistake I ever made." Stanford won three straight Pacific Coast titles, 1933-35, becoming first team to play in three Rose Bowls. Indians were known as "Vow Boys" because, as freshmen, they vowed they'd never lose to Southern Cal. They never did.

THORP, EDWARD J. Official. B. 6/5/1886, New York, N.Y. D. 6/23/34, Port Chester, N.Y. Manhattan College graduate. Gained no fame as player but did as football official. Came to be regarded as penultimate authority on rules. Respected not only for ability but also for size — he towered over 6', weighed over 200. Helped organize Eastern Association of Football Officials in 1923. Promoted college basketball in addition to football. At NYU, 1920, developed AAU national champions. Howard Cann, now in Basketball Hall of Fame, was

NYU Star. Thorp was great storyteller, popular with both players and coaches. Officiated last time in 1934 Rose Bowl, Columbia (7) vs. Stanford (0). Died of cerebral hemorrhage at age 48, two weeks after suffering stroke.

THORPE, JAMES F. Running Back. B. 5/28/1888, Prague, Okla. D. 3/28/53, Lovita, Calif. 6'1", 185. Legendary all-round athlete. Of American Indian descent. Born in one-room cabin on banks of Oklahoma's North Canadian River. Great-grandfather was Black Hawk, Sac and Fox war chief. Twin brother, Charles, died in boyhood. Acquired strength, stamina, speed by doing farmwork and hunting. Played for Pop Warner at Carlisle, 1908, 11-12. All-America, 1911, 12. In 1911 scored all Carlisle's points in 18-15 victory over Harvard. In 1912 scored 198 points, including 25 TDs. Same year scored on runs of 60, 75, 85 yds. vs. Penn; netted 28 points vs. Pitt. Overpowering runner, tackler. Excelled in all phases of football. Won both pentathlon and decathlon in Stockholm Olympic Games, 1912. King Gustavus of Sweden, presenting trophies to Thorpe, made historic remark: "You, sir, are the greatest athlete in the world." Year later forfeited prizes after AAU discovered he played minor league baseball in 1909-10. Sixty years later, 1973, trophies and medals were restored. Played pro baseball, 1913-19, with New York Giants, Cincinnati Reds, Boston Braves. Elected president of American Professional Football Association, 1920. In 1950 voted greatest football player and male athlete of first half century in A.P. poll. Movie of life, starring Burt Lancaster as Thorpe, was made in 1951. Early-Day All-Time All-America team. Citizens Savings Hall of Fame, National Football Foundation Hall of Fame, Pro Football Hall of Fame.

THURSTON, FREDERICK C. (Fuzzy) Guard. B. 11/29/33, Altoona, Wis. 6'1", 250. Attended Valparaiso. Didn't play football competitively until junior year in college. Went to Valparaiso originally to play basketball. Blossomed into All-Indiana Collegiate Conference offensive guard. Related in *Saturday Evening Post* article: "I'm lucky that I went to a smaller school. Otherwise, I would never have gotten a chance to play football at all." Had tryout with Philadelphia Eagles, then played one season with Baltimore Colts, 1958, before he found home at Green Bay. In nine seasons with Packers, 1959-67, Fuzzy was twice All-Pro and mainstay of club's offensive line. Played on five NFL championship teams. Now restaurateur in Neenah, Wis.

TIBBOTT, FREDERICK M. Running Back. B. 12/11/1885, Indianapolis, Ind. D. 8/20/65, Farmington, Maine. 5'9", 149. All-America at Princeton, 1908. That season spurred bid for upset vs. Yale. Gave Tigers 6-0 1st-half lead with TD, but Ted Coy rallied Elis for 11-6 verdict. Also ran track at Princeton. 1st Lt. Army Corps of Engineers, World War I. From 1922 until death managed lumber and plywood tracts in Farmington. Also authored articles for periodicals.

TIGERT, JOHN J., JR. Running Back. B. 2/11/1882, Nashville, Tenn. D. 1/12/65, Gainesville, Fla. Vanderbilt, 1902-03. Born on Vanderbilt campus. Father, John Sr., was Bishop of Methodist Episcopal Church. Played on 14-2-1 teams.

Failed to make All-America — big reason was that Walter Camp ignored players below Mason-Dixon line at turn of century. First Rhodes Scholar from Tennessee. President of Kentucky Wesleyan at age 27, 1909. U.S. commissioner of education, 1921-28. President, U. of Florida, 1928-47. Also served on Central (Mo.) College and Kentucky faculties. Grandfather, Bishop Holland McTyeire, was Vanderbilt's first executive head and one of its founders. National Football Foundation Hall of Fame.

TIMBERLAKE, ROBERT W. Quarterback. B. 10/18/43, Middletown, Ohio. 6'4", 215. Michigan, 1962-64. Playing and Academic All-America, 1964. Guided Michigan to '65 Rose Bowl victory (34-7) over Oregon State. Scored 24-yd. TD run and completed 7 of 10 passes against Ducks. During Wolverine career passed for 1579 yds., rushed for 910 more and kicked 37 of 37 PATs. Also returned six kickoffs and caught 10 passes. Author Ivan N. Kaye named book on college football, *Good Clean Violence,* after Timberlake comment. Preministerial student at Michigan, Timberlake was asked how he justified playing football. His reply: "What's wrong with a little good clean violence?" Played lone pro football campaign with New York Giants, 1965. Pastor, Heritage United Presbyterian Church, Hales Corners, Wis.

TINGLEHOFF H. MICHAEL (Mick) Center. B. 5/22/40, Lexington, Neb. 6'2", 235. Nebraska. 1959-61. Played linebacker and center. Achieved outstanding success with Minnesota Vikings after signing as free agent in 1962. Vikings, 1962-73. Pro Bowl, 1965, 66, 67, 68, 69, 70. NFL championship game, 1969. Super Bowl, 1970, 74. All-NFL, 1964, 65, 66, 67, 68, 69. In 12 seasons played in 168 straight league games. Operates summer football camp for boys.

TINSLEY, GAYNELL C. (Gus) End. B. 2/1/15, Ruple, La. 6'1", 195. Louisiana State, 1934-36. Played baseball and football. Captained both sports. Football All-America, 1935, 36. Played offense and defense. Chicago Cardinals, 1937-38. LSU end coach, 1939-42; head coach, 1948-54. National Football Foundation Hall of Fame.

TIPTON, ARTHUR C. Center. B. 6/5/1882, Las Vegas, N.M. D. 1/15/42, Gainesville, Fla. 5'11", 197. Attended Sacred Heart College, Denver, and New Mexico Normal before going to West Point. Army varsity, 1903-04. All-America, 1904. Served in World War I. Achieved rank of Lt. Col. Was commandant of U. of Florida ROTC unit. Assistant coach Army, 1908; Florida, 1924-26.

TIPTON, ERIC G. (The Red) Running Back. B. 4/20/15, Parkersburg, W. Va. 5'11", 190. Best known for punting skills. Was also fine runner, passer, defender. Played three years at Duke, 1936-38. Teamed sophomore season with Ace Parker. Against Pittsburgh, in 1938, enjoyed greatest game. Seven of his punts left Pitt inside 10-yd. line, another seven rolled dead or went out of bounds between 10 and 20. Clark Shaughnessy praised: "It is unlikely that any big game in history ever was so completely dominated by remarkable punting — in which Eric Tipton proved the deciding factor in a punting performance that is still talked about wherever football men gather." Duke blanked Pitt, 7-0. Tipton played seven seasons of major league baseball. He batted .270 lifetime with Philadelphia A's and Cincinnati Reds. Formerly coached at William & Mary. National Football Foundation Hall of Fame. Varsity baseball and lightweight football coach at Army.

TITTLE, YELBERTON A. (Y.A.) Quarterback. B. 10/24/26, Marshall, Tex. 6'1", 190. Antithesis of handsome hero. Was big-eared, bony-faced, prematurely bald (hence "Bald Eagle"). 23-11-2 playing record at Louisiana State, 1944-47. Threw for 2576 yds. but was overshadowed for national recognition by Johnny Lujack (Notre Dame), Charlie Trippi (Georgia), Charlie Conerly (Mississippi). Played with Baltimore Colts, 1948-50; San Francisco 49ers, 1951-60; New York Giants 1961-64. Colts were in AAFC, 1948-49. Baltimore franchise folded after 1950 season and Tittle ended up with 49ers. Traded to Giants in 1961 for lineman Lou Cordileone ("Me for Tittle? You mean, just me?"). At San Francisco developed "alley-oop" pass with receiver R.C. Owens. Enjoyed greatest prosperity with Giants, leading team to three Eastern Conference titles. Bitterly disappointed that he was never able to win NFL championship. Against Redskins in 1962, completed 27 of 39 passes for 505 yards, record-tying seven touchdowns. "That," exclaimed Giant coach Allie Sherman, "was the finest passing exhibition I've ever seen." Led league with 60.1%, 3145 yards, 36 TDs, 1963. NFL career completed 55.5% for 28,339 yds., 212 TDs. Three times All-Pro, 1957, 62, 63. Tremendous competitor. Pro Football Hall of Fame.

TOLAR, CHARLES G. (Cannonball) Running Back. B. 9/5/37, Natchitoches, La. 5'7", 195. Attended Louisiana State, freshman year, 1955. Rushed for 2194 yds. on 316 carries (6.9 average) at Northwestern Louisiana, 1956-58. Still holds school records for TDs, career, 29; TDs, season, 12; points, career, 182; points season, 79. Dropped after tryout with Steelers, went on to play seven seasons for Houston Oilers in 1960-66. Owns Oiler record for most TDs rushing, career, 20. Played fullback. Crashed into foes with abandon, delighting fans. Knee injury cut short career. Works in public relations in Houston.

TONEFF, ROBERT Tackle. B. 6/23/30, Detroit, Mich. 6'3", 270. Notre Dame, 1949-51. All-America, 1951. Teammate of Jim Mutscheller, Johnny Lattner, Ralph Guglielmi, Dick Syzmanski. San Francisco 49ers, 1952, 54-58; Washington Redskins, 1959-64. Corner linebacker, defensive end and tackle, offensive guard for 49ers; defensive tackle at Washington. All-Pro, 1955. Aggressive, fast, strong.

TONNEMAKER, F. CLAYTON Center. B. 6/8/28, Ogilvie, Minn. 6'3", 240. Unanimous All-America at Minnesota, 1949. Co-captain that season with George Brennan. Green Bay Packers, 1950, 53-54. All-Pro, 1950. Served 32 months in army, 1951-53. Discharged as 1st Lt. Now vice president of Cargill, Inc.

TORGESON, LaVERN (Torgy) Linebacker. B. 2/28/29, LaCrosse, Wis. 6', 222. Washington State captain, 1950. Detroit Lions, 1951-54; Washington Redskins, 1955-58. All-Pro five times, playing despite injuries in 94 of 96 games. Since retiring as player has coached Washington, Pittsburgh Steelers, Los Angeles Rams. Currently Redskin defensive coordinator.

TORREY, ROBERT G. Center. B. 7/12/1878, Henrico County, Va. D. 1/11/41, Philadelphia, Pa. 5'11", 186. Played at Pennsylvania. Middle name "Grant" was given for Dr. James A. S. Grant, uncle by marriage and British physician who practiced in Cairo. Dr. Grant was personal physician to Khedive who ruled Egypt many years. Grew up and attended high school in Montclair, N.J. Captained two Penn teams. All-America, 1905. Helped develop "roving center" technique. Enjoyed long association with Philadelphia General Hospital as physician, secretary of medical board and its president. Spent 33 years in fight against tuberculosis. National Football Foundation Hall of Fame.

TOWLER, DANIEL L. (Deacon Dan) Running Back. B. 3/6/28, Donora, Pa. Shares same Pennsylvania hometown with baseball immortal Stan Musial. Played at Washington & Jefferson, 1947-50. Los Angeles Rams, 1950-55. All-NFL, 1951, 52, 53. League rushing champion with 894 yds. on 156 carries, 1952. During pro playing days became ordained minister. First Black named to Los Angeles Board of Education. Received honorary degree from Washington & Jefferson and Ph.D. from UCLA. Currently campus pastor at California State (Los Angeles).

TRACY, J. THOMAS Running Back. B. 2/21/33, Birmingham, Mich. 5'9", 205. Attended Tennessee. All-SEC, 1954. Known as Tom (The Bomb) Tracy. Detroit Lions, 1956-57; Pittsburgh Steelers, 1958-63; Washington Redskins, 1964. NFL championship game, 1957. Workhorse runner and receiver; also effective pass-option man and part-time placement kicker. Finished among NFL's top 10 ground gainers twice, 1959, 60. Resident of Pontiac, Mich.

TRAFFORD, BERNARD W. Running Back. B. 7/2/1871, Dartmouth, Mass. D. 1/2/42, Milton, Mass. Harvard fullback, 1889-92. Forerunner of Charley Brickley as dropkicking artist. Walter Camp once wrote of Trafford: "It is extremely dangerous to give him even a single chance for a drop kick at a distance of 35 yards." Had Camp chosen All-America specialists in 1890s, Trafford would have been easy selection as kicker. In 1891 scored 270 points (24 TDs, 77 PATs, 4 FGs) including 64 vs. Wesleyan (7 TDs, 18 PATs). Both totals are pre-1937 records. In Trafford's day TDs were valued at four points each, PATs two, FGs five. Baseball was another specialty. Long remembered for game-saving catch vs. Yale in last collegiate game. Playing right field, he speared ball over his head at top speed with two out and two Yalies on base. Was president of First National Bank of Boston; retired in 1941 as chairman of the board.

TRAFTON, GEORGE Center. B. 12/6/1896, Chicago, Ill. D. 9/5/71. Rates with Mel Hein and Clyde (Bulldog) Turner as pro football's greatest centers. Many colleges sought Trafton after he played at Oak Park H.S. in Chicago and Camp Grant, Ill. Selected Notre Dame but stay was short. Coach Knute Rockne caught Trafton playing semipro football on Sunday and had him expelled. Joined Decatur Staleys, 1920, beginning 13-year pro career with one franchise. Staleys moved to Chicago in 1921, and one year later were renamed Bears. Roughhouse player deluxe, Trafton was called "the toughest, meanest, most ornery critter alive" by teammate Red Grange. Once knocked out four opponents in stretch of 12 plays. Briefly pursued boxing career while playing for Bears. It ended when he was kayoed by Primo Carnera, 54 seconds into 1st-round match. Assistant coach for world champion Green Bay Packers, 1944; Cleveland Rams, 1945. Pro Football Hall of Fame. All-Pro Squad of the 1920s.

TRIPLETT, MELVIN Running Back. B. 12/24/31, Indianola, Miss. 6'1", 215. Son of sharecropper, one of 17 children. Working plow with four mules by age 9. Moved to Ohio when tornadoes ruined cotton crop. Married, father of two children when accepted scholarship to Toledo. New York Giants, 1955-60; Minnesota Vikings, 1961-62. Scored two TDs in New York's 47-7 romp over Chicago Bears, deciding NFL championship. Lost in two other title game appearances, 1958, 59. Gained 2865 yds., 14 TDs rushing in eight seasons. Punishing runner, but temperamental and inconsistent.

TRIPPI, CHARLES L. (Charlie) Running Back. B. 12/14/22, Pittston, Pa, 5'11", 185. Georgia 1942, 45-46. Combined defensive safety work with punting and offensive duties. Substituting for injured All-America Frankie Sinkwich, Trippi gained 115 yds. rushing and 88 passing as Georgia won Rose Bowl, 9-0, over UCLA in 1943. Also victorious in Oil Bowl (20-6 over Tulsa, 1946) and Sugar Bowl (20-10 over North Carolina, 1947). 28-3 playing record. Unanimous All-America, Maxwell Award winner and Hiesman Trophy runnerup, 1946. Named to All-Time Rose Bowl team. Signed out of college for $100,000 (four-year contract) with Chicago Cardinals. Played entire pro career with Cards, 1947-55. Paul Christman, Marshall Goldberg, Elmer Angsman, Trippi formed Chicago's "Dream Backfield." Member NFL champions, 1947. Led NFL in rushing with 5.4-yd. Led punt returners with 239 yds., 11.4 average, 1953. Finished pro career with 3506 yds. on 687 carries for 5.4 average, scored 22 TDs. Blindsided by John Henry Johnson in exhibition game, 1955 — event precipitated retirement from football. When he did retire, Trippi held almost all team rushing, punting and punt-return records. Citizens Savings Hall of Fame, National Football Foundation Hall of Fame. Called "Scintillating Sicilian" and "Triple-threat Trippi." Now in private business in Athens, Ga.

TRIPUCKA, FRANK Quarterback. B. 12/8/27, Bloomfield, N.J. 6'2", 205. Notre Dame, 1945-48. Played only two losing games in Irish career, both in 1945. Understudied Johnny Lujack until senior year. Suffered broken bone against USC in final collegiate game. Trojans tied N.D. at Los Angeles, 14-14, before 100,571 fans. Philadelphia Eagles, 1949; Detroit Lions, 1949; Chicago Cardinals,

1950-52; Dallas Texans, 1952; Denver Broncos, 1960-63. Played five years in CFL. Led AFL with 248 completions, 3038 yds., 1960. Tossed five TD passes vs. Buffalo Bills, 1962. Same year vs. Bills threw for 447 yds., hit Al Frazier for 96-yd. completion. In career gained 7676 yds. passing, made 51 TD strikes.

TRULL, DONALD Quarterback. B. 10/20/41, Oklahoma City. 6'1", 179. All-State prep QB at Southeast H.S. of Oklahoma City. Baylor, 1961-63. Completed 325 of 593 passes during collegiate career for 4143 yds. Led nation twice in passing, 1962, 63. All-America and 4th in Heisman Trophy voting, 1963. Academic All-America twice, 1962, 63. Played in Gotham Bowl, 1961; Astro-Bluebonnet, 1963; Hula, 1964. East-West Shrine and All-America Bowl games, 1964. Houston Oilers, 1964-66; 68-69; Boston Patriots, 1967; Edmonton Eskimos, 1970-71. Now freshman coach at Arkansas.

TRUMPY, ROBERT T., JR. Tight End. B. 3/6/45, Springfield, Ill. 6'6", 228. Attended Springfield H.S., U. of Illinois, U. of Utah. Prep All-America in football and basketball. Also broad-jumped 23'4" and high-jumped 6'4". Graduated from Utah. 12th-round draft choice of Cincinnati Bengals in 1968. Scored 24 TDs in first five years as Bengal pass receiver, 1968-73. Scored nine touchdowns and averaged 22.6 yds. per reception, 1969. Caught 44 passes for career best, 1972. All-AFC, 1970. Blessed with excellent hands and speed. AFL All-Star game, 1969. Pro Bowl, 1971, 74.

TRYON, J. EDWARD (Eddie) Running back. B. 7/25/1900, Medford, Mass. 180. Played four years at Colgate, 1922-25. Scored three TDs against Niagara on runs of 50, 95, 97 yds., 1923. Led Colgate to undefeated season, 1925. Red Raider coach Dick Harlow appraised slippery halfback: "Tryon was the answer to a of 50, 95, 97 yds, 1923. Led Colgate to undefeated season, 1925. Red Raider coach Dick Harlow appraised slippery halfback: "Tryon was the answer to a coach's fondest dream. He could do everything and in addition was a wonderful boy to handle." Graduate work at NYU and Springfield in physical education. New York Yankees, 1926-27. Head coach and physical education instructor at Hobart. Member of NCAA Rules Committee, 1960-63. Citizens Savings Hall of Fame, National Football Foundation Hall of Fame.

TUBBS, GERALD (Jerry) Linebacker. B. 1/23/35, Breckenridge, Tex. 6'2", 205. Played three years at Oklahoma for Charles (Bud) Wilkinson, never losing varsity game, 1954-56. Played on two consecutive national championship teams, 1955-56. All-America, Knute Rockne Trophy recipient, 1956. Also played with All-Americas Bo Bolinger and Tommy McDonald. Drafted No. 1 by Chicago Cardinals. Cards, 1957-58; San Francisco 49ers, 1958-59; Dallas Cowboys, 1960-68. Two-way player in college, specialized as middle linebacker in pros. Assistant coach Dallas Cowboys.

TUCKER, ROBERT Tight End. B. 6/8/45, Hazleton, Pa. 6'3", 230. Attended Bloomsburg State. Of Tyrolean-Polish descent. Small-college pass-receiving champion with 77 catches, 1325 yds. and 147.2-yd. average per game, 1967. Little All-America, 1967. Played both ways. Signed with New York Giants as free agent, 1970. Previously had trials with Philadelphia Eagles and Boston Patriots. Played in minors with Lowell, Mass., and Pottstown, Pa. Immediate starter with Giants, beating out Aaron Thomas for tight end post. First tight end in NFL history to win receiving title, with 59 receptions for 791 yds., in 1971. All-NFC, 1972.

TUNNELL, EMLEN Defensive Back. B. 3/29/25, Byrn Mawr, Pa. 6′1″, 200. Graduated from Radnor (Pa.) H.S. Suffered broken neck in his one football season at U. of Toledo. Recuperated to play basketball, helping Rockets gain NIT berth. Coast Guard service interrupted collegiate career, resumed schooling at Iowa. New York Giants, 1948-58, and Green Bay Packers, 1959-61. First Black to sign with Giants. Played in 167 NFL games, 158 consecutively, both were records at one time. Still holds pro marks for interceptions (79), interception yardage (1282), punt returns (258), punt-return yardage (2209). Named All-Pro four times. Eight Pro Bowl games. Gained 924 all-purpose yds. in 1952, surpassing 894 of running back Dan Towler who led NFL offensively. Rated with all-time best safetymen. Pro Football Hall of Fame. Assistant coach for Giants, 1963-73. First full-time Black coach in NFL.

TURNER, JAMES A. Quarterback-Kicker. B. 3/28/41, Martinez, Calif. 6′2″, 205. QB for John Ralston at Utah State, 1960-62. Played in Sun, 1960, and Gotham, 1962, Bowls. Attended graduate school at California State College. 6th leading NFL career scorer with 993 points. Thru 1973 had longest PAT string among actives with all straight. In career has connected on 220 of 356 field goals. Shares AFL FG record of six in one game. Played with New York Jets, 1964-70, and Denver Broncos, 1971-73. Played briefly with Jets as quarterback, throwing four passes. Likes to fish and hunt. AFL championship game, 1968. Super Bowl, 1969. Booted one PAT, three FGs in New York's 1607 Super Bowl victory. AFL All-Star games, 1969, 70.

TWOMBLY, HENRY B. (Deacon) Quarterback. B. 11/10/1862, Albany, N.Y. D. 2/28/55. Football fanatic. Yale quarterback, 1881-83. Fondest recollection of grid career were words of praise from Walter Camp following scrimmage against scrubs: "Twombly, those runs of yours were as good as any I have seen on the field this year." Acquired nickname as class deacon. Member Yale lacrosse team, 1882-84. Member Harvard's U.S. amateur lacrosse champions, 1885. Graduated from Harvard Law School, 1886. Played football for Gentlemen of Boston, 1888-89. Maintained lifetime interest in recreation, outdoor life. Was senior member Putney, Twombly & Putney law firm, New York City.

TYRER, JAMES E. Tackle. B. 2/25/39, Newark, Ohio. 6′6″, 270. Ohio State, 1958-60. Received B.A. degree in zoology. All-America, 1960. Drafted on 3rd round by Dallas Texans. Texans, 1961-63; Kansas City Chiefs, 1964-73. Has started throughout career. Played in nine AFL All-Star games and two Pro

Bowls. Highly regarded for strength and consistency at offensive tackle. All-AFL seven times, All-AFC twice. Member Super Bowl champions, 1970. Also played in 1962, 66, 69 AFL championship games; Super Bowl I, 1967. President of own company, Pro Forma. It represents pro athletes in commercial ventures. Co-captain of Chiefs. Member of All-Time AFL team.

UNITAS, JOHN C. Quarterback. B. 5/7/33, Pittsburgh, Pa. 6'1", 196. Attended St. Justin's H.S., Pittsburgh. Wanted scholarship to Notre Dame but coaches there thought he was too small (5'11", 140). Grew to 6'1", 190 at U. of Louisville. Drafted on 9th round by Pittsburgh Steelers, 1955; they released him before regular season began. Joined semi-pro Bloomfield Rams. One year later he joined Baltimore Colts as free agent, launching incredible career. Thru 1973 had attempted more passes (5186), completed more passes (2830) for more yds. passing (40,239), more TDs passing (290) than any player in NFL history. Holds numerous other pro records. In 1969 named greatest QB ever in conjunction with NFL's 50th anniversary. Named 1960s Player of the Decade by AP. Holds league record for 300-yd. passing games (27). In 1956-60 threw touchdown pass 47 consecutive games, streak comparable to DiMaggio's 56-game hitting streak. All-Pro six times, NFL's MVP thrice. Gave memorable performance in 1958 championship game, throwing for 349 yds. as Colts won 23-17 in sudden death. Raymond Berry, Lenny Moore were favorite targets. Jim Thorpe Trophy, 1957, 67. In 1970 league's first Man of the Year, awarded to top citizen-athlete. Relegated to backup duty in youth movement by Colt general manager Joe Thomas, 1972. Sold, 1973, to San Diego Chargers for $150,000. Made No. 19 legendary. Noted for coolness, consistency. According to Sid Luckman: "John Unitas is the greatest quarterback ever to play the game — better than me, better than Sammy Baugh, better than anyone." NFL championship games, 1958, 59, 64, 68, 70. Super Bowl, 1969, 71. Ten Pro Bowls.

UPSHAW, EUGENE Guard. B. 8/15/45, Robstown, Tex. 6'5", 255. Played tackle, center and end at Texas A. & I. NAIA All-America, 1966. Senior Bowl, Coaches All-America, College All-Star games. Earned three track letters, setting Texas A. & I. shot-put record with 57' toss. No. 1 draft choice of Oakland Raiders, 1967. Played in 98 straight games with Raiders, 1967-73. All-AFL, 1967, 68, 69, and All-AFC, 1970, 71, 72. Pro Bowl, 1973, 74. Leads impressive Raider sweeps. Older brother of Marv Upshaw, defensive end for Kansas City Chiefs. Operates two night clubs in Oakland, active in charity fundraising drives around Bay Area. AFL All-Star game, 1969. AFL championship games, 1967, 68, 69. Super Bowl, 1968.

UREMOVICH, EMIL P. Tackle. B. 9/29/16, Gary, Ind. Indiana tackle, 1939-41. All-America, 1940. B.S. degree. Detroit Lions, 1941-42, 45-46; Chicago Rockets (AAFC), 1948. All-Pro, 1945. Served U.S. Army in European theater. Now deputy sheriff for Lake County (Ind.) Police Dept.

UTAY, JOE Administrator. B. 5/2/1887, St. Louis, Mo. Texas A. & M. letterman, 1905-07. Athletic director and assistant football coach under Charley Moran, both in 1912 at A. & M. Same year helped organize Southwest Football Officials Association. Was organization chairman for over 20 years. Officiated more than 100 SWC games from 1912-36. Southwest editor for *Spalding Football Guide* during 1915-41 period. Promoted first post-season game in Southwest, arranging Dixie Classic between Centre College and Texas A. & M. In that game Aggies upset Praying Colonels, 22-14. Dixie Classic was forerunner of Cotton Bowl, which Utay also pioneered. Charter member of National Football Foundation and Hall of Fame. Graduate of Michigan School of Law. 87-year-old Utay is still practicing law today in Fort Worth, Tex. Elected to National Football Foundation Hall of Fame in 1974.

VAN BROCKLIN, NORMAN (Dutchman) Quarterback. B. 3/15/26, Eagle Butte, S.D. Pocket passer personified. Hated to lose more than anything. "Defeat used to drive him stark, raving mad," said Les Richter, Los Angeles Ram teammate. "He'd beat his bare fist against the walls of the dressing room, kick the bench, scream like a banshee and cry like a baby." Watchmaker's son and 8th of nine children. Started athletic life at Acalanes H.S. in Walnut Creek, Calif. Only 4th-string tailback at U. of Oregon until new coach Jimmy Allen switched Ducks to T. Event launched Van Brocklin's passing career. Led Oregon to perfect conference record, 1948, capped by appearance in Cotton Bowl. Played 12 years professionally, not all happy ones. In nine seasons with Rams, 1949-57, forced to alternate with Bob Waterfield and Billy Wade but still managed to lead NFL three times in passing. Spent last three years with Philadelphia Eagles, 1958-60. NFL championship games, 1949, 50, 51, 55, 60. Nine Pro Bowls. Went out winner as Eagles defeated Green Bay Packers, 17-6, in NFL championship game in 1960. For efforts Van Brocklin was named league MVP. All-NFL same year. In 1951 he threw for 554 yds., one-game passing record which still stands. Completed 1553 of 2895 (53.6 percent) pro passes for 23,611 yds., 173 TDs. NFL head coach with Minnesota Vikings, 1961-66, and Atlanta Falcons, 1968-73. National Football Foundation Hall of Fame, Pro Football Hall of Fame. Volatile and acerbic personality, owing somewhat to his background. "I was a Depression kid," Van Brocklin said. "It was never easy. Anything I wanted I had to work for."

VAN BUREN, STEVE W. Running Back. B. 12/28/20, La Ceiba, Honduras.

6'1", 205. Consummate runner, possessing both speed and power. Could also catch passes, punt and even placekick. He wouldn't throw pass, however, disdaining it as offensive weapon — "The fellow who threw the first pass must have been someone too tired to run with the ball." Best remembered for pro career, though he was first-rate college halfback. Grew up in New Orleans with grandparents, both parents having died when he was very young. Louisiana State, 1941-43. Blocking back first two years. Coach Bernie Moore turned him loose as rusher in 1943. Accounted for all three LSU TDs as Tigers whipped Texas A. & M., 18-13, in 1944 Orange Bowl. Victory capped 847-yd., 14-TD season for Van Buren who still holds LSU one-year TD record. Philadelphia Eagles, 1944-51. All-Pro, 1945, 47, 48, 49. NFL rushing leader four times, exceeding 200 yds. once in one game. Retired as pro's greatest rusher, with 5860 yds. on 1320 carries (4.1-yd. average). Gave brilliant performance, despite weather adversities, in back-to-back NFL championship games, 1948, 49. Eagles stopped St. Louis, 7-0, 1948, as Van Buren scored only TD during one of Philadelphia's worst snowstorms. Following year, in torrential Los Angeles rain, sloshed thru Rams for 196 yds. on 31 carries — Eagles prevailed, 14-0, for unprecedented 2nd straight championship game shutout. Many of his offensive thrusts were aimed at right side of line. He was powerful enough to shed defensive front and swift enough (9.8 for 100 yds.) to run with any defensive back. Career declined after 1950. It ended in 1952 pre-season practice when he tore knee ligament. Played long enough for Philadelphia coach Greasy Neale to call him "the best offensive halfback who ever lived." Scored 71 pro TDs. All-Pro Squad of the 1940s. Pro Football Hall of Fame.

VANDERKELEN, RONALD Quarterback. B. 11/6/39, Green Bay, Wis. 6'1", 190. Played at Wisconsin. Big 10 passing (1009 yds.) and total offense (1237 yds.) leader, 1962. Engineered amazing comeback in '63 Rose Bowl, electrifying huge national TV audience. Badgers, trailing USC 42-14 in 4th quarter, rallied for three quick TDs. Two of them came on VanderKelen passes, last to All-America Pat Richter. Score thus read: USC 42, Wisconsin 37, with 1:19 to play. Unfortunately for Badgers, they were never able to gain possession again and lost by that 5-point margin. VanderKelen completed record 33 of 48 passes against Trojans for 401 yds. His 406 yds. total offense is also Rose Bowl record. Not drafted by NFL and only 21st-round pick of AFL New York Titans. Signed as free agent with Minnesota Vikings in 1963. Understudied Fran Tarkenton for five years before brief trials with Buffalo Bills, Atlanta Falcons, CFL. Retired in 1968. Now advertising account executive in Minneapolis. Rose Bowl remains biggest thrill — "It was the most fantastic experience of my life."

VAN SURDAM, HENDERSON (Dutch) Quarterback. B. Hoosick Falls, N.Y. 5'6", 165. Wesleyan (Conn.), 1902-05. One of best quarterbacks of era, earning high rating from Walter Camp. Coached at Marietta, Sewanee and Texas School of Mines. Active football official in East for 42 years, 1920-61. Professional fund raiser and musician. Lt. and balloon observer in World War I. Active in American Football Coaches Association, given bronze plaque for 37 years service. National Football Foundation Hall of Fame.

VARRICHIONE, FRANK Tackle. B. 1/14/32. 6'2", 235. Played at Notre Dame under Frank Leahy, 1952-53, and Terry Brennan, 1954. All-America, 1954. Pittsburgh Steelers, 1955-60; Los Angeles Rams, 1961-65. Pro Bowl, 1956, 57, 58, 59, 63. Fine pass-blocker. Expert at "legal holding." No. 1 draft choice of Steelers in '55.

VATAHA, RANDY End. B. 12/4/48, Santa Monica, Calif. 5'10", 170. Attended Golden West (Calif.) J.C. before playing two years at Stanford. Caught 83 Jim Plunkett passes for 1535 yds. One went for 97 yds. All-Pacific 8 twice, 1969, 70. Major role in Stanford's 27-17 upset of Ohio State in Rose Bowl, 1971. Drafted on 17th round and signed by Los Angeles Rams, who released him. Then signed as free agent with New England Patriots. Led Patriots in receiving (3rd in AFC) with 51 catches, 872 yds. and 9 TDs, 1971. Johnny Unitas Award winner same season. As Pat reunited with Plunkett. Slumped to 25 receptions in 1972, 20 in '73.

VAUGHT, JOHN H. Coach. B. 5/6/08, Olney, Tex. Attended Polytechnic H.S. in Fort Worth; was class valedictorian. Played left guard for Texas Christian under Francis Schmidt. Captained TCU's Southwest Conference champions, 1932. All-SWC twice, 1931, 32. North Carolina line coach, 1936-41. Mississippi head coach, 1947-70. Record: 185-85-12 (.749). Won more Southeastern Conference championships (6) than any other coach. Took Ole Miss to 18 bowl games, 14 in succession, 1957-70, for national record. Second SEC coach to win conference title in first year as head coach. His All-Americas include Charlie Conerly, Barney Poole, Charlie Flowers, Jim Dunaway, Archie Manning. Retired due to heart condition in 1970, but returned to post when Billy Kinard was fired as Ole Miss coach after three games (1-2). Vaught finished out season with 6-5 record, making lifetime 190-88-12.

VESSELS, BILLY W. (Curly) Running Back. B. 3/22/31, Cleveland, Okla. 6', 185. Oklahoma, 1950-52. Overshadowed by Leon Heath in 1950, and injured much of junior season. Enjoyed brilliant senior year. Won Heisman Trophy, A.P. and UPI Player of the Year awards. Had greatest day that year in losing effort against Notre Dame. Scored 3 TDs, rushed for 195 yds. and 11.5 average. In 24-game career scored 35 TDs, netted 2085 yds. rushing, caught 21 passes for 391 yds. First Heisman winner to sign with CFL, winning Schenley Award as league's best back in 1953. Injured knee in subsequent service hitch. Tried to make comeback with Baltimore Colts in 1956. Gained 244 yds. in only NFL season. National Football Foundation Hall of Fame. Now prominent real estate developer in Florida.

VIDAL, EUGENE L. Running Back. B. 4/13/1895, Madison, S.D. D. 2/20/69, Palos Verdes, Calif. Graduated from South Dakota, 1916. Lettered in four sports: basketball, baseball, track, football. Army, 1917-18. Captain and All-America nominee, 1918. Played halfback. West Point teammate of Red Blaik, Elmer Oliphant, Biff Jones. "One of the best backs and all-around athletes in

Academy annals," Blaik later wrote of him. Finished 2nd in pentathlon at Antwerp Olympics, 1920. Coached U.S. pentathlon entries at Paris in 1924. Volunteer Cadet coach in three sports until 1926 when resigned from army. Director of air commerce for Department of Commerce, 1933-37. Developed process for making airplane fuselages, tails and wings from molded plywood. Also affiliated with Northeast Airlines. Gore, his son, is famous writer.

VILLAPIANO, PHILIP J. Linebacker. B. 2/26/49, Long Branch, N.J. 6'1", 222. Attended Bowling Green. Mid-American Conference Defensive Player of the Year, 1970. All-Conference defensive end, 1969, 70. Blue-Gray, Senior Bowl, College All-Star games. Member *Omicron Delta Kappa,* national honorary leadership fraternity. All-Rookie NFL, 1971, with Oakland Raiders. Moved to linebacker in pros. Ran 82 yds. for TD on interception, 2nd-longest return in Raider history, 1972. Plays accordion and tuba. Brother, John, also played for Bowling Green. Phil also spent 1973 with Raiders.

VOGEL, ROBERT L. Tackle. B. 9/23/41, Columbus, Ohio. 6'5", 250. Another in long line of great Ohio State linemen produced by Woody Hayes. Played for Buckeyes, 1960-62. Opened holes for such runners as Bob Ferguson, Tom Matte, Paul Warfield, Matt Snell. Baltimore Colts, 1963-72. All-NFL, 1968. Played in four Pro Bowls, 1965, 66, 68, 72. Member of winning Super Bowl team, 1971. Lost Super Bowl in 1969, NFL title game in 1964.

VOLK, RICHARD R. (Rick) Defensive Back. B. 3/15/45, Toledo, Ohio. 6'3", 195. College: Michigan, 1964-66. Nephew of Bob Chappuis, who played pro ball with Brooklyn Dodgers and Chicago Hornets. Rick was switched to defensive back in college after career as high school QB. Member of Michigan's Rose Bowl team which defeated Oregon State, 34-7, in 1965. All-Big 10 and All-America, 1966. No. 2 draft choice of Baltimore Colts. Intercepted 28 passes for Colts in first six seasons, 1967-72, but only one in 1973. Considered one of hardest hitters and best tacklers in game. All-AFC, 1971. Made nine tackles in AFC championship game against Oakland, 1970. Pro Bowl, 1968, 70, 72. NFL championship game, 1968. Super Bowl, 1969, 71.

VON EVERY, HAROLD Running Back. B. 2/10/18, Minnetonka Beach, Minn. Minnesota halfback. All-Big 10, 1939. National interception leader that year with eight. Flew B-17s in World War II before crashing over Germany. Sustained back injury which is still bothersome. Great success as Minnesota insurance salesman. In 1964 named to *Sports Illustrated* Silver Anniversary All-America team. Credits coach Bernie Bierman with instilling philosophy of success — "He made us do things we didn't want to do in practice, and later made us see how they paid dividends. The common denominator of success is making a habit of doing what unsuccessful men don't like to do."

WADE, WILLIAM J., JR. (Billy) Quarterback. B. 10/4/30, Nashville, Tenn. 6'2", 205. Vanderbilt, 1951-53. Began playing football at Woodmont grammar school in Nashville. Went to Vanderbilt hoping to be single-wing tailback for Red Sanders. Bill Edwards replaced Sanders as head coach, however, before Wade's sophomore season and switched Commodores to T formation. Under T system Wade completed 201 of 437 passes for 3397 yds. and 31 TDs. In 13 years of pro ball played for Los Angeles Rams, 1954-60, and Chicago Bears, 1961-66. Threw for 466 yds. against Dallas Cowboys, 1962. NFL title games, 1955, 63. Scored two TDs as Bears stopped New York Giants, 14-10, for NFL championship, 1963. Tossed 124 TD passes in pro career, made 1370 completions, amassed 18,530 yds. Serious student of football, and deeply religious. "Football stresses the great lessons of life," Wade said. "It makes a man humble. It unites people. It teaches value and self-discipline." Now bank vice president in Nashville.

WALDEN, ROBERT E. (Bobby) Kicker. B. 3/9/38, Boston, Ga. 6', 190. Georgia, 1958-60. Collegiate punting champion in 1958 with 45.3-yd. average. Played in Blue-Gray and Senior Bowl games. Edmonton Eskimos, 1961-63; Minnesota Vikings, 1964-67; Pittsburgh Steelers, 1968-73. CFL punting leader with 46.8-yd. average, 1961. Signed with Vikings as free agent in 1964. Topped NFL in punting that year with 46.4-yd. average. His 72-yarder was longest of 1972 NFL season. Had first punts (two) of career blocked in '72. Was running back in college and CFL. Pro Bowl, 1970. Owns farm, works for Kaiser Aluminum in off-season.

WALDORF, LYNN O. (Pappy) Coach. B. 10/3/02, Clifton Springs, N.Y. Attended Syracuse U. 2nd-team All-America tackle, 1922, 24. Syracuse was 22-4-3 when Waldorf played. Varsity crew, 1923. Coached Oklahoma City, 1926-27; Oklahoma State, 1929-33; Kansas State, 1934; Northwestern, 1935-46; California, 1947-56. Won national Coach of the Year Award first year at Northwestern. Year later won Big 10 title and lost only to Notre Dame. Northwestern All-Americas included Stephen Reid, Max Morris, Bob Voigt and Otto Graham. Took three straight California teams to Rose Bowl, 1949-51. Great fundamentals teacher. 170-94-22 record overall. National Football Foundation Hall of Fame. Upon coaching retirement joined San Francisco 49ers as personnel director.

WALKER, DOUGLAS C. (Peahead) Coach. B. 1899, Birmingham, Ala. D. 7/16/70. Baseball, football, basketball standout at Howard, 1918-21. Played 12 years of pro baseball with Rochester of International League, Wilson and Norfolk of Piedmont League. Also managed in minors. Football coach at Atlantic Christian, 1926; Elon, 1927-36; Wake Forest, 1937, 49. Coached Montreal Alouettes of CFL. Compiled record of 77-51-6 at Wake Forest, best in school history. Produced Deacons' only two bowl teams: Dixie, 1949, and Gator, 1956. Well known for storytelling ability. On retiring from baseball said: "I decided it was time to quit when the Yankees made Casey Stengel manager. That was the job I shoulda had."

WALKER, EWELL DOAK, JR. (Doaker) Running Back. B. 1/1/27, Dallas, Tex. 5'11", 170. No man ever played with more all-round skill and was worshipped more for it than Doak Walker, scion of Davy Crockett, Sam Houston, Davey O'Brien, Sammy Baugh and other Texas heroes. "Some called it luck, others called it destiny," said Southern Methodist coach Matty Bell. "But Doak had a natural knack of pulling off great deeds." He was good enough, as 1945 freshman, to make SMU varsity. Good enough, in fact, for All-Conference honors. On 1/1/46, his 19th birthday, Doak quarterbacked West in East-West Shrine game. For next three years was premier halfback in nation. In 1947 brought Mustangs back in last minute to tie TCU, 19-19. During that game ripped off runs of 80, 61 and 56 yds., amassing 471 yds. total offense. Made 79-yd. punt against Oregon in 1949 Cotton Bowl (SMU 21, Oregon 13). Also played in '48 Cotton classic (13-13 tie with Penn State). Cotton Bowl was doubledecked thanks to his heroics at SMU. Name was common in newspaper headlines, picture graced numerous magazine covers, fan letters reached him at rate of 200-300 week. Took it all in stride and never lost natural modesty. Career statistics: 3582 yds. total offense (1928 rushing, 1654 passing), 52 TDs-accounted-for (38 rushing, 14 passing), 8 interceptions, 27 pass receptions (16.8-yd. average), 80 punts (39.3-yd. average), 50 punt returns (15-yd. average), 26 kickoff returns (29.4-yd. average). Unanimous All-America, 1948; consensus, 1947, 49. Heisman Trophy, 1948; 3rd, 1947, 49. Probably would have won Heisman in '49 but injured much of season. Watched last college game vs. Notre Dame in street clothes.

Despite slight build for pros game, Walker was immediate star with Detroit Lions in 1950. Received reported $25,000 contract for three years, mighty substantial in those days. Reunited with Bobby Layne, former high school teammate at Highland Park of Dallas. Duo led Lions to world titles in 1952, 53. 1952 marked club's first championship in 17 years. Walker was All-Pro four times, 1950, 51, 53, 54. League scoring leader twice, 1950, 55. Still owns Detroit career scoring record with 563 points. Retired at youthful age of 28 — "I wanted to get out while I had all my teeth and both my knees." Today, he's sales executive in Detroit. Citizens Savings Hall of Fame, National Football Foundation Hall of Fame.

WALKER, WADE H. Tackle. B. 11/29/23, Gastonia, N.C. 6', 203. Recruited for Oklahoma by Jim Tatum, who subsequently went to North Carolina as head coach. Played one year under Tatum, 1946, and three under Bud Wilkinson, 1947-49. All-America, 1949. All-Big 6, 1946, 47; All-Big 7, 1948, 49. Co-captain, 1947, 48. Regarded as one of greatest blocking tackles of his era. Starred in 1949 Orange Bowl, winning 14-6 over North Carolina. Head coach at Mississippi State, 1956-61. Record: 22-32. Mississippi State athletic director, 1959-66. Won first annual Football Coaches Association golf tournament, 1965. Now Oklahoma athletic director.

WALSH, ADAM J. Center. B. 12/4/01, Churchville, Iowa. 6', 190. Four-sport letterman at Hollywood (Calif.) H.S. Notre Dame center, 1922-24. Captained football's most celebrated team — "Four Horsemen" and "Seven Mules," 1924. Inspiring leader, vicious tackler, excellent blocker. Performed 58 minutes against Army despite two broken hands. Also won letters in track and basketball. Coached Santa Clara, Yale, Harvard, Bowdoin and Los Angeles Rams. As Yale assistant was first non-Yale graduate hired to coach football at New Haven. Named Santa Clara head coach at age 23. Served two terms in Maine House of Representatives and as U.S. marshal for District of Maine. Citizens Savings Hall of Fame, National Football Foundation Hall of Fame.

WALSTON, ROBERT (Bobby) End-Placekicker. B. 10/17/28. 6', 195. Georgia, 1947-50. Played with Philadelphia Eagles, 1951-62. Led league scorers with 114 points, 1954. In career scored 881 points (46 TDs, 80 FGs, 365 conversions). Also caught 311 passes for 5363 yds., 17.2 average. At one time was all-time NFL scoring leader. Caught many timely passes for Eagles. Now assistant to president and player personnel director, Chicago Bears.

WALTON, CHARLES R. (Chuck) Guard. B. 7/7/41, Canon City, Colo. 6'3", 250. Iowa State, 1960-62. Three-year regular. All-Big 8, 1962. All-CFL in three of four years with Montreal Alouettes, 1963-64, and Hamilton Tiger-Cats, 1965-66. Detroit Lions, 1967-73. Respected for speed and blocking ability at offensive guard. Originally drafted by Detroit and San Diego Chargers.

WALTON, JOSEPH Tight End. B. 12/15/35, Beaver Falls, Pa. 5'11", 195.

Attended U. of Pittsburgh. Unanimous All-America, 1956. From same town that produced Joe Namath. Washington Redskins, 1957-60; New York Giants, 1961-63. Caught 95 passes for 1321 yds., 17 TDs with Giants, playing on three straight divisional winners. Overall: 178 receptions for 2623 yds., 28 TDs. Despite small dimensions for tight end, he was regarded as one of game's best blockers. Also "the best third-down receiver in the game, bar none" according to Giant quarterback Y. A. Tittle. Joe's father, Frank, was Redskin three years. Giant assistant coach, 1969-73.

WARBURTON, IRVINE E. (Cotton) Quarterback. B. 10/8/11, San Diego, Calif. 5'7", 146. Played under Howard Jones at Southern California, 1932-34. Resourceful little runner, especially effective on punt returns. Broke open 1933 Rose Bowl with pair of touchdowns. Trojans went on to blank Pitt, 35-0. Unanimous All-America, 1933. Southern Cal's 27-game defeatless string was snapped by Stanford in 1933, 13-7. Warburton played in fast company. Teammates Ernie Smith, Tay Brown, Aaron Rosenberg also were All-Americas. Now film editor for Walt Disney Studios. Won Oscar in 1964 for best editing, of *Mary Poppins*.

WARD, JOHN H. Guard. B. 5/27/48, Enid, Okla. 6'4", 260. Attended Oklahoma State. Consensus All-America offensive tackle, 1969. Two-time Big 8 heavyweight wrestling champ, finishing 3rd once in NCAA tournament. Minnesota Vikings, 1970-73. Was Vikings' 1st-round draft choice. Suffered broken bone in foot against Detroit Lions, 1973. Fishing guide during off-season.

WARD, ROBERT R. Guard. B. Elizabeth, N.J. 5'10",189. Army paratrooper before enrolling at Maryland. All-America and outstanding player in Southern Conference, 1951. Played four years with Maryland varsity, 1948-51. As senior named Lineman of the Year by Washington Touchdown Club and Philadelphia Sportswriters Association. Majored in real estate and insurance, graduating in upper third of class. Joined Maryland coaching staff after graduation. Owns retail liquor business near Annapolis.

WARFIELD, PAUL D. End. B. 11/28/42, Warren, Ohio. 6', 188. Attended Warren Harding H.S. in Warren, starred in three sports. Turned down several lucrative bonus offers to play pro baseball. Played offensive and defensive back at Ohio State 1961-63. All-America, 1963. All-Big 10, 1962, 63. Played in East-West, All-America, Hula Bowl and College All-Star games. Cleveland Browns, 1964-69; Miami Dolphins, 1970-73. Was No. 1 draft choice of Browns. Scored 75 TDs in first 10 seasons as pro flanker. Compiled season highs of 1067 yds. and 12 TDs, 1968. Pro Bowl, 1965, 69, 70, 71, 72, 73, 74. One of premier NFL receivers. Also excellent blocker. NFL championship games, 1964, 65, 68, 69. Super Bowl, 1972, 73, 74. All-NFL, 1968. All-AFC, 1970, 71, 72, 73. Thru 1973 caught 344 passes for 7169 yds. Looking to broadcasting career.

WARMATH, MURRAY A. Coach. B. 12/26/11, Humboldt, Tenn. Tennessee end and tackle, 1932-34. Learned under single-wing perfectionist, Bob Neyland. Served two stints as Neyland's assistant, 1935-39; 45-49. Line coach at Mississippi State, 1939-42; Army, 1949-51. Head coach, Mississippi State, 1952-53; Minnesota, 1954-71. Suffered number of improprieties at hands of Minnesota fans during several lean years (1-8 in 1958, 2-7 in 1959). Garbage was thrown on lawn, bribes were offered to leave, children were threatened. Answered critics in 1960 with 8-1 season and Big 10 title. Repeated in 1961 and won subsequent Rose Bowl over UCLA, 21-3. Had lost earlier Rose Bowl to Washington, 17-7. Perfectionist, fine tutor. Utilized conservative brand of football, often punting on 3rd down and playing for field position. Minnesota record: 83-72-5; overall: 93-78-8. Developed All-Americas Tom Brown, Sandy Stephens, Bobby Bell, Carl Eller, Aaron Brown, Bob Stein. Coach of the Year, 1960.

WARNER, GLENN S. (Pop) Coach. B. 4/5/1871, Springville, N.Y. D. 9/7/54. Acquired "Pop" because he was older than most Cornell students during undergraduate days. School's heavyweight boxing champion, 1893. Football guard with no previous training, 1892-94. Won more games (313) than any other college coach except Amos Alonzo Stagg (314). Warner lost 106, tied 32 for .729 percentage. Coached Georgia, 1895-96; Cornell, 1897-98, 04-06; Carlisle, 1899-1903, 07-14; Pittsburgh, 1915-23; Stanford, 1924-32; Temple, 1933-38. He and Stagg are thought to be football's greatest innovators. Warner introduced single-, double-wingback formations, numbering of players, huddle, rolling body block, headgear, spiral punt, blocking dummy. His 1916 Pittsburgh team rates with all-time best. Took Stanford to three Rose Bowls, Temple to first Sugar Bowl. Developed 47 All-Americas, including backfield immortals Jim Thorpe (Carlisle) and Ernie Nevers (Stanford). In 1925 Rose Bowl used double-wingback formation first time exclusively, against Notre Dame. Three years later unveiled formation in East as Stanford blanked Army, 26-0, at Yankee Stadium. It was widely imitated in 1930s. Master of deceptive football, but never unsportsmanlike. He said, "You cannot play two kinds of football at once, dirty and good... There is no system of play that substitutes for knocking an opponent down. When you hit hard, hit hard... You play the way you practice. Practice the right way and you will react the right way in a game." Received $34 a week for first coaching job; left $500,000 estate. Citizens Savings Hall of Fame, National Football Foundation Hall of Fame.

WARNER, WILLIAM J. Guard. B. Springdale, N.Y. D. 2/12/44, Portland, Ore. 6'4", 210. Younger brother of Glenn S. (Pop) Warner. Cornell All-America, 1901; 2nd team, 1902. 1901 team, which he captained, was school's first to beat Penn. Unusually fast for big man. Coached Cornell for one season, 1903, and was then succeeded by Pop. Earned LL.B. degree. Later coached at North Carolina, Colgate, St. Louis U., Oregon and Sherman Indian School, Riverside, Calif. Became U.S. commissioner at Hermiston, Ore. National Football Foundation Hall of Fame.

WASHINGTON, EUGENE Wide Receiver. B. 1/25/44, LaPonte, Tex. 6'3", 208. Michigan State, 1964-66. All-America, 1966. Won three Big 10 hurdles championships, one NCAA title. Minnesota Vikings, 1967-72; Denver Broncos, 1973. No. 1 draft choice of Vikings. Broke in with bang, catching 13 passes for 384 yds., 29.5 average, 1967. Hit peak of 46 receptions in 1968. Gained 821 yds. receiving in 1969. Made 44 catches, 1970. Underwent surgery after both 1971, 72 seasons for old track injury. Made 10 receptions for Broncos in 1973, lowest output of career. In seven years caught 182 passes for 3237 yds. and 26 TDs. Pro Bowl, 1970, 71. NFL championship game, 1969. Super Bowl, 1970. Big, fast with good hands.

WASHINGTON, GENE A. End. B. 1/14/47, Long Beach, Calif. 6'2", 185. Attended Long Beach Poly H.S. and Stanford. QB and split end at Stanford. During senior year captained football and basketball teams, was student body president. San Francisco 49ers, 1969-73. Pro Bowl each of first four seasons. Led NFL in reception yds. (1100, 1970) and TDs (12, 1972). Considered one of game's premier pass catchers. All-NFC, 1970, 72.

WASHINGTON, KENNETH S. (Kenny) Running Back. B. 8/31/18. D. 6/27/71. 6'1", 195. Attended Lincoln H.S., Los Angeles. All-time UCLA rushing leader with 1914 yds., 1937-39. Accounted for 3182 yds. total offense, scored 19 TDs. Led UCLA to 6-0-4 season, becoming school's first All-America, 1939. Played in same backfield with Jackie Robinson. Washington and another UCLA teammate, Woody Strode, became first Blacks in NFL after World War II when they signed with Los Angeles Rams, 1946. Played with Rams, 1946-48. Was Los Angeles businessman, civic leader. Citizens Savings Hall of Fame, National Football Foundation Hall of Fame.

WASHINGTON, RUSSELL Tackle. B. 12/17/46, Kansas City, Mo. 6'6", 289. Missouri, 1965-67. All-Big 8 each year. All-America, 1967. Played offensive tackle, defensive end, fullback. Nicknamed "Mt. Washington." Picked No. 1 by San Diego Chargers in 1968, No. 4 player taken in entire draft. Chargers, 1968-73. Extremely mobile despite massive size. All-AFC, 1973. Pro Bowl, 1974. Named Charger MVP in '73. Outstanding pass blocker, can lead sweeps. Sings, interested in acting.

WATERFIELD, ROBERT S. (Rifle) Quarterback. B. 7/26/20, Elmira, N.Y. 6'1", 205. Moved to Van Nuys, Calif., at early age and attended Van Nuys H.S., then UCLA. MVP in East-West Shrine game, 1945. Played eight years with NFL Rams, 1945-52, first year in Cleveland, last seven in Los Angeles. Renowned for versatile skills, was NFL passing leader twice, FG champion thrice and PAT leader four times. As punter averaged 44.7 yds. in 1946, and twice recorded 88-yd. punts during career. In four title games completed 46 passes for 672 yds., including 312 yds. Played on two NFL championship teams, 1945, 52. Cleveland Browns in 1950. MVP, All-Pro and Rookie of the Year, 1945. All-Pro also in 1946. During early part of pro career developed "bomb", or long TD pass, which became one of football's most powerful weapons. Had outstanding receivers in Elroy (Crazylegs) Hirsch and Tom Fears. In eight seasons threw for 11,849 yds., 98 TDs. Ram head coach, 1960-62. Formerly married to actress Jane Russell. They met at Van Nuys H.S. Pro Football Hall of Fame. Sportswriter Vincent Y. Flaherty, Los Angeles *Examiner,* once wrote of Waterfield: "No other athlete ever embodied so many different football skills and qualities. Waterfield is the finest all-around football player of the generation, and perhaps of all time."

WAY, CHARLES A. Running Back. B. 12/29/1897, Howningtown, Pa. 5'7", 140. Attended Penn State. Graduated from Howningtown H.S. All-America, 1920. Canton Bulldogs, 1921; Frankford Yellowjackets, 1924; Philadelphia Quakers, 1926. Coached Haydon College, 1921; Allentown (Pa.) H.S., 1922-23; Virginia Tech, 1925. Retired after 27 years with Internal Revenue Service.

WEATHERALL, JAMES P. Tackle. B. 10/26/29, White Deer, Tex. 6'4", 230. Played at Oklahoma on three straight Big 7 championship teams, 1949-51. Successful on 76 of 94 extra point atttempts, 1950-51. Consensus All-America, 1950, 51. Oklahoma co-captain, 1951. Co-captain of North in Senior Bowl and West in East-West Shrine game, 1951. Outland Trophy winner, 1951. Philadelphia Eagles, 1955-57; Washington Redskins, 1958; Detroit Lions, 1959-60. Owns insurance agency in Oklahoma City.

WEBSTER, ALEX Running Back. B. 4/19/31, Kearney, N.J. 6'3", 235. Attended North Carolina State. Starred in Canada before joining New York Giants in 1955. Spent 10 years with Giants, 1955-64, helping to fuel their greatest prosperity. With Webster in lineup, New York played in six championship games. They won only once, however, as Chicago Bears were 47-7 victim in 1956. In that game Webster scored two TDs. Suffered from shoulder and leg ailments in 1961 and was almost cut in pre-season camp. Made remarkable comeback in 1962. That year gained 1241 yds. as rusher and receiver. Still holds New York career records for rushing attempts (1213), rushing yardage (4638), TDs rushing (39). Was bruising runner. Giant head coach, 1969-73. Record: 31-39. In 1970 season voted NFL Coach of the Year by UPI and Washington Touchdown Club — N.Y. finished 9-5. Announced resignation prior to last game of 1973; thus was lame-duck coach in finale against Minnesota Vikings. He said, "I felt the season was gone and it was time for a change."

WEBSTER, GEORGE Linebacker. B. 11/25/45, Anderson, S.C. 6'4", 220. Michigan State, 1964-66. Three-year letterman for Duffy Daugherty. Played defensive end as sophomore. Last two seasons was roverback, position which allowed him freedom to find the action. Consensus All-America twice, 1965, 66. 19-1-1 record covering junior and senior years. Daugherty termed Webster "the finest defensive back I've ever seen." Named outstanding player in both East-West Shrine and Hula Bowl games, 1966. State retired his jersey (No. 90). Played in 1966 Rose Bowl. Houston Oilers, 1967-71, and Pittsburgh Steelers, 1972-73. AFL Rookie of the Year. All-AFL three times, 1967, 68, 69. Traded to

Pittsburgh in 1972 for wide receiver Dave Smith. AFL All-Star games, 1968, 69. AFL championship game, 1967. Full-time linebacker in pros. Known as powerful, deadly tackler. Bothered by knee injuries in recent years. Named to All-Time AFL team.

WEDEMEYER, HERMAN C. Quarterback. B. Honolulu, Hawaii. 5'10", 173. Attended St. Louis H.S. of Honolulu and St. Mary's (Calif.). Unanimous All-America, 1945; All-America, 1946. Chosen All-America QB, though actually played halfback in old single wing. Was 4th in Heisman Trophy voting, 1945. Played four years under Jimmy Phelan, 1943, 45-47. Amassed 4061 total-offense yds. and accounted for 40 TDs. Led St. Mary's to 1946 Sugar Bowl and 1947 Oil Bowl. Lost them both, to Oklahoma State and Georgia Tech. Los Angeles Dons (AAFC), 1948; Baltimore Colts, 1949. Public relations work in travel industry, 1951-68. Later elected to Hawaii House of Representatives.

WEEKES, HAROLD H. Running Back. B. 4/2/1880, Oyster Bay, N.Y. D. 7/26/50, New York, N.Y. 5'10", 178. Columbia, 1899-1901. Ran 55 yds. for game's only TD as Columbia beat Yale first time in 26 years, 1899. All-America, 1901; 2nd team, 1900; 3rd team, 1899. Utilized "flying hurdle" play. In this maneuver Weekes, carrying football, was mounted on shoulders of two teammates and thrown across scrimmage line. When he landed, took off for daylight. Injured most of senior season but still scored six TDs against Fordham, returned kickoff 107 yds. vs. Hamilton. Strong, fleet runner. Stockbroker in New York City prior to death. Citizens Savings Hall of Fame, National Football Foundation Hall of Fame.

WEHRLI, ROGER R. Defensive Back. B. 11/26/47, New Point, Mo. 6', 190. Prep sprinter and hurdler at King City (Mo.) H.S. U. of Missouri, 1966-68. Consensus All-America as he led NCAA in punt returns with 11.7-yd. average, 1968. Intercepted 10 passes same season. No. 1 draft pick of St. Louis Cardinals in 1969. Played first three seasons for Cards as cornerback, then switched to free safety in 1973. Intercepted six passes, including two in 38-0 win over Dallas, en route to All-NFC honors, 1970. All-NFC again in 1971.

WEINMESITER, ARNOLD Tackle. B. 3/23/23, Rhein, Sask., Canada. 6'4", 250. Spent boyhood in Portland, matriculated at U. of Washington. Coach: Ralph (Pest) Welch. Collegiate career interrupted by service in army field artillery. Returned to school in 1946. Injured knee twice playing fullback and thought he would never play again. Bounced back, however, after surgery and played in 1948 College All-Star game. New York Yankees (AAFC), 1948-49; New York Giants, 1950-53. All-Pro defensive tackle each year with Giants. So fast he could outrun most backs, often matched in training squad races. His rumblings about pay and expenses demoralized '53 Giants. Concern for worker rights and wages took him into union work. Now vice president with International Brotherhood of Teamsters.

WEIR, ED S. Tackle. B. 3/14/03, Superior, Neb. 5'9", 181. Nebraska, 1923-25. Lived first 16 years of his life on farm near Superior, developing stamina by running four miles to and from school each day. Played on Nebraska teams that defeated Knute Rockne - coached Notre Dame elevens, 1923, 35. Rockne called Weir "the best tackle I have ever seen." Unanimous All-America, 1925; All-America, 1924. Lettered three years in football and track. Was exceptional hurdler; edged Olympic gold medalist Dan Kinsey in high hurdles at Kansas Relays, 1925. Frankford Yellowjackets, 1926-28. After pro career returned to Nebraska to coach. His track teams won 10 outdoor and indoor titles. Citizens Savings Hall of Fame, National Football Foundation Hall of Fame. Retired, lives in Lincoln.

WELLER, JOHN A. C. (Jac) Guard. B. 1/6/13, Atlanta, Ga. 6', 195. Played under Fritz Crisler at Princeton, 1933-35. Lost only once during 26-game career. That was to Yale, 7-0. Highlight of perfect 1935 season was 26-6 victory over Dartmouth, played before 50,000 fans in blizzard at Princeton's Palmer Field. Game became known as "Rape in the Snow." Line coach Tad Wieman said, "I have coached several All-America linemen. Weller is the best." Extremely accomplished post-football career. Author of numerous books and articles on history, military weapons and tactics. Is graduate and licensed engineer. Currently manages insurance company in Princeton, N.J. National Football Foundation Hall of Fame.

WELSH, GEORGE T. Quarterback. B. 8/26/33, Coaldale, Pa. 5'10", 164. Navy, 1953-55. All-America, 1954, 55. 3rd in Heisman Trophy voting, 1955. In career completed 172 passes in 313 attempts for 2335 yds., 20 TDs. Led Middies to 1955 Sugar Bowl victory, 21-0, over Mississippi. Major-college leader in completions (94), passing yds. (1319), and percentage (.627). On active duty with U.S. Navy, 1956-62. Assistant coach at Penn State, 1962-73. On 2/15/73 named Navy head coach.

WENDELL, PERCY L. (Bullet) Running Back. B. 7/16/1889, Roxbury, Mass. D. 3/13/32, Boston, Mass. 5'5", 174. Prepped at Roxbury Latin School where he lettered in four sports. 23-2-2 playing record at Harvard, 1910-12. Led Harvard to 9-0 season senior year, including 20-2 win over Yale. Coach George Trevor called him "concentrated dynamite." Built low to ground, was exceptionally strong and fast. Head coach at Boston U., Williams and Lehigh. Resigned from latter post after disagreement with faculty over support for college athletics. Fought long battle against danger of blindness, and eventually succumbed to pneumonia. Upon his passing Spalding's official *Football Guide* commented: "Percy Wendell was one of the Homeric heroes of American football. So deeply and distinctly are his exploits imprinted upon the sagas and chronicles of the sport, that his name for many years will come to stand for all that is best and brilliant in the game." Citizens Savings Hall of Fame, National Football Foundation Hall of Fame.

WEST, D. BELFORD (Belf) Tackle. B. 5/7/1896, Hamilton, N.Y. 6'2", 195. Grandson of Civil War general and founder of National Hamilton (N.Y.) Bank. Lettered in five sports at Colgate: football, basketball, baseball, tennis, hockey. Football All-America twice, 1916, 19. In West's 21 varsity games, Colgate held foes scoreless 14 times. Kicked 52-yd. field goal against rival Syracuse en route to 15-0 victory, 1916. Member Colgate class of '18, his graduation was deferred 1½ years due to overseas service with 307th Field Artillery. Canton Bulldogs, 1921. Received Alumni Award for Distinguished Service to Colgate, 1953. National Football Foundation Hall of Fame. Retired as partner of Smith-West Co. (machinery and industrial equipment) in Buffalo. Citizens Savings Hall of Fame, National Football Foundation Hall of Fame.

WEST, MELVIN G. Running Back. B. 1/14/39, Columbia, Mo. 5'11", 195. Grew up and attended high school in Jefferson City, Mo., where he was All-State, All-America fullback. U. of Missouri's top rusher three straight years, 1958-60. 3rd-leading ground gainer in Tiger history with 1993 yds. All-Big 8 for Missouri's only unbeaten and untied team (11-0, 1960). Tigers subdued Navy, 21-14, in '61 Orange Bowl. Boston Patriots, 1961, and New York Titans, 1961-62. Halfback in college, defensive back in pros. Owns master's degree from Missouri. Now junior high school principal in Minneapolis.

WEYAND, ALEXANDER M. (Babe) Tackle. B. 1/10/1892, Jersey City, N.J. 6'2", 198. Army, 1913-15. All-America 2nd team, 1913; 3rd team, 1914, 15. Captained Army eleven, 1915. West Point's heavyweight wrestling champion three years, member of U.S. Olympic wrestling team in 1920. Launched military career on Mexican Border Patrol. Served in both world wars, receiving numerous decorations including Silver Star, Purple Heart, Bronze Star and Army Commendation with Oak Leaf Cluster. Retired as colonel, 1946. Devoted much of life to historical study of amateur sports. Authored *The Saga of American Football, The Olympic Pageant, The Cavalcade of Basketball* and *Football Immortals.* "Babe" was given to him by Army teammate Dwight D. Eisenhower. Resident of Cornwall-on-Hudson, N.Y., 10 miles from West Point. National Football Foundation Hall of Fame.

WHARTON, CHARLES M. (Buck) Guard B. 1868, Magnolia, Del. D. 11/15/49, Dover, Del. 6'3", 210. Won 52 of 56 games at Pennsylvania under George Woodruff, 1893-96. All-America, 1895, 96; 2nd team, 1894. Captain senior year. Earned nickname "Buck" from ability at cracking line. Took D.D.S. and M.D. degrees from Penn. Organized with Walter Camp physical training program for navy and air service during World War I. Delaware state senator, 1914-17. Unsuccessful Democratic candidate in Delaware gubernatorial race, 1928. Associated with Penn athletic and physical education departments for 30 years. National Football Foundation Hall of Fame.

WHEELER, ARTHUR L. (Beef) Guard. B. 5/12/1872, Philadelphia, Pa. D. 12/20/17. 6'1", 200. Second Princeton player to win 1st-team All-America honors thrice, 1892, 93, 94. Other was Phil King, two-year teammate of Wheeler. In junior year Orange and Black defeated outstanding Harvard and Yale teams, both 6-0, and won 11 straight games. Yale's defeat was only loss in four-year career of Frank Hinkey. National Football Foundation Hall of Fame.

WHEELER, WAYNE (Grayhound) End. B. 3/28/50, Orlando, Fla. 6'1½", 185. All-State at W. R. Boone H.S. in Orlando. Caught 13 passes in 4th quarter of one game. Also played basketball and ran track as schoolboy. U. of Alabama, 1971-73. All-SEC, 1972, averaging 19.1 yds. per catch on 30 receptions. Twice winner at Alabama of Ray Perkins Most Improved Receiver Award for spring drills excellence. Averaged 27.9 yds. per catch in 1973, received All-America recognition. In Alabama career caught 55 passes for 1246 yds. "As good a receiver as we've had here," claimed coach Bear Bryant. Orange Bowl, 1972; Cotton Bowl, 1973; Sugar Bowl, 1974.

WHITE, BYRON R. (Whizzer) Running Back. B. 6/8/17, Ft. Collins, Colo. 6'1", 185. Attended Wellington (Colo.) H.S. and U. of Colorado. Consensus All-America, 1937, as he led nation in scoring (119 points on 16 TDs, 23 PATs) and rushing (1121 yds. on 181 carries). Also completed 22 of 44 passes for 314 yds. and returned 36 punts for 731 yds., playing 60 minutes almost every game of season. Longest gainer of career was 102-yd. kickoff return against Denver, 1936. All-Conference in three sports: baseball, basketball and football. Scored TD on interception return and threw TD pass in 28-14 losing effort against Rice in Cotton Bowl, 1938. Graduated *Phi Beta Kappa* from Colorado. Received Rhodes Scholarship to Oxford. Played with Pittsburgh Steelers, 1939-40. First player in NFL to receive five-figure salary ($15,000). Rushing leader and All-Pro, 1940. Served in Naval Air Combat Intelligence during World War II. Graduated from Yale Law School with honors. Citizens Savings Hall of Fame, National Football Foundation Hall of Fame. White is United States Supreme Court Justice, appointed by President John Kennedy.

WHITE, DARYL Guard. B. East Orange, N.J. 6'4", 247. Nebraska, 1971-73. Recruited out of New Jersey with Rich Glover. They played together two years at Nebraska. All-State first baseman in high school, scouted heavily by Baltimore Orioles and Pittsburgh Pirates. Redshirted in 1970. Consensus All-America, 1973; All-America, 1972. Played in 1972 Orange Bowl, '73 Orange Bowl, '74 Cotton Bowl. Won them all. Cornhuskers were national champions in 1971. Outstanding pass blocker. Ran 40-yd. dash in 4.9.

WHITE, EDWARD A. Guard. B. 4/4/47, LaMesa, Calif. 6'2", 268. California defensive lineman. Twice winner of school's Brick Muller Award. Consensus All-America, 1968. Won two track letters. Honor student in landscape architecture. Minnesota Vikings, 1969-73. Made switch to offense. Became starter in 1971. Extremely strong. NFL championship game, 1969. Super Bowl, 1970, 74. Hobbies are painting, sculpting and arm-wrestling.

WHITE, HAROLD A. (Babe) Guard. B. 1894. D. 5/4/73, Thomasville, Ga. 6'6", 265. Syracuse All-America, 1915. Also starred in track, specializing in shotput and discus events. Played pro football for Akron Pros, 1919, after serving as intelligence officer in World War I. Was accomplished big-game hunter and explorer. Represented Emperor Haile Selassie at old League of Nations in Geneva.

WHITE, JAN Tight End. B. 10/6/48, Harrisburg, Pa. 6'2", 212. State hurdles champion at John Harris H.S. in Harrisburg. Lost only two games at Ohio State, 1968-70. Teamed with Rex Kern, Jim Stillwagon and Jack Tatum, leading Buckeyes to two Rose Bowls, 1969, 71. Extremely fast for tight end. Clocked in 4.4 for 40-yd. dash. 2nd-round draft choice of Buffalo Bills. Caught 25 passes in two years with team, 1971-72. Walked out of Buffalo training camp, 1973, citing no incentive to play football and said he would work with youth programs.

WHITE, L. ROBERT (Bob) Running Back. B. 8/22/38, Portsmouth, Ohio. 6'2", 212. Ohio State, 1957-59. 17-7-3 playing record. Rushed for 93 yds. in 10-7 victory over Oregon in '58 Rose Bowl. Consensus and Academic All-America, 1958. Punted 25 times his junior year for 40.7-yd. average. Played in East-West Shrine game, 1960. Houston Oilers, 1960. Director of admissions and registrar at Cedarville College in Ohio.

WHITE, SANFORD B. (Sam) End. B. 5/4/1888, Fall River, Mass. D. 4/21/64, Chicago, Ill. 6'1", 180. Graduate of Princeton. All-America for 8-0-2 national championship team, 1911. Tied by Navy (0-0), Lehigh (6-6). Scored winning points against both Harvard and Yale. Vs. Harvard scooped up loose ball after blocked dropkick and ran 85 yards for TD. Later dropped Harvard back for safety. Princeton won, 8-6. Seized another loose ball vs. Yale and on muddy field lumbered 60 yds. to score; Princeton prevailed, 6-3. Coached by Bill Roper. Was Princeton baseball captain. Business career culminated as secretary of International Harvester Co., Chicago.

WHITE, SHERMAN E. Defensive End. B. 10/6/49, Manchester, N.H. 6'5", 255. Played just two games of organized football before entering U. of California. Attended Portsmouth (N.H.) H.S. School and Laney (Calif.) J.C. where he concentrated on baseball. All-Pacific 8, 1970, 71. Consensus All-America at defensive tackle, 1971. Played in East-West Shrine and College All-Star games. Ran 40-yd. dash in 4.8. 1st-round draft choice of Cincinnati Bengals in 1972. Won starting job as rookie at defensive end.

WHITE, WILFORD (Whizzer) Running Back. B. Mesa, Ariz. 5'9", 161. Arizona State, 1947-50. All-round performer. Played offense and defense, punted, returned kicks, caught and threw passes. Rushed for 3173 yds. in four years. Senior year compiled 1502 yds. rushing and 7.5 average, leading nation in both departments. Arizona State lost 1951 Salad Bowl, 34-21, to Miami (Ohio) despite White heroics. Rushed for 106 yds., caught 4 passes, completed 1 pass, returned 3 kickoffs, punted for 33.2 average, scored 1 TD. Also played in 1950 Salad Bowl. Sun Devils retired No. 33 jersey. Chicago Bears, 1951. Son, Danny, maintained family tradition by starring for Sun Devils in 1971-73.

WHITMIRE, DONALD B. Tackle. B. 7/1/22, Giles County, Tenn. 5'11", 215. Played two years at Alabama, 1941-42, and Navy, 1943-44. Winner in two bowl games with 'Bama: 29-21 over Texas A. & M. (Cotton, 1942) and 37-21 over Boston College (Orange, 1943). Both bowls subsequently named him all-time tackle for their events. Unanimous All-America, 1944; Consensus, 1943. Received Knute Rockne Trophy, 1944. Citizens Savings Hall of Fame, National Football Hall of Fame. Rear Adm. in U.S. Navy; resides in Annandale, Va.

WHITTENTON, URSHELL (Jesse) Defensive Back. B. 5/9/34, Big Spring, Tex., 6', 182. Attended Texas Western, now Texas (El Paso). Los Angeles Rams, 1956-57; Green Bay Packers, 1958-64. Had speed to run with any receiver or halfback in league. Great student of opponents, kept complete "book" on all veterans. Stole ball from Alex Webster (New York Giants) to set up winning TD as Packers clinched 1961 Western Conference title. "The trouble with this job," he once said, "is that it's all out in the open where everyone can see it. You make one mistake and they complete a pass for a TD and millions watch you running behind the other guy, looking like a fool." Considered Pete Retzlaff (Philadelphia Eagles) toughest to cover. All-Pro defensive halfback, 1961. Packers were NFL champions twice with Whittenton in lineup, 1961, 62. Became Green Bay restaurateur during playing career. Later became golf pro in Texas.

WICKHORST, FRANK H. Tackle. B. 3/18/06, Aurora, Ill. 6', 218. Played freshman year at Illinois with Harold (Red) Grange, 1923. Then transferred to Navy to great dissatisfaction of Illinois coach Bob Zuppke who realized Wickhorst's potential. Navy, 1924-26. Captain and All-America of Navy's unbeaten '26 team—tied only by Army (21-21) in William (Navy Bill) Ingram's first season as head coach. Known for speed and power around line of scrimmage. Assistant coach 15 years at Iowa and California. National Football Foundation Hall of Fame. Retired as Director of Civic Affairs for Kaiser Industries Corp., Oakland, Calif.

WIEMAN, E. E. (Tad) Coach. B. 1896, Orosi, Calif. *Phi Beta Kappa* at Michigan. Assistant coach, Michigan, 1921-26; Minnesota; 1930-31; Princeton, 1932-37. Head coach, Michigan, 1927-28; Princeton, 1938-42. 1927 Michigan team, featuring Bennie Oosterbaan, outscored eight opponents 137-39. At Princeton defeated Yale four out of five years. 29-24-4 overall record. Recognized as great organizer, line play tutor. Was president of American Football Coaches Association. National Football Foundation Hall of Fame.

WIGGIN, PAUL Defensive End. B. 11/8/34, Modesto, Calif. 6'3", 245. Scholastic rugby and shot-put star. Attended Modesto J.C. before transferring to Stanford in 1953. In 1955 enjoyed one of best games against Ohio State and its

All-America, Hopalong Cassady. Buckeyes' 11-game winning streak was ended (6-0), Cassady was held to 37 yds., 11 carries. Played tackle at Stanford. Defensive end for Cleveland Browns, 1957-67. Browns won NFL title, 1964. Pro Bowl, 1966, 68. Always in shape, strong, resourceful.

WILCE, JOHN W. Coach. B. 5/12/1888, Rochester, N.Y. D. 5/17/63. Wisconsin fullback. Spent entire coaching career at Ohio State, 1913-28. 78-33-9 record. Coached immortal running back, Charles (Chic) Harley. Also tutored All-America Gaylord Stinchcomb and Wes Fesler. Produced school's first unbeaten, untied season in 1916—not repeated for 28 years. Won three Western Conference (Big 10) titles, 1916, 17, 20. In resignation statement complained, "They're taking the game away from the boys." Victim of California, 28-0, in 1921 Rose Bowl. Citizens Savings Hall of Fame, National Football Foundation Hall of Fame.

WILCOX, DAVID Linebacker. B. 9/29/42, Ontario, Ore. 6'2", 239. Attended Boise J.C. and U. of Oregon. San Francisco 49ers, 1964-73. Was 3rd-round draft choice. "I wait until he (rusher) stops screwing around," philosophized Wilcox on tackling. Utilizes long arms to snare runners. In 10 seasons intercepted 13 passes for 128 yds. Yet to score TD. Pro Bowl, 1967, 69, 70, 72, 73, 74. Tremendous hitter. All-NFC, 1971, 72, 73. Outside linebacker. Known as "Intimidator."

WILDUNG, RICHARD K. Tackle. B. 1921, St. Paul, Minn. 6', 215. Prepped at Laverne (Minn). H.S. U. of Minnesota, 1940-42. Consensus All-America twice, 1941, 42. Was three-year starter. Played under Bernie Bierman. Gophers were national champions in 1940, 41. Navy Lt. in World War II. Green Bay Packers, 1946-53. Citizens Savings Hall of Fame, National Football Foundation Hall of Fame.

WILKIN, WILBUR (Wee Willie) Tackle. D. 5/16/73, Palo Alto, Calif. 6'6", 280. Attended St. Mary's (Calif.). Considered one of great tackles in NFL history. Played with Washington Redskins, 1938-43, and Chicago Rockets (AAFC), 1946. Saw Marine Corps duty in World War II. Chosen game's best lineman despite Washington's 73-0 loss to Chicago Bears in 1940 title match. Night-life lover who spent money faster than he earned it. Often in debt to Washington owner George P. Marshall. Victim of tragedy and illness. His 21-year-old twin sons, John and Christopher, were killed in car accident in 1965; Willie was stricken with stomach cancer in 1971. Taught math and social studies to retarded children for several years in Deer Lodge, Mont.

WILKINSON, CHARLES B. (Bud) Coach. B. 4/23/16, Minneapolis, Minn. Graduate of Shattuck Military Academy, Faribault, Minn. Minnesota quarterback and guard under Bernie Bierman, 1934-36. Also played varsity hockey. Coached Oklahoma, 1947-63. Compiled 145-29-4 record for .826 percentage. Known for outstanding ground attack teams. Popularized many split-T innovations. Three of Wilkinson's Oklahoma clubs won national championships, three won national scoring titles. Produced four backs who scored more than 100 points in one season: George Thomas, Billy Vessels, Clendon Thomas, Tommy McDonald. Sooners scored in 123 straight games, 1946-57; compiled win streaks of 31 and 47 games. NCAA Coach of the Year, 1949. Had 6-2 bowl record, winning four times in Orange Bowl. Developed fierce pride and desire in players. Headed Physical Fitness Program for President John Kennedy. Also served in executive post for President Richard Nixon. Lost U.S. senatorial race in Oklahoma, 1964. Citizens Savings Hall of Fame, National Football Foundation Hall of Fame. Coordinates activities, which include announcing NCAA Game of the Week for ABC, thru Bud Wilkinson Associates in Oklahoma City.

WILLARD, KENNETH H. Running Back. B. 7/14/43, Richmond, Va. 6'1", 219. Won 16 letters at Varina (Va.) H.S. Turned down pro baseball offer from Ted Williams, representing Boston Red Sox, for $100,000. Gained 2023 yds. rushing for U. of North Carolina, 1962-64. MVP in Gator Bowl (beat Air Force, 35-0) and Coaches All-America game (rushed for 133 yds.). San Francisco 49ers, 1965-73. Was 1st-round draft choice. Best season, 1971, rushed for 855 yds., caught passes for 202 more. Four Pro Bowls, 1966, 67, 69, 70. Big, strong fullback. In nine seasons accumulated 5930 yds. rushing on 1582 carries, added 2156 yds. on 273 pass receptions. Scored 61 TDs. Grew bitter over lack of playing time with 49ers. Asked to be traded before 1973 season but wish not granted until 5/74. Was sent to St. Louis Cardinals.

WILLIAMS, CLARENCE (Clancy) Defensive Back. B. 9/24/42, Renton, Wash. 6'2", 194. Washington State running back and defensive back. Also 9.6 sprinter. Gained 783 yds with 5.3 average as junior, 1963. All-America cornerback, 1964. Played in East-West, Hula Bowl and College All-Star games. Los Angeles Rams, 1965-72, and Washington Redskins, 1973. Rams' 2nd-leading career thief with 28 interceptions.

WILLIAMS, HENRY L. (Doc) Coach. B. 7/26/1869, Hartford, Conn. D. 6/14/31, Minneapolis, Minn. Yale, 1888-91. Football halfback and track hurdler. Set world 120-yd. high-hurdle record with 15.8 clocking, 1891. Same meet set intercollegiate mark of 21.2 in 220-yd. low hurdles. Editor of Yale *Daily News* in junior and senior years. First Army coach to beat Navy, 1891. Graduate of Pennsylvania Medical School. Compiled 143-14-12 record at Minnesota, 1900-21. Five squads went undefeated. Known as outstanding innovator, originated Minnesota shift and tackle-back formation (at William Penn Charter School). His .788 percentage is still 10th best in college football history. Citizens Savings Hall of Fame, National Football Hall of Fame.

WILLIAMS, JAMES (Froggy) End. B. 3/18/28, Waco, Tex. 6', 197. Attended Waco H.S. and Rice. 28-10-2 Rice playing record, 1946-49. Consensus All-America, 1949. Played in 1947 Orange Bowl (beat Tennessee, 8-0); 1950 Cotton Bowl (beat North Carolina, 27-13). Scored one TD and kicked three PATs in

Cotton Bowl. During career scored 13 TDs and kicked 75 PATs for 156 points. "He was as good an end as I ever coached," claimed Rice coach Jess Neely. "Jim was strong, fast, competitive, a real leader and a fine student." National Football Foundation Hall of Fame. Marketing manager for The Western Co., Fort Worth.

WILLIAMS, ROBERT (Bobby) Quarterback. B. 1/2/30, Cumberland, Md. 6'1", 185. Older brother, Hal, introduced Bobby to Notre Dame coach Elmer Layden in 1937. Predicted kid brother would someday play QB for Irish. He was right. Learned under Frank Leahy, 1948-50. Consensus All-America, 1949. Played greatest game that year vs. Michigan State. Completed 13 of 16 passes (Notre Dame record .813 percent) for 2 TDs, ran 6 times for 49 yds. on "bootleg," averaged 42 yds. on 3 punts, made many tackles in 34-21 victory that preserved Irish four-year winning streak. Finally lost, 28-14, to Purdue in 1950. Chicago Bears, 1951, 52, 54. In advertising business. Hal became newspaper editor, foreign correspondent.

WILLIAMS, SAMUEL F. End. B. 3/9/31, Dansville, Mich. 6'5", 225. Played four sports at Dansville H.S. Enrolled at Michigan State in 1949 but stayed only six weeks, leaving for full-time work and subsequent naval service. Played three years for Pensacola (Fla.) Naval Air Station, 1952-54. Passed up offer from Los Angeles Rams to enroll for second time at Michigan State in 1955. Developed into consensus All-America, 1958. Two-way player. Won E. Jack Spaulding Trophy, 1958.

WILLIAMS, TRAVIS Running Back. B. 1/14/46, El Dorado, Ark. 6'1", 210. Briefly, one of pro football's most dangerous runners. Born in Arkansas but moved to Sacramento, Calif., during infancy. Attended Contra Costa J.C., San Pueblo, Calif. Then Arizona State, 1965-66. Ran 100-yd. dash in 9.3. Instant sensation as rookie with Green Bay Packers, 1967. Set NFL records for kickoff-return average (41.1 yds) and TDs (4). Included was fabulous 104-yd. kickoff return TD vs. Rams. In 1969 won Wisconsin Pro Football Writers MVP award. Traded to Los Angeles Rams, 1971, and signed by San Diego Chargers as free agent in 1973. 105-yd kickoff return vs. New Orleans Saints tied NFL record for career kickoff return TDs (6). Early comparisons to such pro greats as Gale Sayers and Jim Brown never realized. After 1969 just another NFL halfback and kickoff-return specialist, though occasionally brilliant with Rams.

WILLIAMSON, FRED R. (Hammer) Defensive Back. B. Gary, Ind. 6'3", 215. Fred Williamson — extravagant, loud-mouthed, arrogant — wasn't popular player. Yet outlasted many detractors; obviously had some talent. His father went to Harvard and became civil engineer, brother attended Yale prior to law career. Fred studied architecture at Northwestern. Enjoyed life of dandy. Smoked pipe, wore ascots and drove white Cadillac convertible. Played flanker for football Wildcats, then signed with Pittsburgh Steelers in 1960. After one year with Steelers joined Oakland Raiders. Spent remainder of pro career with

Oakland, 1961-64, and Kansas City Chiefs, 1965-68. Considered fine tight end prospect early in pro career but became full-fledged defensive back with Raiders. Ideally suited to cornerback. Possessed speed, size, intelligence. Invented the "Hammer," right forearm chop with whole arm very stiff. It was deadly, controversial weapon. Broke Howard Twilley's cheekbone, Frank Jackson's nose, and gave several others concussions. All-AFL, 1962, 63, 64, 65. Now prospering in movie career.

WILLIAMSON, IVAN B. (Ivy) Coach. B. 2/4/11, Wayne, Ohio. D. 2/19/69, Madison, Wis. Attended Bowling Green (Ohio) H.S. U. of Michigan end, 1930-32. All-Conference three years. Captain senior year on national championship team. Michigan coach Harry Kipke said of him: "Ivan Williamson is the smartest player I have ever had or hope to have." Yale assistant, 1934-41, 45-46; head coach at Lafayette, 1947-48, and Wisconsin, 1949-55. 54-24-4 coaching record. Shared Big 10 title with Purdue, 1952. Lost 7-0 to USC in Rose Bowl, 1953. Tutored Alan Ameche, Wisconsin All-America and Heisman Trophy winner. Wisconsin athletic director 14 years, 1955-68.

WILLINGHAM, LARRY L. Defensive Back. B. 12/22/48, Birmingham, Ala. 6', 180. Auburn, 1968-70. Played on three bowl teams (Sun, Astro-Bluebonnet, Gator). 22-8 playing record. Twice All-SEC, 1969, 70. Consensus All-America, 1970. Intercepted 11 career passes, returning 2 for TDs. Went 70 yds. for score with first collegiate punt he ever returned. St. Louis Cardinals, 1971-73. Spot starter at safety, key reserve with Cards. Still lives in Birmingham.

WILLIS, FREDERICK F., III Running Back. B. 12/9/47, Natick, Mass. 6', 212. Prepped at Kimball Union Academy, Meriden, Mass. Subsequently captained Boston College football and hockey teams. Rushed for 2115 yds. and scored 30 TDs in B.C. career, 1968-70. 19-9 playing record. Won All-New England and All-East honors. Cincinnati Bengals, 1971, and Houston Oilers, 1972-73. Leading Cincinnati rusher with 590 yds., scoring 7 TDs. Traded to Oilers after six games of '72 season. Caught 45 passes, 1972. Led AFC in receiving with 57 catches, 1973.

WILLIS, WILLIAM Guard. B. Columbus, Ohio. 6'4", 205. First Black signed to play pro football after World War II, with AAFC Cleveland Browns, 1946. Marion Motley was second when Browns signed him soon afterwards. Willis and Motley thereby ushered integration into modern-day pro football. Began celebrated career at East H.S. in Columbus. Then on to Ohio State where he played tackle for Paul Brown, 1942-43, and Carroll Widdoes, 1944. Latter wartime team, composed of freshmen, deferred students and 4-Fs, was unbeaten and untied (9-0-0). It finished No. 2 in national rankings to Army. Willis received 1944 All-America recognition along wtih teammates Les Horvath, Jack Dugger, Bill Hackett. Converted to guard with Browns and played eight years, 1946-53. Won All-AAFC and/or All-NFL honors seven times. Was simply overwhelming on line play. Extremely powerful, fast, quick. "Speed was my greatest asset," he claims and anyone who saw him roaming in foe's backfield would probably agree. Citizens Savings Hall of Fame, National Football Foundation Hall of Fame. Has devoted much of life working with troubled youngsters. Now deputy director of Ohio State Youth Commission in Columbus.

WILSON, HARRY E. (Lighthorse Harry) Running Back. B. 8/6/02, Mingo Junction, Ohio. 170. Called "Lighthorse" after Revolutionary War cavalry general, Henry (Light-Horse) Lee. Was tremendously elusive, possessed unusual balance. Attended Sharon (Pa.) H.S., Penn State and Army. Played at Penn State under Hugo Bezdek, 1921-23. Then transferred to Army, playing four more years. Most productive seasons were spent with Nittany Lions. In 1923 scored three TDs against both Navy and Penn. Navy scores were 95-yd. kickoff return, 80-yd. run and 55-yd. interception return. Against Penn tallied on runs of 49, 45 and 25 yds. Lost only once in seven games with Navy. 2nd-team All-America, 1923, 26. Also basketball All-America and lacrosse star. Citizens Savings Hall of Fame, National Football Foundation Hall of Fame. Retired Col., USAF.

WILSON, JERRELL D. Running Back-Kicker. B. 10/4/41, New Orleans, La. 6'4", 222. Southern Mississippi center and linebacker. Kansas City Chiefs, 1963-73. In brief running back career rushed 21 times for 53 yds. AFL's leading punter, 1965, 68. NFL's leading punter with 44.8-yd. average, 1972; again in '73 with 45.5 average. Powerful and consistent kicker. Averaged 44.4 yds. on 728 career punts. Owns career best of 72 yds. Best average, 45.1, 1968. Pro Bowl, 1971, 72, 73. Named to All-Time AFL team by Pro Football Hall of Fame. Enjoys fishing, hunting, golf and playing guitar. AFL championship games, 1966, 69. Super Bowl, 1967, 70. Owns Super Bowl punting record with 61-yarder, 1967. Puts every ounce of energy into every kick. Unorthodox style, both feet leaving ground when ball is delivered.

WILSON, KIRK Defensive Back-Kicker. B. 8/4/36, Venice, Calif. 6'2", 205. UCLA, 1956-58. "It was the first play of my college career—and I thought it would be my last," recalls Wilson about his three-yard punt in UCLA's 1956 season opener. He recovered to average 49.3-yds. per punt that year, all-time major college mark. Suffered knee injury senior season but still finished career with 45.2 average, another major college standard. His form was far from classic. Held hands underneath ball, used one hand and low leg kick. Most successful kickers hold ball on both sides, use two hands and high leg kick. Recreation superintendent in West Covina, Calif.

WILSON, LAWRENCE F. (Larry) Defensive Back. B. 3/24/38, Rigby, Idaho. 6', 190. Utah running back. Switched to free safety when he joined St. Louis Cardinals in 1960. Played 13 seasons with Cards, 1960-72. Intercepted 52 passes during pro career, for 800 yds., 5 TDs. Stole three passes, including one for 96 yds. and TD against Cleveland, 1965. Led NFL in interceptions (10), 1966, and tied league mark with thefts in seven straight games. Holds 10 St. Louis records. Famous for safety blitz—devised by late Cardinal assistant coach Chuck Drulis.

Wore No. 8. Played in eight Pro Boels. All-NFL, 1963, 66, 67, 68, 69. All-NFC, 1970. Fearless competitor. Now scouting for Cardinals. Named to All-Pro Squad of the 1960s.

WILSON, ROBERT E. (Bobby) Running Back. B. Corsicana, Tex. 5'10", 148. Southern Methodist, 1933-35. Called "Mighty Midget of Corsicana." Tailback in SMU's single-wing formation. Poor punter and passer, yet tremendously effective. Great on buck lateral, as runner and pass receiver. Scored winning TD on pass from Bob Finley in 20-14 verdict over TCU, 1935. Billed as "Game of the Year," teams entered 10-0 and matched two notable coaches—Dutch Meyer (TCU), Matty Bell (SMU). Win sent SMU to Rose Bowl where they lost to Stanford, 7-0. Consensus All-America, 1935. Resident of Anchorage, Alaska. Employed 35 years by Sun Oil Co. National Football Foundation Hall of Fame.

WINSTON, ROY C. (Moonie) Linebacker. B. 7/15/40, Baton Rouge, La. 5'11", 224. Attended Istrouma H.S., Baton Rouge, and Louisana State. Unanimous All-America and SEC Lineman of the Year, 1961. Also played baseball at LSU. Has spent entire pro career with Minnesota Vikings, 1962-73. Was 4th-round draft choice. Shares Viking record with three interceptions in one game. Played in Super Bowl IV against Kansas City Chiefs, 1970; Super Bowl VIII vs. Miami Dolphins, 1974. Likes to hunt and fish.

WISTER, L. CASPAR End. B. 2/4/1888, Germantown, Pa. D. 10/1/68. 6', 175. Princeton All-America, 1906; 3rd team, 1907. Excellent baseball player, too. Teammate of All-Americas James Cooney, Edward Dillon, Edward Harlan, James McCormick. Infantry Capt. with AEF in France, 1918-19. Engaged both as investment banker and broker until retirement.

WISTERT, ALBERT A. (Ox) Tackle. B. 12/18/20, Chicago, Ill. 6'2", 215. Played no prep football— Chicago's Foreman H.S. didn't field team. Left tackle for Michigan and Fritz Crisler, 1940-42. Second of three Wistert brothers to make consensus All-America, 1942. Whitey made it in 1933, Alvin in 1949. Co-captain of 1943 College All-Star team that bumped Washington Redskins, 27-7. Philadelphia Eagles, 1943-51. All-Pro five straight years, 1944-48. Eagle captain, 1946-50. Played on two NFL championship teams, 1948, 49. Wistert and Philadelphia coach Greasy Neale were mutual admiration society. Citizens Savings Hall of Fame, National Football Foundation Hall of Fame. Active in many church, civic and Michigan alumni affairs. Affiliated with Bankers Life Nebraska. In 1951 was company's "Leading Salesman;" in 1967 qualified for "Wall of Fame."

WISTERT, FRANCIS M. (Whitey) Tackle. B. 2/20/12, Chicago, Ill. 6'3", 212. A.B. degree Michigan, LLB. Michigan Law School. Oldest of three brothers to make consensus All-America, 1933; first of two to make National Football Foundation Hall of Fame. Also three-year baseball letterman. Conference's baseball MVP, 1934. Played in Cincinnati Reds organization, 1934-36. Assistant football coach Michigan, 1934-39. Achieved rank of senior lieutenant in Navy during World War II. Practiced law 11 years in New York City. Author of *Fringe Benefits*. Citizens Savings Hall of Fame. Vice president and director of industrial relations, Eltra Corporation, Toledo, Ohio.

WITHAM, MYRON E. Quarterback. B. 10/29/1880, Pigeon Cove, Mass. D. 3/8/73, Burlington, Vt. 173. One of famed Dartmouth ball carriers who inspired school fight song, *When the Backs Go Tearing By*. 2nd-team All-America, 1903. Season was highlighted by Dartmouth's 10-0 victory vs. Harvard. It came on day that Crimson christened new football stadium on banks of Charles River. Indians savored victory for years. Witham recalled: "That win is firmly embedded in Harvard history. One of the consulting engineers for the stadium was a Dartmouth man. The stadium, one of the first of its kind in the country, wasn't quite finished for the game. So afterwards, the final score was scraped into the wet cement high up in the stand." Coached Purdue, 1906; Colorado, 1920-31. Record: 63-31-7. While at Colorado taught engineering. Assistant professor of mathematics at Vermont, 1933-46. Ninety-two when he died.

WITTUM, THOMAS H. Kicker. B. 1/11/50, Berwyn, Ill. 6'1", 185. Graduate of Northern Illinois. Signed as free agent with San Francisco 49ers, 1972. Spent that year on taxi squad. In 1973 led NFC punters with 43.7-yd. average, on 79 punts for 3455 yds. Longest was 62 yds. Pro Bowl, 1974.

WOJCIECHOWICZ, ALEXANDER (Wojie) Center. B. 8/12/15, South River, N.J. 6', 235. Fordham, 1935-37. Center for Fordham's famous "Seven Blocks of Granite." Two-time consensus All-America, 1936, 37. 18-2-5 playing record — Fordham opponents scored only 90 points in those 25 games. Three scoreless ties were registered against Pitt; Wojie credited with stopping long Panther drives in each game. 1937 Blocks allowed no touchdowns and only 16 points entire season. Played alongside Vince Lombardi (guard). Detroit Lions, 1938-45; Philadelphia Eagles, 1946-50. Drafted on 1st round by Lions. Sixty-minute performer in both college and pros. Devastating blocker, tackler. Once described as "one thousand elbows put together without a plan." Citizens Savings Hall of Fame, National Football Foundation Hall of Fame, Pro Hall of Fame. Named to All-Pro Squad of the 1940s. Affiliated with State of New Jersey Real Estate Department.

WOOD, WILLIAM B. (Barry) Quarterback. B. 5/4/10, Milton, Mass. D. 3/9/71. 6'1", 173. Harvard All-America and captain, 1931. Also played baseball and hockey. Selected to U.S. Davis Cup team, 1932. Professor and bacteriologist at Johns Hopkins prior to death.

WOOD, WILLIAM V. (Willie) Defensive Back. B. 12/23/36, Washington, D.C. 5'10", 190. Attended Armstrong H.S., Washington, D.C., Coalinga (Calif.) J.C., and Southern California. Quarterback at USC. Following college wrote to Green Bay Packers for tryout, then signed as free agent. Became one of pro football's most feared defensive backs. Intercepted 48 passes as free safety during

12-year career with Packers, 1960-71. Also returned punts, totaling 187 for 1391 yds. Led NFL in returns with 16.1-yd. average, 1961. Owns three Super Bowl punt-return records. Played in eight Pro Bowls, six NFL championship games and two Super Bowls. All-NFL, 1964, 65, 66, 67, 68. All-NFC, 1970. Defensive back coach of San Diego Chargers, 1972-73.

WOODRUFF, GEORGE C. Coach. B. 11/29/1889, Columbus, Ga. From prominent Columbus family. Captain and star quarterback for Georgia Bulldogs, 1911. Older brother, Harry, also played for Georgia. Jim, another brother for whom Woodruff Dam is named, played at Auburn. In 1923, George became head coach of his alma mater. Being wealthy businessman and not planning to make career of coaching, he charged only one dollar per year for services. Coached thru 1927. Compiled 30-16-1 record. "Dream and Wonder Team" of 1927 lost only to Georgia Tech in 10 games. That defeat, in final game of season, knocked Georgia from Rose Bowl contention. Introduced Notre Dame formation to South and brought in two Knute Rockne disciples, Harry Mehre and Frank Thomas, as assistant coaches. Both Mehre and Thomas became successful head coaches.

WOODRUFF, GEORGE R. Coach. B. Athens, Ga. Tennessee tackle, 1936-38. 23-5 playing record. Assistant coach at Tennessee, Army, Georgia Tech; head coach at Baylor, 1948-50; Florida (also athletic director), 1950-59. 73-52-8 record as head coach. Helped Army win two national titles under Earl Blaik, 1944-45. Tennessee athletic director, 1963-73. Under his aegis Vols won two SEC football championships, made eight straight bowl appearances, 1965-72. Also captured conference titles in basketball, tennis, cross-country, track, swimming, and baseball.

WOODRUFF, GEORGE W. Coach. B. 2/22/64, Dimmock, Pa. D. 3/23/34. Wore straw hat and sported black whiskers when first reported for football at Yale in 1885. Subsequently played right guard for four years, 1885-88. Originated "guards-back" attack, predecessor of "tackle-back," which was designed to knock out defensive ends. Head coach at Pennsylvania, 1892-1901; Illinois, 1903; Carlisle, 1905. His Penn teams compiled 124-15-2 record. Won 54 of 55 games in four-year period, 1894-97, and outscored opponents 1777-88. Only loss was 6-4 to Lafayette. Overall record: 142-25-2 (.846). Turned to legal career after retiring from football and served four years as Pennsylvania attorney-general. Citizens Savings Hall of Fame, National Football Foundation Hall of Fame.

WOODSON, ABRAHAM B. (Abe) Running-Defensive Back. B. 2/15/34, Jackson, Miss. 6'1", 188. Track, football, basketball star at Austin H.S. in Chicago. U. of Illinois, 1954-56. Was versatile gridiron performer, excelling on both offense and defense. In career rushed for 1276 yds. and caught 31 passes for 571 more. Scored three TDs, including decisive 82-yd. screen pass as Illinois came from 13 points behind to upend Michigan State (20-11) in 1956. Twice tied world indoor record for 50-yd. high hurdles. Defensive and kickoff-punt return specialist as pro with San Francisco 49ers, 1958-64; St. Louis Cardinals, 1965-66. Averaged 28.7 yds. during career on kickoffs, 3rd best in NFL history. Returned kickoff 105 yds. against Los Angeles Rams, 1959, one short of pro record. "I just run," Woodson said trying to explain effectiveness. But if I see something, I react instinctively. I'll cut or pivot or even stop, but it's not a conscious manuever. I just seem to do what's called for." Four times All-Pro. Resides today in San Francisco.

WOODSON, WARREN B. Coach. B. 2/24/03, Fort Worth, Tex. Graduated from Baylor, 1924. Saw first football game atop bicycle at TCU's old Clark Field. All-SWC in basketball, captain of tennis team. From Baylor went to Springfield College and earned degree in physical education. At Springfield learned T-formation fundamentals from Knute Rockne. Coached Texarkana (Tex.) J.C., 1927-34; Arkansas State, 1935-40; Hardin-Simmons, 1941-42, 46-51; Arizona, 1952-56; New Mexico State, 1958-67; Trinity, 1972-73. Thru 1972 had 247-112-20 record. Total victories made him 3rd winningest college coach, behind Amos Alonzo Stagg and Pop Warner, until NCAA discounted 52 wins because they were gained at junior college (Texarkana). Father of "Woodson T formation with a wingback" attack. In 1960 named college division Coach of the Year after directing New Mexico State to 11-0 season, including Sun Bowl victory. Citizens Savings Hall of Fame.

WORLEY, AL Defensive Back. B. 8/8/46, Chelan, Wash. 6', 175. Washington, 1966-68. As freshman was told by assistant coach he'd never play varsity football. After mediocre sophomore and junior years, Worley proved his worth, as senior, 1968. Intercepted major-college record 14 passes and was selected All-America. His 14th came in season's last game, helping to preserve 6-0 victory over UCLA. Explained his sudden success this way: "I was one of 10 children — five girls and five boys. At the dinner table, you had to be able to intercept to eat." Now assistant coach at Northern Arizona.

WORSTER, STEPHEN C. Running Back. B. 7/8/49, Rawlins, Wyo. 6', 210. Had phenomenal career at Bridge City, Tex. Gained 5422 yds., scored 79 TDs and 38 PATs. Texas won out over 80 colleges. When queried by writers where Worster would play coach Darrell Royal said, "He's like that 400-pound go-rilla. He'll play anywhere he likes." In 1968 joined stellar backfield of Ted Koy, Chris Gilbert, Bill Bradley. Devastating runner, helped make wishbone T powerful weapon. Consensus All-America, 1970. Worster, Jim Bertelsen powered '70 team. Played in three Cotton Bowl games, 1969, 70, 71. Texas fumbled away '71 Cotton Bowl to Notre Dame, ending 30-game winning streak. Had brief fling in CLF. Now realtor in Austin.

WRAY, JAMES R. LUDLOW (Lud) Center. B. 2/7/1894, Philadelphia, Pa. D. 7/24/67. Attended Chestnut Hill (Pa.) Academy. Played six years at U. of Pennsylvania, 1914-19. Massillon Tigers, 1919; Buffalo Bisons, 1920-21;

Rochester Jeffersons, 1922. Penn assistant coach, 1924-28. In 1933 Wray and Bert Bell bought Frankford Yellowjackets and moved franchise to nearby Philadelphia — Eagles they have been ever since. Wray coached Eagles, 1933-35 (9-21-1); prior to that spent one year with Boston Redskins, 1932 (4-4-2).

WRIGHT, ELMO (Dancer) End. B. 7/3/49, Brazoria, Tex. 6′, 190. Houston, 1968-70. Consensus All-America, 1970. Established two NCAA records: career TDs (34) and best per-catch average, season (20.2 yds.). Runnerup nationally to Jim O'Brien in best per-catch average for career (21.9 yds.). No. 1 draft choice of Kansas City Chiefs, 1971. Kansas City, 1971-73. Won Mack Lee Hill Award as team's top rookie. Hampered by injuries sophomore year, playing only seven games. Took nickname from dance he performs in end zone after scoring TD. Accomplished saxophone player.

WRIGHT, ERNIE H. Tackle. B. 11/6/39, Toledo, Ohio. 6′4″, 257. Attended Scott H.S. in Toledo before playing under Woody Hayes at Ohio State. Signed, as free agent, by San Diego Chargers in 1960. Ensuing 11 years missed only one game due to injury. Went to Cincinnati Bengals in AFL allocation draft of 1968. Returned to Chargers via trade for Bob Bruggers, 1972. Played in three AFL All-Star games, 1962, 64, 66. Outstanding pass blocker. During off-season manages financial company. AFL championship games, 1961, 63, 64, 65.

WYANT, ANDREW R. E. (Polyphemus) Center-guard. B. 1873, Chicago, Ill. D. 6/17/64, Chicago, Ill. 6′3″, 180. Initials R. E. stand for Robert Elmer. Started playing at Bucknell Academy prep school. Never substituted for in four seasons at Bucknell, 1888-91, and three at U. of Chicago, 1892-94, comprising 98 games. Bucknell contemporary of baseball's Christy Mathewson. Wyant was first elected captain at Chicago. Played for Amos Alonzo Stagg's first organized team there. In multi-faceted career was minister, physician, author, teacher, financier. Long-time minister at Morgan Park Baptist Church in Chicago. Just prior to his death in 1964, Wyant visited coach Stagg on West Coast. Wyant was 91 and Stagg 102. Held following college degrees: B.A., M.D., B.D., Ph.D. and M.D. National Football Foundation Hall of Fame.

WYATT, BOWDEN End. B. 10/4/17, Kingston, Tenn. D. 1/21/69, Kingston, Tenn. 6′1″, 190. Tennessee, 1936-38. Two-way end for Robert Neyland. Consensus All-America and captain for No. 2 ranked Vols, 1938. Defeated Oklahoma 17-0, in 1938 Orange Bowl. Coached Wyoming, 1947-52; Arkansas, 1953-54; Tennessee, 1955-63. Won titles in three major conferences: Skyline, 1949, 50; Southwest, 1954; Southestern, 1956. Wyatt's teams played in Cotton Bowl, 1955, and Sugar Bowl, 1957, losing both. Coaching record: 104-61-5. Died of viral pneumonia. National Football Foundation Hall of Fame.

WYCOFF, S. DOUGLAS (Doug) Quarterback. B. 9/6/03, St. Louis, Mo. Member W. A. Alexander Era team, 1920-44, at Georgia Tech. All-Southern fullback, 1923-25. Captain, 1925. Quarterbacked Newark Bears (AFL), 1926; New York Giants, 1927, 31; Staten Island Stapletons, 1929-30, 32; Boston Redskins, 1934; New York Yanks (AFL), 1936. Giants were 1927 pro champs. Wycoff was player-coach of Stapletons, 1929 (3-4-3).

YARY, A. RONALD Tackle. B. 8/16/46, Chicago, Ill. 6'6", 256. Attended Bellflower (Calif.) H.S., Cerritos (Calif.) J.C., Southern California. Unanimous All-America, 1967; consensus All-America, 1966. Outland Trophy winner, 1967. First player selected in NFL draft, 1967. Member Minnesota Vikings, 1968-73. Pro Bowl, 1972, 73, 74. All-NFC, 1970, 71, 72, 73. Much in demand as after-dinner speaker. Rated with best offensive tackles. NFL championship game, 1969. Super Bowl, 1970, 74.

YEOMAN, WILLIAM F. Coach. B. 12/26/27, Elnora, Ind. Attended Glendale (Ariz.) H.S., Texas A. & M. and Army. A. & M. football and basketball letterman in 1945, then received appointment to West Point. Played three years there under Earl (Red) Blaik, 1946-48. Captain and All-America, 1948. Was 6'2", 200-pound center. Assistant at Army and Michigan State before taking Houston head post in 1960. Since then has developed some of nation's most powerful offensive teams. Famous for veer-T system, featuring triple option. Citadel coach Red Parker called option "the greatest innovation in football since the forward pass." 1968 Cougars set NCAA total-offense record (broken by Oklahoma) with 562.0 yds. per game. Houston defense, nicknamed "Mad Dog", has also been nationally ranked. Developed All-Americas Warren McVea, Paul Gipson, Royce Berry, Elmo Wright, Riley Odoms, Robert Newhouse, Rich Stotter. West coach in 1973 East-West Shrine game. Three bowl games, winning two and losing one. Annually ranked in top 20.

YEPREMIAN, GARABED S. (Garo) Kicker. B. 6/2/44, Larnaca, Cyprus. 5'8",

175. Played soccer and tennis for American Academy in Larnaca. Never graduated from high school but speaks four languages. Fled Cyprus in 1960 when fighting broke out between Turks and Greeks. Went to London, spent five years hustling fabrics in Carnaby Street. Joined Detroit Lions as free agent in 1966. Alternated with Wayne Walker, 1966, 67, then released by Lions. Out of football in 1968, 69. Signed by Miami Dolphins, 1970, though coach Don Shula had never seen him kick. Missed no PATs next two seasons. Had two blocked in 1972. Led NFL in scoring with 117 points, Won football's longest game, at 22:40 of overtime, with 37-yd. FG vs. Kansas City Chiefs in AFC playoff, 1971. Super Bowl, 1972, 73, 74. Had disconcerting moment in Super Bowl VII, 1973. Recovered own blocked FG attempt and attempted to throw pass. Ball was taken by Mike Bass (Washington Redskins) and returned for TD. Had trouble kicking long ones as Lion, but no such trouble with Miami. Manufactures ties and owns two tire stores. Known for quick wit.

YOST, FIELDING H. (Hurry Up) Coach. B. 4/30/1871, Fairview, Neb. D. 8/20/46, Ann Arbor, Mich. Lafayette and West Virginia tackle. Coached Ohio Wesleyan, 1897; Nebraska, 1898; Kansas, 1899; Stanford, 1900; Michigan, 1901-25. Famous for Michigan's "point-a-minute" teams, 1901-05. During five-year stretch Wolverines were tied only by Minnesota (6-6), lost only to Chicago (2-0). Chicago's victory, in 1905, broke Michigan's 56-game winning streak. During same five-year period Michigan outscored its opponents, 2821 to 42. Juggernaut allowed no points while scoring 550 in 1901. Overall record: 196-36-12 (.828); Michigan record: 164-29-10. Coached Wolverines to 49-0 win over Stanford in first Rose Bowl game, 1902. Michigan athletic director, 1921-41. Also developed prominent law practice. Acquired nickname during first year of coaching at Michigan. He yelled, "You'll have to hurry-up" to players after almost every play. Popular after dinner speaker, was apostle of "four-sided" men — comprising brains, heart, courage and character. These men he believed made best athletes and best citizens. Citizens Savings Hall of Fame, National Football Foundation Hall of Fame.

YOUNG, CHARLES Tight End. B. 2/5/51, Fresno, Calif. 6'4", 230. Five-sport star at Edison H.S. in Fresno. Southern California, 1970-72. Consensus All-America for USC's national championship team, 1972. 12-0 Trojan season included 42-17 thrashing of Ohio State in Rose Bowl. All-time reception leader at USC. Played in Coaches All-America, Hula Bowl and College All-Star games. One of two 1st-round draft choices (with Texas' Jerry Sisemore) of Philadelphia Eagles, 1973. In '73 rookie season caught 55 passes for 854 yds., 6 TDs. Longest was 80-yarder from QB Roman Gabriel. Pro Bowl. Tremendous future barring injury.

YOUNG, CLAUDE H. (Buddy) Running Back. B. 1926, Chicago, Ill. 5'5", 163. Attended Wendell Phillips H.S. in Chicago. U. of Illinois halfback, 1944, 46. Compensated for lack of size with outstanding speed. Ran 100-yd. dash in 9.5, tied world indoor 60-yd. dash record of 6.1. Tied Red Grange's school mark with

13 TDs, 1944. All-America same season, averaging 8.9 yds. per carry, 2nd best nationally. Rushed for 103 yds. on 20 carries, scored 2 TDs in Illini's 45-14 Rose Bowl victory, 1947. MVP for College All-Stars vs. Chicago Bears, 1947. New York Yankees (AAFC), 1947-49; New York Yanks, 1950-51; Dallas Texans (1952); Baltimore Colts, 1953-55. As pro scored 44 TDs and compiled 9419 all-purpose yds. Retired with record 27.9-yd. average on kickoffs. National Football Foundation Hall of Fame. Administrative aid to NFL Commissioner Pete Rozelle.

YOUNG, M. ADRIAN (Ado) Linebacker. B. 1/31/46, Dublin, Ireland. 6'1", 232. Attended Bishop Amat Memorial H.S. LaPuente, Calif., and Southern California. Majored in business management at USC. Consensus All-America and co-captain of Trojans' national championship team, 1967. Capped season with 14-3 Rose Bowl victory over Indiana. Drafted on 3rd round by Philadelphia Eagles in 1968. Eagles, 1968-71; Detroit Lions, 1972; New Orleans Saints, 1973. Missed 11 games due to knee surgery, 1971.

YOUNG, WALTER R. (Waddy) End. B. 9/4/16, Ponca City, Okla. D. 1/9/45, Tokyo, Japan. 6'2", 203. Played at Oklahoma. All-America, 1938. Member of Oklahoma's losing Orange Bowl team, 1939. In that game played head-to-head against Tennessee All-America Bowden Wyatt. Brooklyn Dodgers, 1939-40. In first raid over Tokyo Young was killed when his B-29 was shot down.

YOUNGBLOOD, JACK Defensive End. B. 1/26/50, Jacksonville, Fla. 6'4", 250. Attended Jefferson County H.S., Monticello, Fla., and U. of Florida. All-America and Most Valuable Defensive Lineman in SEC, 1970. Participated in College All-Star and Senior Bowl games. Los Angeles Rams, 1971-73. Was 1st-round draft choice. Sacked QBs six times as nine-game starter with Rams, 1972. Full-time starter in 1973.

YOUNGER, PAUL (Tank) Running Back. B. 6/25/28, Grambling, La. 6'3", 226. First from Black school (Grambling) to play pro football. Tank's godfather, Dr. Ralph Jones, who has been Grambling president since 1936, negotiated contract — with Los Angeles Rams. Terms were $6,000 for rookie season, 1949. Went on to play nine years with Rams, distinguishing himself as linebacker and fullback. There have been few better two-way players. Also Pittsburgh Steelers, 1958. Was powerful, fast and savage. George Halas once remarked after game, "Tank, you're the greatest, dirtiest, best football player in the league. I just wish we (Chicago Bears) had you." Played in three Pro Bowls. Gained 3640 yds. rushing, 3296 with Rams. Career total placed him among top five NFL rushers when retired. Scout for Rams since 1966.

YOUNGSTROM, ADOLPH F. (Swede) Guard. B. 5/24/1897, Waltham, Mass. D. 8/5/68, Boston, Mass. 6'1", 181. Dartmouth All-America, 1919. Blocked nine punts that season, three against Colgate and two against Cornell. Played service ball in 2nd Naval District with other Ivy League greats; and with Buffalo All

Americans, 1921-25; Frankford Yellowjackets, 1926-27. After real estate career was named review appraiser for Commonwealth of Massachusetts, 1961. Suffered declining health following 1958 operation for stomach ulcers.

YOWARSKY, WALTER Tackle. B. 5/10/28, Cleveland, Ohio. 6'2", 235. Played at Kentucky. MVP in Sugar Bowl, 1951. Kentucky defeated Oklahoma, 13-7, to end Sooners' 33-game win streak. Pro experience with Washington Redskins, 1951, 54; Detroit Lions, 1955; New York Giants, 1955-57; San Francisco 49ers, 1958. Played on Giants' NFL title team, 1956. Yowarsky was two-way tackle. Currently defensive line coach with San Diego Chargers. Former coach with Giants, Minnesota Vikings, Atlanta Falcons, New Orleans Saints, Houston Oilers.

YUNEVICH, ALEX J. Coach. B. 12/8/09. Purdue fullback, 1929-31. 23-3 playing record. Tutored by Jimmy Phelan, 1929, last two years by Noble Kizer. Coached Central Michigan, 1934-36; Alfred, 1937-41; 46-73. Record: 172-90-11. Six unbeaten teams at Alfred, 1937, 40, 52, 55, 56, 71. Thru 1973 ranked 3rd in wins among active college-division coaches. 1973 was 34th year at Alfred, 37th in coaching. Citizens Savings Hall of Fame.

ZABEL, STEVE G. (Zabe) Linebacker. B. 3/20/48, Minneapolis, Minn. 6'4", 235. Attended Thornton (Colo.) H.S. and U. of Oklahoma. Captain, All-Big 8 and All-America tight end, 1969. Tutored by Chuck Fairbanks. Played in East-West and Hula Bowl games. Business administration major. Philadelphia Eagles, 1970-73. Moved to linebacker in 1972. Was No. 1 draft selection. Limited to action in seven games by knee surgery, 1972.

ZIMMERMAN, DONALD G. Running Back. B. 1/19/12, Houston, Tex. 5'10", 190. Tulane, 1930-32. Perhaps Tulane's most versatile player. Ranked among top three in 26 different school marks, covering most offensive and defensive categories. During Zimmerman's career Green Wave compiled 25-4-1 record. Amassed 3733 yds. as all-purpose runner (525 plays), 4657 in total performance (764 plays). Rushed 27 times, returned 6 punts and 3 kickoffs, threw 7 passes and punted 9 times as Tulane whipped Georgia Tech, 20-14, in 1932. Threw one TD pass in Tulane's losing Rose Bowl effort against Southern Cal, 1932. Consensus All-America his senior year, one of four such honorees in Tulane history.

ZIMMERMAN, H. LEROY Quarterback. B. Tonganoxie, Kan. Attended San Jose State. Washington Redskins, 1940-42; Philadelphia Eagles, 1942, 44-46; Phil-Pitt Stegles, 1943; Detroit Lions, 1947; Boston Yanks, 1948. NFL leader in interceptions with seven, 1945. Washington Touchdown Club's outstanding player, 1944. Coached six championship prep teams in 15 years. Softball pitcher 34 years. Member Softball Hall of Fame. Five-handicap golfer. Teacher at Madera (Calif.) H.S.

ZOOK, JOHN E. End. B. 9/24/47, Garden City, Kan. 6'5", 248. All-State in football and basketball at Larned (Kan.) H.S. End, fullback as prep. U. of Kansas, 1966-68. All-Big 8 twice, 1967, 68. Consensus All-America, 1968. Conference Lineman of the Year, same season. Played with Kansas in Orange Bowl, 1969. Atlanta Falcons, 1969-73. Originally 4th-round draft choice of Los Angeles Rams. Was traded same day twice, 7/7/69, to Philadelphia Eagles and then on to Atlanta. Recorded first safety in Falcon history when he trapped Green Bay's Scott Hunter in end zone, 1971. Scored first pro TD by recovering fumble and running 26 yds. against Chicago Bears, 1972. He and Claude Humphrey gave Atlanta outstanding defensive end tandem. Pro Bowl, 1974.

ZUPPKE, ROBERT C. (Zupp) Coach. B. 7/2/1879, Berlin, Germany. D. 12/22/57. Came to America at age 2. Fell in love with football, but later was too small for Wisconsin varsity. So he settled for being scrub quarterback, 1903-04. Member league championship basketball team with Hall of Famer Christian Steinmetz, 1905. Coached Muskegon (Mich.) H.S., 1905-09; Oak Park (Ill.) H.S., 1910-12; U. of Illinois, 1913-41. Developed Hall of Famers Bart Macomber and Red Grange. Contended, "I will never have another Red Grange, but neither will anybody else." Won or shared seven Western Conference (Big 10) championships. Illinois record: 131-81-12. Told his players prior to 1916 game with heavily favored Minnesota: "I am Louis XIV, and you are my court. After us the deluge." Whatever it meant Illini players were inspired to stunning 14-9 upset, ranking with greatest surprises in collegiate history. Introduced "Flea Flicker," onside kick, screen pass, modern huddle, spiral pass from center, guards pulling back to protect passer. Was intellectually curious, complex — artist (gave gallery exhibitions), philosopher (student of Schopenhauer, Kant), psychologist, humorist. Called "Rembrandt of the Prairies." Authored numerous funny stories. "Never let hope elude you. That is life's biggest fumble" — one of many original Zuppke aphorisms. Raised prized hogs and painted when retired from coaching. Citizens Savings Hall of Fame, National Football Foundation Hall of Fame.

ADDENDA

BATTLE, WILLIAM R. Coach. B. 12/8/41, Birmingham, Ala. Alabama end, 1960-62. Duting playing career won one national championship and lost only two games. Earned master's degree from Oklahoma, 1963. Assistant coach Oklahoma, 1963-64; Army, 1964-65; Tennessee, 1966-69. Became youngest head coach (age 28) in nation when named to guide Tennessee Volunteers, 1970. Logged 39-9 record first four years. Won 11 of 12 games, 1970, capping season with 34-13 decision over Air Force in Sugar Bowl. 8-3 mark, in 1973, "worst" to date.

BERGEY, BILL Linebacker. B. 2/9/45, South Dayton, N.J. 6'3", 243. Little All-America at Arkansas State, 1968. Helped school gain national recognition. Cincinnati Bengals, 1969-73. Was 2nd-round draft pick. Rugged, exceptionally hard-hitting middle linebacker. After '73 season signed with WFL, angering coach Paul Brown. Tried to get court order to stop Bergey from switching. Denied — Bergey then traded to Philadelphia Eagles.

DAVIS, AL Owner. B. 7/4/29, Brockton, Mass. Attended Wittenberg College and Syracuse U. Played three sports. Assistant coach at Adelphi College, Baltimore Colts, The Citadel, USC, Los Angeles-San Diego Chargers. In 1963 hired to rehabilitate Oakland Raiders. He did. As head coach won 23, lost 16, tied 3, 1963-65. Since then has been Oakland general manager, AFL commissioner (eight weeks), principal owner of Raiders. AFL-NFL merger completed during his brief tenure as commissioner. In Davis era Raiders have won six western Division titles in AFL-AFC; AFL championship, 1967.

DOOLEY, VINCENT J. Coach. B. 9/4/32, Mobile, Ala. Auburn tailback-defensive back, 1951-53. Career hampered by knee injury. Still managed to lead Auburn to 7-2-1 record in 1953, its first winning season in 17 years. Played in 1954 College All-Star game vs. Detroit Lions. Coached Georgia, 1964-73. Record of 73-32-5 puts him among top 10 in winning percentage among actives. Has produced seven bowl teams and two SEC co-championships. Thrice named SEC Coach of the Year. Developed All-Americas Jake Scott and Bill Stanfill. His teams epitomize offensive and defensive balance. State chairman, Georgia Easter Seal campaign, eight consecutive years.

EVASHEVSKI, FOREST (Evy) Coach. B. 2/19/18, Detroit, Mich. Graduated from Michigan, 1940. In USNR, 1942-46. Coached Hamilton College, 1941-42; Washington State, 1950-51; Iowa, 1952-60. Using winged-T offense developed many exciting teams at Iowa. Won three Big 10 championships and two Rose Bowl games between 1956-60. Hawkeye record: 52-27-4. Iowa has had only one winning season, and that in 1961, since he retired from coaching. Received numerous Coach of the Year honors. Delegate to Democratic National Convention, 1964. Author of *Scoring Power With the Winged-T Offense* and *The Modern Winged T Play Book*. Iowa athletic director, 1960-70.

FORD, GERALD R. Center. B. 7/14/13, Omaha, Neb. All-State at South High in Grand Rapids, Mich. Recruited by Michigan, Michigan State, Northwestern, Harvard. Impressed with coach Harry Kipke, so enrolled at Michigan. Played there three years, 1932-34. College All-Star game, 1935. Turned down offers from Chicago Bears and Detroit Lions. Coached at Yale, 1935-40. Received A.B. from Michigan, 1935; LL.B. from Yale, 1941. Member 81st-92nd Congresses. Elected House minority leader, 1965. *Sports Illustrated* Silver Anniversary All-America team, 1959. Recipient of Gold Medal award from National Football Foundation in 1972. Appointed U.S. vice president in 1973. Succeeded Richard M. Nixon as President of the United States of America, August 9, 1974.

HICKERSON, R. GENE Guard. B. 2/15/36, Trenton, Tenn. 6'2", 252. Mississippi, 1955-57. Co-captain and All-SEC, 1957. Cleveland Browns, 1958-73. Pro Bowl, 1966, 67, 68, 69, 70, 71. NFL championship games, 1964, 65, 68, 69. All-NFL, 1967, 68, 69. Blocked for such luminaries as Jim Brown, Bobby Mitchell, Leroy Kelly. Fluid, quick, efficient. Played primarily at right guard. Retired from pros with 16 years service. Among Browns, only Lou Groza (17 years) surpassed him in longevity.

HUBBARD, MARVIN R. Running Back. B. 5/7/46, Salamanca, N.Y. 6'1", 225. Colgate, 1965-67. Rushed for 1891 yds. in three seasons. Gained 897 yds. rushing, scored 88 points in 1966. Won Atlantic Coast League rushing title with Hartford in '68, amassing 899 yds. Oakland Raiders, 1969-73. AFL championship game, 1969. Strong, competitive, dependable. Oakland rushing leader three straight years, 1971-73. Had 1100 yds. on ground in 1972. Pro Bowl, 1972-74.

HUNT, LAMAR Owner. B. Dallas, Tex. Pro sports entrepreneur. Bespectacled, soft-spoken, industrious, rich. Son of H. L. Hunt, oil multimillionaire. Lamar played end at Southern Methodist behind Raymond Berry. Frustrated in bid to land NFL franchise, so formed own league (AFL) in 1959. Only 26 at time. Became league's first president in 1960 and obtained own franchise, Dallas Texans. Moved franchise to Kansas City in 1963, renamed club Chiefs. Kansas City was first AFL team to participate in Super Bowl, 1967. Hunt and Dallas Cowboy executive Tex Schramm, 11/66, began talks which eventually led to AFL-NFL merger. Has numerous sports and business interests. Is vice president of Hunt Oil Co. Pioneered World Championship Tennis. Named to Pro Football Hall of Fame in 1973. At induction friend Billy Sullivan, of New England Patriots, paid tribute: "It is entirely appropriate that Lamar Hunt should be the first American Football League man to be enshrined in the Hall of Fame. He is the architect, designer and builder of an impossible dream."

JONES, CALVIN J. Guard, B. 2/7/33, Steubenville, Ohio. D. 12/56, Canada. 6', 200. Iowa standout under Forest Evashevski. Consensus All-America, 1954, 55. Outland Trophy winner, 1955. CFL, 1956. Jones, like Iowa immortal Nile Kinnick, met death in airplane crash. Was en route to watch alma mater play in Rose Bowl when plane ploughed into isolated Canadian mountainside. His body and other victims never recovered.

KASSULKE, KARL O. (Cowboy) Defensive Back. B. 3/20/41, Milwaukee, Wis. 6', 195. Marquette running back and safety, 1960-61. Transferred to Drake in '62 when Marquette dropped football. Minnesota Vikings, 1963-72. Originally drafted by Detroit Lions in '63, then sold to Vikes. Intercepted 19 passes in 10 seasons as strong safety. Career ended prematurely. Was critically injured in motorcycle accident, 7/73. Will likely never walk again. Honored by Vikings with Karl Kassulke Day, 11/25/73, as club played Chicago Bears. Over $200,000 donated to special fund for him. Remains cheerful, optimistic. Owns group of saloons in Twin Cities.

LARSEN, GARY L. Tackle. B. 3/13/40, Fargo, N.D. Spent three years in Marine Corps after high school. Graduated from Concordia (Minn.) College in 1964. Los Angeles Rams, 1964; Minnesota Vikings, 1965-73. Forgotten man of Viking front four, called "Purple People Eaters." Helped Vikes to Super Bowl appearances in 1970, 74. Pro Bowl, 1971.

McCAULEY, DONALD F., JR. Running Back. B. 5/12/49, Garden City, N.Y. 6'1", 214. North Carolina, 1968-70. All-America, 1970. Rushed for 1720 yds. in senior year to break O. J. Simpson's NCAA yardage record (1709). In three years picked up 3172 yds. on ground. Set 26 ACC and North Carolina records, four NCAA marks. Baltimore Colts, 1971-73. Drafted No. 1 by Colts. Returned kickoff 93 yds. vs. New York Jets, 1972.

McKENZIE, REGGIE Guard B. 7/27/50, Detroit, Mich. 6'4", 237. Michigan, 1969-71. Consensus All-America, 1971. Participated in Rose Bowl, Hula Bowl, College All-Star games. Buffalo Bills, 1972-73. All-Pro, 1973. Opened holes that led to O. J. Simpson's record-breaking season, 1973.

MARSALIS, JIM Defensive Back. B. 10/10/45, Pascagoula, Miss. 5'11", 194. Tennessee State, 1965-68. All-America, 1968. During collegiate career had only one TD pass thrown against him. Only defensive back ever selected by Kansas City Chiefs on 1st round, in 1969. Chiefs, 1969-73. Immediate regular at cornerback. Rookie of the Year in several polls. All-AFC, 1970. Intercepted 11 passes first four years as pro. Lost his job at left corner to Nate Allen in '73. Expert at bump-and-run.

MILDREN, L. JACK, JR. Quarterback-Defensive Back. B. 10/10/49, Abilene. Tex, ,6'1'" 199. Tremendously spirited, intelligent athlete. Oklahoma QB, 1969-71. All-America, 1971. Unsurpassed as wishbone-T field general. Led Oklahoma to 11-1 season in senior year, including Sugar Bowl win over Auburn. Same season gained 1140 yds. rushing — better than any QB in history. In three years gained 4787 yds. total offense. Baltimore Colts, 1972-73.

Switched to defensive back. Now plays safety, on special teams.

PYLE, CHARLES C. (Cash and Carry) Promoter. B. 1881, Van Wert, Ohio. D. 2/3/39. Sports profiteer. Name usually linked with Red Grange. Negotiated Grange's first pro contract — with Chicago Bears in 1925. It was good for half of Bear gate receipts and, for Grange, would amount to about $125,000. Following year Pyle sought NFL franchise but was refused. As alternative he took Grange and formed own league (original American Football League). Folded after only one season. Grange went back to NFL minus business manager. Pyle, who began business career as small-town theatre owner, promoted other sports besides football. Organized first professional tennis tour, which led to formation of Professional Lawn Tennis Association in 1927. "Bunion Derby" proved his Waterloo. Was scheduled 2500-mile marathon between Los Angeles and Passaic, N.J. Pyle lost $50,000 on event, faded from limelight.

RICE, H. GRANTLAND (Granny) Sportswriter. B. 11/1/1880, Murfreesboro, Tenn. D. 7/13/54. Beloved figure in American sports journalism. Was gentleman and scholar. Writer for more than half-century. Turned out 67,000,000 words; more than 22,000 columns, 7000 sets of verse, 1000 magazine articles. Also announced games on radio and narrated short movie features. Had been baseball and football player at Vanderbilt. Writing career launched in 1901 as general reporter for Nashville *News*. Worked way to national prominence. Named 1924-24 Notre Dame backfield "Four Horsemen"; and Jack Dempsey "Manassa Mauler." Composed poetry "by ear." His most famous lines were: "When the Last Great Scorer comes/To mark against your name,/He'll write not 'won' or 'lost'/But how you played the game." Almost fittingly, he died while sitting at typewriter working on syndicated column. Rice's close friend, Gene Fowler, author and movie writer, eulogized: "Granny didn't preach The Sermon on the Mount. He *lived* it."

SULLIVAN, PATRICK J. Quarterback. B. 1/18/50, Birmingham, Mich. 6', 195. Auburn, 1969-71. 25-5 playing record. Unanimous All-America and Heisman Trophy winner, 1971. Numerous other honors. Responsible for 71 career TDs, tying NCAA mark. Ranks 3rd in TD passes with 53. Completed 454 of 817 tosses for 6284 yds. Atlanta Falcons, 1972-73. Was 2nd-round draft choice.

TWILLEY, HOWARD J., JR. End. B. 12/25/43, Houston, Tex. 5'10", 185. Tulsa, 1963-65. Set 10 NCAA pass-receiving records. Finished collegiate career 1st in catches (261), 1st in receiving yds. (3343), 1st in TD catches (32). Consensus All-America and Heisman Trophy runnerup, 1965. Academic All-America, 1964, 65. Miami Dolphins, 1966-73. Joined Dolphins in team's maiden season. Super Bowl, 1972, 73, 74. After eight pro seasons had 150 receptions for 2228 yds. Career lows — two catches, 30 yds. in '73. Deceptive — small and not particularly fast — but great hands, moves.

WIDBY, G. RONALD (Ron) Kicker. B. 3/9/45, Knoxville, Tenn. 6'4", 210. Tennessee football and basketball star. Received All-American mention in both sports. NCAA punting leader with 43.8-yd. average on 48 punts. Dallas Cowboys, 1968-71; Green Bay Packers, 1972-73. Super Bowl, 1971, 72. Pro Bowl, 1972. Booted 84-yd. punt in 1968. Played pro basketball with New Orleans Buccaneers, 1968.

Notes On The Authors

RONALD L. MENDELL is a free lance sports editor and writer. He authored *Who's Who in Basketball* (Arlington House, 1973). Born in 1947 in Ottawa, Kansas, he graduated *cum laude* from Wichita State University in 1969 where he subsequently served as assistant sports information director. He also worked on the sports desk of the *Wichita Eagle*. He and wife Dene reside in Lenexa, Kansas.

TIMOTHY B. PHARES studied at Hillsdale College, Hillsdale, Michigan. A resident of New York's Westchester County, he has contributed articles on sports to numerous academic publications.